Policy Analysis

Fourth Edition

Policy Analysis

Concepts and Practice

David L. Weimer
University of Wisconsin-Madison

Aidan R. Vining
Simon Fraser University

PEARSON
Prentice Hall

Upper Saddle River, New Jersey 07458

Library of Congress Cataloging-in-Publication Data

WEIMER, DAVID LEO.
Policy analysis: concepts and practice / David L. Weimer, Aidan R. Vining.—4th ed.
p. cm.
Includes indexes.
ISBN 0–13–183001–5 (pbk.)
1. Policy sciences. I. Vining, Aidan R. II. Title.

H97.W45 2004
320.6—dc22

2003062694

Acquisitions Editor: Glenn Johnston
Editorial Director: Charlyce Jones Owen
Assistant Editor: John Ragozzine
Editorial Assistant: Suzanne Remore
Marketing Manager: Kara Kindstrom
Marketing Assistant: Jennifer Lang
Production Editor: Joan Stone
Manufacturing Buyer: Sherry Lewis
Cover Art Director: Jayne Conte
Cover Design: Bruce Kenselaar
Composition: Emilcomp
Cover Printer: Phoenix Color Corp.
Typeface: 10/11 Palatino

Pearson Education LTD.
Pearson Education Singapore, Pte. Ltd
Pearson Education, Canada, Ltd
Pearson Education—Japan
Pearson Education Australia PTY, Limited
Pearson Education North Asia Ltd
Pearson Educación de Mexico, S.A. de C.V.
Pearson Education Malaysia, Pte. Ltd
Pearson Education, Upper Saddle River, NJ

PEARSON
Prentice Hall

10 9 8 7 6 5 4
ISBN 0–13–183001–5

To Rhiannon, Rory, and Eirian

Contents

List of Figures xiii
List of Tables xv
Preface xvii

PART I: INTRODUCTION TO PUBLIC POLICY ANALYSIS

1 *Preview: The Canadian Salmon Fishery* 1
Increasing the Social Value of the Canadian Salmon Fishery 2
Postscript and Prologue 22
For Discussion 22

2 *What Is Policy Analysis?* 23
Policy Analysis and Related Professions 24
Policy Analysis as a Profession 31
A Closer Look at Analytical Functions 35
Basic Preparation for Policy Analysis 37
For Discussion 38

3 *Toward Professional Ethics* 39
Analytical Roles 40
Value Conflicts 43
Ethical Code or Ethos? 51
For Discussion 53

PART II: CONCEPTUAL FOUNDATIONS FOR PROBLEM ANALYSIS

4 *Efficiency and the Idealized Competitive Model* 54

The Efficiency Benchmark: The Competitive Economy 55
Market Efficiency: The Meaning of Social Surplus 57
Caveats: Models and Reality 69
Conclusion 70
For Discussion 70

5 *Rationales for Public Policy: Market Failures* 71

Public Goods 72
Externalities 91
Natural Monopoly 97
Information Asymmetry 104
Conclusion 112
For Discussion 112

6 *Rationales for Public Policy: Other Limitations of the Competitive Framework* 113

Thin Markets: Few Sellers or Few Buyers 114
The Source and Acceptability of Preferences 115
The Problem of Uncertainty 119
Intertemporal Allocation: Are Markets Myopic? 124
Adjustment Costs 128
Macroeconomic Dynamics 129
Conclusion 130
For Discussion 131

7 *Rationales for Public Policy: Distributional and Other Goals* 132

Social Welfare Beyond Pareto Efficiency 133
Substantive Values Other Than Efficiency 142
Some Cautions in Interpreting Distributional Consequences 147
Instrumental Values 153
Conclusion 154
For Discussion 155

8 *Limits to Public Intervention: Government Failures* 156

Problems Inherent in Direct Democracy 157
Problems Inherent in Representative Government 163
Problems Inherent in Bureaucratic Supply 179
Problems Inherent in Decentralization 187
Conclusion 190
For Discussion 191

9 *Policy Problems as Market and Government Failure: The Madison Taxicab Policy Analysis Example* 192

Regulation of the Madison Taxi Market 193
The Relationship between Market and Government Failures 204
Conclusion 208
For Discussion 208

PART III: CONCEPTUAL FOUNDATIONS FOR SOLUTION ANALYSIS

10 *Correcting Market and Government Failure: Generic Policies* 209

Freeing, Facilitating, and Simulating Markets 210
Using Subsidies and Taxes to Alter Incentives 218
Establishing Rules 234
Supplying Goods through Nonmarket Mechanisms 246
Providing Insurance and Cushions 253
Conclusion 259
For Discussion 260

11 *Adoption and Implementation* 261

The Adoption Phase 263
The Implementation Phase 274
Thinking More Strategically about Policy Design 284
Conclusion 294
For Discussion 294

12 *Government Supply: Drawing Organizational Boundaries* 295

Production Costs, Bargaining Costs, and Opportunism Costs 297
Predicting Bargaining and Opportunism Costs 302
Can Opportunism Be Controlled by the Use of Not-for-Profits? 306
Assessing and Building Capacity 307
Conclusion 307
For Discussion 308

PART IV: DOING POLICY ANALYSIS

13 *Gathering Information for Policy Analysis* 309

Document Research 310
Field Research 318
Putting Document Review and Field Research Together 321
Conclusion 322
For Discussion 323

14 *Landing on Your Feet: How to Confront Policy Problems* 324

Analyzing Yourself: Meta-Analysis 325
The Client Orientation 326
Steps in Rationalist Policy Analysis 327
Problem Analysis 329
Solution Analysis 343
Communicating Analysis 357
Meta-Analysis Once Again: Combining Linear and Nonlinear Approaches 361
Conclusion 362
For Discussion 362

15 *Goals/Alternatives Matrices: Some Examples from CBO Studies* 363

Setting Out Broad Options: Auctioning Radio Spectrum Licenses 364
Quantitative Predictions: Restructuring the Army 366
Comparing Proposed Alternatives: Launching Digital Television 370
Combining Policy Alternatives: Improving Water Allocation 376
Conclusion 379
For Discussion 379

16 *Cost-Benefit Analysis* 380

A Preview: Increasing Alcohol Taxes 381
Identifying Relevant Impacts 382
Monetizing Impacts 384
Discounting for Time and Risk 399
Choosing among Policies 410
An Illustration: Taxing Alcohol to Save Lives 413
Conclusion 425
For Discussion 425

PART V: CASE STUDIES OF POLICY ANALYSIS

17 *Cost-Benefit Analysis in a Bureaucratic Setting: The Strategic Petroleum Reserve* 426

Background: Energy Security and the SPR 427
Analytical Approaches to the Size Issue 432
The Role of Analysis in the SPR Size Controversy 443
Postscript 450
Conclusion 450
For Discussion 451

18 *When Statistics Count: Revising the Lead Standard for Gasoline* 452

Background: The EPA Lead Standards 453
Origins of the 1985 Standards 455
Pulling the Pieces Together 456
A Closer Look at the Link between Gasoline Lead and Blood Lead 460
Finalizing the Rule 472
Conclusion 475
For Discussion 476

PART VI: CONCLUSION

19 *Doing Well and Doing Good* 477

Name Index 479
Subject Index 489

List of Figures

Figure 3.1 Alternative Responses to Value Conflicts 46
Figure 4.1 Pareto and Potential Pareto Efficiency 57
Figure 4.2 Consumer Values and Surpluses 58
Figure 4.3 Changes in Consumer Surplus 60
Figure 4.4 Money Metrics for Utility 61
Figure 4.5 Average and Marginal Cost Curves 63
Figure 4.6 Monopoly Pricing, Rents, and Deadweight Loss 65
Figure 4.7 A Supply Schedule and Producer Surplus 67
Figure 4.8 Inefficiencies Resulting from Deviations from the Competitive Equilibrium 68
Figure 5.1 Demand Summation for Rivalrous and Nonrivalrous Goods 75
Figure 5.2 A Classification of Goods: Private and Public 78
Figure 5.3 Toll Goods 80
Figure 5.4 Private Provision of a Public Good: Privileged Group 83
Figure 5.5 Overconsumption of Open-Access Resources 87
Figure 5.6 Choice of Herd Size as a Prisoner's Dilemma 88
Figure 5.7 Overproduction with a Negative Externality 94
Figure 5.8 Underproduction with a Positive Externality 95
Figure 5.9 Social Surplus Loss from Natural Monopoly 99
Figure 5.10 Shifting Demand and Multiple Firm Survival 101
Figure 5.11 *X*-Inefficiency under Natural Monopoly 103
Figure 5.12 Consumer Surplus Loss from Uninformed Demand 105
Figure 6.1 Utility Function Showing Loss Aversion 123
Figure 7.1 Lorenz Curve and Geni Index of Income Inequality 151
Figure 8.1 Agenda Control in a Two-Dimensional Policy Space 161
Figure 8.2 Surplus Transfers and Deadweight Losses under Price Supports 168
Figure 8.3 Surplus Transfer and Deadweight Losses under Price Ceilings 171
Figure 9.1 A Procedure for Linking Market and Government Failure to Policy Interventions 205
Figure 10.1 The Effect of a Matching Grant on Provision of Targeted Good 225
Figure 10.2 The Effect of an In-Kind Subsidy on Consumption 229
Figure 11.1 Equilibria in a Repeated Game 292
Figure 13.1 A Strategy for Combining Literature Review and Field Research 322
Figure 14.1 A Summary of Steps in the Rationalist Mode 328
Figure 14.2 Goal Trade-Offs and Feasibility 336
Figure 14.3 Choosing a Solution Method 339
Figure 16.1 Measuring Opportunity Cost in Efficient Factor Markets 386
Figure 16.2 Opportunity Cost in a Factor Market with a Price Floor 389

Figure 16.3 Measuring Benefits in an Efficient Market 391
Figure 16.4 Social Benefits of a Subsidy for a Good with a Positive Externality 393
Figure 16.5 Valuation of Effects in Secondary Markets 395
Figure 16.6 The Present Value of Production and Consumption 400
Figure 16.7 Social Surplus Loss in the Beer Market from a 30 Percent Tax 415
Figure 17.1 Measuring the Direct Economic Benefits of an SPR Drawdown 434
Figure 17.2 A Simple Decision Tree for the Stockpiling Problem 440
Figure 17.3 A Sample Node in the Expanded Decision Tree for the Stockpiling Problem 442
Figure 18.1 Lead Used in Gasoline Production and Average NHANES II Blood Lead Levels 458
Figure 18.2 Data Samples with Identical Correlations but Different Regression Lines 461

List of Tables

Table 1.1 A Summary of Fishery Alternatives in Terms of Policy Goals 21
Table 2.1 Policy Analysis in Perspective 26
Table 3.1 Three Views on the Appropriate Role of the Policy Analyst 42
Table 5.1 Examples of Externalities 93
Table 6.1 A Summary of Market Failures and Their Implications for Efficiency 130
Table 7.1 Alternative Social Welfare Functions 134
Table 7.2 Impact of Different Definitions of Income on Measures of Poverty and Distribution (United States, 2000) 149
Table 8.1 An Illustration of the Paradox of Voting 158
Table 8.2 Sources of Inefficiency in Representative Government: Divergences between Social and Political Accounting 178
Table 8.3 Sources of Government Failure: A Summary 191
Table 10.1 Freeing, Facilitating, and Simulating Markets 211
Table 10.2 Using Subsidies and Taxes to Alter Incentives 220
Table 10.3 Establishing Rules 235
Table 10.4 Supplying Goods through Nonmarket Mechanisms 248
Table 10.5 Providing Insurance and Cushions 254
Table 10.6 Searching for Generic Policy Solutions 260
Table 11.1 A Political Analysis Worksheet: Feasibility of a Ban on Random Drug Testing in the Workplace 265
Table 11.2 Thinking Systematically about Implementation: Forward Mapping 282
Table 12.1 When Are Incremental Costs Likely to Favor Contracting Out? 298
Table 14.1 The Simple Structure of a Goals/Alternatives Matrix 344
Table 14.2 Worksheet for Predicting Impacts of Alternative Policies for Dealing with Central Business District (CBD) Traffic Congestion 351
Table 14.3 Communicating Policy Analyses 360
Table 15.1 License Assignment Methods Compared 365
Table 15.2 Changes in Force Structure under the Army's Plan and Four Alternatives 367
Table 15.3 Effect of the Army's Plan and Four Alternatives on Annual Costs, Deployment Times, and Number of Forces 369
Table 15.4 Summary of Plans for Introducing Digital TV 371
Table 15.5 Summary Evaluation of Plans for Introducing Digital TV 374
Table 15.6 Estimated Benefits and Costs of a Shorter Transition to Digital TV 376
Table 15.7 Effect of the Central Valley Improvement Act on Agricultural Water Use, Urban Water Use, and Revenues 378

Table 16.1 Present Value of the Net Benefits of Investment in New Garbage Trucks 403
Table 16.2 Choosing among Projects on the Basis of Economic Efficiency 410
Table 16.3 Costs and Benefits of a 30 Percent Tax on Alcohol (billions of dollars) 422
Table 16.4 Net Benefits of Alcohol Taxes (billions of dollars) 423
Table 17.1 Impacts of a Public Oil Stockpiling Program 433
Table 18.1 Basic Regression Model for Estimating the Effects of Gasoline Lead on Blood Lead 467
Table 18.2 Present Value of Costs and Benefits of Final Rule, 1985–1992 (millions of 1983 dollars) 475

Preface

When we began our study of policy analysis at the Graduate School of Public Policy (now the Goldman School), University of California at Berkeley, the field was so new that we seemed always to be explaining to people just what it was that we were studying. It is no wonder, then, that there were no textbooks to provide us with the basics of policy analysis. More than a dozen years later we found ourselves teaching courses on policy analysis but still without what we considered to be a fully adequate text for an introductory course at the graduate level. Our experiences as students, practitioners, and teachers convinced us that an introductory text should have at least three major features. First, it should provide a strong conceptual foundation of the rationales for, and the limitations to, public policy. Second, it should give practical advice about how to *do* policy analysis. Third, it should demonstrate the application of advanced analytical techniques rather than discuss them abstractly. We wrote this text to have these features.

We organize the text into six parts. In Part I we begin with an example of a policy analysis and then emphasize that policy analysis, as a professional activity, is client-oriented, and we raise the ethical issues that flow from this orientation. In Part II we provide a comprehensive treatment of rationales for public policy (market failures, broadly defined) and we set out the limitations to effective public policy (government failures). In Part III we set out the conceptual foundations for solving public policy problems, including a catalogue of generic policy solutions that can provide starting points for crafting specific policy alternatives. We also offer advice on designing policies that will have good prospects for adoption and successful implementation and how to think about the choice between government production and contracting out. In Part IV we give practical advice about doing policy analysis: structuring problems and solutions, gathering information, and measuring costs and benefits. In Part V we present several extended examples illustrating how analysts have approached policy problems and the differences that their efforts have made. Part VI briefly concludes with advice about doing well and doing good.

We aim our level of presentation at students who have had, or are concurrently taking, an introductory course in economics. Nevertheless, students without a background in economics should find all of our general arguments and most of our technical points accessible. With a bit of assistance from an instructor, they should be able to understand the remaining technical points.

We believe that this text has several potential uses. We envision its primary use as the basis of a one-semester introduction to policy analysis for students in graduate programs in public policy, public administration, and business. We believe that our emphasis on conceptual foundations also makes it attractive for courses in graduate programs in political science and economics. At the undergraduate level, we think our chapters on market failures, government failures, generic policies, and cost-benefit analysis are useful supplements, and perhaps even replacements, for the commonly used public finance texts that do not treat these topics as comprehensively.

Acknowledgments

A reviewer of the first edition of this text told us that we had expounded what he takes to be the "Graduate School of Public Policy approach to public policy." His comment surprised us. We had not consciously attributed our peculiar views of the world to any particular source. But in retrospect, his comment made us realize how much our graduate teachers contributed to what we have written. Although they may wish to disavow any responsibility for our product, we nevertheless acknowledge a debt to our teachers, especially Eugene Bardach, Robert Biller, Lee Friedman, C. B. McGuire, Arnold Meltsner, William Niskanen, Philip Selznick, and the late Aaron Wildavsky.

We offer sincere thanks to our many colleagues in Rochester, Vancouver, B.C., and elsewhere who gave us valuable comments on the drafts of the first edition of this text: Gregg Ames, David Austen-Smith, Judith Baggs, Eugene Bardach, Larry Bartels, William T. Bluhm, Gideon Doron, Richard Fenno, Eric Hanushek, Richard Himmelfarb, Bruce Jacobs, Hank Jenkins-Smith, Mark Kleiman, David Long, Peter May, Charles Phelps, Paul Quirk, Peter Regenstreif, William Riker, Russell Roberts, Joel Schwartz, Fred Thompson, Scott Ward, Michael Wolkoff, Glenn Woroch, and Stephen Wright. A special thanks to Stanley Engerman, George Horwich, and John Richards, who went well beyond the call of duty in offering extensive and helpful comments on every chapter. We thank our research assistants, Eric Irvine, Murry McLoughlin, Katherine Metcalfe, and Donna Zielinski. We also thank Betty Chung, Mary Heinmiller, Jean Last, Dana Loud, Karen Mason, and Helaine McMenomy for logistical assistance at various times during preparation of the first edition.

We wish to thank the following people who helped us make improvements in the second, third, and fourth editions: Theodore Anagnoson, Eugene Bardach, William T. Bluhm, Wayne Dunham, Stanley Engerman, Richard C. Feiock, David

Greenberg, Catherine Hansen, Eric Hanushek, Robert Haveman, Bruce Jacobs, Renee J. Johnson, Kristen Layman, Marv Mandell, William H. Riker, Ulrike Radermacher, Richard Schwindt, Danny Shapiro, and Itai Sened. We thank our research assistants Shih-Hui Chen, Christen Gross, and Ga-der Sun, and Ruth Krasner for their help. Finally, we thank our students at the University of Rochester, Simon Fraser University, Lingnan College, and the Robert M. LaFollette School of Public Affairs at the University of Wisconsin for many useful suggestions regarding presentation.

David L. Weimer

Madison, Wisconsin

Aidan R. Vining

Vancouver, British Columbia

Policy Analysis

1

Preview

The Canadian Salmon Fishery

The product of policy analysis is advice. Specifically, it is advice that informs some public policy decision. Policy advice comes in many forms, but to give you the tenor of advice-giving, we begin with an example that illustrates many of the concepts and ways of organizing policy analysis that you will encounter in this book. Its purpose is to show you a comprehensive policy analysis that includes a description and analysis of the problem, specific policy alternatives, an evaluation of the alternatives, and a policy recommendation.

Imagine that you have been asked by the new Minister of the Department of Fisheries and Oceans of the Canadian government to conduct an analysis of the commercial "small-boat" salmon fishery in the province of British Columbia. Does the current Canadian federal policy promote effective management of the fishery? The minister wants you to help answer this question by providing an assessment of current policy in comparison with possible alternative policies.

The term "small-boat" fishery is used to distinguish this type of fishery from the commercial aquaculture (or farmed) salmon fishery, which is regulated by the provincial, rather than the federal, government. The minister has instructed you to consider the salmon sports fishery only to the extent that it directly affects the commercial fishery. (Another analysis is examining the larger trade-offs between the commercial and sports fisheries.) The minister has also instructed you to ignore for the purposes of this analysis current negotiations with the United States over the division of salmon stocks between the two countries. (Again, a separate analysis of this issue has been commissioned.) He has instructed you to treat the current law on the Aboriginal (or "First Nations") salmon food fishery as a given but does not wish to preclude you from considering policy alternatives that might transfer to the Aboriginal community a greater share of the commercial fishery harvest.

As the minister hopes to propose new policy initiatives early in his term, he has given you one month to produce your analysis. Although you are new to the Ministry, and therefore have no background in fisheries, your training as a policy analyst should enable you to gather relevant information quickly from already available research and organize it effectively to provide a useful answer to the minister's question. An example of the sort of report you might produce follows.

Increasing the Social Value of the Canadian Salmon Fishery

Prepared for
the Minister of the Department of Fisheries and Oceans
April 2003

EXECUTIVE SUMMARY

The salmon fishery of British Columbia faces serious challenges. The evidence suggests that, as currently organized, the fishery represents a net drain on the wealth of Canadians. This will remain the case for the foreseeable future, in spite of costly reforms instituted between 1995 and 2001. While some of the problems associated with the fishery can be attributed to inherent market failures, most are attributable to ineffective or, indeed, counterproductive government interventions. Although the current regime probably does not threaten the viability of most salmon runs, it does endanger some of the smaller runs and subspecies. On balance, it is desirable to replace the current regulatory regime with a policy based on exclusive ownership of salmon fishing rights for specific rivers.

This analysis examines four policy alternatives: (1) the status quo policy, (2) harvesting royalties and license auction, (3) river-specific, exclusive ownership and harvesting rights (with cooperative ownership on the Fraser River), and (4) individual transferable quotas. All four alternatives are evaluated in terms of their ability to meet the following four goals: *efficiency* (primarily reduce rent dissipation, the unnecessary expenditure of resources to secure the catch); *biodiversity preservation* (primarily maximize the number of viable river runs); *equitable distribution* of the economic value of the harvest (to current license holders, to Aboriginal fishers, and to taxpayers); and *political feasibility*. On the basis of this evaluation, the analysis concludes that the minister should move toward the adoption of river-specific, exclusive ownership and harvesting rights (with cooperative ownership on the Fraser River). Individual transferable quotas (ITQs) also have the potential to improve significantly the efficiency and equity of the fishery. While it would probably not be as efficient as the preferred alternative, it is probably more politically feasible, as indicated by recent implementation of ITQs for other British Columbia fisheries.

River-specific exclusive ownership rights would ensure efficient resource use through incentives to use the lowest-cost fishing technology. It would also eliminate most public costs. As designed here, this alternative should ensure biodiversity protection. With compensation to incumbents (as described), it should be equitable to the major relevant constituencies.

Experience in other countries over the last decade suggests that boat-based ITQs would largely eliminate rent dissipation (although it is not the lowest-cost harvesting method for catching salmon). Effective implementation of the quotas would probably be the greatest challenge (poor implementation would reduce many of the benefits of the structural efficiency improvements). Nevertheless, a study of experiences in other countries (particularly New Zealand and Iceland) suggests that ITQs can be implemented in such a way that efficiency is substantially improved. This alternative could also be designed and implemented so that salmon biodiversity is maintained (provided share catches rather than fixed quotas are utilized), and it would be equitable to relevant groups.

INTRODUCTION

A recent review of commercial fisheries around the world concludes: "The world's fisheries face the crises of dwindling stocks, overcapitalization, and disputes over jurisdiction."[1] In Canada, the collapse of the Atlantic cod fishery dramatically illustrated the risks of mismanagement: losses to the Canadian economy, personal hardship to those in the fishing and related industries, and the adverse fiscal impacts of adjustment expenditures by the government. Does current policy provide an adequate basis for effective management of the British Columbia (BC) salmon fishery? Do alternative policies offer the prospect for better management? In addressing these issues, this analysis draws on numerous previous analyses of the BC salmon fishery as well as on theoretical and empirical analyses of salmon fisheries and other fisheries worldwide.

THE BC SALMON FISHERY

The commercial salmon fishery on the west coast is an important Canadian industry, especially for the province of British Columbia. The average value of the commercial salmon harvest over a recent twenty-year period was approximately $260 million (in 1995 Canadian dollars) but has dropped considerably in the last five years.[2] The fishery, if effectively managed, has the potential to generate benefits considerably in excess of the costs required to harvest the fish. This value is known as economic, or scarcity, rent. However, mismanagement of the fishery can potentially dissipate some, or even all, of this rent by encouraging too much investment in fishing effort. The evidence suggests that dissipation of the economic rent offered by fisheries is a common worldwide phenomenon.[3] Indeed, mismanagement

[1] R. Quentin Grafton, Dale Squires, and James Kirkley, "Private Property Rights and Crises in World Fisheries: Turning the Tide?" *Contemporary Economic Policy* 14(4) 1996, 90–99, at p. 90.

[2] Richard Schwindt, Aidan Vining, and David Weimer, "A Policy Analysis of the BC Salmon Fishery," *Canadian Public Policy* 29(1) 2003, 1–22, Figure 1, at p. 2.

[3] Jeffrey Sachs and Andrew Warner, "The Curse of Natural Resources," *European Economic Review* 45(4–6) 2001, 827–39.

combined with other misguided policies could lead to social costs in excess of total economic rent.[4] To what extent are potential rents from the BC salmon fishery being dissipated?

ECONOMICS OF THE FISHERY: THE OPEN-ACCESS CASE

It is useful to contrast the current state of the salmon fishery with what would likely occur if it were to operate as an unregulated resource. In the unregulated fishery, we assume that individual fishers cannot be excluded from access to fish until the fish are actually appropriated in the process of fishing—in other words, there is competitive "open access" and a "law of capture" applies. An open-access salmon fishery can be best understood and analyzed as a public goods problem, that is, one in which the good is rivalrous in consumption (if one individual captures and consumes a salmon, that particular fish is not available to any other individual) but in which exclusion is not economically feasible. Extensive theoretical and empirical research on open-access resources in general, and on fisheries in particular, characterizes the consequences of open access: most importantly, too much of the resource will be harvested from the social perspective.[5] Fishers will find it in their individual self-interest to fish until the costs they see of catching an additional fish (their marginal cost) just equal the price of the fish (their marginal benefit). Their individual efforts, however, increase the marginal costs of all other fishers by reducing the stock of fish available for catching.

Before the arrival of Europeans, open access of the salmon fishery as just described may not have presented an economic problem because supply exceeded demand at zero price. It is certainly plausible to posit that there was an Aboriginal fishery in the distant past before the arrival of Europeans in which salmon were essentially "free goods," so that the catches of individuals did not increase the marginal costs borne by other fishers. In such circumstances, the indigenous peoples of the northwest coast would have been free to exploit the salmon fishery fully without depleting the resource in any meaningful economic sense.[6]

There is, however, considerable historical evidence that, even before the European incursion, increasing demand for fish had moved much of the Aboriginal salmon fishery beyond the status of a free good. However, rather than allowing an open-access situation to arise, the indigenous population had developed a system of private and common property ownership.[7] The northwest coast Aboriginal salmon

[4] Robert Deacon, "Incomplete Ownership, Rent Dissipation, and the Return to Related Investments," *Economic Inquiry* 32(4) 1994, 655–83; Richard Schwindt, Aidan Vining, and Steven Globerman, "Net Loss: A Cost-Benefit Analysis of the Canadian Pacific Salmon Fishery," *Journal of Policy Analysis and Management* 19(1) 2000, 23–45.

[5] See H. Scott Gordon, "The Economic Theory of a Common-Property Resource: The Fishery," *Journal of Political Economy* 62, 1954, 124–42; and Anthony Scott, "The Fishery: The Objectives of Sole Ownership," *Journal of Political Economy* 63(2) 1955, 116–24.

[6] Robert Higgs, "Legally Induced Technical Regress in the Washington Salmon Fishery," 247–79, in Lee Alston, Thrainn Eggertsson, and Douglass North, eds., *Empirical Studies in Institutional Change* (New York: Cambridge University Press, 1996).

[7] Anthony Netboy, *Salmon of the Pacific Northwest: Fish vs. Dams* (Portland, OR: Binfords and Mort, 1958); Russell Barsh, *The Washington Fishing Rights Controversy: An Economic Critique* (Seattle: University of Washington Graduate School of Business Administration, 1977).

fishery was generally a terminal, or river, fishery that caught fish in an efficient manner using weirs and traps.[8] Most importantly, the fishery was efficient in a temporal sense; the aboriginal population had both the incentives and social organization to allow sufficient spawning fish through to replenish the stock.[9]

The influx of the nonindigenous Europeans, who, in practice, were not subject to the extant indigenous property rights, created an open-access regime. Not only were the new users not excluded from the river-mouth fishery, they also introduced technology that allowed them to leapfrog Aboriginal riverine fisheries by fishing in the open sea.[10] This leapfrogging created an open-access environment and it introduced less cost-effective fishing methods. One estimate is that in the 1930s, traps in neighboring Washington State were approximately two-thirds more cost-effective than the emerging small-boat fishery, and that, without the interception of fish by the small-boat fishers, the traps could have been five-sixths more cost-effective.[11] The history of the regulation of the fishery makes clear that the incentive to leapfrog with new technology has remained strong.

A BRIEF HISTORY OF GOVERNMENT REGULATION OF THE FISHERY

The history of the salmon fishery has been well documented.[12] For this analysis, it is sufficient to review briefly four eras of policy development: the early fishery, the Sinclair Report/Davis Plan, the Pearse Commission, and the 1996 Mifflin Plan and subsequent buy-backs up to the year 2001.

Early History: Open Access

By the 1880s, there were already signs of overfishing in BC, especially on the Fraser River. The overfishing paralleled problems experienced on the Columbia and Sacramento rivers.[13] It appears that open access had begun to lead to reductions in returning stocks. Licenses were introduced, but as much for their revenue potential as to deter entry. In 1887, the first formal attempts were unsuccessfully made to restrict entry. The first restrictions on entry were made in 1908, but new licenses

[8]Richard Schwindt, "The Case for an Expanded Indian Fishery: Efficiency, Fairness, and History," in Helmar Drost, Brian Lee Crowley, and Richard Schwindt, eds., *Market Solutions for Native Poverty* (Toronto: C. D. Howe Institute, 1995); Higgs, "Legally Induced Technical Regress in the Washington Salmon Fishery."

[9]Higgs, "Legally Induced Technical Regress in the Washington Salmon Fishery."

[10]Fay Cohen, Treaties on Trial: The Continuing Controversy over Northwest Indian Fishing Rights (Seattle: University of Washington Press, 1986).

[11]Higgs, "Legally Induced Technical Regress in the Washington Salmon Fishery," pp. 273–74.

[12]These sources include Sol Sinclair, *Licence Limitation—British Columbia: A Method of Economic Fisheries Management* (Ottawa: Department of Fisheries, 1960); Alex Fraser, *Licence Limitation in the British Columbia Salmon Fishery*, Technical Report Series No. PAC/T-77-13 (Vancouver: Department of the Environment, Fisheries and Marine Services, 1977); Daniel Boxberger, *To Fish in Common: The Ethnohistory of Lummi Indian Salmon Fishing* (Lincoln: University of Nebraska Press, 1989); Schwindt, "The Case for an Expanded Indian Fishery"; Higgs, "Legally Induced Technical Regress in the Washington Salmon Fishery"; Schwindt, Vining, and Weimer, "A Policy Analysis of the BC Salmon Fishery."

[13]Fraser, *Licence Limitation in the British Columbia Salmon Fishery*.

were issued in 1914, and limitations on licenses were suspended completely in 1917. Effective entry restrictions were not implemented again until the late 1960s.

Between the end of the First World War and the 1950s, pressure on the fish stocks increased both from new entrants and increased investments in capital and labor by both incumbents and new entrants. The growing problem of overcapitalization had long been recognized. The 1917 report of the BC Commissioner of Fisheries noted, "The solution of this problem would not seem to be found in encouraging or permitting the employment of more capital or more labour than can efficiently perform the work. ... If the cost of production becomes too great all hope of advantage to the public as consumers will disappear."[14]

The Sinclair Report/Davis Plan

With pressure on the fish stocks continuing to mount, the federal government commissioned Sol Sinclair, an economist, to provide a detailed report on the fishery and to make recommendations for improving its management. Sinclair identified three policy alternatives: creating exclusive property rights to the resource through a monopoly; using taxes to discourage overcapitalization; and closing entry.[15] In spite of these recommendations, the federal government was reluctant to stop entry: "a policy of restricted entry would run counter to the popular notion that participation by any citizen in the fishery was a natural right."[16] Rather than directly challenging this popular view, government chose to restrict fishing incrementally, especially through restrictions on fishing times and locations: "Resource rents were dissipated as before, but the danger of physical exhaustion of the stocks was lessened."[17] The other alternatives were even less politically popular, as they would directly harm incumbent fishers—the most organized and vocal group. In 1968, license limitation was introduced under the Davis Plan (named after the then–Minister of Fisheries) to little opposition: "incumbent vessel owners generally approved of the plan ... the revocation of rights provoked no public outcry ... the interest group adversely affected (potential participants) was dispersed, unorganized, and undoubtedly incapable of calculating the loss."[18]

The Davis Plan also included the first effort to reduce the size of the fleet by a voluntary buy-back. But this aspect of the plan suffered from a "vicious circle" syndrome that has also affected subsequent voluntary buy-back efforts: the buy-back raises the market value of all remaining licenses (the anticipated fishing effort reduction "capitalizes" into the remaining licenses); this, in turn, raises the cost of the buy-back and quickly exhausts the buy-back budget. Clearly, even after the buy-back, there remained many more than the number of vessels that would max-

[14]Ibid., p. 5.

[15]Sinclair, *Licence Limitation—British Columbia: A Method of Economic Fisheries Management*, pp. 101–106.

[16]Don DeVoretz and Richard Schwindt, "Harvesting Canadian Fish and Rents: A Partial Review of the Report of the Commission on Canadian Pacific Fisheries Policy," *Marine Resource Economics* 1(4) 1985, 5–23, at p. 130.

[17]Ibid., p. 131.

[18]Schwindt, "The Case for an Expanded Indian Fishery," p. 106.

imize rent.[19] A final important consequence of the Davis Plan was that it effectively "froze" vessel types to seine, gillnet, troll, and gillnet-troll boats, which have very different capabilities and efficiencies.

Apart from failing to eliminate excess incumbent boats, the Achilles heel of the Davis Plan was that it did nothing to curb overcapitalization unrelated to entry. Indeed, it worsened the problem. Incumbents were now relatively fixed in number and therefore only had to compete with each other for the rents. They did this by replacing older boats with newer ones and purchasing ancillary technology, a process known as *capital-stuffing*. This is a widely occurring problem in fisheries with entry restrictions.[20] The buy-back was somewhat effective through most of the 1970s as salmon prices rose, but landed values dropped substantially between 1978 and 1983. New entrants who gained access by purchasing licenses from incumbents found themselves facing a financial crisis (many "old" incumbents who had held licenses when the Davis Plan was implemented had become rich enough to retire on their windfall gains). These conditions led to the 1982 Pearse Commission.

The Pearse Commission

The Pearse Commission, after extensive hearings, again noted the disastrous state of the fishery: "the economic circumstances of the commercial fisheries are exceptionally bleak ... [and] ... there is growing concern about the precarious condition of many of our fish stocks."[21] In spite of this situation, economist Peter H. Pearse pointed out that the primary problem was *not* the size of the harvest, which had remained relatively stable for approximately 50 years, whether measured in terms of number of fish or landed weight. The combination of restricted openings, gear restrictions, riverine protection, and salmon enhancement were generally succeeding in protecting the viability of the stocks. However, Pearse argued that the catch was still considerably below the potential sustainable yield. This was partly because of degradation of fish habitat by the forest industry and other land-based developments that are subject to provincial jurisdiction.

The Pearse Commission concluded that previous efforts to limit boat length and tonnage alone had not successfully restricted capital-stuffing: "when one or more inputs in the fishing process are restricted, the capacity of the fleet can continue to increase by adding other unrestricted inputs."[22] While regulators could conceivably continue to place more input dimensions under restriction, "such restrictions would have to be so numerous and diverse (covering vessel size, power, crew, time spent fishing, gear for finding, catching and holding fish, and so on) that they would be virtually impossible to administer and enforce."[23]

The Pearse Commission's recommendations are comprehensive and complex. The most important recommendation was that royalty taxes be imposed on the

[19]See Peter H. Pearse, *Turning the Tide*; see also Diane Dupont, "Rent Dissipation in Restricted Access Fisheries," *Journal of Environmental Economics and Management* 19(1) 1990, 26–44.

[20]Ralph Townsend, "Entry Restrictions in the Fishery: A Survey of the Evidence," *Land Economics* 66(4) 1990, 359–78.

[21]Pearse, *Turning the Tide*, p. vii.

[22]Ibid., 83; see also R. Rettig, "License Limitation in the United States and Canada: An Assessment," *North American Journal of Fisheries Management* 4(3) 1984, 231–48

[23]Pearse, *Turning the Tide*, p. 83.

salmon catch: "a realistic portion of revenues derived from commercial fisheries should now be directed away from excess catching capacity toward recouping these costs to the public, reducing bloated fleets and enhancing the resource."[24] Note that although the distributional consequences of the tax are emphasized in this quote, such a tax would also be efficiency-enhancing because the revenues that would now go to government previously represented economic waste. Thus, such a tax both preserves and transfers the rent. Pearse recommended that a royalty rate of between 5 and 10 percent of the gross value of the harvest be imposed on buyers (that is, mostly on the fish processors). Pearse did not discuss the incidence of this royalty tax, but subsequent analysis suggests that it would be spread among foreign consumers, domestic consumers, processors, and fishers.[25]

Pearse also recommended reducing the fishing capacity of the fleet by approximately 50 percent by buying back licenses and by auctioning licenses for ten-year periods. The major features of the proposed auction were as follows: in the first year, ten-year licences representing 10 percent of the target capacity of the fleet would be competitively auctioned. In each of the nine subsequent years, a further 10 percent would be auctioned. During the first ten-year period only existing license holders would be allowed to bid. Bids would be in sealed envelopes and would be ranked from the highest offer downward. The bid value of the lowest accepted bid would determine the price to be paid by all successful applicants. Each license would specify the gear, vessel capacity, and zone from which fish could be taken. Bids would be expressed in dollars per ton of vessel capacity sought. No individual or corporation would be allowed to acquire new licenses if, as a result, they would hold more than 5 percent of the total available licenses. Finally, during the initial ten-year period incumbent fishers could sell their license to a buy-back authority at market value.

Pearse acknowledged that the proposal to reduce fishing capacity by 50 percent was greater than apparent excess capacity. But he argued that "many underestimate the *potential* capacity of the fleet unencumbered by many of the restrictions on time, location and gear that have been imposed to constrain fishing power."[26]

The major Pearse Commission recommendations relating to the salmon fishery were not implemented.

1996–2001: The Mifflin Plan and Subsequent Restructuring

At the end of 1995, the size of the fleet was much as it had been in 1982, at the time of the Pearse Commission. In 1982, there had been 4,470 extant salmon licenses; in 1995, the number was 4,367.[27] However, fishing power had increased enormously over this period because of continued capital-stuffing. The then Minister of Fisheries summarized the problem succinctly: "a fundamental cause of the increased difficulty in managing the salmon fishery is that the size of the fleet has remained static while its fishing power has increased dramatically."[28] The fishing power of the fleet meant

[24]Ibid., p. 93.
[25]DeVoretz and Schwindt, "Harvesting Canadian Fish and Rents."
[26]Pearse, *Turning the Tide*, p. 111.
[27]Schwindt, Vining, and Globerman, "Net Loss."
[28]Brian Tobin, "Statement in Response to the Report of the Fraser River Sockeye Public Review Board," Montreal, March 7, 1995.

that the major mechanism available for protecting fish stocks was strong restrictions on the time in which the fishery was open. While this approach generally protected the viability of stocks, for many river runs there was little margin for error given the immense fishing capacity that could be deployed. This, in turn, put tremendous pressure on marine scientists in the Department of Fisheries and Oceans to get their estimates of specific run sizes right. Many marine biologists feared that one or more runs were vulnerable: "Our current fishery … will very likely go the same way as [the] Atlantic Canada [cod fishery] within the next few decades if profound steps are not taken to restructure and protect it."[29]

In March 1996, the federal government introduced the Pacific Salmon Revitalization Strategy, known as the Mifflin Plan, after the DFO minister at the time. The plan proposed to reduce the fleet in two ways. First, $80 million was allocated to a voluntary license buy-back program. Under this buy-back the total fleet was reduced by 1,173 vessels, or approximately 27 percent of the extant capacity. Second, "area licensing" was imposed, consisting of two geographic regions for seine vessels and three regions for gillnet and troll vessels. Existing license holders had to select one geographic area. However, they could "stack" licenses by purchasing them from other license holders. The Mifflin Plan did not address other aspects of capital-stuffing. For example, because of technological advances, seine vessels that in the past were only capable of making four "sets" a day now make more than twenty-five sets a day.[30] Area licensing was a further attempt to reduce congestion externalities, but given the large number of vessels remaining in each area, the impact has been small.

In the following years, there was widespread recognition that the fleet was still too big. In 1998 and 1999, the federal government committed an additional $400 million to the fishery, with approximately half budgeted for further buy-backs.[31] By 2002, the fleet was down to 1,881 vessels, a 57 percent reduction.[32] The Mifflin Plan and its immediate successors represent the current salmon fishery regime. The next section of this report summarizes the evidence on the current state of the fishery, and projects the probable impacts these changes will have in the future.

THE CURRENT AND EXPECTED STATE OF THE FISHERY

Will the 1996–2001 fleet reductions eliminate or substantially reduce rent dissipation? Will they adequately protect salmon stocks? The buy-backs have resulted in a substantial short-run reduction in capacity. Yet the historical experience suggests that the remaining incumbents will be tempted into a new round of capital-stuffing. In order to assess the current state of the fishery, it is useful to ask: what is the economic cost of rent dissipation, and how might buy-backs and other forms of cost reduction mitigate it?

[29]Carl Walters, *Fish on the Line* (Vancouver: David Suzuki Foundation, 1995), at p. 4.

[30]R. Quentin Grafton and Harry Nelson, "Fisher's Individual Salmon Harvesting Rights: An Option for Canada's Pacific Fisheries," *Canadian Journal of Fisheries and Aquatic Sciences* 54(2) 1997, 474–82.

[31]See Schwindt, Vining, and Weimer, "A Policy Analysis of the BC Salmon Fishery," Table 1, p. 5.

[32]Ibid., p. 6, and Table 2.

A recent cost-benefit analysis of the BC salmon fishery can serve as a basis for answering some of these questions, although it was conducted before both the most recent buy-backs and the recent decline in salmon volume and value of landings. The analysts estimated annual costs and benefits for specific elements of the fishery: value of the harvest, harvesting costs of participants in the industry, government expenditures on management, enhancement, enforcement, and unemployment insurance payments.[33] The *net present value (NPV)*, a measure of the stream of net benefits of the fishery expressed in terms of an equivalent amount of current consumption, under various assumptions, was estimated using a twenty-five-year time horizon and a base-case (real) discount rate of 5 percent (sensitivity analysis was also carried out using 3 and 7 percent).

The analysis assumed that the fishery was being managed close to its maximum sustainable yield. The initial estimate of the NPV of the fishery assumed no Mifflin Plan. Under one assumption, unemployment insurance (UI) payments were treated as a cost of the fishery, and under another assumption they were treated as not relevant.[34] Under either assumption, the NPV was *negative*, indicating net social losses in terms of current consumption equivalents. The NPV of the fishery was estimated at either –$783.6 million (UI not included) or –$1,572.9 million (UI included). Thus, its operation prior to the Mifflin Plan appeared to involve a substantial net loss to the Canadian economy.

What has been the impact of the Mifflin Plan? It was primarily a buy-back plan, but it also increased locational constraints through area licensing. Subsequent buy-backs also involved some other relatively minor policy changes. One optimistic assumption is that all of the boat retirements induced by the buy-backs will go straight to "the bottom line" *and stay there*. In other words, the boat retirements will represent capital permanently removed from the fishery. The authors of the cost-benefit analysis present a number of alternative estimates of the impact that the Mifflin buy-back (but not the subsequent buy-backs) might have on both private and public costs. They estimate that if private costs are reduced by 27 percent, approximately equivalent to the percentage of the fleet that has been retired under Mifflin, and public costs are unchanged, then the NPV would be $101 million.[35] This is obviously a significant improvement over the pre-Mifflin NPV and indicates net economic benefits (albeit small) from operation of the fishery. However, significant economic rents would still be forgone.

In order to estimate the value of the forgone rents, the projected net benefits of the current fishery should be compared to the potential benefits of an efficiently organized fishery. In order to do this, one must make a number of assumptions about what an "efficient salmon fishery" means.

Schwindt, Vining, and Globerman argued that the fishery, even organized as a post-Mifflin small-boat fishery, could be fully exploited with approximately half the extant resources that were employed at that time. They based this estimate on the costs of the more efficient Alaskan salmon fishery, which had a lower-cost fleet. If the fishery were managed in this way, and assuming that public costs remained

[33]Schwindt, Vining, and Globerman, "Net Loss."
[34]Ibid., Table 8, p. 37.
[35]Ibid., Table 9.

the same, they estimated that the NPV of the fishery would increase to $1,140 million.[36]

In 2003, Schwindt, Vining, and Weimer provided NPVs that take into account the probable impact of subsequent buy-backs on private costs. Using all other Schwindt, Vining, and Globerman assumptions, they concluded that if "private costs are reduced (approximately equivalent to the percentage of the fleet that has been retired through buy-backs or stacking) and public costs remain the same ... the NPV of the fishery would be about $1,258 million."[37] Although this NPV of $1,258 million represents some improvement over $1,140 million, it is not much higher because the increased benefits of further fleet buy-backs are offset by new, less optimistic price and volume predictions.

Schwindt, Vining, and Weimer concluded that even this NPV is a very optimistic scenario, for two reasons. First, there are still private rents, and expected private rents are increased (because of the fleet reduction). As a result, the industry will remain attractive to most participants. Incumbents are likely to engage in a new round of capital-stuffing. This is foreshadowed in higher asking prices for licenses in 2002, which exceeded the prices paid in the last round of buy-backs. Second, even without capital-stuffing, the most plausible current prediction is that harvest volumes will only reach 75 percent of their 1995–2001 levels in the future and that prices will remain at recent (lower) levels. Given these assumptions (but still assuming a 60 percent sustained reduction in private costs), the analysts estimated that the NPV is –$951 million, a substantial loss to the Canadian economy.

It is useful to have some handle on the sources of rent dissipation in thinking about policy alternatives. Analysis based on 1982 harvest figures suggests that fleet composition is probably the major source of rent dissipation, with excess boats second and other margins of input substitution third.[38] The recent buy-backs did not directly address these issues, although more troll and gillnet boats were retired than the more efficient (in terms of effort-to-catch ratio) seiners. This suggests that incremental reform that does not alter, or eliminate, boat types will not be able to realize the largest potential rent gains.

In spite of the introduction of area licensing, current policy is also unlikely to protect vulnerable fishing runs adequately, especially if there is renewed capital-stuffing. There will still be huge capacity hovering over particular runs. The number of salmon can vary greatly from year to year, from area to area, and from species to species—sometimes by twenty- or thirty-fold. Under these conditions, incorrect volume and escapement estimates by the DFO could be catastrophic for preservation of runs.

POLICY GOALS

What policies should govern the BC salmon fishery? An answer to this question requires the specification of policy goals that provide an appropriate basis for comparing current policy with possible alternatives. The preceding discussion of problems inherent in the status quo immediately suggests a number of important goals.

[36]Schwindt, Vining, and Globerman, "Net Loss," Table 9, p. 38.
[37]Schwindt, Vining, and Weimer, "A Policy Analysis of the BC Salmon Fishery," p. 7.
[38]Dupont, "Rent Dissipation in Restricted Access Fisheries."

First, although the salmon fishery is a potentially valuable resource, because of rent dissipation it is currently a net drain on the wealth of the people of British Columbia and Canada. A primary policy goal, therefore, should be *economically efficient use* of the fishery. The primary measure of the projected impact of each alternative in terms of this goal is the *extent of rent dissipation*. It is important to note that merely achieving a positive NPV is not equivalent to eliminating rent dissipation. Additionally, we are interested in realizable rents. Therefore, implementation feasibility is an important dimension of efficiency. The two impacts used for assessing implementation feasibility are the *ease of enforcement* of regulations and the *degree of flexibility* to allow the policy to accommodate the dynamic and cyclical nature of salmon stocks.

Second, the current policy poses a risk to the preservation of salmon runs. Most Canadians place a positive value on preserving the fishery for multiple uses and future generations.[39] *Preservation of the fishery* should, therefore, be a policy goal. (We treat it as a separate goal, although it could be treated as a dimension of efficiency.) The primary criterion for measuring progress toward this goal is the impact on the *number of viable runs*.

Third, the costs and benefits of the fishery should be fairly distributed among important stakeholders. *Equitable distribution* should be a policy goal. Fairness requires that current license holders, who have made investment decisions based on a reasonable expectation that current policy will continue, receive explicit consideration. As current license holders, who may or may not themselves be fishers, are likely to be highly attentive to proposed policy changes and very vocal in opposition to changes they view as harmful, consideration of their interests is likely to contribute to the political feasibility of any policy alternative, an instrumental value beyond fairness itself. Aboriginal peoples have cultural, economic, and constitutionally protected stakes in the use of the salmon fishery. Any policy change should at least protect their interests. As alternative policies have implications for government revenues and expenditures, fairness to Canadian taxpayers should be a concern. (In this analysis, therefore, we treat impact on government revenues as a fairness issue, although it is certainly reasonable to consider it as a goal in its own right.) Although the federal government is just now getting its fiscal house in order, it still faces a large accumulated debt that burdens Canada with one of the worst ratios of national debt to gross domestic product among industrialized countries. Therefore, reducing subsidies from taxpayers to the fishery, or even capturing some fishery rent for the public treasury, is desirable. These considerations suggest that for assessing progress toward achieving an equitable distribution, we are interested in the impact on three groups: *fairness to current license holders*, *fairness to aboriginal fishers*, and *fairness to taxpayers*.

Fourth, *political feasibility* is always relevant to some degree. Radical alternatives are usually more politically difficult to achieve than more incremental change. There is more uncertainty as to the impacts of more radical policy alternatives, especially distributional impacts.

[39]This is known as existence value. See Aidan Vining and David Weimer, "Passive Use Benefits: Existence, Option, and Quasi-Option Value," 319–45, in Fred Thompson and Mark Green, eds., *Handbook of Public Finance* (New York: Marcel Dekker, 1998).

It is important to note that these goals are often in conflict. For example, while allowing small salmon runs to be extinguished might be consistent with a narrow definition of economic efficiency, it would conflict with the goal of preserving the fishery. Therefore, selecting the most socially desirable policy involves making trade offs among the goals.

SOME NEW WAYS OF ORGANIZING THE SALMON FISHERY

The analysis presented in the remainder of this report compares the status quo policy to the following three alternatives.

The Pearse Commission Proposal: Harvesting Royalties and License Auction

This alternative recycles the Pearse Commission recommendations. Specifically, it includes a royalty tax of 10 percent, the ten-year rolling license auction, and the 50 percent buy-back, as described above. The Pearse Commission also proposed providing financial assistance to the Aboriginal bands to further their participation in license purchases ($20 million over five years) and a ban on licenses that were held by Aboriginal fishing corporations from being sold to non-Aboriginals. As described earlier, extensive buy-backs have now taken place (although not in the manner recommended by Pearse), but most of the other recommendations of the Pearse Commission were never adopted. Many fisheries experts regard the Pearse Commission recommendations as exemplary.

River-Specific Exclusive Ownership (with Cooperative Ownership on the Fraser)

This alternative largely follows the proposal put forward by Schwindt, Vining, and Weimer.[40] Under this alternative the right to catch all salmon entering each river system would be allocated to a single owner for a period of twenty-five years ("single" ownership could include corporate or nonprofit ownership). During the last five years incumbents would only be allowed to catch the same average number of fish as in the first five years of their tenure. The small-boat fishery would be bought out and disbanded. Owners would almost certainly adopt fish traps and weirs, the lowest cost method of catching salmon.[41] Current incumbents of the small-boat fishery would receive compensation for their withdrawn licenses from the government equal to license market value plus a 50 percent premium. It is proposed that payments would be annualized over fifteen years; the payments would include interest at market rates.

[40]Schwindt, Vining, and Weimer, "A Policy Analysis of the BC Salmon Fishery," pp. 10–20.

[41]Some analysts have argued that in-river fish are inherently of lower quality that those caught out to sea, but this is unlikely to be an issue with modern technology (Schwindt, "The Case for an Expanded Indian Fishery").

Compensation necessarily has some element of arbitrariness. The rationale for a level of compensation greater than license value is that market value would fully compensate marginal fishers (who, with the payments, would be indifferent between staying in or leaving the fishery) but not fishers who would not be willing to sell at market prices (whether because of superior skill, utility from the fishing lifestyle, or other reasons). First Nations would receive a percentage of the ownership rights at least equal to their current (approximate) 19 percent of commercial fishing licenses. Fish hatcheries would be included in the ownership rights, and owners would have the right to continue using them or closing them down.

The only river system in BC where it will be impossible from a practical standpoint to sell rights to a single owner is the Fraser River. The Fraser accounts for more than 50 percent of the sockeye, pink salmon, and chinook originating from Canadian Pacific waters.[42] Sockeye (approximately 30 percent of the total catch) and pink (approximately 48 percent of the total catch) are the most important species in commercial fishery by a considerable margin. While there are other important rivers for particular species (for example, the Skeena accounts for approximately 12 percent of Pacific sockeye runs), no other single river presents insurmountable "single-owner" problems. On the Fraser, a cooperative would be established by the federal government.[43] It is important that this cooperative be organized so that it is not subject to its own set of open-effort problems. In view of the number of appropriators involved and the other characteristics of the Fraser fishery, a reasonably efficient fishery should be achievable.[44]

Individual Transferable Quotas

One widely recommended regime for fisheries is *individual transferable quotas (ITQs)*. ITQs are now widely used in New Zealand, Iceland, Australia, South Africa, the United States, and Canada.[45] Specifically, they have been used with some evidence of success in both the BC halibut fishery[46] and the BC sablefish fishery.[47] A recent volume published by the Fraser Institute considers ITQs among several possible alternatives for improving the BC salmon fishery.[48] A tremendous amount has been learned over the last decade from the experiences in New Zealand and Iceland as to the appropriate structure of ITQs in fisheries with high stock variability.[49]

[42]Pearse, *Turning the Tide*, Appendix D.

[43]Schwindt, Vining, and Weimer, "A Policy Analysis of the BC Salmon Fishery," pp. 11–12, describe how such a cooperative could be organized.

[44]See Elinor Ostrom, *Governing the Commons: The Evolution of Institutions for Collective Action* (Cambridge: Cambridge University Press, 1990).

[45]Grafton, Squires, and Kirkley, "Private Property Rights and Crises in World Fisheries"; see also R. Quentin Grafton, "Individual Transferable Quotas: Theory and Practice," *Reviews in Fish Biology and Fisheries* 6(1) 1996, 5–20.

[46]Keith Casey, Christopher Dewees, Bruce Turris, and James Wilen, "The Effects of Individual Vessel Quotas in the British Columbia Halibut Fishery," *Marine Resource Economics* 10(3) 1995, 211–30.

[47]Grafton, "Individual Transferable Quotas."

[48]Laura Jones and Michael Walker, eds., *Fish or Cut Bait!* (Vancouver: The Fraser Institute, 1997).

[49]See John Annala, "New Zealand's ITQ System: Have the First Eight Years Been a Success or Failure?" *Reviews in Fish Biology and Fisheries* 6(1) 1996, 43–62; and Ragnar Arnason, "On the ITQ Fisheries Management System in Iceland," *Reviews in Fish Biology and Fisheries* 6(1) 1996, 63–90.

ITQs would be allocated to percentage shares of the salmon total annual catch (TAC). Government biologists would continue to predict the TAC and would have the power to adjust it throughout the harvesting season. Fixed quotas offer more certainty and, therefore, value to fishers, but allocation of shares rather than a number or weight of fish ensures that fishers bear the risks associated with the large temporal fluctuations in the salmon harvest.[50] The fishery would remain a small-boat fishery. Once allocated, quotas would be transferable to other incumbents or to potential new entrants. The quotas would be allocated to incumbents in the small-boat fishery based on previous average catch history.[51] The government would also collect a tax from each share owner based on the amount of quota held rather than on fish caught. The proposed fee would equal 5 percent of the value of the TAC. While it is not possible to discuss all the details of this alternative here, it would operate very much like the current New Zealand regime, which is explained in depth elsewhere.[52]

A COMPARISON OF THE ALTERNATIVES

The following discussion compares the status quo, harvesting royalties and license auction, river-specific auctioned monopolies, and individual transferable quotas in terms of economically efficient use, preservation of the fishery, equitable distribution, and political feasibility.

Status Quo: The Mifflin Plan and Subsequent Restructurings

Efficiency. The status quo will perform poorly in terms of efficiency, especially over the longer term. Over time, new capital-stuffing will negate any short-term benefits in regard to capacity reduction. Within five to ten years, there will probably be little difference in effective capacity compared to that at the time of the 1996–2001 buy-backs. At best, there would be approximately a net 10 percent decrease in capacity. Also, as with all the small-boat alternatives, the status quo does not move toward the lowest-cost catch technology. It is an inflexible regulatory regime. Experience with it helps counter its inherent difficulties to some extent. Therefore, in NPV terms, the status quo will probably turn out to be essentially no different from the pre-Mifflin situation from an efficiency perspective.

Preservation. This is probably the most difficult consequence of the status quo policy to predict. Much depends on specific decisions made by DFO biologists. The outcome could range from "poor" (where small, variable stocks are continually under threat) to "reasonable" (where these stocks are protected). However, it is

[50]For a discussion of the trade-offs between shares and fixed quota under ITQs, see Carl Walters and Peter Pearse, "Stock Information Requirements for Quota Management Systems in Commercial Fisheries," *Reviews in Fish Biology and Fisheries* 6(1) 1996, 21–42.

[51]For example, see Arnason, "On the ITQ Fisheries Management System in Iceland," p. 73.

[52]For an analysis of the New Zealand model, see Annala, "New Zealand's ITQ System"; and Laura Jones, "A Pilot Project for Individual Quotas in the Salmon Fishery," in Jones and Walker, *Fish or Cut Bait!*, pp. 115–24.

impossible to be optimistic under the status quo because of the tremendous fishing power that continues to "hover" at every opening river and the continued incentive to "race to fish" (although the situation has been somewhat improved by the introduction of area licensing that reduces excess fishing capacity at particular river openings). Any miscalculation by DFO, whether by the biologists, by more senior officials succumbing to political pressure, or from enforcement difficulties, could lead to small-run extinctions.[53] Thus, at best, the status quo must be rated as medium on this goal.

Equity. In one sense, the status quo can be thought of as being very generous to incumbents: it provides them with de facto property rights to the resource at nominal prices. On the other hand, if the rent is largely dissipated, this is not the "bargain" it seems to be. The situation is approximately the same for Aboriginal fishers. The current system, however, is very inequitable to taxpayers: as documented earlier in the analysis, rather than collecting resource rents, taxpayers end up paying a large net subsidy to the fishery.

Political Feasibility. Absent reductions in viable runs or a Supreme Court of Canada–imposed reallocation of fishing rights to First Nations, keeping the current regulatory regime in place is politically feasible.

The Pearse Commission Proposal: Harvesting Royalties and License Auction

Efficiency. A major advantage of this policy alternative relative to the status quo is in terms of efficiency: it would preserve more of the potential rent. The proposed license buy-back would have considerably reduced excess fishing capacity. Although almost twenty years late, the percentage reduction recommended by Pearse has now been achieved. It is, of course, impossible to know what further reductions Pearse would now regard as appropriate, given technological progress in the intervening twenty years. Equally important, this regime would eliminate incentives (through royalties and the license auction) to begin another round of capital-stuffing to replace the retired capacity. Because the Pearse Commission proposal retains the small-boat fishery, it probably only has the potential to reduce fishing costs approximately halfway to their lowest potential level (that is, costs under an efficiently organized terminal fishery). However, how much rent is preserved crucially depends on the extent to which the combination of royalty rate and auction would actually extract rents. A 5 percent royalty rate would not preserve and extract much of the rent, but the auction license, if competitive and appropriately designed, should preserve and extract most of it.[54] We know a great deal more about the practical issues involved in running public sector auctions than was known in 1982, at the time of the Pearse Commission.[55] This proposal would also

[53]On these problems in the Atlantic fishery, see A. Bruce Arai, "Policy and Practice in the Atlantic Fisheries: Problems of Regulatory Enforcement," *Canadian Public Policy* 40(4) 1994, 353–64.

[54]DeVoretz and Schwindt, "Harvesting Canadian Fish and Rents."

[55]R. Preston McAfee and John McMillan, "Analyzing the Airways Auction," *Journal of Economic Perspectives*, 10(1) 1996, 159–75.

encourage the gradual transfer of licenses to fishers who can exploit the resource most efficiently. The primary efficiency weakness of this alternative is that it takes the small-boat fishery as a given, so that the harvest cannot be taken at lowest cost (similarly, see discussions of status quo above and ITQs below).

Enforcement under this regime would be more complex than under the status quo, as taxing on the basis of catch volume would require extensive monitoring of all boats because incentives for "highgrading" (discarding overboard of less valuable fish and the substituting of more valuable fish to stay within catch limits—it is individually rational, but socially wasteful) and "quota-busting" (smuggling) would be much greater. Threat of license loss should be the major deterrent to such behaviors.[56] Nevertheless, the need for more extensive monitoring makes enforcement more difficult than under the status quo.

Preservation. A weakness of this alternative is that it can endanger specific fish stocks and thus is weak in terms of resource conservation. Indeed, this is probably its major weakness. The reason is that a royalty tax is inherently a price mechanism rather than a quantity (restriction) mechanism. There are risks in using price mechanisms when there is uncertainty over stocks and the costs of being wrong are potentially high in terms of species, or subspecies, extinction.[57] Quantity mechanisms, such as quotas and opening restrictions, lower the risk of catch "overshooting" that can threaten stock viability. Of course, it is possible to design an intermediate alternative that incorporates opening (that is, quantity) restrictions, but this raises (public) expenditures on the fishery. Such a proposal is not examined here.

Equity. The major concession to existing fishers in the Pearse proposal was the ongoing buy-back of licenses. This would allow those who were prepared to leave the industry to avoid capital losses. Remaining fishers would have greatly reduced incentives to engage in overcapitalization because the government would be extracting the rent from the fishery—partly in royalties but largely through the license auction. However, if the license auction process is reasonably competitive, all expected rents would be transferred to the government. It is, therefore, remaining fishers who would suffer the loss of economic rents. There is some justice in this in that they are presumably those who would get the most utility from actually fishing.

Pearse proposed some financial assistance to Aboriginals to acquire licenses over a five-year period (see above). It is fair to say that perceptions have changed since 1982 as to what would be fair to Aboriginals and that many would now argue that Pearse's subsidy to the First Nations population was low. The Supreme Court of Canada might well take that view. On the other hand, it would still place Aboriginals in a considerably better position than the status quo.

[56]Rick Boyd and Christopher Dewees, "Putting Theory into Practice: Individual Transferable Quotas in New Zealand's Fisheries," *Society and Natural Resources* 5(2) 1992, 179–98; Annala, "New Zealand's ITQ System."

[57]See Wallace Oates and Paul Portney, "Economic Incentives and the Containment of Global Warming," *Eastern Economic Journal* 18(1) 1992, 85–98.

This alternative would generate extensive (new) government revenues (probably more through the auction than the royalties) and might reduce government expenditures slightly. The reduced government expenditures should occur because fishing capacity would be reduced, thus reducing fleet monitoring costs. In general, the taxpayers' position would be much improved. Estimating the exact size of the benefit is difficult, though, because auction receipts are difficult to predict.

Political Feasibility. The loss of rents by remaining fishers would likely mobilize them in opposition to the plan.

River-Specific Exclusive Ownership Rights (with Cooperative Ownership on the Fraser)

Efficiency. The advantage of this alternative is that it is the *lowest-cost* fish-catching regime and, therefore, offers the potential of being the most efficient—at least 50 percent lower cost than the small-boat fishery alternatives. As owners would have long-term property rights, they would have the correct conservation incentives. It is important to emphasize that the term *monopoly* as used here is only a monopoly to a single river system and, therefore, does not imply the inefficiencies society would normally incur from monopoly supply of a good. This form of monopoly would be efficiency-enhancing because much of the open effort associated with the small-boat fishery would be eliminated, without creating any effective market power. Indeed, even if a single owner controlled all of the BC monopolies, that owner would be unable to exercise much monopoly pricing power, because salmon are sold into a competitive, global market. (Provided, of course, the government continues to allow free trade in salmon.)

The major problem with this alternative, from an efficiency perspective, is that, as discussed above, it would not be possible to have a single monopoly owner on the Fraser River. It is important that the regime proposed for the Fraser eliminate capital-stuffing and other forms of open effort. In order to ensure this, it is proposed that there would be a fixed, relatively small number of license holders.[58]

Preservation. This alternative also is likely to do well in terms of resource conservation, for two reasons. First, the monopoly owners have strong and unambiguous incentives to maximize the NPV of their stocks. Second, information is clearer as to the link between escapement and specific stock preservation. This may be somewhat more difficult in the Fraser context and may require a more extensive government oversight role.

Equity. Under this alternative, the small-boat fishery is retired; on the face of it, this does not look good for incumbent fishers. However, because this alternative is so efficient, it offers the potential for considerable rent, presumably well in excess of the $2 billion NPV estimated as being the best-case scenario under an ef-

[58]See Ostrom, *Governing the Commons;* and Elinor Ostrom and Roy Gardner, "Coping with Asymmetries in the Commons: Self-Governing Irrigation Systems Can Work," *Journal of Economic Perspectives* 7(4) 1993, 93–112.

ficiently organized small-boat fishery. Some of this rent could be used to compensate existing fishers—either in the form of direct payments, as described above, or by offering them preferential bidding rights (for example, by allowing them to bid with a 50-cent-per-dollar subsidy).

This alternative allocates a fixed percentage of monopolies to First Nations. It is, therefore, equitable to them relative to the status quo. The alternative would also enhance government revenues considerably, especially after small-boat license holders have been reimbursed. Overall, it would probably generate the largest benefit to taxpayers. The reason is that the river monopolies would be extremely valuable resources because they offer a low-cost regime for catching the fish. Licenses, therefore, would likely be auctioned for high prices; the total revenue from all river auctions should exceed considerably the total revenue from auctions of small-boat fishery licenses as proposed by Pearse.

Political Feasibility. This alternative is the most radical departure from the existing regulatory regime. It would induce a complete restructuring of the industry, which, along with its novelty, would make it politically difficult to achieve.

Individual Transferable Quota Scheme

Efficiency. Provided that fishers are reasonably certain that they can make their quota using current levels of inputs, ITQs should reduce incremental overcapitalization incentives, although not congestion externalities at specific river mouths. While, as yet, there have been no reported evaluations of ITQ fisheries based on actually realized costs and benefits, detailed reviews of both the New Zealand and Icelandic experiences with ITQs are now available. Annala concludes that the efficiency impacts have been positive and that "the economic performance of the industry has improved."[59] Arnason has similarly examined the impact of ITQs on the Icelandic fisheries. In general, he finds that total catches have increased and capital investment has been reduced, resulting in greatly improved "catch per unit effort."[60] Given that the small-boat fishery would remain, and given the other factors discussed here, this alternative would reduce, but not minimize, rent dissipation, because it would not induce a switch to the lowest-cost technology.

There is some disagreement on the administrative costliness of ITQs. Incentives to engage in both quota-busting and highgrading are inherent to ITQs.[61] However, Annala, based on the New Zealand experience, considers one of the major gains from ITQs to be "minimal government intervention."[62] Grafton, on the other hand, concludes on the basis of a multi-country review that "an essential component to the success of ITQs, therefore, is adequate monitoring and enforcement."[63] On balance, the evidence from other countries suggests that these problems should be solvable in the salmon fishery without imposing massive public costs.

[59] Annala, "New Zealand's ITQ System."
[60] Arnason, "On the ITQ Fisheries Management System in Iceland," pp. 77–80, 83–84.
[61] Lee Anderson, "Highgrading in ITQ Fisheries," *Marine Resource Economics*, 9(3) 1994, 209–26.
[62] Annala, "New Zealand's ITQ System," p. 46.
[63] Grafton, "Individual Transferable Quotas," p. 18.

Preservation. ITQs regimes have generally been successful at preserving and, in many cases, enhancing, stocks. Resource conservation problems have occurred when total allocated catch has been set too high: this is an endemic problem that has little to do with ITQs, per se. In these cases biological preservation (or recovery) has remained a problem.[64] The salmon fishery is probably more vulnerable in this regard than most other fisheries where ITQs are being utilized (although some of these fisheries, such as the Icelandic capelin, also experience high stock variability). One advantage that ITQs would have in the salmon fishery is that the TAC under the new regime would not be very different from the current catch. In many other fisheries, ITQs have been introduced in open-access contexts or other situations in which the resource was in serious danger and resource-conserving TACs needed to be set considerably lower than current catches.[65]

Equity. Because the proposed regime allocates ITQs to incumbents with relatively low tax rates, it would be generous to those currently in the fishery. As rent dissipation would be considerably curbed, the rents would largely accrue to incumbents who would be substantially enriched. This has been the main criticism of the ITQ system in Iceland, where quota fees only amount to approximately 0.5 percent of estimated catch value: "Why, it is asked, should a relatively small group of fishing firms and their owners be handed, more or less free of charge, the extremely valuable property rights to the Icelandic fisheries?"[66] The proposal here is a considerable improvement on the Icelandic regime, as it would introduce a 5 percent quota fee.

This alternative does nothing for Aboriginal fishers, except to the extent that they hold commercial fishing licenses. Additionally, this alternative does relatively less for taxpayers, as the only rents transferred to them would result from the 5 percent quota fee. It is not clear that current government expenditures would be reduced either, because of the potential for high administrative costs.

Political Feasibility. The generosity of this plan for incumbent fishers, the most attentive stakeholder group, makes it the most political feasible alternative to the status quo.

EVALUATION AND RECOMMENDATION

The issues discussed in this section of the report are summarized in a simple matrix (Table 1.1) that presents policy alternatives on one dimension and the goals for assessing them on the other. It should be stressed that these are predictions, based on the extant research, of how each of the alternatives would perform in terms of the stated goals. Of course, the preferred alternative depends on how the minister

[64]Annala, "New Zealand's ITQ System"; Arnason, "On the ITQ Fisheries Management System in Iceland," comments on the Icelandic cod TAC: "The catches have simply been excessive compared with the reproductive capacity of the fish stocks ... [because] ... the TACs have been set too high" (p. 83).

[65]R. Francis, D. Gilbert, and J. Annala, "Rejoinder—Fishery Management by Individual Quotas: Theory and Practice," *Marine Policy* 17(1) 1993, 64–66.

[66]Annala, "New Zealand's ITQ System," p. 88.

Table 1.1 *A Summary of Fishery Alternatives in Terms of Policy Goals*

		Policy Alternatives			
Goals	**Impact Category**	**Current Policy: Continued Implementation of the Mifflin Plan**	**Harvesting Royalties and License Auction (Pearse Plan)**	**River-Specific Auctioned Monopolies (Schwindt Plan)**	**Individual Transferable Quotas to Current License Holders**
Economically Efficient Use	**Impact on Rent Dissipation**	Poor—large negative net present value	Good—considerable improvement over status quo	Excellent—major improvement over status quo, lowest-cost technology	Good—considerable improvement over status quo
	Ease of Enforcement	Medium—inherent difficulties offset by much experience	Low	High, except on Fraser	Medium—but requires close attention to incentives
	Flexibility	Low	Medium—good price flexibility	Medium—good price flexibility	Medium—with "shares" system
Preservation of the Fishery	**Impact on the Number of Viable Runs**	Very poor—high risks	Poor—continued risk for vulnerable runs	Good—very good except for Fraser River	Good—provided "share" quotas used
Equitable Distribution	**Fairness to Current License Holders**	Nominally fair, but not so in practice because rent is dissipated	Good—generous to existing fishers but less so to remaining incumbents	Very good	Excellent
	Fairness to Aboriginal Fishers	Nominally fair, but not so in practice because rent is dissipated	Good	Good	Excellent for Aboriginal incumbents
	Fairness to Taxpayers	Poor, large net costs	Excellent	Excellent	Acceptable, improvement over status quo
Political Feasibility	**Likelihood of Successful Adoption**	High—in place	Low—not attractive to remaining fishers	Medium—large potential gains, but radical change	High—attractive to incumbent fishers

weights the goals described above. But, because the minister has instructed us to make a recommendation, we do so based on the following comparisons.

Table 1.1 summarizes the major impacts described in the previous section. It is clear that all three alternatives are superior to the status quo in terms of almost all the goals except political feasibility. The River-Specific Exclusive Ownership Rights (with Cooperative Ownership on the Fraser) is the highest-ranked alternative in terms of reversing and eliminating rent dissipation, because it would result in the small-boat fishery being replaced with fish traps and weirs, the lowest-cost fishing technology. The Pearse Commission Proposal and ITQs probably do equally well in preserving rent, offering more modest gains in the reduction of rent dissipation than the River-Specific Ownership Rights, because they each maintain the small-boat fishery. They would encourage license utilization by those who could exploit the resource most efficiently.

It is a close call in choosing among these three alternatives. Our recommendation is that the minister adopt the River-Specific Exclusive Ownership Rights (with Cooperative Ownership on the Fraser). This is, however, a radical departure from the status quo, and it would be politically difficult to implement. ITQs are a close second. It is especially important, however, that share quotas (rather than fixed number of fish or weight of fish) be adopted in the salmon fishery because of the cyclical stock variability. The only weakness of the particular ITQ scheme outlined here is that it does not generate a high degree of equity for taxpayers: rent transfers are modest and reduced by monitoring and enforcement costs. However, it would be the most politically feasible of the three alternatives.

Postscript and Prologue

The chapters that follow provide you with the concepts and tools to perform an analysis such as the one you have just reviewed. Not all policy analysis takes this form: it can be as informal as spoken advice in a corridor to a policymaker or as formal as a legislatively required regulatory impact analysis. But all good policy analysis necessarily includes the sort of thinking that this report represents. Read on. Enjoy. Or, at least endure!

For Discussion

1. Think back to the research papers you have written for undergraduate courses. In what ways are your papers similar in content and structure to the sample policy analysis of the BC salmon fishery? In what ways do your papers differ?
2. Now think about articles you have read in scholarly journals. How does the sample policy analysis differ in content and structure from published academic research?

2

What Is Policy Analysis?

The product of policy analysis may be advice as simple as a statement linking a proposed action to a likely result: passage of bill *A* will result in consequence *X*. It may also be more comprehensive and quite complex: passage of bill *A*, which can be achieved with the greatest certainty through legislative strategy *S*, will result in aggregate social costs of *C* and aggregate social benefits of *B*, but with disproportionate costs for group 1 and disproportionate benefits for group 2. At whatever extremes of depth and breadth, policy analysis is intended to inform some decision, either implicitly (*A* will result in *X*) or explicitly (support *A* because it will result in *X*, which is good for you, your constituency, or your country).

Obviously, not all advice is policy analysis. So to define it, we need to be more specific. We begin by requiring that the advice relate to public decisions and that it be informed by social values. That is not to say that policy analysts do not work in private organizations. Businesses and trade associations often seek advice about proposed legislation and regulations that might affect their private interests—when their employees or consultants consider the full range of social consequences in giving such advice they are providing policy analysis. Of course, the majority of policy analysts are to be found in government and nonprofit organizations where day-to-day operations inherently involve public decisions, as well as in consultancies that serve these public and private organizations. Because our interest centers on policy analysis as a professional activity, our definition requires that policy analysts, in either public or private settings, have clients for their advice who can participate in public decision making. With these considerations in mind we hazard the following simple definition: *policy analysis* is client-oriented advice relevant to public decisions and informed by social values.

A plethora of definitions of policy analysis already exists.[1] Why introduce another one? One reason is that it helps us keep our focus on the purpose of this book: developing the practical approaches and conceptual foundations that enable the reader to become an effective producer and consumer of policy analysis. We emphasize development of a professional mind-set rather than the mastering of technical skills. If we keep central the idea of providing useful advice to clients, then an awareness of the importance of learning the various techniques of policy analysis and of gaining an understanding of political processes will naturally follow.

Another reason is that this definition also emphasizes the importance of social values in policy analysis. Social values can come into play even when advice seems purely predictive. By looking at consequences of policies beyond those that affect the client, the analyst is implicitly placing a value on the welfare of others. Good policy analysis takes a comprehensive view of consequences and social values. As will become clear in subsequent chapters, we believe that economic efficiency deserves routine consideration as a social value not only because it measures aggregate welfare fairly well but also because it tends to receive inadequate weight in political systems.

An appropriate starting place for our study is an overview of the emerging profession of policy analysis. How does policy analysis differ from the older professions to which it is related? Where are policy analysts to be found, and what do they do? What skills are most essential for success?

Policy Analysis and Related Professions

If you are a student in a public policy analysis program, then you probably already have a good sense of what policy analysis is all about—you have, by your educational choice, purposely selected the profession. Yet you may instead aspire to another profession, such as public administration, business management, city and regional planning, law, or public health, in which you may, nevertheless, be required to play the role of policy analyst from time to time. Perhaps you are reading this book as a student in an academic program in political science, economics, or political economy. We hope to put policy analysis in perspective by comparing it with some of the related professions and activities with which you may be more familiar.

[1]Some examples: "Policy analysis is a means of synthesizing information including research results to produce a format for policy decisions (the laying out of alternative choices) and of determining future needs for policy relevant information." Walter Williams, *Social Policy Research and Analysis* (New York: American Elsevier, 1971), xi; and "Policy analysis is an applied social science discipline which uses multiple methods of inquiry and argument to produce and transform policy-relevant information that may be utilized in political settings to resolve policy problems." William N. Dunn, *Public Policy Analysis* (Englewood Cliffs, NJ: Prentice Hall, 1981), ix. These definitions, as do most, lack the client orientation that distinguishes policy analysis as a professional activity. Descriptions of policy analysis closest to our definition are given by Arnold J. Meltsner, *Policy Analysts in the Bureaucracy* (Berkeley: University of California Press, 1976); and Norman Beckman, "Policy Analysis in Government: Alternatives to 'Muddling Through'," *Public Administration Review* 37(3) 1977, 221–22. For an extended discussion of the policy sciences, a broader conception of policy analysis, see Garry D. Brewer and Peter deLeon, *The Foundations of Policy Analysis* (Homewood, IL: Dorsey Press, 1983), 6–17.

A comparison of policy analysis with five other paradigms—academic social science research, policy research, classical planning, the "old" public administration, and journalism—appears in Table 2.1. We focus our attention on similarities and differences in such characteristics as major objectives, client orientation, common style, time constraints, and general weaknesses. The comparison of paradigms emphasizes differences. As our discussion indicates, however, the professions of planning and public administration have moved much closer to the policy analysis paradigm in recent years.

Academic Research

The common experience of higher education gives us all at least some familiarity with *academic research* in the social sciences. Its major objective is the development of theories that contribute to a better understanding of society. Because the client for the research is "truth," at least as recognized by other scholars, the social science disciplines have attempted to develop rigorous methods for logically specifying theories and empirically testing hypotheses derived from them. Progress in the social sciences proceeds as much from the idiosyncrasy of researchers as from the demands of the larger society. The new theory or clever empirical test earns respect from social scientists whether or not it is immediately relevant to public policy. Nevertheless, the accumulation of empirical evidence, and the associated rise and fall of competing theories, eventually influence the "worldviews" of policymakers outside of the academy.[2] Although academic research only fortuitously contributes to the debate over any particular policy issue, the development of social science knowledge forms a base for more narrowly specified research of greater potential relevance.

Policy Research

This research, which often directly employs the methods of the social science disciplines, can be described as *policy research*.[3] Whereas academic research looks for relationships among the broad range of variables describing behavior, policy research focuses on relationships between variables that reflect social problems and other variables that can be manipulated by public policy. The desired product of policy research is a more or less verified hypothesis of the form: if the government does *X*, then *Y* will result. For example, academic research into the causes of crime might identify moral education within the family as an important factor. Because our political system places much of family life outside the sphere of legitimate public intervention, however, there may be little that the government can do to foster moral education

[2]Within disciplines, acceptance of new theories that better explain empirical anomalies often occurs only after repeated failures of the older theories over an extended period. See Thomas S. Kuhn, *The Structure of Scientific Revolutions* (Chicago: University of Chicago Press, 1970). For a discussion of a paradigm shift in political context, see Peter A. Hall, "Policy Paradigms, Experts, and the States: The Case of Macroeconomic Policy-Making in Britain," in Stephen Brooks and Alain-C. Gagnon, eds., *Social Scientists, Policy, and the State* (New York: Praeger, 1990), 53–78.

[3]For a discussion of policy research, see James S. Coleman, *Policy Research in the Social Sciences* (New York: General Learning Press, 1972). Policy research, expanded to include the study of the policy process, is sometimes referred to as policy science. Harold D. Lasswell, "The Emerging Conception of the Policy Sciences," *Policy Sciences* 1(1) 1970, 3–30.

Table 2.1 *Policy Analysis in Perspective*

Paradigms	Major Objective	"Client"	Common Style	Time Constraints	General Weakness
Academic Social Science Research	Construct theories for understanding society	"Truth," as defined by the disciplines, other scholars	Rigorous methods for constructing and testing theories; usually retrospective	Rarely external time constraints	Often irrelevant to information needs of decision makers
Policy Research	Predict impacts of changes in variables that can be altered by public policy	Actors in the policy arena; the related disciplines	Application of formal methodology to policy-relevant questions; prediction of consequences	Sometimes deadline pressure, perhaps mitigated by issue recurrence	Difficulty in translating findings into government action
Classical Planning	Defining and achieving desirable future state of society	"Public interest," as professionally defined	Established rules and professional norms; specification of goals and objectives	Little immediate time pressure because deals with long-term future	Wishful thinking in plans when political processes ignored
Public Administration	Efficient execution of programs established by political processes	"Public interest," as embodied in mandated program	Managerial and legal	Time pressure tied to routine decision making such as budget cycles	Exclusion of alternatives external to program
Journalism	Focusing public attention on societal problems	General public	Descriptive	Strong deadline pressure—strike while issue is topical	Lack of analytical depth and balance
Policy Analysis	Systematic comparison and evaluation of alternatives available to public actors for solving social problems	Specific person or institution as decision maker	Synthesis of existing research and theory to predict consequences of alternative policies	Strong deadline pressure—completion of analysis usually tied to specific decision	Myopia resulting from client orientation and time pressure

within the home. The policy researcher, therefore, may take moral education as a given and focus instead on factors partly under government control, such as the certainty, swiftness, and severity of punishment for those who commit crimes. The policy researcher may then be willing to make a prediction (a hypothesis to be tested by future events), say, that if the probability of arrest for a certain crime is increased by 10 percent, then the frequency of that crime will go down by 5 percent.

A fine line often separates policy research and policy analysis. The strength of client orientation distinguishes them in our scheme. Policy researchers are less closely tied to public decision makers. While one or more decision makers may be interested in their work, policy researchers usually view themselves primarily as members of an academic discipline. Sometimes their primary motivation for doing policy research is personal financial gain or the excitement of seeing their work influence policy; perhaps more often they do it to gain resources or attention for their academic research programs. Because they place primary importance on having the respect of others in their academic disciplines, policy researchers are often as concerned with the publication of their work in professional journals as with its use by decision makers.

Disciplinary orientation contributes to a general weakness in policy research because the translation of research findings into policies that can be directly implemented often requires attention to practical considerations of little academic interest. Returning to our example, the policy researcher's prediction that an increase in the probability of arrest will decrease the crime rate is only the first step in developing and evaluating a policy option. How can the arrest rate be increased? How much will it cost? What other impacts will result? How can it be determined if the predicted reduction in the crime rate has actually occurred? The answers to questions such as these require information of a specific nature, often of little disciplinary interest. Consequently, policy researchers often leave these sorts of questions to policy analysts, who will actually craft policy options for decision makers.

Classical Planning

A very different paradigm is *classical planning*, a reaction to the apparent disorder and myopia resulting from private market behavior and pluralistic government. The general approach of planning is, first, to specify goals and objectives that will lead to a better society and, second, to determine ways of achieving them. Necessary for effective planning is a centralization of authority for the creation and execution of the plan.

As extreme cases, the poor performances of the centrally planned economies of Eastern Europe during the Soviet era point to the inherent weaknesses of the planning paradigm. One weakness was the difficulty of specifying appropriate goals and objectives. The five-year plan may clearly specify what is to be produced, but it is unlikely that the products will closely match the wants of consumers. The other was the massive problem of cognition caused by the need to collect and process information for the comprehensive direction and monitoring of numerous economic actors.[4] Although central economic planning has had little currency in the U.S. context, the planning paradigm has been important in narrower applications.

[4]For a discussion of the paradoxes inherent in planning, see Aaron Wildavsky, "If Planning Is Everything, Maybe It's Nothing," *Policy Sciences* 4(2) 1973, 127–53.

Urban planning in Great Britain and the United States developed from the belief that control of the use of land could be an effective tool for improving the aesthetics and efficiency of cities. The comprehensive master plan, which embodied professional norms about appropriate patterns of land use, became the statement of goals and objectives. Zoning and land-use ordinances were to serve as the mechanisms for implementing the master plans.

The impact of urban planning has been limited, however, by the autonomy of local governments that do not fully accept the professionally specified goals and objectives, by the dynamic of local economic growth that often takes unanticipated forms, and by a narrow emphasis on physical structure rather than broader issues of social behavior. Recognizing the incongruence of the classical planning paradigm with the reality of democratic politics, many planners have urged their profession to adopt a more active interventionist role in public decision making.[5] Consequently, many urban and regional planning schools now require coursework in policy analysis.

A more recent manifestation of the planning paradigm is *systems analysis*, which attempts to extend the techniques of *operations research* beyond narrow applications. The basic approach of systems analysis involves the construction of quantitative models that specify the links among the multitude of variables of interest in social or economic systems. The analytical objective is to maximize, or at least achieve lower bounds on, certain variables that represent goals by altering other variables that can be manipulated by government. By identifying the many possible interactions, the systems analyst hopes to avoid the myopia of incremental political decision making.

But systems analysis has tended to be both overambitious and reductionist.[6] Rarely is there adequate theory or data for the construction of reliable comprehensive models. Further, not all important factors are readily subject to quantification. In particular, the appropriate weights to place on the multiple goals that characterize public issues are usually not obvious; the analyst's choice may cloak value judgments in apparent objectivity. Additionally, the mystique of quantification may give simplistic models more attention than they deserve. Witness, for example, the public attention given to the report of the Club of Rome on the limits to world growth[7]—a report based on a model with virtually no empirical links to the real world.[8] An apparently rigorous model purported to show that continued economic

[5]For example, see Jerome L. Kaufman, "The Planner as Interventionist in Public Policy Issues," in Robert W. Burchell and George Sternlieb, eds., *Planning Theory in the 1980s: A Search for Future Directions* (New Brunswick, NJ: Center for Urban Policy Research, 1978), 179–200.

[6]For critiques of systems analysis, see Ida R. Hoos, *Systems Analysis in Public Policy: A Critique* (Berkeley: University of California Press, 1972); and Aaron Wildavsky, "The Political Economy of Efficiency: Cost-Benefit Analysis, Systems Analysis, and Program Budgeting," *Public Administration Review* 26(4) 1966, 292–310. For a comparison of systems analysis and policy analysis, see Yehezkel Dror, "Policy Analysts: A New Professional Role in Government Service," *Public Administration Review* 27(3) 1967, 197–203.

[7]Donella H. Meadows, Dennis L. Meadows, Jorgen Randers, and William W. Behrens III, *The Limits to Growth: A Report for the Club of Rome's Project on the Predicament of Mankind* (New York: Universe Books, 1974).

[8]For critiques of the Club of Rome approach, see William D. Nordhaus, "World Dynamics: Measurement without Data," *Economic Journal* 83(332) 1973, 1156–83; Chi-Yuen Wu, "Growth Models and Limits-to-Growth Models as a Base for Public Policymaking in Economic Development," *Policy Sciences* 5(2) 1974, 191–211; and Julian L. Simon and Herman Kahn, eds., *The Resourceful Earth: A Response to Global 2000* (New York: Basil Blackwell, 1984).

growth would soon be unsupportable, leading to a dramatic decline in world living standards. Despite numerous arbitrary and questionable assumptions, the Club of Rome report was embraced by many whose worldview associated continued economic growth with unavoidable environmental degradation. The formality of the model tended to divert attention from its implicit assumptions.

A more focused application of systems analysis is the *planning, programming, budgeting system (PPBS)*, which shares some characteristics with policy analysis. The basic approach of PPBS is to identify all programs that have common objectives so that budget allocations to those programs can be compared in terms of their effectiveness in achieving the objectives. PPBS is like policy analysis in that it is directed at influencing specific decisions in the budget cycle. It differs in its attempt to force comprehensive and quantitative comparisons over a wide range of programs. After some apparent success in the Defense Department, President Lyndon Johnson ordered its use throughout the federal government in 1965. In 1971, however, its use was formally abandoned by President Richard Nixon's Office of Management and Budget. Even this limited form of planning placed too great a strain on available knowledge and analytical resources.[9]

Public Administration

The goal of the *"old" public administration* was more modest than that of planning: the efficient management of programs mandated by the political process. Its advocates sought to separate the management function from what they saw as the corruption of politics. The words of Woodrow Wilson provide an unequivocal statement of the basic premise of the old public administration: "... administration lies outside the proper sphere of politics. Administrative questions are not political questions. Although politics sets the tasks for administration, it should not be suffered to manipulate its offices."[10] The ideal is a skillful and loyal civil service free from political interference and dedicated to the implementation and efficient administration of politically mandated programs according to sound principles of management. In other words, the science of management should be insulated from the art of politics.

Both the old public administration and policy analysis are intended to bring greater expertise into public endeavors. Once organizational structures for programs have been created, public administrators turn their attention to the routine decisions concerning personnel, budgets, and operating procedures that help determine how well the programs will meet their mandated goals. Although policy analysts must concern themselves with questions of organizational design and administrative feasibility, they seek to influence the choice of programs by the political process. One focuses exclusively on doing well what has been chosen; the other also considers the choice of what is to be done.

[9]Consider the following assessment: "Although it may fail for many other reasons, such as lack of political support or trained personnel, it always fails for lack of knowledge, when and if it is allowed to get that far," in Aaron Wildavsky, *Budgeting: A Comparative Theory of Budgetary Processes* (Boston: Little, Brown, 1975), 354. Also see Allen Schick, "A Death in the Bureaucracy: The Demise of Federal PPB," *Public Administration Review* 33(2) 1973, 146–56.

[10]Woodrow Wilson, "The Study of Administration," *Political Science Quarterly* 2(1) 1887, 197–222.

Public administration has gradually come to include policy analysis among its professional activities. One reason is that the large bureaus and vague legislative mandates associated with an expanded public role in society require administrators to choose among alternative policies—they thus become consumers and producers of policy analysis relevant to their own agencies. Another reason lies in the usual absence of a clean separation between politics and administration, Woodrow Wilson's vision not withstanding. The administrator must be able to secure resources and defend implementation decisions within the political process. Policy analysis may help accomplish these tasks.

The *"new" public administration* explicitly abandons the notion that administration should be separate from politics.[11] Its practitioners seek to influence the adoption as well as the implementation of policies. Professional training, therefore, must include methods both for predicting the consequences of alternative policies so that informed choices can be made and for effectively participating in the political process so that the choices can be realized. Training in public administration thus often includes coursework in policy analysis, even though its primary focus remains management and operational decision making.

The newest formulation of public administration has been labeled *public management*.[12] It has taken several forms, including an empirical emphasis on discovering best practice from the observation of practicing managers. More recently, however, it has been framed within the study of governance, "… regimes of laws, rules, judicial decisions, and administrative practices that constrain, prescribe, and enable the provision of publicly supported goods and services."[13] Although this broader perspective encompasses managerial practices, it explicitly deals with the choice of organizational forms, a decision appropriately informed by policy analysis.

Journalism

The comparison of policy analysis with *journalism* may at first seem strange. Journalists typically concern themselves with recent events; they are rarely called upon to make predictions about the future. When they write about public policy, the need to attract a wide readership often leads them to focus on the unusual and the sensational rather than the routine and the mundane. Narratives with victims, heros, and villains catch readers' interest more effectively than nuanced discussions of competing social values. Their contribution to the political process, therefore, is more often introducing policy problems to the public agenda than providing systematic comparisons of alternative solutions. Nevertheless, policy analysts and journalists share several goals and constraints.

Tight deadlines drive much of journalists' work. Because news quickly becomes stale, they often face the prospect of not being able to publish unless they make the next edition. Similarly, the advice of policy analysts, no matter how sophisticated

[11]Consider the following: "New Public Administration seeks not only to carry out legislative mandates as efficiently and economically as possible, but to both influence and execute policies which more generally improve the quality of life for all." H. George Frederickson, "Toward a New Public Administration," in Frank Marini, ed., *Toward a New Public Administration* (Scranton, PA: Chandler, 1971), 314.

[12]See Donald F. Kettl and H. Brinton Milwood, eds., *The State of Public Management* (Baltimore: Johns Hopkins University Press, 1996).

[13]Laurence E. Lynn, Jr., Carolyn J. Heinrich, and Carolyn J. Hill, *Improving Governance: A New Logic for Empirical Research* (Washington, DC: Georgetown University Press, 2001), 7.

and convincing, will be useless if it is delivered to clients after they have had to vote, issue regulations, or otherwise make decisions. Rarely will it be the case of better late than never.

Tight deadlines lead journalists and policy analysts to develop similar strategies for gathering information. Files of background information and networks of knowledgeable people are often extremely valuable resources. They may enable journalists to put events quickly in context. They play a similar role for policy analysts but may also provide information useful for assessing technical, political, and administrative feasibility of policy alternatives when time does not permit systematic investigation.[14] Policy analysts, like journalists, wisely cultivate their information sources.

Finally, communication is a primary concern. Journalists must be able to put their stories into words that will catch and keep the interest of their readers. Policy analysts must do the same for their clients. Effective communication requires clear writing—analysts must be able to explain their technical work in language that can be understood by their clients. Also, because the attention and time of clients are scarce resources, writing must be concise and convincing to be effective.

In summary: we gain a perspective on policy analysis by comparing it to related professions. Like policy research, policy analysis employs social science theory and empirical methods to predict the consequences of alternative policies. Like journalism, policy analysis requires skills in information gathering and communication. Policy analysis is neither so narrow in scope as the old public administration nor so broad in scope as classical planning. Yet planners and public administrators who explicitly recognize participation in the political process as professionally legitimate may at times become advice givers to various political actors, thus playing the role of policy analysts.

Policy Analysis as a Profession

Until the 1980s, few of those actually doing policy analysis would have identified themselves as members of the policy analysis profession; even fewer were filling positions labeled "policy analyst." Many who do policy analysis held, and continue to hold, positions as economists, planners, program evaluators, budget analysts, operations researchers, or statisticians. In recent years, however, the policy analysis profession has emerged as an established profession.[15] Positions called policy analyst are now more common in government agencies, and often these positions are filled by people who have been trained in graduate programs in policy analysis. Many practicing analysts trained in a variety of disciplines have joined with academics to form a professional organization, the Association for Public Policy Analysis and Management.[16] Nevertheless, the profession is still young, and those who

[14] On the value of accumulated studies, see Martha Feldman, *Order by Design* (Palo Alto, CA: Stanford University Press, 1989).

[15] For an excellent overview, see Beryl A. Radin, *Beyond Machiavelli: Policy Analysis Comes of Age* (Washington, DC: Georgetown University Press, 2000).

[16] Association for Public Policy Analysis and Management, Box 18766, Washington, DC 20036-8766. Information about membership and annual conferences can be obtained at the following World Wide Web address: www.appam.org

consider themselves members represent only a fraction of those actually practicing the craft of policy analysis.

Practicing policy analysts work in a variety of organizational settings, including federal, state, and local agencies and legislatures; consulting firms; research institutes; trade associations and other organizations representing interest groups; and business and nonprofit corporations. We focus here primarily on the U.S. context, but policy analysts can be found in similar settings in all the major industrialized countries.[17] The way analysts practice their craft is greatly influenced by the nature of their relationships with their clients and by the roles played by the clients in the political process. Because these relationships and roles vary greatly across organizations, we should expect to see a wide range of analytical styles. We consider the various analytical styles and their ethical implications in detail in Chapter 3. For now, let us look at a few examples of organizational settings in which policy analysts work.

First, consider the U.S. federal government. Where would we find policy analysts? Beginning with the executive branch, we could start our search right in the White House, where we would find small but influential groups of analysts in the National Security Council and Domestic Policy staffs. As presidential appointees in politically sensitive positions, they generally share closely the philosophy and goals of their administration. Their advice concerns the political, as well as the economic and social, consequences of policy options. They often coordinate the work of policy analysts in other parts of the executive branch.

The Office of Management and Budget (OMB) and, to a lesser extent, the Council of Economic Advisers (CEA) also play coordinating roles in the federal government. Analysts in OMB are responsible for predicting the costs to the federal government of changes in policy. They also participate in the evaluation of particular programs. The major role that OMB plays in the preparation of the administration budget gives its analysts great leverage in disputes with the federal agencies; it also often leads the analysts to emphasize budgetary costs over social costs and benefits.[18] Analysts on the CEA do not play as direct a role in the budgetary process and, therefore, retain greater freedom to adopt the broad perspective of social costs and benefits. Without direct leverage over the agencies, however, their influence derives largely from the perception that their advice is based on the technical expertise of the discipline of economics.[19]

Policy analysts work throughout the federal agencies. In addition to small personal staffs, agency heads usually have analytical offices reporting directly to them.[20] These offices have a variety of names that usually include some combina-

[17]For international comparisons, see William Platen, ed., *Advising the Rulers* (New York: Basil Blackwell, 1987).

[18]For a discussion of the institutional role of OMB, see Hugh Heclo, "OMB and the Presidency: The Problem of Neutral Competence," *Public Interest* 38, 1975, 80–98. For a history of OMB, see Larry Berman, *The Office of Management and Budget and the Presidency 1921–1979* (Princeton, NJ: Princeton University Press, 1979).

[19]Herbert Stein, "A Successful Accident: Recollections and Speculations about the CEA," *Journal of Economic Perspectives*, 10(3) 1996, 3–21.

[20]For example, on the role of analysis at the State Department, see Lucian Pugliaresi and Diane T. Berliner, "Policy Analysis at the Department of State: The Policy Planning Staff," *Journal of Policy Analysis and Management* 8(3) 1989, 379–94. See also Robert H. Nelson, "The Office of Policy Analysis in the Department of the Interior," 395–410, in the same issue.

tion of the words "policy," "planning," "administration," "evaluation," "economic," and "budget."[21] For example, at various times the central analytical office in the Department of Energy has been called the Office of the Assistant Secretary for Policy and Evaluation and the Policy, Planning, and Analysis Office. Often, the heads of agency subunits have analytical staffs that provide advice and expertise relevant to their substantive responsibilities. Later in this chapter we briefly consider policy analysis in the Department of Health and Human Services to illustrate the sorts of functions analysts perform in federal agencies.

Policy analysts also abound in the legislative branch. Both the Congress as a whole and its individual members serve as clients. Policy analysts work for Congress in the General Accounting Office (GAO),[22] the Congressional Budget Office (CBO), the Congressional Research Service (CRS), and, until its recent elimination, the Office of Technology Assessment (OTA).[23] The analytical agendas of these offices are set primarily by the congressional leadership but sometimes also by individual members of Congress as well. Of course, members have their own personal staffs, including legislative analysts. Most of the analysis and formulation of legislation, however, is done by committee staffs that report to committee chairs and ranking minority members.[24] Committee staffers, often recruited from the campaign and personal staffs of members of Congress, must be politically sensitive if they are to maintain their positions and influence. Congressional staff involved with legislation—and, therefore, to some extent working as policy analysts, even though often trained as lawyers—number in the thousands.[25]

How influential is policy analysis in policy formation and choice in Congress? Based on his detailed study of communication surrounding four policy issues in the areas of health and transportation, David Whiteman concludes: "The results ... clearly indicate that policy analysis clearly does flow through congressional communication networks. In three of the four issues examined, analytic information played a significant role in congressional deliberations."[26] Much of the communication takes place through discussions between congressional staffers and analysts in government offices and think tanks rather than as formal written reports.

[21]As recently as the mid-1970s, only a small fraction of the offices responsible for doing policy analysis actually had "policy" or "policy analysis" in their names. Arnold J. Meltsner, *Policy Analysts in the Bureaucracy* (Berkeley: University of California Press, 1976), 173–77.

[22]The General Accounting Office and the Bureau of the Budget, the forerunner of OMB, were established in 1921 with the creation of an executive budget system. During much of its history, GAO devoted its efforts primarily to auditing government activities. In the late 1960s, however, GAO became a major producer of policy analysis in the form of program evaluations with recommendations for future actions. Because GAO must serve both parties and both legislative houses, and because its reports are generally public, it faces stronger incentives to produce politically neutral analyses than OMB. For a comparative history of these "twins," see Frederick C. Mosher, *A Tale of Two Agencies: A Comparative Analysis of the General Accounting Office and the Office of Management and Budget* (Baton Rouge: Louisiana State University Press, 1984).

[23]For an account of the elimination of the OTA and a comparison with the larger congressional support agencies that survived, see Bruce Bimber, *The Politics of Expertise in Congress: The Rise and Fall of the Office of Technology Assessment* (Albany: State University of New York Press, 1996).

[24]See Carol H. Weiss, "Congressional Committees as Users of Analysis," *Journal of Policy Analysis and Management* 8(3) 1989, 411–31. See also Nancy Shulock, "The Paradox of Policy Analysis: If It Is Not Used, Why Do We Produce So Much of It?" *Journal of Policy Analysis and Management* 18(2) 1999, 226–44.

[25]Michael J. Malbin, *Unelected Representatives* (New York: Basic Books, 1980), 252–56.

[26]David Whiteman, *Communication in Congress: Members, Staff, and the Search for Information* (Lawrence: University of Kansas Press, 1995), 181.

Turning to state governments, we find a similar pattern. Governors and agency heads usually have staffs of advisers who do policy analysis. Most states have budget offices that play roles similar to that of OMB at the federal level.[27] Personal and committee staffs provide analysis in the state legislatures; in some states, such as California, the legislatures have offices much like the Congressional Budget Office to analyze the impact of proposed legislation.

At the county and municipal levels, legislative bodies rarely employ persons who work primarily as policy analysts. Executive agencies, including budget and planning offices, usually do have some personnel whose major responsibility is policy analysis. Except in the most populous jurisdictions, however, most analysis is done by persons with line or managerial duties. Consequently, they often lack the time, expertise, and resources for conducting analyses of great technical sophistication. Nevertheless, because they often have direct access to decision makers, and because they can often observe the consequences of their recommendations firsthand, policy analysts at the local level can find their work professionally gratifying despite the resource constraints they face.

What do public agencies do if their own personnel cannot produce a desired or mandated analysis? If they have funds available, then the agencies can purchase analysis from consultants. Local and state agencies commonly turn to consultants for advice about special issues, such as the construction of new facilities or major reorganizations, or to meet evaluation requirements imposed by intergovernmental grant programs. Federal agencies not only use consultants for special studies, but also as routine supplements to their own staff resources. In extreme cases consulting firms may serve as "body shops" for government offices, providing the services of analysts who cannot be hired directly because of civil service or other restrictions.[28]

The importance of the relationship between client and analyst is extremely apparent to consultants. Usually, the consultants are paid to produce specific products. If they wish to be rehired in the future, then they must produce analyses that the clients perceive as useful. Consultants who pander to the prejudices of their clients at the expense of analytical honesty are sometimes described as "hired guns" or "beltway bandits." Consultants best able to resist the temptation to pander are probably those who have a large clientele, provide very specialized skills, or enjoy a reputation for providing balanced analysis; they will not suffer greatly from the loss of any one client and they will be able to find replacement business elsewhere if necessary.

Researchers in academia, think tanks, and policy research institutes also provide consulting services. Although their work is usually not directly tied to specific policy decisions, researchers at places like the Rand Corporation, the Brookings Institution, the American Enterprise Institute for Public Policy Research, the Cato Institute, the Urban Institute, Resources for the Future, the Institute for Defense Analyses, and the Institute for Research on Public Policy (Canada) sometimes do produce analyses of narrow interest for specific clients. It is often difficult in practice to determine whether these researchers better fit the policy analysis or the pol-

[27]For a survey, see Robert D. Lee Jr., and Raymond J. Staffeldt, "Executive and Legislative Use of Policy Analysis in the State Budgetary Process: Survey Results," *Policy Analysis* 3(3) 1977, 395–405.

[28]For a study of the use of consultants by the federal government, see James D. Marver, *Consultants Can Help* (Lexington, MA: Lexington Books, 1979).

icy research paradigms presented above. Ever-more issues are attracting policy analyses from the growing number of think tanks.[29] Many of the newer think tanks with strong ideological identifications, however, have predispositions toward particular policies that often interfere with the professional validity of the analyses they provide.

Finally, large numbers of analysts neither work for, nor sell their services to, governments. They often work in profit-seeking firms in industries heavily regulated by government, in trade associations and national labor unions concerned with particular areas of legislation, and in nonprofit corporations that have public missions in their charters. For example, consider a proposal to make health insurance premiums paid by employers count as taxable income for employees. Private firms, trade associations, and labor unions would seek analysis to help determine the impact of the proposed change on the pattern and cost of employee benefits. The American Medical Association would seek analysis of the impact on the demand for physician services. Health insurance providers, such as Blue Cross and Blue Shield, commercial insurers, and health maintenance organizations, would want predictions of the effect of the change on the demand for their plans and the cost of medical care. These interests might also ask their analysts how to develop strategies for supporting, fighting, or modifying the proposal as it moves through the political process.

It should be obvious from our brief survey that policy analysts work in a variety of organizational settings on problems ranging in scope from municipal refuse collection to national defense. But what sorts of functions do analysts actually perform in their organizations?

A Closer Look at Analytical Functions

At the beginning of this chapter we pointed out that the nature of policy analysis can vary widely. In subsequent chapters we set out a framework for doing comprehensive policy analysis—how an individual analyst should go about producing a structured analysis that assesses problems presented by clients and systematically compares alternatives for solving them. This is the most appropriate pedagogic approach because it encompasses the range of functions that analysts commonly perform. By mastering it, analysts not only prepare themselves for performing the inclusive functions but also gain a useful framework for putting what they are doing into perspective.

Rather than describe these inclusive functions in the abstract, we present a brief overview of some of the policy analytical functions identified by the Department of Health and Human Services (DHHS). We single out DHHS for two reasons. First, it is a very large federal agency with responsibilities that demand the full range of analytical functions. Second, DHHS has written down what it sees to be the important functions of its policy analysts.

DHHS is very large by any measure. It oversees many specialized agencies, such as the Food and Drug Administration, the National Institutes of Health, the

[29]For instance, *The Capital Source* (Washington, DC: The National Journal, Fall 1997) lists 114 think tanks in the Washington area (pp. 73–75), from the Alan Guttmacher Institute, which focuses on population issues, to the Worldwatch Institute, which focuses on environmental issues.

Health Care Financing Administration, and Centers for Disease Control and Prevention, to name just a few. In fiscal year 2002, it administered spending of over $460 billion, issued more grants than any other federal agency, and employed more than 65,000 people nationwide in its constituent units. As such, it is one of the largest and most complex bureaus in the world. DHHS is of such size and scope that the Office of the Secretary (OS), the central coordinating office for DHHS, itself employs approximately 2,400 people. The purpose of the OS includes providing independent advice and analysis concerning program issues, analyzing trade-offs among programs, and developing common policies across agencies. While much of what the OS does involves administration and monitoring, there is no clear separation of these tasks from policy analysis.

Although policy analysts can be found throughout DHHS, we focus on the Office of the Assistant Secretary, Planning and Evaluation (ASPE), because it has the clearest and most direct mandate for doing policy analysis.[30] (The Office of the Assistant Secretary, Management and Budget has closely related policy analysis responsibilities but with greater emphasis on budgetary and cost issues; the two offices often work together on policy analysis projects.)

ASPE analysts perform a variety of functions. An ASPE orientation document specifically alerts new analysts to four major functions that they will be likely to perform.[31] First, analysts play a "desk officer" function that involves coordinating policy relevant to specific program areas and serving as a contact for the line agencies within DHHS that have responsibilities in these areas. For example, a desk officer might cover biomedical research issues and work closely with analysts and other personnel at the National Institutes of Health. Desk officers serve as the eyes and ears of the department, "going out to the agency, talking with the staff about issues and options before they reach decision points, and knowing what issues are moving and what are not."[32] Desk officers are also expected to reach outside of DHHS to identify concerns and ideas from academics and those who deal with the programs in the field. By staying on top of issues, desk officers can provide quick assessments of proposed policy changes in their areas.

Second, analysts perform a policy development function. This is important to DHHS because ASPE resources "constitute some of the few flexible analytic resources in the Department."[33] Policy development often involves special initiatives within DHHS but can also be done through task forces that include personnel from other departments. These initiatives often result in policy option papers or specific legislative proposals.

Third, analysts perform a policy research and oversight function. "ASPE spends approximately $20 million a year in both policy research and evaluation funds" to carry out this core function.[34] It is important to emphasize that DHHS, like many other government agencies, contracts out a considerable amount of policy-relevant research. Therefore, analysts at ASPE are both consumers and producers of policy research and analysis. ASPE analysts also participate in reviews of the research plans of other agencies, help formulate and justify plans for allocating evaluation funds, and serve on agency panels that award research contracts and grants.

[30]For a long-term view of analysis at ASPE, see George D. Greenberg, "Policy Analysis at the Department of Health and Human Services," *Journal of Policy Analysis and Management* 22(2) 2003, 304–07.

[31]Assistant Secretary, Policy and Evaluation, "All about APSE: A Guide for APSE Staff," no date.

[32]Ibid., E-1.

[33]Ibid., E-2.

[34]Ibid.

Fourth, analysts perform a "firefighting" function. Fires can be "anything from a request from the White House to review the statement of administration accomplishments on welfare reform … to preparing an instant briefing for congressional staff because a key committee is preparing to mark up a bill, to helping … [the] Office of the Secretary prepare for a meeting with a key outside group tomorrow."[35] The term *firefighting* conveys the urgency of the task—analysts drop whatever else they are doing until the fire is put out!

These four categories of functions illustrate the great variety of tasks that analysts are routinely called upon to perform. Some of these tasks are on-going, others are episodic. Some have short deadlines, others extend for long periods. Some are internal to the analysts' organizations, others require interaction with external analysts and decision makers. Some involve topics of great familiarity, others present novel issues. What sorts of basic skills help analysts prepare for this diversity of tasks?

Basic Preparation for Policy Analysis

Policy analysis is as much an art and a craft as a science.[36] Just as the successful portraitist must be able to apply the skills of the craft of painting within an aesthetic perspective, the successful policy analyst must be able to apply basic skills within a reasonably consistent and realistic perspective on the role of government in society. In order to integrate effectively the art and craft of policy analysis, preparation in five areas is essential.

First, analysts must know how to gather, organize, and communicate information in situations in which deadlines are strict and access to relevant people is limited. They must be able to develop strategies for quickly understanding the nature of policy problems and the range of possible solutions. They must also be able to identify, at least qualitatively, the likely costs and benefits of alternative solutions and communicate these assessments to their clients. Chapters 13 and 14 focus on the development of these basic informational skills.

Second, analysts need a perspective for putting perceived social problems in context. When is it legitimate for government to intervene in private affairs? In the United States, the normative answer to this question has usually been based on the concept of *market failure*—a circumstance in which the pursuit of private interest does not lead to an efficient use of society's resources or a fair distribution of society's goods. But market failures, or widely shared normative claims for the desirability of social goals other than efficiency, such as greater equity in the distributions of economic and political resources, should be viewed as only necessary conditions for appropriate government intervention. Sufficiency requires that the form of the intervention not involve consequences that would inflict greater social costs than social benefits. Identification of these costs of intervention is facilitated by an understanding of the ways collective action can fail. In other words, the analyst needs a perspective that includes *government failure* as well as market failure. The chapters in Parts II and III provide such a perspective. Chapters 4, 5, 6, and 7 analyze the various market failures and other rationales that have been identified; Chapter 8 discusses the systematic ways that government interventions tend to lead to undesirable

[35] Ibid.

[36] For a strong statement of this viewpoint, see Aaron Wildavsky, *Speaking Truth to Power: The Art and Craft of Policy Analysis* (Boston: Little, Brown, 1979), 385–406.

social outcomes; Chapter 9 considers the interaction between market and government failures; and Chapters 10, 11, and 12 set out conceptual foundations for developing policies to correct market and government failures. These chapters provide a "capital stock" of ideas for categorizing and understanding social problems and proposing alternative policies for dealing with them.

Third, analysts need technical skills to enable them to predict better and to evaluate more confidently the consequences of alternative policies. The disciplines of economics and statistics serve as primary sources for these skills. Although we introduce some important concepts from microeconomics, public finance, and statistics in the following chapters, those readers who envision careers in policy analysis would be well advised to take courses devoted to these subjects.[37] Even an introduction to policy analysis, however, should introduce the basics of benefit-cost analysis, the subject of Chapter 16. Chapters 17 and 18 illustrate the application of benefit-cost analysis and related techniques.

Fourth, analysts must have an understanding of political and organizational behavior in order to predict, and perhaps influence, the feasibility of adoption and successful implementation of policies. Also, understanding the worldviews of clients and potential opponents enables the analyst to marshal evidence and arguments more effectively. We assume that readers have a basic familiarity with democratic political systems. Therefore, practical applications of theories of political and organizational behavior are integrated with subject matter throughout the text but particularly in the context of thinking about policy adoption and implementation (Chapter 11), government failure (Chapter 8), and in the case studies (especially Chapter 17).

Finally, analysts should have an ethical framework that explicitly takes account of their relationships to clients. Analysts often face dilemmas when the private preferences and interests of their clients diverge substantially from their own perceptions of the public interest. Approaches to the development of professional ethics for policy analysts is the subject of Chapter 3.

For Discussion

1. The Legislative Analyst's Office, which functions as the "eyes and ears" of the California legislature, was founded in 1941. It served as a model for the federal Congressional Budget Office. Visit its Website (www.lao.ca.gov) to view its history and samples of its products. Would you expect the analysis produced by the Legislative Analyst's Office to be more or less politically neutral than analytical offices within the California executive branch?
2. Think tanks differ in a variety of ways, including their areas of specialization and the degree to which they advocate specific policies. Characterize the following think tanks after visiting their Website: Cato Institute (www.cato.org), Fraser Institute (www.fraserinstitute.ca), Progressive Policy Institute (www.ppion.org), RAND Corporation (www.rand.org), and Resources for the Future (www.rff.org).

[37]There are three reasons why a solid grounding in economics and statistics is important for the professional policy analyst: (1) the techniques of these disciplines are often directly applicable to policy problems; (2) researchers who use economic models and statistical techniques are important sources of policy research—the ability to interpret their work is, therefore, valuable; and (3) analytical opponents may use or abuse these techniques—self-protection requires a basic awareness of the strengths and limitations of the techniques.

3

Toward Professional Ethics

The policy analyst with a philosopher-king as a client would be fortunate in several ways. The analyst could prepare advice with the knowledge that it would be thoughtfully evaluated on its merits by a wise leader who placed the welfare of the kingdom above considerations of private or factional interest. Good advice would be adopted and implemented solely on the word of the king, without resort to complicated political or organizational strategies. Thus, as long as the king truly had wisdom, benevolence, and power, the analyst could expect that only reasoned and reasonable differences of opinion would come between recommendations and action. In other words, the analyst would not have to fear conflict between the professional ideal of promoting the common good and the practical necessity of serving a client.

Although we often discuss policy analysis as if all clients were philosopher-kings, reality is never so kind. History offers many examples of despots and few examples of consistently benevolent autocrats. Representative government seeks to limit the damage that can be done by abusive leaders by providing opportunities to replace them without resort to revolution. Yet, in regimes of representative government, many cooks contribute to the policy broth. The distribution of authority by constitution or tradition to elected officials, bureaucrats, legislators, and magistrates guarantees many their place at the kettle. Prevailing norms of democratic participation ensure that they receive a variety of advice and demands from their fellow citizens to whom they are accountable, either directly or indirectly, at the ballot box. Presidents and prime ministers may enjoy more favored positions than other participants; but, except for very mundane or exceptional circumstances, even they generally lack authority to select and to implement policies by simple directive.[1] Even in political systems where the authority of the chief executive verges on the dictatorial, the limits of time and attention imposed by nature necessitate the delegation of discretion over many routine decisions to other officials.

Analysts must expect, therefore, that their clients will be players in the game of politics—players who not only have their own personal conceptions of the good society but who also must acknowledge the often narrow interests of their constituencies if they hope to remain in the game. The reality that, outside the classroom, policy analysis cannot be separated from politics has important practical and ethical implications. Analysis that ignores the interests of the client may itself be ignored; recommendations that ignore the interests of other key players are unlikely to be adopted or successfully implemented. In the extreme, if efficacy were the only professional value, "good" analysts would be those who helped their clients become better players in the game of politics. But other values, not always explicitly stated, lead to broader ethical considerations. Analysts should not only care that they influence policy, but also that they do so for the better.

Much of the growing literature in the area of ethics and public policy concerns the values that we should consider in attempting to select better policies.[2] It reminds analysts that no single value, such as economic efficiency, can provide an adequate basis for all public decision making. We focus here on professional ethics rather than the comparative merits of substantive policies. Our objective in the following sections is to sketch a framework for thinking about the ethical responsibilities of the professional policy analyst. To do so, we must pay attention to the nature of the relationships between analysts and clients and the various contexts in which they evolve.[3] Even if we fail to develop explicit and universally accepted ethical guidelines, we will at least become acquainted with the most common analytical environments and the dilemmas they sometimes raise for practitioners.

Analytical Roles

Policy analysis, like life itself, forces us to confront conflicts among competing values. Often conflicts arise inherently in the substantive question being considered. For example, should a policy that would yield a great excess of benefits over costs for society as a whole be selected even if it would inflict severe costs on a small group of people? Our answers will depend on the relative weights we give to the

[1]Commenting on the U.S. executive, Richard E. Neustadt concludes, "Command is but a method of persuasion, not a substitute, and not a method suitable for everyday employment." Richard E. Neustadt, *Presidential Power* (New York: John Wiley, 1980), 25.

[2]See, for example, Charles W. Anderson, "The Place of Principles in Policy Analysis," *American Political Science Review* 74(3) 1979, 711–23; Robert E. Goodin, *Political Theory and Public Policy* (Chicago: University of Chicago Press, 1982); Peter G. Brown, "Ethics and Policy Research," *Policy Analysis* 2(2) 1976, 325–40; Joel L. Fleishman and Bruce L. Payne, *Ethical Dilemmas and the Education of Policymakers* (New York: Hastings Center, 1980); Douglas J. Amy, "Why Policy Analysis and Ethics Are Incompatible," *Journal of Policy Analysis and Management* 3(4) 1984, 573–91; and Daniel Callahan and Bruce Jennings, eds., *Ethics, the Social Sciences, and Policy Analysis* (New York: Plenum, 1983).

[3]For the contrast between a genuine discourse about values in a consensual environment and the potential manipulation of this discourse in adversarial processes, see Duncan MacRae, Jr., "Guidelines for Policy Discourse: Consensual versus Adversarial," in Frank Fischer and John Forester, eds., *The Argumentative Turn in Policy Analysis and Planning* (Durham, NC: Duke University Press, 1993), 291–318.

values of efficiency (getting the greatest aggregate good from available resources) and equity (fairness in the way it is distributed). These values, along with others, such as the protection of human life and dignity and the promotion of individual choice and responsibility, provide criteria for evaluating specific policy proposals.

Rather than focusing on values from the unique perspectives of particular policy issues, here we consider values relevant to the general question of how analysts should conduct themselves as professional givers of advice. Three values seem paramount: *analytical integrity*, *responsibility to client*, and *adherence to one's personal conception of the good society*. Conflicts among these values raise important ethical issues for analysts.

To understand better the nature of these values and the contexts in which they become important, we consider three conceptions of the appropriate role of the analyst.[4] Each role gives priority to one of the three values, relegating the remaining two to secondary status. We can anticipate, therefore, that none of the three roles provides an adequate ethical standard in its pure form in all circumstances. Our task will be to search for appropriate balance.

Objective technicians hold analytical integrity as their fundamental value. They see their analytical skills as the source of their legitimacy. The proper role for the analyst, in their view, is to provide objective advice about the consequences of proposed policies. Objective technicians feel most comfortable applying skills within recognized standards of good practice. Therefore, they often prefer to draw their tools from the disciplines of economics, statistics, and operations research, all of which employ well-established methods. They realize that they must often work under severe time constraints and data limitations. Nevertheless, they want to believe that researchers in the disciplines would approve of their work as methodologically sound under the circumstances.

As asserted in Table 3.1, objective technicians view clients as necessary evils. Clients provide the resources that allow objective technicians to work on interesting questions. In return, clients deserve the most accurate predictions possible. The political fortunes of clients should take second place behind analytical integrity in the preparation, communication, and use of analyses. Analysts should try to protect themselves from interference by not becoming too closely associated with the personal interests of their clients. In general, they should select institutional clients, because such clients are likely to provide greater opportunities for preparing and disseminating objective analyses. For example, one is likely to face fewer interferences with analytical integrity working for the Congressional Budget Office, which must be responsive to Congress as a whole as well as anticipate changes in partisan control, than working directly for a member of Congress who must run for reelection every two years.

The objective technician believes that values relevant to the choice of policies should be identified. When no policy appears superior in terms of all the relevant values, however, trade-offs among competing values should be left to the client rather than be implicitly imposed by the analyst. The analyst contributes to the good society, at least in the long run, by consistently providing unbiased advice, even when it does not lead to the selection of personally favored policies.

[4]Our approach here benefits from Arnold J. Meltsner, *Policy Analysts in the Bureaucracy* (Berkeley: University of California Press, 1976), 18–49, who developed a classification of styles to understand better how analysis is actually practiced; and from Hank Jenkins-Smith, "Professional Roles for Policy Analysts: A Critical Assessment," *Journal of Policy Analysis and Management* 2(1) 1982, 88–100, who developed the three roles we use.

Table 3.1 *Three Views on the Appropriate Role of the Policy Analyst*

	Fundamental Values		
	Analytical Integrity	**Responsibility to Clients**	**Adherence to One's Conception of Good**
Objective Technician	Let analysis speak for itself. Primary focus should be predicting consequences of alternative policies.	Clients are necessary evils; their political fortunes should be secondary considerations. Keep distance from clients; select institutional clients whenever possible.	Relevant values should be identified, but trade-offs among them should be left to clients. Objective advice promotes good in the long run.
Client's Advocate	Analysis rarely produces definitive conclusions. Take advantage of ambiguity to advance clients' positions.	Clients provide analysts with legitimacy. Loyalty should be given in return for access to privileged information and to political processes.	Select clients with compatible value systems; use long-term relationships to change clients' conceptions of good.
Issue Advocate	Analysis rarely produces definitive conclusions. Emphasize ambiguity and excluded values when analysis does not support advocacy.	Clients provide an opportunity for advocacy. Select them opportunistically; change clients to further personal policy agenda.	Analysis should be an instrument for progress toward one's conception of the good society.

The *client's advocate* places primary emphasis on his or her responsibility to the client. He or she believes that analysts derive their legitimacy as participants in the formation of public policy from their clients, who hold elected or appointed office or who represent organized political interests. In return for access, clients deserve professional behavior that includes loyalty and confidentiality. Like physicians, analysts should "do no harm" to their clients; like attorneys, they should vigorously promote their clients' interests.

To some extent the client's advocate views analytical integrity in the same way attorneys view their responsibility in an adversarial system. Analysts have a primary responsibility never to mislead their clients through false statements or purposeful omissions. Once clients have been fully informed, however, analysts may publicly interpret their analyses in the best possible light for their clients. Because analysis rarely produces definitive conclusions, analysts can emphasize the possible rather than the most likely when doing so favors their clients. The client's advocate believes that analytical integrity prohibits lying, but it requires neither full disclosure of information nor public correction of misstatements by clients.

Clients' advocates must relegate their policy preferences to a secondary position once they make commitments to clients. Therefore, their selection of clients matters greatly. When analysts and clients share similar worldviews, less potential exists for situations to arise that require analysts to help promote policies that are inconsistent with their own conceptions of the good society. Upon discovering that their clients hold very different worldviews, analysts may nevertheless continue such relationships if they believe that they will be able to make their clients' outlooks more like their own over periods of extended service. In fact, they may believe that they have a responsibility to try to change their clients' beliefs before switching to new clients.

Issue advocates believe that analysis should be an instrument for making progress toward their conception of the good society. They focus on values inherent in policy outcomes rather than on values, like analytical integrity and responsibility to the client, associated with the actual conduct of analysis. They see themselves as intrinsically legitimate players in the policy process. They may also see themselves as champions for groups or interests, such as the environment, the poor, or the victims of crime, that they believe suffer from underrepresentation in the political process.

Issue advocates select clients opportunistically. Clients unable or unwilling to promote the advocates' personal policy agendas should be abandoned for clients who can and will. Analysts owe their clients only those duties spelled out in the contractual arrangements defining the relationships; loyalty to one's conception of the good society should take priority over loyalty to any particular client.

Like the client's advocate, the issue advocate believes in taking advantage of analytical uncertainty. When analysis does not support one's policy preferences, the issue advocate questions the simplifying assumptions that must inevitably be employed in dealing with complex issues, or challenges the choice of criteria used to evaluate alternatives. (The latter will almost always be a possible strategy when one does not agree with conclusions.) Though issue advocates desire the respect of other analysts, especially when it contributes to effectiveness, they may be willing to sacrifice respect to obtain important policy outcomes.

Value Conflicts

One can imagine each of these extreme roles being ethically acceptable in specific circumstances. For example, analysts on the White House staff enjoy privileged positions with respect to information and political access. An important factor in their selection was, undoubtedly, their perceived loyalty to the president. In accepting these positions, they were implicitly if not explicitly committing themselves to a high degree of discretion in confidential matters. Except in the most extreme cases where failure to act would lead with reasonable certainty to significant violations of human rights or constitutional trust, honoring confidentiality and otherwise behaving as clients' advocates seem to be ethically defensible. In contrast, a consultant hired by the Nuclear Regulatory Commission to analyze the risks associated with alternative policies for nuclear waste disposal might appropriately act as an objective technician, placing analytical integrity above the political interests of the commission. One might even argue that the consultant has an ethical duty to speak out publicly if the commission were to misrepresent the study to obtain a political outcome radically different from that which would otherwise have resulted.

In general, however, the analyst need not adopt any of the three roles in its extreme form. Rather than selecting one of the three fundamental values as dominant and sacrificing the other two as circumstances demand, the analyst should attempt to keep all three under consideration. The ethical problem, then, involves deciding how much of each value can be sacrificed when conflicts arise.

In any situation the range of ethical behavior will be bounded by the minimal duties the analyst owes to each of the values. The development of professional ethics, either collectively or individually, may be viewed as an attempt to discover these minimal duties. In the discussion that follows, we consider some of the common situations in which value conflicts arise and minimal duties must be determined. We begin by considering the range of actions the analyst has available for responding to severe conflicts in values.

Responses to Value Conflicts: Voice, Exit, and Disloyalty

The most serious ethical conflicts for policy analysts usually pit responsibility to the client against other values. A variety of factors complicate ethical judgment: continued access to the policy issue, the status of current and future employment, the personal trust of the client, and the analyst's reputation. Many of these factors involve implications that go well beyond the particular ethical issue being considered. For example, loss of employment directly affects the economic and psychological well-being of analysts and their families, as well as the sort of advice that will be heard on the issue at hand. It will also contribute to the sort of advice that will be offered in the analysts' organizations on similar issues in the future. We must be careful, therefore, to look for consequences beyond the particular issue at stake.

So far we have spoken of the analyst as if he or she were the direct employee of the client. Some analysts, such as consultants reporting directly to project managers or political appointees on the personal staffs of administrators and legislators, have clearly defined persons as clients. Analysts usually have immediate supervisors who can generally be thought of as clients. These supervisors, however, often operate in organizational hierarchies and, therefore, often have their own clients, who will also be consumers of the analysts' advice. Limiting the definition of the client to the immediate supervisor would unreasonably absolve analysts from responsibility for the ultimate use of their products. At the same time, we do not want to hold analysts accountable for misuse totally beyond their control. For our purposes, we consider the client to be the highest-ranking superior who receives predictions, evaluations, or recommendations attributable to the analyst. Thus, an analyst working in a bureau may have different persons as clients at different times. Sometimes the client will be the immediate supervisor; other times the client will be a higher-ranking official in the bureau.

Note that we have purposely adopted a narrow, instrumental conception of the client. There is some temptation to look for an ultimate client: analysts themselves as moral persons, the social contract as embodied in the constitution, or the public interest as reflected in national laws.[5] To do so, however, would assume away the essence of the professional role. Instead, we see personal morality, the constitution,

[5]Many writers have chosen to approach professional ethics with the question: Who is the real client? See, for example, E. S. Quade, *Analysis for Public Decisions* (New York: American Elsevier, 1975), 273–75.

and laws as the sources of other values that often conflict with responsibility to client.[6]

What are the possible courses of action for analysts when demands by their clients come in conflict with their sense of analytical integrity or their conception of the good society? We can begin to answer this question by considering the concepts of voice and exit developed by Albert O. Hirschman. In his book, *Exit, Voice, and Loyalty*, Hirschman explores how people can react when they are dissatisfied with the organizations in which they participate.[7] They may exercise voice by working to change the organization from within, or they may simply exit, leaving the organization for another. For example, parents dissatisfied with the quality of education provided by their local school district might exercise voice by attending school board meetings or even by standing for election to the board. Alternatively, they may put their children in private schools or move to another community with a better school district. In Hirschman's framework, loyalty helps determine how much voice is exercised before exit is chosen. Attachment to the community and commitment to public education, for example, will influence the parents' choice between voice and exit.

We find it useful to use Hirschman's concepts of voice and exit and to add a third concept, disloyalty. An action is disloyal when it undercuts the political position or policy preferences of the client. Note that we thus abandon Hirschman's use of loyalty. Rather than being a contributing factor to the choice between voice and exit, we specify loyalty as another dimension of action.

Analysts can exercise various combinations of voice, exit, and disloyalty when they confront value conflicts. The logical possibilities are presented in Figure 3.1, where voice, exit, and disloyalty are represented by circles. Actions involving more than one of the dimensions are represented by intersections of circles. For example, we label voice alone as "protest," whereas "leak" combines protest with disloyalty. We specify seven different actions for purposes of discussion.

Consider the following situation: you work in a government agency as a policy analyst. You have just been assigned the job of developing an implementation strategy for a policy that you believe is bad. After careful deliberation, you decide that the policy is sufficiently bad that you feel it would be morally wrong for you simply to follow orders. Under what conditions might you feel ethically justified in choosing each of the actions listed in Figure 3.1?

You might try to change the policy through *protest* within the agency. You would probably begin by informally discussing your objections to the policy with your supervisor. If your supervisor lacks either the inclination or the authority to reverse the policy, then you might next make your objections formally through memoranda to your supervisor, your supervisor's supervisor, and so forth, until you reach the lowest-ranking official with authority to change the policy. At the same time, you might speak out against the policy at staff meetings whenever you have the opportunity. You might also request that the assignment be given to someone else, not only because you would feel morally absolved if someone else did it, but because the request helps to emphasize the intensity of your objections. At some

[6]John A. Rohr argues that public officials have a responsibility to inform their actions by studying the constitutional aspects of their duties through relevant court opinions and the substantive aspects through legislative histories. John A. Rohr, "Ethics for the Senior Executive Service," *Administration and Society* 12(2) 1980, 203–16; and *Ethics for Bureaucrats: An Essay on Law and Values* (New York: Marcel Dekker, 1978).

[7]Albert O. Hirschman, *Exit, Voice, and Loyalty* (Cambridge, MA: Harvard University Press, 1970).

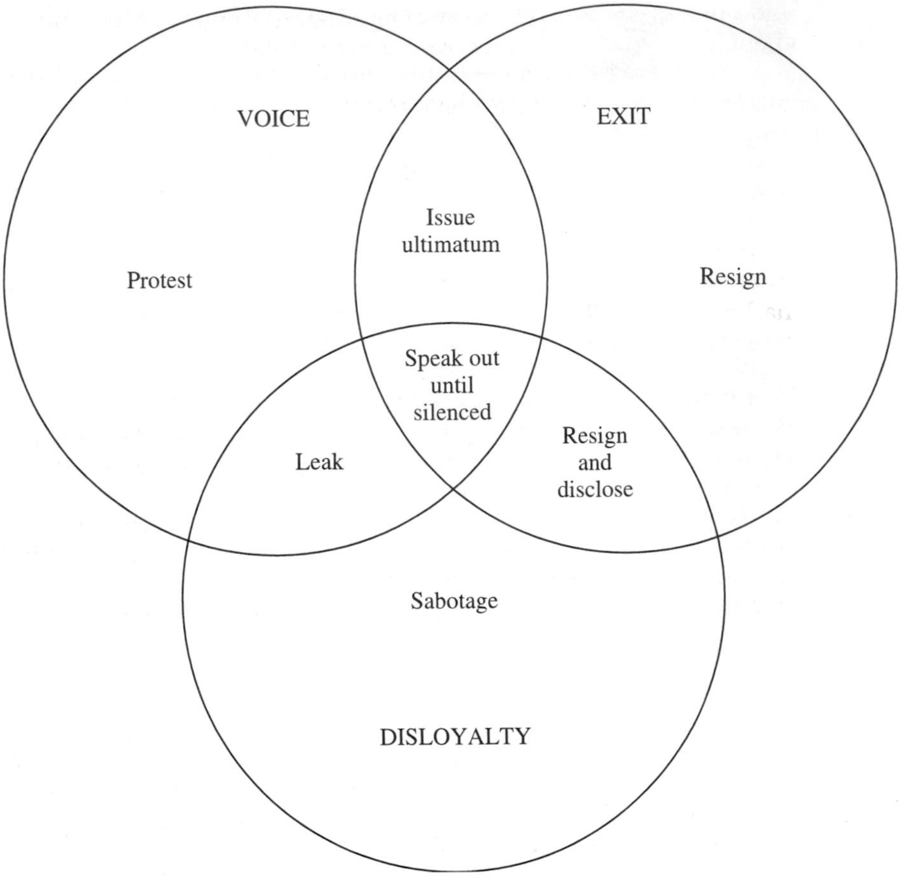

Figure 3.1 Alternative Responses to Value Conflicts

point, however, you will have exhausted all the avenues of protest within the agency that are recognized as legitimate.

Although you remained loyal to the agency, your protest probably involved personal costs: the time and energy needed to express your opinions, the personal offense of your superiors, perhaps the loss of influence over the policy in dispute, and the potential loss of influence over other issues in the future. If you were successful in reversing the policy, then at least you can take comfort in having disposed of your ethical problem. If you were unsuccessful, then you must make a further assessment by comparing the values you can achieve by remaining loyal to the agency with the values you give up by participating in the implementation of the bad policy.

A very different approach would be to *resign* when asked to prepare the implementation strategy.[8] You decide that contributing to implementation would be so ethically objectionable that it justifies your leaving the agency. Your personal

[8]For an overview of the practical and ethical issues, see J. Patrick Dobel, "The Ethics of Resigning," *Journal of Policy Analysis and Management* 18(2) 1999, 245–63.

costs will depend largely on your employment opportunities outside the agency. If you are highly skilled and have a good reputation, then it may be possible for you to move directly to a comparable position. If you are less skilled and not well regarded in the professional network, then you may face unemployment or underemployment for a time.

But what are the ethical implications of your action? Only if your skills were essential to implementation would resigning stop the bad policy. If the policy goes forward, then the ethical value of your resignation is questionable. Although you were able simultaneously to remain loyal to the agency and to avoid contributing directly to the implementation, you forfeited whatever influence you might have had within the agency over the policy. You also may have betrayed the terms of your employment contract as well as some of the personal trust placed in you by your superiors and colleagues, and you may have jeopardized other worthy projects within the agency by withdrawing your contributions. If you believe either that the policy is very bad or you would have had a good prospect of overturning it from within the agency, then running away by resigning seems to lack fortitude.

Combining voice with the threat of exit by *issuing an ultimatum* is likely to be ethically superior to simply resigning. After employing the various avenues of protest within the agency, you would inform your superior that if the policy were not reversed you would resign. Of course, you must be willing to carry out your threat, as well as bear the costs of greater personal animosity than you would face from simple resignation. You gain greater leverage in your protest against the policy, but you lose influence over future decisions if you actually have to execute your threat.

Beyond your personal decision to resign, there may be a larger social issue at stake. Why do you find the policy so objectionable while others approve of it? Perhaps the answer is that you have a better developed ethical sense; you are more principled. Is it good for society in the long run to have people such as yourself leave important analytical positions?[9] On the other hand, the reason for disagreement may be that both you and your superiors hold morally justifiable values that happen to conflict. Although we may have some concern about maintaining diversity within our public agencies, the danger of selective attrition seems less serious when it results from legitimate differences of moral opinion rather than from a clash between expediency, say, and basic principles.

Now consider actions that involve *disloyalty* to your client. You might *leak* your agency's plans to a journalist, congressman, interest group leader, or other person who can interfere with them.[10] You are taking your protest outside the agency, and doing so surreptitiously. Even if you are not a pure Kantian, anytime

[9]For an elaboration of this point, see Dennis F. Thompson, "The Possibility of Administrative Ethics," *Public Administration Review* 45(5) 1985, 555–61.

[10]In our discussion, *leaking* refers to the sharing of confidential information with the intention of undermining the client's decision or political position. The sharing of confidential information can also be instrumental in good analysis and to furthering the client's interest in systems where information is decentralized. Analysts may be able to increase their efficacy by developing relationships with their counterparts in other organizations—the exchange of information serves as the instrumental basis of the relationships. For a discussion of the importance of these professional relationships in the U.S. federal government, see William A. Niskanen, "Economists and Politicians," *Journal of Policy Analysis and Management* 5(2) 1986, 234–44. Even when the analyst believes that the revelation is instrumental to the client's interests, however, there remains the ethical issue of whether the analyst should take it upon himself to break the confidence.

you do not act openly and honestly, you should scrutinize closely the morality of your actions. Further, an important moral tenet is that one take responsibility for one's actions.[11] By acting covertly, you hope to stop the bad policy without suffering any adverse personal consequences from your opposition beyond the moral harm you have done to yourself by betraying the trust of your client and by acting dishonestly.

You should not view the violation of confidentiality, by the way, solely as a betrayal of personal trust. Confidentiality often contributes to organizational effectiveness. The expectation of confidentiality encourages decision makers to seek advice beyond their closest and most trusted advisers and to consider potentially desirable alternatives that would attract political opposition if discussed publicly.[12] Your decision to violate confidentiality has implications not just for your client but also for the expectations others have about the confidentiality they will enjoy when considering good as well as bad policies.

You can at least avoid the dishonesty by speaking out publicly. One possibility is that you *resign and disclose* your former client's plans to potential opponents. Although you are being honest and taking responsibility for your actions, disclosure, by violating the confidentiality you owe to your client, is still disloyal. You also forfeit the opportunity of continuing your protest within the agency. Another possibility is that you *speak out until silenced.* This approach, often referred to as *whistle-blowing,* keeps you in your agency for at least a while. Your agency will probably move quickly to exclude you from access to additional information that might be politically damaging. You must expect that eventually you will be fired, or, if you enjoy civil service protection, exiled to some less responsible assignment that you will ultimately wish to leave.[13] Therefore, your approach combines voice and disloyalty with eventual exit.

Under what conditions is whistle-blowing likely to be ethically justified? Peter French proposes four necessary conditions: first, you must exhaust all channels of protest within your agency before bringing your objections to the attention of the media, interest groups, or other units in the government. Second, you must determine that "procedural, policy, moral, or legal bounds have been violated." Third, you must be convinced that the violation will "have demonstrable harmful immediate effects upon the country, state, or citizens." Fourth, you must be able to support specific accusations with "unequivocal evidence."[14]

French's conditions limit justifiable whistle-blowing to fairly exceptional circumstances. We might question whether they should all be viewed as necessary. For example, if great harm were at stake, we might view whistle-blowing as ethical

[11]We might think of leaking as a form of civil disobedience, a type of protest often considered ethically justified. The classification fails, however, because most definitions of civil disobedience include the requirement that the acts be public. See Amy Gutmann and Dennis F. Thompson, eds., *Ethics & Politics* (Chicago: Nelson-Hall, 1984), 79–80. For a thoughtful discussion of personal responsibility in the bureaucratic setting, see Dennis F. Thompson, "Moral Responsibility of Public Officials: The Problem of Many Hands," *American Political Science Review* 74(4) 1980, 905–16.

[12]For a discussion of this point and whistle-blowing, see Sissila Bok, *Secrets: On the Ethics of Concealment and Revelation* (New York: Pantheon, 1982), 175, 210–29.

[13]Whistle-blowing is likely to be personally and professionally costly. Federal programs intended to provide financial compensation to whistle-blowers may not fully compensate these costs and, further, may induce socially undesirable behaviors in the organizations covered. See Peter L. Cruise, "Are There Virtues in Whistleblowing? Perspectives from Health Care Organizations," *Public Administration Quarterly* 25(3/4) 2001/2002, 413–35.

[14]Peter A. French, *Ethics in Government* (Englewood Cliffs, NJ: Prentice Hall, 1983), 134–37.

even if the evidence brought forward falls short of unequivocal. We should also recognize that the conditions call for great judgment on the part of the potential whistle-blower, especially with respect to anticipating the harmful effects of inaction, and therefore constitute only general guidelines. Nevertheless, they seem appropriately to demand a careful weighing of all values, including loyalty.

Consider again the appropriateness of leaking. In addition to whatever conditions you believe justify whistle-blowing, you must also have a moral reason for acting covertly. In some extreme situations, perhaps involving the reporting of criminal acts in democracies or the supporting of human rights in totalitarian states, you might feel justified in acting covertly because your life or that of your family would be jeopardized by open protest. You might also be justified acting covertly if you were convinced that you could prevent serious harm that might occur in the future by remaining in your position.

Finally, you might consider *sabotage*—disloyalty without voice or exit. In designing the implementation plan for the policy you abhor, you might be able to build in some subtle flaw that would likely force your agency to abandon implementation at some point. For example, you might select a pilot site in the district of a powerful congresswoman who will strongly oppose the policy once it becomes apparent. But such sabotage is morally suspect, not only because it involves covert action but also because it operates through obstruction rather than persuasion. Only the most extreme conditions, including all those needed to justify leaking plus the absence of any reasonable avenues for protest, justify sabotage. It is hard to imagine situations in democratic regimes that produce these conditions.

Some Examples of Value Conflicts

Clients, because they have political interests related to their own policy preferences, the missions of their agencies, or their own personal advancement, may refuse to accept the truthful reports of their analysts. In some situations clients may put pressure on analysts to "cook up" different conclusions or recommendations. In other situations the clients may simply misrepresent their analysts' results to other participants in the decision-making process. What are the minimal duties of analysts in these situations?

Demands for Cooked Results. Most analysts desire at least the option to act as objective technicians. Faced with the task of evaluating alternative courses of action, they want the freedom to make reasonable assumptions, apply appropriate techniques, report their best estimates, and make logical recommendations. Unfortunately, clients sometimes hold strong beliefs that lead them to reject their analysts' findings, not on the basis of method but solely on the basis of conclusions. If the client simply ignores the analysis, then the analyst will undoubtedly be disappointed but generally faces no great ethical problem—the analyst is simply one source of advice and not the final arbiter of truth. The ethical problem arises when the client, perhaps feeling the need for analytical support in the political fray, demands that the analyst alter the work to reach a different conclusion. Should the analyst ever agree to "cook" the analysis so that it better supports the client's position?

A purist would argue that analytical integrity requires refusal; issue an ultimatum and resign if necessary. Can less than complete refusal ever be ethical?

We should keep in mind that, because analysis involves prediction, analysts rarely enjoy complete confidence in their conclusions. Careful analysts check the sensitivity of their results to changes in critical assumptions and convey the level of confidence they have in their conclusions to their clients. We can imagine analysts developing plausible ranges of results. For example, although the analyst believes that the cost of some program is likely to be close to $10 million, the most conservative assumptions might lead to an estimate of $15 million and the most optimistic assumptions to an estimate of $5 million. After making the range and best estimate clear to the client, would it be ethical for the analyst to prepare a version of the analysis for public distribution that used only the most optimistic assumptions?

Analysts who view themselves as clients' advocates might feel comfortable preparing the optimistic analysis for public use; those who see themselves as issue advocates might also if they share their clients' policy preferences. After all, analysis is only one of many political resources, and it rarely encompasses all the relevant values. For analysts viewing themselves as objective technicians, however, the question is more difficult. Limiting the analysis to optimistic assumptions violates their conception of analytical integrity: in honest analysis, the assumptions drive the results rather than vice versa. Nevertheless, objective technicians may feel justified in going along if they are confident that their clients' political opponents will draw attention to the slanted assumptions.[15] When objective technicians believe that the aggregate of analysis reaching the political forum will be balanced, their acquiescence appears less serious in terms of ethics and more serious in terms of professional reputation.

Indeed, if we focus solely on consequences, might not analysts have a responsibility to slant their analysis to counter the slanted analyses of others? Imagine that the person making the final decision lacks either the time or the expertise to evaluate the technical validity of the analyses that are presented. Instead, the decision maker gives the results of each analysis equal weight. In our example, the final decision would be based on the average of the cost estimates presented by the various analysts. If one analyst gives a pessimistic estimate and another gives a realistic estimate, then the final decision will be biased toward the pessimistic. If the second analyst gives an optimistic estimate instead, then the final decision may be less biased. The broader consequences of compromising the procedural value of analytical integrity, however, may be to increase the professional acceptability of slanted analyses, and thus make it less likely that analysts will adopt the role of neutral technician in the future. Perhaps attacking the methodology of the slanted analysis directly rather than counterslanting, even if less effective for the issue at hand, would be better in the long run from the perspective of the social role of the professional policy analyst.

Misrepresentation of Results. Analysts have less ethical room in which to maneuver when their clients try to force them out of the range of the plausible. Defense of analytical integrity would seem generally to require protest backed up with

[15]More generally, this example suggests that the appropriate role for the analyst will depend on the policy environment. In closed fora where the analysis is most likely to be decisive, the role of neutral technician seems most socially appropriate. In more open fora where all interests are analytically represented, advocacy may be the most socially appropriate role. For a development of this line of argument, see Hank C. Jenkins-Smith, *Democratic Politics and Policy Analysis* (Pacific Grove, CA: Brooks/Cole, 1990), 92–121.

the threat of resignation. The analysts' predicament, however, becomes much more complicated when their clients do not actually try to force them to cook up results but, rather, misrepresent what they have already done.

An analyst facing such misrepresentation is in a position similar to that of the defense attorney in a criminal case in which the client insists on being given the opportunity to commit perjury as a witness. By actively participating in the perjury, the attorney would be clearly violating his or her responsibility as an officer of the court. A more interesting problem arises if the client switches attorneys, conceals the truth, and then commits the perjury. Hearing of the testimony, the first attorney knows that perjury has been committed. Must he or she inform the court? One value at stake is the integrity of judicial fact-finding. Another is the confidentiality of the communication between defendant and attorney that encourages defendants to be truthful so that their attorneys can give them the most vigorous defense. Although there seems to be a consensus in the U.S. legal profession that actually participating in perjury is unethical, there does not appear to be a consensus about the responsibility of attorneys when they know that former clients are committing perjury.[16]

Confidentiality probably plays a more important social role in the relationship between defense attorney and defendant than between analyst and client. The former contributes to a system of justice that rarely convicts or punishes the innocent; the latter to more inquisitive and open public officials. Further, the public official's obligation to honesty arises from a public trust as well as private virtue so that public dishonesty, unjustified by other overriding values, lessens the force of confidentiality. Therefore, the analyst's ethical burden seems to go beyond refusal to participate actively in the misrepresentation of the analysis.

Before taking any action, however, the analyst should be certain that the misrepresentation is intentional. Usually this involves confronting the client privately. Upon hearing the analyst's concern, the client may voluntarily correct the misrepresentation through private communication with relevant political actors or take other remedial action. The client might also convince the analyst that some other value, such as national security, justifies the misrepresentation. If the analyst becomes convinced, however, that the misrepresentation is both intentional and unjustified, then the next step (following the guidelines for whistle-blowing) should be to determine the amount of direct harm that will result if the misrepresentation is left unchallenged. If little direct harm is likely to result, then resignation alone may be ethically acceptable. If the direct harm appears substantial, then the analyst bears a responsibility to inform the relevant political actors as well.

Ethical Code or Ethos?

Professions often develop ethical codes to guide the behavior of their members. The codes typically provide guidelines for dealing with the most common ethical predicaments faced by practitioners. The guidelines usually reflect a consensus of

[16]For general background, see Phillip E. Johnson, *Criminal Law* (St. Paul, MN: West, 1980), 119–32.

beliefs held by members of professional organizations.[17] Established and dominant professional organizations with homogeneous memberships enjoy the best prospects for developing ethical codes that provide extensive and detailed guidance.[18] Although a professional organization for policy analysts exists (the Association for Public Policy Analysis and Management), it is young, still relatively small, and seeks to serve a very diverse membership with strong ties to other, more established, professions. Not surprisingly, it has not yet tried to develop an ethical code. Even when it becomes more established, the great diversity of its members and the organizational contexts in which they work suggest the difficulty of developing a code that directly addresses a wide range of circumstances.[19]

Students of the policy sciences, however, have suggested some general guidelines that deserve consideration. For example, Yehezkel Dror proposes that policy scientists not work for clients who they believe have goals that contradict the basic values of democracy and human rights, and that they should resign rather than contribute to the realization of goals with which they fundamentally disagree.[20] Obviously, the analyst who chooses only clients with similar worldviews and value systems is less likely to face conflicts between the values of responsibility to client and adherence to one's conception of good than the analyst who is less selective. Unfortunately, analysts often find themselves in situations where selectivity is impractical. All analysts face the problem of inferring the values and goals of potential clients from limited information; in addition, analysts employed in government agencies may find themselves working for new clients when administrations change. We have already discussed the reasons why resignation is not always the most ethical response to value conflicts between analysts and clients.

Most of Dror's other proposals seem relevant to policy analysis. For example, he proposes that clients deserve complete honesty, including explicated assumptions and uncensored alternatives, and that analysts should not use their access to information and influence with clients to further their own private interests. But these sorts of admonitions would follow from the moral system most of us would accept as private persons. In fact, some would argue that the moral obligations in most professions are not strongly differentiated from those of the nonprofessional.[21] A reasonable approach to professional ethics for policy analysts, therefore, may be to recognize responsibility to the client and analytical integrity as values that belong in the general hierarchy of values governing moral behavior.

[17]For empirical assessments of the degree of consensus over what constitutes ethical behavior within two policy-related professions, see Elizabeth Howe and Jerome Kaufman, "The Ethics of Contemporary American Planners," *Journal of the American Planning Association* 45(3) 1979, 243–55; and James S. Bowman, "Ethics in Government: A National Survey of Public Administrators," *Public Administration Review* 50(3) 1990, 345–53.

[18]The American Society for Public Administration adopted a general set of moral principles that evolved into a code of ethics for members in 1984. The code, which was revised in 1994, can be found on the back cover of *Public Administration Review*. It provides specific admonitions relevant to policy analysts under five general headings: Serve the Public Interest, Respect the Constitution and the Law, Demonstrate Personal Integrity, Promote Ethical Organizations, and Strive for Professional Excellence.

[19]For a discussion of some of the problems of developing an ethical code, see Guy Benveniste, "On a Code of Ethics for Policy Experts," *Journal of Policy Analysis and Management* 3(4) 1984, 561–72, which deals with the conduct of scientists and others who provide expert advice on policy questions.

[20]Yehezkel Dror, *Designs of Policy Science* (New York: American Elsevier, 1971), 119.

[21]See, for example, Alan H. Goldman, *The Moral Foundations of Professional Ethics* (Totowa, NJ: Rowman and Littlefield, 1980).

Rather than waiting for a code of ethics, perhaps we should, as Mark Lilla argues, work toward an ethos for the new profession of policy analysis.[22] As teachers and practitioners of policy analysis, we should explicitly recognize our obligations to protect the basic rights of others, to support our democratic processes as expressed in our constitutions, and to promote analytical and personal integrity.[23] These values should generally dominate our responsibility to the client in our ethical evaluations. Nevertheless, we should show considerable tolerance for the ways our clients choose to resolve difficult value conflicts, and we should maintain a realistic modesty about the predictive power of our analyses.

For Discussion

1. Imagine that you are a policy analyst working as a budget analyst for your state's department of education. You have made what you believe to be a fairly accurate prediction of the cost of a statewide class-size reduction program for elementary schools. You just discovered that your supervisor is planning to testify before a committee of the state assembly that the cost would be less than half of what you predicted. What factors would you consider in deciding on an ethical course of action?
2. Imagine that you are an analyst in a public agency. Think of a scenario in which you would feel compelled to resign. Avoid extreme scenarios—merely a situation that would just push you over the edge. (Thanks to Philip Ryan, "Ethics and Resignation: A Classroom Exercise," *Journal of Policy Analysis and Management* 22(2) 2003, 313–18.)

[22]Mark T. Lilla, "Ethos, 'Ethics,' and Public Service," *Public Interest* (63) 1981, 3–17.

[23]See J. Patrick Dobel, "Integrity in the Public Service," *Public Administration Review* 50(3) 1990, 354–66, for a discussion of commitments to regime accountability, personal responsibility, and prudence as moral resources for exercising discretion.

4

Efficiency and the Idealized Competitive Model

Collective action enables society to produce, distribute, and consume a great variety and abundance of goods. Most collective action arises from voluntary agreements among people—within families, private organizations, and exchange relationships. The policy analyst, however, deals primarily with collective action involving the legitimate coercive powers of government: public policy encourages, discourages, prohibits, or prescribes private actions. Beginning with the premise that individuals generally act in their own best interest, policy analysts bear the burden of providing rationales for any governmental interference with private choice. The burden applies to the evaluation of existing policies as well as new initiatives. It is an essential element, if not the first step, in any analysis, and will often provide the best initial insight into complex situations.

Our approach to classifying rationales for public policy begins with the concept of a perfectly competitive economy. One of the fundamental bodies of theory in modern economics deals with the properties of idealized economies involving large numbers of profit-maximizing firms and utility-maximizing consumers. Under certain assumptions, the self-motivated behaviors of these economic actors lead to patterns of production and consumption that are efficient in the special sense that it would not be possible to change the patterns in such a way so as to make some person better off without making some other person worse off.

Economists recognize several commonly occurring circumstances of private choice, referred to as *market failures*, that violate the basic assumptions of the idealized competitive economy and, therefore, interfere with efficiency in production or consumption. The traditional market failures, which we discuss in Chapter 5, provide widely accepted rationales for such public policies as the provision of goods and the regulation of markets by government agencies. Economists, until recently, have paid less attention, however, to the plausibility of some of the more fundamental assumptions about the behavior of consumers. For example, economic models usually treat the preferences of consumers as unchanging. Is this reasonable? Do consumers always make the right calculations when faced with decisions involving such complexities as risk? Negative answers to these questions, which we consider in Chapter 6, may also provide rationales for public policies.

Of course, efficiency is not the only social value. Human dignity, distributional equity, economic opportunity, and political participation are values that deserve consideration along with efficiency. On occasion, public decision makers or ourselves, as members of society, may wish to give up some economic efficiency to protect human life, make the final distribution of goods more equitable, or promote fairness in the distribution process. As analysts, we have a responsibility to address these multiple values and the potential conflicts among them. We discuss distributional and other values as rationales for public policies in Chapter 7.

The Efficiency Benchmark: The Competitive Economy

Imagine a world where each person derives *utility* (one's perception of one's own well-being) from personally consuming various quantities of all possible goods, including things, services, and leisure. We can think of each person as having a utility function that converts the list of quantities of the goods consumed into a utility index such that higher numbers imply greater well-being. We make several basic assumptions. First, other things equal, the more of any good a person has, the greater that person's utility. (We can incorporate unpleasant things such as pollution within this framework by thinking of them as "goods" that decrease utility.) And, second, additional units of the same good give ever-smaller increases in utility; in other words, we have what economists call *declining marginal utility.*

Now make the following assumptions about the production of goods: Firms attempt to maximize profits by buying factor inputs (such as labor, land, capital, and materials) to produce goods for sale. The technology available to firms for converting factor inputs to final goods is such that, at best, an additional unit of output would require at least as many units of inputs to produce as the preceding unit; in other words, it becomes more costly in terms of resources to produce each additional unit of the good. Firms behave competitively in the sense that they believe that they cannot change the prices of factor inputs or products by their individual actions.

Each person has a budget derived from selling labor and his or her initial endowments of the other factor inputs like capital and land. People maximize their well-being by using their incomes to purchase the combinations of goods that give them the greatest utility.

In this simple world, a set of prices arises that distributes factor inputs to firms and goods to persons in such a way that it would not be possible for anyone to find a reallocation that would make at least one person better off without making at least one person worse off.[1] Economists refer to such a distribution as being *Pareto efficient.* It is a concept with great intuitive appeal: wouldn't, and shouldn't, we be dissatisfied with an existing distribution if we could find an alternative distribution that would make someone better off without making anyone else worse off? Although we would need other criteria for choosing between two distributions that were each Pareto efficient, we should, unless we are malevolent, always want to make Pareto-improving moves from inefficient distributions to efficient ones.

Figure 4.1 illustrates the concept of Pareto efficiency involving the allocation of $1,000 between two people. Assume that the two people will receive any mutually agreed-upon amounts of money that sum to no more than $1,000. The vertical axis represents the allocation to person 1 and the horizontal axis represents the allocation to person 2. An allocation of all of the money to person 1 would appear as the point on the vertical axis at $1,000; an allocation of all of the money to person 2 would appear as the point on the horizontal axis at $1,000. The line connecting these two points, which we call the *potential Pareto frontier*, represents all the possible allocations to the two persons that sum exactly to $1,000. Any point on this line or inside the triangle it forms with the axes would be a technically feasible allocation because it gives shares that sum to no more than $1,000.

The potential Pareto frontier indicates all the points that fully allocate the $1,000. Any allocation that does not use up the entire $1,000 cannot be Pareto efficient, because it would be possible to make one of the persons better off by giving her the remaining amount without making the other person worse off. The actual Pareto frontier depends on the allocations that the two people receive if they reach no agreement. If they each receive nothing in the event they reach no agreement, then the potential Pareto frontier is the *actual Pareto frontier* in that any point on it would make at least one of the persons better off without making the other person worse off.

Now imagine that, if these two people reach no agreement about an allocation, person 1 receives $100 and person 2 receives $200. The point ($100, $200) can be thought of as the status quo—it indicates how much each person gets in the absence of an agreement. The introduction of this status quo point reduces the Pareto frontier to the line segment between ($100, $900) and ($800, $200). Only moves to this segment of the potential Pareto frontier actually guarantee that each person is no worse off than under the status quo.

Note that whether or not a particular point on the potential Pareto frontier is actually Pareto efficient depends on the default allocations that comprise the status quo. More generally, Pareto efficiency in an economy depends on the initial endowments of resources to individuals.

The idealized competitive economy is an example of a *general equilibrium model*—it finds the prices of factor inputs and goods that clear all markets in the sense that the quantity demanded exactly equals the quantity supplied. Although general equilibrium models can sometimes be usefully applied to policy problems, limitations in data and problems of tractability usually lead

[1]For an overview of the history of general equilibrium theory, see E. Roy Weintraub, "On the Existence of a Competitive Equilibrium: 1930–1954," *Journal of Economic Literature* 21(1) 1983, 1–39.

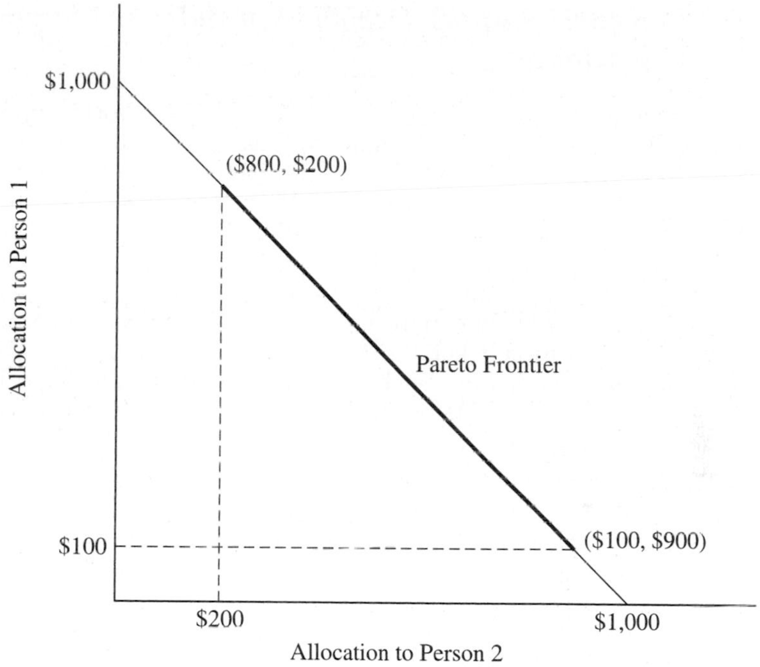

Status quo: Point ($100, $200)
Potential Pareto Frontier: Line segment connecting ($1,000, $0) and ($0, $1,000)
Pareto Frontier: Line segment connecting ($800, $200) and ($100, $900)

Figure 4.1 Pareto and Potential Pareto Efficiency

economists to evaluate policies in one market at a time.[2] Fortunately, a well-developed body of theory enables us to assess economic efficiency in the context of a single market.

Market Efficiency: The Meaning of Social Surplus

We need a yardstick for measuring changes in efficiency. Social surplus, which measures the net benefits consumers and producers receive from participation in markets, serves as an appropriate yardstick. In the context of the ideally competitive economy, the Pareto-efficient allocation of goods also maximizes social surplus. When we look across markets, the set of prices and quantities that give the greatest social surplus is usually Pareto efficient. Moreover, differences in social surplus between alternative market allocations approximate the corresponding sum of differences in individual welfares. As social surplus is the sum of consumer surplus and producer surplus, we consider each in turn.

[2]For a review of general equilibrium models used in policy analysis, see John B. Shoven and John Whalley, "Applied General-Equilibrium Models of Taxation and International Trade: An Introduction and Survey," *Journal of Economic Literature* 22(3) 1984, 1007–51.

Consumer Surplus: Demand Schedules as Marginal Valuations

Imagine that you have the last five tickets to the World Cup Soccer final match. You walk into a room and announce to those present that you own all the remaining tickets to the event and that you will sell these tickets in the following manner: Starting with a high stated price, say, $500, you will keep lowering it until someone agrees to purchase a ticket. You will continue lowering the stated price until all five tickets are claimed. (An auction such as this with declining prices is known as a Dutch auction; in contrast, an auction with ascending prices is known as an English auction.) Each person in the room decides the maximum amount that he or she is willing to pay for a ticket. If this maximum amount must be paid, then each person will be indifferent between buying and not buying the ticket. Figure 4.2 displays the valuations for the persons in descending order from left to right. Although the stated prices begin at $500, the first acceptance is at $200. The purchaser obviously values this ticket at least at $200. Value in this context means the maximum

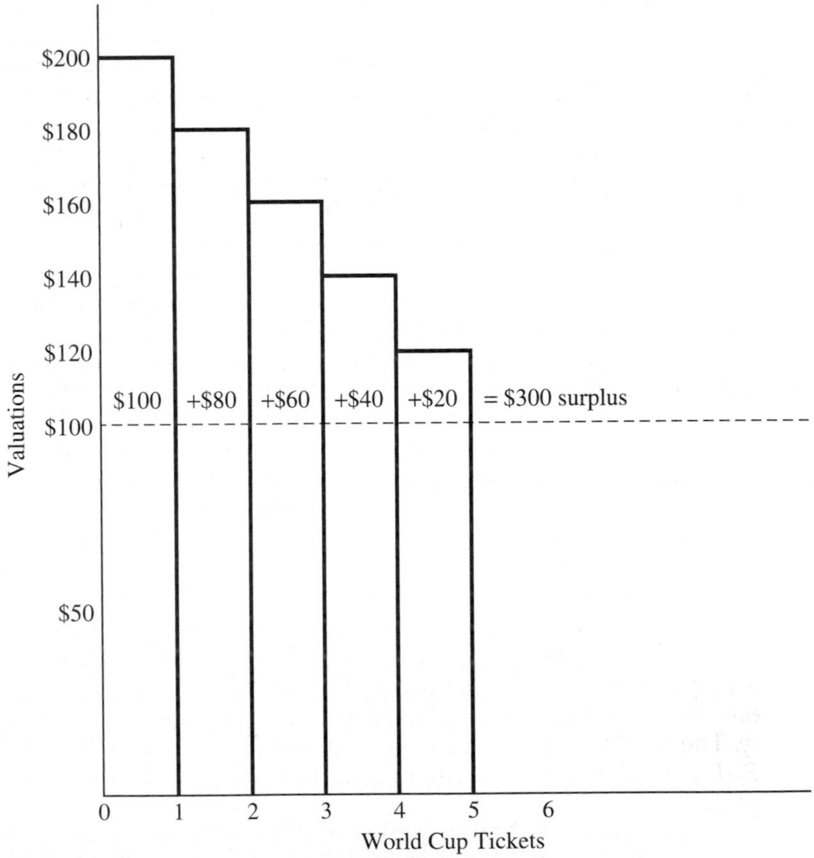

Figure 4.2 Consumer Values and Surpluses

amount the person is willing to pay, given his or her budget and other consumption opportunities. You now continue offering successively lower stated prices until you sell a second ticket, which a second person accepts at $180, the second-highest valuation. Repeating this process, you sell the remaining three tickets at $160, $140, and $120, respectively.

You were happy as a seller to get each person to pay the amount that he or she valued the ticket. If, instead, you had announced prices until you found one (specifically, $100) such that exactly five people wanted to buy tickets, then some of the purchasers would get tickets at a price substantially lower than the maximum amounts that they would have been willing to pay. For example, the person with the highest valuation would have been willing to pay $200 but only has to pay your set price of $100. The difference between the person's dollar valuation of the ticket and the price that he or she actually pays ($200 – $100) is the surplus value that the person gains from the transaction. In a similar way, the person with the second-highest surplus gains $80 ($180 – $100). The remaining three purchasers receive surpluses of $60 ($160 – $100), $40 ($140 – $100), and $20 ($120 – $100). Adding the surpluses realized by these five purchasers yields a measure of the *consumer surplus* in this market for World Cup tickets of $300.

The staircase in Figure 4.2 is sometimes called a *marginal valuation schedule* because it indicates how much successive units of a good are valued by consumers in a market. If, instead of seeing how much would be bid for successive units of the good, we stated various prices and observed how many units would be purchased at each price, then we would obtain the same staircase but recognize it as a *demand schedule*. Of course, we would also get a demand schedule by allowing individuals to purchase more than one unit at the stated prices. If we had been able to measure our good in small enough divisible units, or if demanded quantities were very large, the staircase would smooth out to become a curve.

How do we move from this conceptualization of consumer surplus to its measurement in actual markets? We make use of demand schedules, which can be estimated from observing market behavior.

Line D in Figure 4.3 represents a person's demand schedule for some good X. (Later we will interpret the curve as the demand schedule for all persons with access to the market.) Note that this consumer values all units less than *choke price*, P_c, the price that "chokes off" demand. The horizontal line drawn at P_0 indicates that she can purchase as many units of the good as she wishes at the constant price P_0. At price P_0 she purchases a quantity Q_0. Suppose, however, she purchased less than Q_0; then she would find that she could make herself better off by purchasing a little more because she would value additional consumption more than its cost to her. (The demand schedule lies above price for quantities less than Q_0.) Suppose, on the other hand, she purchased more than Q_0; then she would find that she could make herself better off by purchasing a little less because she would value the savings more than the lost consumption. At given price P_0, the quantity Q_0 is an *equilibrium* because the consumer does not want to move to an alternative quantity. The area of the triangle under the demand schedule but above the price line, $P_c a P_0$, represents her consumer surplus from purchasing Q_0 units of the good at price P_0.

Changes in consumer surplus are often the basis for measuring the relative efficiencies of alternative policies. For example, how does consumer surplus change in Figure 4.3 if a government policy increases price from P_0 to P_1? The new consumer

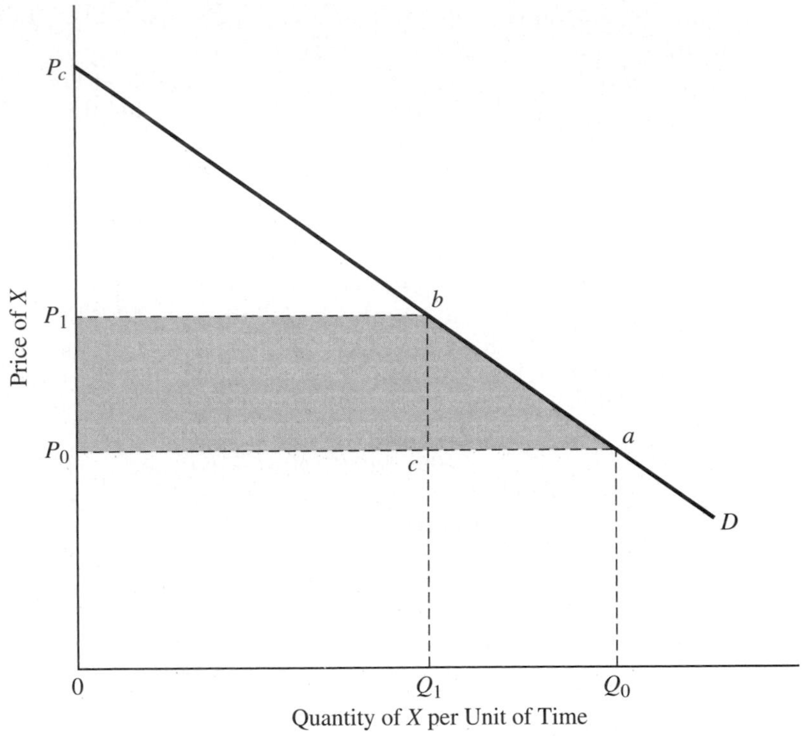

Loss in consumer surplus:	P_1baP_0
Revenue collected by government:	P_1bcP_0
Deadweight loss:	*abc*

Figure 4.3 Changes in Consumer Surplus

surplus is the area of triangle P_cbP_1, which is smaller than the area of triangle P_caP_0 by the area of the trapezoid inscribed by P_1baP_0 (the shaded region). We interpret the area of the rectangle P_1bcP_0 as the additional amount the consumer must pay for the units of the good that she continues to purchase and the area of the triangle *abc* as the surplus the consumer gives up by reducing consumption from Q_0 to Q_1.

As an example of a government policy that raises price, imagine the imposition of an excise (commodity) tax on each unit of the good in the amount of the difference between P_1 and P_0. Then the area of rectangle P_1bcP_0 corresponds to the revenue raised by the tax, which, conceivably, could be rebated to the consumer to offset exactly that part of the consumer surplus lost. The consumer would still suffer the loss of the area of triangle *abc*. Because there are no revenues or benefits to offset this reduction in consumer surplus, economists define this loss in surplus due to a reduction in consumption as the *deadweight loss* of the tax. The deadweight loss indicates that the equilibrium price and quantity under the tax are not Pareto efficient—if it were possible, the consumer would be better off simply giving the tax collector a lump–sum payment equal to the area of P_1bcP_0 in return for removal of the excise tax and its associated deadweight loss.

The loss of consumer surplus shown in Figure 4.3 approximates the most commonly used theoretical measure of changes in individual welfare: *compensating variation.* The compensating variation of a price change is the amount by which the consumer's budget would have to be changed so that he or she would have the same utility after the price change as before. It thus serves as a dollar measure, or *money metric,* for changes in welfare. If the demand schedule represented in Figure 4.3 were derived by observing how the consumer varied purchases as a function of price, holding utility constant at its initial level (it thus would be what we call a *constant-utility demand schedule*), then the consumer surplus change would exactly equal the compensating variation.

Figure 4.4 illustrates how compensating variation can be interpreted as a money metric for utility. The vertical axis measures expenditures by a person on all goods other than good X; the horizontal axis measures how many units of X she consumes. Imagine initially that she has a budget, *B*, but that she is not allowed to purchase any units of X, say, because X is manufactured in another country and imports of it are prohibited. She will, therefore, spend all of *B* on other goods. The *indifference curve* I_0 indicates all the combinations of expenditures on other goods and units of *X* that would give her the same utility as spending *B* on other goods and consuming no units of X. Now imagine that the import ban is lifted so that she can purchase units of *X* at price P_x. She can now choose any point on the line connecting *B* with the point on the horizontal axis indicating how many units of *X* she

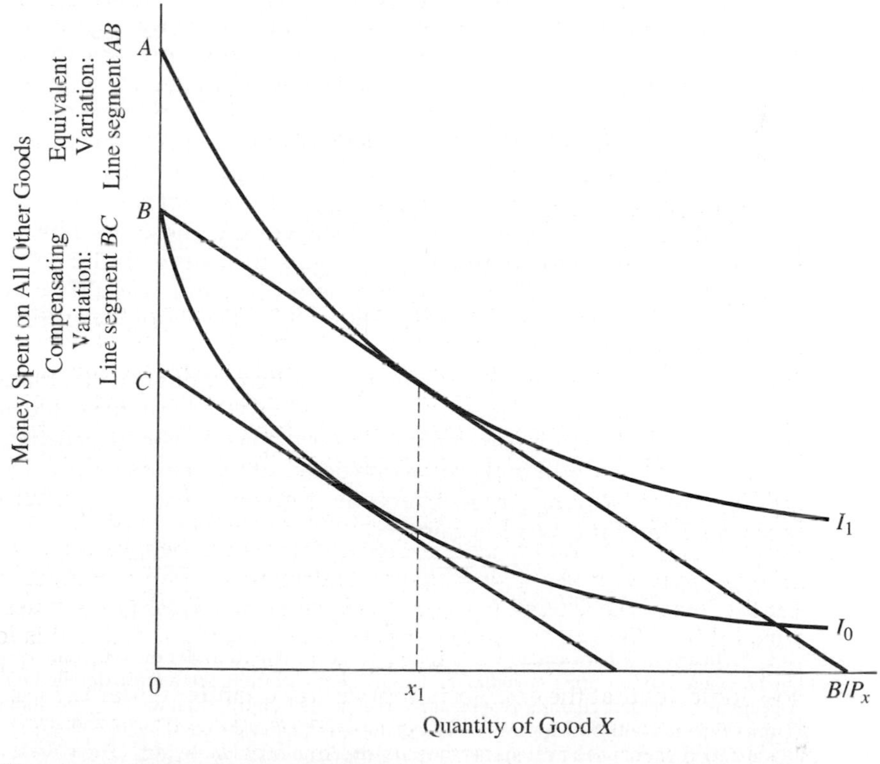

Figure 4.4 Money Metrics for Utility

could purchase if she spent zero on other goods, B/P_x. Once this new budget line is available, she will maximize her utility by selecting a point on the highest feasible indifference I_1, by purchasing x_1 units of X and spending her remaining budget on other goods. Once X is available, it would be possible to return her to her initial level of utility by reducing her initial budget by the distance between B and C on the vertical axis. This amount is her compensating variation associated with the availability of X at price P_x. It is a dollar value, or money metric, for how much value she places on being able to consume X.

Instead of asking how much money we could take away to make the person as well off after introduction of imports of X as before, we could ask how much money we would have to give her if X were not available so that she is as well off as she would be with imports of X. This amount, called *equivalent variation*, is shown as the distance between A and B on the vertical axis—if her budget were increased from B to A, then she could reach indifference curve I_1 without consuming X.

In practice, we usually work with empirically estimated demand schedules that hold constant the consumer's *income* (rather than utility) and all other prices. This *constant income*, or *Marshallian*, *demand schedule* involves decreases in utility as price rises (and total consumption falls) and increases in utility as price falls (and total consumption rises). In comparison with a demand schedule holding utility constant at the initial level, the Marshallian demand schedule is lower for price increases and higher for price reductions. Fortunately, as long as either the price change is small or expenditures on the good make up a small part of the consumer's budget, the two schedules are close together and estimates of consumer surplus changes using the Marshallian demand schedule are close to the compensating variations.[3]

Now, moving from the individual to society, consider the relationship between price and the quantity demanded by all consumers. We derive this *market demand schedule* by summing the amounts demanded by each of the consumers at each price. Graphically, this is equivalent to adding horizontally the demand schedules for all the individual consumers. The consumer surplus we measure using this market demand schedule would just equal the sum of the consumer surpluses of all the individual consumers. It would answer the questions: How much compensation would have to be given in aggregate to restore all the consumers to their original utility levels after a price increase? How much could be taken from consumers in the aggregate to restore them all to their original utility levels after a price decrease?

Thus, if we can identify a change in price or quantity in a market that would produce a net positive increase in social surplus, then there is at least the potential for making a Pareto improvement. After everyone is compensated, there is still something left over to make someone better off. Of course, the change is not actually Pareto improving unless everyone is given at least his or her compensating variations from the surplus gain.

[3]In any event, the consumer surplus change measured under the Marshallian demand curve will lie between compensating variation and equivalent variation. For a more detailed discussion of the use of consumer surplus changes as a measure of changes in individual welfare, see Robert D. Willig, "Consumer Surplus without Apology," *American Economic Review* 66(4) 1976, 589–97. For a more intuitive justification of the use of consumer surplus, see Arnold C. Harberger, "Three Basic Postulates for Applied Welfare Economics," *Journal of Economic Literature* 9(3) 1971, 785–97.

Our primary use of consumer surplus in the next chapter is to illustrate the inefficiencies associated with the various market failures. For this purpose, an exclusive focus on the potential for Pareto improvement is adequate. In the context of benefit-cost analysis, the Kaldor-Hicks compensation principle advocates a similar focus on net positive changes in social surplus as an indication of the potential for Pareto improvements. When we consider benefit-cost analysis as a tool for evaluating policies in Chapter 16, we discuss the implications of focusing on potential rather than actual improvements in the welfare of individuals.

Producer Surplus: Background on Pricing

In the ideal competitive model, it is standard to assume that marginal costs of production for individual firms are rising with increases in output beyond equilibrium levels. Because firms have some fixed costs that must be paid before any production can occur, the average cost of producing output first falls as the fixed costs are spread over a larger number of units, then rises as the increasing marginal cost begins to dominate, because the use of some input, such as labor, becomes less efficient. Consequently, some output level minimizes the average cost of the firm. The curve marked AC in Figure 4.5 represents a U-shaped *average cost* curve for the firm. The *marginal cost* curve is labeled MC. Note that the marginal cost curve crosses the average cost curve at the latter's lowest point. When marginal cost is lower than average cost, the latter must be falling. When marginal cost is higher than average cost, the latter must be rising. Only when marginal cost equals average cost

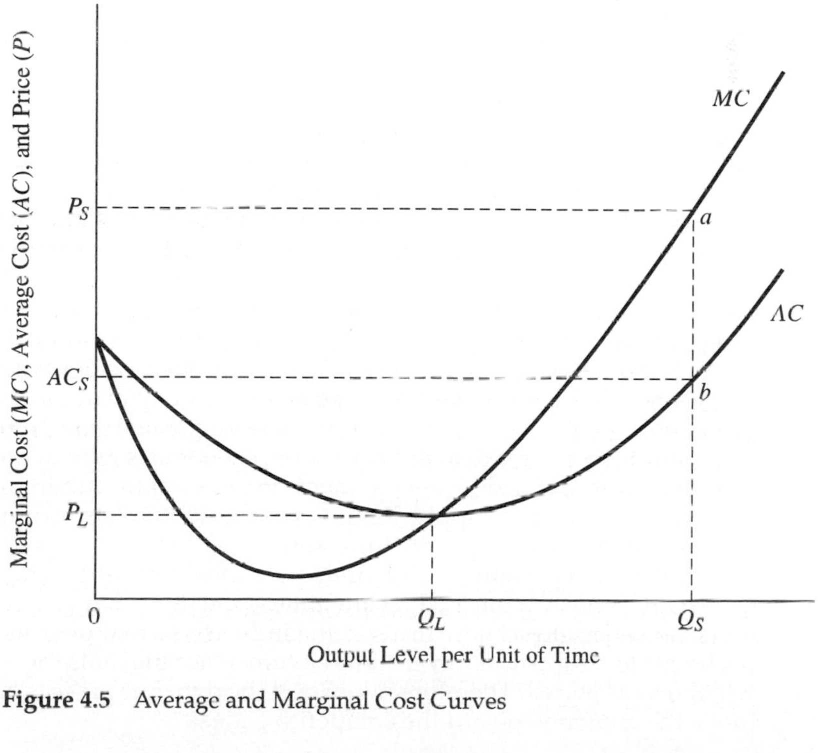

Figure 4.5 Average and Marginal Cost Curves

does average cost remain unchanged. This is easily grasped by thinking about your average score for a series of examinations—only a new score above your current average can raise your average.

The total cost of producing some level of output, say, Q_S, can be calculated in one of two ways. First, because average cost is simply total cost divided by the quantity of output, multiplying average cost at this quantity (AC_S in Figure 4.5) by Q_S yields total cost as given by the area of rectangle AC_SbQ_S0. Second, recalling that marginal cost tells us how much it costs to increase output by one additional unit, we can approximate total cost by adding up the marginal costs of producing successive units from the first all the way up to Q_S. The smaller our units of measure, the closer will be the sum of their associated marginal costs to the total cost of producing Q_S. In the limiting case of infinitesimally small units, the area under the marginal cost curve (*MC* in Figure 4.5) from zero to Q_S exactly equals total cost. (Those familiar with calculus will recognize marginal cost as the derivative of total cost, so that integrating marginal cost over the output range yields total cost; this integration is equivalent to taking the area under the marginal cost curve between zero and the output level.)

Now imagine that the market price for the good produced by the firm is P_S. The firm would maximize its profits by producing Q_S, the quantity at which marginal cost equals price. Because average cost is less than price at output level Q_S, the firm would enjoy a profit equal to the area of rectangle P_SabAC_S. Profit equals total revenue minus total cost. (Total revenue equals price, P_S, times quantity, Q_S, or the area of rectangle P_SaQ_S0; the total cost of producing output level Q_S is the area of rectangle AC_SbQ_S0.) In the competitive model, profit would be distributed to persons according to their initial endowments of ownership. But these shares of profits would signal to others that profits could be made simply by copying the technology and input uses of the firm. As more firms enter the industry, however, total output of the good would rise and, therefore, price would fall. At the same time the new firms would bid up the price of inputs so that the entire marginal and average cost curves of all the firms would shift up. Eventually, price would fall to P_L, the level at which the new marginal cost equals the new average cost. At P_L profits fall to zero, removing any incentive to enter the industry.

With no constraints on the number of identical firms that can arise to produce each good, the Pareto-efficient equilibrium in the idealized competitive model is characterized by zero profits for all firms. (Note that we are referring to economic profits, not accounting profits. *Economic profit* is total revenue minus payments at competitive market prices to all factors of production, including an implicit rental price for capital owned by the firm. *Accounting profit* is simply revenue minus expenditures.) If the firm does not make an explicit payment to shareholders for the capital it uses, then accounting profits may be greater than zero even when economic profits are zero. To avoid confusion, economists refer to economic profits as *rents*, which are defined as any payments in excess of the minimum amounts needed to cover the cost of supply. Rents can occur in markets for inputs such as land and capital as well as in product markets.

In the real economic world, unlike our ideal competitive model, firms cannot be instantaneously replicated; at any time some firms may thus enjoy rents. These rents, however, attract new firms to the industry, so that over the long run we expect rents to disappear. Only if some circumstance prevents the entry of new firms will the rents persist. Therefore, we expect the dynamic process of profit seeking to move the economy toward the competitive ideal.

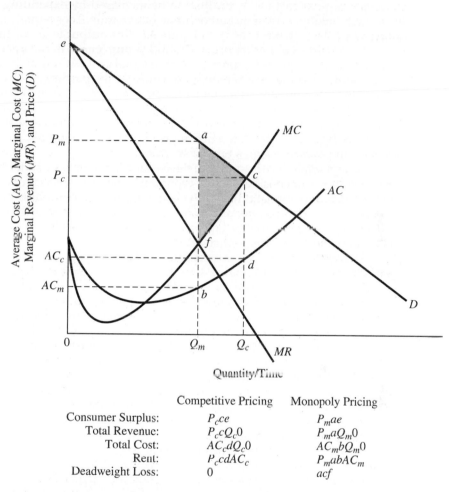

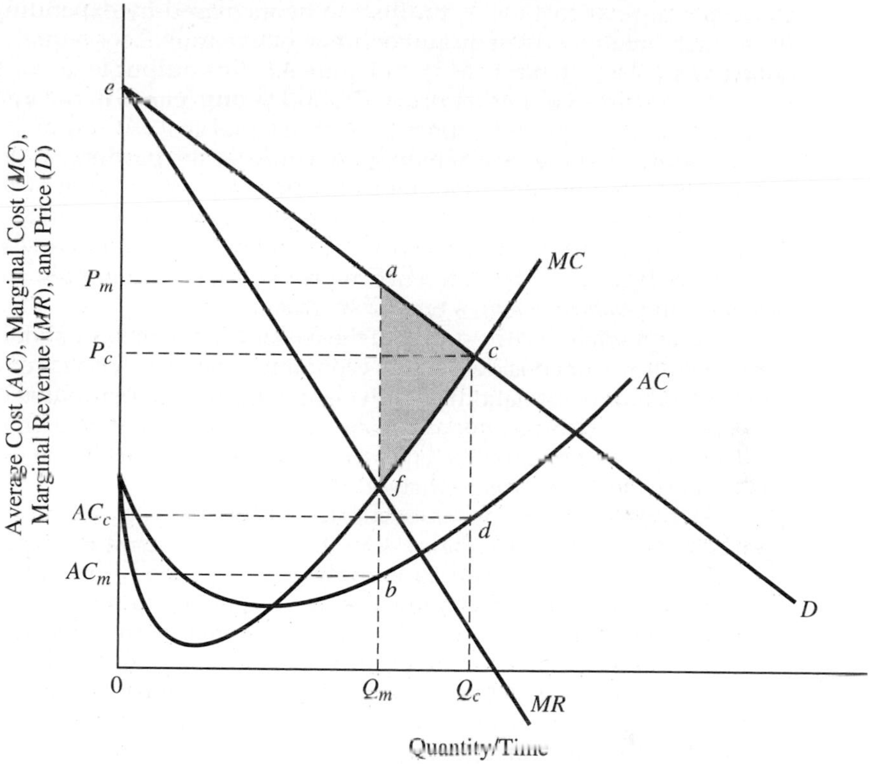

	Competitive Pricing	Monopoly Pricing
Consumer Surplus:	$P_c ce$	$P_m ae$
Total Revenue:	$P_c cQ_c 0$	$P_m aQ_m 0$
Total Cost:	$AC_c dQ_c 0$	$AC_m bQ_m 0$
Rent:	$P_c cdAC_c$	$P_m abAC_m$
Deadweight Loss:	0	acf

Figure 4.6 Monopoly Pricing, Rents, and Deadweight Loss

To understand better the concept of rent, it is useful to contrast pricing in a monopolistic industry with one that is competitive. To begin, consider the case of an industry with a single firm that does not have to worry about future competition. This monopoly firm sees the entire demand schedule for the good, labeled D in Figure 4.6. It also sees a *marginal revenue curve* (MR), which indicates how much revenue increases for each additional unit offered to the market. The marginal revenue curve lies below the demand schedule because each additional unit offered lowers the equilibrium price not just for the last but for all units sold. For example, imagine that by increasing supply from 9 to 10 units decreases the market price from $100/unit to $99/unit. Revenue increases by $90 (10 times $99 minus 9 times $100). The height of the marginal revenue curve above 10 units is thus $90, which is less than the height of the demand schedule, $99. As long as marginal revenue exceeds marginal cost (*MC*), profits can be increased by expanding output. The profit-maximizing level of output occurs when marginal cost equals marginal revenue (where *MC* intersects *MR*). In Figure 4.6, this output level for the monopoly firm, Q_m, results in a market price, P_m, and profits equal to the area of rectangle $P_m abAC_m$: total revenue (P_m times Q_m) minus total cost (AC_m times Q_m).

In contrast to the case of monopoly, consider the production decisions of one of the firms in a competitive industry. Because it provides a small part of the total industry supply, it ignores the effects of its supply on market price and, therefore, equates marginal cost with price (the intersection of *MC* and *D*), yielding price P_C and profits $P_C cdAC_C$. The difference in profit between monopoly and competitive pricing is the *monopoly rent*, a type of economic rent.

Remembering that the profits of the firm go to persons, we should take account of these rents in our consideration of economic efficiency. A dollar of consumer surplus (compensating variation) is equivalent to a dollar of distributed economic profit. If we set the price and quantity to maximize the sum of consumer surplus and rent, then we will generate the largest possible dollar value in the market, creating the prerequisite for a Pareto-efficient allocation.

The largest sum of consumer surplus and rent results when price equals marginal cost. A comparison in Figure 4.6 of the sums of consumer surplus and rent between the competitive and monopoly pricing cases illustrates this general proposition. The sum in the monopoly case, where marginal cost equals marginal revenue ($MC = MR$), is the area between the demand schedule and the marginal cost curve from quantity zero to Q_m. The sum in the competitive case, where marginal cost equals price ($MC = P$), is the area between the demand schedule and the marginal cost curve from quantity zero to Q_C. Obviously, the sum of consumer surplus and rent under competitive pricing exceeds that under monopoly pricing by the shaded area between the demand schedule and the marginal cost curve from Q_m to Q_C. This difference, the area of triangle acf, is the deadweight loss caused by monopoly pricing. That this area is the deadweight loss follows directly from the observation that the marginal benefit (D) exceeds the marginal cost (MC) for each unit produced in expanding output from Q_m to Q_C.

Producer Surplus: Measurement with Supply Schedules

We usually deal with markets in which many firms offer supply. Therefore, we desire some way of conveniently summing the rents that accrue to all the firms supplying the market. Our approach parallels the one we used to estimate compensating variations. First, we introduce the concept of a supply schedule. Second, we show how the supply schedule can be used to measure the sum of rents to all firms supplying the market.

Imagine constructing a schedule indicating the number of units of a good that firms offer at each of various prices. Figure 4.7 shows the common case of firms facing increasing marginal costs. Firms offer a total quantity Q_2 at price P_2. As price increases, firms offer successively greater quantities, yielding an upward-sloping *supply schedule.* The schedule results from the horizontal summation of the marginal cost curves of the firms. (For example, see *MC* in Figure 4.5.) Each point on the supply curve tells us how much it would cost to produce another unit of the good. If we add up these marginal amounts one unit at a time, beginning with

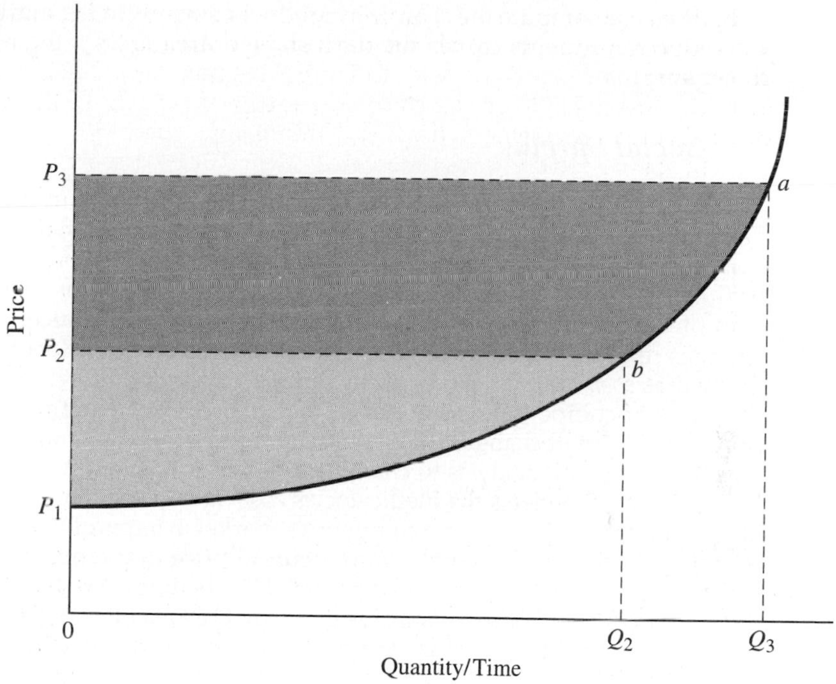

Loss in producer surplus resulting from a fall in price from P_3 to P_2: P_3abP_2

Figure 4.7 A Supply Schedule and Producer Surplus

quantity equal to zero and ending at the quantity supplied, then we arrive at the total cost of producing that quantity. Graphically, this total cost equals the area under the supply curve from quantity zero to the quantity supplied.

Suppose the market price is P_3 so that the quantity supplied is Q_3. Then the total cost of producing Q_3 is the area P_1aQ_30. The total revenue to the firms, however, equals price times quantity, given by the area of rectangle P_3aQ_30. The difference between total revenue and total cost equals the total rent accruing to the firms. This difference, called *producer surplus*, is measured by the total shaded area in Figure 4.7 inscribed by P_3aP_1.

Producer surplus need not be divided equally among firms. Some firms may have unique advantages that allow them to produce at lower cost than other firms, even though all firms must sell at the same price. For instance, a fortunate farmer with very productive land may be able to realize a rent at the market price, while another farmer on marginal land just covers total cost. Because the quantity of very productive land is limited, both farmers face rising marginal costs that they equate with market price to determine output levels. The general point is that unique resources—such as especially productive land, exceptional athletic talent, easy-to-extract minerals—can earn rents even in competitive markets. Excess payments to such unique resources are usually referred to as *scarcity rents.* Unlike monopoly rents, scarcity rents do not necessarily imply economic inefficiency.

Changes in producer surplus represent changes in rents. For example, if we want to know the reduction in rents that would result from a fall in price from P_3

to P_2, then we compute the change in producer surplus in the market. In Figure 4.7 the reduction in rents equals the dark shaded area P_3abP_2, the reduction in producer surplus.

Social Surplus

We now have the basic tools for analyzing efficiency in specific markets. A necessary condition for Pareto efficiency is that it not be possible to increase the sum of compensating variations and rents through any reallocation of factor inputs or final products. We have shown how changes in consumer surplus measure the sum of compensating variations and how changes in producer surplus measure changes in rents. The sum of consumer and producer surpluses in all markets is defined as *social surplus*. Changes in social surplus, therefore, measure changes in the sums of compensating variations and rents. For evaluating the efficiency implications of small changes in the price and quantity of any one good, it is usually reasonable to limit analysis to changes in social surplus in its market alone.

Figure 4.8 reviews the inefficiencies associated with deviations from the equilibrium price and quantity in a competitive market in terms of losses of social surplus. The efficient competitive equilibrium occurs at price P_0 and quantity Q_0, the point of intersection of the supply (S) and demand (D) schedules. A policy that increases price to P_1 involves a loss of social surplus given by the area of triangle *abc*—each forgone unit between Q_1 and Q_0 yields marginal value (as given by the height of the demand

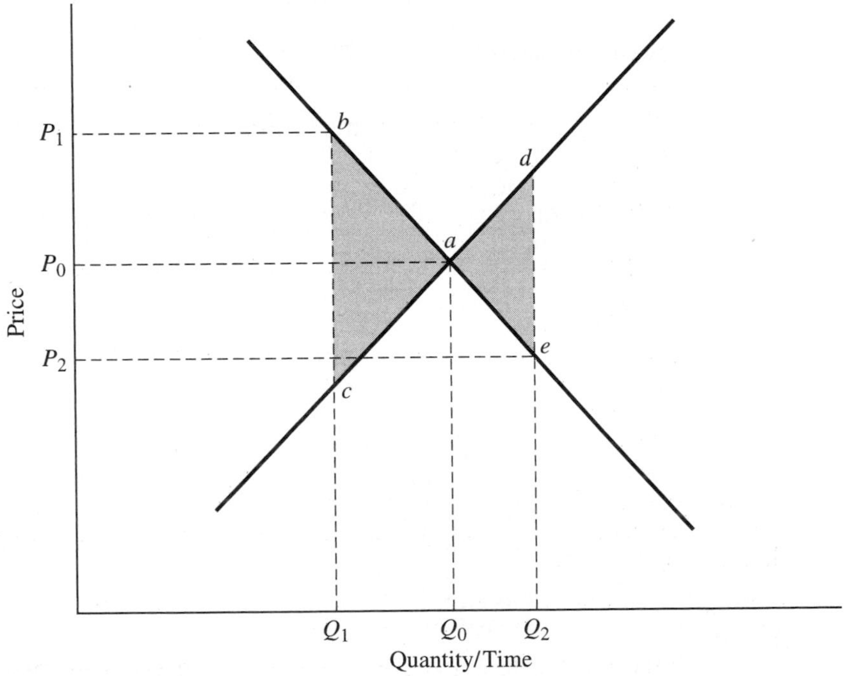

Figure 4.8 Inefficiencies Resulting from Deviations from the Competitive Equilibrium

schedule) in excess of marginal cost (as given by the height of the supply schedule). Consequently, social surplus can be increased by lowering price so that the quantity supplied and demanded moves closer to Q_0. A policy that decreases price to P_2 involves a loss of social surplus given by the area of triangle *ade*—each additional unit supplied and demanded between Q_0 and Q_2 yields marginal cost (as given by the height of the supply schedule) that is in excess of marginal benefit (as given by the height of the demand schedule). Consequently, raising price to move the quantity supplied and demanded closer to Q_0 increases social surplus.

Caveats: Models and Reality

The general equilibrium model helps us understand a complex world. As is the case with all models, however, it involves simplifications that may limit its usefulness. It is worth noting three such limitations.

First, the general equilibrium model is static rather than dynamic. Real economies constantly evolve with the introduction of new goods, improvement in technologies, and changes in consumer tastes. An amazing feature of the price system is its capacity for conveying information among decentralized producers and consumers about such changes, which F. A. Hayek refers to as "the particulars of time and place."[4] The equilibria of the competitive framework give us snapshots rather than videos of the real world. Usually, the snapshot is helpful and not too misleading. Nevertheless, policy analysts should realize that substantial gains in social welfare result from innovations that were not, and perhaps could not, have been anticipated. Policy analysts should be careful not to take too static a view of markets. Large rents that seem well protected by barriers to entry, for example, may very well spur innovative substitutes. In discussing each of the market failures in the next chapter, we consider some of the market responses that may arise to reduce social welfare losses.

Second, the general equilibrium model can never be complete—modelers simply do not have enough information to incorporate all goods and services. If they could, then it would be unlikely they could solve the model for its equilibrium. Our switching from the general equilibrium model to models of individual markets is a purposeful restriction of the model so that it can be usefully applied. In most applications it is a reasonable approach, though sometimes goods are such strong complements or substitutes that it is not reasonable to look at them separately.[5]

Third, the assumptions of the general equilibrium model are often violated in the real world. In the two chapters that follow, we consider the most important of these violations of assumptions. We do so in the context of specific markets, acknowledging that doing so may not fully capture all their implications in the wider economy.[6] Nonetheless, we see this analysis as highly valuable in helping policy analysts get started in understanding the complexity of the world in which they work.

[4] F. A. Hayek, "The Use of Knowledge in Society," *American Economic Review* 35(4) 1945, 519–30, at p. 522.

[5] See Anthony E. Boardman, David H. Greenberg, Aidan R. Vining, and David L. Weimer, *Cost-Benefit Analysis: Concepts and Practice* (Upper Saddle River, NJ: Prentice Hall, 2001), Chapter 5.

[6] R. G. Lipsey and Kelvin Lancaster, "General Theory of the Second Best," *Review of Economic Studies* 24(1) 1956–57, 11–32.

Conclusion

The idealized competitive economy provides a useful conceptual framework for thinking about efficiency. The tools of applied welfare economics, consumer and producer surplus, give us a way of investigating efficiency within specific markets. In the next chapter, we explicate four situations, the traditional market failures, in which equilibrium market behavior fails to maximize social surplus.

For Discussion

1. Assume that the world market for crude oil is competitive, with an upward-sloping supply schedule and a downward-sloping demand schedule. Draw a diagram that shows the equilibrium price and quantity. Now imagine that one of the major oil exporting countries undergoes a revolution that shuts down its oil fields. Draw a new supply schedule and show the loss in consumer surplus in the world oil market resulting from the loss of supply. What assumptions are you making about the demand for crude oil in your measurement of consumer surplus?
2. Now assume that the United States is a net importer of crude oil. Show the impact of the price increase resulting from the loss of supply to the world market on social surplus in the U.S. market.

5

Rationales for Public Policy

Market Failures

The idealized competitive model produces a Pareto-efficient allocation of goods. That is, the utility-maximizing behavior of persons and the profit-maximizing behavior of firms will, through the "invisible hand," distribute goods in such a way that no one could be better off without making anyone else worse off. Pareto efficiency thus arises through voluntary actions without any need for public policy. Economic reality, however, rarely corresponds perfectly to the assumptions of the idealized competitive model. In the following sections we discuss violations of the assumptions that underlie the competitive model. These violations constitute market failures, that is, situations in which decentralized behavior does not lead to Pareto efficiency. Traditional market failures are shown as circumstances in which social surplus is larger under some alternative allocation to that resulting under the market equilibrium. Public goods, externalities, natural monopolies, and information asymmetries are the four commonly recognized market failures. They provide the traditional economic rationales for public participation in private affairs.

Public Goods

The term *public*, or *collective*, *goods* appears frequently in the literature of policy analysis and economics. The blanket use of the term, however, obscures important differences among the variety of public goods in terms of the nature of the market failure and, consequently, the appropriate public policy response. We begin with a basic question that should be raised when considering any market failure: Why doesn't the market allocate this particular good efficiently? The simplest approach to providing an answer involves contrasting public goods with private goods.

Two primary characteristics define private goods: rivalry in consumption and excludability in ownership and use. *Rivalrous consumption* means that what one consumes cannot be consumed by another; a perfectly private good is characterized by complete rivalry in consumption. *Excludable ownership* means that one has control over use of the good; a perfectly private good is characterized by complete excludability. For example, shoes are private goods because when one wears them no one else can (rivalrous consumption) and, because when one owns them, one can determine who gets to wear them at any particular time (excludable ownership).

Public goods, on the other hand, are, in varying degrees, *nonrivalrous* in consumption, *nonexcludable* in use, or *both*. In other words, we consider any good that is not purely private to be a public good. A good is nonrivalrous in consumption when more than one person can derive consumption benefits from some level of supply at the same time. For example, a particular level of national defense is nonrivalrous in consumption because all citizens benefit from it without reducing the benefits of others—a new citizen enjoys benefits without reducing the benefits of those already being defended. (Each person, however, may value the commonly provided level of defense differently.) A good is nonexcludable if it is impractical for one person to maintain exclusive control over its use. For example, species of fish that range widely in the ocean are usually nonexcludable in use because they move freely among regions such that no individual can effectively exclude others from harvesting them.

In practice, a third characteristic related to demand, the potential for congestion, or congestibility, is useful in describing public goods. (The term *crowding* is often used interchangeably with congestion.) Levels of demand for a good often determine the extent to which markets supply public goods at inefficient levels. A good is *congested* if the marginal social cost of consumption exceeds the marginal private cost of consumption. For example, a considerable number of people may be able to hike in a wilderness area without interfering with each other's enjoyment of the experience (a case of low demand) so that the marginal social cost of consumption equals the marginal private cost of consumption and there is no congestion. However, a very large number of hikers may reduce each other's enjoyment of the wilderness experience (a case of high demand) such that the marginal social cost of consumption exceeds the marginal private cost of consumption and, therefore, the wilderness is congested. The key point to recognize is that some goods may only be nonrivalrous over some range of usage, but at some higher level of use, consumers begin to impose costs on each other. Later we interpret the divergence between social and private marginal costs as an externality.

Excludability and Property Rights

Excludability implies that some individual can exclude others from use of the good. In most public policy contexts in developed democracies, power to exclude others from use of a good is dependent on property rights granted and enforced by the state and its (judicial) organs. *Property rights* are relationships among people concerning the use of things.[1] These relationships involve claims by rights holders that impose duties on others. In contrast to political systems in which institutional arrangements create and enforce property rights, there are anarchic, or Hobbesian, situations with no government and no constraining norms or conventions where physical force alone determines the power to exclude.

Property rights can be partitioned in complex ways beyond what we think of as simple ownership.[2] For example, a farmer may have a property right that allows using water from a river only during specific months of the year. However, for the purposes of a discussion of excludability, we treat goods as being controlled or "owned" by a single actor. Effective property rights are characterized by clear and complete allocation of claims and high levels of compliance by those who owe the corresponding duties. In this context, where the claim is to exclusive use of the good, compliance simply means accepting exclusion. De jure property rights, which are granted by the state, are typically clear though sometimes incomplete. These de jure property rights, however, may be attenuated, or in some cases superseded, by extra-legal behaviors such as trespass, squatting, poaching, or custom. Behaviors such as these may give rise to de facto property rights, the claims that actually receive compliance from duty bearers. Sometimes de jure property rights do not exist because changes in technology or relative prices create new goods that fall outside of existing allocations. For example, advances in medical technology have made fetal tissue valuable, but the right to its use is yet unclear. Note that de facto property rights may or may not present excludability problems, though often they involve substantial costs to the claimants if they must employ physical protection systems, vigilance, stealth, or retaliation to enforce them. If these costs become too high, then individuals may abandon attempts to exclude others from use of the good. In these cases, the good is effectively nonexcludable.

Nonrivalrous Goods

As we concluded in our discussion of efficient pricing, the production of a private good, involving rivalrous consumption, will be in equilibrium at a level where price equals marginal cost ($P = MC$). On the demand side, the marginal benefits consumers receive from additional consumption must equal price ($MB = P$) in equilibrium. Therefore, marginal benefits equal marginal cost ($MB = MC$). Essentially the same principle applies to nonrivalrous goods. Because all consumers receive marginal benefits from the additional unit of the nonrivalrous good, however, it should be produced if the sum of all individual consumers' marginal benefits

[1]For a seminal discussion of property rights, see Eirik Furubotn and Svetozar Pejovich, "Property Rights and Economic Theory: A Survey of Recent Literature," *Journal of Economic Literature* 10(4) 1972, 1137–62. For a review of property right issues, see David L. Weimer, ed., *The Political Economy of Property Rights: Institutional Change and Credibility in the Reform of Centrally Planned Economies* (New York: Cambridge University Press, 1997), 1–19.

[2]Yoram Barzel, *Economic Analysis of Property Rights* (New York: Cambridge University Press, 1989).

exceeds the marginal cost of producing it. Only when output is increased to the point where the sum of the marginal benefits equals the marginal cost of production is the quantity produced efficient.

The sum of marginal benefits for any level of output of a purely nonrivalrous public good (whether excludable or not) is obtained by vertically summing the marginal benefit schedules (demand schedules) of all individuals at that output level.[3] Repeating the process at each output level yields the entire social, or aggregate, marginal benefit schedule. This contrasts with the derivation of the social marginal benefit schedule for a private good—individual marginal benefit schedules (demand schedules) are added horizontally because each unit produced can only be consumed by one person.

Figure 5.1 illustrates the different approaches. Panel (a) represents the demand for a rivalrous good, and panel (b) the demand for a nonrivalrous good. In both cases the demand schedules of the individual consumers, Jack and Jill, for the good appear as D_1 and D_2, respectively. The market demand for the rivalrous good, the downward-sloping dark line, results from the horizontal addition of individual demands D_1 and D_2 at each price. For example, at price P_0, Jack demands Q_1 and Jill demands Q_2, so that the total quantity demanded is Q_0 (equal to $Q_1 + Q_2$). Repeating this horizontal addition at each price yields the entire market demand schedule. Note that at higher prices, above P_{c1}, Jack's choke price, only Jill is willing to purchase units of the good, so that the market demand schedule follows her demand schedule. If there were more consumers in this market, then the quantities they demanded at each price would also be included to obtain the market demand schedule.

Panel (b) presents the parallel situation for the nonrivalrous good, with the caveat that we are unlikely to be able to observe individual demand schedules for public goods (for reasons we discuss below). Here, the social marginal benefit at Q_0 (MB_{0S} corresponding to the point on D_S above Q_0) is the sum of the marginal benefits enjoyed by Jack (MB_{01} corresponding to the point on D_1 above Q_0) and Jill (MB_2 corresponding to the point on D_2 above Q_0). The social marginal valuation at this point is obtained by summing the amounts that Jack and Jill would be willing to pay for the marginal unit at Q_0. The entire social marginal valuation schedule (MB_S) is obtained by summing Jack and Jill's marginal valuations at each quantity. Note that for quantities larger than Q_{c1} Jack places no value on additional units so that the social demand (social marginal benefit) schedule corresponds to the demand schedule of Jill.

Notice that in this example the upward-sloping supply schedule indicates that higher output levels have higher marginal costs (a brighter streetlight costs more to operate than a dimmer one); it is only the marginal cost of consumption that is equal, and zero, for each person (they can each look at what is illuminated by the light without interfering with the other). In other words, there are zero marginal social costs of consumption but positive marginal costs of production at each level of supply.

A crucial distinction between rivalrous and nonrivalrous goods is that the valuations of individual consumers cannot directly tell us how much of the nonrivalrous good should be provided—only the sum of the valuations can tell us that. Once an output level has been chosen, every person must consume it. Therefore, the various values different persons place on the chosen output level are not revealed

[3]Paul A. Samuelson, "Diagrammatic Exposition of a Theory of Public Expenditure," *Review of Economics and Statistics* 37(4) 1955, 350–56.

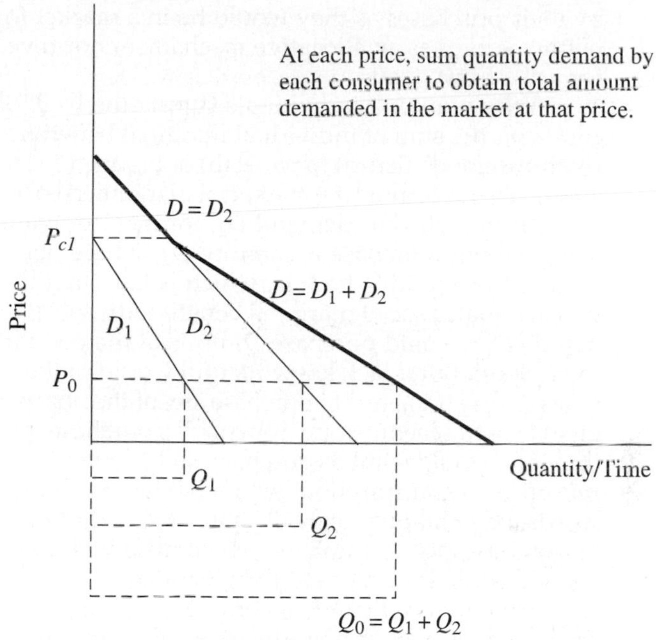

(a) Rivalrous Good
(Horizontal Summation)

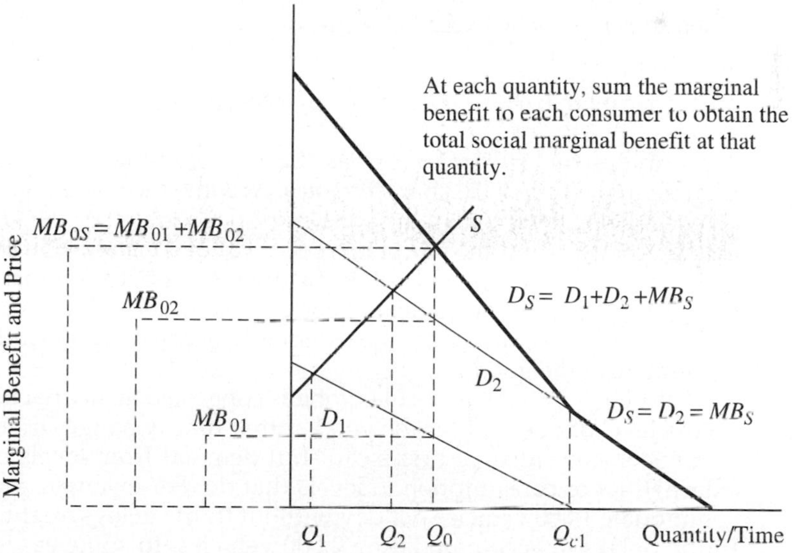

(b) Nonrivalrous Good
(Vertical Summation)

Figure 5.1 Demand Summation for Rivalrous and Nonrivalrous Goods

by their purchases as they would be in a market for a rivalrous good. Thus, price neither serves as an allocative mechanism nor reveals marginal benefits as it does for a rivalrous good.

Why wouldn't individuals supply the level of output that equates marginal cost with the sum of individual marginal benefits as they would in a market for a rivalrous good? Return to panel (b) of Figure 5.1. There, the supply schedule for the good, labeled S, indicates the social marginal cost of producing various levels of the good. If Jill, who has demand D_2, for the nonrivalrous good makes her own decision, she will purchase a quantity Q_2, where her own marginal benefit schedule crosses the supply schedule, which is less than the socially optimal quantity, Q_0, which equates social marginal benefit with social marginal cost. Jack, who has demand (D_1), would purchase Q_1 units of the good if he were the only demander in the market. But if Jack knew that Jill would make a purchase, he would not find it in his own self-interest to purchase any of the nonrivalrous good because, as the marginal benefit schedules are drawn, Jill's purchase quantity would exceed the amount that Jack would want to purchase on his own. He would have an incentive to *free-ride* on Jill's consumption, which he gets to enjoy because of nonrivalry. In other words, once Jill purchases Q_2 units, Jack would not find it in his personal interest to purchase any additional units on his own because each unit he purchases gives him less individual benefit than its price.

A market could still generate the optimal amount of the nonrivalrous good if all consumers would honestly reveal their marginal valuations. (Notice that one of the great advantages of the market for rivalrous goods is that consumers automatically reveal their marginal valuations with their purchases.) Consumers do not normally have an incentive to reveal honestly their marginal valuations, however, when they cannot be excluded from consumption of the good.

Congestibility: The Role of Demand

An economically relevant classification of public goods requires attention to more than their physical characteristics. At some level of demand, consumption of a good by one person may raise the marginal costs other persons face in consuming the good, so that the marginal social cost of consumption exceeds the marginal private cost. Later we will define the divergence between social and private costs as an externality. In the context of congestion, or crowding, we are dealing with a particular type of externality—an externality of consumption inflicted only on other consumers of the good.

Whether or not a particular good is congested at any particular time depends on the level of demand for the good at that time. Changes in technology, population, income, or relative prices can shift demand from levels that do not involve externalities of consumption to levels that do. For example, a road that could accommodate 1,000 vehicles per day without traffic delays might sustain substantial traffic delays in accommodating 2,000 vehicles. In some cases, seasonal or even daily shifts in demand may change the externalities of consumption, making a good more or less congested. For example, drivers may face substantial traffic delays during rush hour but no delays during midday.

We must be careful to distinguish between the marginal social cost of consumption and the marginal cost of production. A purely nonrivalrous and noncongestible good exhibits zero marginal costs of consumption. Yet increments of the good (unless they occur naturally) require various factor inputs to produce. For instance, one way to increase the level of defense is to increase readiness, say, by shooting off more ammunition in practice. But it takes labor, machines, and materials to produce the ammunition, things that could be used to produce other goods instead. Thus, the marginal cost of production of defense is not zero; the marginal cost of consumption is likely to be zero, however, for a given level of supply.

Some care is required in thinking about congestion in cases in which supply cannot be added in arbitrarily small units. Many goods that display nonrivalry in consumption also display "lumpiness" in supply. For example, one cannot simply add small units of physical capacity to an existing bridge. To provide additional units of capacity, one must typically either build a new bridge or "double-deck" the existing one. Either approach provides a large addition to capacity. But this "lumpiness" is irrelevant to the determination of the relevance of congestion. The important consideration is whether or not the external costs of consumption are positive at the available level of supply.

To summarize, three characteristics determine the specific nature of the public good (and hence the nature of the inefficiency that would result solely from market supply): the degree of rivalry in consumption; the extent of excludability, or exclusiveness, in use; and the existence of congestion. The presence of nonrivalry, nonexcludability, or congestion arising from changes in levels of demand can lead to the failure of markets to achieve Pareto efficiency. The presence of either nonrivalry or nonexcludability is a necessary condition for the existence of a public good market failure.

A Classification of Public Goods

Figure 5.2 presents the basic taxonomy of public goods with the rivalrous/nonrivalrous distinction labeling the columns and the excludability/nonexcludability distinction labeling the rows. Additionally, the diagonals within the cells separate cases where congestion is relevant (congested) from those cases where congestion is not relevant (uncongested). By the way, note that the definitions of public goods that we provide differ starkly from a common usage of the term *public good* to describe any good provided by government. In fact, governments, and indeed markets, provide both public and private goods as defined in this taxonomy.

Rivalry, Excludability: Private Goods. The northwest (NW) cell defines private goods, characterized by both rivalry in consumption and excludability in use: shoes, books, bread, and the other things we commonly purchase and own. In the absence of congestion or other market failures, the self-interested actions of consumers and firms elicit and allocate these goods efficiently so that government intervention would have to be justified by some rationale other than the promotion of efficiency.

When the private good is congested (that is, it exhibits externalities of consumption), market supply is generally not efficient. (In competitive markets the marginal social cost of the good equals not just the price—the marginal cost of production—but the sum of price and the marginal social costs of consumption.) Rather than consider such situations as public goods market failures, it is more

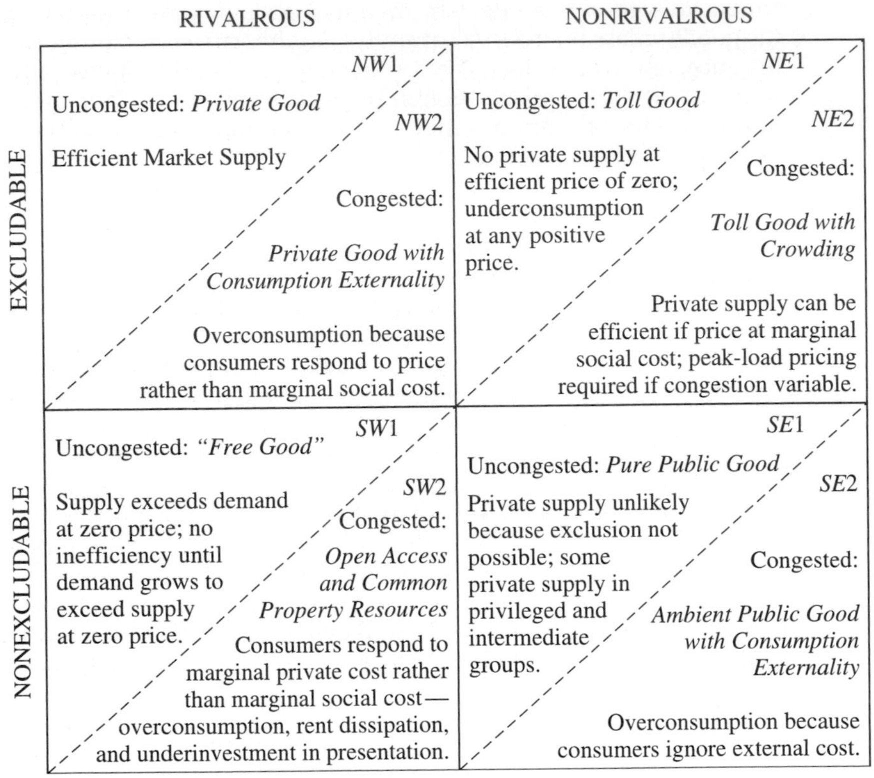

Figure 5.2 A Classification of Goods: Private and Public

common to treat them under the general heading of externality market failures. Consequently, we postpone consideration of category NW2 in Figure 5.2 to our discussion of externalities.

Nonrivalry, Excludability: Toll Goods. The northeast cell (NE) includes those goods characterized by nonrivalry in consumption and excludability. Such goods are often referred to as *toll goods*. Prominent examples include bridges and roads that, once built, can carry significant levels of traffic without crowding. Other examples include goods that occur naturally, such as wilderness areas and lakes. Because exclusion is economically feasible, a private supplier might actually come forward to provide the good. For example, an enterprising individual might decide to build a bridge and charge a crossing toll that would generate a stream of revenue more than adequate to cover the cost of construction—hence, the label toll good. Clearly, in these situations the problem is not supply, per se. Rather, the problem is twofold. First, the private supplier may not efficiently price the facility that is provided. Second, the private supplier may not provide the correct facility size to maximize social surplus [Q_S in Figure 5.1(b)].

With respect to the pricing problem, first consider the case of nonrivalrousness and no congestion (NE1), one in which we can be certain that the private supplier will not charge the efficient price, which is zero. In the absence of congestion, the social marginal cost of consumption is zero, so that any positive price inappropriately discourages use of the bridge. The shaded triangular area *abc* in panel (a) of Figure 5.3 represents the deadweight loss that results from a positive price (or toll) P_1 with the demand schedule for crossings given by *D*. From the diagram we can see that any positive price would involve some welfare loss. The reason is that if a positive price is charged, some individuals who, from the social perspective, should cross the bridge will be discouraged from doing so. Why? Because those individuals who would receive marginal benefits in excess of, or equal to, the marginal social cost of consumption should cross. As the marginal social cost of consumption is zero (that is, lies along the horizontal axis), any individual who would derive any positive benefit from crossing should cross. Those who obtain positive marginal benefits less than the price, however, would not choose to cross. The resulting deadweight loss may seem nebulous—the lost consumer surplus of the trips that will not take place because of the toll—but it represents a misallocation of resources that, if corrected, could lead to a Pareto improvement.

The analysis just presented is complicated if the good displays congestion over some range of demand (NE2). Return to the bridge example. We assumed that capacity exceeded demand—this need not be the case. Consumption is typically uncongested up to some level of demand, but as additional people use the good, the marginal social costs of consumption become positive. Goods such as bridges, roads, and parks are potentially subject to congestion because of physical capacity constraints. Whether or not they are actually congested depends on demand as well as capacity. Panel (b) of Figure 5.3 shows the marginal social costs of consumption for goods that are congested. At low demand levels (for example, D_L), the marginal cost of consumption is zero (in other words, consumption is uncongested), but at high levels of demand (for example, D_H), consumption at a zero toll imposes marginal costs on all users of the good. Line segments $0f$, fg, and gh trace out the marginal social cost of consumption for the good over the range of possible consumption. Notice that these costs are imposed by the marginal consumer, not by the good itself. In the case of the bridge, for instance, the costs appear as the additional time it takes all users to cross the bridge. If additional users crowd onto the bridge, then quite conceivably marginal costs could become almost infinite: "gridlock" prevents anyone from crossing the bridge until some users withdraw. The economically efficient price is shown in panel (b) as P_C.

Let us take a closer look at the incentives that lead to socially inefficient crowding. Suppose that there are 999 automobiles on the bridge experiencing an average crossing time of ten minutes. You are considering whether your auto should be number 1,000 on the bridge. Unfortunately, given the capacity of the bridge, your trip will generate congestion—everyone crossing the bridge, including yourself, will be slowed down by one minute. In other words, the average crossing time of the users rises by one minute to eleven minutes. You will cross if your marginal benefits from crossing exceed your marginal costs (which in this case equal the new average consumption cost of eleven minutes for the group of users). If you decide to cross, however, the marginal social costs of your decision will be 1,010 minutes! (the eleven minutes you bear plus the 999 additional minutes your use inflicts on the other users). Thus, from the social perspective, if everyone places the same value on time as you, then you should cross only if the benefits that you receive from crossing exceed the cost of 1,010 minutes of delay.

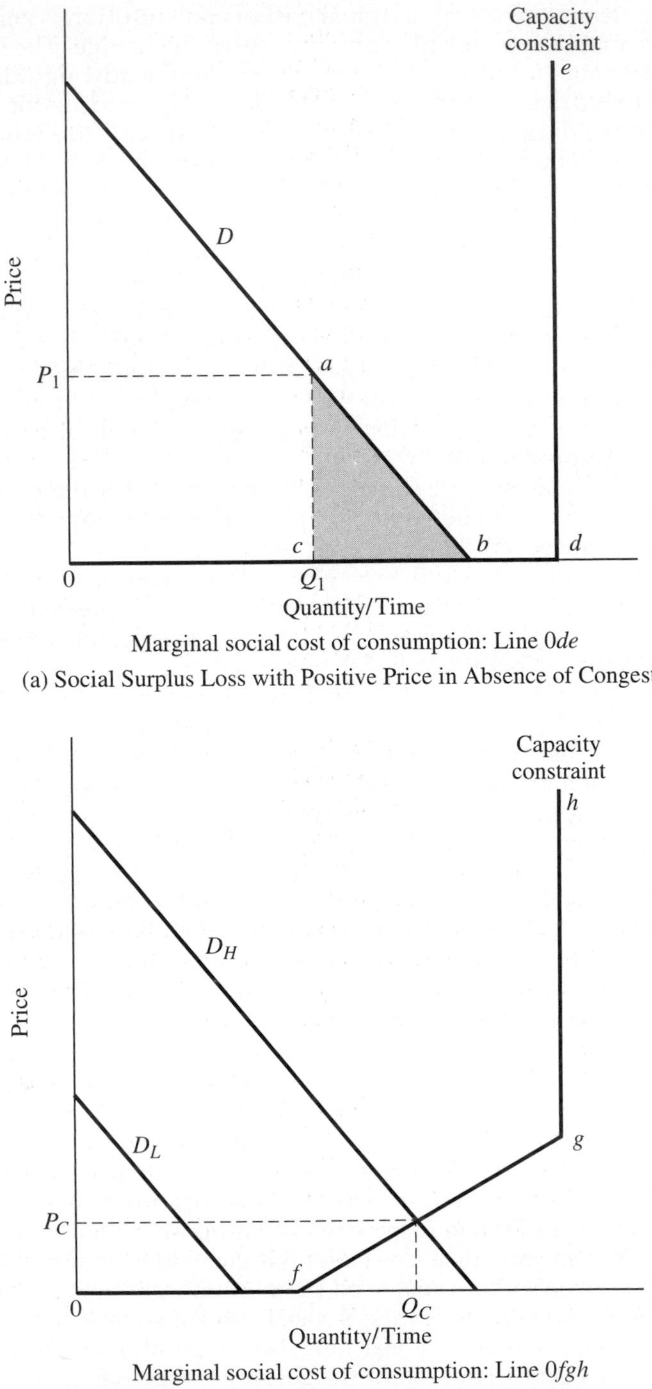

Marginal social cost of consumption: Line 0*de*

(a) Social Surplus Loss with Positive Price in Absence of Congestion

Marginal social cost of consumption: Line 0*fgh*

(b) Appropriate Positive Price in Presence of Congestion

Figure 5.3 Toll Goods

In practice, nonrivalrous, excludable public goods that exhibit congestion involve quite complex pricing problems; however, the basic principle follows readily from the above discussion. Let us assume that the congestion occurs at regular time periods as demand shifts over times of the day or seasons of the year (roads at rush hour, for instance). Efficient allocation requires that the price charged users of the good equal the marginal costs imposed on other users during each period of the day, implying a zero price during uncongested periods (more generally, price should equal the marginal cost of production in the absence of congestion) and some positive price during congested periods (so-called peak-load pricing).

Many toll goods are produced by private firms. The firms must pay the cost of producing the goods with revenues from user fees. That is, the stream of revenues from the fees must cover the cost of construction and operation. To generate the necessary revenues, firms must usually set the tolls above the marginal social costs of consumption. Indeed, as profit maximizers, they set tolls at levels that maximize their rent [the area of rectangle P_1aQ_10 in Figure 5.3 (a)], given the demand schedule they face. Thus, market failure results because the fees exclude users who would obtain higher marginal benefits than the marginal social costs that they impose. The magnitude of the forgone net benefits determines the seriousness of the market failure.

The problem of inefficient scale arises in the case of private supply because firms seeking to maximize profits anticipate charging tolls that restrict demand to levels that can be accommodated by smaller facilities. The result is that the facilities built are too small from a social perspective. Further, the choice of facility size determines the level of demand at which congestion becomes relevant.

Nonrivalry, Nonexcludability: Pure and Ambient Public Goods. We now turn to those goods that exhibit nonrivalrous consumption and where exclusion is not feasible—the southeast (SE) quadrant of Figure 5.2. When these goods are uncongested, they are *pure public goods*. The classic examples of such public goods are defense and lighthouses. One of the most important public goods in modern societies is the generally available stock of information that is valuable in production or consumption. With certain exceptions, to be discussed below, pure public goods will not be supplied at all by markets because of the inability of private providers to exclude those who do not pay for them. Contrast this with the NE quadrant, where there is likely to be market provision, but at a price that results in deadweight losses.

The number of persons who may potentially benefit from a pure public good can vary enormously, depending on the good: ranging from a particular streetlight, with only a few individuals benefiting to national defense, where all members of the polity presumably benefit. Because benefits normally vary spatially or geographically (that is, benefits decline monotonically as one moves away from a particular point on the map), we commonly distinguish among local, regional, national, international, and even global public goods.[4] While this is a convenient way of grouping persons who receive benefits, it is only one of many potential ways. For example, persons who place positive values on wilderness areas in the Sierras may be

[4]For an interesting discussion and classification of global public goods in health, see Todd Sandler and Daniel G. Arce, "A Conceptual Framework for Understanding Global and Transnational Public Goods for Health," *Fiscal Studies* 23(2) 2002, 195–222.

spread all over North America—indeed, all over the world. Some, or even most, of those who actually reside in the Sierras may not be included in this category because their private interests depend upon commercial or agricultural development of the area rather than upon preservation.

We have already touched briefly on the major problem in the SE quadrant. People who would actually receive some level of positive benefits, if the good is provided, often do not have an incentive to reveal honestly the magnitude of these benefits: if contributions for the public good are to be based on benefit levels, then individuals generally have an incentive to understate their benefit levels; if contributions are not tied to benefit levels, then individuals may have an incentive to overstate their benefit levels to obtain a larger supply. Typically, the larger number of beneficiaries, the less likely is any individual to reveal his or her preferences. In such situations, private supply is unlikely. As Mancur Olson has pointed out, however, two specific situations can result in market supply of pure public goods.[5] He labels these situations the *privileged group* and the *intermediate group* cases.

The privileged group case is illustrated in Figure 5.4, where three consumers receive benefits from the good according to their marginal benefit schedules. For example, the three might be owners of recreational facilities in a valley and the good might be spraying to control mosquitoes. The marginal benefit schedule of person 3 (D_3) is high relative to the marginal benefit schedules of persons 1 and 2. (By relatively high, we mean that at any quantity, person 3 places a much higher marginal value on having an additional unit than do the other two persons.) In fact, it is sufficiently high that person 3 will be willing to purchase Q_3 of the good if the other two persons purchase none. (Person 3's demand schedule intersects with the supply schedule at quantity Q_3.) Of course, once person 3 purchases Q_3, neither person 1 nor person 2 will be willing to make additional purchases. In effect, they free-ride on person 3's high demand. (We can speak of person 3's marginal benefit schedule as a demand schedule because she will act as if the good were private, revealing her demand at various prices.) Despite the provision of Q_3 units of the public good, compared to the socially efficient level Q_0, social surplus is lower by the area of triangle *abc*.

In this case the demand of person 3 makes up such a large fraction of total demand that the amount purchased (Q_3) is fairly close to the economically efficient level (Q_0). In this sense, the three persons form a privileged group. Even when no one person has a sufficiently high demand to make a group privileged, however, *some* provision of the good may result if the group is sufficiently small so that members can negotiate directly among themselves. We recognize such a group as "intermediate" between privileged and unprivileged: two or more members may, for whatever reasons, voluntarily join together to provide some of the good, although usually at less than the economically efficient level. Intermediate groups are generally small, or at least have a small number of members who account for a large fraction of total demand.

The situation just described closely resembles a positive externality (benefits accruing to third parties to market transactions), which we discuss in detail in the next section. Clearly, if persons 1 and 2 did not agree to finance jointly the public good at the efficient level (Q_0), they would nevertheless receive benefits from Q_3,

[5]Mancur Olson, *The Logic of Collective Action* (Cambridge, MA: Harvard University Press, 1973), 43–52.

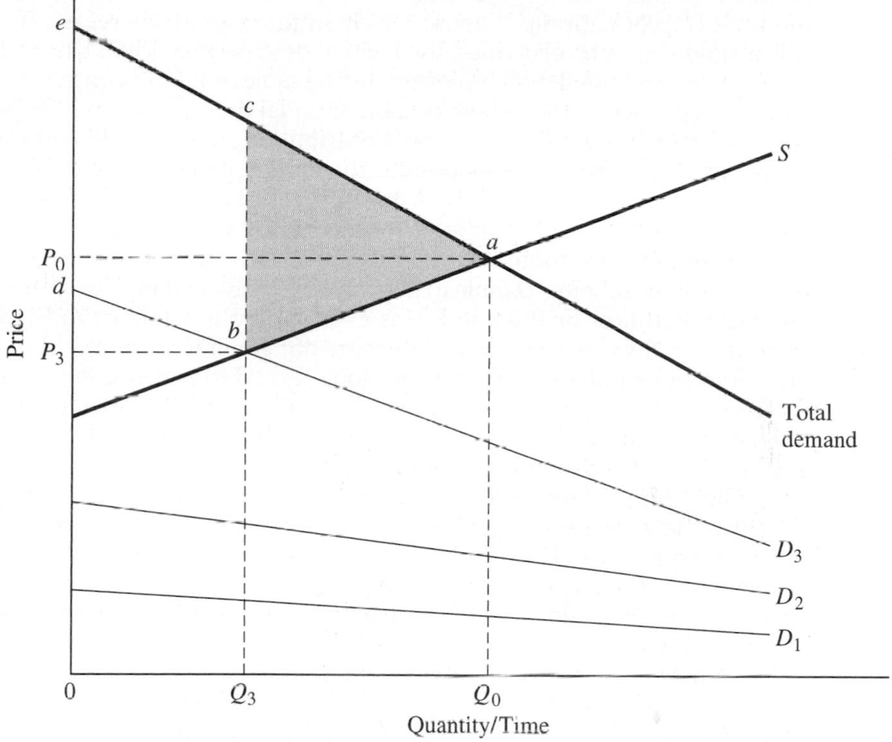

Socially optimal level of provision: Q_0
Private provision by person 3: Q_3
Deadweight loss from underprovision: *abc*

Figure 5.4 Private Provision of a Public Good: Privileged Group

the amount purchased by person 3. Through the purchase of Q_3, person 3 receives the private consumer surplus benefit given by the area of triangle P_3bd and confers an external (to herself) consumer surplus benefit of area *bced* on the other group members. For analytical convenience, however, we maintain a distinction between public goods and positive externalities. We restrict the definition of an externality to those situations where provision of a good necessarily requires the joint production of a private good and a public good. We reserve the public good classification for those cases where there is no joint production. So, for example, mosquito control poses a public good problem, while chemical waste produced as a by-product of manufacturing poses an externality problem.

In many situations large numbers of individuals would benefit from the provision of a public good where no small group receives a disproportionate share of total benefits. Such cases of large numbers raise the free-rider problem with a vengeance. In situations involving large numbers, each person's demand is extremely small relative to total demand and to the cost of provision. The rational individual compares his individual marginal benefits and costs. Take as an example national defense. The logic is likely to be as follows: my monetary contribution to the financing of national defense will be infinitesimal; therefore, if I do not contribute and everyone else does, the level of defense provided, from which I cannot be effectively excluded, will be essentially the same as if I did contribute. On the other hand, if I contribute and others do not, national defense will not be provided anyway. Either way I am better off not contributing. (As we will discuss below, free riding arises in other contexts besides the market provision of public goods; it can also occur when attempts are made to supply the economically efficient quantity of the public good through public sector mechanisms.)

To summarize, then, the free-rider problem exists in the large-numbers case because it is usually impossible to get persons to reveal their true demand (marginal benefit) schedules for the good (it is even difficult to talk of individual demand schedules in this context because they are not generally observable). Even though all would potentially benefit if all persons agreed to contribute to the financing of the good so that their average contributions (in effect, the price they each paid per unit supplied) just equaled their marginal benefits, self-interest in terms of personal costs and benefits discourages honest participation.

The concept of free riding plays an important role in the theory of public goods. Recently, there has been considerable debate among economists about the practical significance of free riding. Both observational and experimental evidence, however, suggest that free riding occurs, but perhaps not to the level predicted by theory.[6] John Ledyard, in a summary of the experimental literature, concludes: "(1) In one-shot trials and in the initial stages of finitely repeated trials, subjects generally provide contributions halfway between the Pareto-efficient level and the free riding level, (2) contributions decline with repetition, and (3) face-to-face communication improves the rate of contribution."[7] Another survey concludes that higher individual marginal per capita returns from the public good raises contributions, but that free-ride problems tend to be worse in larger groups than in smaller groups.[8] In the context of relatively small groups that permit face-to-face contact, such as neighborhood associations, social pressure may be brought to bear, ensuring that failure to contribute is an unpleasant experience.[9] More generally, we would expect a variety of voluntary organizations with less individual anonymity to arise to combat free riding. There has also been considerable theoretical interest in pricing mechanisms that encourage people to reveal their preferences truthfully, though they have as yet been little used in practice.[10]

Thus far we have not considered the issue of congestion in the SE quadrant in Figure 5.2. Some goods are simply not congestible and can be placed to the left

[6]See, for example, Linda Goetz, T. F. Glover, and B. Biswas, "The Effects of Group Size and Income on Contributions to the Corporation for Public Broadcasting," *Public Choice* 77(20) 1993, 407–14. For a review of the experimental evidence, see Robert C. Mitchell and Richard T. Carson, *Using Surveys to Value Public Goods: The Contingent Valuation Method* (Washington, DC: Resources for the Future, 1989), 133–49.

[7]John Ledyard, "Public Goods: A Survey of Experimental Research," in John H. Kagel and Alvin E. Roth, eds., *The Handbook of Experimental Economics* (Princeton, NJ: Princeton University Press, 1995), 111–94, at p. 121.

[8]Douglas D. Davis and Charles A. Holt, *Experimental Economics* (Princeton, NJ: Princeton University Press, 1993), 332–33.

[9]Thomas S. McCaleb and Richard E. Wagner, "The Experimental Search for Free Riders: Some Reflections and Observations," *Public Choice*, 47(3) 1985, 479–90.

[10]For an overview of Vickrey, Clarke-Groves, and other demand revelation mechanisms, see Dennis C. Mueller, *Public Choice II* (New York: Cambridge University Press, 1995), 124–34.

of the diagonal (SE1) within the SE quadrant. For instance, mosquito control, a local public good, involves nonexcludability, nonrivalry in consumption, and noncongestibility; no matter how many people are added to the area, the effectiveness of the eradication remains the same. Similarly, national defense, a national or international public good, in general is not subject to congestion. In contrast, nature lovers may experience disutility when they meet more than a few other hikers in a wilderness area.

We label nonrivalrous and nonexcludable goods that exhibit congestion—and thus are appropriately placed into SE2—as *ambient public goods with consumption externality.* Air and large bodies of water are prime examples of public goods that are exogenously provided by nature. For all practical purposes, consumption (use) of these goods is nonrivalrous—more than one person can use the same unit for such purposes as disposing of pollutants.[11] In other words, consumption of the resource (via pollution) typically imposes no Pareto-relevant impact until some threshold, or ambient-carrying capacity, has been crossed. Exclusion in many market contexts is impossible, or at least extremely costly, because access to the resources is possible from many different locations. For example, pollutants can be discharged into an air shed from any location under it (or even upwind of it!).

Relatively few goods fall into category SE2. The reason is that as congestion sets in, it often becomes economically feasible to exclude users so that goods that might otherwise be in SE2 are better placed in NE2 instead. For example, to return to wilderness hiking: once the density of hikers becomes very large, it may become economically feasible for a private owner to issue passes that can be enforced by spot checks. Wilderness in this context is an ambient public good only over the range of use between the onset of crowding and the reaching of a density where the pass system becomes economically feasible. The efficiency problems associated with many of the goods that do fall into category SE2 can alternatively be viewed as market failures due to externalities. So, for example, the carrying capacity of a body of water can be viewed as an ambient public good that suffers from overconsumption. Alternatively, the pollution that the body of water receives can be viewed as an externality of some other good that is overproduced.

Rivalry, Nonexcludability: Open Access, Common Property Resources, and Free Goods. Consider goods in the SW quadrant, where consumption is rivalrous, but where exclusion is not economically feasible—in other words, there is open access to the good. We should stress that in this quadrant we are dealing with goods that are rivalrous in consumption. Trees, fish, bison, oil, and pastureland are all rivalrous in consumption: if I take the hide from a bison, for instance, that particular hide is no longer available for you to take. Specifically, open access means that anyone who can seize units of the good controls their use. We normally think of open access in terms of unrestricted entry of new users. However, open access also involves unrestricted use by a fixed number of individuals who already have access. But, in these circumstances it is plausible to talk in terms of ownership—

[11]Other sorts of consumption may be rivalrous. For example, taking water from a river for irrigation is rivalrous—assuming congestion (positive marginal social costs of consumption), the water should be treated as a common property resource (SW2 in Figure 5.2) rather than as an ambient public good. The same river, however, might be nonrivalrous with respect to its capacity to carry away wastes. See Robert H. Haveman, "Common Property, Congestion, and Environmental Pollution," *Quarterly Journal of Economics* 87(2) 1973, 278–87.

a fixed number of users may share collective property rights to the good. With this property right, they have an incentive and, possibly, the means to reduce or eliminate overconsumption.

No immediate market failure appears in those cases in which the good is naturally occurring and where supply exceeds demand at zero price. As anyone can take these goods without interfering with anyone else's use, we refer to them as *free goods* (SW1). Thus, although they are theoretically rivalrous in consumption, from an efficiency perspective they are not because of the excess supply.

In situations in which demand is higher so that there is no excess supply at zero price, we have what is usually referred to as an *open access resource* (SW2). When access is limited to a defined group of potential users (in other words, entry is restricted), and the users own the good in common, there is *common property ownership*. The distinction between open access and common property situations requires some elaboration. In the case of common property, the limiting of access to a defined set of persons opens the possibility of self-governance among them that reduces or eliminates inefficiencies.[12] In the case of open access, however, the threat of new entrants effectively eliminates the possibility of self-governance. Even in cases of common property, individual rational behavior by members of the defined group can lead to inefficiency in a way that may end up being indistinguishable from open access—in such cases common property results in a *common property resource problem*. Consequently, although much of the following discussion is framed in terms of open access, it is generally relevant to common property as well.

Market failure arises in the open access case from the "infeasibility" of exclusion. Why the quotation marks? Because, as we will see, open access problems often occur in situations in which institutional features rather than the inherent nature of the goods make exclusion infeasible. For example, in most countries oil does not suffer from open access because their governments have adopted laws that keep and enforce exclusive property rights to subsurface resources for the governments themselves. In the United States, however, oil has often suffered from the open access problem because of the "rule of capture," a legal doctrine that gives most subsurface rights to the owner of the surface property. When different people own separate pieces of property over the same pool of oil, the rule of capture prevents exclusion. Unless all the owners agree to treat their combined property as a unit, the common reservoir of oil will be extracted too quickly.

Nonexcludability leads to economically inefficient overconsumption of rivalrous goods. It can also lead to underinvestment in preserving the stock of goods or to overinvestment in capital used to capture the good.[13] Naturally occurring resources are especially susceptible to the open access problem. Persons with access to the resource realize that what they do not consume will be consumed by someone else. Each person, therefore, has an incentive to consume the resource at a faster rate than if he or she had exclusive ownership. For instance, deforestation often results when a population relies on a forest as a source of firewood. Further, the availability of underpriced firewood does not give users the appropriate incentive to

[12]Gary D. Libecap, *Contracting for Property Rights* (New York: Cambridge University Press, 1989); and Elinor Ostrom, *Governing the Commons: The Evolution of Institutions for Collective Action* (New York: Cambridge University Press, 1990).

[13]See Michael B. Wallace, "Managing Resources That Are Common Property: From Kathmandu to Capitol Hill," *Journal of Policy Analysis and Management* 2(2) 1983, 220–37.

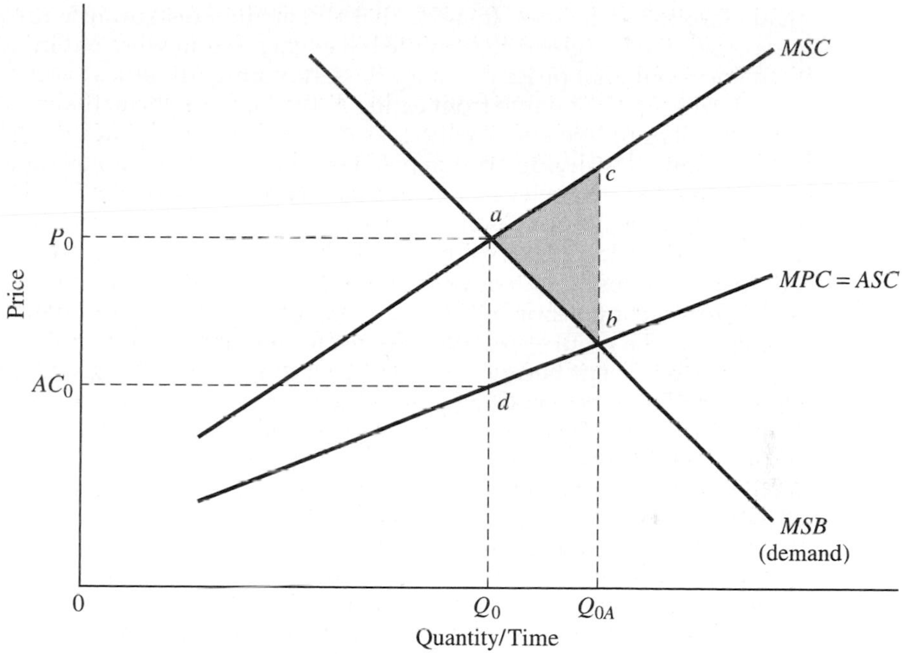

MPC = Marginal private cost
MSC = Marginal social cost
ASC = Average social cost

Socially optimal level of consumption: Q_0 ($MSB = MSC$)
Open access resource level of consumption: Q_{0A}
Deadweight loss from overconsumption: *abc*

Figure 5.5 Overconsumption of Open Access Resources

invest in stoves that use less wood, and the fact that anyone can cut and gather wood discourages individuals from replanting or nurturing trees.

Figure 5.5 illustrates the efficiency losses associated with overconsumption when there is open access to a resource. The marginal social benefit schedule (MSB) represents the horizontal summation (remember, we are dealing with a rivalrous good) of all the demand schedules of individuals. The economically efficient level of consumption, Q_0, results when marginal social cost (MSC) equals marginal social benefit ($MSC = MSB$). Each individual, however, takes account of only the costs that he or she directly bears, that is, marginal private costs (MPC). This private marginal cost turns out to be the average cost for all demanders (ASC) if marginal social cost is borne equally (that is, averaged) among consumers. With everyone rationally treating average group cost as their marginal cost, equilibrium consumption will be at Q_{OA}, which is greater than the economically efficient level Q_0. The shaded triangle *abc* measures the loss in social surplus that results from the overconsumption.

A simple example may help clarify why individuals in open access and common property situations have an incentive to respond to marginal private cost rather than marginal social cost. Imagine that you are in a restaurant with a group of ten people who have agreed to split the bill evenly. If you were paying your own tab, then you would not order the fancy dessert costing $10 unless you expected to get at least $10 worth of value from eating it. But because the actual cost to you of the dessert will be $1 (the average increase in your bill, and for the bills of everyone else in the group—$10 divided by ten people), you would be rational (ignoring calories, your remaining stomach capacity, and social pressure) to order it as long as it would give you at least one more dollar in value. You might continue ordering desserts until the value you placed on one more fell to $1, your marginal private cost and the group average cost. In other words, your out-of-pocket cost for an additional dessert is the increment to your bill. It is the cost of the dessert split equally among the members of the group—the average cost for members of the group. But this result is clearly inefficient because you and everyone else in the group could be made better off if you refrained from ordering the last dessert in return for a payment from the others of any amount between $1 (your marginal private cost) and $9 (the difference between the marginal social cost and your marginal private cost). Remember that the problem arises here because you have access to items on the menu at below their real social (in this case, group) cost.

Note two things about this example. First, as the number of people in the group is restricted to ten, this is a common property situation in that membership in the group is closed. However, remember that we defined open access as including "unrestricted use by those who already have access." If anyone could freely join the group and join in the tab splitting, then it would be a pure open access situation. As group size increases, the divergence between marginal private and marginal group (social) costs increases, so that overordering increases. Second, in this example, overordering is mitigated by the fact that participants must consume the food at the table. If the participants could take doggie bags, or even resell ordered food, then the incentives to overorder would be even greater. Natural resource extractors, who typically sell seized units rather than consume them, are thus like those who take doggie bags.

Modeling common property as a game between two potential users makes clear how individual incentives lead to overexploitation from a social perspective. Imagine that two ranchers have access to a grassland. Each must decide how many head of cattle to graze on the grassland not knowing how many head the other will graze. For simplicity, imagine that the choices are either 50 or 100 head of cattle. These choices are the "strategies" available to the ranchers in this game. Each pair of strategies, shown as the cells in Figure 5.6, yields pairs of payoffs to the two ranch-

		Rancher 2: 50 Head	Rancher 2: 100 Head
Rancher 1	50 Head	($1,000, $1,000)	($600, $1,200)
Rancher 1	100 Head	($1,200, $600)	($700, $700)

Figure 5.6 Choice of Herd Size as a Prisoner's Dilemma

ers given as (payoff to rancher 1, payoff to rancher 2). If each chooses to graze 50 head, then each earns a profit of $1,000 because the total herd size of 100 can be accommodated by the field. If each chooses to graze 100 head, then each earns a profit of only $700 because the total herd size is much too large for the field so that the cattle gain too little weight. If rancher 1 grazes 100 head and rancher 2 grazes 50 head, then rancher 1 earns a profit of $1,200 and rancher 2 a profit of only $600. If rancher 1 grazes 50 and rancher 2 grazes 100, then it is rancher 2 who earns the $1,200 and rancher 1 the $600. In these strategy combinations, the herd size is too big for the field, but the lost weight per head does not offset the advantage to the more aggressive rancher of grazing the extra 50 head.

A prediction of behavior in a game is the *Nash equilibrium*. In a two-person game, a pair of strategies is a Nash equilibrium if, given the strategy of the other player, neither player wishes to change strategies. In the game at hand, it is clear that each rancher restricting his herd size to 50 head is not a Nash equilibrium—either rancher could raise his profit from $1,000 to $1,200 by switching to 100 head. But if only one switched to 100 head, the other could raise his profits from $600 to $700. Only when both choose 100 head would neither player have an incentive to move back to 50 head. Thus, the only Nash equilibrium in this game is for both to choose herds of 100 head. That this equilibrium is Pareto inefficient is clear—each would be made better off if they chose herds of 50 head.

Games with similar structure, called *Prisoner's Dilemmas*, are widely used by social scientists to model problems of cooperation.[14] They are called *noncooperative games* because of the assumption that the players cannot make binding commitments to strategies before they must be chosen. If it were possible to make binding commitments, then we could imagine the ranchers cooperating by agreeing to limit their herd sizes to 50 head before strategies are chosen. As this game is only played one time, it is called a *single-play game*. One could imagine that the ranchers faced the problem of choosing herd sizes each year. It might then be reasonable to model their interaction as a *repeated game* consisting of successive plays of the single-play, or *stage*, game. If the repeated game consists of an infinite, or uncertain, number of repetitions, and players give sufficient weight to future payoffs relative to current payoffs, then cooperative equilibria may emerge that involve each repeatedly choosing strategies that would not be equilibria in the stage game. (We return to these ideas when we discuss corporate culture and leadership in Chapter 11.)

Natural resources (both renewable and nonrenewable) have the potential for yielding scarcity rents—returns in excess of the cost of production. With open access, these rents may be completely dissipated. In Figure 5.5, for instance, consumption at the economically efficient level Q_0 would yield rent equal to the area of rectangle P_0adAC_0. The economically efficient harvesting of salmon, for example, requires catch limits that keep the market price above the marginal costs of harvesting. In the absence of exclusion, however, these rents may well be completely dissipated.[15] (At consumption level Q_{OA} in Figure 5.5, there is no rent.) The reason is that fishers will continue to enter the industry (and those already in it will fish more intensively) as long

[14]For introductions to game theory, see James D. Morrow, *Game Theory for Political Scientists* (Princeton, NJ: Princeton University Press, 1994); and Martin J. Osborne and Ariel Rubenstein, *A Course in Game Theory* (Cambridge, MA: MIT Press, 1994).

[15]See, for example, L. G. Anderson, *The Economics of Fishery Management* (Baltimore: Johns Hopkins University Press, 1977).

as marginal private benefits—the rents they can capture—exceed marginal private costs. Just as in the restaurant example, each fisher will ignore the marginal costs that his behavior imposes on other fishers. If every fisher is equally efficient, then his marginal private cost equals the average cost for the fishers as a group.

The question of how rent should be distributed is usually one of the most contentious issues in public policy. For example, how should the catch limits for salmon be divided among commercial, sport, and Native fishers? Nevertheless, from the perspective of economic efficiency someone should receive the scarcity rent rather than allowing it to be wasted. Indeed, economic efficiency as measured by reductions in the dissipation of rent was one of the goals of the regulatory alternatives for the British Columbia salmon fishery analyzed in Chapter 1.

Note that demand for a resource may be sufficiently low so that it remains uncongested at zero price. Increases in demand, however, may push the resource from a free good (SW1) to an open access good (SW2). A number of free goods, including such resources as buffalo, forests, aquifer water, and rangeland, have been historically important in North America. Typically, however, the free goods eventually disappeared as demand increased and excess supply was eliminated.[16] Open access often led to rapid depletion and, in some cases, near destruction of the resource before effective exclusion was achieved. For example, open access permitted destruction of the Michigan, Wisconsin, and Minnesota pine forests.[17] Nonexcludability continues to be at the heart of many water use problems in the western United States.[18] When animal populations are treated as open access resources, the final result of overconsumption may be species extinction; such a result has already occurred with certain birds and other animals with valuable organs or fur.

Thus far we have not specified the meaning of "feasible" exclusion. Many of the goods we have given as examples appear not to be inherently nonexcludable. Indeed, one of the most famous historical examples of open access resource—sheep and cattle grazing on the medieval English pasture—was "solved," willy-nilly, without overt government intervention, by the enclosure movement, which secured property rights for estate holders. Similar enclosures appear to be currently taking place on tribal, historically open access, lands in parts of Africa.

It is useful to dichotomize open access and common property problems into those that are *structural* (where aspects of the goods preclude economically feasible exclusion mechanisms) and those that are *institutional* (where economically efficient exclusion mechanisms are feasible but the distribution of property rights precludes their implementation). The averaging of restaurant bills, which we previously discussed, serves as an excellent illustration of an institutional common property problem. We can imagine an obvious exclusion mechanism that we know from experience is economically feasible: separate bills for everyone. Institutional common property resource

[16]In the case of the buffalo, the opening of the railroad facilitated the hunting and transportation of hides at much lower costs, so that what had previously been a free good became an open access resource. See John Hanner, "Government Response to the Buffalo Hide Trade, 1871–1883," *Journal of Law and Economics* 24(2) 1981, 239–71.

[17]Andrew Dana and John Baden, "The New Resource Economics: Toward an Ideological Synthesis," *Policy Studies Journal* 14(2) 1985, 233–43.

[18]B. Delworth Gardner, "Institutional Impediments to Efficient Water Allocation," *Policy Studies Review* 5(2) 1985, 353–63; and William Blomquist and Elinor Ostrom, "Institutional Capacity and the Resolution of a Commons Dilemma," *Policy Studies Review* 5(2) 1985, 283–93.

problems are usually not fundamentally market failures. Rather, they are most often due to the failure of government to allocate enforceable property rights.

Typically, the crucial factor in making a distinction between structural and institutional problems is whether or not the good displays *spatial stationarity.* Trees are spatially stationary, salmon are not, and bodies of water may or may not be. When resources are spatially stationary, their ownership can be attached to the ownership of land. Owners of the land are usually able to monitor effectively all aspects of their property rights and, consequently, ensure exclusive use. Given exclusion, common property resources become private resources that will be used in an economically efficient manner. Without spatial stationarity, ownership of land is not a good proxy for low monitoring costs and the viability of enforcing exclusion. It does not necessarily follow that the open access or common property problem could not be dealt with by some form of private ownership, but it does suggest that ownership of a defined piece of land or water will not be adequate to ensure exclusion. Allocating fishing rights to specific water acreage where the fish stock moves over considerable distances, or associating the rights to oil extraction to ownership of land when the oil pool extends under a large number of parcels, illustrate the difficulty of creating effective property rights for nonstationary resources.

In summary, a stationary good may have common property resource characteristics simply because its ownership is not well defined, perhaps because of the historical accident that at one time supply exceeded demand at zero price. Nonstationary goods generally require more complex policy interventions to achieve efficiency because the linking of property rights to landownership will not serve as an effective proxy for exclusive resource ownership of the resource.

Reprise of Public Goods

Returning to Figure 5.2, we summarize the efficiency implications of the various types of market failures involving public goods. To reprise, the major problem with toll goods (NE quadrant—nonrivalry, excludability) is underconsumption arising from economically inefficient pricing rather than a lack of supply, per se. Congestion usually further complicates these problems by introducing the need for variable pricing to achieve efficiency. In the case of pure and ambient public goods (SE quadrant—nonrivalry, nonexcludability), the pervasiveness of free riding generally leads to no market supply at all. In specific circumstances (a privileged or intermediate group in which one or a few persons account for a large fraction of demand), however, there may be some, and perhaps even nearly efficient, market supply. In the case of open access resources (SW quadrant—rivalry, nonexcludability), inefficiency results because individuals do not equate marginal social costs with marginal benefits but, rather, marginal private costs with marginal benefits. Hence, they inefficiently overconsume and inefficiently underinvest in enhancing open access resources.

Externalities

An *externality* is any valued impact (positive or negative) resulting from any action (whether related to production or consumption) that affects someone who did not fully consent to it through participation in voluntary exchange. Price changes in competitive markets are not relevant externalities because buyers and sellers are engaging voluntarily in exchange. We have already encountered a variety of externalities in our discussion of public goods—private supply of nonrivalrous goods by privileged and intermediate groups (a positive externality) and the divergence between marginal private and marginal social costs in the use of congested resources (a negative externality). We reserve the label *externality problem* for those situations in which the good conveying the valued impact on nonconsenting parties is the by-product of either the production or consumption of some good.

As is the case with open access resources and ambient public goods, externality problems involve attenuated property rights because either the rights to exclusive use are incompletely specified or the costs of enforcing the rights are high relative to the benefits. Secure and enforceable property rights often permit private transactions to eliminate the economic inefficiency associated with an externality by opening up the possibility for markets in the external effect. Indeed, one can think of an externality problem as a *missing market*. We will return to this point after discussing a few examples.

Common examples of negative externalities include the air and water pollution generated by firms in their production activities, the cigarette smoke that nonsmokers must breathe in public places, and the unsightliness generated by a dilapidated house in a well-kept neighborhood. Persons who suffer these externalities place different values on them. For instance, I may simply dislike the smell of cigarette smoke, but you may be allergic to it. Whereas I would be willing to pay only a small cost to avoid sitting near a smoker—say, waiting an extra ten minutes for a restaurant table in the nonsmoking section—you might be willing to pay considerably more—say, waiting thirty minutes or leaving the restaurant altogether. Note that we can think of placing a value on these externalities in the same way we do for the goods we voluntarily consume.

Common examples of positive externalities include vaccinations that reduce everyone's risk of infectious disease (so-called herd immunity) and the benefits that neighbors receive from a homeowner's flower garden and nicely painted house. An important category of positive externality arises in the context of communication networks. One more person connecting to a Web-based digital music exchange provides marginal social benefits that exceed marginal private benefits because everyone already on the network has one more interface for potential exchange.[19] Such positive externalities are usually referred to as *network*, or *adoption*, *externalities*.

Externalities can arise in either production or consumption. Production externalities affect either firms (producer-to-producer externalities) or consumers (producer-to-consumer externalities); consumption externalities may also affect the activities of firms (consumer-to-producer externalities) or those of other consumers (consumer-to-consumer externalities). In this context, the category consumers as

[19]For an analysis of network externalities, see Hal R. Varian, *Intermediate Economics: A Modern Approach* (New York: W. W. Norton, 1999), 606–12.

Table 5.1 *Examples of Externalities*

	Positive	Negative
Producer-to-Producer	Recreational facilities attracting people who purchase from nearby businesses	Toxic chemical pollution harming downstream commercial fishing
Producer-to-Consumer	Private timber forests providing scenic benefits to nature lovers	Air pollution from factories harming lungs of people living nearby
Consumer-to-Consumer	Immunization by persons against contagious disease helping to reduce risk to others	Cigarette smoke from one person reducing enjoyment of meal by another
Consumer-to-Producer	Unsolicited letters from consumers providing information on product quality	Game hunters disturbing domestic farm animals

recipients of externalities includes everyone in society. Table 5.1 provides simple examples of each type of externality. (Keep in mind that sometimes the same activity may constitute a positive externality for some but a negative externality for others.) Classifying a situation that potentially involves an externality is often a good way to begin considering its efficiency implications, distributional impacts, and, most important, possible remedies.

Efficiency Losses of Negative and Positive Externalities

Figure 5.7 illustrates the resource allocation effects of a negative externality in production. In the presence of a negative externality, firms will produce too much of the private good that generates the externality. The market supply schedule for the private good, *MPC*, indicates the marginal costs borne directly by the firms producing it. For example, if the private good were electricity, *MPC* would represent the marginal amounts firms have to pay for the coal, labor, and other things that show up in their ledgers. But *MPC* does not reflect the negative impacts of the pollution that results from burning the coal. If somehow we could find out how much each person in society would be willing to pay to avoid the pollution at each output level, then we could add these amounts to the marginal costs actually seen by the firms to derive a supply schedule that reflected total social marginal costs. We represent this more inclusive supply schedule as *MSC*.

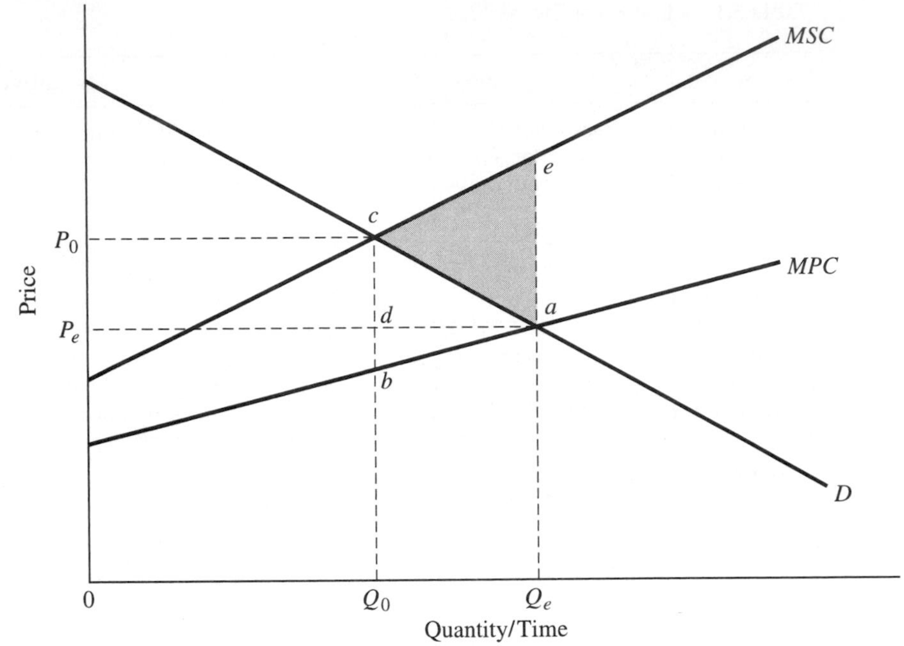

Social Surplus at Q_e relative to Q_0

Consumer surplus from private good:	larger by P_0caP_e
Producer surplus of firms producing private good:	smaller by $(P_0cdP_e - abd)$
Losses to third parties bearing externality:	larger by *abce*
Social surplus:	smaller by *ace*

Figure 5.7 Overproduction with a Negative Externality

Economic efficiency requires that social marginal benefits and social marginal costs be equal at the selected output level—this occurs at quantity Q_0, where marginal social cost (*MSC*) and demand (*D*) intersect. But because firms do not consider the external costs of their output, they choose output level Q_e at the intersection of *MPC* and *D*. Relative to output level Q_0, consumers of the private good being produced gain surplus equal to area P_0caP_e (because they get quantity Q_e at price P_e rather than quantity Q_0 at price P_0), and producers lose surplus equal to area P_0cdP_e minus area *abd* (the first area captures the effect of the lower price, the second the effect of greater output). Those who bear the external costs, however, suffer a loss given by the area *abce* (the area between the market and social supply curves over the output difference—remember, the vertical distance between the supply curves represents the external marginal cost). The net loss in social surplus is the area of triangle *ace*, the algebraic sum of the surplus differences for the consumers and producers of the private good and the bearers of the externality. (This net social surplus loss is simply the deadweight loss due to the overproduction—the area between *MSC* and *D* from Q_0 to Q_e.) In other words, Pareto efficiency requires a reduction in output from the equilibrium level in the market (Q_e) to the level at which marginal social costs equal marginal social benefits (Q_0).

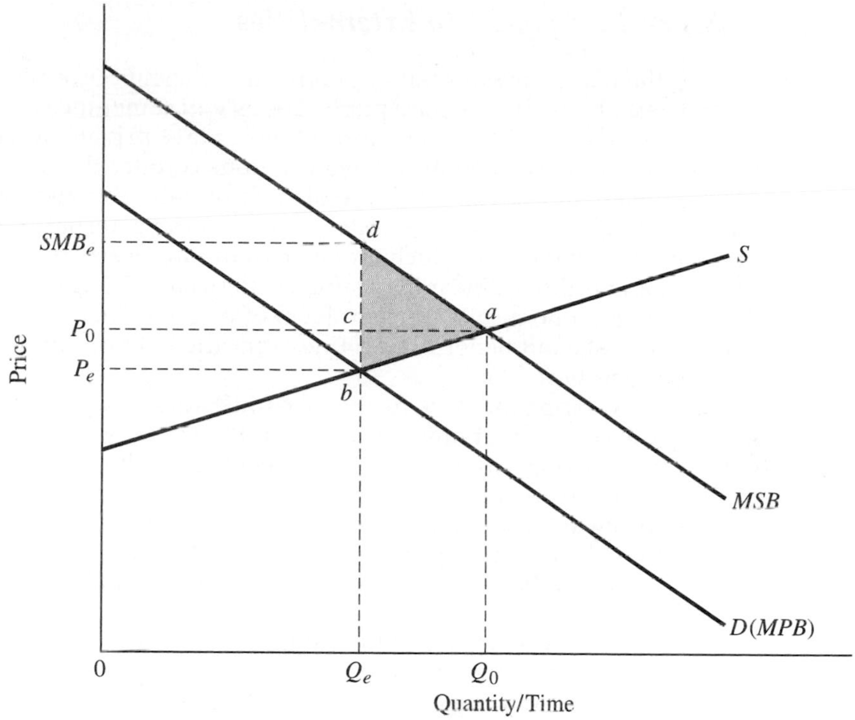

Social Surplus at Q_e relative to Q_0

Consumer surplus: smaller by $(acd - P_0cbP_e)$
Producer surplus: smaller by P_0abP_e
Social surplus: smaller by abd

Figure 5.8 Underproduction with a Positive Externality

Turning to positive externalities, we can think of the private good generating benefits that cannot be captured by the producer. For example, firms that plant trees for future harvesting may provide a scenic benefit for which they receive no compensation. In Figure 5.8 we illustrate the demand schedule for the private good (trees for future harvest) as D, which also gives the marginal private benefits (MPB). At each forest size, however, the social marginal benefit schedule would equal the market demand plus the amounts that viewers would be willing to pay to have the forest expanded by another unit. MSB labels the social marginal benefit schedule, which includes both the private and external marginal benefits. Market equilibrium results at output level Q_e, where the market demand schedule and the supply schedule intersect. But if output were raised to Q_0, consumer surplus would increase by area acd (resulting from increased consumption from Q_e to Q_0) minus area P_0cbP_e (due to the price rise from P_e to P_0), and producer surplus would increase by area P_0abP_e. The net increase in social surplus, therefore, would be area abd. Again, we see that in the case of an externality, we can find a reallocation that increases social surplus and thereby offers the possibility of an increase in efficiency.

Market Responses to Externalities

Will the market always fail to provide an efficient output level in the presence of externalities? Just as pure public goods will sometimes be provided at efficient, or nearly efficient, levels through voluntary private agreements within intermediate groups, so too may private actions counter the inefficiency associated with externalities. The relevance of such private responses was first pointed out by Ronald Coase in a seminal article on the externality problem.[20] He argued that in situations in which property rights are clearly defined and costless to enforce, and utility is linear in wealth, costless bargaining among participants will lead to an economically efficient level of external effect. Of course, the distribution of costs and benefits resulting from the bargaining depends on who owns the property rights.

Before exploring the issue further, we must stress a very restrictive assumption of Coase's model that limits its applicability to many actual externality situations. Namely, Coase assumes zero transaction costs in the exercise of property rights.[21] In many real-world situations, transaction costs are high usually because those producing and experiencing the externality are numerous. With large numbers of actors, the bargaining that produces the Coasian outcome becomes impossible because of the high costs of coordination in the face of opportunities for a free ride.

Nevertheless, Coase's insight is valuable. He pointed out that in the case of small numbers (he assumes one source and one recipient of the externality), the allocation of property rights alone would lead to a negotiated (that is, private) outcome that is economically efficient in the sense of maximizing the total profits of the parties. Assuming that individuals make decisions based on the dollar value rather than the utility value of external effects, efficiency results whether a complete property right is given to the externality generator (one bears no liability for damages caused by one's externality) or to the recipient of the externality (one bears full liability for damages caused by one's externality). Either rule should lead to a bargain being reached at the same level of externality; only the distribution of wealth will vary, depending on which rule has force. Assuming that individuals maximize utility rather than net wealth, however, opens the possibility for different allocations under different property rights assignments.[22]

A moment's thought should suggest why large numbers will make a Coasian solution unlikely. Bargaining would have to involve many parties, some of whom would have an incentive to engage in strategic behavior. For example, in the case of a polluter with no liability for damages, those experiencing the pollution may fear free riding by others. In addition, firms may engage in opportunistic behavior, threatening to generate more pollution to induce payments. Under full liability, individuals would have an incentive to overstate the harm they suffer. Other things

[20]Ronald Coase, "The Problem of Social Cost," *Journal of Law and Economics*, 3(1) 1960, 1–44.

[21]For a conceptual discussion of transaction costs that takes account of bargaining, see Douglas D. Heckathorn and Steven M. Maser, "Bargaining and the Sources of Transaction Costs: The Case of Government Regulation," *Journal of Law, Economics, and Organization* 3(1) 1987, 69–98.

[22]For a discussion of this point and a general overview of Coase, see Thrainn Eggertsson, *Economic Behavior and Institutions* (New York: Cambridge University Press, 1990), 101–10.

equal, we expect that the greater the number of parties experiencing the externality, the greater will be the costs of monitoring damage claims.

Nevertheless, private cooperation appears effective in some situations. For instance, neighborhood associations sometimes do agree on mutually restrictive covenants, and individual neighbors occasionally do reach contractual agreements on such matters as light easements (which deal with the externalities of the shadows cast by buildings).

Moreover, there is an important case where Coase-like solutions do arise, even with large numbers of parties—namely, where (1) property rights become implicitly established by usage; (2) the value of the externality (whether positive or negative) is captured by (more technically, "capitalized into") land values; (3) considerable time has passed such that the initial stock of external parties has "rolled over"; and (4) externality levels remain stable. The relevance of these conditions can best be explained with an example. Suppose that a factory has been polluting the surrounding area for many years without anyone challenging its owner's right to do so. It is probable that the pollution will result in lower property values.[23] Residents who bought before the pollution was anticipated will have to sell their houses for less—reflecting the impact of the pollution. New homeowners, however, will not be bearing any Pareto-relevant externality, because the negative impact of the pollution will be capitalized into house prices. The lower prices of the houses will reflect the market's (negative) valuation of the pollution. In other words, through the house price it is possible to get a proxy dollar measure of the disutility of pollution. Notice that a second generation of homeowners (that is, those who bought houses after the pollution was known and capitalized into prices) would receive a bonus if the existing allocation of property rights were changed so that the factory had to compensate current homeowners for existing levels of pollution. Of course, if there are unexpected changes in the level of pollution (or new information about the harmful impacts of the pollution—see our discussion of information asymmetry below), there will be, in effect, new (either positive or negative) impacts; in these situations, considerable argument is likely to occur over who has rights to compensation for the changes.

Natural Monopoly

Natural monopoly occurs when average cost declines over the relevant range of demand. Note that this definition is in terms of both cost and demand conditions. In the case of natural monopoly, a single firm can produce the output at lower cost than any other market arrangement, including competition.

While the cost-and-demand conditions establish the existence of a natural monopoly situation, the *price elasticity of demand* determines whether or not the natural monopoly has important implications for public policy. The price elasticity of demand measures how responsive consumers are to price changes. Specifically, the

[23]Indeed, changes in property values provide a basis for empirically estimating the social costs of externalities. For example, with respect to air pollution, see V. Kerry Smith and Ju-Chin Huang, "Can Markets Value Air Quality? A Meta-Analysis of Hedonic Property Value Models," *Journal of Political Economy* 103(1) 1995, 209–27.

price elasticity of demand is defined as the percentage change in the quantity demanded that results from a 1 percent change in price.[24] If the absolute value of the price elasticity of demand is less than one (a 1 percent change in price leads to less than a 1 percent reduction in the quantity demanded), then we say that demand is inelastic and an increase in price will increase total revenue. A good is unlikely to have inelastic demand if there are other products that, while not exactly the same, are close substitutes. In such circumstances, the availability of substitutes greatly limits the economic inefficiency associated with natural monopoly. For example, although local cable television markets have the cost-and-demand characteristics of natural monopolies, many substitute products, including conventional over-the-air television, direct satellite dishes, and DVD players, may prevent cable television companies from realizing large monopoly rents in their local markets.

We should also keep in mind that, although we stated the basic definition of natural monopoly in static terms, markets in the real world are dynamic. Technological change may lead to different cost characteristics, or high prices may bring on close or even superior substitutes. The result may be the elimination of natural monopoly or the supplanting of one natural monopoly technology by another.[25] For example, especially in developing countries, cellular phones may be direct substitutes for line-connected phones, providing competition for traditional telephone systems.

Allocative Inefficiency under Natural Monopoly

We show a cost structure leading to natural monopoly in Figure 5.9. Marginal cost (MC) is shown as constant over the range of output. Fixed cost (FC), which is not shown in the figure, must be incurred before any output can be supplied. Because of the fixed cost, average cost (AC) starts higher than marginal cost and falls toward it as the output level increases. ($AC = FC/Q + MC$, where Q is the output level.) Although marginal cost is shown as constant, the same analysis would apply even if marginal cost were rising or falling, provided that it remains small relative to fixed cost.

Figure 5.9 shows the divergence between the firm's profit-maximizing behavior and economic efficiency. Let us first consider the economically efficient price and output. Efficiency requires, as we discussed in the previous chapter, that price be set equal to marginal cost ($P = MC$). Because marginal cost is below-average cost, the economically efficient output level Q_0 results in the firm suffering a loss equal to FC. Obviously, the firm would not choose this output level on its own. Instead, it would maximize profits by selecting output level Q_m, which equates marginal revenue to marginal cost ($MR = MC$). At output level Q_m, the market price will be P_m and profits equal to the area of rectangle $P_mcbP_0 - FC$ will result. Relative to output

[24]Mathematically, if the demand schedule is continuous, the price elasticity of demand at some quantity equals the slope of the demand schedule at that quantity times the ratio of quantity to price. For example, with linear demand schedule, $Q = a - bP$, the slope of the demand schedule (the derivative dQ/dP) is $-b$. Therefore, the price elasticity of demand is $e = -bP/Q$. Note that the elasticity of a linear demand schedule varies with quantity.

[25]For an example of a case study that finds that technological change significantly reduced economies of scale and eliminated natural monopoly, see Stephen M. Law and James F. Nolan, "Measuring the Impact of Regulation: A Study of Canadian Basic Cable Television," *Review of Industrial Organization* 21(3) 2002, 231–49.

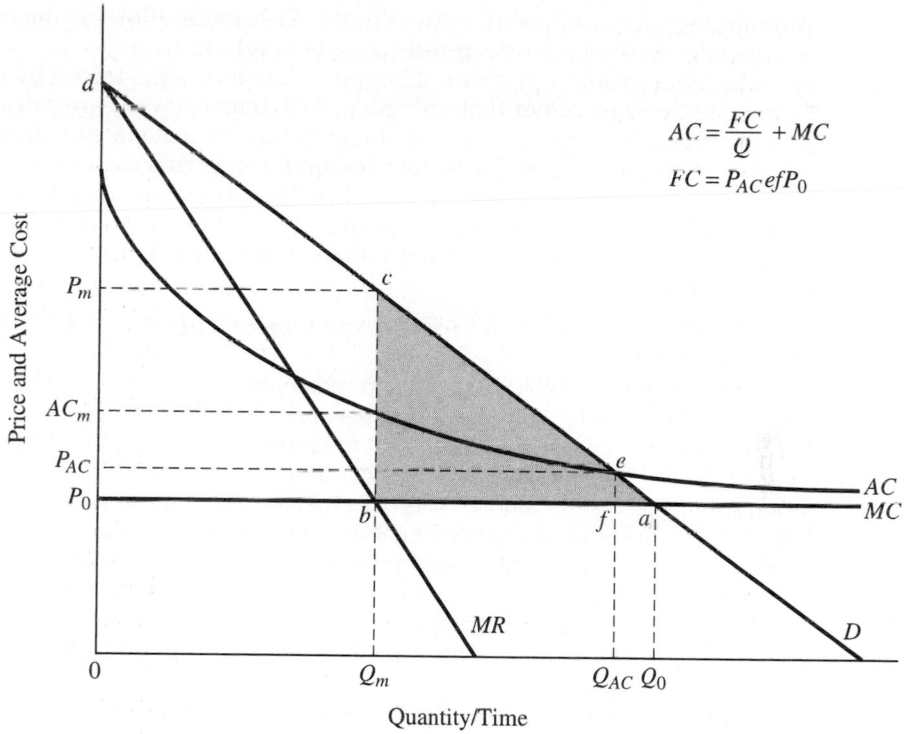

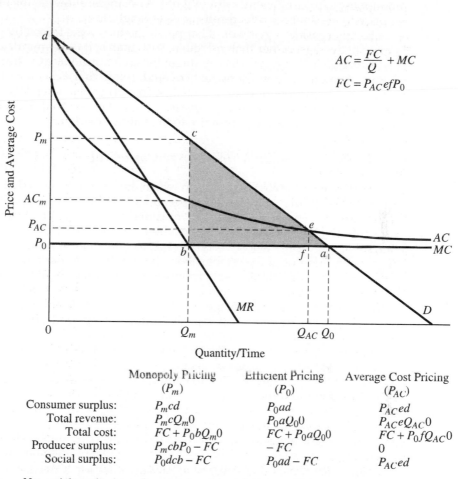

	Monopoly Pricing (P_m)	Efficient Pricing (P_0)	Average Cost Pricing (P_{AC})
Consumer surplus:	P_mcd	P_0ad	$P_{AC}ed$
Total revenue:	P_mcQ_m0	P_0aQ_00	$P_{AC}eQ_{AC}0$
Total cost:	$FC + P_0bQ_m0$	$FC + P_0aQ_00$	$FC + P_0fQ_{AC}0$
Producer surplus:	$P_mcbP_0 - FC$	$-FC$	0
Social surplus:	$P_0dcb - FC$	$P_0ad - FC$	$P_{AC}ed$

Net social surplus loss of monopoly pricing relative to efficient pricing: *abc*
Net social surplus loss of average cost pricing relative to efficient pricing: *aef*

Figure 5.9 Social Surplus Loss from Natural Monopoly

level Q_0, consumer surplus is lower by the area of P_mcaP_0, but the profit of the firm is larger by P_mcbP_0. The net loss in social surplus due to the underproduction equals the area of the shaded triangle *abc*, the deadweight loss to consumers. (As noted in our discussion of Figure 4.5, units of forgone output would have offered marginal benefits in excess of marginal costs—a total loss equal to the area between the marginal benefit, or demand schedule, and the marginal cost curve. Again, in Figure 5.9, this loss is the area of triangle *abc*.)

Imagine that public policy forced the natural monopolist to price at the economically efficient level (P_0). The monopolist would suffer a loss of *FC*. Consequently, the monopolist would go out of business in the absence of a subsidy equal to offset the loss. Notice the dilemma presented by natural monopoly: forcing the monopolist to price efficiently drives it out of business; allowing the monopolist to set price to maximize profits results in deadweight loss.

Briefly consider what would happen if the firm were forced by public policy to price at average, rather than marginal, cost; that is, if the firm priced at P_{AC} and produced Q_{AC} in Figure 5.9. Clearly, under these circumstances the firm can survive because its costs are now being just covered. (Note that *FC* equals $P_{AC}efP_0$.) Although the deadweight loss under average cost pricing is much lower than under monopoly pricing (area *aef* versus area *abc*), it is not eliminated. Therefore, average cost pricing represents a compromise to the natural monopoly dilemma.

Restraints When Markets Are Contestable

We can imagine circumstances in which the natural monopoly firm might, in fact, be forced to price at average cost because of the threat of competition from potential entrants. The crucial requirement is that entry to, and exit from, the industry be relatively easy. Whether or not the firm has in-place capital that has no alternative use, capital whose costs are *sunk*, usually determines the viability of potential entry and exit. If the established natural monopoly has a large stock of productive capital that cannot be sold for use in other industries, it will be difficult for other firms to compete because they must first incur cost to catch up with the established firm's capital advantage. The in-place capital serves as a barrier to entry; the greater the replacement cost of such capital, the higher the barrier to entry. For example, once a petroleum pipeline is built between two cities, its scrap value is likely to be substantially less than the costs a potential competitor would face in building a second pipeline. The greater is the difference, the greater is the ability of the established firm to fight off an entry attempt with temporarily lower prices. Of course, keep in mind that the ability of the firm to charge above the marginal cost level will be influenced by the marginal costs of alternative transportation modes, such as truck and rail, that can serve as substitutes.

Much economic research considers industries with low barriers to entry and decreasing average costs, which, because of the threat of potential entry, are said to be in *contestable markets*.[26] We expect markets that are contestable to exhibit pricing closer to the efficient level. One of the most important debates in the literature arising from the contestable market framework concerns the empirical significance of in-place capital as effective barriers to entry.[27] Most natural monopolies appear to enjoy large advantages in in-place capital, raising the question of whether or not they should be viewed as being in contestable markets.

As we have seen, the "naturalness" of a monopoly is determined by decreasing average cost over the relevant range of output. In many situations it appears that

[26]William J. Baumol, John C. Panzar, and Robert D. Willig, *Contestable Markets and the Theory of Industry Structure* (New York: Harcourt Brace Jovanovich, 1982); and William J. Baumol, "Contestable Markets: An Uprising in the Theory of Industry Structure," *American Economic Review* 72(1) 1982, 1–15. For a discussion of *imperfect contestability*, see Steven A. Morrison and Clifford Winston, "Empirical Implications and Tests of the Contestability Hypothesis," *Journal of Law and Economics* 30(1) 1987, 53–66.

[27]For evidence that the U.S. Postal Service, for example, may have few natural monopoly characteristics, see Alan L. Sorkin, *The Economics of the Postal Service* (Lexington, MA: Lexington Books, 1980), Chapter 4; and Leonard Waverman, "Pricing Principles: How Should Postal Rates Be Set?" in *Perspectives on Postal Services Issues*, Roger Sherman, ed. (Washington, DC: American Enterprise Institute, 1980), 7–26.

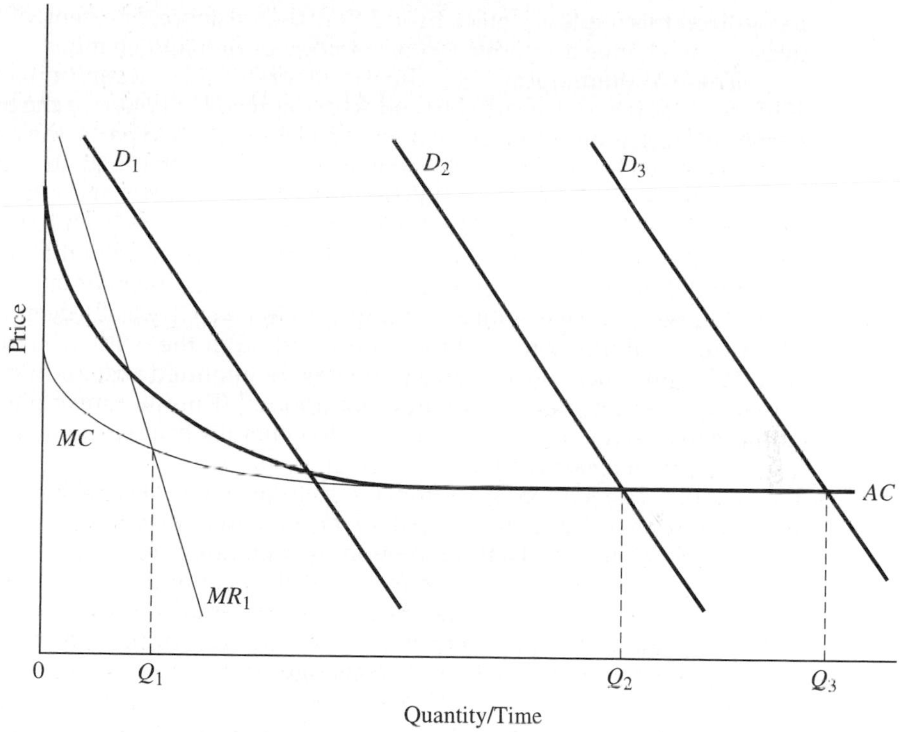

Figure 5.10 Shifting Demand and Multiple Firm Survival

Source: William G. Sheperd, *The Economics of Industrial Organization* (Upper Saddle River, NJ: Prentice Hall, 1979), fig, 3.4, p. 59.

average cost declines over considerable ranges of output but then flattens out. In other words, initial economies of scale are exhausted as output increases. What happens if demand shifts to the right (for example, with population increases) such that the demand curve intersects the flat portion of the average cost curve? There may be considerable room for competition under these circumstances. Figure 5.10 illustrates such a situation. If demand is only D_1 (the "classic" natural monopoly), only one firm can survive in the market. If demand shifts outward beyond D_2 to, say, D_3, then two or more firms may be able to survive because each can operate on the flat portion of the average cost curve.

Simply because two firms could survive at D_3 does not mean that two competing firms will actually emerge as demand expands. If the original natural monopoly firm expands as demand moves out, it may be able to forestall new entrants and capture all of the market. Nevertheless, we are again reminded of the importance of looking beyond the static view.

When considering natural monopoly from a policy perspective, we often find that legal and regulatory boundaries do not correspond to the boundaries delineating natural monopoly goods. Most discussion of industrial issues tends to be within the framework of product "sectors," such as the electric and the telephone industries. Unfortunately, the economic boundaries of natural monopolies are not likely to conform to these neat sectoral boundaries. Historically, regulation has often not recognized this unpleasant fact. In addition, the existence, or extent, of a natural monopoly can change as production technology or demand changes.

The telecommunications industry illustrates these definitional problems. In 1982, the U.S. Justice Department and AT&T agreed on a plan for the breakup of the corporation. The agreement called for a division into two parts: the part that could be expected to be workably contestable and the part that had strong natural monopoly elements. Both long-distance services (contestable) and equipment manufacture and supply (competitive) were largely deregulated, while local telephone exchanges were deemed to be regional natural monopolies.[28] Similar problems with sectoral definitions have not been well recognized in other contexts, however. For example, electricity generation and transmission have typically been treated as part of an electrical utility natural monopoly, although the evidence suggests that in many circumstances only transmission has the required cost and demand characteristics to be considered a natural monopoly.[29] (Running multiple sets of transmission lines across the countryside would generally be inefficient; having multiple firms generating electricity would not be.)

Another dimension, apart from the sectoral, where the problem of defining natural monopoly arises is the spatial. Over what spatial area does the natural monopoly exist? Almost all natural monopoly regulation corresponds to existing city, county, state, and federal boundaries; but the economic reality of a natural monopoly knows no such bounds—it is purely an empirical question how far (spatially) the natural monopoly extends. Again, the appropriate spatial boundaries of a natural monopoly can change with changes in technology.

X-Inefficiency Resulting from Limited Competition

Thus far we have described the potential social costs of natural monopoly, whether it prices to either maximize profits or cover cost, in terms of deadweight loss caused by allocational inefficiency. The social costs, however, may be larger because natural monopolies do not face as strong incentives as competitive firms to operate at minimum cost. One of the greatest advantages of a competitive market is that it forces firms to keep their costs down—in other words, the whole average and marginal cost curves are as low as they can possibly be. In the absence of competition, firms may be able to survive without operating at minimum cost. Harvey Leibenstein coined the phrase *X-inefficiency* to describe the situation in which a monopoly does not achieve the minimum costs that are technically feasible.[30] (As we shall see, X-inefficiency is not fully descriptive because transfers as well as technical inefficiencies are often involved.) One also sometimes finds the terms *cost inefficiency*, *operating inefficiency*, or *productive inefficiency* to describe the same phenomenon.

[28]Kenneth Robinson, "Maximizing the Public Benefits of the AT&T Breakup," *Journal of Policy Analysis and Management* 5(3) 1986, 572–97. For discussion of technological change that eroded the natural monopoly characteristics of telephone services, see Irwin Manley, *Telecommunications America: Markets without Boundaries* (Westport, CT: Quorum, 1984).

[29]For the case against treating any aspects of the electric industry as a natural monopoly, see Robert W. Poole, Jr., *Unnatural Monopolies: The Case for Deregulating Public Utilities* (Lexington, MA: Lexington Books, 1985).

[30]See Harvey J. Leibenstein, *Beyond Economic Man* (Cambridge, MA: Harvard University Press, 1976); and Roger S. Frantz, *X-Efficiency: Theory, Evidence and Applications* (Boston: Kluwer, 1988).

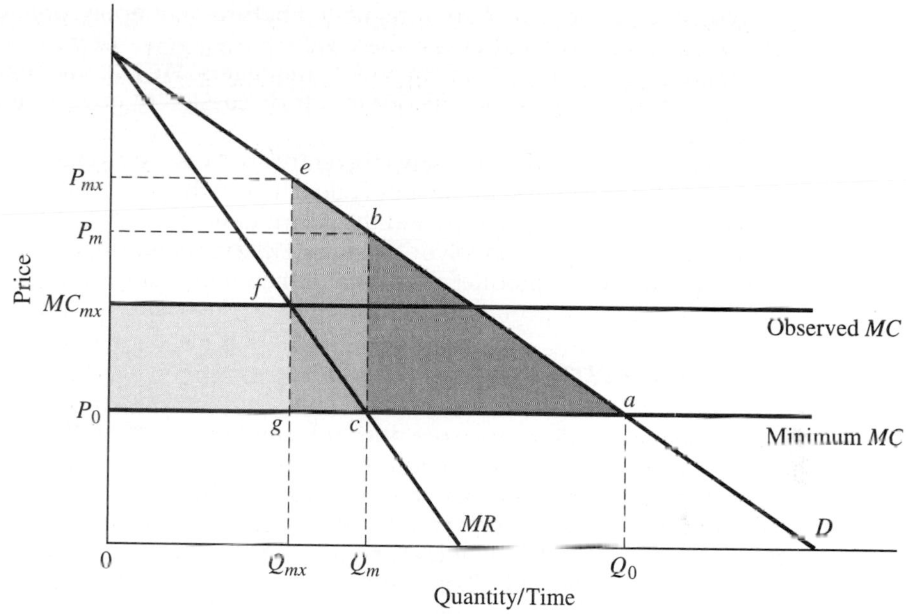

Social surplus loss from efficient monopoly:	*abc*
Minimum social surplus loss from inefficient monopoly:	*aeg*
Maximum social surplus loss from inefficient monopoly:	$aeg + MC_{mx}fgP_0$

Figure 5.11 X-Inefficiency under Natural Monopoly

In Figure 5.11 we incorporate X-inefficiency into the basic analysis of monopoly pricing. But first suppose that we ignore X-inefficiency for a moment. The deadweight loss associated with a profit-maximizing natural monopoly is the darkly shaded triangular area *abc* (already discussed in Figure 5.9). If we take X-inefficiency into account, however, the minimum possible marginal cost curve is lower than that observed from the behavior of the firm. The actual deadweight loss, therefore, is at least equal to the larger triangular *aeg*—the additional loss of *cbeg* results because output is Q_{mx} rather than Q_m.

Some or all of the very lightly shaded area $MC_{mx}fgP_0$ represents unnecessary cost that should be counted as either producer surplus or deadweight loss. If marginal costs are higher than the minimum because the managers of the firms employ more real resources such as hiring workers who stand idle, then the area $MC_{mx}fgP_0$ should be thought of as a social surplus loss. If, on the other hand, costs are higher because the managers pay themselves and their workers higher than necessary wages, we should consider this area as rent—it represents unnecessary payments rather than the misuse of real resources.[31] If, however, potential employees and managers spend time or other resources attempting to secure the rent (say, by enduring periods of unemployment while waiting for one of the overpaid jobs to open up), then the rent may be dissipated and thus converted to deadweight loss.

[31] For evidence that unions are successful in capturing some of this rent in the presence of monopoly, see Thomas Karier, "Unions and Monopoly Power," *Review of Economics and Statistics* 67(1) 1985, 34–42.

Note that in the case of an unregulated natural monopoly, one would not expect X-inefficiency to occur unless there were a divergence of information and interests between owners of the firm and its managers. We put this type of problem into the perspective of agency theory in our discussion of government failures in Chapter 8.

In summary, natural monopoly inherently involves the problem of undersupply by the market. The extent of undersupply depends on the particular cost-and-demand conditions facing the monopolist and the extent to which the market can be contested. Natural monopoly may involve additional social surplus losses because the absence of competition permits production at greater than minimum cost to persist.

Information Asymmetry

Please note that we do not use the title "information costs" or "imperfect information" in this section. The reason is that information is involved in market failure in at least two distinct ways. First, information itself has public good characteristics. Consumption of information is nonrivalrous—one person's consumption does not interfere with another's; the relevant analytical question is primarily whether exclusion is or is not possible. Thus, in the public goods context we are interested in the production and consumption of information itself. Second, and the subject of our discussion here, there may be situations where the amount of information about the characteristics of a good varies in relevant ways across persons. The buyer and the seller in a market transaction, for example, may have different information about the quality of the good being traded. Similarly, there may be differences in the level of information relating to the attributes of an externality between the generator of the externality and the affected party. Workers, for instance, may not be as well informed about the health risks of industrial chemicals as their employers. Notice that in this context we are not primarily interested in information as a good but in the degree of asymmetry in the information that relevant parties have about any good. We thus distinguish between information *as* a good (the public good case) and information *about* a good's attributes as distributed between buyer and seller or between externality generator and affected party (the *information asymmetry* case).

Inefficiency Due to Information Asymmetry

Figure 5.12 illustrates the potential social surplus loss associated with information asymmetry.[32] D_U represents the quantities of some good that a consumer would purchase at various prices in the absence of perfect information about its quality. It can, therefore, be thought of as the consumer's uninformed demand schedule. D_I represents the consumer's informed demand schedule—the amounts of the good that would be purchased at various prices if the consumer were perfectly informed about its quality. The quantity actually purchased by the uninformed con-

[32]The basic analysis was introduced by Sam Peltzman, "An Evaluation of Consumer Protection Legislation: The 1962 Drug Amendments," *Journal of Political Economy* 81(5) 1973, 1049–91. For a discussion of the empirical problems in using this approach when some consumers overestimate and others underestimate the quality of some good, see Thomas McGuire, Richard Nelson, and Thomas Spavins, "'An Evaluation of Consumer Protection Legislation: The 1962 Drug Amendments': A Comment," *Journal of Political Economy* 83(3) 1975, 655–61.

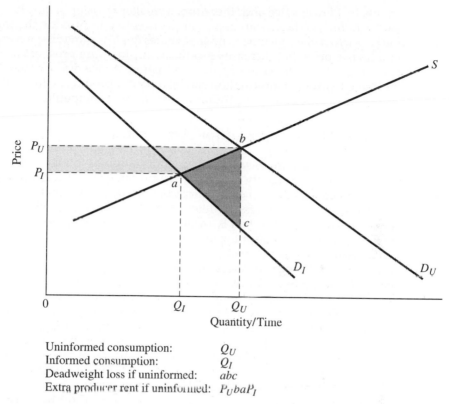

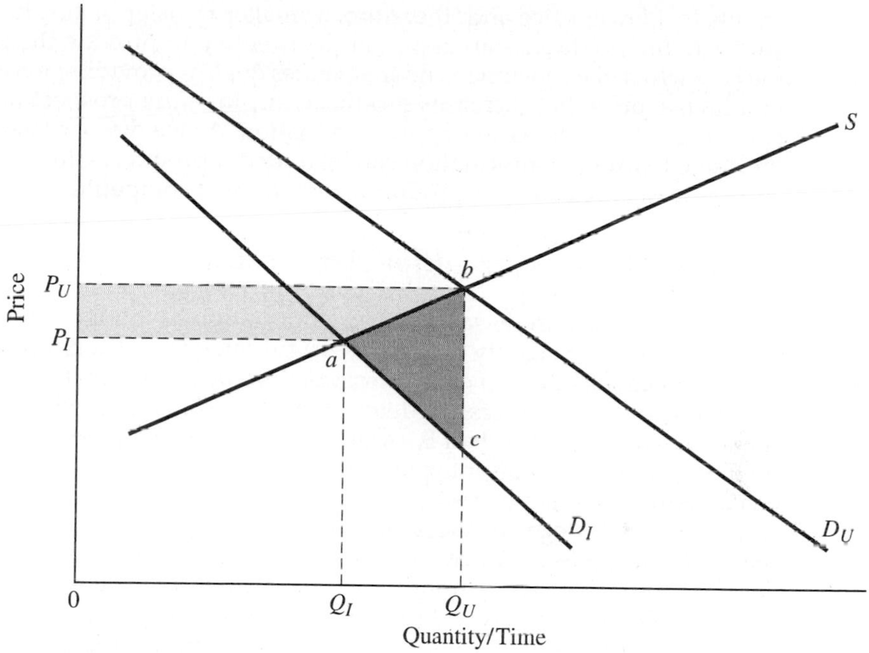

Uninformed consumption:	Q_U
Informed consumption:	Q_I
Deadweight loss if uninformed:	*abc*
Extra producer rent if uninformed:	$P_U baP_I$

Figure 5.12 Consumer Surplus Loss from Uninformed Demand

sumer is determined by the intersection of D_U with the supply schedule, *S*. This amount, Q_U, is greater than Q_I, the amount that the consumer would have purchased if fully informed about the quality of the good. The darkly shaded area *abc* equals the deadweight loss in consumer surplus resulting from the overconsumption. (For each unit purchased beyond Q_I, the consumer pays more than its marginal value as measured by the height of the informed demand schedule.) This excess consumption also results in a higher equilibrium price (P_U), which transfers surplus equal to the area $P_U baP_I$ from the consumer to the producer of the good. Figure 5.12 signals the presence of information asymmetry if the producer could have informed the consumer about the true quality of the good at a cost less than the deadweight loss in consumer surplus resulting when the consumer remains uninformed. More generally, we have market failure due to information asymmetry when the producer does not supply the amount of information that maximizes the difference between the reduction in deadweight loss and the cost of providing the information.

The same sort of reasoning would apply if the consumer underestimated rather than overestimated the quality of the good. The consumer would suffer a deadweight loss resulting from consuming less than Q_I. The incentives that the producer faces to provide the information, however, can be quite different in the two cases. In the case where the consumer overestimates quality, providing information results in a lower price and, therefore, a smaller transfer of surplus from the consumer to the producer—an apparent disincentive to provide the information. In the case where the consumer underestimates quality, providing information results in a higher price that increases producer surplus—the prospect of this gain may encourage the producer to supply information. As we discuss later, however, this incentive to provide information can be muted if producers are unable to get consumers to distinguish their products from those of competitors.

Diagnosing Information Asymmetry

Our first task in deciding when information asymmetry is likely to lead to market failure is to classify goods into useful categories. Economists have generally divided goods into two categories: *search goods* and *experience goods*.[33] A good is a search good if consumers can determine its characteristics with certainty prior to purchase. For example, a chair is a search good because consumers can judge its quality through inspection prior to purchase. A good is an experience good if consumers can determine its characteristics only after purchase; examples include meals, hairstyling, concerts, legal services, and used automobiles. We add a third category, which we call *post-experience goods*, to distinguish those goods for which it is difficult for consumers to determine quality even after they have begun consumption. For example, people may fail to associate adverse health effects with drugs that they are consuming. Experience goods and post-experience goods differ primarily in terms of how effectively consumers can learn about quality through consumption. After some period of consumption, the quality of the experience goods generally becomes apparent; in contrast, continued consumption does not necessarily reveal to consumers the quality of the post-experience good.[34]

Within these three categories, a number of other factors help determine whether information asymmetry is likely to lead to serious market failure. The effectiveness of any information-gathering strategy, other things equal, generally depends on the *variance in the quality* of units of a good (heterogeneity) and the *frequency* with which consumers make purchases. The potential costs of the information asymmetry to consumers depend on the extent to which they perceive the *full price* of the good, including imputed costs of harm from use.[35] The *cost of searching* for candidate purchases and the full price determine how expensive and potentially beneficial it is for consumers to gather information.

Search Goods. Searching can be thought of as a sampling process in which consumers incur costs to inspect units of a good. A consumer pays a cost C_S to see a particular combination of price and quality. If the price exceeds the consumer's marginal value for the good, no purchase is made and the consumer either again

[33]The distinction between search and experience goods was introduced by Philip Nelson, "Information and Consumer Behavior," *Journal of Political Economy* 78(2) 1970, 311–29.

[34]See Aidan R. Vining and David L. Weimer, "Information Asymmetry Favoring Sellers: A Policy Framework," *Policy Sciences* 21(4) 1988, 281–303.

[35]A formal specification of the concept of full price is provided by Walter Oi, "The Economics of Product Safety," *Bell Journal of Economics and Management Science* 4(1) 1973, 3–28. He considers the situation in which a consumer buys X units of a good at price P per unit. If the probability that any one unit is defective is $1 - q$, then, on average, the consumer expects $Z = qX$ good units. If each bad unit inflicts, on average, damage equal to W, then the expected total cost of purchase is $C = PX + W(X - Z)$, which implies a full price per good unit of $P^* = C/Z = P/q + W(1 - q)/q$.

pays C_S to see another combination of price and quality or stops sampling. If the consumer's marginal valuation exceeds price, then the consumer either makes a purchase or pays C_S again in expectation of finding a more favorable good in terms of the excess of marginal value over price. When C_S is zero, the consumer will find it advantageous to take a large sample and discover the complete distribution of available price and quality combinations so that the pre-search information asymmetry disappears. For larger C_S, however, the consumer will take smaller samples, other things equal, so that information asymmetry may remain. Additionally, because the range in price for a given quality is likely to be positively correlated with price, optimal sample sizes will be smaller the larger the ratio of C_S to expected price.

The more heterogeneous the available combinations of price and quality, the more likely that the consumer will fail to discover a more favorable choice for any given sample size. In contrast, even small samples will eliminate information asymmetry if the price and quality combinations are highly homogeneous. Once consumers realize that nearly identical units are offered at the same price, the optimal sample size falls to one.

Going beyond a static view, the frequency of purchase becomes important in determining whether information asymmetry remains. If the frequency of purchase is high relative to the rate at which the underlying distribution of combinations of price and quality changes, then consumers accumulate information over time that reduces the magnitude of the information asymmetry. If the frequency of purchase is low relative to the rate of change in the underlying distribution, then accumulated information will not necessarily lead to reductions in information asymmetry. In either case, however, frequent purchasers may become more experienced searchers so that C_S falls and larger samples become efficient.

Thus, if search costs are small relative to the expected purchase price *or* the distribution of price and quality combinations is fairly homogeneous *or* the frequency of purchase is high relative to the rate of change in the distribution of price and quality combinations, then information asymmetry is unlikely to lead to significant inefficiency. In the case where search costs are high relative to the expected purchase price, the distribution of price and quality combinations is very heterogeneous, and the frequency of purchase is relatively low, information asymmetry may lead to significant inefficiency. But, if it is possible for producers to distinguish their products by brand, they have an incentive to undertake informative advertising that reduces search costs for consumers. When brands are difficult to establish, as in the case of, say, farm produce, retailers may act as agents for consumers by advertising prices and qualities. Because the veracity of such advertising can be readily determined by consumers through inspection of the goods, and because retailers and firms offering brand name products have an incentive to maintain favorable reputations, we expect the advertising generally to convey accurate and useful information. Reputation is likely to be especially important in emerging electronic commerce markets because consumers cannot directly examine goods before purchasing them. For example, one recent study found that sellers' reputation had a statistically significant, albeit small, positive impact on price for an Internet auction good.[36]

In summary, search goods rarely involve information asymmetry that leads

[36]Mikhail I. Melnik and James Alm, "Does a Seller's Ecommerce Reputation Matter? Evidence from Ebay Auctions," *Journal of Industrial Economics* 50(3) 2002, 337–49.

to significant and persistent inefficiency. When inefficiency does occur, it takes the form of consumers' forgoing purchases that they would have preferred to ones that they nevertheless found beneficial. From the perspective of public policy, intervention in markets for search goods can rarely be justified on efficiency grounds.

Experience Goods: Primary Markets. Consumers can determine the quality of experience goods with certainty only through consumption. To sample, they must bear the search costs, C_S, and the full price, P^* (the purchase price plus the expected loss of failure or damage collateral with consumption).[37] The full price of consuming a meal at an unfamiliar restaurant, for instance, is the sum of purchase price (determined from the menu) and the expected cost of any adverse health effects (ranging from indigestion to poisoning) from the meal being defective. Of course, even when the expected collateral loss is zero, prior to consumption, the marginal value that the consumer places on the meal is not known with certainty.

In contrast to search goods, where, holding search costs constant, consumers optimally take larger samples for more expensive goods, they optimally take smaller samples for more expensive experience goods. Indeed, for all but the very inexpensive experience goods, we expect sampling (equivalent to the frequency of purchase for experience goods) to be governed primarily by durability. For example, sampling to find desirable restaurants will generally be more frequent than sampling to find good used automobiles.

As is the case with search goods, the more heterogeneous the quality of an experience good, the greater is the potential for inefficiency due to information asymmetry. The consumption of an experience good, however, may involve more than simply forgoing a more favorable purchase of the good. Once consumption reveals quality, the consumer may discover that the good provides less marginal value than its price and therefore regret having made the purchase regardless of the availability of alternative units of the good. The realized marginal value may actually be negative if consumption causes harm.

Learning from the consumption of experience goods varies in effectiveness. If the quality of the good is homogeneous and stable, then learning is complete after the first consumption—consumers know how much marginal value they will derive from their next purchase, including the expected loss from product failure or collateral damage. If the quality is heterogeneous or unstable, then learning proceeds more slowly. Unless consumers can segment the good into more homogeneous groupings, say, by brands or reputations of sellers, learning may result only in better ex ante estimates of the mean and variance of their ex post marginal valuations. When consumers can segment the good into stable and homogeneous groupings, repeated sampling helps them discover their most preferred sources of the good in terms of the mean and variance of quality. For example, national motel chains with reputations for standardized management practices may provide travelers with a low-variance alternative to independent motels in unfamiliar locales.

In what situations can informative advertising play an important role in reducing information asymmetry? Generally, informative advertising can be effective when consumers correctly believe that sellers have a stake in maintaining

[37]In our discussion of information asymmetry, we assume that consumers cannot sue producers for damages (in other words, they do not enjoy a property right to safety.) As we discuss in Chapter 10 under "framework regulation," tort and contract law often reduce the inefficiency of information asymmetry by deterring parties from withholding relevant information in market transactions.

reputations for providing reliable information. A seller who invests heavily in developing a brand name with a favorable reputation is more likely to provide accurate and useful information than an unknown firm selling a new product or an individual owner selling a house or used automobile.

When consumers perceive that sellers do not have a stake in maintaining a good reputation, and marginal cost of supply rises with quality, then a "lemons" problem may arise: consumers perceive a full price based on average quality so that only sellers of lower than average quality goods can make a profit and survive in the market.[38] In the extreme, producers offer only goods of low quality.[39]

When reliability is an important element of quality, firms may offer warranties that promise to compensate consumers for a portion of replacement costs, collateral damage, or both. The warranties thus provide consumers with insurance against low quality: higher purchase prices include an implicit insurance premium, and the potential loss from product failure is reduced. The quality of a warranty may itself be uncertain, however, if consumers do not know how readily firms honor their promises. Further, firms may find it impractical to offer extensive warranties in situations where it is costly to monitor the care taken by consumers. Nevertheless, warranties are a common device for reducing the consequences of information asymmetry for experience goods.

Experience Goods: The Role of Secondary Markets. Producers and consumers often turn to private third parties to help remedy information asymmetry problems. Certification services, agents, subscription services, and loss control by insurers are the most common market responses that arise.

Certification services "guarantee" minimum quality standards in processes or products. Professional associations, for instance, often set minimum standards of training or experience for their members—the board-certified specialties in medicine are examples. Perhaps closer to most people's experience, the Better Business Bureau requires members to adhere to a code of fair business practices. Underwriters Laboratories tests products against minimum fire safety standards before giving its seal of approval.[40] When such services establish their own credibility, they help producers to distinguish their goods satisfying the minimum standards from goods that do not.

Agents often sell advice about the qualities of expensive, infrequently purchased, heterogeneous goods. These agents combine expertise with learning from being participants in a large number of transactions between different pairs of buyers and sellers. For example, most people do not frequently purchase houses, which are expensive and heterogeneous in quality. Because owners typically enjoy an informational advantage by virtue of their experiences living in their houses, prospective buyers often turn to engineers and architects to help assess structural integrity. Art and antique dealers, jewelers, and general contractors provide similar services.

[38]The "lemons" argument originated with George Akerlof, "The Market for Lemons," *Quarterly Journal of Economics* 84(3) 1970, 488–500.

[39]Economists have recently considered the role of expenditures to establish reputation as a means for high-quality producers to distinguish themselves. See, for instance, Benjamin Klein and Keith B. Leffler, "The Role of Market Forces in Assuring Contractual Performance," *Journal of Political Economy* 89(4) 1981, 615–41; and Paul Milgrom and John Roberts, "Price and Advertising Signals of Product Quality," *Journal of Political Economy* 94(4) 1986, 796–821.

[40]For an overview of private organizations that set quality standards, see Ross E. Cheit, *Setting Safety Standards: Regulation in the Public and Private Sectors* (Berkeley: University of California Press, 1990).

The problem of excluding nonpaying users limits the supply of agents for goods that are homogeneous—one consumer can easily pass along information that the agent provides to prospective purchasers of similar units of the good. Inexpensive goods are unlikely to provide an adequate incentive for consumers to pay for the advice of agents. (Note that the full price is the relevant measure—one might very well be willing to pay for a visit to a doctor to get advice about a drug with a low purchase price but a high potential for harm to one's health.) Finally, agents are less likely to be relatively attractive for goods with high frequencies of purchase because consumers can often learn effectively on their own.

Consumers often rely on the experiences of friends and relatives to gather information about the quality of branded products. They may also be willing to pay for published information about such products. But such subscription services, which have public good characteristics, are likely to be undersupplied from the perspective of economic efficiency because nonsubscribers can often free-ride on subscribers by interrogating them and by borrowing their magazines. (The very existence of subscription services such as *Consumer Reports* suggests that a large number of consumers see the marginal costs of mooching or using a library as higher than the subscription price.)

Insurers sometimes provide information to consumers as part of their efforts to limit losses. For example, health maintenance organizations, which provide medical insurance, often publish newsletters that warn members of potentially dangerous and unhealthy goods such as diet products and tanning salons. Casualty insurers may signal warnings through their premiums as well as through direct information. Fire insurance underwriters, for instance, set premiums based on the types of equipment that businesses plan to use; they also often inspect commercial properties to warn proprietors of dangerous equipment and inform them about additions that could reduce their risks of fire.

Experience Goods: Summary. By their very nature, experience goods offer the potential for serious inefficiency caused by information asymmetry. Secondary markets, however, limit the inefficiency for many experience goods by facilitating consumer learning and providing incentives for the revelation of product quality. Nevertheless, problems are likely to remain in two sets of circumstances: first, when quality is highly heterogeneous, branding is ineffective, and agents are either unavailable or expensive relative to the full price of the good; and second, where the distribution of quality is unstable, so that consumers and agents have difficulty learning effectively. In these fairly limited circumstances, market failure may justify public intervention on efficiency grounds.

Post-Experience Goods. Consumption does not perfectly reveal the true quality of post-experience goods.[41] Quality remains uncertain because the individual consumer has difficulty recognizing the causality between consumption and some of its effects. For example, consumers may not recognize that the fumes of a

[41]Our category of post-experience goods shares characteristics with Arrow's "trust goods" and captures Darby and Karni's "credence qualities." Kenneth J. Arrow, "Uncertainty and the Welfare Economics of Medical Care," *American Economic Review* 53(5) 1963, 941–73; and Michael R. Darby and Edi Karni, "Free Competition and the Optimal Amount of Fraud," *Journal of Law* and *Economics* 16(1) 1973, 67–88.

cleaning product increase their risks of liver cancer because they do not expect the product to have such an effect. Often, the effects of consumption only appear after great delay so that consumers do not connect them with the product. An extreme example is DES, a drug that increases the risk of cancer in mature daughters of women who used it during pregnancy. Many other drugs require extended periods before all their effects are manifested. Young smokers, for instance, may fully appreciate the addictive power of tobacco only after they are addicted. Beyond drugs, many medical services appear to be post-experience goods—patients often cannot clearly link the state of their health to the treatments that they have received.

In terms of our earlier discussion, the consumer of a post-experience good may not have sufficient knowledge of the product to form reasonable estimates of its full price even after repeated consumption. In other words, whereas experience goods involve risk (known contingencies with known probabilities of occurrence), post-experience goods involve uncertainty (unknown contingencies or unknown probabilities of occurrence). Further, repeated consumption of a post-experience good does not necessarily lead to accurate estimates of risk.

Obviously, the potential for substantial and persistent inefficiency due to information asymmetry is greater for post-experience than experience goods. Other things equal, frequent purchases are less effective in eliminating information asymmetry for post-experience goods. In contrast to the case of experience goods, information asymmetry can persist for an extended period for even homogeneous post-experience goods.

Turning to private responses to the information asymmetry inherent in the primary markets for post-experience goods, we expect secondary markets in general to be less effective than they are for experience goods because of learning problems. Nevertheless, secondary markets can play important roles. For example, consider the services that are or have been privately offered to provide information about pharmaceuticals. The *Medical Letter on Drugs and Therapeutics*, one of the few medical periodicals that covers its costs through subscriptions rather than advertising, provides independent assessments of all new drugs approved by the FDA. Many hospitals, and some insurers, have formulary committees that review information about drugs for participating physicians. Between 1929 and 1955, the American Medical Association ran a seal of acceptance program that subjected all products advertised in the *Journal of the American Medical Association* to committee review. The National Formulary and the United States Pharmacopoeia were early attempts at standardizing pharmaceutical products. Of course, most of these information sources are directed at physicians and pharmacists who commonly serve as agents for consumers of therapeutic drugs. Although their learning from direct observation may not be effective, they can often determine if advertising claims for products are based on reasonable scientific evidence.

Reprise of Information Asymmetry

The potential for inefficiency due to information asymmetry between buyers and sellers can be found in many markets. There is some evidence that Internet, or e-commerce, markets will be particularly prone to information asymmetry on some dimensions; for example, consumers cannot touch or feel goods and are, therefore, less likely to be able to assess directly their quality.[42] The potential is rarely great for search goods, often great for experience goods, and usually great for post-experience goods. The extent to which the potential is actually realized, however, depends largely on whether public goods problems hinder the operation of secondary market mechanisms that provide corrective information. Thus, market failure is most likely in situations where information asymmetry in primary markets occurs in combination with public goods problems in secondary markets.

Conclusion

Traditional market failures involve circumstances in which the "invisible hand" fails to produce Pareto efficiency. They thus indicate possibilities for improving the efficiency of market outcomes through collective action. Along with the pursuit of distributional values, which we consider in Chapter 7, they constitute the most commonly advanced rationales for public policy. But other, less easily accommodated discrepancies between the competitive framework and the real world also suggest opportunities for advancing efficiency through collective action. These discrepancies, the subject of the next chapter, provide additional rationales for public policy.

For Discussion

1. Imagine that you and two friends are going to share a house. You have to decide whether each of you will purchase your own groceries and cook your own meals, or whether you will purchase groceries and cook meals as a group. What factors might make you more or less likely to choose the group option? Would you be more or less likely to choose it if there were five in the group rather than three?
2. Consider a developing country with a single railroad between the primary port and the most populous city. Under what conditions might the railroad have natural monopoly characteristics?
3. Under what conditions is the market for vaccination against a communicable disease likely to be inefficient?
4. Show the social surplus loss in a situation in which a consumer's uninformed demand schedule lies below her informed demand schedule.

[42]For discussions of this issue, see Severin Borenstein and Garth Saloner, "Economics and Electronic Commerce," *Journal of Economic Perspectives* 15(1) 2001, 3–12; and James V. Koch and Richard J. Cebula, "Price, Quality, and Service on the Internet: Sense and Nonsense," *Contemporary Economic Policy* 20(1) 2002, 25–37.

6

Rationales for Public Policy

Other Limitations of the Competitive Framework

Although the four traditional market failures—public goods, externalities, natural monopolies, and information asymmetries—represent violations of the ideal competitive model, we nevertheless were able to illustrate their efficiency consequences with the basic concepts of producer and consumer surplus. The consequences of relaxing other assumptions of the competitive model, however, cannot be so easily analyzed with the standard tools of microeconomics. This in no way reduces the importance of considering them. They often serve as rationales, albeit implicitly, for public policies.

We begin by considering two of the most fundamental assumptions of the competitive model—that participants in markets behave competitively and that individual preferences can be taken as fixed, exogenous, and fully rational. We then look at the assumptions that must be made to extend the basic competitive model to uncertain and multiperiod worlds. We then consider the assumption that the economy can costlessly move from one equilibrium to another. Finally, we briefly address the role of macroeconomic policy in managing aggregate economic activity.

Thin Markets: Few Sellers or Few Buyers

Participants in markets behave competitively when they act as if their individual decisions do not affect prices. In other words, they take prices as given. It is reasonable to assume competitive behavior when no seller accounts for a noticeable fraction of supply and no buyer accounts for a noticeable fraction of demand, which is usually the case when there are many buyers and many sellers. In *thin markets*, markets with either few sellers or few buyers, imperfect competition can lead to prices that differ from the competitive equilibrium and hence result in Pareto-inefficient allocations of inputs and goods.

We have already considered one important example of noncompetitive behavior—*natural monopoly*. In the case of natural monopoly, declining average cost over the relevant range of demand makes supply by more than one firm inefficient. Yet the single firm, if allowed to maximize its profits, will produce too little output from the perspective of economic efficiency. Whether or not a firm is a natural monopoly, it can at least temporarily command monopoly rents when it is the only firm supplying a market. The monopoly rents, however, will attract other firms to the market.[1] Unless technological, cost, or other barriers block the entry of new firms, the monopoly will eventually lose its power to set price and command rents.

Noncompetitive behavior can also occur on the demand side of the market. In the case of pure *monopsony*, a single buyer faces competitive suppliers and, therefore, can influence price by choosing purchase levels. When supply is not competitive, the monopsonist may be able to extract some of the rents that would otherwise go to suppliers. The resulting allocation of rents, however, will not necessarily be more efficient than that without the exercise of monopsony power.

Intermediate between cases of perfect competition and monopoly is *oligopoly*. In an oligopolistic industry, two or more firms account for a significant fraction of output. (A common rule of thumb is that when the four-firm concentration ratio—the percentage of industry sales by the four leading firms—reaches about 40 percent, the leading firms begin to realize their mutual dependence.[2]) The belief that oligopoly often leads to monopoly pricing, either through collusive agreements to limit output (*cartelization*) or through cutthroat competition to drive firms from the industry to obtain an actual monopoly, has motivated much of antitrust law. A full evaluation of antitrust policy requires a critical review of the various models of oligopoly, a task beyond the scope of this text.[3] It is sufficient for our purposes to note that imperfect competition often serves as a rationale for public intervention.

[1]Of course, firms are always looking for opportunities to be able to price above competitive levels. An extensive literature on business strategy analyzes the ways in which firms can create and preserve rents. See, for example, David Besanko, David Dranove, and Mark Shanley, *The Economics of Strategy*, 2nd ed. (New York: John Wiley, 2000).

[2]F. M. Scherer, *Industrial Pricing: Theory and Evidence* (Chicago: Rand McNally, 1970), 3. Some economists have argued that high concentration, per se, does not necessarily lead to collusion. For a review of this argument, see Yale Brozen, *Concentration, Mergers, and Public Policy* (New York: Macmillan, 1982), 9.

[3]For an overview, see W. Kip Viscusi, John M. Vernon, and Joseph E. Harrington, Jr., *Economics of Regulation and Antitrust*, 3rd ed. (Cambridge, MA: MIT Press, 2000). For an advanced treatment, see Jean Tirole, *The Theory of Industrial Organization* (Cambridge, MA: MIT Press, 1989).

The Source and Acceptability of Preferences

In the basic competitive model, we assume that each person has a fixed utility function that maps his or her consumption possibilities into an index of happiness. We make no assumption about how the particular utility functions arise, just that they depend only on the final bundles of consumed goods. But the preferences underlying the utility functions must come from somewhere. Either people have fully developed preferences at birth, or preferences are formed through participation in society.[4] If the latter, then they either arise in a sphere of activity totally independent of all economic exchange, or, in violation of the assumption of fixed preferences, depend on what goes on in the economic world.

Endogenous Preferences

Historically, the perception that preferences can be changed has been the basis for many public policies. The specific rationales usually involved arguments that, without instruction or correction, certain persons would engage in behavior that inflicted costs on others. In other words, the outcomes of certain preferences had negative external effects. Such policies as universal education, which was supposed to supplement the formation of values in the home and community, and criminal rehabilitation, which was intended to alter the willingness of some to harm others, were responses to the external effects of preferences. Although we may now despair in finding particular education and rehabilitative programs that actually impart values in the intended ways, we may nevertheless continue to view these public efforts as conceptually, if not always practically, valid.

The question of preference stability also arises in debates over the social implications of private advertising. Does advertising ever actually change preferences, or does it simply provide information that helps people better match available goods to the preferences they already hold? If advertising actually does change preferences, then we can imagine situations in which private advertising leads to economic inefficiency. For example, if advertising convinced me that, holding other consumption and my income constant, I now additionally need a digital camera to maintain my level of happiness, I have been made worse off by the advertising. Further, the gains to the makers of digital cameras cannot be large enough to make the advertising even potentially Pareto-improving.

Can advertising actually change preferences? At one time, economists generally viewed the empirical evidence as suggesting that advertising primarily affects market shares for different brands rather than the total quantity of the good

[4]Gary Becker proposes that we think of persons as having fairly stable and uniform utility functions over the direct consumption of fundamental "household goods," such as health and recreation, that result when market goods and time are combined according to individual production functions: Gary Becker, *The Economic Approach to Human Behavior* (Chicago: University of Chicago Press, 1976). Although this formulation preserves the properties of a competitive equilibrium, it begs the question of how the different production functions arise. For a discussion of the normative implications of Becker's approach, see Alexander Rosenberg, "Prospects for the Elimination of Tastes from Economics and Ethics," *Social Philosophy & Policy* 2(2) 1985, 48–68. For an example of an explicit model of utility change, see Michael D. Cohen and Robert Axelrod, "Coping with Complexity: The Adaptive Value of Changing Utility," *American Economic Review* 74(1) 1984, 30–42.

demanded.[5] More recently, however, empirical evidence suggesting quantity effects from advertising has been accumulating for goods, such as tobacco and alcohol, that have particular relevance to public policy.[6] In cases in which advertising does appear to increase market demand, however, we often have no empirical basis for clearly separating behavior that results from better information about available choices from behavior that results from changes in preferences. Only the latter potentially involves economic inefficiency.

Preferences may also change as a result of the consumption of addictive goods. Repeated use of cocaine and tobacco, for example, may produce physical dependencies that increase the relative importance of these goods in people's utility functions. People who are not able to appreciate fully the consequences of the dependency may overconsume to the detriment of their future happiness. In a sense, we encounter the sort of information asymmetry that we have already discussed. The addictive substance is a post-experience good, perhaps with an irreversible consequence—namely, a change in the person's utility function.[7] Thus, public intervention offers at least the potential for Pareto improvement.[8]

Utility Interdependence: Other-Regarding Preferences

Going beyond the question of how preferences arise, we next confront the implications of relaxing the assumption that the utility of individuals depends only on the goods that they personally consume. Such preferences are *self-regarding*. Most of us are also *other-regarding* in the sense that we do care about the consumption of at least some others: we give gifts to those we know and donations to charities that help those we do not know. This sort of altruistic behavior is most obvious in the context of the family. Parents typically care deeply about the goods their children consume. We can accommodate this interdependence in the competitive model by taking the household, rather than the individual, as the consuming unit. As long as we are willing to think of the household as having a utility function that appropriately reflects the preferences of household members, the competitive equilibrium will be economically efficient. Unfortunately, parents are not always adequately paternal. In cases of abuse, for instance, most of us would agree that public intervention is justified to ensure that the utilities of the children are being adequately taken into account in the distribution of goods (including especially safety).

Interdependence causes much greater conceptual difficulty when utilities depend not only on the absolute quantities of goods people consume but also on the

[5] William S. Comanor and Thomas A. Wilson, "The Effect of Advertising on Competition: A Survey," *Journal of Economic Literature* 17(2) 1979, 453–76; Mark S. Albion and Paul W. Farris, *The Advertising Controversy: Evidence on the Economic Effects of Advertising* (Boston: Auburn House, 1981).

[6] For example, see Henry Saffer and Dhaval Dave, "Alcohol Consumption and Alcohol Advertising Bans," *Applied Economics* 34(11) 2002, 1325–34; and Wei Hu, Hai-Yen Sung, and Theodore E. Keeler, "The State Antismoking Campaign and Industry Response: The Effects of Advertising on Cigarette Consumption in California," *American Economic Review* 85(2) 1995, 85–90.

[7] For economic models of addiction, see Athanasios Orphanides and David Zervos, "Rational Addiction with Learning and Regret," *Journal of Political Economy* 103(4) 1995, 739–58; and Gary S. Becker, *Accounting for Tastes* (Cambridge, MA: Harvard University Press, 1996).

[8] For an application to smoking, see Fritz M. Laux, "Addiction as a Market Failure: Using Rational Addiction Results to Justify Tobacco Regulation," *Journal of Health Economics* 19(4) 2000, 421–37.

relative amounts.[9] In the basic competitive model, increasing the goods available to one person without decreasing the goods available to anyone else is always a Pareto-efficient redistribution. The redistribution may not be Pareto improving, however, if some people care about their relative consumption positions. For instance, if your happiness depends to some extent on your income being higher than that of your brother-in-law, then, when your brother-in-law receives a salary increase that puts his income above yours, you will feel worse off even though your consumption possibilities have not changed. Although many people undoubtedly do care to some extent about their relative standings among colleagues, friends, or some other reference group, the implications of such interdependence for the economic efficiency of the competitive economy are as yet unclear. If nothing else, preferences based on relative consumption limit the straightforward, intuitive interpretation of the Pareto principle.

Taste for Fairness: Process-Regarding Preferences

In addition to the possibility that people are other-regarding in important ways, they may be *process-regarding* as well.[10] People often care not just about the distribution of goods but also about how the distributions were produced. Both people waiting for transplant organs and the general public, for example, may have a preference for allocation by medical criteria rather than by celebrity status. Laboratory experiments involving ultimatum games often suggest the process-regarding preferences.[11] In ultimatum games, one player proposes a split of a fixed amount of money and the other player either accepts the split or rejects it. As rejecting the split results in a zero payment for the proposer and the rejecter, a prediction of the equilibrium if both players are only self-regarding and do not expect to interact again in the future is that the proposer offers the smallest possible positive amount and the other player accepts the proposal. Often, however, the proposer offers substantially more than the minimum amount, and, if offered a very small share, the other player rejects it. Unfortunately, the stakes in these experiments, typically involving college students, tend to be low, leaving open the question if process-regarding preferences would dominate self-regarding preferences in more realistic situations. For example, you might prefer to reject a split that gives you only $1 out of a possible $10, but not to reject a split that gives you only $1,000 out of a possible $10,000.

Some evidence of the existence of relevant process-regarding has been found in public policy applications. For example, a study of attitudes toward the siting of nuclear waste repositories in Switzerland found that, in addition to expected

[9]For a provocative discussion of the implications of this sort of interdependence, see Robert H. Frank, *Choosing the Right Pond: Human Behavior and the Quest for Status* (New York: Oxford University Press, 1985).

[10]Avner Ben-Nur and Louis Putterman, "Values and Institutions in Economic Analysis," in Avner Ben-Nur and Louis Putterman, eds., *Economics, Values, and Organization* (New York: Cambridge University Press, 1998), 3–69.

[11]For a review, see Colin Camerer and Richard H. Thaler, "Ultimatums, Dictators and Manners," *Journal of Economic Perspectives* 9(2) 1995, 209–19.

economic impacts and risks, respondents' perceptions of the acceptability of the siting rules affected their willingness to accept facilities near their hometowns.[12] Perceived fairness was the major determinant of acceptability.

Legitimacy of Preferences

This brings us to an important general question about preferences: Are all preferences equally legitimate?[13] In the competitive model we treat all preferences as legitimate, all consumers as sovereign. Almost all would agree, however, that certain preferences leading to behaviors that directly harm others should not be considered legitimate from the social perspective. For example, our criminal laws prohibit us from taking out our anger on others through assault on their persons. Of course, we can think of this as simply prohibiting one from inflicting involuntary transactions, which directly violate the Pareto principle, on others.

But our laws and customs also prohibit the exercise of other preferences that do not seem to harm others directly. For instance, some people get pleasure from having sexual intercourse with animals, an activity that, if carried out in private with one's own animal, would seem not to influence directly the utility of others. Why is it not, therefore, Pareto inefficient to prohibit bestiality? Although the reason may not be obvious, in most societies there is a consensus favoring prohibition. Sometimes we can identify external effects that seem to justify such prohibitions. For example, rationales presented for restrictions on prostitution include preventing such external effects as the undermining of family stability, the exploitation of prostitutes by pimps, and the spread of venereal diseases. Perhaps disease and family stability are also relevant to the prohibition of bestiality. It may also be, however, that the prohibition rests as much on some widely shared conception of what behaviors violate human dignity. Of course, even accepting the undesirability of the behavior, the question still remains as to whether public restriction or private suasion is more appropriate.

Reprise of Preference Problems

Preferences in the real world are neither as stable nor as simple as assumed in the competitive model. The extent to which this divergence keeps the economy from achieving Pareto efficiency remains unclear, however. Yet, while we recognize the limitations of the standard assumptions, our relatively poor understanding of preferences should lead us to tread carefully in using perceived problems with them to justify public policies.

[12]Bruno S. Frey and Felix Oberholzer-Gee, "Fair Siting Procedures: An Empirical Analysis of Their Importance and Characteristics," *Journal of Policy Analysis and Management* 15(3) 1996, 353–76.

[13]Peter Brown sees this question, along with ones concerning whose utilities should count and how much, as providing the basic framework for the consideration of the ethics of substantive public policy: Peter G. Brown, "Ethics and Education for the Public Service in a Liberal State," *Journal of Policy Analysis and Management* 6(1) 1986, 56–68. Also, see Dale Whittington and Duncan MacRae, Jr., "The Issue of Standing in Cost-Benefit Analysis," *Journal of Policy Analysis and Management* 5(4) 1986, 665–82; S. C. Littlechild and J. Wiseman, "The Political Economy of Restriction of Choice," *Public Choice* 51(2) 1986, 161–72; and Cliff Walsh, "Individual Rationality and Public Policy: In Search of Merit/Demerit Policies," *Journal of Public Policy* 7(2) 1987, 103–34.

The Problem of Uncertainty

Without great conceptual difficulty, we can extend the basic competitive model to incorporate multiple periods and uncertainty. Instead of assuming that people have utility functions defined over the goods consumed in a single period with complete certainty, we assume that they have utility functions over all goods in all periods and under all possible contingencies. In effect, we simply distinguish goods by time of consumption and "state of nature" (or *contingency*) as well as by physical characteristics. In a two-period world (this year versus next) with two possible states of nature (heavy versus light snow), for example, a physical commodity such as rented cross-country skis enters the utility functions of consumers as four different goods: skis this year if snow is light, this year if snow is heavy, next year if snow is light, and next year if snow is heavy. With the crucial assumption that efficient markets exist for all these goods at the beginning of the first time period, the resulting equilibrium allocation of goods will be Pareto efficient.[14]

Availability of Insurance

The assumption that efficient markets exist for all goods under all contingencies means that it must be possible to buy actuarially fair insurance so that each person's utility will remain constant no matter what state of nature actually occurs. Insurance is actuarially fair when the premium exactly equals the expected payout. Of course, to know the expected payout, one must know the probabilities of each of the possible contingencies as well as their associated payouts. In standard terminology, *risk* involves contingencies with known probabilities, and *uncertainty* involves contingencies with unknown probabilities.

Do efficient and complete insurance markets exist in the real world? Of course, insurers must routinely charge something more than the actuarially fair price to cover their administrative costs. More important, however, two sets of factors limit the range of contingencies that can be insured at even approximately actuarially fair prices: characteristics of the contingencies themselves and behavioral responses to the available insurance. In order to set actuarially fair prices, insurers must know the probabilities of the covered contingencies. The most common types of casualty insurance protect against contingencies that occur frequently enough to allow reliable estimation of their probabilities from experience. For example, by observing the accident records of a large number of drivers, insurers can make fairly accurate predictions of the probability that anyone with specific characteristics (such as sex, age, and driving environment) will have an accident over the next year. "Experience rating" of this sort, however, is not possible, or at least not accurate, for very rare events such as major earthquakes. Consequently, insurers are unable to offer actuarially fair insurance against rare events. Further, the price of the insurance they do offer will likely include a *risk premium*, which is an addition to the estimated actuarially fair price to reflect their lack of confidence in the estimates of probabilities.

An additional premium above the actuarially fair price may also be demanded in situations in which individual risks are not independent, because after pooling,

[14]This extension of the basic model is in the spirit of Kenneth J. Arrow and Gerard Debreu, "Existence of an Equilibrium for a Competitive Economy," *Econometrica* 22(3) 1954, 265–90.

some collective, or social, risk remains.[15] If the probability that any one policyholder will have an accident is independent of the probabilities that other policyholders will also have accidents, a reasonable assumption with respect to automobile accidents for instance, then as the number of policyholders gets larger, even though the variance in total loss increases, the variance in the average loss per policy falls so that smaller risk premiums per policy are required.[16] The convergence between observed frequencies and underlying probabilities, which is known as the *law of large numbers*, breaks down when individual probabilities are not independent. In the absence of independence, insurers should demand larger risk premiums to guard against the probability that losses in any period will greatly exceed expected losses. For example, the probabilities of individual losses from flooding are clearly not independent if all policyholders live in the same river valley—an insurer would have to hold very large reserves to avoid bankruptcy in years with floods. In order to build these reserves, however, the insurers would have to price their insurance well above actuarially fair levels.

In all but extreme situations, insurers generally are able to mitigate social risk through some sort of diversification. For example, insurers may be able to spread coverage over several different floodplains. When geographic diversification is not possible, insurers may be able to shift some of the risk to reinsurers, who balance it against other types of risk. If the probability of loss correlates negatively with other risky holdings, then the total risk held by the reinsurer will fall. Some social risks, however, such as nuclear war or the presumed melting of the polar icecaps due to the greenhouse effect, would involve sufficiently large and widespread negative impacts so that diversification would not be possible.

Incomplete Insurance Markets: Adverse Selection, Moral Hazard, and Underinsuring

Turning to the behavioral responses to available insurance, we consider adverse selection, moral hazard, and underinsuring of irreplaceable commodities.

We have already encountered the concept of *adverse selection* (of goods) in our discussion of information asymmetry in goods markets. In the insurance context, it pertains to insured individuals and arises when insurers cannot costlessly classify potential policyholders according to risk categories. It therefore involves what is sometimes referred to as *hidden information*. Within each category some individuals will have either higher-than-average or lower-than-average probabilities of loss. Those with higher-than-average probabilities will tend to find the insurance attractive, those with lower-than-average probabilities will not. As more of the former buy policies and more of the latter decline to buy, the average for the group must rise. This in turn drives the insurance price higher above the actuarially fair level

[15]For a discussion and review of the economics of uncertainty, see J. Hirshleifer and John G. Riley, "The Analytics of Uncertainty and Information: An Expository Survey," *Journal of Economic Literature* 17(4) 1979, 1375–1421. On the limitations of insurance markets, see Richard J. Zeckhauser, "Coverage for Catastrophic Illness," *Public Policy* 21(2) 1973, 149–72; and "Resource Allocation with Probabilistic Individual Preferences," *American Economic Review* 59(2) 1969, 546–52.

[16]J. David Cummins, "Statistical and Financial Models of Insurance Pricing and the Insurance Firm," *Journal of Risk and Insurance* 58(2) 1991, 261–301.

for the group as a whole. Eventually, only those with the highest probabilities choose to remain covered. Insurers can sometimes limit adverse selection by offering inclusive policies to groups such as company employees, for which insurance is only one attraction of membership. In general, however, information asymmetries tend to keep the prices of many types of insurance well above actuarially fair levels.[17] One rationale for public insurance programs is that they can be made mandatory so that adverse selection can be avoided.

Moral hazard refers to the reduced incentive that insurees have to prevent compensable losses.[18] If fully insured, then they can make themselves better off, and perhaps society in the aggregate worse off, by spending less of their own resources on loss prevention than they would in the absence of insurance.[19] Actual reductions in loss protection are more likely the more costly it is for insurers to monitor behavior. It is thus sometimes referred to as the problem of *hidden action*. Insurers often try to limit moral hazard by requiring insurees to pay a fraction of the suffered loss through copayments.

People may underinsure for contingencies involving the loss of irreplaceable goods that cannot be exactly replicated. For many plausible utility functions, economically rational people will only wish to purchase actuarially fair insurance to cover the monetary part of their losses.[20] Thus, in a world filled with irreplaceable goods such as good health, beloved spouses, and unique works of art, people will not necessarily choose to purchase adequate insurance to give them constant utility under all contingencies. Of course, in light of the experience rating and moral hazard problems we have already discussed, insurers might not be willing to offer actuarially fair insurance for all irreplaceable goods anyway. For example, insurers might worry about the dangers of moral hazard if you claimed that you needed one million dollars to compensate yourself fully for the supposed accidental death of your dog.

Subjective Perception of Risk

So far we have assumed that people effectively evaluate and use information to arrive at rational decisions in situations involving risk. A large body of experimental research in cognitive psychology and economics, however, suggests that

[17]See, for example, Robert Puelz and Arthur Snow, "Evidence on Adverse Selection: Equilibrium Signaling and Cross-Subsidization in the Insurance Market," *Journal of Political Economy* 102(2) 1994, 59-76. However, one recent study could find no evidence of adverse selection in the French auto insurance market: Pierre-Andre Chiappori and Bernard Salanie, "Testing for Asymmetric Information in Insurance Markets," *Journal of Political Economy* 108(1) 2000, 56–78.

[18]For a theoretical treatment of moral hazard, see Isaac Ehrlich and Gary S. Becker, "Market Insurance, Self-Insurance, and Self-Protection," *Journal of Political Economy* 80(4) 1972, 623–48.

[19]Moral hazard also describes risky actions by the insured to qualify for compensation. See, for example, the study of the behavior of air traffic controllers under the Federal Employees Compensation Act by Michael E. Staten and John R. Umbeck, "Close Encounters in the Skies: A Paradox of Regulatory Incentives," *Regulation*, April/May 1983, 25–31.

[20]See Philip J. Cook and Daniel A. Graham, "The Demand for Insurance and Protection: The Case of Irreplaceable Commodities," *Quarterly Journal of Economics* 91(1) 1977, 141–56; and Richard Zeckhauser, "Procedures for Valuing Lives," *Public Policy* 23(4) 1975, 419–64.

people tend to make several systematic errors in assessing probabilities.[21] In order to deal economically with a great variety of information in a complex world, people tend to employ *heuristics* (rules of thumb) that sometimes lead to correct decisions but nevertheless involve predictable biases. For instance, it appears that people often estimate the probabilities of events by the ease with which instances or occurrences can be brought to mind.[22] Recall, however, depends on a number of factors, such as the personal salience of events, that tend to bias systematically estimates of relative probabilities. For example, in a study of flood and earthquake insurance coverage, Howard Kunreuther and colleagues found that knowing someone who suffered flood or earthquake loss was the single most important factor for distinguishing between purchasers and nonpurchasers.[23]

The growing dissatisfaction among economists with use of the expected utility hypothesis for predicting individual behavior also raises questions about our understanding of the way people make risky choices and hence shakes our confidence somewhat in the rationality of private behavior involving risk.[24] The *expected utility hypothesis* states that people choose among alternative actions to maximize the probability-weighted sum of utilities under each of the possible contingencies. For example, if a person's utility, $U(w)$, depends only on his wealth (w), and the probability that his wealth will be w_A is p and the probability that his wealth will be w_B is $(1 - p)$, then his expected utility is $pU(w_A) + (1 - p)U(w_B)$. The expected utility hypothesis is consistent with the competitive model and lies at the heart of most economic analysis of individual responses to risk. Laboratory experiments have identified several situations in which the expected utility hypothesis seems to be systematically violated. Although individuals tend to underestimate the probabilities of very infrequent events, for instance, they tend to be overly sensitive to small changes in the probabilities of rare events relative to the predictions of the expected utility hypothesis.[25] These findings have led cognitive psychologists and economists to begin to explore other formulations of behavior under uncertainty.[26] As yet, the full implications of the alternative formulations for our evaluation of economic efficiency remain unclear.

[21]For general overviews, see Amos J. Tversky and Daniel Kahneman, "Judgment under Uncertainty: Heuristics and Biases," *Science* (185) 1974, 1124–31; Daniel Kahneman, Paul Slovic, and Amos Tversky, eds., *Judgment under Uncertainty: Heuristics and Biases* (New York: Cambridge University Press, 1982). For an explanation of these misperceptions in terms of Bayesian updating, see W. Kip Viscusi, "Prospective Reference Theory: Toward an Explanation of the Paradoxes," *Journal of Risk and Uncertainty* 2(3) 1989, 235–63.

[22]Tversky and Kahneman call this the *heuristic of availability* (p. 1127). They also identify the *heuristic of representativeness*, which is often used when people have to estimate conditional probabilities (given some observed characteristics, what is the probability that the object belongs to some class); and the *heuristic of anchoring*, which refers to the tendency of people not to adjust their initial estimates of probabilities adequately as more information becomes available (pp. 1124 and 1128).

[23]H. Kunreuther, R. Ginsberg, L. Miller, P. Sagi, P. Slovic, B. Borkin, and N. Katz, *Disaster Insurance Protection: Public Policy Lessons* (New York: John Wiley, 1978), 145–53.

[24]See Kenneth J. Arrow, "Risk Perception in Psychology and Economics," *Economic Inquiry* 20(1) 1982, 1–9.

[25]For an excellent review of these issues, see Mark J. Machina, "'Expected Utility' Analysis without the Independence Axiom," *Econometrica* 50(2) 1982, 277–323.

[26]For a review of variants of the expected utility hypothesis, see Paul J. H. Schoemaker, "The Expected Utility Model: Its Variants, Purposes, Evidence, and Limitations," *Journal of Economic Literature* 20(2) 1982, 529–63. Recently, there have been numerous efforts to develop a broader, more descriptively valid form of expected utility theory. For a brief overview, see Richard A. Chechile and Alan D. J. Cooke, "An Experimental Test of a General Class of Utility Models: Evidence for Context Dependency," *Journal of Risk and Uncertainty* 14(1) 1997, 75–93.

More General Issues Related to the Rationality of Decision Making

In discussing uncertainty, we briefly touched on the issue of decision making and judgment biases that arise in the way people perceive risks. But risk perception is not the only context in which individuals behave in ways that appear to be inconsistent with the tenets of classical utility theory. Considerable experimental evidence suggests that people make very different valuations of gains and losses.

These differences underlie *prospect theory*. Developed by Daniel Kahneman and Amos Tversky, prospect theory suggests that individuals deviate from expected utility maximization in the following systematic ways: they value gains and losses from a reference point, which is, in turn, based on some notion of the status quo (hence this is sometimes called the *status quo effect* or, more commonly, the *endowment effect*).[27] Also, they place more weight on losses than on gains—a simultaneous loss and a gain of the same size would leave an individual worse off. In a context of risky choices, they are risk averse toward gains and risk seeking toward losses. They prefer a smaller certain gain to a larger probable gain when the expected values of the two alternatives are the same, but they exhibit *loss aversion* in that they prefer a larger probable loss to a smaller certain loss when the expected value of the two alternatives is the same.

Figure 6.1 illustrates the shape of the utility function assumed by prospect theory.

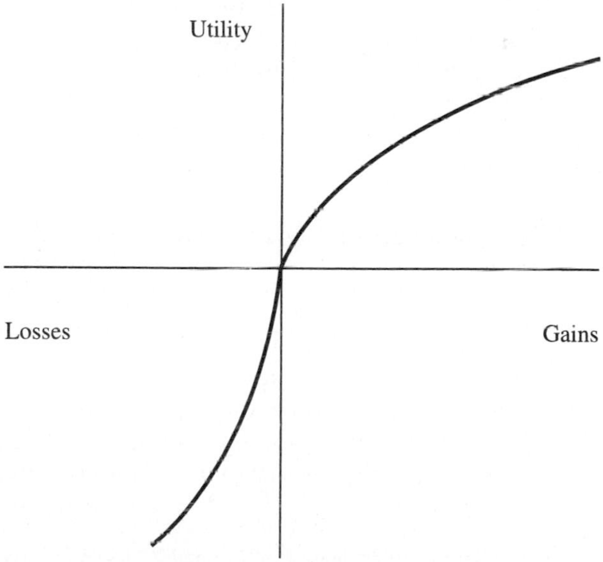

Figure 6.1 Utility Function Showing Loss Aversion

[27]Jack Knetsch argues that the reference point is determined by people's perception of normalcy. It often, but not always, reflects the actual status quo, but in public policy contexts it often is not synonomous with legal entitlement. "Preference States, Fairness, and Choices of Measures to Value Environmental Changes," in Max H. Bazerman, David M. Messick, Ann Tenbrusel, and Kimberly A. Wade-Bensoni, eds., *Environment, Ethics, and Behavior* (San Francisco: Lexington Press, 1997).

Loss aversion is inconsistent with the standard formulations of the competitive framework. To what extent does it pose a problem for public policy? One answer is that it does not. Individuals simply value losses more highly than gains; even though this is inconsistent with a simple utility maximization model, it is not irrational. Unfortunately, however, many public policy issues can be framed as *either* a loss or a gain, especially in the context of political rhetoric, which we discuss in Chapter 8. Most relevant to our discussion of market failures, however, the asymmetry of gains and losses undermines the usefulness of the Coase theorem (Chapter 5), even in the context of small numbers.

More generally, *behavioral economics* seeks to incorporate the findings of cognitive psychology into models of economic behavior.[28] For example, the standard economic approach would predict little difference in participation in company savings plans between those that require employees to "opt in" (affirmatively make a decision to participate) and those that require employees to "opt out" (affirmatively make a decision not to participate). Empirical evidence strongly suggests, however, that participation is much higher in the opt-out plans.[29]

Reprise of Uncertainty Problems

These observations about insurance markets and individual responses to risk suggest that public policies may have potential for increasing economic efficiency in circumstances involving uncertainty. Public assessments of risks, for example, may be an appropriate response when people make important systematic errors in their private assessments, and public insurance may be justified when private coverage is significantly incomplete. Until we have a better understanding of how individuals actually deal with uncertainty, however, our evaluation of economic efficiency in circumstances involving uncertainty must itself remain uncertain.

Intertemporal Allocation: Are Markets Myopic?

As we have already indicated, the competitive model can be extended to the intertemporal allocation of goods. If we assume that it is possible to make contracts in the current period for the production and delivery of goods in all future periods (in other words, forward markets exist for all goods), then the competitive equilibrium will be Pareto efficient.[30] One "price" that emerges in the intertemporal context is the *social marginal rate of time preference*, the rate at which everyone is indifferent between exchanging current for future consumption. For example, if peo-

[28]Matthew Rabin, "Psychology and Economics," *Journal of Economic Literature* 36(1) 1998, 11–46; Jessica L. Cohen and William T. Dickens, "A Foundation for Behavioral Economics," *American Economic Review* 92(2) 2002, 335–38.

[29]Brigitte C. Madrian and Dennis F. Shea, "The Power of Suggestion: Inertia in 401(k) Participation and Savings Behavior," *Quarterly Journal of Economics* 116(4) 2001, 1149–87.

[30]We can distinguish three types of markets: *Spot markets* encompass transactions involving immediate delivery of goods. *Forward markets* encompass contracts that specify future delivery at a specified price. *Futures markets* are specially organized forward markets in which clearinghouses guarantee the integrity and liquidity of the contracts.

ple were indifferent between giving up one unit of current consumption for an additional 1.06 units next year and giving up 1.06 units of consumption next year in return for an additional unit this year, then they would be exhibiting a marginal rate of time preference of 0.06. In the ideal competitive equilibrium, the social rate of marginal time preference will equal the market interest rate, the rate at which people can borrow and lend.

To see why the social rate of time preference and the market rate of interest must be equal in equilibrium, consider what would happen if someone's rate of time preference were either smaller or larger than the market interest rate. If it were smaller (say, 0.06 compared to a market interest rate of 0.08), giving up one unit of current consumption by lending at the interest rate would yield an additional 1.08 units of consumption next year, which is more than the 1.06 needed to keep the consumer as well off as before the temporal reallocation. The consumer would be able to make himself better off by continuing to shift consumption to the future until his time preference has risen to the market rate of interest and no further gains are possible. If the market interest rate were lower than the consumer's rate of time preference, then the consumer could make himself better off by borrowing until his rate of time preference has fallen to the rate of interest.

Capital Markets

What determines the rate of interest? In equilibrium, the demand for borrowing must just equal the supply of loans. The resulting rate of interest is the price that clears this *capital market*. Of course, in the real world the financial institutions that make up the capital market cover their administrative expenses by lending at higher rates than at which they borrow. They may also demand premiums for riskier loans.

Just as the theoretical efficiency of the competitive equilibrium depends on the existence of complete insurance markets to accommodate uncertainty, it depends on complete, or perfect, capital markets to accommodate intertemporal allocation. Perfect capital markets allow anyone to convert future earnings to current consumption through borrowing. But in reality, the anticipation by lenders of moral hazard greatly reduces the amount people can actually borrow against future earnings. Borrowers who owe large percentages of their incomes may be tempted to reduce their work effort because they realize smaller net returns to their labor than if they were debt free. With the now almost universal prohibition against slavery and the existence in most countries of bankruptcy laws, borrowers have no means of convincing lenders that they will maintain full work effort. Therefore, at least with respect to labor income, capital markets appear to be imperfect. It is at least conceivable that some public policies, such as guaranteed loans for education, might be justified on the grounds of imperfect capital markets.

At a more fundamental level, scholars have long debated whether or not capital markets lead to appropriate levels of saving and investment for future generations.[31] No one lives forever. How, then, can we expect the decisions of current

[31]For a variety of economic approaches to the issue, see Robert C. Lind, ed., *Discounting for Time and Risk in Energy Policy* (Washington, DC: Resources for the Future, 1982).

consumers to take adequate account of the unarticulated preferences of those yet to be born? One response recognizes that generations overlap. Most of us consider the welfare of our children and our grandchildren, who we hope will outlive us, in our economic decisions. Rather than attempting to consume all of our resources before the instant of death, most of us plan on bequeathing at least some of our savings to family or charity. Even when we do not intentionally plan to leave unconsumed wealth behind, we may do so unintentionally through untimely death.

Despite intentional and unintentional bequests, positive market interest rates prevail in most societies. Some philosophers and economists object on normative grounds to interpreting positive interest rates as appropriate social marginal rates of time preference.[32] They argue that there is no ethical basis for any social marginal rate of time preference other than zero; that is, they argue that consumption by someone in the future should be given the same weight from the social perspective as consumption by someone today. Their argument implies that any investment yielding a positive rate of return, no matter how small, should be undertaken. Because investment in the competitive economy demands rates of return at least as high as the rate of interest, they generally advocate public policies to increase investment.

The underinvestment argument seems to ignore the legacy of capital from one generation to the next. Net investments increase the available capital stock. Most forms of capital do, of course, depreciate over time. A bridge, for instance, needs maintenance to keep it safe, and eventually it may have to be abandoned or rebuilt. But perhaps the most important element of our capital stock is knowledge, which does not depreciate. Improvements in technology not only increase current productive options but those in the future as well. This legacy helps explain the growing wealth of successive generations in countries, like the United States, that rely primarily on private investment. The underinvestment argument loses force, therefore, if the total capital stock, including nontangible capital such as knowledge, can be reasonably expected to continue to grow in the future.

One variant of the underinvestment (or overconsumption of current wealth) argument deserves particular attention. It concerns the irreversible consumption of natural resources such as animal species, wilderness, and fossil fuels. When an animal species becomes extinct, it is lost to future generations. Likewise, fossil fuels consumed today cannot be consumed tomorrow. Although it may be technically possible to restore wilderness areas that have been developed, the cost of doing so may make it practically unfeasible. Will markets save adequate shares of these resources for future generations?

The answer is almost certainly yes for resources, such as fossil fuels, that have value as factor inputs rather than final goods. As long as property rights are secure, owners of resources will hold back some of the resources in anticipation of future scarcity and the higher prices the scarcity will command.[33] As higher prices are actually realized, substitutes will become economically feasible. Although generations in the distant future will be consuming less fossil fuel, they undoubtedly will

[32]For a review of the objections, see Robert E. Goodin, *Political Theory & Public Policy* (Chicago: University of Chicago Press, 1982), 162–83.

[33]The basic model of *exhaustible resources* was first set out by Harold Hotelling, "The Economics of Exhaustible Resources," *Journal of Political Economy* 39(2) 1931, 137–75. For a review of the subsequent literature, see Shantayanan Devarajan and Anthony C. Fisher, "Hotelling's 'Economics of Exhaustible Resources': Fifty Years Later," *Journal of Economic Literature* 19(1) 1981, 65–73.

produce energy from alternative sources and use energy more efficiently to produce final goods. There is no particular reason to believe, therefore, that any collective decision about how much to save for future generations will be any better than allocations made by private markets.

Resources that are themselves unique goods, such as wilderness areas and animal species, raise more serious doubt about the adequacy of market forces to ensure preservation. When owners have secure property rights and can anticipate selling their resource as a private good in the future, they must base their decisions about the extent of development on their estimates of future demand. But this can only happen if a market mechanism exists for articulating the demand. This is often not the case for natural areas, even when exclusion is possible, because there is usually no way to secure contributions from people who would be willing to pay something to keep the resource in place so as to retain the option of visiting it sometime in the future. This willingness of nonusers to contribute to maintenance of the resource for their own possible use in the future is called *option demand*; their willingness to pay something for the preservation of the resource for use by future generations or for its own intrinsic worth is called *existence value*.[34] If owners maximize the expected value of profits, the standard assumption of the competitive model, then they may develop too much of the resource from the social perspective.[35] This is because as more information becomes available about future demand, and hence about the opportunity cost of development, it will be possible for the owners to increase the extent of development, but not decrease it because restoration of the unique asset is unfeasible. Errors of underdevelopment are correctable; errors of overdevelopment are not. From the social perspective, somewhat slower development may be justified to reduce the risk of inappropriately losing in perpetuity the option to preserve.[36]

A final point, which we address more fully later in the context of benefit-cost analysis, concerns the validity of interpreting the market interest rate as the social marginal rate of time preference, even if we accept use of the latter as appropriate when comparing current and future consumption. Lenders generally charge higher rates of interest for riskier investments. But when we look across the full set of investment projects, the aggregate risk will be much less than the risk associated with any individual project because the circumstances that tend to make some projects fail tend to make others succeed. For example, the low energy prices that, ex post, make synthetic fuel plants appear to be bad investments may make recreational facilities requiring long road trips appear to be good investments. The market interest rate, therefore, will tend to exceed the social rate of time preference, which should only reflect the social risk and not the risk to individual lenders. Although

[34]See Burton A Weisbrod, "Collective Consumption Services of Individual Consumption Goods," *Quarterly Journal of Economics* 78(3) 1964, 471–77; John V. Krutilla, "Conservation Reconsidered," *American Economic Review* 57(4) 1967, 777–86; and Aidan R. Vining and David L. Weimer, "Passive Use Benefits: Existence, Option, and Quasi-Option Value," in Fred Thompson and Mark Green, eds., *Handbook of Applied Public Finance* (New York: Marcel Dekker, 1998), 319–45.

[35]Kenneth J. Arrow and Anthony C. Fisher, "Environmental Preservation, Uncertainty, and Irreversibility," *Quarterly Journal of Economics* 88(2) 1974, 312–19; and W. Michael Hanemann, "Information and the Concept of Option Value," *Journal of Environmental Economics and Management* 16(1) 1989, 23–37.

[36]Environmental quality is probably a "normal good"—other things equal, the higher our income the greater the amount of environmental quality we collectively want to consume. Ironically, the larger the legacy of economic wealth we leave to future generations, the less satisfied they may be with the level of environmental quality we bequeath!

a problem caused by public policy rather than inherent in markets, a similar wedge is introduced by taxes on profits. If, for whatever reason, the market interest rate exceeds the social rate of time preference, then private investment will fall short of the economically efficient level.

Reprise of Intertemporal Problems

In summary, specific reservations about the efficiency of capital markets and general concerns about the adequacy of the weight given to the preferences of future generations may serve as plausible rationales for public policies intended to improve the intertemporal allocation of resources and goods.

Adjustment Costs

The competitive model is static. For any given set of assumptions about utilities, production functions, and factor endowments, a unique allocation of factor inputs and goods constitutes an equilibrium in the sense that, at the prevailing prices, no consumers can make themselves better off by changing the quantities of goods they purchase and no firms can increase their profits by changing input mixes or output levels. If any of the assumptions change, then a new equilibrium distribution will arise. We can assess welfare changes by comparing allocations in the two equilibria (economists call this *comparative statics*). In doing so, we implicitly assume, however, that the economy can move costlessly from one equilibrium to another.

In reality, the economy is never static. Changing incomes, the introduction of new products, the growing work force and capital stock, good and bad harvests, and numerous other factors necessitate continual adjustments toward efficient allocation. In most circumstances, as long as prices are free to move in response to changes in supply and demand, the adjustment process itself occurs costlessly: persons change their consumption to maximize utility and firms their factor inputs to maximize profits in response to the new prices. Some persons may be worse off under the new allocation, but this will be fully reflected in the comparison of social surpluses before and after the reallocation. For example, an epidemic that decimates the population of chickens and drives up the price of eggs will, other things equal, make egg consumers worse off. The consumer surplus loss measured in the egg market serves as a good approximation for the reduction in welfare they suffered.

The picture changes if prices are *sticky* because institutional or psychological factors constrain their free movement. Constraints on price movements keep the economy from immediately reaching the new Pareto-efficient equilibrium. As a result, comparing the old and new equilibria may overstate social surplus gains and understate social surplus losses. The larger the needed adjustment and the more rigid are prices, the greater are the adjustment costs that do not show up in the comparative statics.

Consider, for example, the effects of an oil price shock of the sort experienced during the Arab oil embargo (1973–1974) and the Iranian revolution (1979–1980).[37]

[37]For a detailed discussion of how the economy adjusts to oil price shocks, see Chapter 2 of George Horwich and David L. Weimer, *Oil Price Shocks, Market Response, and Contingency Planning* (Washington, DC: American Enterprise Institute, 1984).

A dramatic rise in oil prices makes petroleum a much more expensive factor input. The supply schedules for goods that require petroleum as a factor input will shift up so that marginal costs of production rise. The market clearing product price will be higher and the market clearing quantity will be lower than before the price shock. Therefore, at any wage rate, firms will demand less of all factor inputs, including labor, than before the shock. If all factor prices were flexible, then we would expect this shift to result in reductions in both the quantity of labor demanded and the wage rate. But contracts and custom often keep firms from immediately lowering wage rates. Firms, therefore, will reduce the quantity of labor they use more than they would if wages were free to fall. Either underemployment (employees cannot work as many hours as they want at the prevailing wage rate) or, more likely, again for reasons of contract and custom, involuntary unemployment will result.

Wage rigidities due to either implicit or explicit contracts should not necessarily be interpreted as market failures.[38] They may be the result of attempts by firms and workers to share the risks associated with fluctuations in the demands for products; workers may accept lower than market clearing wages during good times to secure higher than market clearing wages during bad times. The picture is complicated, however, not only by all the limitations to complete insurance markets that we have already discussed but also by the prevalence of collective bargaining that tends to give greater protection to workers with longer tenure. Incomplete markets for risk spreading make it at least possible that public programs, such as unemployment insurance, may contribute to greater economic efficiency.

Macroeconomic Dynamics

The business cycle poses a sort of social risk that may justify public stabilization policies.[39] The economy is dynamic and tends to go through cycles of expansion and recession. During recessions unemployed labor and underutilized capital indicate inefficiency in the economy-wide use of factor inputs. The government may be able to dampen recessions through its fiscal and monetary policies. *Fiscal policies* involve taxation and expenditures. During recessions, for instance, the government may be able to stimulate demand by spending in excess of revenues. *Monetary policy* refers to manipulation of the money supply. In general, the money supply must continually increase to accommodate the growing economy. During recessions, the government may increase the money supply at a faster rate to lower interest rates, at least temporarily, thereby stimulating investment and current consumption.

Unfortunately, there is no consensus among economists about either the causes of business cycles or the most appropriate policies for reducing their adverse

[38]For a review, see Sherwin Rosen, "Implicit Contracts: A Survey," *Journal of Economic Literature* 23(3) 1985, 1144–75. For the argument that labor contracts of long duration involve negative externalities, see Laurence Ball, "Externalities from Contract Length," *American Economic Review* 77(4) 1987, 615–29.

[39]For an overview of economic thought on the business cycle, see Victor Zarnowitz, "Recent Work on Business Cycles in Historical Perspective: A Review of Theories and Evidence," *Journal of Economic Literature* 23(2) 1985, 523–80.

Table 6.1 *A Summary of Market Failures and Their Implications for Efficiency*

Traditional Market Failures (Chapter 5)	
Public Goods	Pure public goods (undersupply) Open access/common property (overconsumption, underinvestment) Toll goods (undersupply)
Externalities (Missing Markets)	Positive externalities (undersupply) Negative externalities (oversupply)
Natural Monopoly	Declining average cost (undersupply) With costly monitoring (undersupply, *X*-inefficiency)
Information Asymmetry	Quality overestimation of experience, post-experience goods (overconsumption) Quality underestimation of experience, post-experience goods (underconsumption)
Other Limitations of the Competitive Framework (Chapter 6)	
Thin Markets	Cartelization (undersupply)
Preference Problems	Endogenous preferences (typically overconsumption) Utility interdependence (distributional inefficiency) Unacceptable preferences (overconsumption)
Uncertainty Problems	Moral hazard, adverse selection, unique assets (incomplete insurance) Misperception of risk (violation of expected utility hypothesis)
Intertemporal Problems	Nontraded assets, bankruptcy (incomplete capital markets)
Adjustment Costs	Sticky prices (underemployed resources)
Macroeconomic Dynamics	Business cycles (underemployed resources)

effects. Although fiscal and monetary policies undoubtedly have potential for improving the dynamic efficiency of the economy, we must await advances in the field of macroeconomics before we can have confidence in anyone's ability to use them for anything approaching fine tuning. Fortunately, in the vast majority of situations, policy analysts can take monetary and fiscal policies as given and still provide good advice about economic efficiency.

Conclusion

Table 6.1 summarizes the traditional market failures presented in Chapter 5 and the other limitations of the competitive framework discussed in this chapter. Together they constitute a fairly comprehensive list of market failures indicating circumstances in which public policy can potentially increase efficiency. Our understanding of their implications varies greatly, however. At one extreme, economics provides well-developed theory and empirical evidence to help us understand and apply the traditional market failures. At the other extreme, economics hardly deals at all with the question of the origins of preferences. Despite these disparities of development, the list in Table 6.1 provides an import stock of ideas for policy analysts. Policies that do not find a basis in one of these market failures must be justified by values other than efficiency. It is to these other values that we next turn.

For Discussion

1. Why is the premium for health insurance provided by an employer typically much lower than the premium for the same coverage purchased by an individual?
2. Why is it that public subsidy programs often result in much higher levels of expenditures than initially estimated?

7

Rationales for Public Policy

Distributional and Other Goals

The traditional market failures and other limitations of the competitive framework discussed in Chapters 5 and 6 identify circumstances in which private economic activity may not lead to Pareto efficiency. Thus, they indicate the potential for Pareto improvements through public policy. As we discuss in the next chapter, correcting government failures also offers opportunities for making Pareto improvements. Values other than efficiency, however, warrant consideration in our assessments of the extent to which any particular combination of private and public activity achieves the "good society." As individuals, we turn to philosophy, religion, and our moral intuition to help ourselves develop systems of values to guide our assessments. Absent a consensus on the values to be considered and their relative importance when they conflict, our political institutions must unavoidably play a role in selecting the specific values that will have weight in collective decision making. Nevertheless, we sketch here some of the more common rationales for public policies that are based on values other than efficiency.

Social Welfare beyond Pareto Efficiency

Before discussing distributional and other important *substantive values* as distinct goals in competition with Pareto efficiency, we present two perspectives for viewing these values as contributing to economic efficiency, more broadly defined. One approach involves the specification of a *social welfare function* that aggregates the utilities of the individual members of society. Another approach shifts the focus from the valuation of particular allocations of goods to the valuation of alternative *institutional arrangements* for making allocations.

Explicit Social Welfare Functions

The concept of Pareto efficiency offers a way of ranking allocations of goods without making explicit comparisons of the utilities of individuals. The avoidance of interpersonal utility comparisons is achieved at the cost of an implicit acceptance of the initial distribution of endowments of productive factors among individuals. The specification of a social welfare function, which converts the utilities of all individuals into an index of social utility, provides an alternative approach to defining economic efficiency and aggregate welfare. Rather than defining efficiency as the inability to make someone better off without making someone else worse off (the Pareto principle), efficiency is defined as the allocation of goods that maximizes the social welfare function (the "greatest good" principle).

To clarify the difference between these definitions, consider a society consisting of three people. Assume that each of these people has a utility function that depends only on wealth, assigns higher utilities to higher levels of wealth, and assigns smaller increments of utility to successive increments of wealth (that is, they exhibit positive but declining marginal utility of wealth). Note that for a fixed quantity of wealth any allocation among the three people would be Pareto efficient—it would not be possible to shift wealth to increase one person's utility without decreasing the utility of at least one of the others. Imagine, however, that these people agree that wealth should be allocated to maximize a social welfare function specified as the sum of the utilities of the three persons. If we assume that the three people have identical utility functions, then the allocation of wealth that maximizes social welfare is exactly equal shares of wealth for each person. (Only when each person has exactly the same marginal utility of wealth would opportunities for increasing the social welfare function disappear—the assumption of identical utility functions implies that the equality of marginal utility can occur only when wealth is equal.) Thus, this social welfare function would identify one of the many Pareto-efficient allocations as socially optimal.

Table 7.1 illustrates socially optimal policy choices under three different social welfare functions for a three-person society. The social welfare function labeled "Utilitarian" simply sums the utilities of the three persons ($U_1 + U_2 + U_3$); it would be maximized by policy C. The social welfare function labeled "Rawlsian" maximizes the utility received by the person deriving the lowest utility—a "maximin" principle, *max*imizing the *min*imum utility realized by anyone. It would identify policy B as the social optimum. The social welfare function labeled "Multiplicative" is proportional to the product of the utilities of the three persons ($U_1 \times U_2 \times U_3$); it indicates policy A as the social optimum. In this example, each of the three social welfare functions identifies a different policy as socially optimal.

Table 7.1 *Alternative Social Welfare Functions*

	Individual Utilities from Alternative Policies			**Alternative Social Welfare Functions**		
	Person 1 U_1	**Person 2** U_2	**Person 3** U_3	**Utilitarian** $U_1 + U_2 + U_3$	**Rawlsian Minimum** (U_1, U_2, U_3)	**Multiplicative** $(U_1 \times U_2 \times U_3)/1{,}000$
Policy A	80	80	40	200	40	**256**
Policy B	70	70	50	190	**50**	245
Policy C	100	80	30	**210**	30	240
				Choose Policy C	Choose Policy B	Choose Policy A

Utilitarianism is an influential welfare function developed by Jeremy Bentham and, especially, John Stuart Mill.[1] It also has attracted modern adherents, such as the Nobel Prize winner John Harsanyi, who argues for a utilitarian based rule of maximizing the expected average utility of all individuals.[2] Utilitarianism is a *consequentialist* philosophy in that actions are to be evaluated in terms of the preferences of individuals for various consequences, which, in turn, can be aggregated. Utilitarianism is sometimes described as the "greatest good for the greatest number," but this is inaccurate. As Table 7.1 demonstrates, utilities are added up; therefore, utilitarianisn is simply the "greatest good." Broadly, utilitarianism underlies the Kaldor-Hicks principle described in Chapter 4 and is the foundation for cost benefit analysis. Although utilitarianism does not differentially weight anyone's utility, whether rich or poor, its founders perceived it to be both egalitarian and democratic. Utilitarianism is egalitarian in spirit because John Stuart Mill argued that individuals exhibit declining marginal utility with respect to wealth, which justifies some level of redistribution from rich to poor. Utilitarianism is democratic in spirit because it posits that the utility of everybody counts—the commoner as well as the king. A common criticism of utilitarianism is that it offers weak protection for fundamental individual rights, because it does not guarantee minimal allocations to individuals.

Rawlsianism, as shown in Table 7.1, is a highly equalizing social welfare function. John Rawls applies the maximin principle—"the greatest benefit of the least advantaged members of society"—on the basis of a provocative thought experiment intended to free us from our particularistic values that may be more driven by self-interest than we are ready to admit.[3] He asks us to imagine people who must decide on a system of social institutions without knowing what their own endowments (such as race, intelligence, and wealth) will be in society. Behind this "veil of ignorance," in an "original position," people would deliberate as equals. Not knowing what one's endowment will be encourages one to consider the overall distribution of opportunities and outcomes. Rawls argues that people would unanimously exhibit risk aversion and would therefore select a social welfare function that raises the position of the least advantaged, leading to greater equality of outcomes. Given that Rawls posits people agreeing to social institutions behind the veil, his philosophical approach is in the spirit of the "social contract" approach developed by John Locke and Jean Jacques Rousseau.[4]

Rawlsianism has been criticized on several grounds.[5] One is that Rawlsianism proposes extreme redistribution that reduces incentives to create wealth. Another

[1]Jeremy Bentham, *An Introduction to the Principles of Morals and Legislation* (1789) (Buffalo, NY: Prometheus Press, 1988); John Stuart Mill, *Utilitarianism* (1861), in Alan Ryan, ed., *Utilitarianism and Other Essays: J. S. Mill and Jeremy Bentham* (New York: Penguin, 1987), 272–338.

[2]John C. Harsanyi. "Morality and the Theory of Rational Behavior," *Social Research* 44(4) 1977, 623–56.

[3]John Rawls, "Justice as Fairness: Political not Metaphysical," *Philosophy & Public Affairs* 14(3) 1985, 223–50, at p. 227; and John Rawls, *A Theory of Justice* (Cambridge, MA: Harvard University Press, 1971).

[4]John Locke, *The Works of John Locke* (1700) (Westport, CT: Greenwood, 1989); Jean Jacques Rousseau, *Of the Social Contract* (New York: Harper & Row, 1984).

[5]See, for example, Harsanyi, "Morality and the Theory of Rational Behavior." Ironically, under some assumptions about the nature of preferences, the two rules become indistinguishable. See Menahem E. Yarri, "Rawls, Edgeworth, Shapley, Nash: Theories of Distributive Justice Re-Examined," *Journal of Economic Theory* 24(1) 1981, 1–39.

criticism is that, in practice, people in the original position would not be as risk averse or as consensual as Rawls suggests. Researchers have tried to address these kinds of questions in a number of experiments that attempt to replicate the original position and the veil of ignorance. One set of experiments, for example, found that most subjects strongly reject Rawls's maximin principle. However, some also reject a Harsanyian "maximizing the average utility" welfare function (although fewer and less strongly). Most subjects preferred an allocation that maximizes average utility with some floor constraint.[6] Notice that these empirical findings are broadly consistent with the muliplicative social welfare function shown in Table 7.1, as it avoids allocations with very low levels of utility to any individuals.

The existence of a universally accepted social welfare function would greatly reduce the complexity of the task that policy analysts face in ranking policy alternatives by eliminating the necessity of making trade-offs among incommensurate values. Analysts would design policy alternatives and predict their consequences, but the social welfare function would mechanically rank the alternatives. The policy analyst would hardly carry a normative burden. A number of conceptual and practical problems, however, prevent the social welfare function from rescuing policy analysts from having to confront trade-offs between efficiency and other values.

First, social welfare functions that directly aggregate the utilities of individuals assume that these utilities can be observed. But utility is a subjective concept that defies measurement.[7] Indeed, most economists eschew any explicit interpersonal comparisons of utilities for this reason. Instead, they usually rely on the principle of "no envy" to define equity: a social allocation is equitable if no one would prefer anyone else's personal allocation to their own.[8] In this formulation, people compare allocations across individuals in terms of their own utility functions. For example, splitting an estate between two heirs by allowing one to divide the assets into two shares and the other to have first choice of shares will result in an equitable allocation in the sense that the chooser will select the allocation that he or she most prefers and, therefore, have no envy, and the divider, not knowing which allocation will be selected, will divide so as to be indifferent between the two allocations and, therefore, also have no envy.

The principle of no envy does not provide a practical basis for constructing social welfare functions, however. The problem of utility measurement can be sidestepped somewhat by relating social welfare to the consumption that produces utility for the members of society.[9] So, instead of social welfare being specified as some function of personal utilities, it is given as a function of either the quantities of goods consumed by each person or the economic resources, such as income or

[6]Norman Frohlich, Joe A. Oppenheimer, and Cheryl L. Eavey, "Choices of Principles of Distributive Justice in Experimental Groups," *American Journal of Political Science* 31(3) 1987, 606–36. We must be cautious, however, in interpreting these results because one recent study found that subjects' responses to redistributive questions are sensitive to the framing of questions and whether redistributive changes are seen as gains or losses. See Ed Bukszar and Jack L. Knetsch, "Fragile Redistribution Choices Behind a Veil of Ignorance," *Journal of Risk and Uncertainty* 14(1) 1997, 63–74.

[7]For a brief overview, see Amartya Sen, *On Ethics and Economics* (New York: Basil Blackwell, 1987). For a more detailed discussion, see Robert Cooter and Peter Rappaport, "Were the Ordinalists Wrong about Welfare Economics?" *Journal of Economic Literature* 22(2) 1984, 507–30.

[8]For an overview, see H. Peyton Young, *Equity: In Theory and Practice* (Princeton, NJ: Princeton University Press, 1994).

[9]See Abram Bergson [as Burk], "A Reformulation of Certain Aspects of Welfare Economics," *Quarterly Journal of Economics* 52(2) 1938, 310–34.

wealth, available to each person for purchasing goods of choice. When the social welfare function depends on the consumption of specific goods, society places values on consumption patterns without direct regard for individual preferences. For example, the social welfare function might place maximum weights on some target level of clothing consumption even though some persons would prefer to consume more, and some persons less, than the target level.

Second, whether the social welfare function depends on individual utilities, wealth levels, incomes, or consumption patterns, it must somehow be specified. Absent unanimity among the members of society over the appropriate social welfare function, no fair voting procedure can guarantee a stable choice.[10] But unanimity is unlikely because individuals can anticipate how they will personally fare under alternative social welfare functions. How, then, would the social welfare function come to be specified? Elevating the preferences of those who happen to be governing at the moment to the status of social welfare function seems presumptuous, especially if current choices will have implications beyond their likely tenures in office. Thus, rather than being an objective starting point for analysis, the social welfare function is more likely to be the product of value judgments made as part of the analysis.

As a society we never explicitly choose the aggregate level of equity—redistributions that have implications for equity are selected sequentially and often delivered through programs bundled with policies seeking other goals, such as efficiency. If we did so, then the process would be subject to some of the preference aggregation problems mentioned above. Therefore, it is extremely difficult to deduce what level and kind of redistribution society would choose if a perfect revelation mechanism did exist. Experiments, however, do provide some hints. Two kinds of experimental "games" are especially useful for this purpose: *ultimatum games* and *dictator games*. In the ultimatum game, introduced in Chapter 6, a Proposer offers a division of a fixed sum of money X to a Responder, who can either accept or reject it. If the Responder accepts the offer, then both the Proposer and the Responder receive their designated percentage of X. If the Responder rejects the offer, then both receive nothing. How often do Responders reject? "Dozens of studies with these games establish that people dislike being treated unfairly, and reject offers of less than 20 percent of X about half the time, even though they end up receiving nothing."[11] In contexts where Proposers can observe acceptances or rejections and respond, they typically offer 40 to 50 percent of X. The ultimatum game tells us about "fairness" rather than equity. The extent of pure redistributive altruism is more clearly revealed in the dictator game. Here, the Proposer can dictate the allocation because the Responder cannot refuse it. Proposers offer considerably less than in the ultimatum game, but still generally offer an average of 20 to 30 percent of the sum to be divided.[12]

Third, even if a social welfare function were somehow to be validly specified, limitations in information and cognition would hinder its practical use. Predicting

[10]This point has been raised as a fundamental criticism of Bergson's approach to social welfare functions. See Tibor Scitovsky, "The State of Welfare Economics," *American Economic Review* 51(3) 1951, 301–15. In the next chapter, we discuss this objection more generally as a fundamental problem inherent in democracy.

[11]Colin Camerer, "Progress in Behavioral Game Theory," *Journal of Economic Perspectives* 11(4)1997, 167–88, at p. 169.

[12]Ibid.

the impacts of policies on the millions of individuals who make up society boggles the mind. It would almost certainly be necessary to divide society into groups to make the application of the social welfare function more tractable, but such grouping risks obscuring important differences among individuals within groups. For example, grouping solely by income level might not be appropriate if people in different life stages, locations, or conditions of health face very different costs in maintaining households.

Fourth, when analysts specify hypothetical social welfare functions to rank alternative policies, perhaps to make explicit the consideration of distributional issues, they tend to make the social welfare functions depend only on immediate consequences so as to keep the burden of prediction manageable. Such myopia can lead to rankings other than those that would be made with greater consideration of consequences occurring in the more distant future. For example, an exclusive focus on the current distribution of income ignores the impacts of policies on investment decisions in physical and human capital that significantly affect the size and distribution of income in the future. Using a myopic social welfare function as an expedient thus risks diverting attention from the full range of appropriate values.

Choosing Institutions versus Choosing Allocations

Several intellectual streams argue for a recasting of the "social welfare problem," from one of choosing distributions of goods to one of choosing the social, economic, and political institutions from which the distributions will actually emerge. The constitutional design perspective focuses on the choice of the fundamental procedural rules governing political decision making.[13] The property rights perspective considers the implications of the rules governing ownership and economic activity, recognizing that they affect how much is produced as well as how it is distributed.[14] Others have sought to understand the significance of social values, norms, habits, conventions, and other informal forces that influence interaction among members of society.[15] An appreciation of the importance of institutions, the relatively stable sets of formal and informal rules that govern relationships among members of society, unifies these otherwise very different perspectives.

The distinction between valuing alternative distributions and valuing alternative institutions is relevant no matter what normative framework underlies the assessment of social welfare. It arises most explicitly, however, in the distinction between *act-utilitarianism* and *rule-utilitarianism*.[16] Under act-utilitarianism, the rightness of an act depends on the utility that it produces. Under rule-utilitarianism,

[13]See, for example, Geoffrey Brennan and James M. Buchannan, *The Reason of Rules: Constitutional Political Economy* (New York: Cambridge University Press, 1985).

[14]For a discussion of institutional arrangements from the perspective of welfare economics, see Daniel W. Bromley, *Economic Interests and Institutions: The Conceptual Foundations of Public Policy* (New York: Basil Blackwell, 1989).

[15]Some recent examples: Amitai Etzioni, *Moral Dimension: Toward a New Economics* (New York: Free Press, 1988); Geoffrey M. Hodgson, *Economics and Institutions: A Manifesto for a Modern Institutional Economics* (Philadelphia: University of Pennsylvania Press, 1988); and James C. March and John P. Olsen, *Rediscovering Institutions: The Organizational Basis of Politics* (New York: Free Press, 1989).

[16]On rule-utilitarianism, see Richard B. Brands, "Toward a Credible Form of Utilitarianism," in Michael D. Bayless, ed., *Contemporary Utilitarianism* (Garden City, NY: Anchor Books, 1968), 143–86. For a full development of institutional-utilitarianism, see Russell Hardin, *Morality within the Limits of Reason* (Chicago: University of Chicago Press, 1988).

the rightness of an act depends on its adherence to general rules or principles that advance social utility; it thus provides a moral basis for the creation and adherence to rights and duties that restrain the expediency of act-utilitarianism.[17] So, for example, giving public relief to people who suffer severe property loss from a flood might be judged under act-utilitarianism as desirable because it results in a more uniform distribution of income. Under rule-utilitarianism, however, the giving of public relief might be viewed as undesirable according to the principle that public policy should not encourage moral hazard—if compensation is given, then others will be encouraged to live in floodplains in anticipation that they, too, will be compensated for losses. Note that if utility interdependence among the population makes relief to the current flood victims a public good that would be underprovided by private charity, act-utilitarianism rather than rule-utilitarianism would be consistent with the common (myopic) interpretation of Pareto efficiency.

Rule-, or institutional, utilitarianism encourages consideration of a variety of values that contribute indirectly to social utility through more effective political, social, and economic institutions. By increasing the chances that dissident views will be heard, for instance, largely unbridled freedom of speech reduces the risks of consistently bad political decisions being made by misguided majorities. Policies that give a major role to parents in the socialization of children help preserve the family as the most fundamental social institution. Maintaining fair procedures for resolving disputes over the enforcement of contracts facilitates efficiency in economic exchange among private parties. Moral and political considerations hinder promotion of institutional values when these values involve immediate consequences that are, in isolation, undesirable: some speech is highly offensive; even intact families sometimes grossly fail children; fair procedures for dispute resolution do not always favor those who would benefit most from compensation. Nonetheless, the focus on institutions deserves consideration because it encourages a broader and less myopic perspective.

Measuring Changes in Social Welfare: Social Indicators

A variety of quantitative measures have been proposed to gauge changes in social welfare when social welfare functions are impractical.[18] Some of these, such as gross national product, substitute for more conceptually appropriate measures of efficiency. Other social indicators, such as the consumer price index, reflect distributional values as well as efficiency. Many other social indicators have been proposed to capture noneconomic dimensions of social welfare. We briefly review here some of the social indicators commonly encountered in policy debates.

Gross and Net National Product. Changes in social surplus provide a conceptually attractive metric for evaluating policies in terms of efficiency. Actually

[17]See John C. Harsanyi, "Rule Utilitarianism, Equality, and Justice," *Social Philosophy & Policy* 2(2) 1985, 115–27. He argues that the rule-utilitarianism provides a rational basis for deontological principles, such as rights and duties, by relating them to the maximization of social utility.

[18]For an excellent review and extension of the literature on policy indicators, see Duncan MacRae, Jr., *Policy Indicators: Links between Social Science and Public Debate* (Chapel Hill: University of North Carolina Press, 1985).

measuring changes in social surplus, however, is often impractical. The effects of policies are sometimes spread so widely in the economy that valuing them in only a few selected markets misses too much. Even when effects are more limited in scope, sufficient information may be unavailable for assessing the magnitudes of the changes in social surplus that they produce. These factors lead to a variety of more easily measured variables as indicators of efficiency and, more generally, social welfare.

The most familiar indicators arise in the context of macroeconomic policy. A central concept is *gross national product* (GNP), the market value of the output of final goods and services produced by a nation's economy. GNP is measured in two ways: first, as the sum of expenditures on final goods and services by consumers, businesses, government, and foreigners; second, as the sum of payments to the factors of production.[19] Economists recognize two obvious limitations of GNP as a welfare measure. First, GNP measures the market value of goods and services in current prices so that increases in general price levels inflate GNP estimates even in the absence of increases in output. Comparisons of policies with effects across different years are, therefore, commonly made in terms of *real GNP*, the value of output measured in prices prevalent in some base year. Second, GNP does not account for the depreciation of plants, equipment, and residential structures that offsets the addition to productive capacity resulting from new investment. Adjusting GNP for depreciation leads to *net national product (NNP)*, which can be measured in base year dollars for multiperiod comparisons. In practice, however, skepticism about the way depreciation is actually measured in national income accounts leads many economists to use real GNP as an indicator of welfare in policy evaluations despite the greater conceptual attractiveness of real NNP.

Changes in either GNP or NNP, however, only roughly approximate changes in social welfare. Consider a reduction in GNP that took away two units of some good from a consumer. The GNP loss and the social surplus loss associated with the removal of the first unit of the good from the consumer would be its price. The GNP loss from removal of the second unit would also be its price. But the social surplus loss would be greater than price if the consumer has a downward-sloping demand schedule. In general, GNP changes reflecting large adjustments in specific markets do not correspond closely to changes in social surplus.

Many other objections have been raised to the use of GNP as an indicator of social welfare.[20] Most are related to items, such as environmental quality and household labor by non-employed spouses, that are not traded in markets and hence not counted as part of GNP. A variety of adjustments have been suggested to deal with some of these objections: better accounting of the investment levels needed to sustain growth; imputations of value for capital services, leisure, and nonmarket work; and the imputation of lost welfare due to environmental disamenities.[21] Other problems arise in comparing real GNP across years because of changes in the composi-

[19]Increasingly, aggregate economic income is being reported as *gross domestic product* (GDP) rather than GNP. GDP measures the output of goods and services produced by labor and property located within the country. Unlike GNP, it does not include net factor income from the rest of the world, a component of GNP particularly difficult to measure. For the United States, GNP and GDP tend to be very close.

[20]For an overview, see Dan Usher, *The Measurement of Economic Growth* (New York: Columbia University Press, 1980).

[21]These adjustments were suggested by William D. Nordhaus and James Tobin, "Is Growth Obsolete?" in Milton Moss, ed., *The Measurement of Economic Performance* (New York: National Bureau of Economic Research, 1973), 509–31.

tion of output: new goods enter the market (hand-held calculators replace slide rules) and improve dramatically in quality (personal computers become faster and easier to use).[22]

Though these problems suggest caution in interpreting GNP as a measure of social welfare, there is a reasonable presumption that, other things equal, the larger the real GNP, the better off are the people living in the economy. Several other politically salient economic indicators, however, have more ambiguous interpretations.

Unemployment, Inflation, and the Balance of Payments. Unemployment rates have both efficiency and distributional dimensions. Involuntary unemployment involves a loss of productive resources for society and personal hardship for those who cannot find employment. A lower unemployment rate is generally desirable. But if it falls too low, overall efficiency may suffer because labor cannot as easily move to jobs where it is valued the most. The economically efficient unemployment rate, therefore, may be larger than zero to accommodate the movement of labor among jobs. The efficient rate may not be consistent with distributional objectives, however, especially if certain segments of the population are more prone to long periods of involuntary unemployment than others.

The rate of inflation involves similar problems of interpretation. Changes in the *consumer price index* (CPI), an index of how much it costs in current dollars to buy a fixed basket of market goods relative to its cost in some base year, commonly serve as measures of inflation rates. Lower rates of inflation are usually viewed as more desirable than higher rates, for several reasons: higher rates generally are associated with greater uncertainty about the future, slowing investment and saving by making anticipation of future prices more difficult; inflation has unequal impacts on real incomes—those who own real property, like houses, and those whose incomes have automatic "cost of living adjustments," generally do relatively better than those who do not own real property or those whose incomes do not have automatic adjustments; and high rates of inflation risk creating "inflationary expectations" that undermine confidence in the monetary system and lead to disruptive hyperinflation.[23] But a zero rate of inflation is not necessarily desirable. During supply-side shocks to the economy such as sudden increases in world oil prices, for instance, inflation may help reduce adjustment costs by loosening the constraints imposed on the economy by "sticky" nominal wages and other price rigidities.

There is a growing consensus among economists that the measurement of the CPI overstates the rate of inflation in the U.S. economy by between 0.3 and 1.4 percentage points per year.[24] Overestimation of the rate of inflation helps explain how standards of living during the 1980s increased despite the apparent stagnation of real wages. It also suggests that government transfer programs with automatic cost of living adjustments, such as social security payments to the elderly, are actually growing in terms of their real value.

[22]See, for example, Jack F. Triplett, "Concepts of Quality in Input and Output Price Measures: A Resolution of the User-Value and Resource-Cost Debate," in Murray F. Fass, ed., *The U.S. National Income and Product Accounts* (Chicago: University of Chicago Press, 1983), 269–311.

[23]For an overview, see Edward Foster, *Costs and Benefits of Inflation* (Minneapolis, MN: Federal Reserve Bank of Minneapolis, March 1972).

[24]David E. Lebow and Jeremy B. Rudd, "Measurement Error in the Consumer Price Index: Where Do We Stand?" *Journal of Economic Literature* 41(1) 2003, 159–201.

Perhaps the most ambiguous of the politically salient economic indicators is the *balance of payments in the current accounts*, the difference between the dollar value of goods and services exported and the dollar value of goods and services imported. A negative balance of payments implies a "trade deficit," which is usually taken in the United States as a sign of weakness in the economy. Such an interpretation, however, is not so clear-cut. Foreigners must do something with the dollars that they accumulate from the trade deficit. That something is investing in the U.S. economy. Indeed, foreigners as a group cannot realize net investment in the U.S. economy unless they enjoy a trade surplus. When the United States is an especially attractive place to invest, as it was during the westward expansion in the late nineteenth century, the realization of net investment forces a trade deficit. Why should we worry about the trade deficit if it is offset by foreign investment?

One cause of concern is that foreigners gain claims on the future wealth of the United States from their investments. Such claims do not mean that the United States will be poorer in the future as long as the investments are economically sound. To the extent that the foreign investment is simply financing current consumption, however, there is cause for concern. Large federal budget deficits during the 1980s were heavily financed by foreign capital so that by 1988 the U.S. government was paying almost $28 billion annually in interest payments to foreigners. Though such heavy borrowing to fund the budget deficit is worrisome, in general deciding at any particular time whether foreign investment, and hence the trade deficit, is too large or too small from the perspective of economic efficiency is difficult and controversial. So, too, is an assessment of its distributional consequences—looking just at jobs lost in export industries without considering jobs gained in industries benefiting from foreign investment and from low import prices tells an incomplete story.

Noneconomic Indicators. A great variety of indicators not tied to macroeconomic data provide measures of various dimensions of social welfare. Infant mortality rates, for instance, reflect the adequacy of the diets and health care available to pregnant women, mothers, and babies, especially those least advantaged. Other commonly used indicators include crime rates, adult life expectancy, smog-free days in air sheds, and educational achievement. In judging the appropriateness of interpreting such indicators as measures of social welfare, it is important to determine both their conceptual validity and their accuracy of measurement.

Consider, for example, an indicator such as educational achievement. At the conceptual level, it seems reasonably related to the potential of the economy for economic growth and, when compared across individuals, to the distribution of opportunity in society—social values of importance. Its measurement, however, is complicated. Simply using years of schooling as a measure of educational achievement ignores differences in school standards and student performance. Lack of comprehensive data may hinder comparisons, over time or across groups, based on more direct measures of achievement, such as test scores.

Substantive Values Other Than Efficiency

Viewing market failure as a necessary condition for government intervention implies that Pareto efficiency is the only appropriate social value. Strong arguments can be made for always *including* efficiency as a substantive value in policy analysis: only the malevolent would oppose making someone better off without making anyone else worse off; the pursuit of efficiency produces the greatest abundance of goods for society, thereby facilitating the satisfaction of wants through private actions, both self-interested and altruistic; and, given the decision to pursue other substantive values through public policy, doing so efficiently preserves the greatest potential for satisfying material wants. Here we sketch the rationales for some of the more important substantive values that often compete with efficiency.

Human Dignity: Equity of Opportunity and Floors on Consumption

We begin with the premise that all people have intrinsic value, which derives from the very fact that they are human beings rather than from any measurable contribution they can make to society. Our own dignity as human beings requires us to respect the dignity of others. Although the meaning of dignity ultimately rests with the individual, it involves, at least to some extent, one's freedom to choose how one lives. A good society must have mechanisms for limiting the extent to which any person's choices interfere with the choices of others. It also should facilitate broad participation in the institutions that determine the allocation of private and public goods.

We have focused on market exchange as a mechanism for translating the preferences of individuals into allocations of private goods. But to participate in markets one must have something to exchange. In the competitive framework one has a set of endowments—ownership of labor and other factor inputs. Someone who has no endowments would be effectively barred from participating in the market process. With very small endowments, people have very little choice; without any endowments, people cannot express their choices of private goods at all. Because survival depends on the consumption of at least some private goods (food and protection from exposure), we might find a Pareto-efficient allocation that results in the premature deaths of some people.

Most of us would not consider such extreme allocations as appropriate. In many societies, people take it upon themselves to mitigate the most drastic consequences of extreme allocations through voluntary contributions to charities or individuals. For example, until the role of the federal government expanded greatly during the 1930s, private charity was a major source of assistance for widows, orphans, and the disabled in the United States.[25] Concern that charity may not adequately reach these vulnerable populations is a widely accepted rationale for public assistance.

Note that these preferences do not necessarily favor the Rawlsian social welfare function presented in Table 7.1. They might very well be consistent with a utilitarian social welfare function that places lower bounds on consumption levels.

[25]Public transfer programs almost certainly displace private charity. U.S. historical data suggests that the displacement may be as large as dollar for dollar. Russell D. Roberts, "A Positive Model of Private Charity and Public Transfers," *Journal of Political Economy* 92(1) 1984, 136–48. State spending on welfare seems to involve displacement rates of about 30 percent. See Burton Abrams and Mark Schmitz, "The Crowding-Out Effect of Government Transfers on Private Charitable Contributions—Cross-Section Evidence," *National Tax Journal* 37(4) 1984, 563–68. It also appears that public funding displaces fund-raising efforts. See James Andreoni and A. Abigail Payne, "Do Government Grants to Private Charities Crowd Out Giving or Fund-Raising?" *American Economic Review* 93(3) 2003, 792–812.

The essential concern is the absolute rather than the relative consumption of those worse off.

More generally, we might agree that viable participation in market exchange requires some minimal endowment of assets. Because most people have potential to sell their own labor, one approach to increasing the number of people with the minimal endowment is to increase their effectiveness and marketability as workers. Public policies intended to provide remedial education, job training, and physical rehabilitation may play an important role in increasing effective participation in the private sector.[26] So, too, might policies that protect against discrimination by employers on the basis of factors not relevant to performance on the job. Direct public provision of money or in-kind goods, however, may be the only way to ensure minimal participation of those, such as the severely disabled, who have little or no employment potential.

Note that while transfers to ensure floors on consumption would increase the equality of the distribution of goods in society by raising up the least wealthy, this is only a side effect of preserving human dignity. Once everyone reaches some minimum level of consumption, preservation of human dignity does not necessarily call for further redistribution to increase equality.

Increasing participation in decisions over the provision and allocation of public goods also merits consideration as an appropriate value in the evaluation of public policies. As we previously discussed, markets will generally not lead to efficient levels of provision of public goods. Actual choices are made though political processes. Public policies that broaden political participation may be desirable, therefore, in terms of respect for individual preferences for public goods. We support universal adult suffrage, for instance, not because we expect it necessarily to lead to greater efficiency in the provision of public goods but, rather, because it recognizes the inherent value of allowing people some say over the sort of society in which they will live.

Finally, we must consider situations in which people are incapable of rationally exercising choice. For example, most of us would not consider preventing either young children or the mentally impaired from seriously harming themselves to be a violation of their human dignity. (Though we may disagree on the definitions of "young" and "impaired.") On the contrary, we might embrace an affirmative duty to act paternalistically. The problem, from the perspective of public policy, is deciding the point at which individual choices should be overridden.

Increasing the Equality of Outcomes

Respect for human dignity seems to justify public policies that ensure some minimum level of consumption to all members of society. Most of us would agree that the minimum level should be high enough to ensure the commonly recognized needs for dignified survival. The level is absolute but not fixed. It is absolute in the sense that it does not explicitly depend on the wealth, income, or consumption of

[26] Robert Haveman considers ways of redesigning the U.S. system of redistribution so that it is directed more toward equalizing opportunity. For example, he proposes the establishment of capital accounts that youths could use for education, training, and health services. Robert Haveman, *Starting Even: An Equal Opportunity Program to Combat the Nation's New Poverty* (New York: Simon & Schuster, 1988).

others in society. It is not fixed because the collective assessment of what constitutes dignified survival will undoubtedly reflect the aggregate wealth in society. The U.S. government regularly estimates how much income families must have to consume a set of basic goods that were considered necessary for decent survival in 1965. The number of persons in families raised above this "poverty line" often serves as a measure of success of government programs.[27] For instance, in 2003 the poverty line for a family of four with two related children under the age of 18 years was $18,224. As the United States has become wealthier, however, there is a growing tendency to use multiples, such as 125 percent of the poverty line in evaluations, suggesting a change in our collective assessment of the decent minimum.[28]

Rather than looking just at the absolute consumption levels of the poorest members of society, we might also consider the entire distribution of wealth. Personal attributes, family circumstance, and chance lead to a wide dispersion in the levels of wealth enjoyed as outcomes in a market economy. Several conceptual frameworks seem to support greater equality in outcomes as an important social value.

The Rawlsian social welfare function shown in Table 7.1 clearly leads to greater equality of outcomes. As previously noted, even the utilitarian social welfare function shown in Table 7.1 provides an argument for viewing equality of outcomes as a social value if we assume that all individuals have identical utility functions exhibiting declining marginal utility with respect to wealth. That is, individuals get less additional happiness from additional units of wealth as their levels of wealth increase. Under these assumptions, the more equal the distribution of any given level of wealth, the higher the ranking of that distribution by the social welfare function. In terms of tax policy, for instance, this argument leads to the notion of *vertical equity*—those with greater wealth should pay higher taxes so that everyone gives up the same amount of utility.[29] (The related notion of *horizontal equity* requires that those in similar circumstance be treated alike.)

An important consideration arises in thinking about equality of outcomes as a social value. The discussion above implicitly assumes that the amount of wealth to be distributed among individuals is constant. This may be true for a one-time, unanticipated reallocation. Once people anticipate reallocation, however, they will begin to change their behaviors in ways that generally reduce the total amount of wealth that will be available. In the extreme, where everyone received the same share of wealth, the incentives for work, investment, and entrepreneurship would be greatly reduced. Costly and intrusive control mechanisms would have to be put in place to try to get people to work and invest as much as they would have in the absence of

[27]For thorough treatments of the "poverty line" issue, see Patricia Ruggles, *Drawing the Line: Alternative Poverty Measures and Their Implications for Public Policy* (Washington, DC: Urban Institute Press, 1990); and Constance F. Citro and Robert T. Michael, eds., *Measuring Poverty: A New Approach* (Washington, DC: National Academy Press, 1995).

[28]For a discussion of this trend with respect to the economic well-being of the elderly, see Bruce Jacobs, "Ideas, Beliefs, and Aging Policy," *Generations* 9(1) 1984, 15–18.

[29]For a demonstration of the application of various measures of vertical and horizontal equity, see Marcus C. Berliant and Robert P. Strauss, "The Horizontal and Vertical Equity Characteristics of the Federal Individual Income Tax," in Martin David and Timothy Smeeding, eds., *Horizontal Equity, Uncertainty, and Economic Well-Being* (Chicago: University of Chicago Press, 1985), 179–211. See also David F. Bradford, ed., *Distributional Analysis of Tax Policy* (Washington, DC: AEI Press, 1995).

the redistribution. Undoubtedly, the result would be a much less wealthy society, perhaps resulting in lower absolute levels of wealth for most members of society.

In general, we should expect the total available wealth to shrink more, the greater the amount of redistribution attempted. Arthur Okun used the analogy of transferring water with a "leaky bucket."[30] If we try to transfer a little water, we will lose a little; if we try to transfer a lot, we will lose a lot.[31] The key question, therefore, is how much current and future wealth are we as a society collectively willing to give up to achieve greater equality in distribution? In practice, we must rely on the political process for an answer.

Preserving Institutional Values

Historical accident, as well as purposeful individual and collective choices, divides the world into distinct polities. National governments play a dominant role in establishing the terms of political and economic interaction. They draw their legitimacy from *constitutions*, both formal and informal, that define the rights and duties of those who reside within their boundaries and the procedures their officials must follow in the creation and enforcement of laws. Political jurisdictions subordinate to national governments generally have their own constitutions, though often in the form of charters granted by the superior level of government. Whether at the national or subnational level, these constitutions provide essential rules for organizing collective and private decision making.

The constitutions themselves derive legitimacy from a number of sources: the perception that their content provides order in a reasonable and fair way; the nature of their establishment, especially the extent to which they enjoyed the consent of those whom they initially governed; and the ease with which people can choose alternative polities through immigration and emigration.[32] Because constitutions maintain legitimacy through adherence, keeping public policy within the bounds of recognized constitutional principles is a social value. There is also social value in protecting legitimate constitutions from threats external to the polity. Thus policies that promote national security may be justified by a social value other than increasing efficiency through the provision of a public good.

Within constitutional frameworks, societies benefit when people voluntarily comply with laws. Voluntary compliance reduces enforcement costs. It also reflects, and almost certainly enhances, the legitimacy of the political system. One factor that seems to contribute to voluntary compliance is the perception of fairness. For example, surveys and laboratory experiments suggest that taxpayers who view the

[30] Arthur M. Okun, *Equality and Efficiency: The Big Tradeoff* (Washington, DC: Brookings Institution, 1975), 91–100.

[31] For numerical estimates of how leaky the bucket may be, see Edgar K. Browning and William R. Johnson, "The Trade-Off between Equality and Efficiency," *Journal of Political Economy* 92(2) 1984, 175–203; and Charles L. Ballard, "The Marginal Efficiency Cost of Redistribution," *American Economic Review* 78(5) 1988, 1019–33.

[32] For example, public support for the democratic regime in the Federal Republic of Germany has grown steadily since 1951. Russell J. Dalton, *Politics in West Germany* (Boston: Scott, Foresman, 1989), 104–106. Economic success under the regime surely contributed to its legitimacy. Probably the declining percentage of the population who lived through imposition of the regime at the end of the Second World War, and the growing percentage of the population that selected it through immigration, also contributed to growing legitimacy.

tax system as fair are more likely to comply than those who view it as unfair.[33] People who view siting processes as fair are more likely to be willing to accept noxious facilities near their hometowns.[34] More generally, there is social value in making policies correspond to common perceptions of fairness. These perceptions can relate to the procedures embedded in the policies for their implementation as well as the process through which the policies are adopted.[35]

As we previously noted, the perspective of institutional utilitarianism suggests that there is likely to be social value in preserving or strengthening important social institutions such as the family. A difficulty arises, however, because people hold divergent views about the intrinsic value of existing social institutions. For example, some people note the subservient role often played by women in the traditional family and, therefore, would object to viewing its preservation as a social value.

Some Cautions in Interpreting Distributional Consequences

Before relating the distributional consequences of alternative policies to substantive values, we must first answer the question: "What is being distributed to and from whom?"[36] Even putting aside the ever-present difficulty of prediction, answering this question raises many conceptual issues that can lead to dubious assessments of distributional consequences. We outline here some of the more important issues that arise in distributional analysis.

Measurement Issues

In a market economy, money gives access to private goods. Personal income, the flow of payments to persons for use of the input factors (labor, land, capital) they own, provides a conceptually attractive measure of purchasing power. Income as commonly measured, however, deviates from purchasing power in several important ways that complicate distributional analysis.

First, not all wealth is fully reflected in measured income.[37] Consider ownership of housing, for example. If owners rent their houses to others, then the values of the houses will be reflected in their incomes. If they live in the houses instead, then their incomes will not reflect the values of their houses even though they derive

[33]For a review of the evidence, see Keith Snavely, "Governmental Policies to Reduce Tax Evasion: Coerced Behavior versus Services and Values Development," *Policy Sciences* 23(1) 1990, 57–72. See also Robert B. Cialdini, "Social Motivations to Comply: Norms, Values, and Principles," in Jeffrey A. Roth and John T. Scholz, eds., *Taxpayer Compliance: Social Science Perspectives* 2 (Philadelphia: University of Pennsylvania Press, 1989); and Daniel S. Nagin, "Policy Options for Combating Tax Noncompliance," *Journal of Policy Analysis and Management* 9(1) 1990, 7–22.

[34]Douglas Easterling, "Fair Rules for Siting a High-Level Nuclear Waste Repository," *Journal of Policy Analysis and Management* 11(3) 1992, 442–75; Bruno S. Frey and Felix Oberholzer-Gee, "Fair Siting Procedures: An Empirical Analysis of Their Importance and Characteristics," *Journal of Policy Analysis and Management* 15(3) 1996, 353–76.

[35]On the relationship between process and substance, see Jerry L. Mashaw, *Due Process and the Administrative State* (New Haven, CT: Yale University Press, 1985).

[36]See the editors' introductory chapter in Sheldon H. Danziger and Kent E. Portney, eds., *The Distributional Impacts of Public Policies* (New York: St. Martin's Press, 1988), 1–10.

[37]For an overview, see Eugene Steuerle, "Wealth, Realized Income, and the Measure of Well-Being," in David and Smeeding, eds., *Horizontal Equity, Uncertainty, and Economic Well-Being* 91–124.

consumption benefits from living in them. A conceptually correct measure of income would impute rental income to those who live in houses that they own. Not imputing income to such assets can cloud the interpretation of income distributions. For example, many elderly have low incomes but nevertheless have considerable wealth invested in their homes. Should they be viewed as having the same economic circumstances as others with the same measured income who do not own their homes? As shown in Table 7.2, which displays various measures of economic well-being for the United States in 2000 under different definitions of income, the answer to this question has important implications for our assessment of the economic status of the elderly. The row labeled "Percent of Persons over 64 Years in Poverty" reveals that the poverty rate for the elderly falls from 6.8 percent to 4.0 percent when an imputed return on equity in homes is added to income. A comparison of columns (2) and (4) shows the dramatic decline in the incidence of poverty among the elderly that results from Social Security and Medicare.

Second, government tax and transfer programs alter the amount of "disposable" income that people have available to purchase private goods. After-tax income can usually be measured or predicted with relative confidence. Yet deductions and other adjustments made to arrive at taxable income imply that taxpayers with the same pre-tax income may have very different *disposable incomes*. This is illustrated forcefully in the third row of Table 7.2, which shows the upper income limit for the 20 percent of U.S. households with the lowest income (the lowest income quintile). Note that the pre-tax and pre-transfer limit, shown in column (2), is approximately half of the post-tax and post-transfer limit shown in column (4).

With respect to transfer programs, cash benefits are more easily figured into disposable income than in-kind benefits such as subsidized housing and health care that must be assigned an imputed dollar value. Assessing the cumulative effect of transfer programs is especially complicated when eligibility depends on income from other sources. Such *means-testing* can produce situations in which those with pre-transfer incomes just too large to qualify are worse off than those with lower pre-transfer incomes. For example, the array of benefits available to the elderly in the United States leaves those with pre-transfer incomes between one and two times the poverty line more vulnerable to economic and health problems than those with either higher or lower pre-transfer incomes.[38]

Third, individuals usually consume as members of households. Not all members of a household necessarily contribute income toward the consumption. More importantly, the per person cost of providing such basic goods as housing is generally smaller for multimember households than for single-person households. This suggests that comparisons of income better reflect basic consumption opportunities if they are done on the basis of households rather than per capita. But changing family composition and problems of definition make household income a less than ideal basis for measuring economic well-being.[39] Consider an economy with a single household of two wage earners. Simply by splitting into two households, say, because of divorce, the average household income of the economy would fall by half (per capita income would remain unchanged). Such a dramatic fall almost certainly

[38]Timothy M. Smeeding, "Nonmoney Income and the Elderly: The Case of the 'Tweeners'," *Journal of Policy Analysis and Management* 5(4) 1986, 707–24.

[39]For a discussion of these problems and others related to income measurement by the U.S. Census Bureau, see Christopher Jencks, "The Politics of Income Measurement," in William Alonso and Paul Starr, eds., *The Politics of Numbers* (New York: Russell Sage Foundation, 1987), 83–131.

Table 7.2 *Impact of Different Definitions of Income on Measures of Poverty and Income Distribution (United States, 2000)*

Measures	(1) Money Income Excluding Capital Gains but Including Government Cash Transfers (Official Measure)	(2) Column (1) *less* Government Transfers	(3) Column (2) *plus* Capital Gains and Health Insurance Supplements to Wage and Salary Income	(4) Column (3) *plus* Government Transfers and Noncash Benefits *less* Taxes	(5) Column (4) *plus* Imputed Return on Equity in Own Home
Median Household Income	$42,151	$38,915	$41,198	$40,576	$42,814
Mean Household Income	$57,047	$52,932	$59,459	$51,860	$54,227
Upper Limit of Lowest Quintile of Household Income	$17,931	$10,978	$11,366	$20,268	$21,536
Gini Ratio Based on Households	.447	.499	.506	.410	.402
Percent of Persons in Poverty	10.1	17.4	16.7	7.5	6.8
Percent of Persons in Families in Poverty	8.6	14.5	13.7	5.9	5.4
Percent of Persons under 18 Years in Poverty	14.6	17.1	15.8	9.5	9.1
Percent of Persons over 64 Years in Poverty	8.2	46.1	45.6	6.8	4.0
Percent of Persons in Female-Headed Households (with Related Children under 18 and No Husband Present) in Poverty	32.1	38.2	31.7	20.6	20.0

Source: U.S. Bureau of the Census, Experimental Measures of Income and Poverty Table of Contents, Tables 1, 2, and 5. <*http://ferret.bls.census.gov/macro/032001rdcall/toc.htm*> accessed on June 23, 2003.

overstates the reduction in consumption opportunities (though perhaps not the overall reduction in social welfare!). Less hypothetically, changing demographic patterns, such as reductions in average family size and the rate of labor force participation by women, affect comparisons of household income over time. Similarly, these differences may affect comparisons of family income between different groups in a population. With respect to definitional issues, consider a college student with part-time employment who spends most of the year living away from parents. At what point should this student be considered a new household?

Index Issues

Comparing distributions poses the problem of choosing appropriate metrics. Ideally, we would like an index that ranks distributions according to appropriate distributional values. Difficulties arise because no single index can fully summarize a distribution. They also arise because of ambiguity in operationalizing distributional values.

Consider first the problem of characterizing a distribution. The commonly used measures of central tendency, the median (the middle value) and the arithmetic mean (the average), fail as indices for characterizing the degree of equality of distributions. The median of a distribution of income would remain unchanged if everyone with income below the median had his or her income reduced by, say, half. The mean would remain unchanged by taking money from the poorest and giving it to the richest. A measure such as sample variance, based on squared deviations from the mean, comes closer to measuring equality, but does not distinguish between distributions with many people above the mean and distributions with many people below the mean, a difference certainly relevant to almost any assessment of equality.

A commonly used distributional measure is the *Gini index of relative inequality*, which is related to the *Lorenz curve*.[40] A Lorenz curve, shown as the curved line in Figure 7.1, is constructed by ranking the population by income and asking: What percent of income goes to the poorest *X* percent of the population? With percentage of income measured on the vertical axis and percentage of population measured on the horizontal axis, the income distribution will trace out a curve going from the origin to the point representing 100 percent of the income going to 100 percent of the population. A perfectly equal distribution of income would be represented by a straight line connecting these points. Any distribution with imperfect equality would lie entirely below this straight line. The Gini index of relative inequality is proportional to the area in a Lorenz diagram between the line of perfect equality and the Lorenz curve for the distribution. A Gini coefficient of zero implies perfect equality; coefficients closer to one correspond to less equality.

Returning to Table 7.2, the third row shows Gini indexes for several definitions of income. The pre-tax and pre-transfer Gini index is shown in column (2) as .499, which indicates substantially less equality than the post-tax and post-transfer Gini index of .410 shown in column (4). Note that imputing an income to home equity further reduces the Gini index, to .402, indicating that taking account

[40]For a detailed discussion of these concepts and other indices of equality, see Satya R. Charkravarty, *Ethical Social Index Numbers* (New York: Springer-Verlag, 1990).

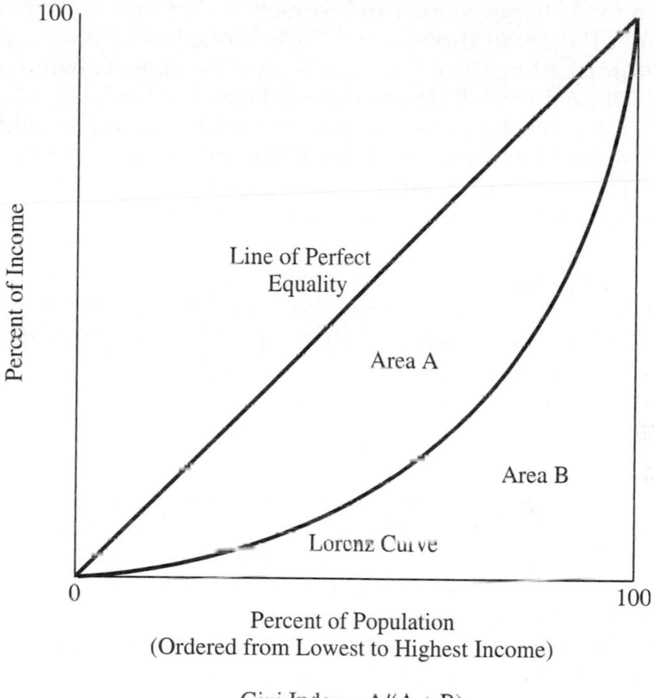

Figure 7.1 Lorenz Curve and Gini Index of Income Inequality

of homeownership makes the income distribution in the United States appear more equitable.

The Gini coefficient provides an attractive measure for comparing the equality of distributions over the entire range of income. If the distributional value of concern is the income of the poorest members of society, however, we may prefer an alternative measure that looks only at the lower end of the distribution. For example, one possibility is the percentage of income going to the lowest income quintile, the 20 percent of households with the lowest incomes. Alternatively, taking an absolute rather than a relative perspective leads to measures such as the sum of payments needed to bring all poor households up to the poverty line. Choosing appropriately among the possible indices that could be constructed requires explicit examination of the values underlying the distributional concern.

Categorization Issues

Indices can be used to provide measures of equality within groups. Yet distributional analysis often deals with equality across identifiable groups defined by characteristics such as sex, race, age, and region. A common approach is to compare mean, or median, income between groups. For example, income comparisons are often made between men and women, whites and nonwhites, and adults under 65 years of age and those older. Care is needed in drawing inferences from such intergroup comparisons because the groups almost always differ in important ways other than their defining characteristics.

Consider, for instance, the observed differences in median household incomes between whites and nonwhites. If the groups were similar with respect to educational achievement, family structure, and age profiles, then the difference would be strong prima facie evidence of racial discrimination in employment. Yet, if the groups differ markedly in terms of these factors, then the inference of discrimination in employment is much weaker. A more appropriate approach would be to compare incomes for households of similar composition and educational achievement. Of course, educational differences themselves might have resulted from racial discrimination.

"Silent Losers" Issues

Distributional analyses often fail to identify all the groups affected by policies. Especially likely to be missed are "silent losers," those who fail to voice protest against the policies causing their losses. In most democratic political systems, complaining increases the chances that losses will at least be considered. Remaining silent risks being overlooked by politicians and analysts alike.

One reason losers fail to protest is that they unexpectedly suffer losses as individuals. At the time of adoption of the policy, they do not anticipate being losers; when they do suffer losses, protest offers little prospect for personal gain. For example, consider residential rent control. The distributional analysis is often cast in terms of current residents versus current landlords. But another group that loses is potential renters, people who sometime in the future desire to live in the community yet cannot because below-market rents "lock-in" long-time residents to rent-controlled units, discourage investors from expanding the rental stock, and encourage landlords to convert rental units to condominiums. Individuals who cannot find apartments have little prospect of personal gain from protest and, therefore, little incentive to bear the cost of protest.

Losers may fail to protest because they do not connect their losses to the policy. For example, petroleum product price controls in the United States and Canada during the oil price shocks of the 1970s were most often justified on distributional grounds—the petroleum industry should not be allowed to gain windfall profits, and higher petroleum product prices hurt low-income consumers more than high-income consumers. This distributional characterization, however, ignores the group that suffers the largest personal losses: those who lose their jobs because of the economic inefficiency caused by the price controls.[41] Yet these people, like many policy analysts at the time, generally failed to make the connection between the inefficiency caused by the price controls and the higher rate of unemployment during oil price shocks.

[41]See George Horwich and David L. Weimer, *Oil Price Shocks, Market Response, and Contingency Planning* (Washington, DC: American Enterprise Institute, 1984), 104–107.

Losers may be silent because they are not yet born! Policies affecting the environment, for instance, may have significant effects on the quality of life of future generations. Usually these effects will begin to occur in the more immediate future so that they have some political saliency. Yet some effects may only become apparent after a considerable period of time. The increasing concentration of carbon dioxide in the atmosphere (a widely accepted empirical observation) may be contributing to substantial global warming in the future through the greenhouse effect (a less widely accepted prediction). The interests of future generations seem to be receiving consideration in discussions of global warming, though not necessarily as fully as they deserve.[42] Advocates of public policies to reduce carbon dioxide emissions dramatically tend to note future environmental effects; advocates of a more cautious approach raise the implications of current policies for the wealth of future generations.

Instrumental Values

The ultimate goal of public policy is to advance the substantive values that define the "good society." Achieving political feasibility and operating within various resource constraints are important as *instrumental values*—things we desire, not necessarily for their own sake but because they allow us to obtain policies that promote substantive values.

Political Feasibility

Public policies cannot directly contribute to substantive values unless they are adopted and successfully implemented.[43] In Chapter 11, we consider in some detail how analysts can assess and increase political feasibility in designing policies. Here we simply outline some of the factors generally relevant to political feasibility that often are treated as values by policy analysts.

The distributional consequences of policies are of fundamental concern to participants in the political process. Public officials draw support from constituencies with strong interests. They tend to support policies favored by their constituencies and oppose policies not favored by them. This often leads to distributional

[42]For very different arguments leading to the conclusion that even if politically accepted as the basis for public policy, welfare economics as currently conceived would not give adequate attention to the interests of future generations, see Peter G. Brown, "Policy Analysis, Welfare Economics, and the Greenhouse Effect," *Journal of Public Policy Analysis and Management* 7(3) 1988, 471–75; and Daniel W. Bromley, "Entitlements, Missing Markets, and Environmental Uncertainty," *Journal of Environmental Economics and Management* 17(2) 1989, 181–94.

[43]Even rejected policies sometimes contribute indirectly to substantive values by serving as vehicles for educating the public and policymakers. See Carol Weiss. "Research for Policy's Sake: The Enlightenment Function of Social Research," *Policy Analysis* 3(4) 1977, 531–45; and Patricia Thomas, "The Use of Social Research: Myths and Models," in Martin Blumer, ed., *Social Science Research and Government: Comparative Essays on Britain and the United States* (New York: Cambridge University Press, 1987), 51–60.

considerations that do not necessarily correspond to substantive values. For example, representatives may be concerned with the quality of some category of public spending across the districts that they represent, even if less equal distributions would contribute more to such values as efficiency or a more equal distribution of wealth across households nationally. Consequently, even when distributional values do not seem substantively relevant, they nevertheless may be instrumentally relevant to political feasibility.

Revenues and Expenditures

Levels of public expenditure, usually through the budgetary process, have political relevance in several ways. First, raising public revenue is generally economically and politically costly, so that, other things equal, policies involving less direct public expenditure tend to receive greater general political support. Second, because the substantive effects of policies are often difficult to predict, expenditure levels often serve as proxies for the level of effort the government is making to solve specific social problems. So, for example, the level of federal expenditure on the "drug war" has symbolic value to many that only very roughly, if at all, corresponds to reductions in drug abuse and the negative externalities associated with it.

Some public decision makers, such as managers of public agencies, face strict budget constraints that they must satisfy in making decisions. For example, a legislature may allocate a fixed level of funding to an agency for launching a new program. Absent a request to the legislature for a supplement, policies for implementing the new program must meet the instrumental goal of costing no more than the allocated budget. The same reasoning would apply to specific categories of resources, such as personnel levels and borrowing authority, that are constrained from the perspective of the decision maker. Expending no more than the available amounts of these resources is instrumental to achieving the substantive values sought by the policy.

Conclusion

We have set out two broad classes of rationales for public policies: the correction of market failures to improve efficiency in the production and allocation of resources and goods and the reallocation of opportunity and goods to achieve distributional and other values. We devoted the majority of our discussion to market failures, not because distributional values are any less important than efficiency but, rather, because the basic analytics of welfare economics serve as useful tools for positive prediction as well as normative evaluation. That is, the various market failures can often serve as models for understanding how unsatisfactory social conditions arise and how they might be remedied.

Market failures and unsatisfied distributional goals are necessary but not sufficient grounds for public intervention. We must always consider the costs of the proposed intervention. Just as markets fail in fairly predictable ways, we can identify generic government failures that either contribute indirectly to the costs of policy interventions or cause them to fail outright. We discuss these limits to public intervention in the next chapter.

For Discussion

1. Almost 5,000 people die in the United States each year waiting for organ transplants. Thus, cadaveric organs are extremely valuable resources whose allocation literally has life and death implications. Which, if any, of the following factors should be relevant to allocation: medical condition, probability of success, geographic location, waiting time, ability to pay, age, family status, and behavioral causes of organ failure?
2. Consider the last three rows of Table 7.2. Do the comparisons among the young, elderly, and female-headed households suggest anything about substantive and instrumental values in the U.S. political system?

8

Limits to Public Intervention

Government Failures

Every society produces and allocates goods through some combination of individual and collective choice. Most individual choice, expressed through participation in markets and other voluntary exchanges, furthers such social values as efficiency and liberty. But some individual choice, like that arising in situations we identify as market failures, detracts from social values in predictable ways. Collective choice exercised through government structures offers at least the possibility for correcting the perceived deficiencies of individual choice. But just as individual choice sometimes fails to promote social values in desired and predictable ways, so, too, does collective choice. Public policy, therefore, should be informed not only by an understanding of market failure but of *government failure* as well.

The social sciences have yet to produce a theory of government failure as comprehensive or widely accepted as the theory of market failure. In fact, we must draw on several largely independent strains of research to piece one together.[1] From social choice theory, which focuses on the operation of voting rules and other mechanisms of collective choice, we learn of the inherent imperfectibility of democracy. From a variety of fields in political science, we learn of the problems of represen-

[1]Charles Wolf, Jr., is one of the few social scientists to develop a theory of government ("nonmarket," in his terms) failure that could complement the theory of market failure. His classification includes problems of bureaucratic supply and policy implementation but largely ignores the more fundamental problems of social choice and representative government. See Charles Wolf, Jr., "A Theory of Nonmarket Failures," *Journal of Law and Economics* 22(1) 1979, 107–39.

tative government. Public choice theory and studies of organizational behavior help us understand the problems of implementing collective decisions in decentralized systems of government and of using public agencies to produce and distribute goods. Together, the insights from these fields help us realize that even governments blessed with the most intelligent, honest, and dedicated public officials cannot be expected to promote the social good in all circumstances.

As policy analysts we should exercise caution in advocating public intervention into private affairs. Some market failures are simply too costly to correct; some distributional goals are too costly to achieve. More fundamentally, we do not know just how government intervention will work out. That government often fails to advance the social good is clear, but the theory of government failure is neither as comprehensive nor as powerful as the theory of market failure. While it raises important warnings about the general problems likely to be encountered in pursuing social values through public policies, the theory of government failure is not yet well developed enough to allow us always to predict the particular consequences of specific government interventions. Enthusiasm for perfecting society through public intervention, therefore, should be tempered by an awareness that the costs may exceed the benefits.

In the following discussion we classify government failures as problems inherent in four general features of political systems: direct democracy, representative government, bureaucratic supply, and decentralized government. In addition to their conceptual importance, these features have varying degrees of practical relevance for policy analysts. At one extreme are the characteristics of direct democracy, which simply warn analysts to be skeptical of claims that the results of elections and referenda provide unambiguous mandates for efficient policies. At the other extreme are the characteristics of bureaucratic supply and decentralized government, which help analysts anticipate the problems likely to be encountered during the implementation of public policies. An understanding of the characteristics of representative government can help analysts determine and improve the political feasibility of their preferred policy alternatives. Although we note some of these practical implications of government failure along the way, our primary purpose in this chapter is to provide a conceptual framework that will be useful for analysts who must operate in a politically complex world.

Problems Inherent in Direct Democracy

Over the course of history, societies have employed a variety of mechanisms for making social choices. Monarchies and dictatorships, in which the preferences of one or a small number of people dominate social choice, have given way in many countries to systems with broader bases of participation. Universal adult suffrage has come to be viewed as an essential element of democracy, which itself is an important social value in many national traditions. In democracies, voting serves as the mechanism for combining the preferences of individuals into social choices.

If voting were a perfect mechanism for aggregating individual preferences, then the job of the policy analyst would be much easier. Questions about the appropriate levels of public goods provision, redistribution, and public regulation of private activity could be answered either directly through referenda or indirectly through the election of representatives who serve as surrogate decision makers.

The vast number of issues arising in a large industrial country, however, makes reliance on referenda impractical for all but the most important issues. Even if improvements in communication technology greatly reduce the logistical costs of voting, the time and other costs citizens face in learning about issues limit the attractiveness of direct referenda. But reliance on referenda for the revelation of social values suffers from a more fundamental problem: no method of voting is both fair and coherent.

The Paradox of Voting

Imagine that a school board holds referenda to determine the size of the budget for its schools. It proposes to base the budget on the results of pairwise voting among three possible budget alternatives: Low (no frills), Medium (similar to other public schools in the region), and High (best of everything). Suppose that three groups of voters can be identified according to their preferences over the three alternative budgets. Moderates are people who have children in school but also see property taxes as burdensome. Their first choice is Medium and their second choice is High; Low is their least preferred budget. Fiscal Conservatives think that the schools are wasting their tax dollars. They prefer Low to Medium and Medium to High. The third group, Effective Schoolers, want their children to receive the best possible schooling. They, therefore, prefer High. If High is not selected, however, then they will send their children to private schools. Therefore, their second choice is Low, and their third choice is Medium.

Table 8.1 summarizes the voters' policy choices under three different agendas. Agenda A offers the voters High versus Low in round 1. As both Moderates and Effective Schoolers favor High over Low, High wins with 65 percent of the vote. In round 2, High, as winner of round 1, now faces Medium. As Moderates and Fiscal

Table 8.1 *An Illustration of the Paradox of Voting*

Voter Group	Preferences over School Budget Levels			Percent of Voters
	First Choice	Second Choice	Third Choice	
Moderates	Medium	High	Low	45
Fiscal Conservatives	Low	Medium	High	35
Effective Schoolers	High	Low	Medium	20

Agenda A (Result: Medium)	
Round 1: High versus Low	High wins 65% to 35%
Round 2: Medium versus High	Medium wins 80% to 20%
Agenda B (Result: High)	
Round 1: Medium versus Low	Low wins 55% to 45%
Round 2: Low versus High	High wins 65% to 35%
Agenda C (Result: Low)	
Round 1: High versus Medium	Medium wins 80% to 20%
Round 2: Medium versus Low	Low wins 55% to 45%

Conservatives favor Medium over High, Medium wins with 80 percent of the vote and is, therefore, the selected alternative. Agenda B pits Medium versus Low in round 1. Low wins with 55 percent of the vote but loses against High in the second round. Consequently, High is the selected budget alternative. Finally, under agenda C, Medium defeats High in round 1, but Low defeats Medium in round 2, so Low is the selected budget alternative. Thus, each agenda results in a different social choice!

The situation is even more perplexing if we allow for the possibility that some people will be opportunistic in their voting. For example, consider how Fiscal Conservatives might try to manipulate the outcome under agenda B. If they have reasonable estimates of the percentages of voters who are Moderates and Effective Schoolers, then they can anticipate that Low will lose overwhelmingly to High in the second round. If, instead, Medium is paired with High in the second round, then Medium would win. The Fiscal Conservatives, who prefer Medium to High, might decide to vote for Medium in the first round over Low even though they prefer Low. If the other voters continued to vote their true preferences, then Medium would be selected in the first round with a majority of 80 percent and defeat High in the second round with a majority of 80 percent. Consequently, by voting in this opportunistic manner, the Fiscal Conservatives would be able to avoid their least preferred alternative, High, which otherwise would have resulted. Because this opportunistic voting requires one to realize that a more favorable final outcome can sometimes be achieved by voting against one's true preferences in the preliminary rounds, political scientists usually refer to it as *sophisticated voting*.

Of course, other voters may also attempt to manipulate the outcome by voting against their true preferences in the first round. The final social choice would depend, therefore, not only on the agenda but also on the extent to which people engage in sophisticated voting. At the heart of this indeterminacy lies what is often referred to as the *paradox of voting*. It brings into question the common interpretation of voting outcomes as "the will of the people."

The paradox of voting was first discovered by the French mathematician and philosopher Condorcet in the eighteenth century. Although later rediscovered by Charles Dodgson (Lewis Carroll) and others, its relevance to the study of democracy was not widely recognized until after the Second World War.[2] As long as the paradox of voting was viewed as a peculiar result of a particular voting scheme, it could be dismissed by scholars as a curiosity. But, in 1951, Kenneth Arrow proved that any voting rule that satisfies a basic set of fairness conditions may produce illogical results.[3]

Arrow's *general possibility theorem* applies to any rule for choice in which a group of two or more persons must select a policy from among three or more alternatives. It assumes that we require any such scheme to satisfy at least the following conditions to be considered fair. First, each person is allowed to have any transitive preferences over the possible policy alternatives (*axiom of unrestricted domain*). *Transitivity* requires that if one alternative is preferred by a person to a second alternative, and the second alternative is preferred by the person to the third

[2]The paradox of voting was rediscovered by Duncan Black in the 1940s. For an overview, see William H. Riker, *Liberalism against Populism* (San Francisco: Freeman, 1982), 1–3.

[3]Kenneth Arrow, *Social Choice and Individual Values*, 2nd ed. (New Haven, CT: Yale University Press, 1963). For a treatment that can be followed with minimal mathematics, see Julian H. Blau, "A Direct Proof of Arrow's Theorem," *Econometrica* 40(1) 1972, 61–67.

alternative, then the first alternative is preferred by the person to the third alternative. Second, if one alternative is unanimously preferred to a second, then the rule for choice will not select the second (*axiom of Pareto choice*). Third, the ranking of any two alternatives should not depend on what other alternatives are available (*axiom of independence*). That is, if the group ranks alternative 1 above alternative 2 in the absence of alternative 3, then it should not rank alternative 2 above alternative 1 when alternative 3 is also available. Fourth, the rule must not allow any one person dictatorial power to impose his or her preferences regardless of the preferences of others (*axiom of nondictatorship*). Arrow's theorem states that any fair rule for choice (one that satisfies the four axioms above) will fail to ensure a transitive social ordering of policy alternatives. In other words, cyclical (intransitive), or incoherent, social preferences like those appearing in the paradox of voting can arise from *any* fair voting system.[4]

What are the implications of Arrow's theorem for the interpretation of democracy? First, because cycles can arise with any fair voting scheme, those who control the agenda will have great opportunity for manipulating the social choice. Referring back to Table 8.1, note that even though only 20 percent of the voters prefer High over the other alternatives, High will result if voting follows agenda B. More generally, it appears that, in a wide range of circumstances involving policy alternatives with more than one dimension (for example, choosing tax rates and deductions in a tax bill), once a cycle arises anywhere in the social ordering, a person with control of the agenda can select a series of pairwise votes to secure any of the alternatives as a final choice.[5] Thus one would have to know how a final vote was reached before one could evaluate the extent to which it reflects the will of the majority.

Figure 8.1 provides an illustration of agenda manipulation in the context of a model that shows policy preferences for three legislators over alternative combinations of social and defense spending.[6] The points labeled B_1, B_2, and B_3 are the *ideal*, or *bliss, points*, respectively for the three legislators. For example, legislator 1 most prefers that S_1 be spent on social programs and D_1 on national defense. If we assume that each legislator prefers points closer to his or her bliss point than farther away, then each will have circular indifference curves. The indifference curves shown in the figure pass through the status quo of S_{SQ} and D_{SQ} and give all the combinations of spending that each legislator finds equally satisfactory to the status quo. Any point inside a voter's indifference curve will be closer to the bliss point than any point on the indifference curve and, therefore, preferred to the status quo. Note that the lens-shaped areas called *win sets* (labeled W_{13}, W_{12}, and W_{23}) represent points that would be favored by a majority of legislators (two out of three) over the status quo. Imagine that legislator 1 has agenda power in the sense that only she can propose an alternative to the status quo. If she proposes her bliss point, B_1,

[4]Further, other scholars have proven that sophisticated voting (manipulation of outcomes by voting against one's true preferences) is an inherent feature of all fair voting systems. Allan Gibbard, "Manipulation of Voting Schemes: A General Result," *Econometrica* 41(4) 1973, 587–601; and Mark Satterthwaite, "Strategy Proofness and Arrow's Conditions," *Journal of Economic Theory* 10(2) 1975, 187–217.

[5]In particular, if the agenda setter has full information about the preferences of the voters who vote sincerely, then she can reach any desired alternative through a series of pairwise votes. Richard D. McKelvey, "Intransitivities in Multidimensional Voting Models and Some Implications for Agenda Control," *Journal of Economic Theory* 12(3) 1976, 472–82; and Norman Schofield, "Instability of Simple Dynamic Games," *Review of Economic Studies* 45(4) 1978, 575–94.

[6]For an introduction to models of this sort, see Keith Krehbiel, "Spatial Models of Legislative Choice," *Legislative Studies Quarterly* 8(3) 1988, 259–319.

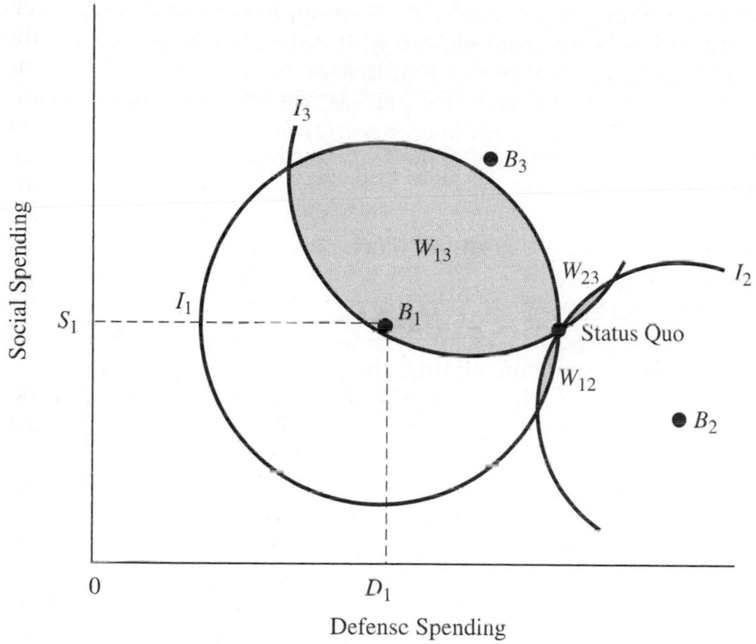

Figure 8.1 Agenda Control in a Two-Dimensional Policy Space

it will win a majority of votes because it is within W_{13}. Consequently, by controlling the agenda she can obtain the spending alternative that she most prefers.

Second, the introduction of alternative policies that create cycles is often an attractive strategy for voters who would otherwise face an undesirable social choice. For instance, William H. Riker argues persuasively that the introduction of slavery as an important national issue in the United States after 1819 can be interpreted as the ultimately successful method in a series of attempts by northern Whigs (later Republicans) to split the nationally strong Democrat Party.[7] Riker goes on to offer a fundamentally important generalization: persistent losers have an incentive to introduce new issues in an attempt to create voting cycles that offer an opportunity to defeat the dominant coalitions during the resulting periods of disequilibrium. Because of this incentive, we should expect voting cycles to be more frequent than if they simply resulted unintentionally from chance combinations of individual preferences. In other words, political disequilibrium, and the attendant problem of interpreting the meaning of social choices, are especially likely when the stakes are high.

Preference Intensity and Bundling

Imagine a society that decides every public policy question by referendum. If people vote according to their true preferences on each issue, social choices may result that are both Pareto inefficient and distributionally inequitable. For example,

[7]William H. Riker, *Liberalism against Populism* (San Francisco: Freeman, 1982), 213–32.

consider a proposal to build an express highway through a populated area. If we were able to elicit truthful answers from everyone about how much they would value the road, we might find that a majority would each be willing to pay a small amount to have the road built, while a minority, perhaps those living along the proposed route, would require a large amount of compensation to be made as well off after the construction of the road as before. If the total amount the majority would be willing to pay falls short of the total amount needed to compensate the minority, then the project is not Pareto efficient, nor even potentially Pareto efficient. Furthermore, most would view the project as inequitable because it concentrates high costs on a minority. Nevertheless, the project would be adopted in a majority rule referendum if all voted their true preferences.

Of course, not everyone in the majority will necessarily vote according to strictly private interests. Some may vote against the project out of a sense of fairness. Others may fear setting a precedent that might be used to justify unfair policies when they are in the minority. Absent these constraints, however, direct democracy can lead to *tyranny by the majority*, whereby either a permanent majority consistently inflicts costs on a permanent minority or a temporary majority opportunistically inflicts very high costs on a temporary minority.

Majorities may also inadvertently inflict high costs on minorities because voting schemes do not allow people to express the intensity of their preferences. No matter how much someone dislikes a proposed project, he or she only gets to cast one vote against it. Even if those in the majority wish to take the interests of the minority into consideration, they have no guarantee that the minority will be truthful in revealing the intensity of their preferences. In fact, those in the minority would have an incentive to overstate the intensity of their dislikes, perhaps checked only by the need to maintain some level of credibility. We can contrast this characteristic of collective choice with markets for private goods that allow people to express the intensity of their preferences by their willingness to purchase various quantities at various prices.

The danger of tyranny by the majority makes democracy by referenda generally undesirable; the complexity of modern public policy makes it impractical. Perhaps the closest a society could come to direct democracy would be the election of an executive who would serve subject to recall. The executive would at least have some opportunity to fashion policies that take into consideration strong preferences of minorities, and would have an incentive to do so if the composition of minorities with strong preferences changed with issues. Otherwise, two or more minorities with strong preferences might form a new majority in favor of recall.

Candidate executives would stand for office on platforms consisting of positions on important policy issues. Voters would have to evaluate the bundle of positions offered by each candidate. Different voters may vote for the same candidate for different reasons. In fact, a candidate holding the minority position on every important issue may still win the election. For example, free-traders consisting of one-third of the electorate may vote for a candidate because of her position on trade policy, which they believe to be most salient, even if they dislike her positions on all the other issues. Voters consisting of another one-third may dislike her position on trade policy but vote for her because of her position on defense spending, which they view as the most important issue. Thus, she may win the election even though a majority of voters opposes her positions on all issues including trade and defense policies. The general implication for democracy is that whenever people must vote on a bundle of policies, it is not necessarily the case that any particular policy in the winning bundle represents the will of a majority. Even a landslide victory may not represent a "mandate from the people" for the winner's proposed policies.

Democracy as a Check on Power

The paradox of voting, the possibility of minorities with intense preferences, and the problem of bundling show the imperfection, and imperfectibility, of democracy as a mechanism of social choice. As policy analysts, we must recognize that democratic processes do not always give us a true assessment of social values. Perhaps no consistent social values exist; perhaps voting does not discover them. Hence, governments apparently following "the will of the people" will not always be doing good.

Despite these inherent problems, direct democracy offers several advantages. The opportunity for participation encourages citizens to learn about public affairs. Actual participation may make citizens more willing to accept social choices that they opposed because they had an opportunity to be heard and to vote. Indeed, referenda may provide a means of putting divisive political issues at least temporarily to rest. For example, the 1980 and 1995 Quebec referenda on sovereignty seem to have defused, for at least a number of years, what otherwise might have been an explosive issue. The 1975 referendum in Great Britain on the question of membership in the European Economic Community, for instance, seems to have settled the issue in favor of continued participation despite strong opposition.[8]

It is another feature of democracy, however, that makes it preferable to other systems of social choice: it provides a great check on the abuse of power by giving the electorate the opportunity to overturn onerous policies and remove unpopular decision makers. It is this ability to "throw the rascals out" that fundamentally gives democracy its intrinsic social value. Democracy does not always lead to good, let alone the best, policies, but it provides an opportunity to correct the worst mistakes. Although we cannot count on democratic processes to produce enlightened public policies, as policy analysts we should, nevertheless, recognize their essential role in the preservation of liberty. They may deny us the full benefits of a truly benevolent and wise government, but they help protect us from the harm of one that is either evil or foolish.

Problems Inherent in Representative Government

In modern democracies, representatives of the electorate actually make and execute public policy. Although the particular constitutional arrangements vary considerably across countries, in most democratic systems voters choose representatives to legislative or executive and sometimes judicial branches. The legislature typically plays a dominant role in establishing public policy by passing laws but also

[8]Austin Ranney, ed., *The Referendum Device* (Washington, DC: American Enterprise Institute, 1981), xii, 1–18. See also Richard Johnston, Andre Blais, Elisabeth Gidengil, and Neil Nevitte, *The Challenge of Direct Democracy* (Montreal: McGill-Queen's University Press, 1996), 9–41.

often plays an administrative role by monitoring budgets and overseeing government operations. The chief executive exercises administrative responsibility, including the appointment of high-ranking officials in government agencies. Members of the executive branch make public policy when they interpret legislation, as, for example, when agency heads issue rules under broadly delegated authority to regulate some aspect of commerce. In addition, they may make proposals that influence the legislative agenda. The members of the judicial branch also interpret laws as well as determine their constitutionality. These legislators, executives, and judges, often referred to as "public servants," represent the rest of society in the numerous government decisions that constitute public policy.

Representatives often face the dilemma of choosing between actions that advance their conception of the good society and actions that reflect the preferences of their constituencies.[9] For example, a legislator may believe that construction of a safe nuclear waste facility is socially desirable and that the best location for society as a whole would be in her district. Should she support construction of the facility even if the residents of her district are almost unanimously opposed to it? On the one hand, we might approve of her support of the facility as consistent with increasing aggregate social welfare. On the other hand, we might approve of her opposition as consistent with protecting a segment of society from bearing disproportionate costs of collective action. The very fact that we have no clear-cut way of resolving this sort of dilemma suggests the difficulty we face in evaluating the behavior of representatives.

Three factors greatly influence the way representatives actually behave. First, representatives have their own private interests. It would be naive to believe that they do not consider their own well-being and that of their families. Elected representatives, motivated perhaps by the status and perquisites of office, usually seek either reelection or election to higher office. Candidates often behave as if they were trying to maximize the percentage of votes they would receive. This strategy, which maximizes the probability that they will actually gain a majority, requires them to pay more attention to the interests of the most responsive citizens than to those who are either unlikely to vote or who are likely to vote according to party, ethnicity, or other general considerations. Public executives, elected and appointed, similarly seek career security and advancement as well as circumstances that make it easier to manage their agencies. In general, the personal interests of representatives tend to push them toward responsiveness to their constituencies and away from concern for broader social welfare. Legislators tend to emphasize benefits to their districts over social costs; public executives tend to value resources for use by their agencies beyond their contribution to social benefits.

Self-interest also raises the question of the relationship between the voting behavior of the individual representatives and financial (or in-kind) campaign contributions by interest groups. Driven by the desire to advertise through costly media, representatives in the United States seek to raise money to engage in political campaigns. If financial contributions alter representatives' voting patterns, most citi-

[9]Political philosophers distinguish between the roles of the representative as a *trustee* (who should act on behalf of what he believes to be his constituency's interest) and as a *delegate* (who should act in accordance with the desires of a majority of his constituency). They also distinguish between representation of a local constituency and the entire nation. For a review, see J. Rolland Pennock, *Democratic Political Theory* (Princeton, NJ: Princeton University Press, 1979), 321–34. Pennock argues that the proper role of a representative falls somewhere between that of trustee and delegate (p. 325).

zens and ethicists would regard such behavior as a source of government failure (although a few have argued that as long as the purchased votes are bought by constituents it simply represents the expression of intense preferences.) Certainly, if vote-buying becomes endemic, it is likely to have negative consequences for aggregate (especially dynamic) efficiency.[10] It is important to recognize that in-kind payments may be as important as direct financial campaign contributions.[11] Political corruption threatens confidence in property rights, leading to costly adaptive behavior by citizens. More fundamentally, corruption threatens the legitimacy of all institutions of the state.

Yet determining the actual impact of financial contributions on political behavior is problematic because it is difficult to separate from an alternative, more benign hypothesis: financial contributors support like minded politicians. Both hypotheses are consistent with a positive correlation between financial contributions and voting behavior.

Some researchers have certainly found correlations between voting patterns and financial contributions.[12] Others have simply noted that contributions do buy access to representatives and argue that the access must be purchasing something tangible.[13] One suggested strategy for separating the two hypotheses is to examine the behavior of incumbents after they have announced that they will not be running for reelection. If representatives are voting their preferences, then they should not change their behavior after their retirement announcement; if they have been influenced by contributions, then they should revert to voting their preferences. Using such data, Stephen Bronars and John Lott report: "Our tests strongly reject the notion that campaign contributions buy politicians' votes."[14]

Second, individuals must incur costs to monitor the behavior of their representatives. Given financial and time constraints, people usually do not find it in their private interests to articulate policy preferences or to monitor closely the actions of their representatives. The broader the scope of government, the more costly is comprehensive articulation and monitoring. Those who do monitor typically have strong policy preferences based on either ideology or financial interests. Consequently, representatives tend to be most closely evaluated by groups that have preferences very different from their broader constituencies. Thus, these *interest groups* may enjoy more influence with representatives than they would in a world with perfect information and costless monitoring.

Third, party discipline may constrain the self-interested behavior of individual representatives. Both in terms of the federal and state legislatures, the United

[10]Pranab Bardhan, "Corruption and Development," *Journal of Economic Literature* 35(3) 1997, 1320–46.

[11]For evidence on this, see Russell S. Sobell and Thomas A. Garrett, "On the Measurement of Rent Seeking and Its Social Opportunity Cost," *Public Choice* 112(1–2) 2002, 115–36.

[12]Henry W. Chappell, Jr., "Campaign Contributions and Congressional Voting: A Simultaneous Probit-Tobit Model," *Review of Economics and Statistics* 64(1) 1982, 77–83; John R. Wright, "Contributions, Lobbying, and Committee Voting in the U.S. House of Representatives," *American Political Science Review* 84(2) 1990, 417–438.

[13]Janet Grenzke, "PACs and the Congressional Supermarket: The Currency Is Complex," *American Journal of Political Science* 33(1) 1989, 1–24; Richard L. Hall and Frank W. Weyman, "Buying Time: Moneyed Interests and the Mobilization of Bias in Congressional Committees," *American Political Science Review* 84(3) 1990, 797–820.

[14]Stephen Bronars and John Lott, "Do Campaign Donations Alter How a Politician Votes? Or Do Donors Support Candidates Who Value the Same Thing That They Do?" *Journal of Law and Economics* 40(2) 1997, 317–50, at p. 346.

States is generally considered to have weak party discipline. For example, in the 102nd Congress only about 50 percent of the Senate roll-call votes and 60 percent of those in the House had the characteristic that the majority of one party voted contrary to the majority of the other party.[15] In many other countries, especially those with parliamentary systems, party discipline is much tighter. This follows from a number of institutional differences: more centralized control of campaign funds, more centralized control of nomination procedures, and the inherent centralizing character of cabinet government in parliamentary systems.

In the following sections we explore some of the implications of self-interested representatives who are not fully monitored by their constituencies. These implications should be thought of as general tendencies. Not all representatives act in their own narrow self-interest all of the time. Some have strong policy preferences that occasionally lead them to take stands that are politically costly. (Of course, in so doing they run an increased risk of being turned out of office.) Analysts can sometimes make common cause with such representatives on the basis of principle. More generally, however, analysts find allies among representatives whose private interests happen to lead them to what the analysts believe to be good policies.

Rent Seeking: Diffuse and Concentrated Interests

In a world where most people pay little attention to their representatives, the politically active few have an opportunity to wield influence disproportionate to their number. By providing information, activists may be able to persuade representatives to support their positions and advocate them more effectively in the political arena. By promising to help secure the votes of constituency groups and by providing campaign funds, they may be able to alter the way representatives concerned with reelection view the social good—at least as revealed by the representatives' policy choices.

Who is likely to become politically active? Undoubtedly, some people have a strong sense of duty to promote the social good and, therefore, feel obliged to express their views on public policy issues whether they stand to gain or lose personally. In general, however, private self-interest plays an important role in motivating political participation. If we believe that most people are economically rational, then the greater the expected net benefits one expects to reap from some political activity, the more likely that one will undertake the activity. Policies that would spread large aggregate benefits widely and uniformly among the electorate may not elicit active political support because, for any individual, the costs of political activity exceed the expected benefits (which are the individual's private gains if the policy is adopted weighted by the probability that political action will result in adoption). Similarly, no individuals may find it in their own self-interests to protest policies that spread costs widely. In contrast, at least some people will likely find it in their self-interest to become politically active when policies involve concentrated costs or benefits. Assuming that representatives respond at least somewhat to political activity, the consequence of individual rationality will be collective choices biased toward policies with concentrated benefits and away from policies

[15] David P. Baron, *Business and Its Environment*, 2nd ed. (Upper Saddle River, NJ: Prentice Hall, 1996), 136.

with concentrated costs. This bias opens the door for the adoption of policies for which total costs exceed total benefits.

Concentrated economic benefits (and diffuse economic costs) often arise when governments intervene in markets. The interventions generally create economic benefits in the form of *rents*—payments to owners of resources above those which the resources could command in any alternative use. Lobbying for such interventions is called *rent seeking*.[16]

The effort to use government to restrict competition is perhaps the oldest form of rent-seeking. (Securing a legal restriction on competition would allow capture of the monopoly rent shown in Figure 4.6.) In earlier times kings gained revenue by sharing the rents that resulted from monopolies given to favored subjects. In more modern times, bribery by those seeking local monopolies, such as cable television franchises, has contributed to the corruption of local public officials. Professions often attempt to keep wages high by restricting entry through government-sanctioned licensing—if the restricted entry does not provide offsetting benefits, such as reductions in information asymmetry (as described in Chapter 5), the professionals gain rents at the expense of consumers. Domestic manufacturers often lobby for tariffs and quotas on foreign imports so that they can sell their products at higher prices. By limiting foreign competition, tariffs and quotas extract rents for domestic manufacturers (and, ironically, for foreign producers) from domestic consumers.

Firms within an industry may seek regulation as a way of limiting competition.[17] For instance, each of the three major laws that expanded federal regulation of the U.S. pharmaceutical industry was supported by firms that believed they would be able to meet standards more easily than their competitors.[18] Even when industries initially oppose regulation, their concentrated interests give them an incentive to lobby the regulators; the result may be "capture." For example, the U.S. Interstate Commerce Commission was originally created largely in response to anticompetitive practices by the railroads.[19] By the 1920s, however, the ICC so identified with the interests of the railroads that it tried to protect them from the growing competition from trucking.[20]

Sometimes governments generate rents for producers by directly setting prices in markets. For example, many countries set price floors on certain agricultural products like wheat, milk, and honey. Figure 8.2 illustrates the rent transfers and deadweight losses that result. Without a price floor, quantity Q_0 will be supplied and demanded as market clearing price P_0. At an imposed floor price of P_S, the quantity demanded falls to Q_D. Those who are able to sell their output extract a rent

[16]James M. Buchanan, Robert D. Tollison, and Gordon Tullock, eds., *Toward a Theory of the Rent-Seeking Society* (College Station: Texas A&M University Press, 1980).

[17]George Stigler, "The Theory of Economic Regulation," *Bell Journal of Economics and Management Science* 3(1) 1971, 3–21.

[18]David L. Weimer, "Organizational Incentives: Safe—and Available—Drugs," in LeRoy Graymer and Frederick Thompson, eds., *Reforming Social Regulation* (Beverly Hills, CA: Sage Publications, 1982), 19–69.

[19]Some scholars argue that the railroads welcomed regulation as a way of rescuing faltering cartels. See Gabriel Kolko, *Railroads and Regulatian, 1877–1916* (Princeton, NJ: Princeton University Press, 1965); and Paul W. MacAvoy, *The Economic Effects of Regulation: The Trunk Line Railroad Cartels and the Interstate Commerce Commission before 1900* (Cambridge, MA: MIT Press, 1965).

[20]Samuel P. Huntington, "The Marasmus of the ICC: The Commission, the Railroads, and the Public Interest," *Yale Law Review* 61(4) 1952, 467–509.

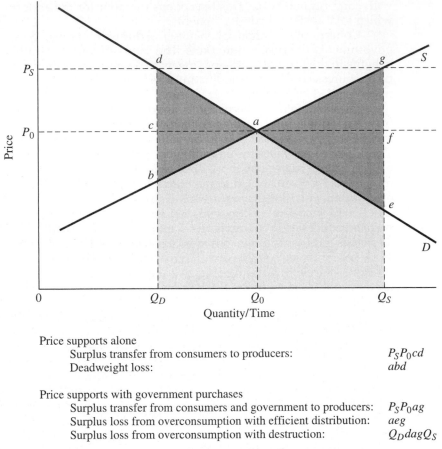

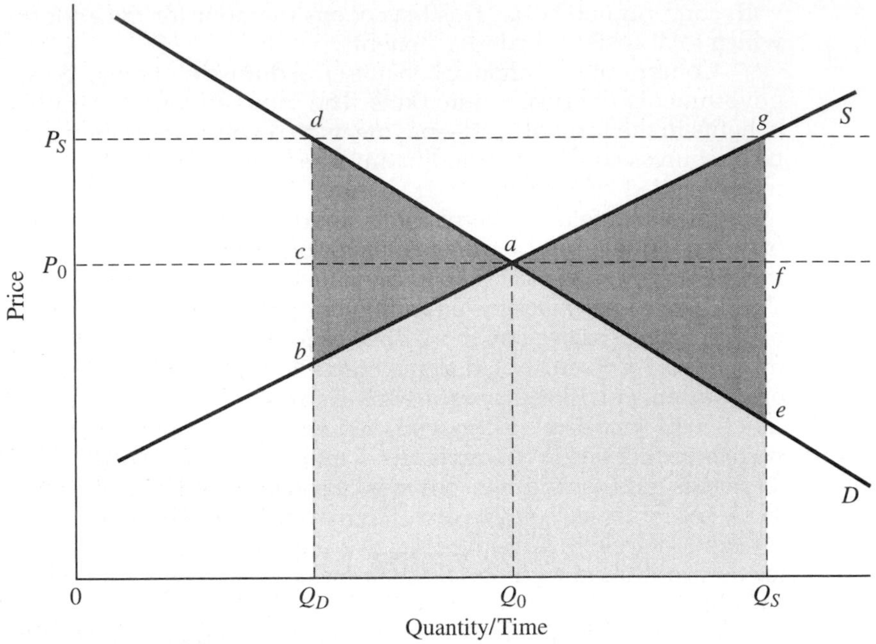

Price supports alone

Surplus transfer from consumers to producers:	P_SP_0cd
Deadweight loss:	*abd*

Price supports with government purchases

Surplus transfer from consumers and government to producers:	P_SP_0ag
Surplus loss from overconsumption with efficient distribution:	*aeg*
Surplus loss from overconsumption with destruction:	Q_DdagQ_S

Figure 8.2 Surplus Transfers and Deadweight Losses under Price Supports

from consumers equal to the area of rectangle P_SP_0cd. A deadweight loss equal to the area of triangle *abd* also results from the losses in consumer and producer surplus associated with lower consumption levels. Of course, at floor price P_S, farmers will want to supply Q_S. To maintain the price floor, therefore, the government must take the excess supply off the market. If it does so by allocating production quotas to the farmers with the lowest marginal costs of production, then the social surplus loss will just equal the deadweight loss, shaded area *abd*. If it purchases and distributes the difference between Q_S and Q_D efficiently to those consumers who value consumption less than the floor price, then the social surplus loss equals the shaded area *aeg*. If the government purchases the excess and destroys it, then the social surplus loss equals the large shaded area Q_DdagQ_S.

The magnitudes of the rent transfers and efficiency losses from price supports in the United States have been at times extremely large. For example, William Rousser reports that during the mid-1980s the price support programs for wheat, corn, cotton, peanuts, and dairy products had the following range of annual economic and fiscal impacts: cost to consumers of between \$3.27 billion and \$4.57 billion; transfers to producers of between $12.8 billion and $14.9 billion; cost to taxpayers of between $13.5 billion and $15.7 billion; and net social losses of between $1.9 billion and $7.4 billion.[21] He also reports that during this period the ratio of public sector assistance to total farmer receipts were 36.5 percent for wheat, 53.9 percent for milk, and a whopping 77.4 percent for sugar.[22] For sugar, milk, and rice, more than 90 percent of these subsidies were predatory (transfers from other sectors), as opposed to productive (reductions in transaction costs, provision of information, research, and the like) forms of government policy.[23]

Programs like price supports often produce only temporary rent transfers. If farmers believe that the government will permanently guarantee a price above the market clearing level, the price of land will rise to reflect the higher value of its output. Specifically, the price of land will reflect the present value of future rents. A farmer who sells land after the introduction of the price supports, therefore, captures all the rent. The new owner, who must service the debt on the purchase amount, does not realize any profits above the normal rate of return. In effect, as the original farmers extract their shares of the rent by selling their land, the supply curve shifts up to the level of the support price. Attempts to regain efficiency and reduce government expenditures through elimination of the price supports will force many of the current owners into bankruptcy.[24]

Even the initial beneficiaries of the market intervention may fail to realize the full rents because of the costs of the rent-seeking activity. Direct lobbying and campaign contributions can be costly, especially if they must be spread over a large number of representatives to secure adoption of the intervention. Most or all of the rents may be dissipated, leaving the rent seekers no better off than they were in the absence of the intervention. In the extreme, expenditures of resources by competing rent seekers may dissipate more than the rents at stake.

Rents can be realized directly from government as well as through the marketplace. Outright grants can sometimes be secured if a plausible public rationale can be offered. Because they tend to be more hidden from public view, exemptions from regulations and taxes are often more attractive targets for rent seekers. Sometimes tax loopholes provide large benefits to small numbers of firms. For example, the transition rules of the 1986 U.S. tax reform law created about $10 billion in loopholes, some written with restrictions so specific that they benefited single companies.[25]

Despite the advantages concentrated interests enjoy in mobilizing for political activity, they do not always prevail over diffuse interests. If those with similar interests are already organized, then they may be able to use the existing organizational structure to overcome the free-riding problem that would keep them from

[21]Calculated from Table 1 of Gordon C. Rausser, "Predatory versus Productive Government: The Case of U.S. Agricultural Policies," *Journal of Economic Perspectives* 6(3) 1992, 133–57.

[22]Ibid., p. 149.

[23]Ibid., pp. 149–50.

[24]For a discussion of the problem of one-time rent gains, see Gordon Tullock, "The Transitional Gains Trap," in Buchanan, Tollison, and Tullock, eds., *Rent-Seeking Society*, pp. 211–21. For a case study that illustrates the transitional gains trap by comparing the highly regulated egg industry in British Columbia with the less regulated industry in Washington State, see Thomas Borcherding (with Gary W. Dorosh), *The Egg Marketing Board: A Case Study of Monopoly and Its Social Cost* (Vancouver, BC: Fraser Institute, 1981).

[25]Mark D. Uehling and Rich Thomas, "Tax Reform: Congress Hatches Some Loopholes," *Newsweek*, September 29, 1986, 22.

expressing their interests individually. For instance, people join the National Rifle Association primarily because of their interests in hunting, shooting, and gun collecting. While very few members would find it in their personal interests to lobby on their own, most support expenditures by the NRA for lobbying on such issues as gun control. In effect, organizations like the NRA provide public goods for their members who join primarily to obtain private benefits.

Diffuse interests may also enjoy access to representatives by virtue of their distribution. For example, the National Education Association appears to enjoy great success in lobbying not only because it has a large, well-educated, and politically active membership, but also because its membership is spread fairly evenly over congressional districts.[26] Similarly, organizations of local governments are often effective at the national level because their members generally have access at least to their own representatives.[27] The extent to which such diffuse interests can become politically effective usually depends on the existence of an organization to mobilize the contributions of individual members.

Even without the advantage of prior organization, however, diffuse interests can sometimes overcome highly concentrated interests. Experience suggests that two factors facilitate the success of diffuse interests: attention to the policy issue from a large segment of the electorate and low public trust in the concentrated interests. These factors often hold in situations in which the prices of key goods rise dramatically. For example, rapidly rising rental prices often attract widespread attention in communities with low rates of homeownership and generate animosity toward landlords who appear to be profiting at the expense of tenants. Representatives may respond with rent control programs that provide modest short-run savings to current tenants at the expense of landlords and potential renters.

The regulation of petroleum prices in Canada and the United States during the 1970s also shows diffuse interests dominating concentrated ones. The quadrupling of world oil prices during the Arab oil embargo in 1974 drew public attention to the so-called energy crisis and raised widespread suspicion that oil companies were profiteering. Each country instituted extensive regulation of its petroleum industry, including price ceilings on petroleum products.

It is worth noting that those who successfully organize diffuse interests may enjoy concentrated private benefits. They may draw salaries as staff members and enjoy access to the political process. These entrepreneurs thus face incentives to search for issues that will enable them to maintain support for their organizations.

Mobilizations of diffuse interests that simply impede rent seeking of concentrated interests probably advance the social good. Sometimes, however, they facilitate rent seeking. When they result in price ceilings, for instance, they generally reduce economic efficiency and rarely lead to greater equity. Figure 8.3 illustrates these points. The price ceiling P_C lies below the unrestrained market price P_0. At price P_C, consumers demand Q_D, but producers supply only Q_S. In the "best case," consumers gain a surplus equal to the area of rectangle, P_0P_Cbc, which corresponds to the producers' loss of rents on the Q_S units they sell; the social cost of the transfer, however, is a deadweight loss of social surplus from reduced consumption equal to the area of triangle *abd*.

[26]Richard A. Smith, "Advocacy, Interpretation, and Influence in the U.S. Congress," *American Political Science Review* 78(1) 1984, 44–63.

[27]Robert H. Salisbury, "Interest Representation: The Dominance of Institutions," *American Political Science Review* 78(1) 1984, 64–76.

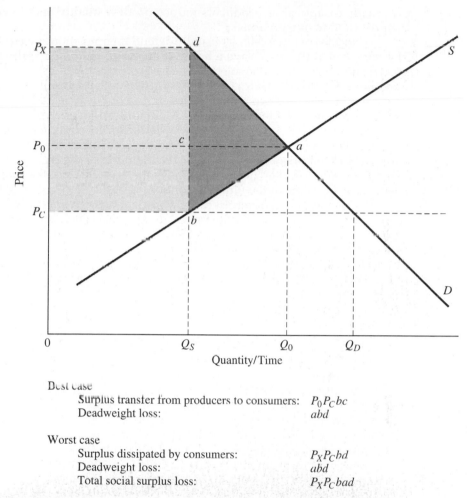

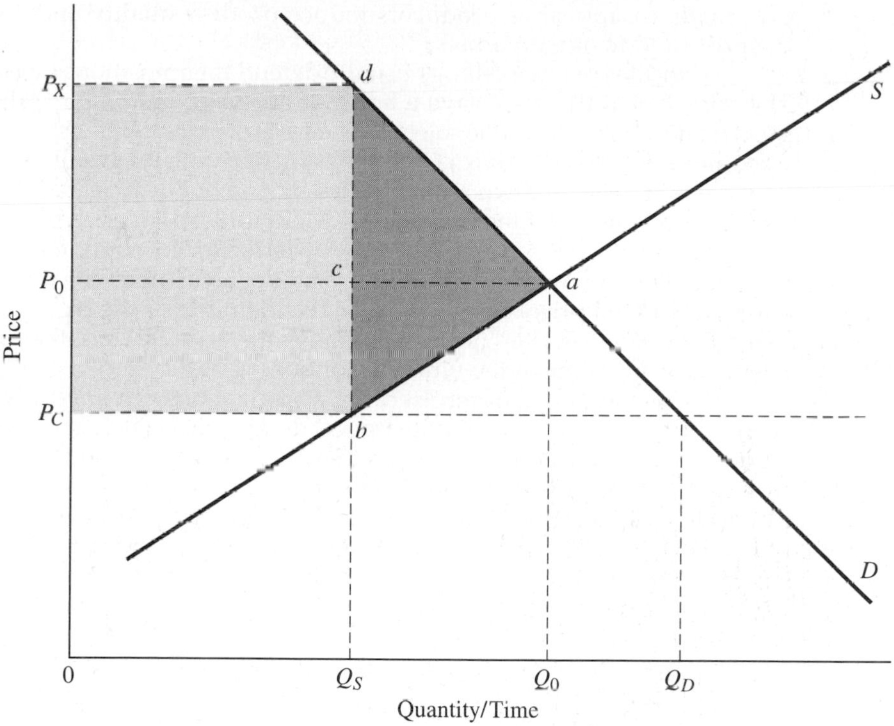

Best case

Surplus transfer from producers to consumers:	P_0P_Cbc
Deadweight loss:	abd

Worst case

Surplus dissipated by consumers:	P_XP_Cbd
Deadweight loss:	abd
Total social surplus loss:	P_XP_Cbad

Figure 8.3 Surplus Transfer and Deadweight Losses under Price Ceilings

In the "worst case," consumers dissipate the surplus they gain from producers as well as surplus equal to the area of rectangle P_XP_0cd. When supply is limited to Q_S, consumers value the last unit available at P_X. Therefore, consumers will be willing to pay up to $P_X - P_0$ in nonmonetary costs, such as queuing, searching, and perhaps even bribing, to obtain shares of the limited supply. These costs have the effect of dissipating the benefits consumers enjoy from the lower monetary cost.

In order to achieve the "best case," an efficient rationing scheme is needed. For example, the distribution of coupons entitling consumers to shares of the available supply, coupled with an efficient "white market" for buying and selling coupons, could secure the surplus transfer for consumers without substantial dissipation. Coupon rationing can be administratively costly, however, because it requires creation and distribution of an entirely new currency. In addition, in most markets rationing schemes become obsolete because the shortages induced by ceiling prices eventually disappear as producers reduce product quality and consumers shift their demand to other markets.[28]

Advocates of price ceilings usually defend their positions on equity grounds. They argue that the poor have a better chance at obtaining a "fair share" of the good if allocation is not done solely on the basis of price. But the mechanisms of non-price allocation do not always favor the poor. Queuing for gasoline, for instance, involves less hardship for two-adult families with flexible professional work hours than for single parents working fixed hours. More important, price ceilings tend to create a number of big losers. For example, by reducing economic efficiency, price ceilings on petroleum products contribute to higher levels of unemployment and lower wages during oil price shocks. Because the identities of the big losers are generally not revealed until after implementation of the price ceilings, their interests rarely receive consideration at the time of adoption.

The accumulation of rent-seeking organizations can have adverse effects on economic growth. Mancur Olson argued that in stable societies rent-seeking "distributional coalitions" shift resources toward cartel activity and lobbying and away from production.[29] Aside from this direct effect on economic efficiency, attempts by coalitions to protect their rents reduce the capacities of societies to adopt new technologies and reallocate resources to meet changing conditions. Consequently, in Olson's view, the greater the accumulation of distributional coalitions, the slower the rate of economic growth.

Problems of Geographic Representation: The District-Based Legislature

Legislatures rely on voting to reach collective decisions. As we have already discussed, no method of voting is both fair and consistent. Procedural rules concerning such things as agenda setting and permissible amendments may prevent cyclical voting, but they cannot eliminate opportunities for sophisticated voting and agenda manipulation.[30] An additional collective choice problem arises in legislatures because the members usually represent constituencies with heterogeneous preferences. Specifically, under majority voting, certain distributions of preferences can result in social choices opposed by a majority of the total electorate.[31]

For example, consider a legislature made up of 100 members, each representing the same number of constituents. Assume that representatives vote according to the preferences of a majority of their constituents. Imagine that 51 percent of the voters in 51 of the constituencies favor a particular policy, while none of the voters in the other 49 favor it. Majority voting in the legislature would result in adoption of the policy, even though it is favored by only a little more than one-quarter of the total electorate.

[28]For a detailed discussion of the impact of price ceilings, see George Horwich and David L. Weimer, *Oil Price Shocks, Market Response, and Contingency Planning* (Washington, DC: American Enterprise Institute, 1984), 57–110.

[29]Mancur Olson, *The Rise and Decline of Nations: Economic Growth, Stagflation, and Social Rigidities* (New Haven, CT: Yale University Press, 1982), 69.

[30]For an overview, see Kenneth A. Shepsle and Mark S. Bonchek, *Analyzing Politics: Rationality, Behavior, and Institutions* (New York: W. W. Norton, 1997).

[31]James M. Buchanan and Gordon Tullock, *The Calculus of Consent* (Ann Arbor: University of Michigan Press, 1962), 220–22.

Because such extreme distributions of preferences are likely to be somewhat rare, the problem of minority choice under representative government probably has limited practical significance in political systems with only two parties.[32] A much more important social choice problem arises from the efforts of representatives to serve the narrow interests of their constituencies.

In most countries legislators represent geographically defined districts. While they may sincerely wish to do what is in the best interests of the entire country, their self-interest in terms of reelection encourages them to pay special attention to the interests of their districts. This often leads to policy choices that do not contribute to aggregate national welfare.

The problem goes well beyond legislators emphasizing the social benefits that accrue to their own constituencies in deciding how to vote. Certain social costs sometimes appear as benefits to districts.[33] For example, a cost-benefit analysis of a weapons system from the social perspective would count expenditures on components as costs. A legislator, however, might very well count expenditures on components manufactured in her own district as benefits because they contribute to the vitality of the local economy. What from the social perspective might be a cost of, say, $10 million might be viewed by the legislator as a benefit of perhaps $5 million. For example, observers have attributed the ultimate political success of the U.S. B-1 bomber program partly to the fact that major subcontractors are located in a large number of congressional districts.[34]

District-oriented valuation of expenditures often leads to adoption of policies with net social costs as legislators bargain with each other to get their share from the "pork barrel." This process, sometimes called *logrolling*, involves assembling a collection of projects that provide sufficient locally perceived benefits to gain adoption of the packages as a whole.[35] When coupled with representatives, unwillingness to bear the political costs of raising taxes, logrolling for district "pork" contributes to deficit spending.

The legislative process generally favors policies that spread perceived benefits over a majority of districts. Although this tendency may contribute to regional equality, it also makes targeting and policy experimentation difficult. Some programs produce net social benefits only in special circumstances and limited scope. For instance, one or two centers for the study of educational innovation might offer positive expected net benefits; on the other hand, because skilled researchers and

[32]In systems with more than two parties, the problem of minority rule is more common. For example, the Conservatives in Great Britain won control of Parliament with a minority of votes in their last three election wins. In the 1987 election, for instance, the Conservatives won 59.4 percent of the seats in Parliament with only 43.3 percent of total votes cast.

[33]For a formal development of this idea, see Kenneth A. Shepsle and Barry R. Weingast, "Political Solutions to Market Problems," *American Political Science Review* 78(2) 1984, 417–34; and Barry R. Weingast, Kenneth A. Shepsle, and Christopher Johnsen, "The Political Economy of Benefits and Costs: A Neoclassical Approach to Distributive Politics," *Journal of Political Economy* 89(4) 1981, 642–64.

[34]Michael R. Gordon, "B-1 Bomber Issue No Longer Whether to Build It but How Many, at What Price," *National Journal*, September 3, 1983, 1768–72. "... Rockwell has aggressively lobbied for the B-1B program, notifying members of Congress about the jobs at stake, many of which are spread among contractors throughout the United States" (p. 1771).

[35]See, for example, William H. Riker and Steven J. Brams,"The Paradox of Vote Trading," *American Political Science Review* 67(4) 1973, 1235–47. Riker and Brams see logrolling as leading to reductions in social welfare. It is worth noting, however, that logrolling can also lead to socially beneficial results by allowing minorities with strong preferences to form majorities.

good ideas are scarce resources, twenty such centers offer net social costs. Nevertheless, legislative approval might be easier to obtain for the more dispersed program because it provides expenditures in more districts. The U.S. Model Cities program fit this pattern.[36] Originally proposed by President Johnson to demonstrate the effects of concentrated and coordinated federal aid on a small number of cities, it was expanded to include a large number of small and medium-sized cities to gain the support of representatives of rural and suburban districts. As a result, resources were widely disbursed so that the effects of concentration could not be determined.

Shortened Time Horizons: Electoral Cycles

Representatives must often make decisions that will have consequences extending many years into the future. From the perspective of economic efficiency, the representatives should select policies for which the present value of benefits exceeds the present value of costs. In making the comparison, each representative should apply the same social discount rate to the streams of benefits as to costs. Self-interest operating in an environment of imperfect monitoring, however, increases incentives for representatives to discount heavily costs and benefits that will not occur in the short run.

Consider a representative who must stand for reelection in, say, two years. Because his constituency does not fully monitor his behavior, he faces the problem of convincing the electorate that his actions have contributed to their well-being. He will undoubtedly realize that it will be easier to claim credit for effects that have actually occurred than for ones expected to occur in the future. Now, imagine him choosing between two projects with different benefit and cost profiles. Project A offers large and visible net benefits over the next two years but large net costs in subsequent years so that, overall, it offers a negative net present value. Project B incurs net costs over the next two years but growing net benefits in subsequent years, so that overall it offers a positive net present value. From the social perspective, the representative should select project B; from the perspective of his own self-interest, however, he can enhance his chances for reelection by selecting project A and claiming credit for the benefits that are realized prior to the election.

Under what circumstances will such myopic judgment be most likely to occur? One factor is the representative's perception of his vulnerability in his reelection bid. The more threatened he feels, the more likely he is to select projects with immediate and visible benefits for which he can claim credit. Representatives either not standing for reelection or running in "safe" districts are likely to place less value on the short-term political gains and, therefore, are more likely to act as "statesmen" with respect to the time horizon they use in evaluating projects. Another factor is the ease with which an opponent can draw the attention of the electorate to the yet-unrealized future costs. The more easily an opponent can alert the electorate to these costs, the less likely is the incumbent to overdiscount the future.

To what extent does the myopia induced by the electoral cycle actually influence public policy? The common wisdom that legislatures rarely increase taxes in the year before an election, for instance, appears to be empirically verified by the

[36] Bryan D. Jones, *Governing Urban America: Policy Approach* (Boston: Little, Brown, 1983), 410.

pattern of tax changes observed across states within the United States.[37] The U.S. picture with respect to macroeconomic policy at the national level is less clear, suggesting that electoral cycles interact importantly with the partisan preferences of incumbents.[38] These latter findings raise at least some concerns about the ability of national governments to manage macroeconomic activity efficiently, even when reliable policy tools are available.

Posturing to Public Attention: Public Agendas, Sunk Costs, and Precedent

Candidates for public office must compete for the attention of the electorate. Most of us focus our attention on our families, careers, and other aspects of our private lives. While we certainly care about public policy, especially when it directly affects us, we generally do not devote great amounts of our time to learning about issues and about how our representatives handle them. Because gathering and evaluating detailed information on public affairs is costly, we usually rely on newspapers, magazines, radio, and television to do it for us. We should not be surprised, therefore, that representatives consider how their actions and positions will be portrayed in the mass media.

The media offer opportunities for representatives to reach the public. When the news media draw public attention to some undesirable social condition like drug abuse, representatives may be able to share the limelight by proposing changes in public policy. These attempts to convert undesirable and highly visible conditions to public policy problems amendable at least to apparent solution help determine the policy agenda. As newly "discovered" conditions push older ones from the media, the agenda changes. Representatives and analysts who prefer specific policies may have to wait for an appropriate condition to arise to gain a "policy window" into the agenda.[39] For example, advocates of urban mass transit in the United States enjoyed a policy window initially when the media reflected public concern about traffic congestion, another when the environmental movement drew attention to pollution, and a third when the energy crisis raised concern about fuel conservation.[40] They made some progress in spreading their preferred solution when each of these windows opened.

Candidates for elected office view media coverage so highly that they are usually willing, if financially able, to pay large sums for political advertising. In order to be financially able, U.S. candidates typically spend large amounts of time and effort soliciting campaign contributions from those who share similar political views,

[37]The year in the governor's term also appears to influence the pattern of tax changes. John Mikesell, "Election Periods and State Tax Policy Cycles," *Public Choice* 33(3) 1978, 99–105.

[38]The literature on electoral cycles begins with William D. Nordhaus, "The Political Business Cycle," *Review of Economic Studies* 42(2) 1975, 169–90. The partisan model was introduced by Douglas Hibbs, "Political Parties and Macroeconomic Policy," *American Political Science Review* 71(4) 1977, 1467–87. For overviews of more recent wok, which suggests the importance of partisanship, see Alberto Alesina and Howard Rosenthal, *Partisan Politics, Divided Government, and the Economy* (New York: Cambridge University Press, 1995); and William R. Keech, *Economic Politics: The Costs of Democracy* (New York: Cambridge University Press, 1995).

[39]For an excellent treatment of the ideas discussed in this paragraph, see John W. Kingdon, *Agendas, Alternatives, and Public Policies* (Boston: Little, Brown, 1984), 205–18.

[40]Ibid., p. 181.

those who wish to ensure future access to elected candidates, and those who seek to influence decisions on specific policies. In open seats for the House of Representatives, for example, contributions appear to affect the probability of winning.[41] Campaign finance reform intended to reduce the role of campaign contributions in politics often have undesirable and unintended consequences. One undesirable consequence is that they may make it harder for challengers to compete against incumbents who use their positions to remain in the public eye. One unintended consequence is the diversion of contributions from the campaigns of specific candidates to any uncovered categories, such as contributions to parties (so-called soft money contributions) and independent spending that indirectly supports or attacks candidates.

A policy agenda strongly influenced by the pattern of media coverage and political advertising is not necessarily consistent with the concept of public policy as a rational search for ways to improve social welfare. The policy agenda only reflects appropriate priorities if the media happen to cover conditions in proportion to their worthiness as public policy problems—a dubious assumption because undesirable social conditions, no matter how unamenable to correction by public policy, may still make good stories. Street crime, for instance, depends most heavily on local rather than national law enforcement policies. Nevertheless, it may elicit a national response when it commands national media attention, as is the case in the United States repeatedly since the late 1960s.[42]

A media-driven policy agenda discourages the careful evaluation of alternatives. Representatives who take the lead in proposing policy responses are most likely to benefit from the wave of media coverage. Thus, they face an incentive to propose something before the crest passes. If they wait too long, then the policy window may close. Furthermore, adoption of any policy response may hasten the decline in media coverage by giving the appearance that something has been done about the problem. Consequently, more comprehensive and, perhaps, better analyzed policy responses may not have time to surface. Even if they are held in reserve for the next policy window, they may no longer be the most desirable in light of new conditions.

Whether or not representatives are attempting to exploit policy windows, they seek to put their actions and positions in a favorable light.[43] Their previous positions often constrain their current options. For example, politicians and econo-

[41]James M. Snyder, Jr., "Campaign Contributions as Investments: The U.S. House of Representatives, 1980–1986," *Journal of Political Economy* 98(6) 1990, 1195–227; Robert S. Erikson and Thomas R. Palfrey, "Campaign Spending and Incumbency: An Alternative Simultaneous Equations Approach," *Journal of Politics* 60(2) 1998, 355–73.

[42]In the early 1970s, James Q. Wilson reflected, "Nearly ten years ago I wrote that the billions of dollars the federal government was then preparing to spend on crime control would be wasted, and indeed might even make matters worse if they were merely pumped into the existing criminal justice system. They were, and they have." *Thinking about Crime* (New York: Basic Books, 1975), 234.

[43]William Riker coined the word *heresthetics* to refer to the art of political strategy. It includes such things as agenda control, sophisticated voting, and the introduction of new issues to split dominant majorities. It also encompasses rhetoric, the art of verbal persuasion, for political purposes. William H. Riker, *The Art of Political Manipulation* (New Haven, CT: Yale University Press, 1986), ix, 142–52. The limited attention of the electorate gives representatives ample scope for the use of rhetorical heresthetics. See Iain McLean, *Rational Choice & British Politics: An Analysis of Rhetoric and Manipulation from Peel to Blair* (New York: Oxford University Press, 2001).

mists often view *sunk costs* differently.[44] To an economist, resources committed to a project in the past and no longer available for other uses are "sunk" and irrelevant when deciding to either continue or terminate the project. The politician who advocated the project initially, however, may be loath to terminate it for fear that opponents will point to abandonment as an admission of a mistake. He may even use the earlier expenditures as a justification for continuation: "If we stop now, we will have wasted the millions of dollars that we have already spent." While a statement of this sort is true, and perhaps politically significant, it makes a point that is irrelevant from the social perspective when deciding whether additional resources should be invested in the project.

Precedents often provide opportunities for representatives to gain favorable public reaction to their proposals. By pointing to apparently similar policies adopted in the past, representatives can appeal to people's sense of fairness: "We gave a loan guarantee to firm X last year, isn't it only fair that we do the same for firms Y and Z now?" Without close examination, it may not be clear that the circumstances that made the guarantee to firm X good policy do not hold for firms Y and Z. Policy analysts should anticipate the possibility that any new policies they recommend may serve as precedents for actions in the future. A subsidy, waiver, or other action that, when considered in isolation, appears socially desirable, may not actually be so if it increases the likelihood that representatives will inappropriately adopt similar actions in the future.

Posturing also plays a role in competition among representatives over policy choices. As we saw in Chapter 6, the experimental literatures in psychology and economics suggest that the choices people make in experimental settings tend to be sensitive to how alternatives are presented to them.[45] For example, many people show a sufficiently strong preference for certain over risky alternatives that they appear to be minimizing their maximum possible losses rather than maximizing expected utility. Environmental economists attempting to determine the values people place on wildlife through surveys often encounter unexpectedly large differences from a theoretical perspective between stated values for marginal losses and gains—the amount of money that one would have to give people to just compensate them for a small reduction in the whale population (their willingness to accept) might be an order of magnitude larger than the amount that they would pay (their willingness to pay) to obtain a small increase in the whale population. One source of these differences is probably loss aversion on the part of respondents.[46]

Perceptual biases create opportunities for the effective use of rhetoric in debates over policy choices. In particular, they explain why negative campaigns, which emphasize the costs and risks of opponents' proposals, are so common.[47] To the extent that such rhetorical tactics affect public perceptions of alternative policies, they may result in political choices that do not maximize social value.

[44]See Robert D. Behn, "Policy Analysis and Policy Politics," *Policy Analysis* 7(2) 1981, 199–226.

[45]Amos Tversky and Daniel Kahneman, "The Framing of Decisions and the Rationality of Choice," *Science* 211, 1981, 453–58.

[46]Timothy McDaniels, "Reference Point Bias, Loss Aversion, and Contingent Values for Auto Safety," *Journal of Risk and Uncertainty* 5(2) 1992, 187–200.

[47]William H. Riker, *The Strategy of Rhetoric: Campaigning for the American Constitution* (New Haven, CT: Yale University Press, 1996), 49–74.

Representatives and Analysts

The characteristics of representative government that we have described are summarized in Table 8.2. They suggest that the political system generally does not base public policy on the careful weighing of social costs and social benefits. To the extent that these failures either result from, or are facilitated by, limited information, policy analysts may be able to contribute to better social choices by providing more objective assessments of the likely consequences of proposed policies. To the extent that inattention to social costs and benefits is tied to the self-interest of representatives, analysts may be able to contribute to the social good by helping to craft politically feasible alternatives that are better than those that would otherwise be adopted. In any event, analysts should try to anticipate the limitations of representative government when they propose and evaluate public policies.

Table 8.2 *Sources of Inefficiency in Representative Government: Divergences between Social and Political Accounting*

Nature of Interests in Electorate	Concentrated interests have strong incentive to monitor and lobby—too much weight likely to be given to their costs and benefits.
	Diffuse interests generally have weak incentives to monitor and lobby—too little weight likely to be given to their costs and benefits.
	Organized diffuse interests often overcome collective action problem in monitoring and lobbying—too much weight may be given to their costs and benefits.
	Mobilization of diffuse interests through intermittent media attention—too much weight may be given to their costs and benefits when policy windows open.
General Electoral Incentives of Representatives	Attempt to realize tangible benefits before elections—too much weight to short-run benefits and too little weight to long-run costs.
	Emphasize potential costs of opponents' policy proposals to take advantage of loss aversion—too much weight given to potential costs.
Electoral Incentives of District-Based Representatives	Seek positive net benefits for district—positive net benefits for majority of districts may result in negative net social benefits.
	Seek support from factor suppliers in district—expenditures within district may be viewed as political benefits despite being economic costs.

Problems Inherent in Bureaucratic Supply

Governments often create publicly funded organizations to deal with perceived market failures.[48] Armies, court systems, and various other agencies provide public goods that might be undersupplied by private markets. Other agencies regulate natural monopolies, externalities, and information asymmetries. Like private firms, they use labor and other factor inputs to produce outputs. Unlike private firms, however, they need not pass a market test to survive. Consequently, the extent to which their continued existence contributes to aggregate social welfare depends greatly on the diligence and motivations of the representatives who determine their budgets and oversee their operations. The very nature of public agencies, however, makes monitoring difficult and inefficiency likely.

Agency Loss

The monitoring problem is not unique to public agencies. In fact, a growing "principal-agent" literature attempts to explain why principals (such as stockholders) employ agents (such as managers) to whom they delegate discretion.[49] In other words, why do we have firms consisting of hierarchical relationships between principals and agents rather than sets of contracts that specify exactly the services to be provided and the payments to be made by every participant in the productive process? The answer lies in the fact that contracting involves costs. Rather than continuously re-contracting, it may be less costly in terms of negotiation and performance-monitoring activities to secure services under fairly general labor contracts. When this is the case, we expect to observe production organized by hierarchical firms rather than by collections of independent entrepreneurs.[50]

The principal-agent problem arises because employers and employees do not have exactly the same interests and because it is costly for employers to monitor the

[48]We use the term *public agency* to denote organizations that are staffed by government employees and that obtain the majority of their revenues from public funds rather than the sale of outputs. In Chapter 10 we distinguish public agencies from organizations that are owned by governments but generate the majority of their revenues from sales. Such publicly owned corporations appear to suffer from many of the problems we describe in this section. For a review of publicly owned corporations in North America, see Anthony E. Boardman, Claude Laurin, and Aidan R. Vining, "Privatization in North America," in David Parker and David Sallal, eds., *International Handbook on Privatization* (Northampton, MA: Edward Elgar, 2003), 129–60.

[49]For theoretical overviews, see David E. M. Sappington, "Incentives in Principal-Agent Relationships," *Journal of Economic Perspectives* 5(2) 1991, 45–66; and Jeffrey S. Banks, "The Design of Institutions: An Agency Theory Perspective," in David L. Weimer, ed., *Institutional Design* (Boston: Kluwer Academic, 1995), 17–36. For a review of empirical research, see William S. Hesterly, Julia Liebeskind, and Todd R. Zenger, "Organizational Economics: An Impending Revolution in Organization Theory?" *Academy of Management Review* 15(3) 1990, 402–20.

[50]Much of the underpinning for the theory of economic organization was provided by Ronald H. Coase, "The Nature of the Firm," *Economica* 4(16) 1937, 386–405. For a review of the literature that approaches the organization question from the perspective of the distribution of property rights, see Louis De Alessi, "The Economics of Property Rights: A Review of the Evidence," *Research in Law and Economics* 2(1) 1980, 1–47. See also Armen A. Alchian and Harold Demsetz, "Production, Information Costs, and Economic Organization," *American Economic Review* 62(5) 1972, 777–95; and Oliver F. Williamson, *The Economic Institutions of Capitalism* (New York: Free Press, 1985).

behavior of their employees. For example, although employees generally want their firms to do well, they also enjoy doing things like reading the newspaper on the job. Managers must expend time, effort, and goodwill to keep such shirking under control. More generally, because agents have more information about their own activities than do their principals, agents can pursue their own interests to some extent. The principal faces the task of creating organizational arrangements that minimize the sum of the costs of the undesirable behavior of agents and of the activity undertaken to control it. These costs, which are measured relative to a world with perfect information, are referred to as *agency loss*.

As we have just stressed, public executives generally operate in environments characterized by great asymmetry of information, not just with respect to the general public but with respect to other representatives as well. The executive (agent) is generally in a much better position to know the minimum cost of producing any given level of output than either the public or their representatives (principals) who determine the agency's budget. For example, consider the U.S. Department of Defense. The public tends to pay attention primarily to sensational circumstances—the revelation that some toilet seats were purchased at $600 apiece, for instance. The Office of Management and Budget and the relevant congressional oversight committees look at the entire budget, but usually do so in terms of such billion-dollar elements as entire weapon systems. Limitations in time and expertise preclude extensive review of the ways available resources are actually used within the agency.[51] Even the Secretary of Defense suffers from an informational disadvantage relative to the heads of the many units that constitute the department.

We can see the implications of the asymmetry in information by introducing the concept of the "discretionary budget": the difference between the budget that the agency receives from its sponsor and the minimum cost of producing the output level that will satisfy the sponsor.[52] Executives enjoy the greatest freedom of action when the size of the discretionary budget is both large and unknown to the sponsor. It would be economically efficient for executives to produce output at minimum cost so that they can return the discretionary budget to the sponsor. If they do so, however, they reveal information to the sponsor about the minimum cost—information that the sponsor can use in deciding how much to allocate to the agency in next year's budget. The observation that agencies rarely fail to spend their budgets, sometimes exhorting employees to spend faster as the end of the fiscal year approaches, suggests that few executives view revelation of their discretionary budgets as an attractive management strategy.[53]

[51]See William A. Niskanen, *Bureaucracy and Representative Government* (Chicago: Aldine-Atherton, 1971); Albert Breton and Ronald Wintrobe, "The Equilibrium Size of a Budget-Maximizing Bureau," *Journal of Political Economy* 83(1) 1975, 195–207; and Jonathan Bendor, Serge Taylor, and Ronald Van Gaalen, "Bureaucratic Expertise versus Legislative Authority: A Model of Deception and Monitoring in Budgeting," *American Political Science Review* 79(4) 1985, 1041–60.

[52]The concept of the discretionary budget allows Niskanen to generalize his earlier and seminal study of bureaucracy to objective functions beyond simple budget maximization. William A. Niskanen, "Bureaucrats and Politicians," *Journal of Law and Economics* 18(3) 1975, 617–44. For an excellent discussion of how Niskanen's work relates to earlier organizational theory concepts like "organizational slack," see Bruce Jacobs, *The Political Economy of Organizational Change* (New York: Academic Press, 1981), 18–30.

[53]For a brief discussion of the advantages and disadvantages of not spending allocated funds, see Aaron Wildavsky, *The Politics of the Budgetary Process*, 3rd ed. (Boston: Little, Brown, 1979), 31–32.

If the agency were a private firm with sales revenue as the source of its budget, then the owner-executive would simply keep the discretionary budget as profit.[54] In most countries, however, civil service laws and their enforcement keep public executives from converting discretionary budgets to personal income. Executives not wishing to return their discretionary budgets have an incentive to find personally beneficial ways to use their discretionary budgets within their agencies to make their jobs as managers easier. With extra personnel, executives can tolerate some shirking by employees that would be time-consuming and perhaps unpleasant for the executive to eliminate. The added personnel might also make it easier for executives to respond to unexpected demands faced by their agencies in the future. Increased spending on such things as travel and supplies might contribute to morale and thereby make managing more pleasant. These uses of the discretionary budget are the realization of X-inefficiency of the sort analyzed in Chapter 5.

Indeed, the concept of the discretionary budget implies that different individuals within the agency might have different objectives. Anthony Downs, for example, suggests that some bureaucrats are self-interested, while others combine self-interest and altruistic committment to larger values.[55] Similarly, it has been argued that bureaucratic goals vary by level or by role.[56]

The idea that bureaucrats have considerable budgetary discretion has been criticized on a number of grounds. These criticisms have been fueled by the fact that there is quite mixed evidence on the existence of discretionary budget maximization and especially on aggregate budget-maximizing behavior by bureaucrats.[57] A basic assumption of the discretionary budget approach is that the bureau has at least some degree of monopoly power. But, at the limit, an agency may not be able to exercise any monopoly power if it faces a monopoly politician (purchaser) with strong bargaining power.[58]

Agency loss is inherent in all organizations, whether private or public. Three factors, however, typically make agency loss a relatively more serious problem for public bureaus than for privately owned firms: the difficulty of valuing public outputs (and, therefore, performance), the lack of competition among bureaus, and the inflexibility of civil service systems.

[54]In firms where chief executive officers are not the owners, they usually receive part of their compensation in the form of stock options to increase their incentives to maximize the present value of the firm. The design of such contractual arrangements in the face of information asymmetry is an important principal-agent problem. See, for example, Michael C. Jensen and William H. Meckling, "Theory of the Firm: Managerial Behavior, Agency Costs and Ownership Structure," *Journal of Financial Economics* 3(4) 1976, 305–60; and Eugene F. Fama, "Agency Problems and the Theory of the Firm," *Journal of Political Economy* 88(2) 1980, 288–307.

[55]Anthony Downs, *Inside Bureaucracy* (Boston: Little, Brown, 1967).

[56]On the former, see Patrick Dunleavy, *Democracy, Bureaucracy and Public Choice* (Englewood Cliffs, NJ: Prentice Hall, 1992). On the latter, see Anthony Boardman, Aidan Vining, and Bill Waters III, "Costs and Benefits through Bureaucratic Lenses: Example of a Highway Project," *Journal of Policy Analysis and Management* 12(3) 1993, 532–55.

[57]Andre Blais and Stephane Dion, *The Budget-Maximizing Bureaucrat. Appraisals and Evidence* (Pittsburgh: University of Pittsburgh Press, 1991). For a detailed case study, see Lee S. Friedman, *The Microeconomics of Public Policy Analysis* (Princeton, NJ: Princeton University Press, 2002), 432–40.

[58]See Jose Casas-Pardo and Miguel Puchades-Navarro, "A Critical Comment on Niskanen's Model," *Public Choice* 107(1–2) 2001, 147–67.

The Necessity to Impute the Value of Output

In the absence of market failures, the marginal social value of the output of a competitive firm equals the market price. Customers reveal this marginal value by their willingness to pay through purchases. Most public agencies, however, do not sell their output competitively. In fact, many were undoubtedly created in the first place because markets appeared not to be functioning efficiently. Representatives thus face the problem of having to impute values to such goods as national security, law and order, and health and safety. Even when representatives are sincerely interested in estimating the true social benefits of such goods, analysts often cannot provide convincing methods for doing so.

The absence of reliable benefit measures makes it difficult to determine the optimal sizes of public agencies. For instance, most observers would agree that adding an aircraft-carrier battle group to the U.S. Navy would increase national security by some amount. Would it contribute enough, though, to justify its multi-billion-dollar cost? This is a very difficult question to answer. Some progress toward an answer might be made by trying to assess how the additional battle group furthers various objectives of national security such as keeping the sea-lanes open in time of war and projecting military capability to regions where the United States has vital interests. Analysts might then be able to find alternative force configurations that better achieve the objectives or achieve them equally well at lower cost. In the end, however, these analyses do little to address the appropriateness of such politically established input goals as the "600-ship navy."

Often distributional goals further complicate the valuation problem. Private firms generally need not be concerned about which particular people purchase their products. In contrast, public agencies are often expected to distribute their output in accordance with principles such as horizontal and vertical equity. Crime reduction, for example, might be thought of as the major output of a police department. At the same time, however, the distribution of crime reduction across neighborhoods is also important—most of us would not favor aggregate reductions in crime gained at the expense of abandoning crime control in some neighborhoods altogether. The valuation of outputs when goals are multiple and conflicting requires consensus about how progress with respect to one goal should be traded off against retrogression with respect to another. Such consensus rarely exists.

Effects of Limited Competition on Efficiency

Competition forces private firms to produce output at minimum cost. Firms that do not use resources in the most efficient manner are eventually driven from the market by firms that do. Because public agencies do not face direct competition, they can survive even when they operate inefficiently.

We have already considered the consequences of an absence of competition in our discussion of natural monopolies in Chapter 5. Natural monopolies can secure rents even if they operate above the minimum achievable average cost curve. The resulting *X*-inefficiency represents some combination of the opportunity cost of wasted resources and rent transfers in the form of excess payments to factor inputs. Because competition is often absent, most clearly at the nation-state level, X-inefficiency can also arise in public agencies. At the subnational level, studies show that the presence of greater competition can have some impact in reducing X-inefficiency.[59]

The absence of competition also affects the dynamic efficiency of public agencies.[60] Public agencies typically face inappropriate incentives for innovation. Usually public agencies have weaker incentives to innovate than private firms. The profit motive provides a strong incentive for firms to find new production methods (technological innovations) that will cut costs. When one firm in an industry successfully innovates, others must follow or eventually be driven from the industry. Additionally, firms may be able to capture some of the industry-wide benefits of their innovations through patents. In comparison, public agencies are generally neither driven from existence if they do not innovate nor capable of fully capturing the external benefits if they do.

Incentives for innovation do operate. Some agency heads seek the prestige and career advancement that might result from being perceived as innovators. Agency heads may also seek cost-reducing innovations at times of budgetary retrenchment to try to maintain output levels to their clienteles. These incentives, however, do not operate as consistently as the profit motive and threats to firm survival.

Public agency heads who do wish to innovate face several disadvantages relative to their private sector counterparts. They have no competitors to imitate. While they can sometimes look to agencies with similar functions in other jurisdictions, they face the valuation problem in deciding whether a new technology has actually produced net benefits elsewhere. Unlike managers of firms, they cannot borrow funds from banks to cover start-up costs. Instead, they must seek funds from their budgetary sponsors, who may be unwilling to allocate funds for uncertain research and development projects, especially when difficult-to-value improvements in output quality are the anticipated benefits. Finally, as we discuss below, civil service rules may make it difficult to secure specialized expertise needed to implement innovations.

The absence of competition raises the possibility that public agencies can survive even if they fail to operate efficiently. Whether inefficiency actually results or not depends on the system of incentives that budgetary sponsors actually impose on public executives.[61]

[59]See Philip J. Grossman, Panayiotis Mavros, and Robert W. Wassmer, "Public Sector Technical Inefficiency in Large U.S. Cities," *Journal of Urban Economics* 46(2) 1999, 278–99; and Kathy J. Hayes, Laura Razzolini, and Leola B. Ross, "Bureaucratic Choice and Nonoptimal Provision of Public Goods: Theory and Evidence," *Public Choice* 94(1–2) 1998, 1–20. For an overview, see Lori L. Taylor, "The Evidence on Government Competition," *Federal Reserve Bank of Dallas: Economic and Financial Review*, 2nd quarter, 2000, 2–10.

[60]See David L. Weimer, "Federal Intervention in the Process of Innovation in Local Public Agencies," *Public Policy* 28(1) 1980, 83–116.

[61]As with natural monopoly, contestability may limit inefficiency. If privatization, or even transferring funding to another public agency, is a credible threat, then public executives and workers have an incentive to limit X-inefficiency so as to make these alternatives appear less attractive. See Aidan R. Vining and David L. Weimer, "Government Supply and Government Production Failure: A Framework Based on Contestability," *Journal of Public Policy* 10(1) 1990, 1–22.

Ex Ante Controls: Inflexibility Caused by Civil Service Protections

The problems principals face in evaluating the ex post performance of public agencies lead to the introduction of ex ante controls that directly restrict the discretion of agency heads in how they use the resources of the agency.[62] For example, agency heads often cannot make expenditures outside of narrow budgetary categories. Civil service rules place especially severe restrictions on how agency heads hire, fire, reward, and punish employees.

The modern civil service provides career opportunities within public agencies. Typically, only high-ranking officials serve at the pleasure of the ruling political power. The remaining employees belong to the civil service, which, in theory, determines their employment tenure and salary independent of the political parties. This separation of most government employees from partisan politics provides continuity in expertise when ruling parties change, as well as insulation against attempts to use agencies for partisan purposes.

Continuity and nonpartisanship, however, must be purchased at the expense of a certain amount of flexibility in agency staffing.[63] The same rules that make it difficult to fire employees for political purposes make it difficult to weed out the incompetent and unproductive. Fixed pay schedules, which provide less opportunity for undue political leverage over employees, tend to underreward the most productive and overreward the least productive. As the former leave for higher-paying jobs in the private sector, the agencies are left with a higher proportion of the latter.[64]

A civil service system that makes it difficult to fire employees must also take great care in hiring them if quality is to be maintained. But a slow and complicated hiring system reduces the ability of managers to implement new programs quickly. The problem is particularly severe for the public manager who fears losing allocated slots if they are not filled within the budget period. Rather than waiting for the civil service to give approval for hiring the most appropriate employee, the safer course of action may be simply to take someone less qualified who already is in the civil service system. The more often these sorts of decisions are made for expediency, the more difficult it is for agencies to operate efficiently in the long run.

Finally, consider the commonly heard complaints that bureaucracies are unresponsive. Because agencies usually enjoy monopoly status, consumers usually cannot show their displeasure by selecting another supplier. Of course, elected representatives have an incentive to be responsive to their constituent-consumers. Shielding the civil service from undue political interference, however, reduces the role politicians can play in informing agencies about public wants. Threatening budget cuts and badgering agency executives may not be very effective ways of influencing behavior by the employees at the lowest level of the bureau, who, in most

[62]Fred Thompson and L. R. Jones, "Controllership in the Public Sector," *Journal of Policy Analysis and Management* 5(3) 1986, 547–71.

[63]Ronald N. Johnson and Gary D. Libecap, "Bureaucratic Rules, Supervisor Behavior, and the Effect on Salaries in the Federal Government," *Journal of Law, Economics, and Organization* 5(1) 1989, 53–82.

[64]For a brief discussion of the implications of this process for policy analysis offices, see Hank Jenkins-Smith and David L. Weimer, "Rescuing Policy Analysis from the Civil Service," *Journal of Policy Analysis and Management* 5(1) 1985, 143–47.

cases, actually deal with the public. Again, the necessity for some separation between politics and administration limits the capability of public agencies to meet consumer wants effectively.

Bureaucratic Failure as Market Failure

The traditional market failures discussed in Chapter 5 provide useful concepts for understanding bureaucratic failure. We have already discussed how monitoring costs (due to information asymmetry between principals and agents) and limited competition (often making bureaus "natural" monopolies) lie at the heart of bureaucratic failure. But bureaucratic failure often manifests itself as public good and externality problems. In situations in which bureaucratic supply is a conceptually appropriate generic policy, or where political constraints force its acceptance as the policy choice, applying these market failure concepts may help analysts better diagnose organizational problems and design ways of mitigating them. In other words, analysts can take the organization as the "market" and look for ways that rules and incentives lead to inefficiency.[65]

Let us provide some examples.

"Organizational" Public Goods. As discussed in Chapter 5, a public good is one that is nonrivalrous or nonexcludable. All organizations must confront public goods problems. The ex ante rules generally imposed on public organizations to compensate for lack of competition contribute to agency costs throughout the hierarchy. We can think of organizational public goods problems as a particular manifestation of agency costs.

Consider first organizational pure public goods that arise when something produced by one member of the organization can be consumed by all members. For example, all the members of an organization share in the organization's reputation. But building and maintaining a favorable reputation may be costly to individual members because it requires them to expend extra effort to meet clientele demands quickly, effectively, and "cheerfully." In private organizations managers can use a variety of rewards and punishments to try to induce employees to contribute to favorable reputations. Civil service rules (already described) make the task much more difficult for the public executive. Indeed, the public goods problem—in this case, undersupply of reputation-enhancing effort—can be seen as resulting from the inability of the executive to match individual rewards to organizational contributions. Bestowing honors and awards to employees or organizational units, or socializing new employees to have strong feelings of loyalty to the organization, may substitute to some extent for more direct incentives.

Consider next organizational open-access resources. Typically, all sorts of equipment and supplies used within organizations are available from a central stock to employees. If employees have unlimited access to the stock at a price below marginal cost to the organization, then we should expect overconsumption. In response, private organizations usually institute internal transfer prices so that employees see prices closer to marginal costs. But for such a system to be more than an upper limit on total use, employees must be able to react to relative prices by using

[65]These ideas are more fully developed in Aidan R. Vining and David L. Weimer, "Inefficiency in Public Organizations," *International Public Management Journal* 2(1) 1999, 1–24.

funds saved by less use in one category for some other purpose, such as greater use of some other resource or profit sharing. In public organizations, however, profit sharing is usually prohibited, and strict line-item budgets often prevent the moving of funds across categories that make relative prices meaningful. Consequently, we generally expect allocations of such resources as travel funds and computer time to be fully expended, and often misallocated, because ex ante controls prevent the establishment of effective internal transfer prices.

Ex ante controls also interfere with the organizationally beneficial use of toll goods. Firms can sometimes make themselves more attractive to employees by allowing them the personal use of resources at times when their use is nonrivalrous. For example, firms may be happy to have some employees using computing time for personal projects on weekends when marginal costs are close to zero. In public organizations such use is almost always prohibited, reducing the capability of executives to reward employees.

"Organizational" Externalities. Production externalities result when organizations do not see the full social marginal costs and benefits of their actions. Several factors make individual members of public agencies prone to impose negative externalities on fellow employees or on members of the public.

Public organizations often have the legal right to use resources without paying their full marginal social costs. For example, citizens generally have a duty to serve on juries for nominal compensation. Because courts pay less than market prices for the time of people on jury panels, we expect them to overuse jurors' time relative to other inputs, such as paid employees to facilitate the efficient use of jurors. Other examples include the compliance costs that tax agencies impose on businesses and individuals, the exemption of many national defense activities from environmental regulations, and waiting time that bureaus in monopoly positions inflict on clientele.

Public organizations are often exempt by law from torts by those who have suffered damages. The exemption means that legal responsibility for large external costs can be avoided. Even when the exemption does not apply, the polity generally bears some of the financial responsibility. In the extreme case of a bureau providing an essential service financed entirely out of general revenue, the entire loss is shifted to taxpayers. Further, civil service protections often make it difficult for overseers to impose penalties on those in the bureau responsible for the external costs, so that deterrence against activity leading to future torts may be insufficient.

Analysts and Bureaucracy

Policy analysts who do not anticipate the problems inherent in bureaucratic supply risk giving bad advice about policy alternatives. The risk arises not only in considering such fundamental issues as the scope of government, but also in more instrumental issues like the choices of organizational forms for providing public goods. Of course, analysts who work in bureaucratic settings must be careful to keep their personal and organizational interests in perspective when called upon to give advice about the social good. At the same time, an understanding of the incentives others face in their organizational setting is often essential for designing policy alternatives that can be adopted and successfully implemented.

Problems Inherent in Decentralization

Canada, the United States, and many other democratic countries have highly decentralized and complex systems of government. Separate and independent branches exercise legislative, executive, and judicial authorities. Some powers are exercised by the central government and others are reserved for the governments of local jurisdictions such as provinces, states, counties, cities, and towns. Within the executive branches of these various levels of government, agency executives often enjoy considerable discretion over policy and administration.

Strong normative arguments support several forms of decentralization. Distribution of authority among branches of government provides a system of "checks and balances" that makes abuse of authority by any one official less damaging and more correctable, and reduces the opportunity for tyranny by the majority.[66] Assigning different functions to different levels of government facilitates both the production of public goods at efficient levels and the matching of local public goods to local preferences.[67] Decentralization to lower levels of government is generally desirable because it brings citizens closer to public decisions, usually making it easier for them to exercise "voice" about the quantities and qualities of public good. More important, geographic decentralization is generally desirable because it permits citizens to exercise "exit"—those dissatisfied with the policies of a jurisdiction have the opportunity to "vote with their feet" by moving to jurisdictions offering more preferred policies. Adherence to these normative principles, however, leads to governments that are not only decentralized but also complex.

The highly desirable benefits of decentralization come at a price. Decentralization tends to hinder implementation of policies. It also allows for fiscal externalities to occur in association with the supply of local public goods. Thus, while decentralization is a desirable, if not essential, structural feature of government, it sometimes limits the effectiveness of public policies.

The Implementation Problem

Adopted policies gain force through implementation. The passage of a law, the adoption of an administrative rule, or the issuance of a judicial order establishes policies and specifies the means thought necessary to achieve them. *Implementation* describes the efforts made to execute the means—efforts that do not always achieve the intended goals.

Eugene Bardach provides an excellent metaphor for implementation: the process of assembling and keeping in place all the elements needed for a machine.[68] Of course, just as a machine may not work as intended if its design is flawed, a policy based on an incorrect theory may also produce unintended consequences.

[66]James Madison set out the normative arguments for separation of powers in Numbers 47 to 51 of *The Federalist Papers* (New York: New American Library, 1961), 300–25.

[67]See Wallace Oates, *Fiscal Federalism* (New York: Harcourt Brace Jovanovich, 1972), 3–20.

[68]Eugene Bardach, *The Implementation Game: What Happens after a Bill Becomes Law* (Cambridge, MA: MIT Press, 1977), 36–38.

But an effective design (correct theory) is only a necessary, but not a sufficient, condition for a working machine (effective policy). If necessary parts (essential policy elements) are either not available or unreliable, then the machine (policy) will not work effectively.

The essence of the implementation problem lies in the distribution of necessary elements. The greater the potential for either persons or organizations to withhold necessary contributions, the greater is the possibility of failure. Those who oppose the goals of the policy and those who do not view the goals as sufficiently beneficial to justify their own costs of compliance may purposely withhold contributions.[69] Others may do so simply because their resources and competence are too limited to allow them to comply.

In decentralized political systems, many officials have the capability to withhold contributions. They thus enjoy bargaining power that may enable them to extract things from those who need their contributions. For example, consider the implementation of the U.S. strategic petroleum reserve program, which is intended to reduce the vulnerability of the U.S. economy to petroleum price stocks.[70] Approval from the governor of Louisiana was needed for essential facilities; before he would give it, he secured a number of concessions from the Department of Energy, including a promise that nuclear wastes would not be stored in his state. The Department of Energy was also forced to make concessions to the Environmental Protection Agency, another federal agency, even though the petroleum reserve enjoyed the enthusiastic support of the president and Congress.

The problem of interorganizational cooperation also arises when central governments must rely on lower levels of government for contributions. Even when the central government enjoys nominal authority over units of the lower-level government, it faces the problem of monitoring the compliance of multiple jurisdictions that may have very different local conditions. For example, the central government may have the constitutional authority to order local school districts to end racial segregation. Systematic monitoring of compliance, however, may require an extended period of investigation because of the large number of jurisdictions involved. Further, the reasons for noncompliance may vary greatly across jurisdictions, making it difficult for the central government to employ a uniform enforcement strategy.

Implementation of policies requiring cooperation from lower-level governments becomes even more difficult when the central government does not have the authority to coerce. In order to induce cooperation successfully, the central government must offer sufficient rewards to secure voluntary compliance. When the lower-level jurisdictions are highly diverse, the central government may offer more compensation than necessary to some and not enough to others, especially if either norms of fairness or legal restrictions force the central government to offer the same opportunities to all. For example, a grant program intended to induce local governments to improve their sewage treatment plants might very well fund some plants that would have been constructed by local governments anyway (the problem of *displacement*) and some plants that should not be built from the social per-

[69]Pressman and Wildavsky argue that means rather than ends are more likely to be the actual focus of conflicts during the implementation process. Jeffrey L. Pressman and Aaron Wildavsky, *Implementation* (Berkeley: University of California Press, 1973), 98–102.

[70]David L.Weimer, *The Strategic Petroleum Reserve: Planning, Implementation, and Analysis* (Westport, CT: Greenwood Press. 1982), 39–62.

spective (the problem of *targeting*).[71] If the grants are passed through states, then some of the money intended for local use may be captured by the state agencies handling the grants, the so-called flypaper effect.[72]

Finally, we should note that many of the problems inherent in bureaucratic supply contribute to the implementation problem. The difficulty representatives have in monitoring costs often leaves them uncertain about the size of contributions that agencies actually can and do make, and sometimes gives public executives opportunities to avoid compliance that is in conflict with their own interests. When executives do wish to comply, they may have difficulty motivating subordinates who face attenuated rewards and punishments within the civil service. These problems introduce uncertainties that complicate interorganizational bargaining over compliance.

Fiscal Externalities

Decentralization permits the provision of local public goods to be better matched to local demands. It also gives people some opportunity to choose the bundles of public goods they consume through their selections of jurisdictions. The greater the variation in public goods bundles across jurisdictions, the greater is the opportunity for people to exercise choice by voting with their feet.[73] In the extreme we can imagine migration working to sort people into groups with homogeneous preferences for local public goods. Because the number of jurisdictions is always limited, and because people consider private factors, such as employment, as well as public goods in locational choice, the sorting process is never complete in reality. Furthermore, jurisdictions have an incentive to discourage some migrants and encourage others.[74]

Immigrants who pay above-average tax shares and place below-average demands on public services are particularly desirable because they lower tax shares for everyone else in the jurisdiction without reducing service levels. In other words, they impart a positive fiscal externality to the established residents. In contrast, immigrants who pay below-average tax shares and place above-average demands on public services are particularly undesirable because they impart a negative fiscal externality to established residents. Because tax shares are usually linear functions of property values at the local level, jurisdictions have an incentive to try to exclude those who would have below-average property values. The incentive leads to such

[71]For a discussion of the incentives that can operate to lead to inappropriate responses to inducements, see David L. Weimer, *Improving Prosecution? The Inducement and Implementation of Innovations for Prosecution Management* (Westport, CT: Greenwood Press, 1980), 5–26.

[72]Paul Gary Wykoff, "The Elusive Flypaper Effect," *Journal of Urban Economics* 30(3) 1991, 310–28.

[73]The interpretation of locational choice as a method of demand revelation for local public goods was first suggested by Charles M. Tiebout, "A Pure Theory of Local Expenditures," *Journal of Political Economy* 64(5) 1956, 416–24. A similar but more general model of demand revelation through choice of membership was provided by James M. Buchanan, "An Economic Theory of Clubs," *Economica* 32(125) 1965, 1–14.

[74]See James M. Buchanan and Charles J. Goetz, "Efficiency Limits of Fiscal Mobility: An Assessment of the Tiebout Model," *Journal of Public Economics* 1(1) 1972, 25–42. For an application to international migration, see Norman Carruthers and Aidan R. Vining, "International Migration: An Application of the Urban Location Model," *World Politics* 35(1) 1982, 106–20. For an application to metropolitan government in California, see Gary J. Miller, *Cities by Contract: The Politics of Municipal California* (Cambridge, MA: MIT Press, 1981), 183–89.

local policies as minimum lot sizes, restrictions on multiple-unit dwellings, and restrictive building codes that inflate construction costs. One social cost of these policies is a reduction in housing opportunities for low- and middle-income families.

In competing for wealthier residents, local jurisdictions may inflict fiscal externalities on each other—families with low incomes and high service demands tend to be left behind in poorer jurisdictions. Similarly, local jurisdictions often inflict fiscal externalities on each other in competition for industry. Many local jurisdictions offer incentives such as tax reductions and site preparation to lure firms that will provide jobs to residents. These incentives are probably not large enough to influence the level of investment in the country as a whole. Therefore, the jurisdictions compete for a fixed amount of investment. This is especially true for industries, like professional sports, that tightly limit the number of franchises—realistic estimates of the economic benefits provided by municipal subsidies for sports stadiums, for instance, appear to fall far short of their economic costs.[75]

Local jurisdictions face a "Prisoner's Dilemma" in their decisions concerning incentives for industrial development. Consider two similar jurisdictions courting a single firm. If neither offered tax abatements to attract the firm, then one of the jurisdictions would get the firm and receive full tax revenues. If one jurisdiction thought it would lose the competition, however, it might offer a tax abatement to change the firm's decision. Of course, the other jurisdiction would be in the same situation. The result is likely to be both jurisdictions offering abatements up to a level that would leave them indifferent between having and not having the firm. As a consequence, neither jurisdiction actually gains from the competition.

Analysts in Decentralized Political Systems

Political decentralization poses challenges for policy analysts. By complicating the implementation process, it greatly increases the difficulty analysts face in trying to predict the consequences of alternative policies. Because analysts have clients throughout the political system, they often encounter conflicts between their own conception of what promotes the social good and the personal interests of their clients. Even the most basic question of whose costs and benefits should count often arises. For example, how should an analyst who works for the mayor of a city count costs and benefits that accrue outside of the city? From the social perspective, we would generally regard these spillovers as relevant to the determination of net social benefits; but what would be the consequences of taking them into account when other jurisdictions do not take into account the externalities of their policies? We will address these and other questions that arise as a consequence of political decentralization when we study the art and craft of policy analysis in later chapters.

Conclusion

Governments, like markets, sometimes fail to promote the social good. We cannot always accurately predict the exact consequences of government failures. (Indeterminacy itself is sometimes a predictable consequence!) We must be aware, how-

[75]See Roger G. Noll and Andrew Zimbalist, eds., *Sports, Jobs, and Taxes: The Economic Impact of Sports Teams and Stadiums* (Washington, DC: Brookings Institution Press, 1997).

Table 8.3 *Sources of Government Failure: A Summary*

Problems Inherent in Direct Democracy	**Paradox of Voting** (meaning of mandate ambiguous)
	Preference Intensity and Bundling (minorities bear costs)
Problems Inherent in Representative Government	**Influence of Organized and Mobilized Interests** (inefficiency through rent seeking and rent dissipation)
	Geographic Constituencies (inefficient pork-barrel allocations)
	Electoral Cycles (socially excessive discount rates)
	Posturing to Public Attention (restricted agendas and distorted perception of costs)
Problems Inherent in Bureaucratic Supply	**Agency Loss** (X-inefficiency)
	Difficulty Valuing Output (allocative and X-inefficiency)
	Limited Competition (dynamic inefficiency)
	Ex Ante Rules Including Civil Service Constraints (inefficiency due to inflexibility)
	Bureau Failure as Market Failure (inefficient use of organizational resources)
Problems Inherent in Decentralization	**Diffuse Authority** (implementation problems)
	Fiscal Externalities (inequitable distribution of local public goods)

ever, that they *can* occur if we are to avoid the most ineffective and unwise interferences with private choices. Table 8.3 summarizes the basic sources of government failure. Our next task in developing conceptual foundations for policy analysis is to consider how to frame problems using both market and government failures.

For Discussion

1. The last twenty years have witnessed considerable concern in the United States about the quality of public schooling, particularly in urban areas. Apply the government failure concepts to various aspects of the public education problem.
2. If you are a U.S. citizen, pick some public policy issue at the federal level that you find important. Do you know where your representative stands on the issue? Do you know where your senators stand on the issue?

9

Policy Problems as Market and Government Failure

The Madison Taxicab Policy Analysis Example

The theories of market and government failure developed in the previous chapters provide conceptual resources for framing public policy problems. Market and government failure, however, often do not occur in isolation. When they are both present to some degree, they rarely interact in simple and obvious ways. In specific policy contexts, we may observe market failure, with no government response, or we observe no market failure, but extensive government intervention. Quite often, we observe market failure and government failure together. For instance, the analysis of the regulation of the British Columbia salmon fishery in Chapter 1 demonstrated how various government policies related to fishing, intended to correct an open-access resource market failure, resulted in a net loss to society. In this chapter we again attempt to show with an example how real policy analysis works in bringing together the theories of market and government failure. Specifically, we consider how they can be employed to understand public policy problems.

Before setting out general guidelines for using market and government failure to frame policy problems, we provide another illustration of a short but comprehensive policy analysis of a pervasive issue—taxicab regulation. This example shows how public policies, purportedly intended to correct a number of the market failures, primarily information asymmetry, can become barriers to entry by new firms. The analysis also attempts a brief explanation of why this state of affairs may be difficult to change: the existing taxicab firms are a concentrated interest that have a strong incentive to block changes that might benefit consumers and other entrepreneurs.

Regulation of the Madison Taxi Market

To: Mayor David Cieslewicz
From: Molly Askin and Katie Croake
Date: August 18, 2003
Re: Taxi Regulation in Madison

EXECUTIVE SUMMARY

Taxi fares in Madison are well above the national average for cities of comparable size. The primary reason for these high fares appears to be that taxi regulation in the City of Madison restricts entry to the taxi market. Current regulatory policies reflect the fact that city officials are more responsive to the interests of incumbent taxi companies than to the needs and interests of taxi users and potential entrants to the taxi market. This report concludes that the city should remove the primary entry barrier, "the 24/7 rule."

After a discussion of the rationale for regulating the taxi industry, an analysis of Madison's taxi market structure, its taxi operators, and municipal taxi regulations, the current policy and removal of the 24/7 rule are analyzed based on the goals of equity, efficiency, fiscal effects on the municipal government, and political feasibility. Currently, the city requires that taxi companies serve the entire City of Madison and that each company provide service 24 hours per day and 7 days per week. Annual license fees are set at $1,000 per company and $40 per vehicle plus $25 per driver.

Based on this analysis, we recommend that the city eliminate the 24/7 rule. Although the Common Council has opposed elimination of the 24/7 rule in the past, the threat of an adverse ruling in federal court may provide an opportunity for change. We recommend that you use this opportunity to propose the removal of the 24/7 rule to the Common Council.

INTRODUCTION: TAXI SERVICE IN MADISON

Taxi service in Madison, Wisconsin, is among the most expensive in the nation.[1] Municipal regulations require all cab companies to operate 24 hours a day, 7 days a week to provide citizens with constant taxi availability. In addition, every cab company must provide citywide service. Firms wishing to enter the market must pay $1,000 to apply for an operating license from the Traffic Engineering Division of the Department of Transportation. Traffic Engineering Division staff members review the application and make a recommendation to the Transit and Parking Commission, and the commission then makes a recommendation to the Common Council. The final decision to approve or deny an application is made by majority rule in the Common Council.

Despite changes in taxi regulations in the past few years, the combination of the current regulations creates service requirements that pose severe barriers to

[1]Taxicab and Limousine and Para-Transit Association, "Chart Ranking of Metered Taxicab Fares in U.S. Cities," *Taxi Division Fact Book* (Washington, DC, 2001).

entry into the taxi market. Commentators on Madison's taxi market agree that the city's current regulations create significant barriers to entry.[2] These barriers have led to a situation in which no new taxi companies have entered Madison's market in more than seventeen years. Consequently, competition is weak and cab fares are approximately one-third higher than the national average (see the Appendix).

The 24/7 rule, the citywide service requirement, high licensing fees, and the lengthy license approval process all raise the initial capital investment and operational costs of taxi companies. More technically, they artificially raise the minimum efficient scale of operation—meaning taxi companies face higher costs than they would in an unregulated market. Today, high taxicab fares and the absence of market entry over a long period of time indicate a weak competitive environment. This analysis examines whether alternatives for reducing entry barriers would increase competition and benefit taxi riders in Madison.

THE RATIONALE FOR TAXI REGULATION

Because taxis provide door-to-door service, they are a convenient and valuable means of transport for less mobile members of the population. In large- and medium-sized cities, taxi service can eliminate some residents' need for cars, and taxis make travel within cities more convenient for tourists. Many state and city governments have recognized the benefits of taxi service and have adopted various forms of licensing and more extensive regulations to address perceived market failures. London taxis, for example, have been licensed since 1654.[3] Although there has been surprisingly little policy analysis on taxi regulation in the academic literature over the last decade, a review of the extant literature suggests that the most important market failure relating to taxi service results from the information advantage of taxi operators over consumers regarding safety, reliability of service, and prices.[4]

In thinking about potential market failures, it is useful to divide the market for taxis into two submarkets—the "cruising market," where customers hail a taxi on the street, and the "phone reservation market." When hailing a cruising taxicab, potential users are not in a position to compare cab fares, consider the safety records of drivers, or review the mechanical safety record of the particular cab they are hailing. Instead, consumers accept rides from the first taxi that appears. Because in this situation taxi users have a very limited basis for judging the safety and quality of taxi service (including clear information on pricing), there is asymmetric information in the market.[5] Some analysts have also argued that there may be no competitive market equilibrium in the cruising market. Robert Cairns and Catherine Liston-Heyes argue:

> Modeling this industry as competitive would imply large numbers of firms facing large numbers of customers at a given instance at a given place.... [I]n the

[2]For example, see Peter Carstensen, "Madison's Current and Proposed Taxi Regulation: Bad Public Policy and an Open Invitation to Litigation," Statement for Madison Transit and Parking Commission Meeting on September 12, 2000, http://www.taxi-l.org/madison2.htm; and Sam Staley, "Madison's Taxi Regulations Stifle Innovation, Competition," *Capital Times* August 4, 1999.

[3]Andrew Fisher, "The Licensing of Taxis and Minicabs," *Consumer Policy Review* 7(5) 1997, 158–61.

[4]This rationale is explained in detail in Australian Productivity Commission, *Regulation of the Taxi Industry* (Canberra: Ausinfo, 1999), at pp. 9–12.

[5]Paul Stephen Dempsey, "Taxi Industry Deregulation and Regulation: The Paradox of Market Failure," *Transportation Law Journal* 24 (Summer) 1996, 73–120.

> cruising market, it is usual for a single customer to hail a single taxi as it goes by. In this situation, where search may be costly to the consumer, customers who are risk-averse may prefer a somewhat higher fixed fare to a fare established through bargaining with operators accustomed to sizing up customers with a high variance across conditions.[6]

Some of these asymmetric information problems and equilibrium issues also occur in the telephone reservation market, but most of them are likely to be less severe. They are less severe because customers can select the cab company they wish to patronize (provided it is not a monopoly, legislated or otherwise) and can rely to some extent on their previous experience. It is important to note that, with the increasing dissemination of mobile telephones, the cruising market is likely to become relatively less important.

Another potential market failure that affects telephone reservations is the presence of network externalities. Holding other attributes of service such as quality constant, potential riders are most likely to be interested in a company that has a network of cabs throughout the city. If they require immediate service, then the availability of multiple cabs is likely to reduce waiting times for customers. If they require pickup at a specific time, then multiple cabs increase the probability of a booking at the preferred time. The presence of these economies of scale does not necessarily preclude individual operators from entering the market, because such drivers can join, or form, a cooperative. The formation of cooperatives, however, may significantly reduce the number of competing entities in specific markets, especially in smaller jurisdictions.

TYPES OF TAXICAB REGULATION

Governments around the world have adopted a variety of policies in an effort to correct some of the market failures in the taxi market. To address the information asymmetry in both the hail and phone markets, governments generally require insurance, mandate the posting of price information, inspect vehicles for safety, and conduct driver background checks. Madison, like many other cities, requires insurance, maintains safety standards, and mandates that companies must file fare information with the city, post fares inside each cab, and charge a consistent rate for service. Typically, in cities that require posting, cab companies must notify the city of price changes. In Madison, companies must notify the city of fare changes twenty-eight days before the changes are effective.

In addition to basic safety regulations and price information, many governments employ two other types of regulation: price regulation and entry regulation.

Price Regulation

Many jurisdictions not only regulate the provision of pricing information, they also directly regulate prices. Some cities create a maximum (ceiling) fare and allow companies to set prices below the ceiling, while others set uniform fares for

[6] Robert D. Cairns and Catherine Liston-Heyes, "Competition and Regulation in the Taxi Industry," *Journal of Public Economics* 59(1) 1996, 1–15 at p. 5. They also argue that providers may prefer price regulation in the taxi-rank market because there the bargaining advantage is with customers.

all operators. The clearest potential justification for fare regulation occurs in the cruising market. Potential customers are in a relatively weak bargaining position on price during peak demand periods or at other times when demand is inelastic, such as at night or during bad weather.[7] Consumers can, therefore, be subject to a "hold-up" problem. In practice, the posting of fares without directly regulating them serves to establish consistent fares for taxi service on a per-company basis.

Entry Regulation

Many cities and other units of government directly control the number of cabs that can operate in their jurisdictions. The impact of this control on the number of cabs plying their trade can be most directly observed when jurisdictions change to open entry. Roger Teal and Mary Bergland found that in the United States, "the size of the taxi industry in cities freed of entry control has increased by at least 18 per cent in every case, and usually by one-third or more."[8] The recent evidence from other countries that have deregulated entry is similar. For example, when Ireland dropped entry restrictions in October 2000, the number of cabs rose from around 4,000 to about 12,000 by late 2002.[9] New Zealand also experienced a major increase in both cabs and cab companies after entry deregulation in 1989, as did Sweden in 1991.[10] There is also evidence of many illegal service providers in jurisdictions with entry restrictions (responding to the unmet demand).

The impact of entry restrictions is also evident in the sale price of taxi licenses, or "medallions." The more the licensing process restricts the number of cabs below the number that would operate in an open market, the greater will be the license price if it is transferable.[11] In large cities such as New York, where the number of cabs is severely restricted, medallions can sell for several hundred thousand dollars.

Entry Regulation to Ensure Safety?

A market failure argument related to safety may support market entry regulation. Some analysts argue that unrestricted entry results in a flooded market with intense competition, and taxi operators have little incentive to follow safety regulations (because of asymmetric information and the inability of the city to enforce safety requirements and inspect a large number of taxicabs). Profit rates of operators are dri-

[7]Cairns and Liston-Heyes provide an efficiency rationale for pricing regulation. For more on demand elasticities for taxis, see Bruce Schaller, "Elasticities for Taxicab Fares and Service Availability," *Transportation* 26, 1999, 283–97.

[8]Roger F. Teal and Mary Berglund, "The Impact of Taxicab Deregulation in the USA," *Journal of Transport Economics and Policy* 21(1) 1987, 37–56.

[9]Department of Transport (Eire), "New Regulation Requires Taxis to Issue Printed Fare Receipts to Customers," www.irlgov.ie/tec/press02/Sept1st2002.htm (accessed 4/24/2003).

[10]P. S. Morrison, "Restructuring Effects of Deregulation: The Case of the New Zealand Taxi Industry," *Environment and Planning A* 29(3), 1997, 913–28; Tommy Garling, Thomas Laitila, Agneta Marell, and Kerstin Westin, "A Note on the Short-Term Effects of Deregulation of the Swedish Taxi-Cab Industry," *Journal of Transport Economics and Policy* 29(2), 1995, 209–14.

[11]C. Gaunt, "Information for Regulators: The Case of Taxicab Licence Prices," *International Journal of Transport Economics* 23(3), 1996, 331–45.

ven down as the number of cabs increases.[12] By limiting the number of taxis on the road, it is argued that cities are better able to ensure the safety and reliability of taxicabs and can hold taxi owners responsible for safety violations. The Australian Productivity Commission countered this argument and concluded that it is difficult to justify restrictions on entry in order to address safety concerns because safety can be ensured more effectively through direct regulation and taxi inspections.[13] Assuming a city has (or can generate) sufficient resources to monitor and enforce taxi safety, barriers to entry are likely to be a relatively inefficient method to ensure safe taxi service.

The Distributional Argument for Price and Entry Regulation

Although this analysis has focused on the efficiency-related arguments for government intervention, it is important to note that sometimes a distributional, or equity, argument is put forward. The rationale takes the following form: price regulation (or, more indirectly, entry restrictions) ensures that operators make excess returns during high demand periods and locations that enable them to cross-subsidize and provide service during low demand periods (for example, the middle of the night) and locations (for example, low-density neighborhoods). The need for such cross-subsidy mechanisms, of course, can also be directly linked to meeting service requirements.

WHY GOVERNMENTS REGULATE: THE EFFECTS OF CONCENTRATED INTERESTS

Limiting the number of taxis within a jurisdiction concentrates the interests of taxi operators and leads to a situation in which city officials are less responsive to the interests of taxi riders. D. Wayne Taylor offers reasons why certain forms of taxi regulation might persist even though they are inefficient.[14] The first reason he calls the "producer protection" hypothesis ("producers" can be extended to include suppliers of labor, capital, raw materials, and the like). Producers seek to transfer income from consumers to themselves. This is facilitated in the taxi market by the fact that taxi operators are a small group that receives significant benefits from the status quo, while each individual taxi user bears only a small cost. Because of the relatively high fixed cost of lobbying and other actions to change the current system, individual users have little incentive to engage in such costly activity for the potentially small individual benefits they would receive under a reformed system. Potential providers of taxi services are also a diffuse interest group because of uncertainty regarding who might receive a license (in the policy analysis literature, this is often referred to as the "silent loser" syndrome).

The second reason Taylor calls the "regulator protection" hypothesis. The argument here is that regulation persists when it benefits the regulator, or government generally. These benefits could include political donations, bureaucratic empire

[12]Paul Dempsey found that this has occurred in some U.S. cities after deregulation. Dempsey, "Taxi Industry Deregulation and Regulation."

[13]Australian Productivity Commission, *Regulation of the Taxi Industry*, p. 12.

[14]D. Wayne Taylor, "The Economic Effects of the Direct Regulation of the Taxicab Industry in Metropolitan Toronto," *Logistics and Transportation Review* 25(2), 1989, 169–83.

building, and increased government revenues. The third reason he calls the "social welfare" hypothesis. Relatively invisible industry regulation is often a politically low-cost means of providing cross-subsidies to citizens. Presumably, this would mainly serve the interests of particular political constituencies (hence, it is a variant of the regulator protection hypothesis), but producers would go along if regulatory framework provides them with sufficient expected financial benefits.

It is extremely difficult to determine whether any of these "government failure" hypotheses are true in any particular policy context. It is not in the interest of anyone to advertise, or even admit, such motives. As well, it is plausible that politicians have been convinced by the market failure arguments and distributional concerns described above. (Note that this could be the case even if one believes that the regulatory instruments they have chosen to use are not particularly well designed to meet the posited problems.) There does, however, appear to be some evidence in support of the producer protection hypothesis for Madison.[15] The city has been more responsive to the interests of current operators than to the interests of both consumers and potential entrants to the taxi market.

MADISON'S TAXI MARKET

Madison, Wisconsin, is a city of approximately 200,000 people. It is the state capital and home to a large university with 40,000 students. Madison is surrounded by four lakes, and the center of the city is located on a narrow strip of land between two of the lakes.

Madison's unique geography affects the taxi market because all cross-town traffic must pass through one of three main roads that connect the east and west sides of the city. Because of the geographic separation of people and places, taxi operators generally do not wait at taxi stands (with the exception of stands at the airport, bus station, and downtown hotels), and taxi passengers must generally phone ahead to request taxi service. Consumers usually cannot hail a cab on the streets in Madison.

MADISON'S TAXI COMPANIES

To request service, taxi riders must phone one of three companies offering taxi service in Madison. Taxi drivers must be employed by a cab company to operate a cab in Madison. Each company serves passengers traveling within Dane County, where Madison is located. Each cab company offers a dispatch service to connect riders with taxis. The three cab companies offering service in Madison and Dane County are Union Cab, Madison Taxi, and Badger Cab.

Union Cab has provided service since 1979 and is a worker-owned cooperative. Cab rides with Union Cab are unshared and direct, and fares are calculated by meter. Union Cab is busiest during weekday rush hours, from 7 to 9 A.M. and 4 to 6 P.M. It operates forty cabs during these hours. Weekend nights are its second busiest time, and thirty cabs are on the road during these hours. Union Cab has 120 drivers and owns 58 cars. Based on 2001 data, the company accrues 34.8 percent of revenue in the taxi market. Dividing the total number of passenger trips by

[15]Carstensen, "Madison's Current and Proposed Taxi Regulation."

the total number of trips in the market suggests that Union Cab has a 28.4 percent market share.[16]

Pricing: For one rider, a three-mile trip with a three-minute delay costs $9.75. Union Cab monitors its expenditures by maintaining a yearly budget; however, fuel costs often determine if profits are made in any given year. For the past decade, Union Cab rates have increased about once every two years.[17] Union Cab operated in 2001 at a loss and raised fares in 2002.

Madison Taxi is privately owned and began offering cab service in Madison in 1986. In direct competition with Union Cab, Madison Taxi offers unshared, metered rides. Madison Taxi is busiest on weekend nights, when eighteen to thirty cabs are scheduled. Twelve to fifteen cabs are available on weekdays. In total, seventy-five drivers are employed and fifty cars are owned. Madison Taxi brought in 27.3 percent of revenue in 2001.[18] The same estimation method used for Union Cab indicates that Madison Taxi has a 21.6 percent market share.[19]

Pricing: For one passenger, a three-mile trip with a three-minute delay costs $9.50. Madison Taxi uses cost forecasting when considering fare increases.

Badger Cab was founded as a cooperative business in 1946 but is now privately owned. Badger Cab, unlike Madison Taxi and Union Cab, charges fares based on a zone system and offers shared-ride service. Rates between locations are predetermined, but there is an additional charge of $1.00 per passenger in a group. Badger Cab estimates its rates to be 30 to 50 percent lower than either that of Union Cab or of Madison Taxi, but suggests passengers allow an extra ten to fifteen minutes for trips. Badger Cab experiences the highest demand on weekend nights, when thirty-five cabs are available. On weekdays, the same number of cabs is available. Badger Cab employs 125 drivers and owns 43 cars.[20] Drivers pay a flat fee to the company to lease a cab for their shift, and drivers keep all the money they take in. Based on company revenue (not driver profit), Badger Cab has 37.8 percent of total revenue in the market. Its market share is 49.9 percent.[21]

Pricing: A three-mile trip with one person in the cab costs $5.50, and there is no charge for a delay. Badger Cab's shared, zoned cab service is less expensive than its competitors and a large portion of its riders is relatively low-income. This company has not raised fares in the past two years.[22]

THE POLICY GOALS OF TAXI REGULATION

Madison's Traffic Engineering Department seeks "to provide and manage the environmentally sensitive, safe, efficient, affordable, reliable, and convenient movement of people and goods" around the city.[23] Taxi services are deemed to be an essential part of fulfilling these goals. Because city buses have limited routes and cease operation at midnight, taxis provide transportation services not otherwise

[16]City of Madison Traffic Engineering Department, Paratransit Service Survey, 2001.
[17]Carl Shulte, General Manager, Union Cab. Telephone interview, November 11, 2002.
[18]Rick Vesvacil, General Manager, Madison Taxi. Telephone interview, November 14, 2002.
[19]City of Madison Traffic Engineering Department, Paratransit Service Survey, 2001.
[20]Tom Royston, Operations Manager, Badger Cab. Telephone interview, October 31, 2002.
[21]City of Madison Traffic Engineering Department, Paratransit Service Survey, 2001.
[22]Ibid.
[23]Traffic Engineering, "Mission, Goals, and Objectives." http://www.ci.madison.wi.us/transp/trindex.html (accessed April 2, 2003).

available. When considering changes in taxi regulations, the city should consider the effects on community-wide transportation access.

A successful system of cab regulations should promote efficiency, equity, and favorable (or at least neutral) fiscal effects and be politically feasible. An efficient cab market would mean that there are cabs available to passengers who demand cab service at the lowest possible sustainable fares. Equity has two impact categories: the opportunity for new cab operators to enter the industry and the community-wide availability of service to consumers. All qualified entrepreneurs should have access to the market. It is also important that all areas of a city be served by taxi companies (note that we regard this as an equity rather than an efficiency issue). Fiscal effects are another essential consideration because changes in policy can affect costs and revenues to the city. Finally, political feasibility is likely to play a role in the successful adoption of any new policy. If new regulations impose significant costs on politicians and concentrated interest groups, then they are less likely to be adopted. As demonstrated below, however, the history of taxi regulation in Madison does suggest willingness to change even when it may not be in the interest of incumbent companies.

REGULATION AND DEREGULATION IN MADISON

The City of Madison took its first steps to deregulate the taxi market in 1979 when the Common Council agreed to revoke the city ordinance that restricted the issuance of taxi permits. Before this decision, the city would approve licenses only to sustain a taxi-to-population ratio of 1 taxi per 1,000 residents.[24] Since 1979, the city has not considered the ratio of taxis per capita in licensing decisions (there is currently 1 taxi per 1,400 residents).

The regulation of fares was changed in the early 1980s. The Common Council agreed to remove maximum price limits on fares and changed its policy to require that fares be posted in cabs. Taxi companies and drivers cannot charge an amount different than the posted fare. Since this change in 1982, taxi companies in Madison have been free to determine their own fares. Current ordinances require only that companies notify the city of price changes 28 days before they take effect.

Taxi regulation in Madison did not receive much attention again until the late 1990s, when scholars and researchers argued that Madison's regulations limited entrepreneurship and created unfair barriers to entry.[25] An editorial in an area newspaper illustrated the problems with city regulations that forced new applicants for taxi licenses to prove that their service would address "public convenience and necessity," and also attacked the city's "political [licensing] process." The article proposed that deregulation of Madison's market would encourage entrepreneurship and create jobs for low-income and minority residents.[26] In response to an increased public concern after these articles, the Common Council formed the Ad Hoc Subcommittee on Taxicab Deregulation. This group investigated the efficiency and

[24]U.S. Department of Transportation, *Taxicab Regulation in U.S. Cities*, Vol. 2. Document DOT-I-84-36: 39. October 1983, at p. 39.

[25]Samuel R. Staley, Howard Husock, David J. Bobb, H. Sterling Burnett, Laura Creasy, and Wade Hudson, "Giving a Leg Up to Bootstrap Entrepreneurship: Expanding Economic Opportunity in America's Urban Centers," *Policy Study* 277, February 2001. http://www.rppi.org/ps277.html (accessed January 15, 2003).

[26]Staley, "Madison's Taxi Regulations Stifle Innovation, Competition," p. 9A.

equity of taxi regulations, and concluded that some policies were not meeting city goals and should be revoked.

After the subcommittee's report was released in August 2000, the Common Council decided to make several changes to regulations in Madison. In October 2000, the Common Council eliminated the need to prove public convenience and necessity, lowered the initial licensing fee from $1,500 to $1,000, and eliminated public hearings for new licensing.

CURRENT POLICY IN MADISON (STATUS QUO)

Below are the current taxi regulations and a discussion of how they are related to the goals of Madison's transportation policy:

1. *Fees*: The city requires a $1,000 licensing fee for new cab companies in Madison. In addition, there is a yearly renewal fee of $500. Vehicle permits and driver permits must also be obtained from the city. Costs are $40 per vehicle and $25 per driver. The company fees make it less affordable for individuals and small companies to enter the market. Regulations requiring adequate taxi insurance increase the cost of operating a single cab to over $4,900.
2. *Service*: Several requirements address the equity of service in Madison. All cab companies in Madison are required to provide service 24 hours a day, 7 days a week (24/7 rule), and they must serve all parts of the city. No taxi can refuse service to a customer traveling within the city limits. These regulations are intended to ensure that consumers are able to receive taxi service at any time, and they prohibit drivers and companies from discriminating against certain areas of the city. At the same time, these regulations, especially the 24/7 rule, prevent single drivers from operating single-cab companies in Madison.
3. *Other regulations*: Several other types of regulations also affect the taxi market in Madison. Safety regulations enforced by the city include vehicle inspections and driver background checks. The city retains the right to revoke or suspend driver, vehicle, and operating licenses if any city regulations are violated. To protect against tired drivers, the city prohibits taxi drivers from driving more than twelve hours per shift and requires eight hours of time off between shifts. The city also requires companies to post cab fares and to notify the city of their rates. The city must receive notice of any rate changes 28 days before they take effect.

To enforce current regulations and ensure safety, the city divides the responsibilities of taxi regulation among several departments. The Traffic Engineering Department works on cab inspections, the Police Department approves taxi driver licenses, the City Clerk's Office approves company applications for renewal and handles new company applications, the City Attorney is responsible for any litigation resulting from the taxi industry, and the Department of Weights and Measures checks taxi meters each year. The Common Council must approve any changes to city taxicab regulations. The most recent city survey of costs estimated that $33,000 was spent on regulating the taxi market in 1998.[27]

Although some of Madison's current taxi regulations are necessary in order to ensure safety standards, existing regulations continue to act as obstacles to entrepreneurship. High entry costs limit the participation of low-income residents

[27]William Knobeloch, Operations Analyst, Traffic Engineering Department, city of Madison. Telephone interview, November 7, 2002.

and minorities in the taxi industry. Because the same three companies have offered service in Madison for the past seventeen years, lack of competition in the market probably causes taxi fares to be higher than they would otherwise be and this increased cost negatively affects all taxi customers in the city.

Moreover, the 24/7 rule, citywide service requirement, and the twelve-hour driving limit make it impossible for individuals to operate single-cab companies, and they make it extremely difficult for small companies to enter the market because of the high start-up costs of operating at all times. By limiting the number of operators in the market, these regulations permit fares to be set above competitive levels. It appears that certain regulations, especially the 24/7 and citywide service requirements, are not fulfilling the efficiency or equity policy goals as well as they could. High entry costs block entrepreneurs wishing to enter Madison's taxi market.

In the past few years, taxi regulation has been hotly debated in the Common Council. A single prospective taxicab operator has repeatedly petitioned the council for an operating license, but the council has repeatedly rejected his application for a license. Though current companies are not directly involved in the licensing process, Badger Cab and Madison Taxi lobby conservative council members to protect the economic interests of existing companies by blocking market entry. Employees of Union Cab also lobby the council and are active in Progressive Dane, the liberal caucus in the Common Council. Progressive Dane seeks to block entry to the taxi market to protect current taxi drivers.[28]

In the past year, after receiving a consumer complaint, the City's Attorney's Office began researching the possible conflict between Madison's taxi regulations and federal antitrust laws. Currently, attorneys representing a city resident are preparing an antitrust case against the City of Madison, and it is expected to be filed in federal court within three months.[29] This case calls into question whether city regulations have created a de facto taxi cartel within the city. Wisconsin State Statute 133.01 states, "State regulatory agencies shall regard the public interest as requiring the preservation and promotion of the maximum level of competition in any regulated industry consistent with the other public interest goals established by the legislature." The current regulatory regime within Madison may violate this statute because city regulations fail to promote "the maximum level of competition" as required and the city has made decisions that define public interest goals when the legislature legally must determine such goals. If the Common Council does not change its taxi regulations and the court rules against the city, then the Common Council will be forced to change the current regulations.

ELIMINATING THE 24/7 RULE

As already discussed, the 24/7 rule is the most limiting regulation in the Madison taxi market because, in combination with the twelve-hour driving limit, it creates a minimum number of drivers who must be employed by a company to meet city standards. This eliminates the opportunity for single drivers to operate cabs unless they are employed by one of the three existing companies. This policy alternative

[28]Peter Carstensen, Law Professor, University of Wisconsin-Madison. Interview, December 18, 2002.

[29]Ibid.

would remove the 24/7 rule while maintaining all other regulations. We compare its performance to the status quo in terms of each of the goals that we have posited as appropriate:

Efficiency. With the 24/7 rule eliminated, the number of taxi operators would increase. Niche markets would be created as new operators begin to supply cabs during the hours they prefer, whether rush hour, weekend nights, or mid-days. Because Madison does not regulate fares, it is likely that fares are currently at or above the competitive level so that an increase in the number of taxis operating would result in a decrease in fares.

As discussed earlier, under the current policy few hailing taxis are available, and consumers must phone ahead to request service. An additional efficiency benefit of an increased number of taxi operators would be an increase in the hail market for cabs, which would also allow for decreased waiting time for consumers in those areas where hailed taxis are available. Thus, removal of the 24/7 rule would increase the efficiency of the taxi market.

Equity. The removal of this regulation would directly increase market access because single operators would now be able to offer service. However, start-up costs are still high, so it would still be difficult for low-income residents to establish taxi businesses. Because the city-wide rule is still in effect, new operators would be required to pick up any passengers and could not deny passengers service to any part of Madison. Assuming this regulation is enforced, there would be no change in the geographic availability of dispatch service when compared to the status quo policy. Thus, removal of the 24/7 rule would increase equity-of-access for potential operators in the taxi market, but not substantially change equity-of-access to service by consumers.

Fiscal Effects. License fee revenue would increase as more taxis are granted licenses. Regulatory costs would also increase as the number of cabs increases because more time would have to be allotted for city workers to inspect new cabs and to ensure that new drivers meet city safety regulations. Under the retained fee structure, removal of the 24/7 rule would probably result in somewhat higher net costs to the city.

Political Feasibility. As the demand for taxi service appears to be price inelastic, the larger number of taxis available for hire would likely decrease revenue per cab for the companies already in the market, eliciting opposition from them and their drivers. Consequently, a majority of the Common Council would almost certainly continue to oppose elimination of the 24/7 rule under current circumstances. However, the filing of a suit in federal court may create an opportunity to obtain a majority in the Common Council for the removal of the 24/7 rule, because some members may want to avoid a court-imposed change to the current regulatory structure. Thus, although the status quo currently is highly rated in terms of political feasibility, removal of the 24/7 rule might become politically feasible if a successful court challenge is credible.

Overall, removal of the 24/7 rule better promotes the substantive goals of efficiency and equity than the status quo policy. The status quo enjoys at most a small advantage in terms of fiscal effects, and either a large or small advantage in terms of political feasibility, depending on the Common Council's perception of the probability of success of the likely court challenge to the current regulatory regime.

RECOMMENDATION

Removing the 24/7 rule would greatly reduce the regulatory barrier to entry into the Madison taxi market. Lower barriers would increase the number of cabs operating, which in turn would result in lower fares and reduced waiting times. It is possible that the prospect of a successful legal challenge to the current regulatory system will create an opportunity for gaining a majority of the Common Council in favor of elimination of the 24/7 rule. As the elimination of the 24/7 rule is desirable relative to the status quo in terms of efficiency and equity-of-access to the market, we recommend that, as Mayor, you seize this opportunity to propose this regulatory change to the Common Council, before a potentially costly court case forces a change.

APPENDIX: ARE MADISON'S FARES TOO HIGH?

The *Taxi Division Fact Book* gives comparable taxicab fare data for 252 cities around the United States. Madison's cab fare of $9.50 is 34 percent higher than the national average of $7.08. Of the 252 cities in this study, 75 have populations in a range between 100,000 and 500,000. As the City of Madison has a population of approximately 200,000, but the county population (which cab companies in Madison serve) is closer to 400,000, these cities provide the most appropriate comparison for Madison. Madison's fare is more than $2 above the sample average and 34 percent higher than the comparison group.

To allow for a better comparison, these cities were contacted to determine if and how they regulated taxi fares. Of 75 cities, 11 had company-specific fare regulation (cities approve or reject each operator's fare proposal individually), 49 cities had uniform fare regulations (the city sets a single fare that all operators must follow), and 13 cities did not regulate cab fares. Mean fare information is listed below:

Cities with population 100,000–500,000

Type of regulation		Average Fare	Standard Deviation
Company-specific fare regulation	(n = 11)	$7.11	$1.55
Uniform fare regulation	(n = 49)	$6.98	$1.78
No regulation	(n = 13)	$7.58	$1.20
Total	(n = 73)	$7.10	$1.64

Madison's fares are unregulated, and when compared with other cities with unregulated fares, Madison's fare of $9.50 is 25 percent higher and approximately $2 above the average for cities without fare regulation. Furthermore, when population of the sample is limited to 150,000 to 250,000 (n = 27), Madison's fare is 38 percent higher than the average of $6.89.

The Relationship Between Market and Government Failures

The rationale for the analysis of both market and government failure in almost all policy contexts is predicated on the centrality of efficiency to policy analysis. Figure 9.1 summarizes how to approach the question of efficiency through a consideration of the relative contribution of market and government failure to any observed inefficiency.

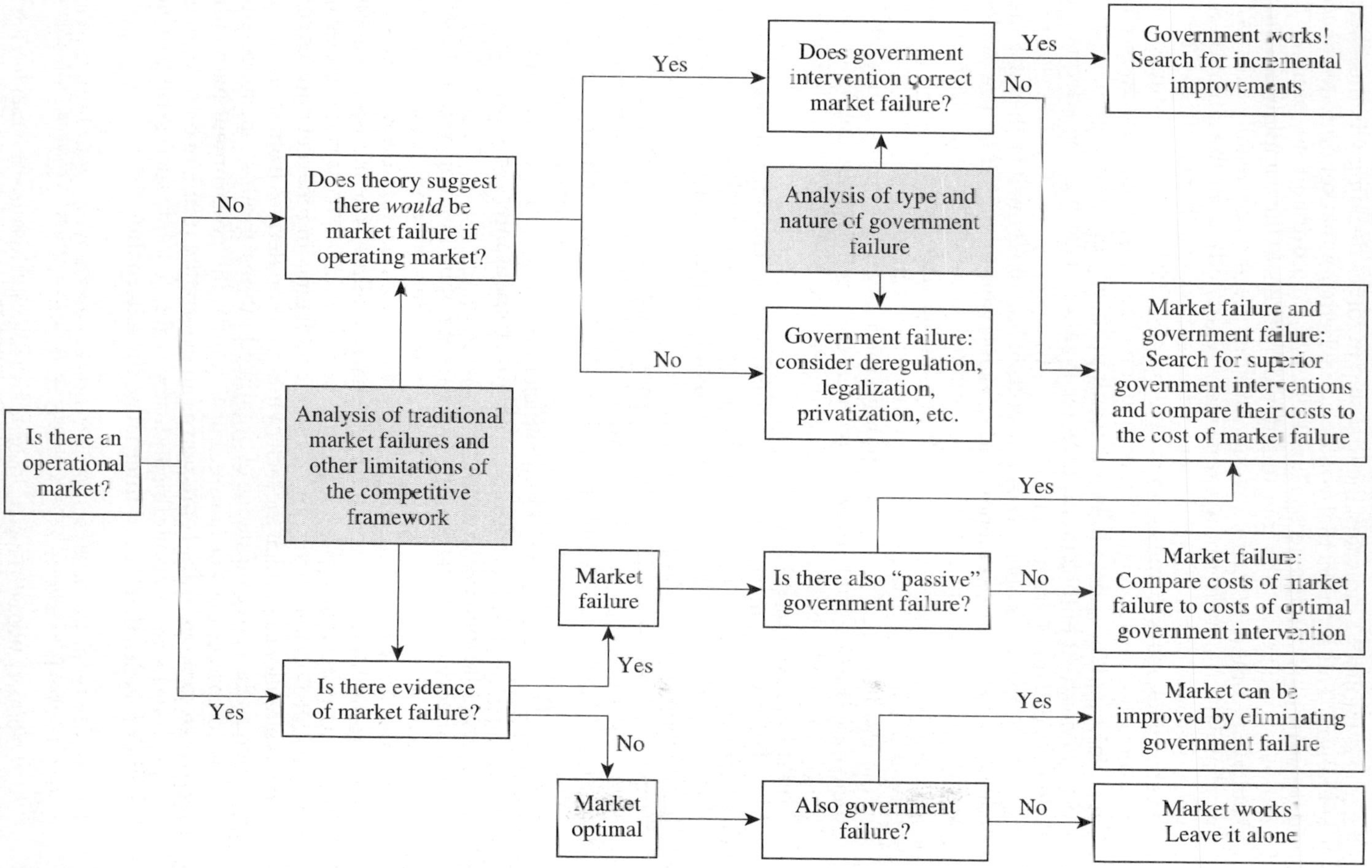

Figure 9.1 A Procedure for Linking Market and Government Failure to Policy Interventions

As Figure 9.1 indicates, the first step involves deciding whether there is market failure. This requires that you decide whether a market operates to accommodate individual preferences. This itself may be a difficult decision, as there is a complex continuum from free, unfettered markets to the complete absence of markets. We recommend the following working rule: if prices legally exist as signaling mechanisms (no matter how extensively regulated), treat the situation as if it involved an *operational market*. Where prices are not legally permitted—for example, if only black market transactions take place—start with the assumption that the market is not operational. Of course, if, on closer inspection, the transaction costs in a black market appear to be the result primarily of enforcement, or the absence of legal contract enforcement, then legalization itself may be adequate to create what we call an operational market.

If the market *is* operational (the bottom half of Figure 9.1), then the analyst next considers the theory, evidence, and facts relevant to market failure. A close familiarity with the content of Chapters 5 and 6 provides a basis for such an investigation. If neither theoretical arguments nor empirical evidence suggests market failure, then it is reasonable to assume that the existing market allocates scarce resources in the most efficient way. Even though there is an operational market, however, there may still be extant government interventions that create inefficiencies; in other words, there may be situations where the elimination of government interventions would improve market allocations.

The housing market illustrates some of these considerations. In any given jurisdiction there may or may not be an operational market. Though rent control regimes in some jurisdictions are so binding that markets cannot function, in most jurisdictions in most Western countries there are operational housing markets. Economists typically conclude that housing markets are not subject to serious market failures,[30] although they do acknowledge the seriousness of distributional problems.[31] But they also frequently argue that housing prices are artificially inflated by inappropriate government interventions such as large-lot zoning. In this case the operational market can be made more efficient by removing the restrictions. If there is no evidence of market failure and no government interventions, then the market works from the perspective of efficiency.

If theory and evidence suggest market failure in an operational market, then there is a prima facie case for government intervention. Furthermore, one could argue that the presence of market failure is evidence that there must also be government failure: the failure to correct market failure. The failure of government to intervene is best described as *passive government failure*. It can include outcomes that are attributable to the government not diagnosing market failures correctly as well as situations in which the lack of intervention derives from more concrete causes, such as the active influence of organized interest groups that successfully block efforts to correct market failure. For example, the government may either fail to recognize some industrial emission as an externality problem or, recognizing it, fail to intervene because a polluting industry is able to lobby successfully to block taxes or other policies that would internalize the externality.

[30]Lawrence B. Smith, "Housing Assistance: A Re-Evaluation," *Canadian Public Policy* 7(3) 1981, 454–63.

[31]Michael J. Wolkoff, "Property Rights to Rent Regulated Apartments: A Path Towards Decontrol," *Journal of Policy Analysis and Management* 9(2) 1990, 260–65.

If a market *is not* operational, then the analyst should work through Figure 9.1, asking if a market could operate efficiently if facilitated by an appropriate framework; in other words, the concept of market failure has relevance here even though no market is currently operational. Notice that, as this is a "what if" question, direct evidence usually does not exist to inform the answer. In these circumstances, the analyst must draw upon the theory of market failure, evidence available from other jurisdictions (for example, other cities, states, and countries), or analogous problems.

If the analysis suggests that a market could operate without serious flaws, then the analyst can assume a priori that significant efficiency losses are associated with the existing government intervention, whether it be an outright prohibition of market activity, a displacement of private supply by public provision, or simply a failure to establish property rights or other rules needed to facilitate private transactions. Thus, if there is no operational market and no evidence of market failure, then one can logically conclude that there is prima facie evidence of government failure. Evidence indicating the cause of government failure, such as interest group rent seeking, further bolsters the case. This line of analysis leads to the examination of such options as deregulation, privatization, and legalization, but keeping in mind that real policy alternatives are rarely as generic as these categories might suggest.

Finally, there may be persuasive evidence that there would be market failure if a market were allowed to operate. The question, then, becomes whether the extant government intervention is efficient. If the intervention is of the appropriate kind, then the conclusion must be that "government works." The only question is whether this intervention can be improved through better implementation or management. Though these incremental questions can have great practical importance, they do not raise the same strategic policy issues. If the intervention appears inappropriate, then the working assumption is that both market failure *and* government failure are relevant. This conclusion indicates the desirability of explaining why the current government intervention fails and to search for alternative interventions that may be superior. In both the salmon fishery example in Chapter 1 and the taxi regulation example in this chapter, market failures require government intervention but the interventions evidence government failure.

If the analyst does not identify a government failure, then she is concluding that the existing government intervention corrects the market failure to the greatest extent practical. In other words, if it is not possible to find changes in current policy that could increase efficiency, don't panic; the current policy is at least efficient. Therefore, the question is whether other values are at stake.

Notice the relative simplicity of the analysis if the only goal is the maximization of aggregate social welfare, that is, efficiency. In the absence of market failure, government intervention will almost always be inefficient. Multiple goals make such a simple analysis inappropriate, however. It may be worth bearing losses in net social surplus (in other words, enduring some inefficiency) in order to achieve other social goals.

Most important, decision makers usually care about distributional considerations, whether in terms of socioeconomic, racial, or other status characteristics. You should explicitly decide whether distributional concerns are relevant to your particular policy problem. While in most situations you will be familiar with client preferences, other times the client may be unaware of the facts and evidence relating to particular target groups. In the latter case, you may wish to argue to the client that greater equity should be a goal. After making a decision on equity, you should consider other goals and constraints. For instance, does the client expect that public revenue would or should be generated? Thus, the absence of market failure is not, in and of itself, determinative. Government intervention that interferes with well-functioning markets is not necessarily undesirable, as other goals may justify the losses in efficiency.

Before considering how to deal with goals, it is worth reiterating that your analysis of market and government (nonmarket) failure plays a vital role in *framing* your subsequent solution analysis. John Brandl, an economist and former member of the Minnesota State Senate, has succinctly summarized the value of such an approach for the decision maker:

> To view an issue as an instance of market (or nonmarket) failure is to transform what was bewildering into a solvable problem. An immense variety of issues can be approached in this fashion. Tuition policy becomes pricing policy, airplane noise is an externality, a utility is a natural monopoly, research yields public goods. This application of economic theory is much more than a translation of English into jargon. In each case the economist has advice to offer aimed at rectifying the wrong implicit in market imperfection. (Currently a new economic theory ... is being created to explain ... nonmarket institutions.)[32]

Conclusion

Theories of market and government failure are valuable for framing public policy problems. Sometimes, as the analysis of Madison's taxicab regulation illustrates, appropriate policy alternatives naturally present themselves. Often, however, a wide range of policy alternatives could reasonably be considered. The next chapter provides a catalogue of generic policy alternatives that can be used as starting points for crafting policy alternatives appropriate for specific contexts.

For Discussion

1. For reasons of brevity and desired pedagogical emphasis, the Madison taxi analysis focused more on the nature of the market and government failure present and less on the development and assessment of policy alternatives. What other policy alternatives might the analysts have considered?
2. Imagine that you are asked to analyze the regulation of taxi service in a city like Madison. Your research, however, leads you to predict that elimination of the 24/7 rule would result in the absence of service during some periods. Design an alternative that permits the entry of single-driver cab companies but also guarantees 'round-the-clock availability of service.

[32]John E. Brandl, "Distilling Frenzy from Academic Scribbling," *Journal of Policy Analysis and Management* 4(3) 1985, 344–53, at p. 348.

10

Correcting Market and Government Failure

Generic Policies

Our discussion of the ways private and collective actions lead to socially unsatisfactory conditions provides a conceptual framework for diagnosing public policy problems. We now turn our attention to policy solutions. We focus on what we call *generic policies*—the various types of actions that government can take to deal with perceived policy problems. They represent a range of general strategies. Because policy problems are usually complex and always contextual, generic policies must be tailored to specific circumstances to produce viable policy alternatives. Nevertheless, familiarity with generic policies encourages a broad perspective that helps the analyst craft specific solutions.

Policy problems rarely have perfect solutions, but some policies are better than others. A primary task of the policy analyst is to identify those policies that have the best prospects for improving social conditions, as measured in terms of specific goals and criteria. To facilitate this task, we indicate the market failures, government failures, or equity concerns that each generic policy most appropriately addresses, as well as the most common limitations and undesirable consequences associated with the use of each. In other words, we provide a checklist for systematically searching for candidate policies.

There are two caveats concerning our discussion of generic policies. First, we do not wish to imply that all policy analyses compare and evaluate across generic policies. Much policy analysis is relatively incremental. For example, you may be asked to compare the efficiency and equity impacts of a variety of voucher schemes. Familiarity with a broad range of generic policies helps you *know* that you are examining relatively incremental alternatives; it may also enable you to exploit opportunities for introducing alternatives that are less incremental. Second, there is an enormous literature on each of the generic policies—too much material for us to review in any depth here. In order to prepare you to examine further the issues relating to each generic policy, however, we provide representative references to relevant literatures.

We group generic policies into five general categories: (1) freeing, facilitating, and simulating markets; (2) using taxes and subsidies to alter incentives; (3) establishing rules; (4) supplying goods through nonmarket mechanisms; and (5) providing insurance and cushions (economic protection). In the following sections we consider specific policies within each of these groups.

Freeing, Facilitating, and Simulating Markets

Market failures, government failures, and distributional concerns underlie perceived policy problems. Markets offer the potential for efficiently allocating goods. Markets, therefore, provide the yardsticks against which to measure the efficiency of government interventions. If we determine that there is no market failure, then we should consider the establishment (or reestablishment) of a market as a candidate solution for our policy problem. Of course, other values besides efficiency may lead us to reject the market solution as a final policy choice. Nevertheless, letting markets work should be among the policies we consider if market failure does not appear inherent in the policy problem.

It is not the case, however, that governments can always create viable markets by simply allowing private transactions. Often, government must play a more affirmative role in enabling the market to function. In other circumstances, although an operational market, per se, cannot be introduced, market outcomes can be simulated with the use of market-like mechanisms.

As shown in Table 10.1, we distinguish three general approaches for taking advantage of private exchange (or market-like exchange between private citizens and governments) in dealing with policy problems: freeing markets, facilitating markets, and simulating markets. The second column of the table notes the perceived problems that the generic policies might appropriately address, while the third column presents the typical limitations and collateral consequences. The second column emphasizes that generic policies are responses to diagnosed market and government failure.

Freeing regulated markets should be considered in those situations in which an effective market can be expected to reemerge with relatively minor efficiency distortions—in other words, where there is no inherent market failure. Keep in mind, however, that there may be large windfall, or distributional, gains or losses once the current government intervention is eliminated. In addition, at this general level of discussion we are not considering the possibility that other goals, such as national security, may be relevant. The absence of markets when there is no inherent market failure suggests either government failure or as yet unaccommodated changes in preferences or technology. Accommodation may require the affirmative establishment of property rights by government, an example of facilitating markets. Finally, even when the complete withdrawal of government may be neither feasible nor desirable, there may be opportunities to simulate markets via various auction processes.

Table 10.1 *Freeing, Facilitating, and Simulating Markets*

Generic Policies	Perceived Problem: Market Failure (MF), Government Failure (GF), Distributional Issue (DI), Limitation of Competitive Framework (LCF)	Typical Limitations and Collateral Consequences
Freeing Markets		
Deregulate	GF: Allocative inefficiency from rent seeking LCF: Technological changes	Distributional effects: windfall losses and gains, bankruptcies
Legalize	LCF: Preference changes	Transitional instability
Privatize	GF: Bureaucratic supply	
Facilitating Markets		
Allocate through property rights	MF: Negative externalities	Distributional effects: windfall gains and losses
Create new marketable goods	MF: Public goods, especially open access	Thin Markets
Simulating Markets		
Auctions	MF: Natural monopolies MF: Public goods DI: Transfer of scarcity rents	Collusion by bidders, opportunistic behavior by winning bidder, political pressure to change rules *ex post*

Freeing Markets

Unfortunately, a wide range of terminology is used to describe the process of freeing markets, the broadest and most popular being deregulation. We distinguish among deregulation, legalization, and privatization.

Deregulation. Clearly, it is difficult to justify government interference with private affairs on efficiency grounds in the absence of evidence of market failure. Historically, in the United States and many other countries, governments have engaged in price, entry, and exit regulation of competitive markets. (We consider these various forms of regulation, themselves generic policy solutions, in a later section.[1]) Economists have been almost uniformly critical of the regulation of competitive industries: "... if economics has any scientifically settled issues, one is surely that price and entry regulation in perfectly competitive industries generates economic inefficiencies."[2]

[1]See W. Kip Viscusi, John M. Vernon, and Joseph E. Harrington, Jr., *Economics of Regulation and Antitrust*, 2nd ed. (Cambridge, MA: MIT Press, 1995), 519–50.

[2]Paul L. Joskow and Roger G. Noll, "Regulation in Theory and Practice: An Overview," in Gary Fromm, ed., *Studies in Public Regulation* (Cambridge, MA: MIT Press, 1981), 4.

We can usually identify various forms of government failure, especially legislators responding to rent seeking by industries, along with sometimes legitimate distributional concerns, as the primary explanations for government regulation of competitive markets. In other cases, changes in technology or patterns of demand may have radically altered the structure of an industry and, therefore, the need for regulation. As we saw in Chapter 5, the natural monopoly characteristics of an industry that justify regulation may erode over time with new technology. Computer advances are facilitating competition in telecommunications, for instance. In such situations, the efficiency rationale for regulation may no longer hold at some point.

Whatever the putative rationale for regulation, deregulation almost inevitably involves complex efficiency and distributional issues. This should not be surprising in light of our discussions of market failure in Chapter 5, related failures in Chapter 6, and rent seeking in Chapter 8. One-shot, complete deregulation may be problematic from an efficiency perspective in those industries in which only a small number of firms operate, either because the legacy of regulation may have entrenched incumbent firms with a competitive advantage or because the industry may be incompletely contestable or otherwise imperfectly competitive. Deregulation in these contexts usually means the removal of formal entry barriers, but continuing regulatory oversight of one kind or another. The Federal Communications Commission, for example, has issued numerous regulations in its implementation of the Telecommunications Act of 1996, which permits competition in local telephone service.[3] Similarly, while many states have now allowed entry into local telephony, they have continued to regulate pricing and service quality.

Martha Derthick and Paul Quirk, among others, have pointed out that efficiency alone is rarely the determinative issue in deregulation. Vested interests—the workers and managers of protected firms, consumers enjoying cross-subsidies, sometimes the regulators themselves—have an incentive to fight to retain the advantages they enjoy under regulation. Consequently, successful deregulation often requires vigorous advocacy that details the failures of the regulatory regime and allays fears about distributional effects.[4] However, in the last decade the potential efficiency gains from deregulation have become widely known; deregulation, or at least more nuanced regulation, is now a worldwide phenomenon.

Evidence from the deregulation of the U.S. trucking, banking, railroad, airline, and other industries suggests that, as expected, large gains in social surplus result.[5] Similar evidence on the deregulation of competitive industries has emerged from other countries. New Zealand, for example, engaged in a broad range of regulatory reforms, including deregulation, during the 1980s and 1990s. While, not surprisingly, some income groups experienced a lowered living standard, the overall process appears to have substantially raised living standards.[6] One note of

[3]Robert G. Harris and C. Jeffrey Kraft, "Meddling Through: Regulating Local Telephone Service in the United States," *Journal of Economic Perspectives* 11(4) 1997, 93–112. For a review of some other countries' experience, see Pablo T. Spiller and Carlo G. Cardilli, "The Frontier of Telecommunications Deregulation: Small Countries Leading the Pack," *Journal of Economic Perspectives* 11(4) 1997, 127–38.

[4]Martha Derthick and Paul Quirk, *The Politics of Deregulation* (Washington, DC: Brookings Institution, 1985). On trucking deregulation, see Dorothy Robyn, *Braking the Special Interests: Trucking Deregulation and the Politics of Regulatory Reform* (Chicago: University of Chicago Press, 1987).

[5]For a review of the evidence, see Clifford Winston, "U.S. Industry Adjustment to Economic Deregulation," *Journal of Economic Perspectives* 12(3) 1998, 89–110.

[6]Atsushi Maki, "Changes in New Zealand Consumer Living Standards during the Period of Deregulation 1984–1996," *The Economic Record* 78(243) 2002, 443–50.

caution: in many countries it is difficult to disentangle the benefits arising from deregulation from those arising from privatization (discussed below), as these often occur simultaneously.[7] There is also evidence of efficiency gains in sectors, such as communications, which may be duopolistic or oligopolistic, rather than competitive, in structure. In sectors with these structural characteristics, however, the changes were rarely simply from regulation to no regulation, even though these changes were often summarized as deregulation. As we discuss later in this chapter (under price regulation), the switch was more often from highly intrusive regulation to more market-oriented, less intrusive regulation. Here, again, it is difficult to disentangle the benefits that arose from less intrusive, more efficient regulation from those arising from privatization.[8]

It is also apparent that deregulation has been traumatic and costly for many of the *stakeholders* (those with a direct, especially economic, interest) in these industries. Remember, however, that firm failure is not synonymous with market failure; the evidence suggests that consumer gains more than offset employee and shareholder losses.[9] Furthermore, keep in mind that industries may be subject to more than one type of regulation, so that deregulation need not apply to all the activities of the industry—pricing, entry, and scheduling within the U.S. airline industry were largely deregulated, while safety, traffic control, and landing rights were not.

Legalization. *Legalization* refers to freeing a market by removing criminal sanctions. There are intermediate steps toward legalization, such as *decriminalization*, through which criminal penalties are replaced by civil penalties, such as fines.[10] Decriminalization reduces the stigma and punishment associated with the activity but does not fully sanction the action as socially acceptable. The impetus for legalization and decriminalization often stems from changing social attitudes (for example, in regard to sexual behavior and drug use). Moves to legalize the market for prostitution, for example, fall into this category.[11] It may also flow from government's desire for new sources of tax revenue and economic development. The rapid legalization of gambling in North America over the last two decades appears

[7]See Graeme Hodge, *Privatization: An International Review of Performance* (Boulder, CO: Westview Press, 2000), esp. 198–202.

[8]For example, see Tae Hoon Oum and Yimin Zhang, "Competition and Allocative Efficiency: The Case of the U.S. Telephone Industry," *Review of Economics and Statistics* 77(1) 1995, 82–96; John S. Ying and Richard T. Shin, "Costly Gains to Breaking Up: LECs and the Baby Bells," *Review of Economics and Statistics* 75(2) 1993, 357–61; Preetum Domah and Michael G. Pollitt, "The Restructuring and Privatisation of Electricity Distribution and Supply Businesses in England and Wales: A Social Cost-Benefit Analysis," *Fiscal Studies* 22(1) 2001, 107–46; Bernardo Bortolotti, Juliet D'Souza, and Marcella Fantini, "Privatization and the Sources of Performance Improvement in the Global Telecommunications Industry," *Telecommunications Policy* 26(5, 6) 2002, 243–68.

[9]For a discussion of these distributional impacts in the U.S. trucking industry, see Thomas Gale Moore, "The Beneficiaries of Trucking Regulation," *Journal of Law and Economics* 21(2) 1978, 327–43. For evidence on Canadian deregulation, see Moshe Kim, "The Beneficiaries of Trucking Regulation, Revisited," *Journal of Law and Economics* 27(1) 1984, 227–41.

[10]For a discussion of the complete continuum in the context of drug policy, see Robert J. MacCoun, Peter Reuter, and Thomas Schelling, "Assessing Alternative Drug Control Regimes," *Journal of Policy Analysis and Management* 15(3) 1996, 330–52.

[11]Barbara Yondorf, "Prostitution as a Legal Activity: The West German Experience," *Policy Analysis* 5(4) 1979, 417–33. For a discussion on cannabis, see R. Solomon, E. Sigle, and P. Erickson, "Legal Considerations in Canadian Cannabis Policy Approaches," *Canadian Public Policy* 9(4) 1983, 419–33.

to fall into this category.[12] Finally, change may flow from the realization that criminalization is an ineffective policy with significant unintended negative consequences.

Privatization. The word *privatization* is used in several different ways: (1) the switch from agency subventions to user fees (discussed below as use of subsidies and taxes to alter incentives); (2) the contracting-out of the provision of a good that was previously produced by a government bureau (discussed below as a method of supplying goods through nonmarket mechanisms); (3) denationalization or desocialization, the selling of state-owned enterprises to the private sector; (4) demonopolization, the process by which the government relaxes or eliminates restrictions that prevent private firms from competing with government bureaus or state-owned enterprises.[13] Only these latter two types of privatization are directly related to the freeing of markets. Even denationalization, however, may not result in free market outcomes if other private firms are restricted from competing against the newly privatized firm. The nature of restrictions placed on competitors was one of the major criticisms of the privatization of British Telecom, for instance.[14]

The presence or absence of market failure is the crucial issue in evaluating privatization. Most state-owned enterprises in the United States have been, and are, in sectors for which there is at least some prima facie evidence of market failure. In many other countries, however, the linkage between market failure and the provision of goods via state-owned enterprises was much more tenuous. However, extensive privatization or partial privatization has now taken place in a wide range of countries, including the United Kingdom, France, Canada, and New Zealand, as well as in the former Soviet bloc countries and many parts of South America. At the urging of the World Bank and International Monetary Fund, many developing countries have also engaged in major privatization programs.

The aggregate evidence on privatization is that there have been major efficiency gains, both in allocative and technical efficiency.[15] Although the evidence from the former Soviet bloc countries has been somewhat mixed, considerable evidence is now beginning to emerge concerning the benefits of privatization.[16] The evidence from developing countries is generally positive.[17]

[12]For example, see Earl Grinols, "Gambling as Social Policy: Enumerating Why Losses Exceed Gains," *Illinois Business Review* 52(1) 1995, 6–12 ; Lennart E. Henriksson, "Hardly a Quick Fix: Casino Gambling in Canada," *Canadian Public Policy* 22, 1996, 116–28; and Charles T. Clotfelter and Philip J. Cook, *Selling Hope: State Lotteries in America* (Cambridge, MA: Harvard University Press, 1989).

[13]See E. S. Savas, *Privatization: The Key to Better Government* (Chatham, NJ: Chatham House, 1987).

[14]See Tom Sharpe, "Privatisation: Regulation and Competition," *Fiscal Studies* 5(1) 1984, 47–60.

[15]See, for example, David Parker and Stephen Martin, "The Impact of UK Privatisation on Labour and Total Factor Productivity," *Scottish Journal of Political Economy* 42(2) 1995, 201–20. For a comprehensive overview of the empirical literature, see William Megginson and John Netter, "From State to Market: A Survey of Empirical Studies on Privatization," *Journal of Economic Literature* 39(2) 2001, 321–89. Specifically on the efficiency evidence relating to North America privatization, see Anthony E. Boardman, Claude Laurin, and Aidan R. Vining, "Privatization in North America," in David Parker and David Sallal, eds., *International Handbook on Privatization* (Northampton, MA: Edward Elgar, 2003), 129–60.

[16]See, for example, Daniel Berkowitz and David N. DeJong, "Policy Reform and Growth in Post-Soviet Russia," *European Economic Review* 47(2) 2003, 337–52; and Alexander Pivovarsky, "Ownership Concentration and Performance in Ukraine's Privatized Enterprises," *IMF Staff Papers* 50(1) 2003, 10–42.

[17]Nargess Boubakari and Jean-Claude Cossett, "The Financial and Operating Performance of Newly Privatized Firms: Evidence from Developing Countries," *Journal of Finance* 53(3) 1998, 1081–110.

Facilitating Markets

If a market has not existed previously, then it does not make sense to talk about freeing it. Rather, the process is one of facilitating the creation of a functioning market by either establishing property rights to existing goods or creating new marketable goods.[18]

Allocating Existing Goods. We saw in Chapter 5 that as demand increases a free good can begin to shift into an inefficient open-access situation (or put another way, a move from the SW1 cell to the SW2 cell in Figure 5.2) if comprehensive and effective property rights are not established. Obviously, it may be very costly and, therefore, unfeasible to allocate property rights effectively if the problem is structural in nature, but it may well be possible if the problem is institutional. For example, while a national government cannot allocate effective property rights to internationally migrating fish, it may be possible to allocate effective property rights to stationary shellfish. The allocation of effective property rights is usually extremely contentious, however. Those who previously enjoyed use at below-efficient prices will undoubtedly oppose any distribution of property rights that makes them worse off. Remember, however, that the Coase theorem suggests that from an ex post efficiency point of view it often does not matter who receives a property right, as long as the right is secure and enforceable. From a distributional point of view, however, it does matter who gets a property right. People may, therefore, expend resources on political activity to gain larger allocations (that is, they engage in rent seeking). From an ex ante efficiency perspective, we want allocation mechanisms that limit the political competition for new property rights. Auctions (which we discuss below) and lottery allocation can sometimes serve this purpose.

The allocation of property rights is highly relevant to water policy in the western United States. State legislatures have increasingly come to recognize the importance of establishing property rights. For example, in 1982 the California legislature stated: "The Legislature hereby finds ... that the growing water needs of the state require the use of water in a more efficient manner and that efficient use of water requires greater certainty in the definition of property rights to the use of water and greater transferability of such rights."[19] Several studies have also documented the legal, administrative, political, social, and distributional barriers to the establishment of such property rights.[20]

The Creation of New Marketable Goods. In certain circumstances it is possible for the government to create new marketable goods. The most common form of these goods is tradable permits, usually for environmental emissions.[21] Tradable

[18]For a discussion of this issue in a somewhat broader context, see Elizabeth S. Rolph, "Government Allocation of Property Rights: Who Gets What?" *Journal of Policy Analysis and Management* 3(1) 1983, 45–61.

[19]California Assembly Bill 3491, Chapter 867, Statutes of 1982.

[20]For a sample of the literature on this topic, see Terry L. Anderson, *Water Rights, Scarce Resource Allocation, Bureaucracy and the Environment* (Cambridge, MA: Ballinger, 1983); and B. Delworth Gardner, "Institutional Impediments to Efficient Water Allocation," *Policy Studies Review* 5(2) 1985, 353–63.

[21]Tradable permits in the environmental context were first extensively analyzed by John Dales, *Pollution, Property Rights, and Prices* (Toronto: University of Toronto Press, 1968). Their use in the implementation of import quotas, such as the U.S. Mandatory Oil Import Control Program, is much older. See Craufurd D. Goodwin, ed., *Energy Policy in Perspective* (Washington, DC: Brookings Institution, 1981), 251–61.

permits have been successfully used in the United States for a number of years to allocate the right to emit sulfur dioxide. The first agreement on global tradable permits was tentatively reached in Kyoto in 1997 for greenhouse gases, such as carbon dioxide. In theory, the allocation of tradable permits for emissions ensures that a specified level of air or water quality is achieved at a minimum total cost (including direct abatement costs and regulatory costs). Under such a tradable permit system, firms maximize profits by restricting emissions to the point where the price of an additional emissions permit equals the marginal cost of abatement. If all firms in the industry can buy and sell permits (including potential entrants), then each firm faces the same price for the last unit of pollution produced, and it would not be possible to find a less costly way of meeting the specified level of total emissions.

Thomas H. Teitenberg, among others, concludes that tradable permits are superior to emissions standards in terms of the informational burden, the speed of compliance, and in making appropriate trade-offs between economic growth and environmental protection.[22] Several critics have emphasized the formidable institutional barriers, such as thin markets (few buyers and sellers), to the practical use of tradable permits.[23] Until 1990, emissions trading had seen limited application, mainly in the Los Angeles air shed. The 1990 Clean Air Act Amendments initiated nationwide trading of permits for emissions of hydrocarbons, nitrogen oxides, particulate matter, sulfur oxides, and carbon monoxide.[24] Commenting on the impact of sulfur dioxide emissions trading, Richard Schmalensee and colleagues are quite positive: "We have learned that large-scale tradable permit programs ... can both guarantee emissions reductions and allow profit-seeking emitters to reduce total compliance costs ... and to adapt reasonably efficiently to surprises produced elsewhere in the economy."[25]

Simulating Markets

In situations in which efficient markets cannot operate, it may be possible for the government to simulate market processes. Edwin Chadwick, in 1859, was the first to argue that, even when competition *within* a market cannot be guaranteed, competition *for* the market may be possible.[26] In other words, the right to provide the good can be sold through an auction.[27]

[22]Thomas H. Teitenberg, *Emissions Trading* (Washington, DC: Resources for the Future, 1985).

[23]Robert W. Hahn and Roger G. Noll, "Implementing Tradable Emission Permits" in LeRoy Graymer and Frederick Thompson, eds., *Reforming Social Regulation* (Beverly Hills, CA: Sage, 1982), 125–58. For a more skeptical view of the feasibility of permits, see W. R. Z. Willey, "Some Caveats on Tradable Emissions Permits," pp. 165–70 in the same volume.

[24]See Vivien Foster and Robert H. Hahn, "Designing More Efficient Markets: Lessons from Los Angeles Smog Control," *Journal of Law and Economics* 38(1) 1995, 19–48.

[25]Richard Schmalensee, Paul L. Joskow, A. Danny Ellerman, Juan P. Montero, and Elizabeth M. Bailey, "An Interim Evaluation of Sulfur Dioxide Emissions Trading," *Journal of Economic Perspectives* 12(3) 1998, 53–68. Relatedly, in the same issue, see Robert N. Stavins, "What Can We Learn from the Grand Policy Experiment? Lessons from SO_2 Allowance Trading," 69–88.

[26]Edwin Chadwick, "Research of Different Principles of Legislation and Administration in Europe of Competition for the Field as Compared with Competition within the Field," *Journal of the Royal Statistical Society*, Series A, 22, 1859, 381–420.

[27]It is beyond our scope to look at the design of auctions. For a starting point in the theoretical and experimental literature, see Vernon L. Smith, Arlington W. Williams, W. Kenneth Bratton, and Michael G. Vannoni, "Competitive Market Institutions: Double Auctions vs. Sealed Bid–Offer Auctions," *American Economic Review* 7(1) 1982, 58–77; and R. Preston McAfee and John McMillan, "Auctions and Bidding," *Journal of Economic Literature* 25(2) 1987, 699–738.

One context where it has been suggested that an auction can appropriately simulate a market is in the provision of goods with natural monopoly characteristics—cable television, for example. It is not efficient to auction the right to operate the natural monopoly to the highest bidder, however. In a competitive auction, the winning bidder would be prepared to pay up to the expected value of the excess returns from operating the natural monopoly. The winning bidder would then be forced to price accordingly, resulting in the allocative inefficiency we described in Chapter 5. Rather, a more efficient approach is to require bidders to submit the lowest retail price at which they will supply customers. While no bidder will be able to offer to supply the good at marginal cost (as you saw in Chapter 5, this would result in negative profits), the winning bidder should be forced to bid close to average cost.

Oliver Williamson has pointed out a potentially serious problem with the use of auctions to allocate the right to operate natural monopolies. The winning bidder has both an incentive and an opportunity to cheat by reducing the quality of the good. To avoid this outcome, specifications for the good must be fully delineated and enforced. Yet it is difficult to foresee all contingencies and costly to monitor contract performance. Williamson has documented how many of these specification, monitoring, and enforcement problems actually arose in the case of a cable television network in Oakland, California.[28] The end result of the interaction between government and franchisee may be quite similar to more traditional regulation.[29]

Auctions are used extensively in the allocation of rights for the exploitation of publicly owned natural resources. As described in Chapter 4, these resources often generate scarcity rents. If the government simply gives away exploitation rights, then the rents accrue to the developers rather than the public (of course, we should not forget that who receives the rent is a distributional, rather than an efficiency, issue). Additionally, we should keep in mind that these rents may partly or completely amount to a lottery prize, where the losing (costly) tickets were held by unsuccessful explorers. In such cases, expropriating the rent will discourage future exploration.

An auction also has advantages relative to setting a fixed price for the allocation of exploitation rights. Most importantly, selling at a fixed price requires the government to estimate the value of the resource, which, in turn, requires estimates of the quality of the resource, future demand and prices for the resource, and future demand and prices for substitutes. An auction, on the other hand, allows the market, and therefore all information available in the market, to determine the appropriate value. The U.S. government, for example, underestimated the value of airwave spectrum it auctioned.[30] Problems can arise, however, if there are few bidders. If the number of bidders is small, then there is danger that they will collude to limit price. Even if the number of bidders is fairly large, they may not generate competing bids if the number of units being offered is large. In general, the unsurprising lesson is that unless auctions are skillfully designed, bidders will behave opportunistically.[31]

[28]Oliver E. Williamson, "Franchise Bidding for Natural Monopolies: In General and with Respect to CAVT," *Bell Journal of Economics* 7(1) 1976, 73–104.

[29]This point has been made by Victor Goldberg, "Regulation and Administered Contracts," *Bell Journal of Economics* 7(1) 1976, 426–48.

[30]R. Preston McAfee and John McMillan, "Analyzing the Airways Auction," *Journal of Economic Perspectives* 10(1) 1996, 159–75.

[31]For the sobering stories of the New Zealand spectrum auction and the Australian TV license auction, see John McMillan, "Selling Spectrum Rights," *Journal of Economic Perspectives* 8(3) 1994, 145–62.

Auctions are proving to be useful allocative tools in situations where governments must allocate *any* scarce resource. The Bank of Zambia, for example, allocates foreign exchange to the highest bidders. When the auctions were first started in 1985, the winning bidders had to pay approximately 50 percent more *kwacha* for each dollar, suggesting that the previous allocation system substantially overvalued the local currency.[32] Auctions are increasingly being used in a wide variety of policy areas;[33] they might be usefully employed in other areas as well.[34]

Using Subsidies and Taxes to Alter Incentives

Freeing, facilitating, or simulating markets may prove inadequate if market failure is endemic or values other than efficiency are important. More interventionist approaches may be necessary. The first major class of these more intrusive policies that we examine consists of subsidies and taxes.[35] They aim to induce behavior rather than command it. Subsidies and taxes, therefore, are market-compatible forms of direct government intervention.

In recent years policy analysts, bureaucrats, and politicians have been engaged in a heated debate on the relative merits of incentives versus other generic policies.[36] While policy analysts, especially those trained in economics, generally view incentives favorably, bureaucrats and politicians have tended to be less enthusiastic. In the United States, this debate has primarily focused on the advantages and disadvantages of incentives relative to direct regulation. This terminology is confusing because incentives also require government intervention and, therefore, involve regulation. To clarify, we distinguish between incentives and rules.[37]

We are primarily concerned with using taxes and subsidies in situations in which the intention is to correct market failures or achieve redistribution. We are not concerned with taxation intended mainly to raise revenue—even though these taxes induce behaviors that are relevant to policy issues. Indeed, taxes designed to raise

[32]"The IMF's Africa Model," *Economist*, October 19, 1985, 78–84.

[33]For example, since the 1950s the U.S. government has leased exploration and development rights to offshore oil and gas through *bonus bidding*—cash bids for the right to a lease with fixed royalty shares for the government (usually 12.5 percent). The Outer Continental Shelf Lands Act Amendments of 1978 opened up the possibility of experimentation with other bidding systems: fixed bonus with variable bidding on the royalty rate, fixed bonus and royalty rate with bidding on exploration expenditures, and fixed bonus and royalty rates with bidding on the rate of profit sharing. Obviously, these systems have different implications for the sharing of risk between the government and the bid winner.

[34]For example, emission permits could be distributed by auction. See Randolph Lyon, "Auctions and Alternative Procedures for Allocating Pollution Rights," *Land Economics* 58(1) 1982, 16–32. Also noxious facilities could be "awarded" to the community with the lowest auction bid; see Howard Kunreuther and Paul R. Kleindoefer, "A Sealed-Bid Auction Mechanism for Siting Noxious Facilities," *American Economic Review* 76(2) 1986, 295–99. However, this is only likely to succeed if the participants perceive that it is fair; see Bruno S. Frey and Felix Oberholzer-Gee, "Fair Siting Procedures: An Empirical Analysis of Their Importance and Characteristics," *Journal of Policy Analysis and Management* 15(3) 1996, 353–76.

[35]The basic case for the greater use of incentives can be found in Charles Schultze, *The Public Use of the Private Interest* (Washington, DC: Brookings Institution, 1977), 1–16.

[36]For an overview of the debate, see Steven E. Rhoads, *The Economist's View of the World: Government, Markets, and Public Policy* (New York: Cambridge University Press, 1985), 39–58.

[37]Many writers use the term *command-and-control* to describe rule-oriented policies. Lester C. Thurow distinguishes between *p-regulations* (incentives) and *q-regulations* (rules) in *Zero-Sum Society* (New York: Basic Books, 1980).

revenue inevitably involve economic inefficiency—for example, by altering the trade-off between leisure and labor or the choice between savings and consumption. (The efficiency loss of the last dollar raised by the tax is called its *marginal excess burden.*) The net effect of these taxes on efficiency depends on how the revenues are ultimately used. If they help correct market failures, then the combined tax and expenditure programs may enhance efficiency. We also are not concerned with efforts to raise incomes generally (this is dealt with below under cushions). Our concern here is with taxes and subsidies that change incentives by altering the *relative* prices of goods. Put simply, we are considering the use of taxes to raise the private costs of things that are too abundant from the social perspective and the use of subsidies to lower the private costs of things that are too scarce from the social perspective.

In general, taxes and subsidies can have one of three possible impacts on efficiency. First, where taxes and subsidies are aimed at correcting for externalities in particular markets, their impact may enhance efficiency. It is usually difficult in practice to estimate accurately either social marginal benefits or social marginal costs—measures needed to gauge the magnitude of positive and negative externalities. If social marginal costs and benefits are inaccurately assessed, then there may be no efficiency gains and, indeed, net efficiency losses may occur. Second, where the objective of taxes and subsidies is purely redistributive, there is inevitably some net deadweight loss. Of course, redistribution may itself enhance efficiency if there is utility interdependence between donors and recipients (remember our discussion of preferences in Chapter 6). Rarely, however, do we have sufficient information to make such assessments confidently. Third, taxes may be used in an attempt to extract scarcity rents such as those that arise in the extraction of natural resources such as oil. In theory, such taxes can be designed to transfer rents without losses in efficiency; in practice, limited information about the magnitude of rents generally leads to market distortions.

In order to make our discussion of taxes and subsidies more concrete, we divide them into four general categories: supply-side taxes, supply-side subsidies, demand-side subsidies, and demand-side taxes. These categories are summarized in Table 10.2. Note that some policies fall into more than one category. For example, a tax on gasoline can be thought of as either a supply-side or a demand-side tax—the effect of the tax does not depend on whether it is collected from refiners or consumers. Nevertheless, we find these categories useful because they emphasize the behavior that is the target of the policy.

Supply-Side Taxes

We consider supply-side taxes under two broad categories: output taxes and tariffs.

Output Taxes. As we saw in Chapter 5, markets with negative externalities overproduce goods from the social perspective (see Figure 5.7). When transaction and coordination costs prevent Coasian market solutions through negotiation among the affected parties, government intervention is desirable to equalize marginal social benefits and costs. Theoretically, the appropriate tax raises price to the level of marginal social cost, thereby internalizing the externality.

Table 10.2 *Using Subsidies and Taxes to Alter Incentives*

Generic Policies	Perceived Problem: Market Failure (MF), Government Failure (GF), Distributional Issue (DI), Limitation of Competitive Framework (LCF)	Typical Limitations and Collateral Consequences
Supply-Side Taxes		
Output taxes	MF: Negative externalities DI: Transfer of scarcity rent	Frequent adjustment of tax levels required
Tariffs	LCF: Market power of foreign exporters	Deadweight losses for consumers; rent seeking by producers
Supply-Side Subsidies		
Matching grants	MF: Positive externalities MF: Public goods DI: Increase equity	Diversion to general revenue by reduction in effort
Tax expenditures (business deductions and credits)	MF: Positive externalities MF: Public goods	Misallocation of resources across industries; horizontal tax inequity
Demand-Side Taxes		
Commodity taxes and user fees	MF: Negative externalities MF: Information asymmetries MF: Public goods, especially open access	Deadweight losses and black markets
Demand-Side Subsidies		
In-kind subsidies	MF: Positive externalities LCF: Utility interdependence DI: Floors on consumption	Restricts consumer choice; bureaucratic supply failure; lumpiness leads to inequitable distribution
Vouchers	MF: Positive externalities DI: Increase equity GF: Bureaucratic supply failure	Informational asymmetries; short-run supply inelasticities; institutional resistance
Tax expenditures (personal deductions and credits)	MF: Positive externalities DI: Increase equity	Poor targeting of subsidies; vertical and horizontal tax inequities

The idea that an appropriate per unit tax can lead to an efficient internalization of a negative externality is usually credited to A. C. Pigou and is often referred to as the *Pigovian tax solution*.[38] The major advantage of using taxes to correct for neg-

[38]Arthur Cecil Pigou, *The Economics of Welfare*, 4th ed. (London: Macmillan, 1946). On taxes and subsidies, see Paul Burrows, "Pigovian Taxes, Polluter Subsidies, Regulation, and the Size of a Polluting Industry," *Canadian Journal of Economics* 12(3) 1979, 494–501.

ative externalities is that they allow firms (or consumers) the choice of how much to reduce production (or consumption) to limit their tax payments. As long as each firm sees the same tax, the industry as a whole reduces the quantity of the externality in the least costly way to society.[39]

The implementation of externality taxes has proven to be extremely difficult, however. The major problem is that the government needs to know the shapes of the social benefit and social cost schedules. The estimation of social benefits from the reduction of a negative externality requires the determination of a damage function—a difficult task because it depends on the impact of a complex set of physical and biological forces upon human beings.[40] Information on the marginal costs of firms, needed to determine the difference between private and social marginal costs, may not be easily determined.[41] Many critics have pointed out that if such information *were* available for private and social marginal costs and benefits, the government would be able to specify the appropriate level of production directly without having to deal with taxes at all.[42] (Of course, polluting firms may have this information, but if they have such private information the calculation of efficient taxes is much more complex.[43]) In practice, these problems, along with objections to firms receiving a "license to pollute," have limited the political acceptability of taxes on pollutants.[44]

While lack of information usually makes it impossible to set optimal tax rates initially, it may be possible to approximate such rates by trial and error after observing how firms respond. Trial-and-error experiments have serious drawbacks, however, including uncertainty, opportunistic behavior by externality producers, and political costs.[45] Trial-and-error experiments may also involve substantial monitoring and administrative costs.

Despite these disadvantages, the potential for efficiency gains should be kept in mind: (1) lower cost—the same outcome can be achieved but at lower cost than with standards; (2) innovation—taxes encourage appropriate innovation as innovation continues until the marginal costs of new technology equal the marginal benefits of forgone taxes; (3) informational requirements—firms face incentives to acquire appropriate information; (4) intrusiveness—government intervention is minimized; (5) administrative complexity—economic incentives require the minimum level of administrative intervention; (6) transaction costs—economic incentives avoid many of the hidden costs of bureaucratic regulation, such as negotiation and lobbying.[46]

[39]For a more detailed discussion, see Allen Kneese and Charles Schultze, *Pollution Prices and Public Policy* (Washington, DC: Brookings Institution, 1975).

[40]See Peter Nemetz and Aidan R. Vining, "The Biology-Policy Interface: Theories of Pathogenesis, Benefit Valuation, and Public Policy Formation," *Policy Sciences* 13(2) 1981, 125–38.

[41]For a discussion of this issue, see Thomas C. Schelling, "Prices as Regulating Instruments," in Thomas Schelling, ed., *Incentives for Environmental Protection* (Cambridge, MA: MIT Press, 1983), 1–40.

[42]For a discussion of the administrative problems associated with the use of effluent charges, see Clifford S. Russell, "What Can We Get from Effluent Charges?" *Policy Analysis* 5(2) 1979, 156–80.

[43]Tracy R. Lewis, "Protecting the Environment When Costs and Benefits Are Privately Known," *RAND Journal of Economics* 27(4) 1996, 819–47.

[44]On the importance of this perception to environmentalists, see Steven Kelman, *What Price Incentives? Economists and the Environment* (Boston: Auburn House, 1981), 44.

[45]Russell has reviewed these issues at length; see Russell, "What Can We Get from Effluent Charges?" pp. 164–78.

[46]Stephen L. Elkin and Brian J. Cook, "The Public Life of Economic Incentives," *Policy Studies Journal* 13(4) 1985, 797–813.

Thus far we have discussed supply-side taxes as a way of dealing with externalities. The use of such taxes in transferring rent has been much more common. As we saw in Chapter 4 (and in the policy analysis in Chapter 1), many natural resources generate scarcity rents. The distribution of these rents is often a contentious public issue. Ideally, any efforts to capture these rents for the public would not disturb the harvesting or extraction decisions of the private owners of the resources. Many different types of taxes have been used to transfer scarcity rents: flat-rate gross royalties (on the physical output), profit taxes, resource rent taxes, corporate income taxes, cash flow taxes, and imputed profit taxes.[47] While in theory some of these mechanisms could capture a portion of the scarcity rent without distorting private decisions about the use of the resource, in practice none is likely to be completely neutral because of limited information.[48] For example, a one-time tax on the value of the resource (a resource rent tax) would not interfere with the owners' decisions about future extraction of the existing resource. It would require, however, accurate information about future extraction costs and market prices. Further, its imposition may reduce the incentive for firms to explore for new stocks of the resource.[49]

A potentially important role for output taxes is the preservation of rent in structural open-access situations. Rent capture through unit taxes is efficiency-enhancing policy if it reduces extraction efforts that are dissipating rents.

Tariffs. A *tariff* is a tax on imported, and occasionally exported, goods. A tariff may either be a percentage of the price (an ad valorem tariff) or a fixed dollar amount per unit, independent of the price. Like any other tax, tariffs generate deadweight losses in the absence of market failures. They usually do so because they impose large consumer surplus losses on domestic consumers, in excess of the gains that accrue to domestic (and foreign) producers. They also impede the development of global comparative advantage and specialization based on increasing returns to scale. A vast array of arguments have been put forward in favor of tariffs and other barriers to trade, including the "infant industry" argument, international monopsony or monopoly conditions, "strategic trade policy" reasons, revenue enhancement, cultural protection, retaliation against another country's tariffs, and domestic redistribution.[50] We review two of the most important arguments here that are often used to justify tariffs.

The commonest argument used to justify tariffs is that there are positive externalities from protecting a fledgling industry (the so-called infant industry argument). The idea is that a domestic industry may have a potential comparative

[47]Lawrence Copithorne, Alan MacFadyen, and Bruce Bell, "Revenue Sharing and the Efficient Valuation of Natural Resources," *Canadian Public Policy* 11, Supplement, 1985, 465–78.

[48]For a discussion of the information requirements of the various approaches to rent extraction, see Thomas Gunton and John Richards, "Political Economy of Resource Policy," in Thomas Gunton and John Richards, eds., *Resource Rents and Public Policy in Western Canada* (Halifax, NS: Institute for Research on Public Policy, 1987), 1–57.

[49]For an illustration of the efficiency effects of taxes on natural resources, see Jerry Blankenship and David L. Weimer, "The Double Inefficiency of the Windfall Profits Tax on Crude Oil," *Energy Journal* 6, Special Tax Issue, 1985, 189–202.

[50]For an overview on market structure and trade policy, see James A. Brander, "Strategic Trade Policy," in Gene Grossman and Ken Rogoff, eds., *Handbook of Industrial Economics* 3 (New York: North-Holland, 1995), 1395–454.

advantage that cannot be initially internalized by specific firms because some factor of production such as skilled labor is mobile. Another version of the argument is that with tariff protection domestic firms will have the opportunity to achieve minimum efficient scale. This argument assumes that investors are myopic, that they are not prepared to accept short-term losses for long-term profits. Many studies have argued, however, that the major impetus in the United States for tariffs, and protectionism in general, has stemmed from redistributional politics and is best understood in terms of government failure. One study from the 1980s estimates that the annual welfare losses caused by U.S. import restraints was approximately $8 billion, with the cost to consumers per job saved ranging from a low of approximately $25,000 to a high of approximately $1 million.[51]

Monopsony effects have also been used to justify import tariffs. If a country accounts for a large share of world demand for some good, then that country may be able to affect world price by restricting its demand through tariffs (or quotas).[52] Depending on the magnitude of the domestic and world elasticities of supply and demand, the imposition of a tariff may actually increase domestic social surplus by depressing the world price.[53] The monopsony effect is one of the rationales advanced in support of a U.S. oil import tariff—although recent supporters from oil-producing states seek the higher prices for domestic oil that would result. A similar kind of argument has been used to justify export tariffs where a country produces enough of a good to potentially have monopoly power in the world market. Individual domestic producers competing against each other will not be able to extract monopoly rents, but a government imposing an export tariff might be able to raise the world price and so extract the rent. (Governments may also use more subtle mechanisms, such as commodity pools and joint marketing organizations for the same purpose.) Export taxes are not very common, because producers prefer export quotas (which allow them to capture the rent). However, national governments sometimes preemptively impose export tariffs when another national government is threatening import tariffs.

Generally, the importance of tariffs is decreasing under global international agreements administered by the General Agreement on Tariffs and Trade (GATT) and its successor, the World Trade Organization (WTO). Under GATT, the tariffs of the industrialized countries have fallen from about 40 percent at the end of World War II to approximately 5 percent in the 1990s.[54] Tariffs have also been reduced under regional trade agreements, such as the North America Free Trade Agreement

[51]Gary Clyde Hufbauer, Diane T. Berliner, and Kimberly Ann Elliott, *Trade Protectionism in the United States* (Washington, DC: Institute for International Economics, 1986).

[52]Quotas and tariffs are usually thought of as being equivalent: the same outcome can be achieved by either imposing a tariff or auctioning import permits. The equivalence breaks down, however, if world supply is not competitive. When suppliers have market power, the imposition of a quota may actually result in an increase in world price. See George Horwich and Bradley Miller, "Oil Import Quotas in the Context of the International Energy Agency Sharing Agreement," in George Horwich and David L. Weimer, eds., *Responding to International Oil Crises* (Washington, DC: American Enterprise Institute, 1988), 134–78.

[53]See Douglas R. Bohi and W. David Montgomery, *Oil Prices Energy Security, and Import Policy* (Washington, DC: Resources for the Future, 1982), 20–29.

[54]Douglas A Irwin, "The GATT in Historical Perspective," *American Economic Review* 85(2) 1995, 323–28.

(NAFTA), although it is not as clear that such regional agreements are efficiency-enhancing.[55] Although tariffs are being reduced, in some cases countries are replacing them with less transparent barriers to trade (collectively, these are known as *nontariff barriers*), such as the imposition of standards that favor domestic producers. The Uruguay Round of GATT tried to reduce these barriers with a process called *tariffication*, which assesses all trade barriers in terms of their equivalent tariffs so that national trade policies could be more easily compared and negotiated.

Supply-Side Subsidies

One way to increase the supply of goods is to give direct subsidies to the suppliers of the goods. The subsidies may be directed at either private firms or lower levels of government. Intergovernmental subsidies are usually referred to as *grants-in-aid*, or simply *grants*.[56] In most respects, subsidies to internalize positive externalities are analytically symmetrical with the taxes on negative externalities described above. Broadly speaking, therefore, if there is a positive externality, an appropriately designed per unit subsidy to the supplier generates an increased supply of the good, reducing the undersupply caused by the externality and thereby increasing social welfare.

Matching Grants. In Figure 10.1 we illustrate how a subsidy might be used by a central government to induce a local government to supply more of some public good X. The vertical axis measures the local government's expenditure on all goods other than X. The horizontal axis measures the quantity of X that the local government provides. For example, X might be remedial classes for children who are slow learners. Given a total budget of B, the local government could spend nothing on X and B on other services, nothing on other services and purchase B/P_X of X, where P_X is the price of X, or any point on the line connecting these extremes. Given this budget line, assume that the local government chooses to provide X_0 units of X. The indifference curve labeled I_0 gives all the combinations of X and expenditures on other goods that would be as equally satisfying to the local government (say, the mayor) as X_0 and b_0 spending on other goods.

Now imagine that the central government offers to pay S dollars to the local government for each unit of X that the local government provides. (We refer to this as a *matching grant* because it matches local expenditures at some fixed percentage. It is also *open-ended* because there is no cap on the total subsidy that the local government can receive.[57]) The effective price that the local government sees for X falls from P_X to $P_X - S$ because of the subsidy. As a result, the budget line for the local

[55]The reason is that although such agreements encourage trade between the trade bloc members (trade creation), they relatively discourage trade with nonmembers (trade diversion). For a discussion of these effects, see Jeffrey A. Frankel, Ernesto Stein, and Shang-Jin Wei, "Regional Trading Agreements: Natural or Supernatural?" *American Economic Review* 86(2) 1996, 52–61. See related articles in the same issue by Ronald J. Wonnacott (62–66), Carlo Perroni and John Whalley (57–61), Jagdish Bhagwati and Arvind Panagariya (82–87), Gary P. Sampson (88–92), and Philip I. Levy and T. N. Srinivasian (93–98).

[56]For a review of this topic, see Wallace Oates, *Fiscal Federalism* (New York: Harcourt Brace Jovanovich, 1972), 65–94; and Martin McGuire, "Notes on Grants-in-Aid and Economic Interactions among Governments," *Canadian Journal of Economics* 6(2) 1973, 207–21.

[57]When a central government gives a local government a fixed amount to be spent on some good, it is providing a *block grant*. The in-kind subsidies we analyze in Figure 10.2 can be thought of as block grants to individuals. If a matching grant is closed-ended, it becomes equivalent to a block grant once the cap is reached.

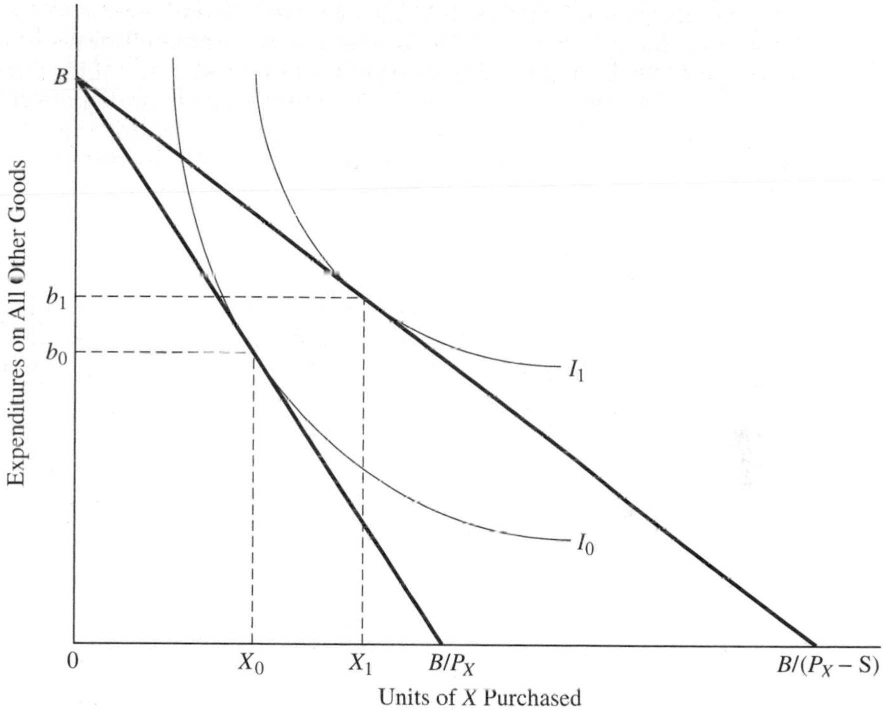

Figure 10.1 The Effect of a Matching Grant on Provision of Targeted Good

government swings to the right. The local government now buys X_1 units of X, reaching the higher level of satisfaction indicated by indifference curve I_1. Note that the local government also spends more on other goods as well—some of the subsidy for X spills over to other goods. In the terminology of grants, part of the categorical grant has been *decategorized*.

To counter this spillover, the subsidy could be given with a *maintenance-of-effort requirement:* only units beyond X_0 would be subsidized. The budget line under the maintenance-of-effort requirement follows the original budget line up to X_0, then rotates to the right so that it becomes parallel to the budget line for the subsidy without maintenance-of-effort requirements. The local government responds by purchasing more units of X and by spending less on other goods than it would in the absence of the subsidy. Thus, maintenance-of-effort provisions may be useful in targeting subsidies so that given expenditure levels have the greatest desired impact. Unfortunately, analysts in central governments do not always have sufficient information to design effective maintenance-of-effort requirements.

Subsidies can also be used to deal with negative externalities.[58] Instead of taxing the good generating the externality, firms can be paid for reducing the level of

[58]Empty containers left in public places are a negative externality of beverage consumption. Many states try to internalize this externality by requiring consumers to pay a deposit at the time of purchase that is refunded when the empty container is returned to the place of purchase. For a discussion of an alternative subsidy program that may offer advantages over deposit systems, see Eugene Bardach, Curtis Gibbs, and Elliott Marseille, "The Buyback Strategy: An Alternative to Container Deposit Legislation," *Resource Recovery and Conservation* 3, 1978, 151–64. See also Peter Bohm, *Deposit-Refund Systems* (Baltimore: Johns Hopkins University Press, 1981).

the externality itself. Such subsidies, however, are vulnerable to opportunistic behavior on the part of suppliers. Unless the government knows how much of the externality the firms would have produced in the absence of the subsidy, the firms have an incentive to increase their externality levels in anticipation of the subsidy. For example, if a firm expects a subsidy program to be implemented for reducing emissions of some pollutant, then it may temporarily increase emissions to qualify for greater levels of future subsidies. It would be particularly difficult to monitor such behavior if the firms simply slowed the introduction of reductions that they were planning to adopt anyway.

Subsidies also have different distributional consequences than taxes. While taxing goods with externalities usually generates revenue, subsidies must be paid for with other taxes. When negative externalities are internalized with taxes, consumers of the taxed good share some of the costs of the reduction in output; when negative externalities are reduced through subsidies, consumers of the good generating the externality generally bear a smaller burden of the reduction. Indeed, sufficiently large subsidies may induce shifts in technology that lead to reductions in the externality without reductions in the supply of the good.

Subsidies can sometimes be effective mechanisms for dealing with market failures other than externalities. For instance, an alternative to auctioning the right to operate a natural monopoly is to induce the natural monopolist to price efficiently (where price equals marginal cost) by providing a subsidy that gives the monopolist a positive rate of return. While this approach has some appeal, it has not been utilized much in practice. One reason is that it requires information about the firm's marginal cost schedule. Another reason is that government has to pay for the subsidy with revenue raised from somewhere.

Skeptics argue that most supply-side subsidies are provided for inappropriate distributional, rather than efficiency-enhancing, reasons. As Gerd Schwartz and Benedict Clements note, "Subsidies are often ineffective (i.e., they fail to benefit their intended target group) and costly (they have adverse real welfare and distributional implications)."[59] While such direct help is relatively uncommon at the federal level in the United States, it is extremely common at the state level and in other countries. Such help may take the form of direct grants, loan forgiveness, loan guarantees, or tax expenditures. Such subsidies are frequently directed at declining, or "sunset," industries. They are likely to be especially inefficient if they simply slow the exit of unprofitable firms from the industry.

Tax Expenditures. Probably the most common form of supply-side subsidy is through *tax expenditures*, such as deductions to taxable income and credits against taxes otherwise owed under corporate income taxes.[60] One can best understand a tax expenditure by realizing that a cash gift and a forgiven debt of the same amount are financially equivalent. If we assume that there is some benchmark tax system (or comprehensive tax base) that treats all taxpayers similarly, no matter what their expenditures, we would have a system without tax expenditures. If one is forgiven a tax payment (that is, debt) from this benchmark rate, it is equivalent to being

[59]"Government Subsidies," *Journal of Economic Surveys* 13(2) 1999, 119–47, at p. 129.

[60]For a general overview, see Stanley S. Surrey and Paul R. McDaniel, *Tax Expenditures* (Cambridge, MA: Harvard University Press, 1985).

given a subsidy of the same amount. We classify tax expenditures as subsidies because they change relative prices by making certain factor inputs less expensive. For example, allowing firms to fully deduct investments in energy-saving equipment from their current tax liabilities makes such equipment appear less expensive than if they had to depreciate it over its useful life as they must for other capital goods. Again, to the extent that the tax expenditures do not correct for market failures, inefficiency results, including interindustry and intraindustry misallocation of resources.

The public good nature of certain aspects of *research and development (R&D)* may also serve as a rationale for subsidies. The U.S. government, as well as the governments of nearly every other industrial nation, directly and indirectly provides R&D assistance. Indeed, these subsidies are viewed as the cornerstones of industrial policies in several countries.

R&D will be supplied at inefficient levels to the extent that they have the characteristics of public goods. First, where exclusion of competitors from access to findings is not possible, private firms tend to underinvest in R&D.[61] The argument is that no market mechanism can ensure that some of the benefits of the innovation will not be captured by other firms. Some of the benefits will accrue to users as consumer surplus, while some of the producer surplus will go to other producers. The typical policy approach has been to subsidize private R&D in an attempt to raise it to socially optimal levels. Second, where exclusion is possible—through patents or effective industrial secrecy—firms tend to restrict the distribution of information concerning their R&D to suboptimal levels. Consequently, private firms may wastefully duplicate research.

There may be underinvestment because of problems hindering the adequate spreading of risks. Research is an inherently risky activity. If the returns on various projects are independent, however, as the number of projects approaches infinity, the risk of a portfolio of projects approaches zero. Research should be conducted to the point where marginal social benefits equal marginal social costs, regardless of the risk of individual projects. Yet, in a competitive market private firms generally cannot hold an adequate portfolio of independent projects.

The underinvestment argument is not without its critics. Gordon McFetridge has questioned whether the public sector is more effective than the private sector in dealing with risk. He argues that risk avoidance is demanded by individuals in the market and that mechanisms, such as venture capital, are available for pooling such risks. He also points out that the stock market itself is a mechanism for risk pooling (of projects) and risk spreading (for individuals).[62]

Do public subsidies actually affect the efficiency and dissemination of R&D? Richard Nelson and a team of researchers conducted case analyses of seven industries: aviation, semiconductors, computers, pharmaceuticals, agriculture, automobiles, and residential construction. Their study attempts to deal with the question of allocative efficiency as well as with distributional and implementation issues. Nelson concludes that government supply or funding of basic and generic research

[61]Kenneth Arrow, "Economic Welfare and Invention," in National Bureau of Economic Research, *Rate and Direction of Inventive Activity* (Princeton, NJ: Princeton University Press, 1962), 609–25.

[62]Gordon McFetridge, *Government Support of Scientific Research and Development: An Economic Analysis* (Toronto: University of Toronto Press, 1977).

incrementally increases the aggregate of R&D activities and encourages the wide dissemination of information. On the other hand, the evidence on applied research and development is less clear.[63]

Demand-Side Subsidies

Demand-side subsidies aim at increasing the consumption of particular goods by reducing their prices to final consumers. There are two basic methods of providing demand-side subsidies: subsidies (vouchers) and personal deductions and credits (tax expenditures). Two major efficiency rationales for intervention, each involving arguments about positive externalities, may be offered for demand-side subsidies. In other cases, demand-side subsidies are justified primarily on redistributional grounds. In many debates about such subsidies, confusion arises because the efficiency and equity dimensions are not clearly distinguished.

The distributional argument alone for such subsidies is weak because the recipients would always be better off (from their own perspective at least) with straight cash transfers (which would not alter relative prices directly). Therefore, the rationale for such transfers is often put in terms of *merit goods*.[64] While the term has no precise and generally accepted meaning, it usually incorporates a mix of redistribution and market failure arguments (most frequently, positive externalities but also information asymmetry and nontraditional market failures such as unacceptable or endogenous preferences).

In-Kind Subsidies. *In-kind grants* subsidize the consumption of specific goods. Strictly speaking, in-kind grants refer to the direct provision of a commodity to consumers. For example, the government may purchase food and distribute it directly to people. In the United States and Canada, however, most in-kind grants are distributed through vouchers that allow recipients to purchase the favored goods in markets. For example, the U.S. food stamp program distributes food vouchers to those meeting income requirements. In contrast, U.S. programs to distribute surplus agricultural products like cheese are literally in-kind grants. So, too, are public housing programs (in contrast to rent and construction subsidies); recipients receive housing services directly from the government at a subsidized rent.

Figure 10.2 illustrates the impact of a lump-sum in-kind subsidy of Z^* units of some good Z. The budget line initially connects the points B and B/P_Z. The introduction of the subsidy shifts the effective budget line to the right by an amount Z^*. If it is possible for the recipient to sell the subsidized good to others, then the effective budget line also includes the dashed line from point *a* to point *b*, which, for purchases of Z greater than Z^*, is identical to the budget line resulting from a cash grant of P_Z times Z^*, where P_Z is the price of the subsidized good. Even if resale were not possible, the subsidy level is sufficiently small so that the

[63]Richard R. Nelson, "Government Support of Technical Progress: Lessons from History," *Journal of Policy Analysis and Management* 2(4) 1983, 499–514. There is a vast literature on the effect of government tax expenditures on R&D; for a sample, see Barry Bozeman and Albert Link, "Public Support for Private R&D: The Case of the Research Tax Credit," *Journal of Policy Analysis and Management* 4(3) 1985, 370–82; Edwin Mansfield and Lorne Switzer, "Effects of Federal Support on Company-Financed R&D: The Case of Energy," *Management Science* 30(5) 1984, 562–71; and by the same authors, "How Effective Are Canada's Direct Tax Incentives for R and D?" *Canadian Public Policy* 11(2) 1985, 241–46.

[64]On merit goods, see J. G. Head, "Public Goods and Public Policy," *Public Finance* 17(3) 1962, 197–220.

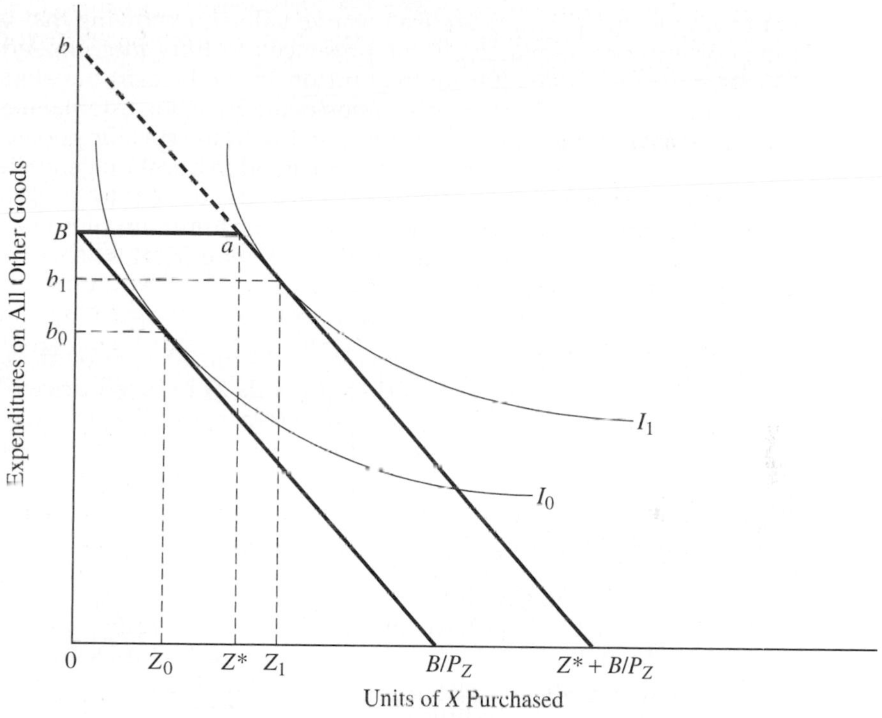

Figure 10.2 The Effect of an In-Kind Subsidy on Consumption

consumption level Z_1 is the same as would result from a cash grant of P_Z times Z^*. Note that in this particular illustration, the equivalence results even though the in-kind subsidy is larger than the presubsidy consumption level. Put bluntly, the disconcerting conclusion under these circumstances is that one may as well give the recipient booze as soup.[65] Giving the grant in-kind rather than as money would only be relevant to consumption if the indifference curve I_1 were tangent to the extension of the budget line (the line segment *ab*).

If the subsidy is sufficiently large, and nonmarketability can be enforced, then consumption of the subsidized good can be increased above the level that would result from an equivalent cash grant. What rationales might justify large in-kind subsidies and the necessary enforcement efforts to prevent trading of the subsidized good in black markets? One putative rationale for effective (large and nontradable) in-kind subsidies based on efficiency grounds is that the givers of the subsidies derive utility from the specific consumption patterns of recipients (another way of describing this interdependence is that taxpayers receive a positive consumption externality from seeing recipients consume particular goods.)[66]

[65] See Mark Pauly, "Efficiency in the Provision of Consumption Subsidies," *Kyklos* 23(Fasc. 1) 1970, 33–57.

[66] See Harold M. Hochman and James D. Rodgers, "Pareto Optimal Redistribution," *American Economic Review* 59(4) 1969, 542–57. The approach has been modified by Russell D. Roberts, "A Positive Model of Private Charity and Public Transfers," *Journal of Political Economy* 92(1) 1984, 136–48. See also Edward M. Gramlich, "Cooperation and Competition in Public Welfare Policies," *Journal of Policy Analysis and Management* 6(3) 1987, 417–31.

For example, many people place a positive value on knowing that the children of the poor are fed adequately. In the presence of utility interdependence, in-kind transfers may be more efficient than unconstrained (cash) transfers. This should not be surprising in light of our discussion of internalizing externalities—cash grants do not internalize the externality associated with the specific goods.

Another possible rationale is that the good in question generates positive externalities. There has been considerable debate about the existence, and magnitude, of positive externalities associated with the consumption of housing, education, health services, and food. Obviously, these are empirical issues that must be considered on a case-by-case basis.

Vouchers. In-kind grants are often administered through *vouchers*, which allow consumers to purchase marketed goods at reduced prices. Typically, the vouchers are distributed to selected consumers at prices lower than their face value. Suppliers who sell the favored goods for vouchers, or consumers with receipts for purchase, then cash the vouchers at their face value. If the vouchers are distributed in fixed quantities at zero price to consumers, then they are conceptually identical to the lump-sum in-kind grants analyzed in Figure 10.2.

The voucher system in the United States with the greatest participation is the food stamp program. Controlled experiments that replaced food stamp coupons with their cash equivalents have found either no statistically significant reductions in total food purchases (Alabama Food Stamp Cash-Out Demonstration) or very small reductions (San Diego Food Stamp Cash-Out Demonstration).[67] Food stamps, therefore, may currently be little more than an administratively costly form of cash transfer that nonetheless seems to enjoy political popularity.

Vouchers are used for subsidizing a wide range of goods such as primary and secondary education, day care, food and nutrition, environmental protection, and housing.[68] If the vouchers provide large subsidies, then they will stimulate market demand for these goods. Because these goods are usually purchased in local markets where short-run supply schedules are upwardly sloping, they may cause the prices of the subsidized goods to rise. For example, if the short-run supply schedule of housing in a locality were perfectly inelastic, the introduction of housing vouchers would simply drive prices up for all renters without increasing supply. These higher prices would, however, eventually induce new construction and the splitting of structures into more rental units. The price effects of housing vouchers were tested through the Housing Allowance Program, a more than $160 million experiment sponsored by the U.S. Department of Housing and Urban Development (HUD).[69] Unfortunately, researchers disagree with the experimental findings that the hous-

[67]David Greenberg and Mark Shroder, *The Digest of Social Experiments*, 2nd ed. (Washington, DC: Urban Institute Press, 1997), 165–70.

[68]For a review of goods and services that are now covered, see Paul Posner, Robert Yetvin, Mark Schneiderman, Christopher Spiro, and Andrea Barnett, "A Survey of Voucher Use: Variations and Common Elements," in C. Eugene Steuerle, Van Doorn Ooms, George Peterson, and Robert D. Reischauer, eds., *Vouchers and the Provision of Public Services* (Washington, DC: Brookings Institution Press/Committee for Economic Development/Urban Institute Press, 2000), 503–39.

[69]For a description, see Harvey S. Rosen, "Housing Behavior and the Experimental Housing Allowance Program: What Have We Learned?" in Jerry A. Hausman and David A. Wise, eds., *Social Experimentation* (Chicago: University of Chicago Press, 1985), 55–75.

ing vouchers did not increase local housing prices.[70] Nevertheless, HUD now assists more households through vouchers or certificates than through the more traditional public housing.[71]

Many analysts have advocated vouchers as devices for increasing access to private primary and secondary education, for increasing parental choice, and for introducing competition among public schools.[72] The primary rationale for public support of education is that individuals do not capture all the benefits of their educations—others benefit from having educated citizens and workers around them. Many see the direct provision of education through public institutions, however, as suffering from the government failures that result from lack of competition. Advocates see vouchers as simultaneously permitting public financing and competitive supply. Critics counter that competitive supply suffers from information asymmetry (parents may not discover the quality of the education their children receive until they have fallen far behind), so that vouchers could not be effectively used without the direct regulation of quality that might reduce the advantages that private schools now enjoy relative to public schools.[73] Yet less intrusive measures, such as regular reporting of average test score gains for students, might deal with the information asymmetry problem without subjecting private schools to excessive regulation.

There are currently a number of experiments with educational vouchers in U.S. cities, including public programs in Milwaukee and Cleveland, and privately funded programs in Dayton, San Antonio, New York, and Washington. Although the results from evaluations of these experiments have been controversial, especially with respect to assessing differences in educational outcomes, it seems to be the case that parents whose children are participating in voucher programs generally have higher levels of satisfaction than they did when their children were in public schools.[74] There is some evidence, although again controversial, that vouchers may be helpful in closing the gap between the educational achievement of African American and white students in urban school districts.[75] Reviewing the overall school voucher evidence, Isabel Sawhill and Shannon Smith conclude: "Whether the education their children receive is of higher quality remains somewhat

[70]For a summary, see Gregory K. Ingram, "Comment," in Hausman and Wise, eds., ibid., pp. 87–94. For an extensive treatment, see Katharine L. Bradbury and Anthony Downs, eds., *Do Housing Allowances Work?* (Washington, DC: Brookings Institution, 1981). However, a recent review concludes that housing vouchers have a negligible impact on U.S. house prices; see George E. Peterson, "Housing Vouchers: The U.S. Experience," in Steuerle et al., *Vouchers and the Provision of Public Services*, 139–75, at p. 165.

[71]Helen F. Ladd and Jens Ludwig, "Federal Housing Assistance, Residential Relocation, and Educational Opportunities: Evidence from Baltimore," *American Economic Review* 87(2) 1997, 272–77.

[72]One of the earliest advocates was Milton Friedman in *Capitalism and Freedom* (Chicago: University of Chicago Press, 1962), 85–107.

[73]Empirical investigations appear to be refuting this assertion: "… we argue that a large enough subset of active and informed parents are driving the demand-side of the market-like setting and pressuring schools to compete. In other words, choice has created the conditions for a corps of marginal consumers to emerge and pressure schools to perform better, a phenomenon that has been documented in many markets for private goods and services." Mark Schneider, Paul Teske, and Melissa Marshall, *Choosing Schools: Consumer Choice and the Quality of American Schools* (Princeton, NJ: Princeton University Press, 2000), pp. 267–68.

[74]John F. Witte, The Market Approach to Education: An Analysis of America's First Voucher Program (Princeton, NJ: Princeton University Press, 2000).

[75]William G. Howell and Paul E. Peterson, *The Education Gap: Vouchers and Urban Schools* (Washington, DC: Brookings Institution, 2002).

unclear, but the results to date are modestly encouraging."[76] In a recent survey of school vouchers globally, Edwin West reports that educational vouchers are being adopted in many countries, including Sweden, Poland, Bangladesh, Chile, and Colombia, usually in the form of a "funds-follow-the-children" model in which governments fund schools of choice in proportion to enrollment.[77] The mere existence of competition may create stronger incentives for public schools to improve.[78]

Tax Expenditures. *Tax expenditures* are commonly used to stimulate individual demand for housing, education, medical care, and child care. Other tax expenditures stimulate demand for goods produced by certain kinds of nonprofit agencies, such as charitable, cultural, or political organizations. Tax expenditures have their effect by lowering the after-tax price of the preferred good. For example, being able to deduct the interest payments on mortgages from taxable income makes homeownership less expensive. In some cases, they may be intended to stimulate aggregate demand during recessions or periods of slow growth. For instance, depreciations rules under individual and corporate taxes may be temporarily reduced in an effort to speed up capital investment.

Tax expenditures are an important source of subsidy in the United States. For example, the forgone revenue from allowing mortgage interest and property tax deductions in 1981 was estimated to be $35 billion; the exclusion of social security and other benefits that could be regarded as income may be in excess of $50 billion in forgone taxes.[79] Additionally, the taxation of imputed income (an increase in wealth that does not directly accrue as a money payment) is not normally treated as a tax expenditure. For example, federal estimates of tax expenditures do not include the imputed income on equity in owner-occupied housing.[80] Most Western countries have come to recognize the importance of the magnitude of tax expenditures. The United States, Germany, Great Britain, Japan, and Canada all now require the annual presentation of tax expenditure accounts.[81]

Critics argue that tax expenditures are less desirable than direct subsidies, for two reasons. First, because tax expenditures emerge from relatively hidden debates on the tax code, their role as subsidies is not rigorously analyzed. Consequently, various forms of government failure like rent seeking are encouraged. Second, tax expenditures are notorious for their inequitable distributional consequences. Higher-income individuals are much more able to take advantage of tax expendi-

[76]Isabell V. Sawhill and Shannon L. Smith, "Vouchers for Elementary and Secondary Education," in Steuerle et al., *Vouchers and the Provision of Public Services*, 251–91, at p. 278.

[77]Edwin G. West, "Education Vouchers in Principle and Practice: A Survey," *The World Bank Research Observer* 12(1) 1997, 83–103.

[78]See Caroline Minter Hoxby, "The Effects of Private School Vouchers on Schools and Students," in Helen F. Ladd, ed., *Holding Schools Accountable* (Washington, DC: Brookings Institution, 1996), 177–208; and Lori L. Taylor, "The Evidence on Government Competition," *Federal Reserve Bank of Dallas—Economic and Financial Review* 2nd quarter, 2000, 2–10, specifically on education pp. 4–5.

[79]Theodore J. Eismeier, "The Power Not to Tax: The Search for Effective Controls," *Journal of Policy Analysis and Management* 1(3) 1982, 333–45.

[80]See Michael Krashinksy, "Limitations on the Use of Tax Expenditures: Some Comments," *Canadian Public Policy* 8(4) 1982, 615–20.

[81]Kevin McLoughlin and Stuart B. Proudfoot, "Given by Not Taking: A Primer on Tax Expenditures, 1971–75," *Policy Analysis* 7(2) 1981, 328–37. For discussion of the tax expenditure reporting system in California, see Karen M. Benker, "Tax Expenditure Reporting: Closing the Loophole in State Budget Oversight," *National Tax Journal* 39(4) 1986, 403–17.

tures than members of lower-income groups, who, not surprisingly, pay little or no tax in the first place.[82] Deductions, which reduce taxable income, avoid tax payments at the payer's marginal tax rate and thus favor higher-income persons in progressive tax systems. Credits, which directly reduce the tax payment, are worth the same dollar amounts to anyone who can claim them. Therefore, credits generally preserve progressivity more than deductions costing the same amount in forgone revenue.

Demand-Side Taxes

We divide demand-side taxes into two major categories: commodity taxes and user fees. Note, however, that other analysts may use other terminology, and even the distinction between these two categories is often unclear.

Commodity Taxes. The terms *commodity tax* and *excise tax* are frequently used interchangeably. We can think of commodity taxes as internalizing the impacts of goods with negative externalities. The most common applications are to reduce consumption of so-called demerit goods like alcohol (see our earlier discussion of merit goods under demand-side subsidies). The use of taxes in these contexts often appears to display a certain amount of schizophrenia. Will taxes only minimally affect demand and raise lots of revenue, or will taxes substantially decrease demand and generate much less revenue? Presumably, the idea in this context is to dampen demand, but the revenue goal often appears to displace it. Obviously, the price elasticity of demand determines the balance between reduced consumption and revenue generation in each particular policy context.[83]

User Fees. The technical terms often used by policy analysts for *user fees* include congestion taxes, marginal social cost pricing, and optimal tolls. In more common bureaucratic parlance, they are usually called license fees, rental charges, or fares. There are two efficiency arguments for user fees: first (once again!), to internalize externalities; second, to price public goods appropriately, specifically in the context of nonrivalrous, excludable, congested public goods (see NE2 in Figure 5.2), like bridges, and open-access resource public goods (see SW2 in Figure 5.2), such as fishing grounds. We already reviewed the appropriate price for excludable public goods in Chapter 5 (see Figure 5.3). Efficient allocation requires that the price charged equal the marginal costs users impose on other users, implying a zero price during noncongested periods and a positive price during congested periods.

[82]For a review of this argument, see Neil Brooks, "The Tax Expenditure Concept," *Canadian Taxation* 1(1) 1979, 31–35. Daniel Weinberg estimates that in FY 1985 over one half of the $250 billion in U.S. tax expenditures given through the individual income tax system went to the one-fifth of families with the highest incomes. Daniel H. Weinberg, "The Distributional Implications of Tax Expenditures and Comprehensive Income Taxation," *National Tax Journal* 40(2) 1987, 237–53.

[83]What, for example, is the effect of high taxes on tobacco consumption? There is evidence that the price elasticity of demand for smoking is somewhat elastic so that higher tobacco taxes would reduce smoking; see Edwin T. Fujii, "The Demand for Cigarettes: Further Empirical Evidence and Its Implications for Public Policy," *Applied Economics* 12(4) 1980, 479–89. For evidence that youth price elasticities are much larger than adult elasticities, see Eugene M. Lewit, Douglas Coate, and Michael Grossman, "The Effects of Government Regulation on Teenage Smoking," *Journal of Law and Economics* 14(3) 1981, 545–69.

Often the central problem faced by policymakers is the feasibility of such peak-load prices. One context in which the feasibility of such pricing may be changing rapidly because of technological advances is road congestion. While road pricing had been considered in many jurisdictions,[84] it was not widely implemented until low-cost electronic monitoring became feasible.[85] It has now been introduced in a number of jurisdictions, including San Diego, Orange County, and Houston in the United Sates and in a number of other urban areas around the world, such as London and Singapore.

Establishing Rules

Rules pervade our lives. Indeed, they are so pervasive that we tend not to think of them as instruments of government policy. Our objective here is to emphasize that rules are like other generic policies, with advantages and disadvantages. Government uses rules to coerce, rather than induce (through incentives), certain behaviors. Compliance may be enforced by either criminal or civil sanctions. We cannot always clearly distinguish between rules and incentives in terms of their practical effect, however. For instance, should one view small fines imposed by the criminal courts as rules or as implicit taxes (in other words, negative incentives)? While it is fashionable to focus on the disadvantages of rules (for example, relative to incentives), rules may provide the most efficient method for dealing with market failures in some contexts.

We divide rules into two major categories: (1) framework rules, encompassing both civil and criminal law; and (2) regulations, including restrictions on price, quantity, quality, and information, as well as more indirect controls relating to registration, certification, and licensing of market participants. Table 10.3 sets out these generic policies.

Frameworks

We should not forget that it is meaningless to talk of competitive markets, *except* within a rule-oriented framework. Lester Thurow states the point strongly:

> There simply is no such thing as the unregulated economy. All economies are sets of rules and regulations. Civilization is, in fact, an agreed upon set of rules of behavior. An economy without rules would be an economy in a state of anarchy where voluntary exchange was impossible. Superior force would be the sole means for conducting economic transactions. Everyone would be clubbing everyone else.[86]

The genesis of this idea goes back to Adam Smith, who recognized the need for frameworks when he pointed out that the first inclination of people in the same line of business when they gather together is to collude and subvert the operation

[84]As long ago as 1964 the Smeed Commission in the United Kingdom recommended road-use pricing, Ministry of Transport, *Road Pricing: The Economic and Technical Possibilities* (London: Her Majesty's Stationery Office, 1964).

[85]For an introduction to the topic of road pricing, see David M. Newbery, "Pricing and Congestion: Economic Principles Relevant to Pricing Roads," *Oxford Review of Economic Policy* 6(2) 1990, 22–38.

[86]Thurow, *The Zero-Sum Society*, p. 129.

Table 10.3 *Establishing Rules*

Generic Policies	Perceived Problem: Market Failure (MF), Government Failure (GF), Distributional Issue (DI), Limitation of Competitive Framework (LCF)	Typical Limitations and Collateral Consequences
Frameworks		
Civil laws (especially liability rules)	MF: Negative externalities MF: Information asymmetries MF: Public goods DI: Equal opportunity LCF: Thin markets	Bureaucratic supply failure; opportunistic behavior; imbalance between compensation and appropriate deterrence
Criminal laws	MF: Negative externalities MF: Public goods LCF: Illegitimate preferences	Costly and imperfect enforcement
Regulations		
Price regulation	MF: Natural monopolies DI: Equity in distribution of scarcity rent DI: Equity in good distribution	Allocative inefficiency; X-inefficiency
Quantity regulation	MF: Negative externalities MF: Public goods, especially open access	Rent seeking; distorted investment; black markets
Direct information provision (disclosure and labeling)	MF: Information asymmetries MF: Negative externalities	Cognitive limitations of consumers
Indirect information provision (registration, certification, and licensing)	MF: Information asymmetries MF: Negative externalities GF: Bureaucratic supply failure	Rent seeking; cartelization

of a competitive market.[87] The competitive market itself, then, can be thought of as a public good that will be undersupplied if left entirely to private activity. Contract law, tort law, commercial law, labor law, and antitrust law can all be thought of as *framework rules*.

Although there is little dispute that a system of criminal and civil rules is in and of itself efficiency enhancing, there is considerable debate over the most efficient structure of such rules. In civil law, for example, the exact nature of optimal liability rules (say, negligence versus strict liability standards) is contentious.[88] Much of

[87]Adam Smith, *The Wealth of Nations*, 1st ed., 1776 (New York: Penguin, 1977), Book One, Chapter X, Pt. II, 232–33.

[88]Much of this literature analyzes the specific nature and extent of market failure in particular contexts, such as product liability, in order to develop optimal liability rules. For a discussion, see Gary Schwartz, "The Vitality of Negligence and the Ethics of Strict Liability," *Georgia Law Review* 15, 1981, 963–1005; and George Priest, "The Invention of Enterprise Liability: A Critical History of the Intellectual Foundations of Modern Tort Law," *Journal of Legal Studies* 14(3) 1985, 461–527. For an overview of the evolution of U.S. tort law, see Richard A. Epstein, *Modern Products Liability Law* (Westport, CT: Quorum Books, 1980).

the burgeoning literature on law and economics is concerned with the specification of such optimal rules in various contexts.

One of the most basic public goods is the establishment and enforcement of property rights, including the rights to health and safety. In the United States, Canada, and other countries with roots in English common law, tort systems allow those who have suffered damages to seek compensation through the courts. Depending on the particular rules in force, the possibility of tort lowers the expected loss that consumers see from collateral damage and deters some risky behavior by producers in situations involving information asymmetry. Because tort often involves substantial transaction costs, however, it may not work effectively as a deterrent or compensation mechanism when the damage suffered by individual consumers is relatively small. (Small claims courts and class action suits are attempts to deal with this problem.) Because the liability of corporations is generally limited to their assets, tort may be ineffective when large losses result from products produced by small corporations. In addition, we expect tort to be least effective in limiting the inefficiency of information asymmetry in cases of post-experience goods because of the difficulty of establishing links between consumption and harmful effects.

Contract law can also be formulated to reduce the consequences of information asymmetry. For example, insurance law places the burden of informing the insured of the nature and extent of coverage on the insurer.[89] Even when contracts state explicit and contradictory limits, the reasonable expectations of the insured are generally taken by the courts in the United States as determining the extent of coverage. Indeed, most insurance agents carry their own "errors and omissions" insurance to cover their liability when the impressions they convey to clients diverge from the coverage implied by contracts. In many jurisdictions, other types of agents, such as those selling real estate, have a duty to disclose certain product characteristics related to quality. Such rules, however, may create an incentive for firms not to discover negative characteristics of their products. To be effective, therefore, they may have to be coupled with "standard of care" rules.

Antitrust law, which can be designed to employ either criminal or civil procedures, seeks to prevent firms from realizing rents through collusive efforts to restrict competition. As briefly discussed in Chapter 6, opportunities for collusion usually arise when an industry is dominated by only a few firms. Firms may form a cartel and attempt to allocate output among members in an effort to achieve the monopoly price. The allocations may be through such mechanisms as explicit quotas, geographic divisions of markets, and bid rigging to rotate contract awards. Where collusion is illegal, these efforts often fail because cartel members cannot make enforceable contracts to prevent cheating. The possibility of entry by new firms and the availability of substitutes also limit the ability of cartels to sustain prices above market levels. Nevertheless, active enforcement of antitrust laws may be necessary to preserve competition in some concentrated industries. One approach is investigation and prosecution under criminal laws by a government agency such as the Antitrust Division of the U.S. Justice Department. Another is the creation of incentives, such as multiple damages, to encourage those who have been harmed by collusion to bring civil suit.

[89]See Kenneth S. Abraham, *Distributing Risk: Insurance, Legal Theory, and Public Policy* (New Haven, CT: Yale University Press, 1986), 31–36.

Framework rules can also be used to counter some of the problems associated with government failures. For example, individual rights given as constitutional guarantees can protect minorities from tyranny of the majority under direct and representative democracy. Similarly, restrictions on gifts and perquisites that can be given to representatives may help avoid the most blatant abuses of rent seeking.

Regulations

Whereas framework rules facilitate private choice in competitive markets, *regulations* seek to alter choices that producers and consumers would otherwise make in these markets. Regulations generally operate through *command and control*: directives are given, compliance is monitored, and noncompliance is punished. Regulation can be extremely costly. One estimate is that in the United States federally mandated annual environmental regulation costs rose from $21 billion in 1972 to $93 billion in 1990 (in 1990 dollars), or approximately 2.1 percent of gross national product.[90] Similarly, the costs of industry-specific economic regulation have been massive.[91] Of course, high cost alone does not imply that regulation is not worthwhile, but it reminds us that it should be rigorously justified.

Price Regulation. In Chapter 8 we analyzed the efficiency costs of imposing either price ceilings or price supports on a competitive market (see Figures 8.2 and 8.3). The conclusion that price regulation leads to inefficiency can be generalized to wage and price controls and income policies, which have frequently been adopted by Western governments, including the United States.[92] The extent of the inefficiency is often difficult to determine, however.

If the quality of a good is variable, then the imposition of price floors often results in firms competing on the basis of quality rather than price. The result may be excessive quality and higher prices but only normal rates of return. In contrast, price ceilings often lead to declines in product quality, enabling firms to sell at a price closer to the competitive level for the lower-quality product. In other words, social surplus analysis that assumes that quality remains constant does not always tell the full story of the impact of price regulation.

Price regulation is frequently used as a method of preventing monopolies from charging rent-maximizing prices. For example, the Cable Television Consumer Protection and Competition Act of 1992 gives the Federal Communications Commission (FCC) authority to regulate cable TV rates. The FCC ordered a 10 percent rate rollback in 1993, and a further 7 percent reduction in 1994. The FCC estimated the competitive price by comparing prices of monopoly cable systems to those with duopoly systems (called "overbuilt" systems in industry parlance). It found that duopoly systems had prices that were, on average, approximately 16 percent lower than

[90]Ralph A. Luken and Arthur G. Fraas, "The US Regulatory Analysis Framework: A Review," *Oxford Review of Economic Policy* 9(4) 1993, 95–111.

[91]Robert Hahn and John A. Hird, "The Costs and Benefits of Regulation: A Review and Synthesis," *Yale Journal of Regulation* 8(1) 1991, 233–78.

[92]See H. Quinn Mills, "Some Lessons of Price Controls in 1971–1973," *Bell Journal of Economics* 6(1) 1975, 3–49; and John Kraft and Blaine Roberts, *Wage and Price Controls: The U.S. Experiment* (New York: Praeger, 1975).

those of the monopoly systems. It is estimated that these price reductions reduced industry revenues by $3 billion.[93] As we saw in Chapter 5, if a natural monopoly can be forced to price at average cost, then deadweight losses are much lower than under rent-maximizing pricing.

Many regulatory regimes attempt to force natural monopolies to price at average cost by regulating prices. Historically, the usual approach has been *rate-of-return* regulation. Large sectors of our energy, transportation, communication, and urban services sectors are, or have been, regulated in this way. Typically, the statutes authorizing regulations speak of "reasonable" prices and profits. In practice, however, it is often not clear what the relative importance of efficiency and equity in defining reasonableness is.

There have been two major lines of criticism to the use of this type of price regulation to limit undersupply by natural monopolies. First, in line with various forms of government failure, George Stigler and others have argued that the regulators are quickly "captured" by the firms that they are supposed to be regulating, such that the outcome may be worse than no regulation at all.[94] Second, such regulation induces inefficient and wasteful behavior. Two well-documented outcomes of such incentives are X-inefficiency and an overuse of capital under rate-of-return regulation.[95]

To counteract these inappropriate incentives, a new form of price regulation, labeled *price cap* regulation, has emerged; it is also referred to as *yardstick competition* regulation. Although largely developed in Great Britain to regulate newly privatized and entry-deregulated industries, it is now being adopted in many countries, including the United States.[96] Over the last fifteen years, almost all states switched their regulation of local exchange telephone companies from rate-of-return regulation to price cap regulation.[97] Price cap regulation is frequently used to regulate industries with natural monopoly characteristics in conjunction with the removal of legal entry barriers, vertical disintegration, and sometimes market share restrictions. In this form of price regulation, the regulatory agency sets an allowed price for a specified time period, such as four years. The allowed price is adjusted annually to take into account inflation but reduced by a percentage to reflect cost reductions that the regulator believes the firm can achieve, based on some notion of the extent of

[93]See Thomas Hazlett, "Duopolistic Competition in Cable Television: Implications for Public Policy," *Yale Journal of Regulation* 7(1) 1990, 65–139; Robert Rubinovitz, "Market Power and Price Increases in Basic Cable Service since Deregulation," *RAND Journal of Economics* 24(1) 1993, 1–18; and Jith Jayaratne, "A Note on the Implementation of Cable TV Rate Caps," *Review of Industrial Organization* 11(6) 1996, 823–40.

[94]George Stigler, "The Theory of Economic Regulation," *Bell Journal of Economics and Management* 2(1) 1971, 3–21; Richard A. Posner, "Theories of Economic Regulation," *Bell Journal of Economics and Management* 5(2) 1974, 335–58; and Sam Peltzman, "Toward a More General Theory of Regulation," *Journal of Law and Economics* 19(2) 1976, 211–40. Their work formalizes an earlier tradition in political science including Samuel P. Huntington, "The Marasmus of the ICC: The Commissions, the Railroads and the Public Interest," *Yale Law Review* 61(4) 1952, 467–509; and Marver H. Bernstein, *Regulating Business by Independent Commission* (Princeton, NJ: Princeton University Press, 1955).

[95]For an extensive discussion of these issues, see Viscusi, Vernon, and Harrington, *Economics of Regulation and Antitrust*. On the overuse of capital, see the seminal article by Harvey Averch and Leland L. Johnson, "Behavior of the Firm under Regulatory Constraint," *American Economic Review* 53(5) 1962, 1052–1069.

[96]Price caps are now extensively used in the United States to regulate long distance telephone rates. See Alan D. Mathios and Robert P. Rogers, "The Impact of Alternative Forms of State Regulation of AT&T on Direct-Dial, Long Distance Telephone Rates," *RAND Journal of Economics* 20(3) 1989, 437–53.

[97]Dennis L. Weisman, "Is There *'Hope'* for Price Cap Regulation?" *Information Economics and Policy* 14(3) 2002, 349–70.

previous X-inefficiency and the extent that new technology may allow cost reductions (that is, the potential for technical efficiency improvements, not related to X-inefficiency). For example, if the rate of inflation is 3 percent annually and the required annual productivity gain is 4 percent, the nominal price allowed would decrease 1 percent annually. Typically, the regulated firm is allowed to reduce prices if it wishes to do so (in other words, there is a ceiling but no floor); as price cap regulation is often accompanied by open entry, incumbents may, in fact, be forced to lower prices more quickly than the cap price.

An advantage of such regulation is that it focuses on dynamic efficiency—managers have an incentive to improve productivity over time because they get to keep the surplus if they can reduce costs faster than the cap price declines. However, price cap regulation requires the regulator to estimate the achievable cost reductions periodically. Ideally, the estimate should provide incentives for firms to reduce cost, but not to allow them to capture too-high profits. This draws the regulator into a process that has some similarities to old-style rate-of-return regulation where the regulators can be influenced by the regulated firms or other interest groups.[98] One important difference, however, remains between price cap regulation and rate-of-return regulation: price cap regulation requires investors in the firm to carry the risk of profit variability.[99] There is evidence that price cap regulation has led to significant efficiency improvements for firms with natural monopoly characteristics. For example, one study found efficiency gains at the British Gas Corporation, even though the firm remained a (vertically integrated) monopoly during this period.[100] Again, though, these regulatory changes have been accompanied by other important changes, such as privatization, so that it is difficult to attribute efficiency improvements to one cause.

Notice that using price regulation to correct for market failure caused by natural monopoly is only one alternative. We have already considered the alternative possibilities of dealing with natural monopoly through auctions and subsidies; we will consider government ownership below. Here we see the substitutability of generic policies. Analysis of the specific context is needed to determine which generic policy is most appropriate.

Price ceilings are sometimes used in an attempt so transfer scarcity rents from resource owners to consumers. For example, during the 1970s ceilings kept the wellhead price of U.S. and Canadian crude oil well below world market levels. While these controls transferred rents from the owners of oil reserves to refiners and consumers, they reduced the domestic supply of oil, increased demand for oil, and contributed to higher world oil prices.[101] In general, the use of price ceilings to transfer scarcity rents involves efficiency losses.

[98]For a discussion of these problems in the context of the water industry in England and Wales, see Caroline van den Berg, "Water Privatization and Regulation in England and Wales," *Public Policy for the Private Sector* 10, June 1997, 9–12.

[99]For an explanation and evidence, see Ian Alexander and Timothy Irwin, "Price Caps, Rate-of-Return Regulation, and the Cost of Capital," *Public Policy for the Public Sector* 8, September 1996, 25–28.

[100]Catherine Waddams Price and Thomas Weyman-Jones, "Malquist Indices of Productivity Change in the UK Gas Industry before and after Privatization," *Applied Economics* 28(1) 1996, 29–39; and Sumit K. Majumdar, "Incentive Regulation and Productive Efficiency in the U.S. Telecommunications Industry," *Journal of Business* 70(4) 1997, 547–76.

[101]For an overview, see Kenneth J. Arrow and Joseph P. Kalt, *Petroleum Price Regulation: Should We Decontrol?* (Washington, DC: American Enterprise Institute, 1979). For a more detailed treatment, see Joseph P. Kalt, *The Economics and Politics of Oil Price Regulation* (Cambridge, MA: MIT Press, 1981). For a discussion of the particular problems associated with domestic oil price ceilings of the context of oil price shocks in the world market, see George Horwich and David L. Weimer, *Oil Price Shocks, Market Response, and Contingency Planning* (Washington, DC: American Enterprise Institute, 1984), 57–110.

Quantity Regulation. We have already mentioned quantity regulation as a means of controlling negative externalities in our discussion of taxes and subsidies. While quantity regulation is less flexible and generally less efficient than market incentives, it usually provides greater certainty of outcome. Therefore, it may be desirable in situations where the cost of error is great. For example, if an externality involves post-experience goods with potentially catastrophic and irreversible consequences, directly limiting it may be the most desirable approach. Should we risk using economic incentives to control the use of fluorocarbons, which have the potential of destroying the ozone layer? If, in the first taxing iteration, we overestimate the price elasticity of demand, the cost and difficulty of achieving reductions later may be great. Other potentially planet-threatening dangers, such as the greenhouse effect, raise similar issues.[102] The relative steepness of the marginal benefit and marginal abatement (cost) curves should determine whether a price or quantity instrument should be used. Suppose that the marginal benefit curve of a given pollutant is quite steep, and the marginal costs are constant. In this situation the benefit from changes in environmental quality vary greatly with changes in pollution levels: the costs from too-high levels of the pollutant will be high. Quantity controls are appropriate. If, on the other hand, the marginal benefit curve is flat but the marginal cost curve is steep, the potential policy problem is the deadweight loss from too-tight regulation. Pollution taxes are appropriate.

In the United States, quantity regulation of pollutants has often taken the form of specifications for the type of technology that must be used to meet standards. For example, the 1977 Clean Air Act Amendments required that all new coal-fired power plants install flue gas scrubbers to remove sulfur emissions, whether the plant used low- or high-sulfur coal.[103] This approach was appealing to representatives from states that produce high-sulfur coal, to owners of old plants whose new competitors would enjoy less of a cost advantage, and to many environmentalists, who saw it as a way of gaining reductions with minimal administrative costs.[104] By raising the cost of new plants, however, the scrubber requirement may actually have slowed the reduction of aggregate sulfur emissions by reducing the speed at which electric utilities replace older plants. In general, regulating how standards are to be met reduces flexibility and thus makes the standards more costly to achieve.

Workplace health and safety regulation in the United States under the administration of the Occupational Safety and Health Administration (OSHA) has also focused on technology-based standards. This is partly because the U.S. Supreme Court explicitly rejected the use of cost-benefit analysis by OSHA in the administration of workplace safety and health.[105] The standard-based approach of OSHA has been controversial, especially among economists. One recent review of the em-

[102]John Houghton, *Global Warming: The Complete Briefing*, 2nd ed. (New York: Cambridge University Press, 1997).

[103]See Robert W. Crandall, "An Acid Test for Congress?" *Regulation* 8, September/December 1984, 21–28. See also, Bruce A. Ackerman and William T. Hassler, *Clean Coal/Dirty Air* (New Haven, CT: Yale University Press, 1981).

[104]Crandall, "An Acid Test for Congress?" 21–22.

[105]*American Textile Manufacturers Institute v. Donovan*, 452 U.S. 490 (1981).

pirical literature concluded with the rather mixed message that " there is no evidence of a substantial impact of OSHA ... [but] ... the available empirical results for the overall OSHA impact ... suggest that OSHA enforcement efforts may be beginning to enhance workplace safety."[106]

It is worth noting that tradable emissions permits (discussed earlier in this chapter under simulating markets), also contain an element of quantity regulation. Before trading begins, a total quantity of allowable pollution must be established. Tradable permits, therefore, combine some of the advantages of quantity control with those of more market-like mechanisms, such as taxes and subsidies.

The use of quotas in international trade is another illustration of quantity regulation, albeit one that has been vigorously criticized.[107] As we have already discussed, tariffs and quotas differ little in theory: in the case of tariffs, prices are raised until imports are reduced to a certain level; in the case of quotas, the government limits the import level directly, and prices adjust accordingly. In practice, tariffs have the advantage of being more accommodating than quotas to changes in supply and demand. Additionally, tariffs are generally easier to implement than quotas because the latter require the government to distribute rights to the limited imports. There are also important distributional differences between quotas and tariffs; quotas transfer rent to foreign producers, whereas tariff revenue is captured by domestic governments.

Jose Gomez-Ibanez, Robert Leone, and Stephen O'Connell have examined the impact of quotas on the U.S. automobile market.[108] Their analysis can be generalized to import quotas for footwear, textiles, steel, and many other products. They estimate that the short-run consumer losses are in excess of $1 billion per annum and that "it is apparent that under most assumptions the economy as a whole is worse off because of restraints."[109] They also point out that the longer-run "dynamic" efficiency costs may be even more significant than the short-run costs, as the Japanese automobile producers adjust their behavior in the face of quotas.

The most extreme form of quantity regulation is an outright ban on usage or ownership, usually enforced via criminal sanctions. For example, in 1984 the U.S. National Organ Transplant Act banned the sale or purchase of human organs.[110] Many countries are currently considering whether to legally ban human cloning. More familiar prohibitions include bans on gambling, liquor, prostitution, and drugs such as heroin and cocaine. Again, countries have chosen to use this policy

[106]Viscusi, Vernon, and Harrington, *Economics of Regulation and Antitrust*, p. 823; see their general evaluation on pp. 814–24. See also W. Kip Viscusi, *Fatal Tradeoffs* (New York: Oxford University Press, 1992). Elsewhere, Viscusi has emphasized that there are two other, more market-like mechanisms to encourage firms to maintain safe workplace: first "compensating wage differentials," whereby risky firms and industries must pay higher wages ("Market Incentives for Safety", *Harvard Business Review* 63(4) 1985, 133–38); and, second, that they must pay higher worker compensation premiums.

[107]For an excellent overview of theory, as well as comprehensive estimates of the deadweight losses from quotas, see Robert C. Feenstra, "How Costly Is Protectionism?" *Journal of Economic Perspectives* 6(3) 1992, 159–78.

[108]Jose Gomez-Ibanez, Robert Leone, and Stephen O'Connell, "Restraining Auto Imports: Does Anyone Win?" *Journal of Policy Analysis and Management* 2(2) 1983, 196–219.

[109]Ibid., p. 205; see Table 2.

[110]National Organ Transplant Act, October 4, 1984, P.L. 98–507, 98 Stat. 2339.

instrument differently. Many countries ban the private ownership of handguns, while most jurisdictions in the United States allow sale and ownership. On the other hand, no country that we know of has banned the use or sale of tobacco.[111] There has not been a consensus on these types of prohibitions among the analytical community. This is not surprising because many of the issues relate to strongly held ethical values. As we saw in our discussion of legalization, changes in such values often lead to calls for freedom of choice. If there is extensive consumer demand for illegal products, then the usual result is black markets, which generate deadweight losses and negative externalities.

One context in which criminal sanctions are now being used more extensively is the regulation of toxic chemicals. In one well-known case, several Illinois businessmen were convicted of murder and sentenced to twenty-five years imprisonment for the toxic-chemical-related death of an employee.[112] While such severe criminal sanctions may provide a powerful deterrent, they may also discourage firms from reporting accidents where they may have been negligent.

The design of efficient standards requires that noncompliance be taken into account. If we want those subject to standards to make efficient decisions, then they should see an expected punishment equal to the external costs of their behavior. For example, if dumping a toxic substance causes $10,000 in external damage, and the probability of catching the dumper is 0.01, then the fine should be on the order of $1 million to internalize the externality. The political system, however, may not be willing to impose such large fines. Nor may it be willing to hire enough inspectors to increase the probability that noncompliance will be detected. In general, the problem of noncompliance limits the effectiveness of standards.[113]

Direct Information Provision. We discussed information asymmetry extensively in Chapter 5. We noted there that the quality of many goods cannot be evaluated until long after they are consumed (for example, post-experience goods like asbestos insulation and certain medical treatments). As products become more technologically complex, product quality is likely to become an increasingly important area of policy concern.

The presence of information asymmetry suggests a relatively simple policy: provide the information! An important question is whether it is more effective for government to supply such information to consumers or to require the suppliers of goods to provide the information. Few studies directly address this important question. In practice, governments tend to engage in both strategies. For instance, the U.S. government, through the National Institutes of Health, provides information concerning the health impact of cigarette smoking as well as requiring cigarette manufacturers to place warning labels on their products.

[111]There have been numerous calls for a ban on advertising, as opposed to selling, cigarettes. See Kenneth E. Warner et al., "Promotion of Tobacco Products: Issues and Policy Options," *Journal of Health Politics, Policy and Law* 11(3) 1986, 367–92; Rebecca Arbogoss, "A Proposal to Regulate the Manner of Tobacco Advertising," ibid., pp. 393–422.

[112]See Daniel Riesel, "Criminal Prosecution and Defense of Environmental Wrong," *Environmental Law Reporter* 15(3) 1985, 10065–81; and Mark Schneider, "Criminal Enforcement of Federal Water Pollution Laws in an Era of Deregulation," *Journal of Criminal Law and Criminology* 73(2) 1982, 642–74.

[113]W. Kip Viscusi and Richard J. Zeckhauser, "Optimal Standards with Incomplete Enforcement," *Public Policy* 27(4) 1979, 437–56. Nonetheless, a recent study has found that compliance is disproportionately high given the low expected costs of noncompliance; see David Well, "If OSHA Is So Bad, Why Is Compliance so Good?" *RAND Journal of Economics* 27(3) 1996, 618–40.

The practice of requiring firms to supply information about various attributes of product quality is becoming increasingly common.[114] Examples include appliance energy efficiency labeling, automobile mileage ratings, clothing care labeling, mortgage loan rate facts, nutrition and ingredient labeling, octane value labeling, truth-in-lending provisions, warranty disclosure requirements, and health warnings on cigarette packages.[115] Additionally, federal, state, and local governments have devoted much effort to instituting so-called plain language laws to make contracts readable.[116]

Another variation on the theme of requiring suppliers of goods to provide information is to facilitate the provision of information by employees.[117] Currently, airline employees can communicate safety problems to federal regulators presumably without being exposed to employer reprisals. Clearly, airline pilots have a more direct incentive to report safety problems than do airline executives. Of course, this policy approach can be applied to government itself by facilitating the protection of whistle-blowing employees who report inefficiency or corruption.

Organizational report cards, which provide consumers comparative information on the performance of organizations, such as schools, health maintenance organizations, and hospitals, are becoming increasingly common.[118] When organizations have a strong incentive to participate, organizational report cards may be provided by private organizations. For example, colleges willingly provide information to *U.S. News & World Report* for its annual report card on colleges, because not being listed would hurt their efforts to compete for students. Many health maintenance organizations participate in report cards at the insistance of large employers that purchase their services. When organizations do not have an incentive to participate, then the government may intervene, either to require the publication of information necessary for private report card makers or to produce the report cards directly. For example, many states now publish report cards on school districts or require the districts to provide parents with comparative information about particular schools.

Direct information provision is likely to be a viable policy response to pure information asymmetry problems. It is an attractive policy option because the marginal costs of both providing the information and enforcing compliance tend to be low. It may be less viable when information asymmetry is combined with other market imperfections, such as limited consumer attention, misperception of risk, endogenous preferences, or addictive products. For example, providing information about the adverse health effects of smoking may not be an adequate policy response because of the addictive properties of tobacco. If we believe that many smokers are

[114]For an overview, see Susan Hadden, *Read the Label: Reducing Risk by Providing Information* (Boulder, CO: Westview Press, 1986).

[115]Joel Rudd, "The Consumer Information Overload Controversy and Public Policy," *Policy Studies Review* 2(3) 1983, 465–73.

[116]For a review of this topic, see Stephen M. Ross, "On Legalities and Linguistics: Plain Language Legislation," *Buffalo Law Review* 30(2) 1981, 317–63.

[117]Eugene Bardach and Robert A. Kagan propose that information provision by employees not just be facilitated but mandated in some circumstances. They also view rules that define the authority of professionals, such as health and safety inspectors, within corporations to be a form of "private regulation" worthy of consideration. Eugene Bardach and Robert A. Kagan, *Going by the Book: The Problem of Regulatory Unreasonableness* (Philadelphia: Temple University Press, 1982), 217–42.

[118]William T. Gormley, Jr., and David L. Weimer, *Organizational Report Cards* (Cambridge, MA: Harvard University Press, 1999).

incapable of rationally evaluating the health risks, then further regulation may be appropriate, including, perhaps, the imposition of quality standards.

Standards provide information to consumers by narrowing the variance in product quality. For example, the Food and Drug Administration (FDA) requires that scientific evidence of efficacy and safety be presented before a new drug can be sold to the public. These quality standards provide at least some information to consumers about marketed drugs.

The effective use of quality standards may be limited by government failure. Regulatory bureaus often lack the expertise to determine appropriate quality standards. Also, they may operate in political environments that undervalue some errors and overvalue others. For example, when the FDA allows a harmful product to reach the market, it is likely to come under severe criticism from members of Congress, who can point to specific individuals who have suffered. In contrast, until recently, the FDA had received virtually no congressional criticism when it prevented a beneficial product from reaching the market, even though large numbers of (generally unidentified) people forwent benefits.[119]

Programs of quality regulation and information disclosure run the risk of regulatory capture. Firms in the regulated industry that can more easily meet quality and disclosure standards may engage in rent seeking by attempting to secure stringent requirements that inflict disproportionate costs on their competitors and increase barriers that make it more difficult for new firms to enter the industry. In addition to reducing competition, stringent standards may also impede innovation by forcing excessive uniformity.[120] The retarding of innovation is likely to be especially serious when the standards apply to production processes rather than to the quality of final products. Delegating standard-setting authority to private organizations may facilitate incremental standard setting that better reflects changing technology.[121]

Indirect Information Provision. Unfortunately, direct information about the quality of services, as opposed to physical products, usually cannot be provided. Typically, service quality is not fixed; it may change over time, either with changes in the level of human capital or the amount of input effort. Because the quality of services may vary over time, providing reliable information about their quality directly may be impractical. The infeasibility of providing such direct information has led policymakers and analysts to search for indirect ways of providing information. A common policy approach is to license or certify providers who meet some standard of skill, training, or experience.

Licensure can be defined as "a regulatory regime under which only the duly qualified who have sought and obtained a license to practice from an appropriate agency or delegate of the state are legally permitted to perform or to take responsibility for given functions."[122] It can be distinguished from *certification* "under

[119]For a more detailed discussion of the asymmetry in oversight of the Food and Drug Administration, see David L. Weimer, "Safe—and Available—Drugs," in Robert W. Poole, Jr., ed., *Instead of Regulation* (Lexington, MA: Lexington Books, 1982), 239–83.

[120]See the discussion of the dairy industry by Bardach and Kagan, *Going by the Book*, pp. 260–62.

[121]Ross E. Cheit, *Setting Safety Standards: Regulation in the Public and Private Sectors* (Berkeley: University of California Press, 1990).

[122]Michael J. Trebilcock and Barry J. Reiter, "Licensure in Law," in Robert G. Evans and Michael J. Trebilcock, eds., *Lawyers and the Consumer Interest* (Toronto: Butterworth, 1982), Chapter 3, 65–103, at p. 66.

which qualified practitioners receive special designations or certifications which other practitioners cannot legally use; however, uncertified practitioners are legally permitted to provide the same functions, provided they do so under some other designation. Certification involves exclusive rights to a professional designation but not to practice."[123]

Milton Friedman has succinctly summarized the weakness of using these approaches: "The most obvious social cost is that any one of these measures, whether it be registration, certification, or licensure, almost inevitably becomes a tool in the hands of a special producer group to obtain a monopoly position at the expense of the rest of the public."[124] Because certification usually does not forestall entry, this criticism has focused particularly on licensure.[125]

While the rationale for providing indirect information through licensure does not necessarily imply *self*-regulation, this is the route that almost all states have gone with occupational licensure. The typical steps are members form a professional association, the association sets up a system of voluntary licensure, and the profession petitions the legislature for mandatory licensure under the auspices of its association.[126]

Occupational licensure suffers from a number of weaknesses: the correlation between training or other measurable attributes and performance may be low; the definition of occupations may lock in skills that become outmoded in dynamic markets; high entry standards deny consumers the opportunity to choose low-quality, but low-price, services; and when professional interests control the licensing standards, the standards may be set unduly high to restrict entry so as to drive up the incomes of the existing practitioners.[127]

While all of these problems deserve serious attention, economists have tended to concentrate on the social costs of entry barriers and the resulting monopoly pricing—perhaps because it is one of the easier licensure impacts to measure. There is certainly strong empirical evidence that professional cartels do indeed raise prices and restrict competition.[128] In light of the existence of these excess returns and what you have already learned about rent seeking, you should not be surprised to hear that many professional and quasi-professional groups continue to seek licensure.[129]

We should, therefore, be cautious in advocating licensure as a policy alternative. When we do, we should consider alternatives to professional *self*-regulation.

[123]Ibid., p. 66.

[124]Friedman, *Capitalism and Freedom*, p. 148.

[125]For one study that finds efficiency benefits from certification, see Bradley S. Wimmer and Brian Chezum, "An Empirical Examination of Quality Certification in a 'Lemons Market'," *Economic Inquiry* 41(2) 2003, 279–91.

[126]William D. White and Theodore R. Marmor, "New Occupations, Old Demands," *Journal of Policy Analysis and Management* 1(2) 1982, 243–56.

[127]We take these points from Trebilcock and Reiter, "Licensure in Law," pp. 67–70. They develop these points in depth and raise a number of others.

[128]For a sample of this large literature, see James W. Begun, "The Consequences of Professionalism for Health Services: Optometry," *Journal of Health and Social Behavior* 20(4) 1979, 376–86; Robert M. Howard, "Wealth, Power, and Attorney Regulation in the U.S. States: License Entry and Maintenance Requirements," *Publius: The Journal of Federalism* 28(4) 1998, 21–33; Morris M. Kleiner and Robert T. Kudrle, "Does Regulation Affect Economic Outcomes? The Case of Dentistry," *Journal of Law and Economics* 43(2) 2000, 547–82; N. J. Philipsen and M. G. Faure, "The Regulation of Pharmacists in Belgium and the Netherlands: In the Public or Private Interest?" *Journal of Consumer Policy* 25(2) 2002, 155–201.

[129]White and Marmor, "New Occupations, Old Demands," pp. 249–52.

Yet we believe it is fair to say that the critics of professional regulation have not been particularly imaginative in proposing alternative policies.[130]

Licensure is now spreading beyond its traditional boundaries. Numerous paraprofessional occupations are winning the right to license and self-regulate. One interesting proposal even suggests that prospective parents should be licensed before having children![131]

Summary: The Wide World of Rules (and Some Checks). As emphasized in the introduction to this section, rules are the most pervasive form of government policy in all our lives. National and subnational (state or provincial, local) regulations continue to multiply. One recent innovation in many jurisdictions such as New York State, however, is the requirement that major regulations be subject to cost-benefit analysis. If this trend continues, then it is likely to have a major impact on the regulatory process.[132]

Supplying Goods through Nonmarket Mechanisms

Surprisingly, policy analysts have had relatively little to say about when government provision of goods through public agencies is an appropriate response to market failure. Peter Pashigian puts it bluntly: "Public production of goods and services is somewhat of an embarrassment to most economists. It exists, and will in all likelihood increase in importance, but it is difficult to explain. An acceptable theory of public production has not yet appeared."[133] Indeed, the choice between government provision and other generic policies is one of the least well understood policy issues. Perhaps the reason is that while we have a convincing theory of market failure and an increasingly convincing theory of government failure, we have no overreaching theory that delineates the efficiency trade-offs between market failure and government failure.[134]

It is tempting to believe that the theory of market failure itself resolves this dilemma: direct government provision is appropriate when there is endemic market failure. This is a weak argument because it ignores the fact that market failures can be addressed with other generic policies. Therefore, market failure provides a rationale generally for government intervention rather than specifically for direct provision by government. For example, consider the possible responses to natural monopoly: auctions to take advantage of competition for markets, subsidies to facilitate marginal cost pricing, and direct regulation. These approaches are alternatives to government ownership of the monopoly.

[130]For one proposal, see Aidan R. Vining. "Information Costs and Legal Services," *Law and Policy Quarterly* 4(4) 1982, 475–500.

[131]John F. Tropman, "A Parent's License," *Journal of Policy Analysis and Management* 3(3) 1984, 457–59.

[132]On the growth of cost-benefit requirements at the state level, see Richard Whisnant and Diane DeWitt Cherry, "Economic Analysis of Rules: Devolution, Evolution, and Realism," *Wake Forest Law Review* 31(3) 1996, 693–743.

[133]Peter Pashigian, "Consequences and Causes of Public Ownership of Urban Transit Facilities," *Journal of Political Economy* 84(6) 1976, 1239–59.

[134]For this argument, see Lee S. Friedman, "Public Institutional Structure: The Analysis of Adjustment," in John P. Crecine, ed., *Research in Public Policy Analysis and Management*, Vol. 2 (Greenwich, CT: JAI Press, 1981), 303–25.

William Baumol provides the beginnings of a moral hazard theory of government production.[135] His insight is best introduced with an example: the provision of national defense. The common rationale for the provision of national defense by government rests on the argument that it is a public good. But this is only an argument for government intervention, not a public army, per se. Baumol's case for a public army is made in terms of moral hazard. A government intends to use its armed forces only when needed for its own purposes. An army provided by the market to the government under contract may have very different incentives that bring into question its loyalty and reliability.

We suggest that the moral hazard problem can be viewed more broadly in the context of opportunism. Again, we can illustrate the crux of the problem using the example of national defense: armies cannot be trusted to carry out the contracts because the government does not have an independent mechanism of enforcement. In other words, the armies are in a position to engage in opportunistic behavior, like the soldiers in the Thirty Years' War who were lured from one side to the other with bonuses and higher wages.[136] Even if a particular private army does not engage in such behavior, the state will inevitably be forced into costly monitoring. For instance, the government would at least have to establish an office of inspector general to make sure that the contractor can actually muster the promised forces.

Although the danger of opportunistic behavior is most starkly revealed in the area of national defense, it is by no means unique to it. The collection of taxes, the printing of money, the administration of justice—all could potentially face serious agency problems if supplied by private firms.

Our analysis suggests a *double market-failure test* for the use of public agencies: first, evidence of market failure or a redistributive goal; second, evidence either that a less intrusive generic policy cannot be utilized or that an effective contract for private production cannot be designed to deal with the market failure (that is, opportunism cannot be reasonably controlled). While we believe that this double market-failure approach provides a rationale for government production, only modest progress has been made in delineating the range of circumstances in which government production is likely to be the best generic policy.[137] The task is especially difficult because public agencies themselves, as we saw in Chapter 8, are prone to serious principal-agent problems.

In spite of these theoretical difficulties, we can at least provide an overview of alternative forms of nonmarket supply. Broadly speaking, once a decision has been made to supply goods publicly, governments can do so either directly or indirectly. Direct supply involves production and distribution of goods by government bureaus. As outlined in Table 10.4, the major means of indirect supply are independent agencies (usually government corporations or special districts) or various forms of contracting out. Although these distinctions are theoretically clear, in practice they are often less so.

[135]William J. Baumol, "Toward a Theory of Public Enterprise," *Atlantic Economic Journal* 12(1) 1984, 13–20.

[136]Andre Corvisier, *Armies and Societies in Europe, 1494–1789*, trans. Abigail T. Siddall (Bloomington: Indiana University Press, 1979), 45.

[137]For general treatments, see David E. M. Sappington and Joseph E. Stiglitz, "Privatization, Information and Incentives," *Journal of Policy Analysis and Management* 6(4) 1987, 567–82; and Aidan R. Vining and David L. Weimer, "Government Supply and Government Production Failure: A Framework Based on Contestability," *Journal of Public Policy* 10, pt. 1, 1990, 1–22.

Table 10.4 *Supplying Goods through Nonmarket Mechanisms*

Generic Policies	Perceived Problem: Market Failure (MF), Government Failure (GF), Distributional Issue (DI), Limitation of Competitive Framework (LCF)	Typical Limitations and Collateral Consequences
Direct Supply		
Bureaus	MF: Public goods MF: Positive externalities MF: Natural monopolies DI: Equity in distribution	Rigidity; dynamic inefficiency; and X-inefficiency
Independent Agencies		
Government corporations	MF: Natural monopolies MF: Positive externalities DI: Equity in distribution GF: Bureaucratic supply failures	Agency loss
Special districts	MF: Natural monopolies MF: Local public goods MF: Negative externalities DI: Universal provision	Agency loss; insensitivity to minorities with intense preferences
Contracting Out		
Direct contracting	MF: Public goods, especially local public goods GF: Bureaucratic supply failures	Opportunistic behavior by suppliers; lock-in and low-balling
Indirect contracting (nonprofits)	MF: Positive externalities GF: Bureaucratic supply failures DI: Diversity of preferences LCF: Endogenous preferences (behavior modification)	Weak coordination of services

Direct Supply by Government Bureaus

The direct production of goods by government bureaus is as old as government itself. Karl Wittfogel argues that the stimulus for the development of many early civilizations in semiarid regions (for example, Egypt, Mesopotamia, and parts of China and India) came from the need to construct and manage water facilities collectively. This, in turn, tended to generate direct government supply of nonhydraulic construction: "under the conditions of Pharaonic Egypt and Inca Peru, direct management prevailed."[138]

The U.S. government provides a vast array of goods through such agencies as the Army Corps of Engineers, the Bureau of the Mint, the National Forest Service, and the Cooperative Extension Service of the Department of Agriculture. Even in the early days of the republic, direct supply was extensive when the activities of the

[138]See Karl Wittfogel, *Oriental Despotism* (New Haven, CT: Yale University Press, 1957), p. 45. See also his Table 1 on government management in agriculture and industry, p. 46.

states are included.[139] Christopher Leman finds that domestic government production can be divided into ten functional categories: facilitating commerce; managing public lands; constructing public works and managing real property; research and testing; technical assistance; laws and justice; health care, social services, and direct cash assistance; education and training; marketing; and supporting internal administrative needs.[140] The "nondomestic" functions of government include national defense and the administration of foreign policy.

A perusal of these categories suggests that all could be justified by some market failure or redistributive rationale. This, however, does not address the question of whether these goods could be efficiently provided by other generic policies or provided *indirectly* by government. Clearly, some of these goods (or at least close substitutes) could be supplied using other generic policies; for instance, elements of health care can be variously provided in free markets, through market incentives, and under rules.

Leman also points out that other interventionist generic policies inevitably involve some level of *direct* government provision.[141] Some examples: the provision of in-kind subsidies requires a bureau to dispense the goods and vouchers; the use of rules requires agencies to monitor and enforce compliance; and even the creation of tradable property rights may require agencies to act as banks and clearinghouses.

Our discussion in Chapter 8 of the various forms of government failure, especially those of bureaucratic supply, suggests that government supply is not a panacea. The policy pendulum appears to have swung against the use of public agencies, as shown by the current interest in privatization and contracting out.

Independent Agencies

The range and types of independent agencies are enormous. The British have coined the term *quango* (quasi-nongovernment organization) to describe the myriad semiautonomous bodies that are not explicitly government departments. Such autonomous "off-budget" agencies have grown explosively in almost all countries around the world. The United States has not been exempt. Ann-Marie Walsh has identified more than 1,000 domestic state and interstate authorities, as well as more than 6,000 substate authorities.[142] These regional, state, and local agencies construct and operate a wide range of facilities, including dams, airports, industrial parks, and bridges, and provide a wide range of services, such as water, gas, and electricity. Because there is no broadly recognized nomenclature, however, even identifying and classifying such entities is problematic. Many authorities have considerable independence but are not corporate in form, while others are corporate but are formally included in government departments. Even more confusingly, formal inclusion

[139]Carter Goodrich, ed., *The Government and the Economy, 1783-1861* (Indianapolis: Bobbs-Merrill, 1967), xv–xviii.

[140]Christopher K. Leman, "The Forgotten Fundamental: Successes and Excesses of Direct Government," in Lester Salamon, ed., *Beyond Privatization: The Tools of Government Action* (Washington, DC: Urban Institute Press, 1989), 53–87.

[141]Ibid.

[142]Ann-Marie H. Walsh, The Public's Business: The Politics and Practices of Government Corporations (Cambridge, MA: MIT Press, 1978), 6. See also Neil W. Hamilton and Peter R. Hamilton, *Governance of Public Enterprises: A Case Study of Urban Mass Transit* (Lexington, MA: Lexington Books, 1981).

in a bureau does not necessarily subject the corporation to departmental supervision or regulation.[143] Here we briefly review two forms of independent agency: government corporations and special districts.

Government Corporations. *Government corporations* are found everywhere, especially in developing countries.[144] In the United States the corporate form tends to be used for the delivery of tangible and divisible goods in sectors that at least appear to be natural monopolies. Government corporations generally operate with their own source of revenue under a charter that gives them some independence from legislative or executive interference in their day-to-day operations. For example, electric utilities owned by municipalities generate revenue from the electricity that they sell. Usually, their charter requires them to do so at the lowest prices that cover operating costs and allow for growth.

Although government corporations are less important in the United States than in many other countries, their presence is not insignificant. The Tennessee Valley Authority had assets of more than $33 billion in 1997, making it the largest electric utility in North America; other important federally owned electricity producers include the Bonneville Power Administration, the Southeastern Federal Power Program, and the Alaska Power Administration. Major federal corporations include the Federal National Mortgage Association, the Postal Service, the Federal Deposit Insurance Corporation, and the Corporation for Public Broadcasting.[145] At the subnational level, major enterprises include the Port Authority of New York and New Jersey, the New York Power Authority, and the Massachusetts Port Authority.

What is the rationale for government corporations? Most government corporations, at least in the United States, meet the *single market-failure test*—that is, they are in sectors in which natural monopoly or other market failure suggests the need for government intervention. In our view, the critics of government corporations are implicitly arguing that few meet the double market-failure test.

The superficial appeal of government corporations is that they can correct market failures while presumably retaining the flexibility, autonomy, and efficiency of private corporations. Are government corporations less prone to principal-agent problems than government bureaus?

Louis De Alessi and other critics contend that government corporations, like government bureaus, are more prone to principal-agent problems than private firms: "The crucial difference between private and political firms is that ownership in the latter effectively is nontransferable. Since this rules out specialization in their ownership, it inhibits the capitalization of future consequences into current transfer prices and reduces owners' incentives to monitor managerial behavior."[146] The theoretical force of this argument is somewhat weakened by the growing realization that large private firms are also subject to principal-agent problems, especial-

[143]See Harold Seidman, "Public Enterprises in the United States," *Annals of Public and Cooperative Economy* 54(1) 1983, 3–18.

[144]Ahmed Galal et al., *Bureaucrats in Business: The Economics and Politics of Government Ownership* (Oxford: Oxford University Press, 1995).

[145]For a discussion of the potential privatization candidates among these corporations, see Anthony E. Boardman, Claude Laurin, and Aidan R. Vining, "Privatization in North America," in David Parker and David Sallal, eds., *International Handbook on Privatization* (Northampton, MA: Edward Elgar, 2003), 129–60.

[146]Louis De Alessi, "The Economics of Property Rights: A Review of the Evidence," in R. Zerbe, ed., *Research in Law and Economics*, Vol. 2 (Greenwich, CT: JAI Press, 1980), 1–47, at pp. 27–28.

ly if shareholding is dispersed.[147] The majority of empirical studies do, indeed, find that dispersed shareholding results in lower profitability and higher costs.[148]

Are public firms less efficient than private firms? Several surveys of cross-sectional empirical studies that compare private and public performance find some edge for the private sector, but several others find no consistent differences.[149] These studies do generally suggest superior private sector performance in competitive sectors, such as oil and gas production and steelmaking. For example, Aidan Vining and Anthony Boardman compared the performances of the largest non-U.S. public, private, and mixed firms operating in competitive environments. After controlling for important variables, such as industry and country, they found that public and mixed firms appeared to be less efficient than the private firms.[150]

The cross-sectional evidence, however, is more mixed in sectors such as electricity, gas, and water collection and distribution where there is little competition (at least historically) and usually extensive (rate-of-return) regulation.[151] In some parts of these industries this may be due to natural monopoly conditions.[152] Here, *X*-inefficiency among private firms resulting from limited competition and rate-of-return regulation is not surprising. Performance differences appear to be small, suggesting that the degree of competition in a given market is a better predictor of efficient performance than ownership, per se.

From the 1990s on, however, a new type of evidence became available on comparative performance: "before-and-after" (that is, time-series) evidence on the privatization of public firms. This evidence strongly suggests large efficiency gains, both *X*-efficiency and allocative efficiency, and is broadly consistent over industrialized countries, former Soviet bloc countries, and developing countries.[153] However, the evidence from the Soviet bloc countries and from developing countries suggests the necessity of appropriate capitalist institutional environments for private corporate entities to create wealth—in other words, framework rules, considered earlier in this chapter, are a

[147]For a comprehensive review of this issue, see the special issue of the *Journal of Law and Economics*, "Corporations and Private Property," 26(2), 1983, esp. Eugene F. Fama and Michael C. Jensen, "Separation of Ownership and Control," 301–26; "Agency Problems and Residual Claims," 327–50, by the same authors; and Oliver E. Williamson, "Organization Form, Residual Claimants, and Corporate Control," 351–66.

[148]For reviews of these studies, see Aidan R. Vining and Anthony E. Boardman, "Ownership versus Competition: Efficiency in Public Enterprise," *Public Choice* 73(2) 1992, 205–39; Helen Short, "Ownership, Control, Financial Structure and the Performance of Firms," *Journal of Economic Surveys* 8(3) 1994, 203–49.

[149]Louis De Alessi makes a strong claim for superior private performance in "The Economics of Property Rights: A Review of the Evidence." Aidan Vining and Anthony Boardman also found superior private sector performance in "Ownership versus Competition." Tom Borcherding found a slight edge for the private sector in "Toward a Positive Theory of Public Sector Supply Arrangements," in J. Robert S. Prichard, ed., *Crown Corporations in Canada* (Toronto: Butterworth, 1983), 99–184. A review that found few differences is Colin C. Boyd, "The Comparative Efficiency of State-Owned Enterprises," in A. R. Negandhi, H. Thomas, and K. L. K. Rao, eds., *Multinational Corporations and State-Owned Enterprises: A New Challenge in International Business* (Greenwich, CT: JAI Press, 1986), 221–44.

[150]Anthony E. Boardman and Aidan R. Vining, "Ownership and Performance in Competitive Environments: A Comparison of the Performance of Private, Mixed and State-Owned Enterprises," *Journal of Law and Economics* 32(1) 1989, 1–34.

[151]Lon L. Peters, "For-Profit and Non-Profit Firms: Limits of the Simple Theory of Attenuated Property Rights," *Review of Industrial Organization* 8(5) 1993, 623–33.

[152]For a recent brief discussion, see Harry M. Trebing, "New Dimensions of Market Failure in Electricity and Natural Gas Supply," *Journal of Economic Issues*, 35(2) 2001, 395–403.

[153]See footnotes and discussion earlier in this chapter under the privatization head.

fundamental requirement. Without such an institutional environment, the corporation is unlikely to be superior to the bureau, even in the absence of market failure.[154]

Certainly, many countries have, at least until recently, utilized government corporations in an extremely broad range of sectors where there is little evidence of underlying market failure. In France, for example, machine tools, automobiles, and watches are all produced by state firms. Until 1987, the French government even controlled one of the largest advertising agencies in the country! In Sweden, there is a government corporation that makes beer.

Special Districts. *Special districts* are single-purpose government entities, usually created to supply goods that are believed to have natural monopoly, public goods, or externality characteristics. Such goods are typically local in nature, but may extend to the state or region. By far the most common use of special districts in the United States is to provide primary and secondary schooling. Other examples include air pollution, water, and transportation districts. What are the advantages and disadvantages of special districts relative to cities and counties? Indeed, we might ask why we have cities at all. One advantage of special districts is that they allow consumers to observe the relationship between service provision and tax-price clearly. Another advantage is that they can be designed to internalize externalities that spill across the historically evolved boundaries of local governments. A major disadvantage is the costs that consumers face in monitoring a whole series of "minigovernments" for different services: "... only for the most important collective functions will wholly independent organization be justified on cost grounds ... the costs of organizing each activity separately would be greater than the promised added benefits from alternative organization."[155]

An important consideration is that collections of special districts prevent logrolling across issue areas. As we discussed in Chapter 8, logrolling often leads to inefficient pork-barrel spending. But it also permits minorities to express intense preferences that are not registered in majority voting on single issues where the social choice only reflects the preferences of the median voter. The more issues that are handled independently in special districts, the fewer that remain for possible inclusion in logrolls. Whether the reduction in logrolling contributes to efficiency and equity depends on the distribution of preferences in the population.

Contracting Out

In the past, private firms mostly provided services *to* government, while government itself provided the final product or service to the public (for example, private firms built the airplanes, but the government provided the army), but increasingly the private sector provides services directly to consumers. The U.S. government, for example, contracts for the construction of almost all military matériel. It also purchases about $36 billion annually in regular commercial ser-

[154]For a general discussion of these issues in the context of developing countries, see Paul Cook, Colin Kirkpatrick, and Frederick Nixson, eds., *Developing and Transitional Economies* (Cheltenham, UK: Edward Elgar, 1998). For empirical evidence, see Scott J. Wallsten, "An Economic Analysis of Telecom Competition, Privatization, and Regulation in Africa and Latin America," *Journal of Industrial Economics* 49(1) 2001, 1–19.

[155]James M. Buchanan and Marilyn R. Flowers, *The Public Finances*, 4th ed. (Homewood, IL: Irwin, 1975), 440.

vices like maintenance.[156] Contracting where the service is delivered to consumers is an important component of the health care system and is becoming increasingly important in some sectors of government activity traditionally associated with direct supply, such as corrections (if the service was previously delivered by government directly, this is a form of privatization).[157] An International City Management Association survey found that contracting for a wide range of services increased rapidly in the 1980s, especially at the local level.[158] The trend continues.

What is the evidence on efficiency of direct supply vis-à-vis contracting out? Here, the empirical evidence does suggest that contracting out is frequently more efficient than either market delivery (private subscription) or direct government supply: "… the empirical studies have found that contracting out tends to be less costly than government provision … cover[ing] a number of distinct services and pertain[ing] to a variety of geographical area."[159] The limitations of these findings, however, should be kept in mind (they are discussed at more length in Chapter 12). First, the services examined usually have tangible, easily measurable outputs, such as are found in highways, garbage disposal, transportation, and food provision. Consequently, monitoring the quality of output is relatively straightforward. Second, for these kinds of services contestability is high; and, third, neither party to the contract has to commit assets that become sunk (asset specificity is low). While opportunistic behavior is possible in such circumstances, even at its worst, it is likely to be limited in nature. (All three concepts—contestability, asset specificity, and opportunism—are explained in Chapter 12.) Additionally, almost all studies have only compared the production costs of contracting out versus in-house production. But contracting out imposes new, more complex contract-monitoring responsibilities on governments; this is costly. Scholars are just beginning to try and measure these costs. As policy analysts increasingly must make recommendations concerning the choice between in-house production and contracting out, we more explicitly address the costs relevant to the governance of government provision in Chapter 12.

Providing Insurance and Cushions

Some government interventions provide shields against the "slings and arrows of outrageous fortune." We divide these into two general categories: insurance and, for want of a better word, cushions. Table 10.5 presents a summary of these generic policies: mandatory and subsidized insurance, stockpiles, transitional assistance, and cash grants.

Insurance

The essence of insurance is the reduction of individual risk through pooling. Insurance can be purchased in private markets to indemnify against loss of life, damage to property, cost of health care, and liability for damages caused to others. As we

[156]Congressional Budget Office, *Contracting Out: Potential for Reducing Federal Costs* (Washington, DC: Congress of the United States, June 1987), vii.

[157]On some of the thorny issues in this particular context, see Ira P. Robbins, "Privatization of Corrections: Defining the Issues," *Federal Probation* September 1986, 24–30; and Connie Mayer, "Legal Issues Surrounding Private Operation of Prisons," *Criminal Law Bulletin* 22(4) 1986, 309–25.

[158]Reported in Robert W. Poole, Jr., and Philip E. Fixler, Jr., "The Privatization of Public Sector Services in Practice: Experience and Potential," *Journal of Policy Analysis and Management* 6(4) 1987, 612–25.

[159]Ibid., p. 615.

Table 10.5 *Providing Insurance and Cushions*

Generic Policies	Perceived Problem: Market Failure (MF), Government Failure (GF), Distributional Issue (DI), Limitation of Competitive Framework (LCF)	Typical Limitations and Collateral Consequences
Insurance		
Mandatory insurance	LCF: Adverse selection	Moral hazard
Subsidized insurance	MF: Information asymmetries DI: Equity in access LCF: Myopia LCF: Misperception of risk	
Cushions		
Stockpiling	LCF: Adjustment costs GF: Price controls	Rent seeking by suppliers and consumers
Transitional assistance (buy-outs, grandfathering)	LCF: Adjustment costs LCF: Macroeconomic dynamics	Inequity in availability
Cash grants	DI: Equality of outcome LCF: Utility interdependence	Reduction in work effort, dependency

discussed in Chapter 6, factors such as moral hazard, adverse selection, and limited actuarial experience can lead to incomplete insurance markets. Furthermore, people do not always make optimal decisions about purchasing insurance coverage because of biases inherent in the heuristics commonly used to estimate and interpret probabilities. Therefore, there may be an appropriate role for public intervention in some insurance markets. More generally, insurance can be used in conjunction with liability laws to deal with problems caused by information asymmetry.

In designing public insurance programs, care must be taken to limit moral hazard. By making certain outcomes less costly, insurance may induce people to take greater risks or bear greater compensable costs than they otherwise would.[160] One way to limit moral hazard is to invest in monitoring systems. Another is to design payment structures that reduce the incentive for beneficiaries to inflate compensable costs. For example, requiring beneficiaries to pay a fraction of their claimed costs through copayments reduces their incentive to incur unnecessary expenses. The general point is that in analyzing proposals for public insurance programs, it is necessary to anticipate how participants will respond to the availability of benefits.

Mandatory Insurance. When people have better information about their individual risks than insurers, adverse selection may limit the availability of insurance. For example, health insurance is sold primarily through group plans because they are less prone to adverse selection than individual policies. Because the pre-

[160]For example, Robert Topel attributes one-third or more of all unemployment spells among full-time participants in unemployment insurance programs to the benefits provided. Robert Topel, "Unemployment and Unemployment Insurance," *Research in Labor Economics* 7, annual, 1985, 91–135.

miums for individual policies are set on the assumption that the worst risks will self-select, good risks who do not have access to group coverage may decide not to insure. Government can use its authority to mandate universal participation in insurance plans to prevent adverse selection from operating.[161] Many proposals for national health insurance in the United States would mandate broader workplace coverage and require those not covered in the workplace to participate in public insurance programs.

Does the mere existence of an incomplete insurance market justify mandatory insurance? Usually, the rationale for mandatory insurance is based on the argument that the losses suffered by those left uncovered involve negative externalities. For example, the personal assets of many drivers are insufficient to cover the costs of property damage and personal injury that they inflict on others in serious accidents. Therefore, many states mandate liability coverage for all drivers so that those injured have opportunities to obtain compensation through tort law.

Paternalism may also serve as a rationale for mandatory insurance. For example, one function of the Old Age, Survivors, Disability and Health Insurance Program, the U.S. Social Security system, is to insure against the possibility that people have insufficient savings for retirement because of myopia, misinformation, miscalculation, bad luck, or simple laziness.[162] People who do not save an adequate amount will either consume at low levels in retirement or receive assistance from private or public charity. It is worth noting that Social Security is not a pure insurance program but, rather, involves considerable transfers from high-income workers to low-income workers and from current workers to current retirees.[163] Mandatory insurance programs typically combine actuarially based risk pooling with income transfers. Of course, if the programs were not mandatory, those paying the subsidies through higher premiums or lower benefits would be unlikely to participate.

Mandatory insurance can also be used to privatize regulation. One reason why legal liability alone cannot fully remedy information asymmetries and negative externalities is that firms often have inadequate assets to pay damages. This is especially likely for the short-lived fly-by-night firms that often exploit information asymmetries. By requiring that they carry minimum levels of liability insurance, the government can guarantee that at least some assets will be available for compensating those who have been harmed. Perhaps more important, the insurance companies have an incentive to monitor the behavior of the firms with an eye to reducing liability.[164]

It is important to note that mandatory insurance does not require that individuals be restricted from purchasing additional, supplementary insurance. Conceptually, mandatory insurance only requires that everyone, no matter what his or

[161]Nicholas Barr, "Social Insurance as an Efficiency Device," *Journal of Public Policy* 9(1) 1989, 35–58.

[162]Laurence J. Kotlikoff, "Justifying Public Provision of Social Security," *Journal of Policy Analysis and Management* 6(4) 1987, 674–89. For a detailed history of analyses dealing with Social Security issues, see Lawrence H. Thompson, "The Social Security Reform Debate," *Journal of Economic Literature* 21(4) 1983, 1425–67.

[163]For calculations for representative age and income groups, see Anthony Pellechio and Gordon Goodfellow, "Individual Gains and Losses from Social Security before and after the 1983 Amendments," *Cato Journal* 3(2) 1983, 417–42.

[164]Paul K. Freeman and Howard Kunreuther, *Managing Environmental Risk through Insurance* (Washington, DC: AEI Press, 1997), 24–25.

her wishes, acquire the core insurance. Monopoly mandatory insurance is normally based on the argument that if individuals are allowed to purchase additional private insurance their support for the publicly financed system will erode or that health care is so important that everybody should be required to utilize approximately the same amount.[165]

Subsidized Insurance. Rather than mandating insurance, the government can provide it at subsidized premiums when myopia, miscalculation, or other factors appear to be contributing to underconsumption. For example, in the United States, the Federal Emergency Management Agency provides subsidized flood insurance under the Flood Disaster Protection Act of 1973. As might be expected, restrictions on coverage are necessary to prevent those who suffer losses from rebuilding in floodplains.

Fairness often serves as a rationale for subsidizing premiums. For example, residents and businesses in poor neighborhoods may find actuarially fair premiums for fire insurance to be so high that they forgo coverage. A perception that they are unable to move to other locations with lower risks may serve as a rationale for subsidy. Rather than pay the subsidies directly, governments often force private insurers to write subsidized policies in proportion to their total premiums. Such *assigned risk pools* have been created to provide subsidized premiums for fire insurance in many urban areas. They are also commonly used in conjunction with mandatory insurance programs.

Cushions

Whereas insurance schemes reduce the variance in outcomes by spreading risk, *cushions* reduce the variance in outcomes through a centralized mechanism. From the perspective of beneficiaries, the consequences may appear identical. The key difference is that with insurance individuals make ex ante preparations for the possibility of unfavorable outcomes, while with cushions they receive ex post compensation for unfavorable outcomes that occur.

Stockpiling. In an uncertain world we always face the potential for supply disruptions or "price shocks," whether as a result of economic or political cartelization, unpredictable cyclicity of supply, or man-made or natural disasters. These shocks are unlikely to cause major problems unless they involve goods without close substitutes that are central to economic activity. In practice, the most serious problems arise with natural resources and agricultural products.

With respect to natural resources, if they are geographically concentrated, then the owners may be able to extract monopoly rents (as well as scarcity rents) from consumers. In a multinational context, cartels, whether they have primarily economic or political motives, may attempt to extract rents. While the long-run prospects for successful cartelization are limited because higher prices speed the introduction of substitutes, cartels may be able to exercise effective market power in the short run. In addition, the supply of concentrated resources may be subject to disruption because of revolution, war, or natural disaster.

[165]For empirical evidence on this issue, see Steven Globerman and Aidan R. Vining, "A Policy Perspective on 'Mixed' Health Care Financing Systems," *Journal of Risk and Insurance* 65(1) 1998, 57–80.

The adverse consequences of these supply disruptions can be dampened with *stockpiling programs* that accumulate quantities of the resource during periods of normal market activity so that they can be released during periods of market disruption. For example, the United States has long maintained government stockpiles of critical minerals like chromium, platinum, vanadium, and manganese, for which production was concentrated in South Africa, the former Soviet Union, and other countries of questionable political reliability.[166] Experience with the program suggests that political pressure from domestic producers tends to keep items in stockpiles long after they have lost their critical nature and that there is a reluctance to draw down stocks at the beginning of supply disruptions when they are most valuable to the economy.[167]

The most prominent U.S. resource stockpiling program is the Strategic Petroleum Reserve (SPR), which stores about 700 million barrels of crude oil for use during oil supply disruptions.[168] Because much of the world's low-cost reserves of crude oil are located in the politically unstable Middle East, the possibility exists for sharp reductions in supply that would cause steep rises in the price of oil and consequent losses to the U.S. economy. Drawdown of the SPR would offset a portion of the lost supply, thereby dampening the price rise and reducing the magnitude of economic losses.

Because private firms could make an expected profit by buying low during normal markets and selling high during disruptions, we might ask why the government should stockpile.[169] One reason is government failure: based on past experience, firms might anticipate the possibility that the government will institute price controls, preventing them from realizing speculative profits. Another is market failure: acquisition and drawdown decisions by private firms have external effects on the economy. (We consider these rationales in more depth in Chapter 17.)

In ancient times agricultural stockpiles served primarily as hedges against scarcity; in modern times they serve mainly as hedges against abundance. For example, the U.S. Commodity Credit Corporation in effect buys surpluses of grain from farmers to help support prices. While stockpiles of agricultural commodities provide security against widespread crop failures, they are costly to maintain. Further, modest price swings can probably be adequately accommodated by private stockpiling and by risk-diversification mechanisms like private futures markets.[170]

State and local governments, which typically must operate with a balanced budget, can prepare for revenue shocks by stockpiling financial resources. These reserves are sometimes called *rainy day funds*.[171] They serve as a form of self-insurance for governments that have difficulty borrowing on short notice. As with stockpilings of physical commodities, an important question is whether political

[166]Michael W. Klass, James C. Burrows, and Steven D. Beggs, *International Mineral Cartels and Embargoes* (New York: Praeger, 1980).

[167]See Glenn H. Snyder, *Stockpiling Strategic Materials: Politics and National Defense* (San Francisco: Chandler, 1966).

[168]For a history of the SPR, see David Leo Weimer, *The Strategic Petroleum Reserve: Planning, Implementation, and Analysis* (Westport, CT: Greenwood Press, 1982).

[169]For a discussion of this question, see George Horwich and David L. Weimer, *Oil Price Shocks, Market Response, and Contingency Planning* (Washington, DC: American Enterprise Institute, 1984), 111–39.

[170]Brian D. Wright, "Commodity Market Stabilization in Farm Programs," in Bruce L. Gardner, ed., *U.S. Agricultural Policy* (Washington, DC: American Enterprise Institute, 1985), 257–76.

[171]Michael Wolkoff, "An Evaluation of Municipal Rainy Day Funds," *Public Budgeting and Finance* 7(2) 1987, 52–63; and Richard Pollock and Jack P. Suyderhud, "The Role of Rainy Day Funds in Achieving Fiscal Stability," *National Tax Journal* 39(4) 1986, 485–97.

interests permit efficient decisions concerning acquisition and use. In particular, we might expect the pressures of the election cycle to lead to inefficient decisions concerning use.

Transitional Assistance. Policy analysts and politicians have increasingly come to realize that efficiency-enhancing policy changes are strongly resisted by those who suffer distributionally. This may result from the elimination of existing benefits or the imposition of new costs. Indeed, if there have only been transitional gains (as discussed in Chapter 8), the elimination of a benefit can impose real economic loss. Resistance to the elimination of benefits is likely to be especially bitter in these circumstances. Government may also wish to pay compensation when its projects would increase aggregate welfare but would impose disproportionate costs on particular individuals or localities.

Compensation may take either monetary or nonmonetary forms. Monetary compensation is typically in the form of a *buy-out*, whereby government purchases, at a fixed price, a given benefit. Examples of cash payments include relocation assistance payments to homeowners and renters displaced by federal urban renewal and highway construction projects.[172] Nonmonetary payment usually takes the form of either a *grandfather clause* or a *hold harmless provision*, both of which allow a current generation to retain benefits that will not be available to future generations. Grandfather clauses can increase political feasibility, but they can also reduce effectiveness.[173]

Cash Grants. The most direct way to cushion people against adverse economic circumstances is through *cash grants*. This generic term covers such programs in the United States as Aid to Families with Dependent Children before 1996 or Temporary Assistance for Needy Families after 1996 (welfare) and Supplemental Security Income (aid to the blind and disabled). The 1974 Health, Education, and Welfare "megaproposal" summarizes the situations in which cash grants are preferable to vouchers: "the provision of cash benefits is an appropriate public action when the objective is to alter the distribution of purchasing power in general and when the recipient of the benefit is to be left free to decide how to spend it ...," while " ... the provision of vouchers is appropriate when the objective is to alter the distribution of purchasing power over specific goods and services when the supply of these can be expected to increase as the demand for them increases."[174]

The advantage (or disadvantage) of cash grants is that they do not interfere with the consumption choices of a target population. Clearly, this is a valuable attribute if the goal is simply to raise incomes. On the other hand, if the objective is to *alter* consumption patterns, then cash grants are less effective instruments. While cash grants do not restrict consumption behavior, they may affect other behavior, most importantly, the "leisure-labor" trade-off. Increases in unearned income, whether through cash grants, in-kind grants, or other subsidies, generally increase the demand for all goods, including leisure, so that the amount of labor supplied falls.[175]

[172]Joseph J. Cordes and Burton A. Weisbrod, "When Government Programs Create Inequities: A Guide to Compensation Policies," *Journal of Policy Analysis and Management* 4(2) 1985, 178–95.

[173]For a discussion of these issues, see Christopher Leman, "How to Get There from Here: The Grandfather Effect and Public Policy," *Policy Analysis* 6(1) 1980, 99–116.

[174]Laurence Lynn and John Michael Seidi, "Policy Analysis as HEW: Story of Mega-Proposal-Introduction," *Policy Analysis* 1(2) 1975, 232–73.

[175]For a review of empirical evidence on the income elasticity of the labor supply, see Robert A. Moffitt and Kenneth C. Kehrer, "The Effect of Tax and Transfer Programs on Labor Supply," *Research in Labor Economics* 4, annual, 1981, 103–50.

A fundamental trade-off between transferring income and discouraging work effort arises in designing cash grant programs. For example, consider the goals of a negative income tax: (1) to make any difference, the transfer should be substantial; (2) to preserve work incentives, marginal tax rates should be relatively low; and (3) the break-even level of income (the point at which the transfer reaches zero) should be reasonably low to avoid high program costs. Unfortunately, at least to some extent, the three are incompatible. For example, if a negative income tax guaranteed every family a floor on income of $8,000 through a cash grant, then a tax rate of 20 percent on earned income would imply that only when earned income reached $40,000 would net payments to families be zero. Raising the tax rate to, say, 50 percent would lower the break-even earned income to $16,000. The higher tax rate, however, would reduce the after-tax wage rate and thereby probably reduce work effort.

If recipients reduce their work effort, then their chances of becoming dependent on the cash grants increase. For some categories of recipients, such as the permanently disabled, the increased risk of dependence may not be a serious concern. For others, however, there may be a trade-off between the generosity of short-term assistance and the long-run economic vitality of recipients. Work requirements may be one way to improve the terms of the trade-off.[176] Unfortunately, they are typically costly and difficult to implement, especially for single-parent families with young children.

Cash grants can also influence choices about living arrangements and family structure. For example, Aid to Families with Dependent Children often made it financially possible for young unmarried mothers to set up their own households. The less generous are state benefit levels, the more likely it is that these mothers will stay with their parents.[177] Indeed, the opportunity to gain independence may encourage some teenage girls to have children. The general point is that the availability of cash grants may influence a wide range of behaviors.

Conclusion

A variety of generic policies can be used to address market and government failures. Table 10.6 indicates the generic policy categories that are most likely to provide candidate solutions for each of the major market failures, government failures, and distributional concerns. In many cases, more than one generic policy can provide potential solutions for the same problem. But the solutions are never perfect. They must be tailored to the specifics of the situation and evaluated in terms of the relevant goals.

Our discussions of general problems and generic policy solutions lay the foundations for actually doing policy analysis. An understanding of market and government failure helps us to understand the nature of public policy problems. Being aware of the generic policies and their collateral consequences helps us to begin our search for solutions to our specific policy problems.

[176]Lawrence W. Mead, "The Potential for Work Enforcement: A Study of WIN," *Journal of Policy Analysis and Management* 7(2) 1988, 264–88.

[177]David T. Ellwood and Mary Jo Bane, "The Impact of AFDC on Family Structure and Living Arrangements," *Research in Labor Economics* 7, annual, 1985, 137–207.

Table 10.6 *Searching for Generic Policy Solutions*

	Market Mechanism	Incentives	Rules	Nonmarket Supply	Insurance and Cushions
Traditional Market Failures					
Public goods	S	S	S	P	
Externalities	S	P	P	S	
Natural monopolies	S	S	P	P	
Information asymmetries			P	S	S
Other Limitations of the Competitive Framework					
Thin markets			P		
Preference-related problems	S	S	P		
Uncertainty problems			P		S
Intertemporal problems			S		P
Adjustment costs					P
Macroeconomic dynamics		P			S
Distributional Concerns					
Equity of opportunity		S	P		S
Equality of outcomes			S	S	P
Government Failures					
Direct democracy			P		
Representative government	P		S		
Bureaucratic supply	P	S	S	S	
Decentralization	S	P		S	

Sources for solutions (though not necessarily most often used!): P—primary; S—secondary.

For Discussion

1. Consider a developing country that has no policies regulating the discharge of pollutants into its surface waters. In the past, there has been some degradation of water quality from agricultural waste. Increasingly, however, factories have begun to discharge industrial wastes into lakes and rivers, raising environmental and health concerns. What are the generic policy alternatives the country might adopt to limit or reverse the reductions in water quality from industrial pollution?
2. Your state or province is concerned that too few children are being immunized against childhood illnesses. What are some of the generic policy alternatives that could be adopted to increase immunization rates?

11

Adoption and Implementation

The adoption and execution of collective decisions inherently involve cooperation. Collective decisions begin as proposals in political arenas and culminate in effects on people. We can divide this process into two phases: adoption and implementation. The *adoption phase* begins with the formulation of a policy proposal and ends, if ever, with its formal acceptance as a law, regulation, administrative directive, or other decision made according to the rules of the relevant political arena. The *implementation phase* begins with the adoption of the policy and continues as long as the policy remains in effect. While policy analysts typically make their contributions by formulating and evaluating proposals during the adoption phase, they cannot do so effectively without anticipating the entire process from proposal to effect.

Yet the distinction between adoption and implementation does not do justice to the complexity that typically characterizes the policy process. Adopted policies, especially laws, rarely specify exactly what is to be done. Instead, they may require policy decisions to be made in other arenas. For example, a county legislature might adopt an ordinance that prohibits smoking in certain public places, makes violations punishable by fines, and delegates enforcement responsibility to the county health department. Now the county's health department must adopt an enforcement policy. Should it simply wait for complaints about violations from the public, or should it institute spot checks? Should it issue warnings, or immediately impose fines? Although the head of the health department may have legal authority to answer these questions as she sees fit, her decisions probably would be influenced by the (perhaps conflicting) advice of her staff. If spot checks are to be instituted, then the chief inspector would face the task of designing a sampling procedure that his deputies could and would execute. Thus, the smoking policy that the public encounters results from a series of decisions following adoption of the ordinance.

We naturally think of values and interests coming into play during the adoption phase, and we are not surprised when those who oppose policies attempt to block their adoption. By thinking of the implementation phase as a series of adoptions, we prepare ourselves for the intrusion of the values and interests of those whose cooperation is needed to move the adopted policy from a general statement of intent to a specific set of desired impacts. In other words, we begin to think strategically about process as well as substance: How can we take advantage of the interests and values of others to further our ends?

As will be obvious by now, good policy analysis requires a great deal of thought. But it does not always require thought that is explicitly strategic. We can often make predictions about the consequences of adopted and fully implemented policies without considering the responses of particular individuals. For example, demand schedules usually allow us to make plausible predictions of the aggregate consequences of taxing goods. When we attempt to predict the prospects for adoption and successful implementation, however, we must think strategically.

Formal models of strategic behavior usually take the form of games that unfold through a series of moves by players. For example, imagine that you are the player who begins by selecting a strategy (move 1). In the case of policy adoption, for instance, your strategy choice may be to convince your client to propose a particular policy. Another player adopts a strategy in response to your first move (move 2), say, by opposing or supporting your client's policy proposal or by suggesting some other policy. Thinking strategically requires you to anticipate the responses that each of your possible strategy choices for move 1 would elicit from the other player in move 2.

When players must choose their strategies not knowing what strategies other players have selected, then we can display the game as a table of payoffs for the various combinations of players' strategy choices as illustrated by the Prisoner's Dilemma displayed in Figure 5.6. The social science literature offers a wealth of formal models for investigating specific sorts of strategic social, political, and economic interactions.[1] Unfortunately, the simplifications necessary for making these formal models tractable often precludes their direct application to the sorts of complex, fluid, and poorly defined situations in which policy analysts typically find themselves. Consequently, except for a brief treatment of social norms in the context of policy design, rather than presenting formal models, we provide general frameworks for helping analysts think strategically.

We believe that our general discussion of strategic thinking in this chapter is valuable for a number of purposes. First, as we discuss in Chapter 14, we cannot make accurate predictions of the consequences of candidate policies without paying careful attention to their implementation. Strategic thinking is valuable, therefore, because it enables us to understand better the implementation process.

Second, clients often want their analysts to consider the political feasibility of adoption of policy alternatives. Sometimes this form of political feasibility is explicitly

[1]For an introduction to formal games in economics, see Robert Gibbons, *Game Theory for Applied Economists* (Princeton, NJ: Princeton University Press, 1992). For an introduction to their use in political science, see James D. Morrow, *Game Theory for Political Scientists* (Princeton, NJ: Princeton University Press, 1994).

treated as one of multiple goals in policy analysis. Other times clients ask analysts to prepare confidential analyses of the political feasibility of getting particular policy alternatives adopted. In either case, good analysis requires strategic thinking.

Third, designing effective policy alternatives requires a certain amount of creativity. Strategic thinking helps us to be more creative by drawing our attention to ways of taking advantage of the self-interested behaviors of others. Similarly, it helps us to be more perceptive about potential problems and opportunities in designing implementation plans.

Fourth, analysts themselves often participate in adoption and implementation efforts. Clients sometimes solicit advice from analysts about day-to-day maneuvering in political arenas, invite them to participate as "technical experts" in negotiations, or send them as representatives to meetings where issues are discussed and perhaps even decided. Analysts are sometimes called upon to advise, direct, oversee, or even manage implementations. These sorts of hands-on activities require analysts to put strategic thinking into practice.

The Adoption Phase

What determines political feasibility? In this context, political feasibility specifically refers to *the feasibility of adoption of the policy*, not to whether citizens, and, more pertinently, voters, will accept the policy once it has been adopted.[2] (When we discuss political feasibility elsewhere, it may mean political feasibility in either sense—or, indeed, both.) Recent work applying expected utility theory to the study of international relations and national coalitions offers promise for making accurate and nonintuitive predictions.[3] In practice, however, politicians and businesspeople who desire political predictions usually turn to *area experts*, people who are familiar with the relevant actors in local, national, or regional settings. For example, someone interested in the prospects for passage of U.S. legislation on trade may hire an expert on Congress. A firm considering capital investments in a particular country may consult someone familiar with the institutions of that country to assess the prospects for political stability. Of course, politicians usually consider themselves to be experts on the particular political arenas in which they operate, and appropriately so. Policy analysts who have long tenure in institutional settings likewise tend to develop contextual knowledge that is useful in predicting the political feasibility of adoption.

Finding the sort of information that an area expert provides is a reasonable starting point for predicting adoption feasibility. But this information by itself is often descriptive and dated. To put it to effective use, we need a theory about how

[2]Indeed, the two types of political feasibility may be negatively correlated. For example, British Prime Minister Margaret Thatcher had relatively little difficulty getting the poll tax adopted because of the centralization inherent in parliamentary government and the weakness of local government opposition, but this almost certainly contributed to her totally underestimating the political unpopularity of the policy. Ultimately, the poll tax was a major factor in driving her from office. See Connor McGrath, "Policy Making in Political Memoirs—The Case of the Poll Tax," *Journal of Public Affairs* 2(2) 2002, 71–85.

[3]For a summary of the expected utility approach, see Bruce Bueno de Mesquita, David Newman, and Alvin Rabushka, *Forecasting Political Events: The Future of Hong Kong* (New Haven, CT: Yale University Press, 1985), 11–54. For an overview, see James Lee Ray and Bruce Russett, "The Future as Arbiter of Theoretical Controversies: Predictions, Explanations and the End of the Cold War," *British Journal of Political Science* 26(4) 1996, 441–70.

people behave so that we can develop strategies for improving the chances of obtaining the outcomes we desire. Hence, after reviewing the sorts of information that are relevant to understanding the political environment, we turn to the basic elements of political strategy.

Assessing and Influencing the Political Feasibility of Adoption

One of the few political scientists to speak directly to the question of how policy analysts can predict and influence the political feasibility of policy proposals is Arnold Meltsner.[4] He provides a checklist of the information needed to assess the political feasibility of adoption: Who are the relevant actors? What are their motivations and beliefs? What are their political resources? In which political arenas will the relevant decisions be made? Although we discuss these questions sequentially, in practice we answer them iteratively, moving among them as we learn more about the political environment.

Identifying the Relevant Actors. Which individuals and groups are likely to voice an opinion on an issue? Two, usually overlapping, sets of actors need to be identified: those with a substantive interest in the issue and those with official standing in the decision arena. For example, imagine a proposal before a city council that would prohibit firms within the city from subjecting their employees to random drug testing. We expect unions to support the measure and business groups to oppose it. Further, we expect unions and business groups that have been politically active in the past to be the ones most likely to become active on this issue—say, the Labor Council and the Chamber of Commerce as shown in Table 11.1. At the same time, we identify the members of the City Council as actors by virtue of their rights to vote on legislation and the mayor by virtue of her veto power.

We expect union and business leaders to be active because their direct interests are at stake. Civil libertarians might become involved because values they perceive as important are at issue. (Some may see the ordinance as necessary to protect the right of workers to privacy; others may view it as an unwarranted interference in the decisions of firms.) Perhaps certain community groups such as the Urban League will become active either because they have a direct interest or because they usually ally themselves with one of the interested parties.

Other public figures besides the members of the City Council may also be relevant. For example, although the city attorney does not have a vote on the council, his opinion on the legality of the proposal may carry considerable weight with council members. The opinion of the director of public health on the accuracy of testing may also be influential. The editor of the local newspaper has no official standing whatsoever, yet may be an important participant by virtue of the editorials she writes and the influence she exerts over the coverage of the news.

How should analysts compile lists of potential actors? Obviously, *assume that anyone with a strong interest, whether economic, partisan, ideological, or professional, will become an actor.* Also, include those in official positions. If you are new to the issue or arena, then try to find an experienced person to be your informant. Use newspapers or other

[4] Arnold Meltsner, "Political Feasibility and Policy Analysis," *Public Administration Review* 32(6) 1972, 859–67.

Table 11.1 *A Political Analysis Worksheet: Feasibility of a Ban on Random Drug Testing in the Workplace*

Actors	Motivations	Beliefs	Resources
Interest Groups			
Labor Council	Protect workers from harassment	Testing would be used unfairly	Large membership; ties to Democratic Party
Chamber of Commerce	Protect firms' rights to weed out dangerous and unproductive workers	Testing may be necessary to detect and deter employee drug use	Influential membership; ties to Republican Party
Civil Liberties Union	Protect rights of individuals	Testing infringes on right to privacy	Articulate spokesperson Vocal membership
Libertarian Party	Protect right of contract	Testing limits should be a matter of negotiation between labor and management	Ideas
Urban League	Protect minority employees	Testing disproportionately hurts minorities	Can claim to speak for minority interests
Daily Newspaper	Support business environment	Testing ban not appropriate at city level	Editorials
Unelected Officials			
City Attorney	Support mayor and protect city from law suit	Ban probably legal	Professional opinion
Director, Public Health	Fight drug abuse	Testing probably desirable if not punitive	Professional opinion; evidence on effectiveness of tests
Elected Officials			
Council Member A (Democrat)	Support labor	Ban desirable	Vote
Council Member B (Democrat)	Support labor	Ban probably desirable	Vote
Council Member C (Democrat) President of Council	Support community groups	Ban probably desirable	Vote; agenda control
Council Member D (Republican)	Support business	Ban probably undesirable	Vote
Council Member E (Republican)	Support business	Ban undesirable	Vote
Mayor (Democrat)	Maintain good relations with labor and business	Ban probably undesirable	Veto power; media attention

written accounts to discover who participated in public debates on similar issues in the past. Finally, when doing so will not adversely affect your client or the future prospects for your proposal, contact potential actors directly to question them about their views and to assess the likelihood that they will become active participants.

Understanding the Motivations and Beliefs of Actors. The motivations and beliefs of organized interest groups will often be apparent. When they are not, you can usually make a reasonable guess about how they will view particular proposals by comparing the costs and benefits that the leaders of the groups are likely to perceive. If their perceptions are based on what you think are incorrect beliefs, then you may be able to influence their positions by providing information.[5] For example, the president of the local Urban League chapter may support a ban on random drug testing because he believes that the ban would protect minority workers, one of his constituencies. He might decide to oppose the ban, however, if he comes to believe that the ban will result in a net loss in minority jobs because some firms will leave the city to avoid its restrictions.

It may be more difficult to determine the relevant motivations and beliefs of those in official positions. Elected officials, political appointees, and members of the civil service all have a variety of motivations. As we discussed in Chapter 8, elected officials are likely to be concerned with reelection or election to higher office as well as with representing the interests of their constituencies and promoting the social good. Political appointees may be motivated by their substantive values as well as by their loyalties to their political sponsors, by their desire to maintain their effectiveness in their current positions, and by their interest in opportunities for future employment. In addition to substantive values, civil servants are often motivated by their sense of professionalism and by their desire to secure resources for their organizational units.

It should not be surprising that it is often difficult to predict which motivations will dominate. Indeed, such conflicting motivations can lead the officials themselves to the sort of personal ethical dilemmas that we described in Chapter 3. How can we understand the relative importance of officials' various motivations concerning a particular issue? We can begin by heeding the insight in the aphorism: *where you stand depends on where you sit.*[6] In other words, put yourself in the position of the relevant officials. What would you want if you were in their place? What actions would you be willing to take to get what you want?

Obviously, the more you know about particular officials, the better you will be able to answer these questions. If an official holds a strong substantive value relevant to the issue, for instance, then she may be willing to act against even vocal constituent interests. On the other hand, she may be willing to go against her own

[5]In their "The Dynamics of Policy-Oriented Learning," Jenkins-Smith and Sabatier identify three important areas in which actors experience policy-oriented learning: "Improving One's Understanding of the Status of Goals and Other Variables Identified as Important by One's Belief System ... Refining One's Understanding of Logical and Causal Relationships Internal to Belief Systems ... Identifying and Responding to Challenges to One's Belief System" (pp. 42–43). Paul A. Sabatier and Hank Jenkins-Smith, eds., *Policy Change and Learning: An Advocacy Coalition Approach* (San Francisco: Westview Press, 1993), 41–56.

[6]Some view this aphorism as the central element of effective strategic thinking. For example, see Donald E. Stokes, "Political and Organizational Analysis in the Policy Curriculum," *Journal of Policy Analysis and Management* 6(1) 1986, 45–55, at p. 52. The aphorism itself is attributed to Rufus E. Miles, Jr., "The Origin and Meaning of Miles' Law," *Public Administration Review* 38(5) 1978, 399–403.

substantive values if the issue is of fundamental concern to one of her important constituencies. Of course, such factors as the electoral competitiveness of her district and the nearness to an election can also affect the position that she takes on the issue.

Assessing the Resources of Actors. Actors have a variety of political resources. Interest groups can claim to speak for a constituency. They may have financial resources that can be used to pay for lobbying, analysis, publicity, and campaign contributions. Their leaders may have ongoing relationships with relevant officials. By virtue of their memberships, analytical capacity, or track record, the information they provide may command attention or carry weight. All these resources can be thought of as potentially relevant. Whether they actually come into play depends on the motivations of the groups and their leaders.

Officials have resources based on their positions and relationships. Legislators can vote, hold hearings, and influence the agenda; elected executives, like mayors, usually have veto power as well as considerable discretion in interpreting laws that are adopted; unelected executives often have influence by virtue of their professional status, programmatic knowledge, and ties to clientele groups. Any of these actors may be able to influence others through personal relationships based on trust, loyalty, fear, or reciprocity.

Table 11.1, which presents a simple worksheet that identifies the actors who may be relevant in predicting the political feasibility of a city ordinance to ban random drug testing of employees, also notes their likely motivations, beliefs, and resources. Many of the entries may be little more than guesses, especially for analysts new to the particular political arena. The entries in the worksheet should be updated as more information becomes available. For example, the actors' actual responses to the proposal once they learn about it may very well change your assessment of their beliefs and their willingness to use resources.

Choosing the Arena. Each political arena has its own set of rules about how decisions are made. The basic rules are generally written—legislatures have "rules of order" and agencies have administrative procedures. But unwritten traditions and standard practices may be just as relevant to understanding how decisions are typically reached. Becoming familiar with these rules, both formal and informal, is important for political prediction and strategy.

To use the information in Table 11.1 to make a prediction about the likelihood of adoption of the drug testing ban, we must first determine the arenas in which the proposal will be considered. As suggested by the entries under "elected officials," we expect that the City Council will be the primary arena. Assuming that the council members vote according to their constituencies' apparent interests, the ban would pass on a party-line vote of three to two. The mayor would then be in a difficult situation. If she vetoes the ordinance, then she may alienate her fellow Democrats. If she does not veto it, then she will alienate business interests.

The mayor might be able to get out of this difficult political position by trying to change the arena. She might argue that, although restrictions on testing are desirable, they are more appropriately imposed at the state level. If she can find a state assembly member or senator to propose the ban in the state legislature, then she could argue that a vote by the City Council should be delayed until the prospects for state action become clear. Perhaps she would ask the council to pass a resolution urging state action. If the council agrees, then she will have been successful in changing arenas.

More generally, we should expect that actors who lose, or anticipate losing, in one arena will try to move the issue to another. As illustrated by the mayor's maneuver, unfavorable outcomes at one level of government can sometimes be avoided by shifting the issue to another level. For example, one reason why labor unions pushed for the federal legislation that became the Occupational Safety and Health Act of 1970 was their dissatisfaction with their ability to influence the setting and enforcement of health standards at the state level.[7] The arena can also shift from one branch of government to another. For instance, when the Food and Drug Administration published a proposed rule that would prohibit the use of saccharin as a food additive, opponents succeeded in getting Congress to pass a moratorium on finalization of the rule.[8] Often those who lose in the legislative and executive branches try to shift the arena to the courts. For instance, during the 1970s, advocates of busing to reduce the racial segregation in schools caused by housing patterns routinely achieved their objectives through the courts. Regulatory agencies that fail to establish strong cases for rule making invite court challenges by those who oppose the rules. Of course, the ability to make a credible threat to move the issue to another arena can itself be a political resource.

Political Strategies within Arenas

Trying to shift issues to more favorable arenas is not the only political strategy that can be used to achieve policy outcomes. We can often use one or more of four other general strategies: co-optation, compromise, heresthetics, and rhetoric. We briefly consider each of these in turn.

Co-optation. People, especially the types with strong egos who typically hold public office (and teach at universities), tend to take pride in authorship. Indeed, we are sometimes reluctant to admit the weaknesses in what we perceive to be *our* ideas. Getting others to believe that your proposal is at least partly their idea is perhaps one of the most common political strategies.[9] In legislative settings it often takes the form of co-sponsorship—across aisles and chambers. In administrative settings, it often involves creating an advisory group that is constituted so as to arrive at the desired recommendation. Potential adversaries who believe that they have contributed to the recommendation as committee members may be less likely to become active opponents. Public officials with strong interpersonal skills can sometimes successfully co-opt potential opponents with as little as a seemingly heart-to-heart conversation or other gesture of personal attention. (Didn't you ever wonder why the dean invited you and the other student leaders to those dinners?)

[7]John Mendeloff, *Regulating Safety: An Economic and Political Analysis of Occupational Safety and Health Policy* (Cambridge, MA: MIT Press, 1979), 15–16.

[8]Richard A. Merrill, "Saccharin: A Regulator's View," in Robert W. Crandall and Lester B. Lave, eds., *The Scientific Basis of Health and Safety Regulation* (Washington, DC: Brookings Institution, 1981), 153–70.

[9]More generally, it may be that radical policy change is possible only when elites from the major political cultures perceive the change as consistent with their fundamental values. For a discussion of such nonincremental change, see Dennis Coyle and Aaron Wildavsky, "Requisites of Radical Reform: Income Maintenance versus Tax Preferences," *Journal of Policy Analysis and Management* 7(1) 1987, 1–16.

Co-optation may be useful when your proposal infringes on the turf of other political actors.[10] Politicians and bureaucrats often stake out areas of interest and expertise. Although some of them may be natural allies by virtue of their interests and beliefs, they may, nevertheless, feel threatened by proposals originating from other people that appear to fall within their areas. Unless you involve them to some extent in the design of policy proposals, they may voice opposition without seriously considering substantive merits. Furthermore, other actors who take their cues on the issue from the recognized experts may decline to give the proposals close attention. For example, council members may not give serious attention to a proposal for the establishment of a particular type of drug rehabilitation program unless the director of public health says that it is worthy of consideration.

Of course, you cannot use co-optation as a strategy unless you are willing to share credit. As an analyst, the nature of your job demands that you allow your client to take credit for your good ideas (and that you save any discredit for bad ideas for yourself)—remember, you earn your keep by providing good ideas. Co-optation strategies, therefore, should be based on your client's explicit willingness to give credit in return for progress toward policy goals.

Compromise. We use the word *compromise* to refer to substantive modifications of policy proposals intended to make them more politically acceptable. When our most preferred policy lacks adequate support, we can consider modifying it to gain the additional support needed for adoption—in terms of policy analysis seeking to promote multiple goals, we trade progress toward some goal to achieve greater political feasibility. Compromise is desirable if we prefer the resulting adoptable proposal over any others that are also feasible. Generally, desirable compromise involves making the smallest modifications necessary to attract the minimal number of additional supporters required for adoption.[11]

One approach to compromising is to remove or modify those features of the proposal that are most objectionable to its opponents. Do any features appear as red flags to opponents? Sometimes offending features can be removed without great change in the substantive impact of the proposal. For example, imagine that you have made a proposal that the county hire private firms to provide educational services to inmates in the county jail. Some opponents, who object on ideological grounds to profit-making activity in connection with criminal corrections, may be willing to

[10]For a discussion of the use of co-optation at the organizational level, see Philip Selznick, *TVA and the Grass Roots* (Berkeley: University of California Press, 1949), 13–16. Harvey M. Sapolsky identifies co-optation of potential critics both inside and outside the navy as one of the factors contributing to the success of the Polaris missile project. See his *The Polaris System Development: Bureaucratic and Programmatic Success in Government* (Cambridge, MA: Harvard University Press, 1972), 15, 47–54.

[11]In arenas where the gains of winners come at the expense of losers (zero-sum games), Riker's size principle predicts such behavior: "In social situations similar to *n*-person, zero-sum games with side-payments, participants create coalitions just as large as they believe will ensure winning and no larger." William H. Riker, *The Theory of Political Coalitions* (New Haven, CT: Yale University Press, 1962), 32–33. In some circumstances, however, compromising more to obtain a broader coalition may be desirable if the greater consensus will deter opponents from seeking to overturn the policy at a later time or in another arena. For example, Justice Felix Frankfurter successfully delayed the Supreme Court decision in *Brown v. Board of Education*, 347 U.S. 483 (1954), so that a unanimous opinion could be achieved. Bernard Schwartz with Stephan Lesher, *Inside the Warren Court* (Garden City, NY: Doubleday, 1983), 21–27.

support your proposal if you specify that only nonprofit organizations can be service providers. With this restriction, you may be able to gain adoption of a policy with most of the benefits of your original proposal.

Another approach to compromising is to add features that opponents find attractive. In Chapter 8 we discussed logrolling, a form of compromise that is characterized by the packaging together of substantively unrelated proposals. The engineering of logrolls is usually the purview of clients rather than analysts. More commonly, analysts are in a position to give advice about the composition of a single proposal. For example, consider again the proposal to ban random drug testing in the workplace. Matched against the status quo, it appears that the ban would be adopted by the City Council. If you opposed the ban, then you might try to stop it by proposing that firms be banned not from testing but from firing, demoting, or disciplining an employee on the basis of a single test. Assuming that the two council members (D and E) who are opposed to the ban would support this compromise position, it might get the necessary votes by attracting the support of one of the less enthusiastic supporters of the stronger ban (B or C). You might be able to get the mayor and the director of public health to support the compromise position and help secure the third vote.

In organizational settings, compromise often takes the form of *negotiation,* whereby interested parties attempt to reach agreement through bargaining. For example, local implementation of a state law requiring teachers and health professionals to report suspected cases of child abuse may require an agreement to be reached between the police chief and the director of social services on how reports are to be investigated.

What factors are likely to influence the character and outcomes of negotiations?[12] One factor is the frequency with which the participants must deal with each other. If they must deal with each other often, then it is likely that they will be more flexible and amicable than they would be in an isolated negotiation. Another factor is the political resources that each brings to the negotiations. Is either one in a better position to appeal to outside parties, such as the county executive or the mayor? Can either one use precedent as an argument? Can either party inflict costs on the other by delaying agreement?

Roger Fisher and William Ury provide a useful practical guide for negotiating effectively.[13] We note here two of their themes that can be thought of as general strategies for successfully negotiating compromise.

First, remember that you are dealing with people who have emotions, beliefs, and personal interests. The presentation as well as the content of proposals can be important for reaching mutually satisfactory agreements. For example, if your counterpart in the negotiation has gone on record as opposing a tax increase, then even if you convince him that additional revenue is needed, he is unlikely to agree to something called a tax increase. Look for a compromise that allows him to save face. Perhaps what we would normally describe as a gasoline tax could be called a "road user's fee" instead. Maybe just substituting the euphemism "revenue enhancement" will be an adequate face saver—perhaps even if everyone knows that it is just a different phrase for the same thing! The general point is to always keep

[12]For a more comprehensive listing, see Howard Raiffa, *The Art and Science of Negotiation* (Cambridge, MA: Harvard University Press, 1982), 11–19.

[13]Roger Fisher and William Ury, *Getting to Yes: Negotiating Agreement without Giving In,* 2nd ed. (New York: Penguin, 1991).

in mind that you are dealing with people, who, like yourself, want to feel good about what they are doing.

Second, try to negotiate interests rather than positions so that mutually beneficial compromises can be found. For example, Fisher and Ury point to the negotiations between Egypt and Israel over the Sinai, which was captured by Israel in the Six-Day War of 1967.[14] As long as both sides approached the issue positionally—Egypt demanding return of the entire Sinai and Israel demanding that the boundary line be redrawn—there was little possibility of agreement. By looking at interests, however, a solution became possible. While Egypt, after centuries of domination, was unwilling to cede sovereignty to any of its territory, Israel did not desire the territory, per se. Rather, it wanted to keep Egyptian forces away from its border. The solution was to return the Sinai to Egyptian sovereignty but to demilitarize those areas that could be used as staging grounds to threaten Israel. The general point to keep in mind is that the ultimate purpose of negotiations should be to satisfy the interests of the parties involved. In other words, approach negotiations as a sort of on-the-spot policy analysis—get agreement on the facts in the dispute (define the problem), identify interests (determine goals), agree on criteria for determining a fair solution (specify evaluation criteria), brainstorm for possible solutions (develop policy alternatives), and only then consider specific solutions (evaluate alternatives in terms of criteria).[15]

Heresthetics. William H. Riker has coined the word *heresthetics* to refer to strategies that attempt to gain advantage through manipulation of the circumstances of political choice.[16] Heresthetical devices fall into two categories: those that operate through the agenda and those that operate through the dimensions of evaluation.

In Chapter 8 we illustrated the paradox of voting with the hypothetical example of pairwise votes on school budgets. The preferences of the voters were such that, if everyone voted his or her true preferences, the order in which policies were considered—the agenda—determined the one that would be selected. Thus, *manipulating the agenda can be a powerful political strategy.*

The holders of specific offices often have the opportunity to manipulate the agenda directly. Such officials as the speaker of the legislature, the committee chair, or the administrator running a meeting may be able to influence the policy outcome by the way they structure the decision process. Sometimes they can bluntly structure the decision process to their advantage by refusing to allow certain alternatives to be considered—perhaps justifying their actions by a call for "further study." Other times they can achieve their ends by determining the order in which the alternatives will be considered.

Obviously, agenda setters are especially important actors in any political arena. If your client is an agenda setter, then you are in an advantageous position for seeing your accepted recommendations adopted as policy. If your client is not an agenda setter, then you must find ways to increase the chances that your client's proposals

[14] Ibid., pp. 40–42.

[15] Ibid., pp. 10–14.

[16] William H. Riker, *The Art of Political Manipulation* (New Haven, CT: Yale University Press, 1986), ix.

receive favorable agenda positions. One approach is to design your proposals so that they appeal to the agenda setters.

Another approach is to mobilize other political actors on your behalf to make it politically costly for agenda setters to block your proposals. For example, in 1962 Senator Estes Kefauver found that the legislation he introduced to amend the laws governing the regulation of pharmaceuticals was stalled in the Judiciary Committee by its chairman, Senator James Eastland, who opposed it. Only by generating criticism of inaction in the press and mobilizing the support of the AFL-CIO did Kefauver succeed in getting President John F. Kennedy to pressure Eastland to report out a version of Kefauver's bill.[17] Obviously, such tactics must be used with care, especially when the goodwill of the agenda setter may be important on other issues in the future.

Once a proposal gets a place on the agenda, its prospects for adoption may be improved by *sophisticated voting,* that is, by someone not voting his or her true preferences at some stage in the voting agenda to achieve a better final outcome. For example, in 1956 the Democratic leadership of the U.S. House of Representatives proposed that federal aid be given directly to local school districts for the first time. If everyone had voted his or her true preference, then the bill would have been passed by the Democratic majority. Representative Adam Clayton Powell introduced an amendment to the bill, however, that would have prevented funds from going to segregated schools. The amendment was supported by northern Democrats, but it was opposed by southern Democrats. Riker argues that a number of Republicans, who preferred no bill to the unamended bill and the unamended bill to the amended bill, nevertheless voted for the amendment because they expected that southern Democrats would vote against the amended bill.[18] Their expectations were correct and the amended bill did not pass.

Assuming that the northern Democrats preferred the unamended bill to no bill, why didn't they counter the Republicans' sophisticated voting with their own by voting against the Powell amendment so that the southern Democrats would join with them to pass the unamended bill? Perhaps, as Riker suggests, the northern Democrats saw taking a stand against segregation as more valuable to them in terms of constituent support than obtaining a more preferred policy outcome. In other words, their position was complicated by the need to consider a second dimension of evaluation.

The situation of the northern Democrats suggests the second category of heresthetical devices: those that alter the *dimension of evaluation.* When you are in a minority position, you can sometimes introduce a new consideration that splits the majority. For example, in 1970 several West Coast senators proposed amendments to the pending military appropriations bill that would have prohibited the Department of Defense from shipping nerve gas from Okinawa to the United States. Although they initially did not have enough votes to prevent the shipments, Senator Warren Magnuson helped them gain a majority by arguing that what really was at stake was the dignity of the Senate. The Senate had earlier passed a resolution

[17] Richard Harris, *The Real Voice* (New York: Macmillan, 1964), 166.
[18] Riker, *Art of Political Manipulation*, pp. 114–28.

saying that the president could not change the status of any territory involved in the peace treaty with Japan without consulting the Senate. Magnuson asserted that the gas shipments were part of preparations to return Okinawa to Japan—an unconstitutional usurpation of the Senate's right to ratify treaties. By casting the issue in terms of the rights of the Senate, Magnuson was able to gain passage of the amendment by attracting enough votes from those who would otherwise have favored the gas shipments.[19]

Rhetoric. Perhaps the most common political strategy is *rhetoric*, the use of persuasive language. At one normative extreme, rhetoric provides correct and relevant information that clarifies the probable impacts of proposed policies. At the other normative extreme, it provides incorrect or irrelevant information that obfuscates the probable impacts of proposed policies. As a policy analyst, you are likely to face ethical questions concerning the extent to which you should participate in your client's use of rhetoric that obfuscates rather than clarifies.

As an illustration of the ethical use of rhetoric, return to the proposal to ban random testing for drug use. In Table 11.1, council member C is listed as likely to vote for the ban because she sees her major constituency as community groups, which favor the ban. The director of the Urban League, for instance, favors the ban because he believes that testing might be used unfairly against minority workers. If you opposed the ban, then you might provide information to the Urban League director indicating that the ban would discourage some employers from staying or expanding in the city—the net effect on minority employment may actually be negative. If convinced, the director might then convince council member C to change her position so that the ban would not pass.

Often the most effective rhetoric influences political actors indirectly through public opinion rather than directly through persuasion. As we discussed in Chapter 8, there seem to be policy windows—periods when public opinion and media attention are sensitive to political initiatives in specific policy areas. Public figures may be moved to act by the opportunity to gain publicity.[20] To keep policy windows open, or perhaps even to create them, policy advocates can provide information to the media through such mechanisms as press conferences, news releases, hearings, planted stories, and leaks. Obviously, information that can be portrayed as sensational will be more likely to be reported by the media than information that appears mundane.

A common, but ethically questionable, rhetorical strategy is to emphasize very negative, but unlikely, consequences.[21] As noted in Chapter 8, this strategy takes advantage of the findings of psychologists that people have a tendency to overestimate

[19]Ibid., pp. 106–13.

[20]For a general overview on how federal officials interact with the press, see Martin Linsky, *Impact: How the Press Affects Federal Policymaking* (New York: W. W. Norton, 1986), 148–68.

[21]Riker labels this strategy *induced dread* and explains how it operates in "Rhetoric in the Spatial Model," paper presented to the Conference on Coalition Government, European Institute, Florence, Italy, May 28, 1987. For fuller development of these ideas, see William H. Riker, *The Strategy of Rhetoric: Campaigning for the American Constitution* (New Haven, CT: Yale University Press, 1996). See also R. Kent Weaver, "The Politics of Blame Avoidance," *Journal of Public Policy* 6(4) 1986, 371–98.

the likelihood of certain kinds of very low probability events and to be more sensitive to potential losses than to potential gains. For example, in discussions of health and safety opponents of nuclear power tend to emphasize the consequences of a meltdown in combination with a containment structure failure. Now such an accident would indeed be catastrophic. But it is hard to imagine peacetime scenarios that would result in the failure of a containment structure.[22] Despite the very low probability of such a disaster, the public tends to focus on it in discussions of nuclear safety to the exclusion of more mundane risks inherent in the mining and transportation of fuels and the disposal of wastes.

In Chapter 3 we discussed analytical integrity as one of the values that should be considered by policy analysts. We argued that the professional ethics of policy analysts should generally preclude participation in the injection of false or grossly misleading information into public debates. If you decide to place responsibility to your client or the furtherance of your conception of the good society above analytical integrity, then you might still want to avoid rhetorical dishonesty in most circumstances so that you will be credible when you do sacrifice analytical integrity. As Machiavelli suggests, for political actors the appearance of honesty is more important than the virtue itself.[23] But, generally, *the best way to appear honest is to be honest.*

The Implementation Phase

If policy adoption is courtship, then implementation is marriage. Courtship is a sort of coalition building—in times gone by, the couple maneuvered to gain the support of their parents; now they often must seek the support of their own children from previous marriages. Not all courtships are successful. Those that are, however, have a formal conclusion (the wedding). With the wedding begins implementation of the marriage agreement. Unless the couple admits failure and divorce, implementation goes on and on. The couple must constantly work to keep the marriage healthy in an ever-changing environment. At some point, however, they may become so accommodated to each other that the marriage stays healthy with little conscious effort. Perhaps achieving this latter condition, though not always permanent, represents the closest we can come to declaring a successful implementation.

In drawing the analogy between implementation and marriage, we hope that we have inspired neither dread of marriage among our single readers nor dread of implementation among our married readers. We hope that we have conveyed the generally open-ended nature of implementation and the need to think seriously about it when proposals are being developed.

[22]For a discussion of the possibilities, see Bernard L. Cohen, *Before It's Too Late: A Scientist's Case for Nuclear Energy* (New York: Plenum Press, 1983), 62–68; and Nigel Evans and Chris Hope, *Nuclear Power: Futures, Costs and Benefits* (New York: Cambridge University Press, 1984), 4–5. For a highly partisan but nevertheless provocative view on the public debate over nuclear power, see Samuel McCracken, *The War against the Atom* (New York: Basic Books, 1982).

[23]Niccolo Machiavelli, *The Prince* (New York: Appleton-Century-Crofts, 1947), Chapter XVIII, 50–52.

Implementation: Factors Affecting Success and Failure

What factors influence the likelihood of successful implementation? A large literature attempts to answer this question.[24] We consider three general factors that have been the focus of much of this literature: the logic of the policy, the nature of the cooperation it requires, and the availability of skillful and committed people to manage its implementation. An awareness of these factors is the first step toward designing policies that can be successfully implemented.

Logic of the Policy: Is the Theory Reasonable? Compatibility is important in marriage. We often question the logic of marriages between people who appear to be incompatible. We should do the same for policies. What theory underlies the connection between policy and intended outcomes? Is the theory reasonable?

We can think of the logic of a policy as a chain of hypotheses. For example, consider a state program to fund locally initiated experiments intended to identify promising approaches to teaching science in high schools. For the program to be successful, the following hypotheses must be true: first, that school districts with good ideas for experiments apply for funds; second, that the state department of education selects the best applications for funding; third, that the funded school districts actually execute the experiments they proposed; fourth, that the experiments produce valid evidence on the effectiveness of the approaches being tested; and fifth, that the department of education be able to recognize which successful approaches can be replicated in other jurisdictions.

Now it is easy to imagine that any of these hypotheses could be false, or at least not universally true. For instance: applicants may be predominantly school districts with experience in applying for grants rather than school districts with good ideas; the education department may face political pressure to distribute funds widely rather than to the school districts with the best ideas; school districts may divert some of the funds to other uses—say, paying for routine classroom instruction; school districts may lack skilled personnel to carry out evaluations or they may be reluctant to report evaluation results that do not support the efficacy of their approaches; the department of education may not have sufficient personnel to look closely at the evaluations to determine which ones are valid. The more likely it is that these hypotheses are false, the less likely it is that the program will produce useful information about how to do a better job teaching science in high schools.

The characteristics of the policy, and the circumstances of its adoption, determine the hypotheses underlying implementation and the likelihood that they will be true. In general, the greater the legal authority the adopted policy gives implementors, the greater their capacity to compel hypothesized behavior. Similarly, the stronger the political support for the adopted policy and its putative goals, the

[24]The seminal work in the literature is Jeffrey L. Pressman and Aaron Wildavsky, *Implementation* (Berkeley: University of California Press, 1973). For overviews of the literature that followed, see Paul A. Sabatier, "Top-Down and Bottom-Up Approaches to Implementation Research: A Critical Analysis and Suggested Synthesis," *Journal of Public Policy* 6(1) 1986, 21–48; and Robert Nakamura and Frank Smallwood, *The Politics of Policy Implementation* (New York: St. Martin's, Press, 1980), 12–18.

greater the capacity of the implementors to secure hypothesized behavior. For example, a department of education is in a better position to get school districts to provide competent evaluations of their experiments if it can require selected grant recipients to hire external evaluators. With respect to political support for policy goals, this department of education is in a better position to ward off pressure for widespread distribution of grants if most of the supporters of the program in the legislature hold the putative goal of improving high school science education as more important than using program funds to provide general aid to school districts.[25]

Obviously, we should view a policy as illogical if we cannot specify a plausible chain of behaviors that leads to the desired outcomes.[26] Later we discuss scenario writing as a way of discovering plausible chains. But first, we turn to the other factors that affect the likelihood that the hypothesized behaviors will occur.

Assembly: Who Has the Essential Elements? As we noted in Chapter 8, Eugene Bardach provides a useful metaphor for implementation: an assembly process involving efforts to secure essential elements from those who control them.[27] His metaphor suggests the generalization that the more numerous and varied are the elements that must be assembled, the greater is the potential for implementation problems. More usefully, it suggests important questions to ask when considering the prospects for successful implementation: Exactly what elements (the hypotheses linking policy to desired outcomes) must be assembled? Who controls these elements? What are their motivations? What resources does the implementor have available to induce them to provide the elements? What consequences will result if the elements cannot be obtained either on a timely basis or at all?

These questions are essentially the same ones we ask in order to determine the political feasibility of adoption. Indeed, the efforts to secure the elements needed for implementation typically involve politics—although rarely decided by votes, those controlling the necessary elements must, nevertheless, be convinced to provide them. In other words, as we noted at the beginning of this chapter, we can think of implementation as a series of adoptions.

Clear legal authority is almost always a valuable resource for implementors. It may not be sufficient by itself to guarantee cooperation, however. For example, imagine a mayor opposed to the transportation of nuclear wastes on the railroad running through her city. Assume that she is required by law to prepare a plan for the evacuation of her city in the event of an accident involving the release of nuclear waste into the environment. Also assume that the transportation through the city cannot begin until an evacuation plan is accepted. The mayor might hinder imple-

[25]As Pressman and Wildavsky note, it is not clear what successful implementation means without specification of a goal: "Implementation cannot succeed or fail without a goal against which to judge it." Jeffrey L. Pressman and Aaron Wildavsky, *Implementation*, p. xiv. In practice, we often face the problem that policies are adopted without explicit agreement about their goals. See Charles Lindblom, "Some Limitations on Rationality: A Comment," in Carl J. Friedrich, ed., *Rational Decision* (New York: Atherton, 1964), 224–28.

[26]Note that politicians sometimes support policies as symbolic statements and really do not expect the putative consequences to result. For a discussion of position taking by members of Congress, see David R. Mayhew, *Congress: The Electoral Connection* (New Haven, CT: Yale University Press, 1974), 61–73.

[27]Eugene Bardach, *The Implementation Game: What Happens after a Bill Becomes a Law* (Cambridge, MA: MIT Press, 1977), 57–58.

mentation of the shipment program by following one of three tactics: tokenism, delayed compliance, or blatant resistance.[28]

The mayor might intentionally have her staff prepare an evacuation plan that meets the letter of the law but falls short substantively. If the implementor—say, the state public utilities commission—accepts the inadequate plan, then it risks not only public safety but also bad publicity and a court challenge from interest groups who oppose the shipment program. Of course, if the implementor does not accept the evacuation plan, then the program cannot go forward. Because the mayor has complied in form, the implementor may have difficulty gaining the political or legal support needed to force the mayor to comply in spirit. Indeed, tokenism is so difficult to deal with because the implementor generally bears the burden of showing that the compliance was inadequate.

The mayor might have her staff prepare the required evacuation plan but have them delay completing it as long as they can without inviting a legal challenge from the implementor. During the period of delay, the mayor may be able to mobilize political support to block the program from shipping through her city. Perhaps an intervening election or change in public opinion will make it possible to repeal the legislation that authorized the program. Or perhaps the implementor will give up and choose another shipment route. In any event, the mayor probably has little to lose from a strategy of delay and at least some hope of a favorable change in political circumstances.

Finally, instead of making a token response, the mayor might simply refuse to allow her staff to prepare an evacuation plan. Such blatant resistance may be costly for the mayor if the implementor decides to seek legal sanctions. But taking the mayor to court may be politically costly for the implementor and would probably involve considerable delay. On the other hand, not challenging the mayor's noncompliance might encourage other mayors also to refuse to prepare evacuation plans, throwing the whole shipment program into jeopardy.

While massive resistance is generally rare—it takes fortitude and works best from a position that makes it costly for the implementor to force compliance—tokenism and purposeful delay are common tactics for those who oppose the policy being implemented. Employees, especially those with civil service protection, can often slow, or even stop, implementation with halfhearted or leisurely contributions.[29] Their ability to impede implementation is particularly great when they must be relied upon to make continuing contributions over an extended period. For instance, management information systems typically require a steady and accurate flow of input data to provide information benefits—delays or inattention to accuracy by a few data providers may be enough to undermine the value of the entire system.[30]

So, even when implementors have the legal authority to demand compliance, they will not necessarily get it at levels adequate for successful implementation.

[28]For excellent discussions of tokenism and massive resistance and ways to counter them, see ibid., pp. 98–124.

[29]On the resources available to employees and lower-level managers, see David Mechanic, "Sources of Power of Lower Participants in Complex Organizations," *Administrative Science Quarterly* 7(3) 1962, 348–64.

[30]For a discussion of the problems encountered in implementing information systems, see David L. Weimer, "CMIS Implementation: A Demonstration of Predictive Analysis," *Public Administration Review* 40(3) 1980, 231–40.

Implementors should expect that their efforts to secure program elements will be political—allies must be mobilized and agreements must be reached with people who have contrary interests. Therefore, implementors should be prepared to use political strategies, especially co-optation and compromise, to assemble program elements and keep them engaged. For example, to increase the chances that mayors will produce acceptable evacuation plans on a timely basis, the implementors might offer to discuss limitations on the frequency and circumstances of the shipments before the mayors commit themselves to noncompliance through their public stands. Perhaps the implementor can offer a concession on an entirely different issue of mutual concern.[31]

Noncompliance need not be purposeful to hinder the implementation process. Someone holding a necessary program element may have every intention of providing it but fail to do so because of incompetence or an inability to get others to provide necessary support. For example, the mayor may believe that the preparation of an evacuation plan as required by law is a duty that should be discharged. Yet her staff may lack the necessary skills to produce an adequate plan. Or perhaps the staff is competent but cannot complete their task quickly because local procedure requires that the plan be discussed in public hearings and reviewed by the city attorney, the city and county planning boards, and the city council. Even without strong opposition to the plan, scheduling problems and routine delays may prevent the plan from being approved in what the implementor considers a reasonable period of time.

Diversity among those providing similar elements makes it difficult to estimate how much inadvertent noncompliance will be encountered. For example, imagine that the shipment program requires that evacuation plans be prepared by twenty cities. Perhaps most have staffs with adequate skills to comply. But even if only a few are incapable of complying, the implementation may be jeopardized—because, say, the authorization for the program requires that all evacuation plans be filed before shipments can begin.

In summary, legal authority alone may not be sufficient to guarantee the compliance of those who control necessary program elements. If they view the program, or their specific contributions to it, as contrary to their interests, then the implementor should expect them to try to avoid full compliance through tokenism, delay, or even blatant resistance. Furthermore, the implementor should hold realistic expectations about the capabilities of those who nominally control the elements to provide them.

Availability of "Fixers": Who Will Manage the Assembly? So far we have been vague about the identity of the implementor. Our examples suggest someone who favors the policy and is willing to expend time, energy, and resources to see it put into effect—in other words, someone who behaves as we think we would. But as policy analysts, we rarely are in a position to manage an implementation ourselves. Indeed, if our clients are legislators or high-ranking executives, it is unlikely

[31]For example, when the governor of Louisiana held up construction of facilities for the U.S. Strategic Petroleum Reserve Program by objecting to the issuing of permits by the Army Corps of Engineers, the Department of Energy got the governor to drop his objections by making several concessions, including a promise that DOE would not store nuclear wastes in Louisiana. David L. Weimer, *The Strategic Petroleum Reserve: Planning, Implementation, and Analysis* (Westport, CT: Greenwood Press, 1982), 50–51.

that they will be willing or able to attend to the day-to-day management of implementations. Instead, the responsibility for managing implementations typically goes to the administrators of organizational units that provide related services. For example, the implementor of the nuclear waste shipment program would probably be the director of the office within the public utilities commission that oversees the state's nuclear power plants.

In light of the importance of politics in the implementation process, understanding the motivations and political resources of the implementor is obviously important for predicting the likelihood that the policy will produce the intended consequences. An implementor who views the policy as undesirable or unimportant is less likely to expend personal and organizational resources during the assembly process than one who views the policy more favorably. One reason that organizational units are sometimes created to implement new policies is the perception that the administrators of existing units will not be vigorous implementors because of their commitments to already-existing programs.[32]

The failings of the implementor can sometimes be compensated for by people who Bardach calls *fixers*—those who can intervene in the assembly process to help gain needed elements that are being withheld.[33] For example, the staff of the legislative sponsor of the policy may oversee the implementation process, perhaps helping to negotiate compromises with those who are not complying. Oversight by the staff may also help motivate a less than enthusiastic implementor.

The availability of fixers at the local level can be especially helpful in adjusting centrally managed policies to local conditions. Sometimes local fixers can be found among interest groups who support the policy; sometimes local administrators become effective fixers. In their evaluation of the implementation of youth employment programs, for instance, Martin Levin and Barbara Ferman found that the most successful local programs usually had executives who were willing to intervene in administrative detail to correct problems. Some of these fixers were especially effective in using incentives to turn the mild interest of other local actors into active support. Other fixers had official and personal connections that enabled them to facilitate interorganizational cooperation.[34]

Allies at the local level can also serve as "eyes and ears" for the implementor.[35] Information about local contexts is often costly for a central implementor to gather without willing informants. Local supporters of the policy may be able to provide information that is useful in anticipating and countering noncompliance tactics. For example, if the state attorney general's office is attempting to implement more stringent medical care standards for local jails, it might find local groups interested in judicial reform or county medical societies as sources of valuable information on whether the standards are actually being followed. Such information could help the attorney general's office target limited enforcement resources on the worst offenders.

[32]Erwin C. Hargrove, *The Missing Link: The Study of the Implementation of Social Policy* (Washington, DC: Urban Institute, 1975), 113.

[33]See Bardach, *The Implementation Game*, pp. 273–78.

[34]Martin A. Levin and Barbara Ferman, *The Political Hand: Policy Implementation and Youth Employment Programs* (New York: Pergamon, 1985), 102–04. On approaches for improving interorganizational cooperation, see Eugene Bardach, *Getting Agencies to Work Together: The Practice and Theory of Managerial Craftsmanship* (Washington, DC: Brookings Institution Press, 1998).

[35]Bardach, *The Implementation Game*, pp. 277–78.

In summary, policies do not implement themselves. In assessing the chances for successful implementation, we should consider the motivations and resources of those who will be managing the implementation. We should also look for ways to mobilize potential supporters of the policy who can serve as fixers.

Anticipating Implementation Problems

Despite the extensive literature on implementation, social scientists have offered relatively little practical advice on how to anticipate and avoid implementation problems.[36] Nevertheless, we believe that two general approaches provide useful frameworks for thinking systematically about implementation in practical situations. The most basic is *scenario writing,* which involves specifying and questioning the chain of behaviors that link policies to desired outcomes. Because scenarios move from policies to outcomes, they can be thought of as *forward mapping.* In contrast, the other general approach, *backward mapping,* begins with the desired outcomes, determines the most direct ways of producing them, and then maps actions backward (effects to causes) through the organizational hierarchy to the highest-level policy that must be adopted to realize the desired outcomes. Whereas forward mapping is most useful for anticipating the problems that are likely to be encountered during the implementation of already-formulated policy alternatives, backward mapping is most useful for generating policy alternatives that have good prospects for successful implementation.

Forward Mapping: Scenario Writing. *Forward mapping* is the specification of the chain of behaviors that link a policy to desired outcomes. We emphasize the "specific" in specification: Exactly what must be done by whom for the desired outcomes to occur? We join with Bardach in recommending scenario writing as a method for analysts to organize their thinking about the behaviors that must be realized for successful implementation.[37] Scenario writing helps analysts discover implicit assumptions that are unrealistic. It may also help them discover alternative approaches to implementation with better prospects for success.

Effective forward mapping requires cleverness and a certain amount of courage. Research helps as well. The forward mapper must think about how those involved in the implementation will behave and how their behavior might be influenced. It requires what has been referred to as *dirty mindedness*—the ability to think about what could possibly go wrong and who has an incentive to make it go wrong.[38] In other words, one must be able to visualize the worst case. Research on outcomes in other jurisdictions is a valuable tool for making such predictions. Decentralized countries, such as the United States and Canada, provide many opportunities for comparative outcomes research.[39] Other things equal, observing the

[36]For a review of the prescriptive literature, see Laurence J. O'Toole, Jr., "Policy Recommendations for Multi-Actor Implementation: An Assessment of the Field," *Journal of Public Policy* 6(2) 1986, 181–210.

[37]Bardach, *The Implementation Game*, pp. 250–67.

[38]Martin Levin and Barbara Ferman, "The Political Hand: Policy Implementation and Youth Employment Programs," *Journal of Policy Analysis and Management* 5(2) 1986, 311–25, at p. 322.

[39]There are many examples of such comparative research. For example, Daniel Eisenberg, "Evaluating the Effectiveness of Policies Related to Drunk Driving," *Journal of Policy Analysis and Management* 22(2) 2003, 249–74.

successful implementation of a particular type of policy in a number of jurisdictions makes that policy a more promising candidate elsewhere.

The forward (and backward) mapper must be courageous about making predictions. Many predictions will be incorrect, especially in their details. Much of the value of forward mapping comes from the thinking that goes into being specific. Therefore, the forward mapper must not become paralyzed by fear of being wrong.

We recommend a three-step approach to forward mapping: (1) write a scenario linking the policy to outcomes; (2) critique the scenario from the perspective of the interests of its characters; and (3) revise the scenario so that it is more plausible. Table 11.2 highlights these steps, which we discuss in turn.

1. *Write the Scenario.* Scenarios are stories. They are narratives about futures as you see them. They have beginnings and ends that are linked by plots involving essential actors. Plots should be consistent with the motivations and capabilities of the actors. Plots should also be "rich" in the sense that they convey all the important considerations that are relevant to implementation.[40]

The plot consists of a series of connected actions. Your narrative should answer four questions for each action: What is the action? Who does the action? When do they do it? Why do they do it? For example, suppose that you are writing a scenario for the implementation of a Neighborhood Sticker Plan (NSP) that would limit long-term on-street parking in specified city neighborhoods to residents who purchase stickers annually to identify their automobiles. An element of your plot might read as follows:

> Upon passage of the NSP (the previous "what"), the director of parking in the police department (the "who") designs procedures for verifying that applicants are bona fide residents of participating neighborhoods and that their out-of-town guests qualify for temporary permits (the "whats"). As requested by the police chief (the "why"), he submits an acceptable procedure to the planning department within one month (the "when").

By putting together a series of such elements, you can connect the adopted policy (the NSP) with the desired outcome (neighborhood residents and their out-of-town guests having convenient access to on-street parking).

By writing scenarios that read well, you may be able to get the attention of clients and colleagues who might otherwise be distracted—most people like stories and learn easily from them. You may be able to make your scenarios more convincing and more lively by inserting quotes from interviews and noting past behaviors that are similar to the ones you are predicting. For example, if the director of parking has told you in an interview that his staff could easily design verification procedures, weave his statement into the plot. Even if you are preparing the scenario for your own exclusive use, write it out. It is the discipline of writing a coherent story that forces you to consider the obvious questions about what must happen for the implementation to be successful.

2. *Critique the Scenario.* Is the scenario plausible? Are all the actors capable of doing what the plot requires? If not, your plot fails the basic test of plausibility and

[40]For a discussion of richness and other desirable characteristics of polity narratives, see Thomas J. Kaplan, "The Narrative Structure of Policy Analysis," *Journal of Policy Analysis and Management* 5(4) 1986, 761–78. See also Martin H. Krieger, *Advice and Planning* (Philadelphia: Temple University Press, 1981); and Emery Roe, *Narrative Policy Analysis: Theory and Practice* (Durham, NC: Duke University Press, 1994).

Table 11.2 *Thinking Systematically about Implementation: Forward Mapping*

Scenario:	**Write a narrative that describes all the behaviors that must be realized for the policy to produce desired outcome. Be specific about who, what, when, and why.**
Critique 1:	**Is the scenario plausible?** For each actor mentioned: 1. Is the hypothesized behavior consistent with personal and organizational interests? 2. If not, what tactics could the actor use to avoid complying? 3. What countertactics could be used to force or induce compliance?
Critique 2:	**Thinking of the direct and indirect effects of the policy, what other actors would have an incentive to become involved?** For each of these actors: 1. How could the actor interfere with hypothesized behaviors? 2. What tactics could be used to block or deflect interference?
Revision:	**Rewrite the narrative to make it more plausible.**

should be rewritten. Of course, if you cannot specify a plausible plot, then you can be fairly certain that the policy is doomed to fail.

The more interesting test of plausibility lies in considering the motivations of the actors. Will they be willing to do what the plot requires? For each actor mentioned in the plot, ask yourself if the hypothesized behavior is consistent with personal and organizational interests. If not, what tactics could the actor use to avoid complying? For example, the director of parking may view the verification procedures as an undesirable burden of his already overworked staff. He might, therefore, produce a token plan that will not adequately exclude nonresidents from purchasing stickers. The result could be that parking congestion will remain a problem in the participating neighborhoods. Perhaps he opposed the NSP in the first place and sees inadequate verification procedures as a way of undermining the whole program.

Can you think of any ways of countering the noncompliance? More generally, this raises the issue of providing either positive or negative incentives for compliance. For example, would a memorandum from the police chief clearly stating the director's responsibility for designing effective verification procedures be sufficient to get the director to do a good job? Would he be more cooperative if he were allocated additional overtime hours for his staff? If inducements such as these appear ineffectual, then you should consider writing him out of the plot by assigning the task to some other organizational unit.

After considering the motivations of actors who are in the plot, think about the "dogs that didn't bark." Who not mentioned in the plot will likely view the policy, or the steps necessary to implement it, as contrary to their interests? How might they interfere with the elements of the plot? What tactics could you employ to block or deflect their interference?

For instance, what will the commuters who have been parking in the participating neighborhoods do when they are excluded? Will they park in other residential neighborhoods or on commercial streets closer to the downtown? This might create pressure for the creation of additional sticker-parking areas or lead adversely affected city residents to oppose continued implementation. Perhaps arranging more convenient bus service from parking lots on the outskirts of the city could help absorb the displacement of nonresident parking from the participating neighborhoods.

3. *Revise the Scenario.* Rewrite the scenario in light of the critique. Strive for a plot that is plausible, even if it does not lead to the desired outcome. If it still does lead to the desired outcome, then you have the basis for a plan of implementation. If it does not lead to the desired outcome, then you can conclude that the policy is probably unfeasible and should be replaced with an alternative that can be implemented.

Backward Mapping: Bottom-Up Policy Design. Richard Elmore describes the logic of backward mapping as follows:

> Begin with a concrete statement of the behavior that creates the occasion for a policy intervention, describe a set of organizational operations that can be expected to affect that behavior, describe the expected effect of those operations, and then describe for each level of the implementation process what effect one would expect that level to have on the target behavior and what resources are required for that effect to occur.[41]

In other words, begin thinking about policies by looking at the behavior that you wish to change. What interventions could effectively alter the behavior? What decisions and resources are needed to motivate and support these interventions? The candidate policies are then constructed from alternative sets of decisions and resources that will achieve the interventions and that can be controlled by the policymaker.

Backward mapping is really nothing more than using your model of the policy problem to suggest alternative solutions. It adds something to our thinking about policy alternatives, however, by drawing our attention to the organizational processes that give them form. Also, by focusing initially on the lowest organizational levels, it may help us discover less centralized approaches that we might have otherwise overlooked.

The development of an implementation plan for neighborhood sticker parking in San Francisco provides an example of the usefulness of backward mapping. By the early 1970s, parking congestion had become a serious problem in many San Francisco neighborhoods as single-family homes were split into multiple units and per capita rates of car ownership increased. The congestion was aggravated in many neighborhoods by commuters who parked near access points to public transportation and by users of public facilities like hospitals. Several neighborhood associations and the City Planning Department favored the introduction of neighborhood sticker parking (like the NSP discussed in the previous section). One of the major issues was determining which neighborhoods would participate in the plan. The City Planning Department originally thought in terms of a top-down approach; planners in the department would designate the neighborhoods that would participate as part of the policy proposal. But an analyst convinced

[41]Richard F. Elmore, "Backward Mapping: Implementation Research and Policy Design," *Political Science Quarterly* 94(4) 1979–80, 601–16, at p. 612; Richard F. Elmore, "Forward and Backward Mapping: Reversible Logic in the Analysis of Public Policy," in Kenneth Hanf and Theo A. J. Toomen, eds., *Policy Implementation in Federal and Unitary Systems* (Boston: Martinus Nijholf, 1985). For an application, see Marcia K. Meyers, Bonnie Glaser, and Karin McDonald, "On the Front Lines of Welfare Delivery: Are Workers Implementing Policy Reforms?" *Journal of Policy Analysis and Management* 17(1) 1998, 1–22.

them to use a bottom-up approach instead: establish a procedure for neighborhoods to self-select.[42]

The analyst reached his recommendation through a backward mapping of the political problem faced by the City Planning Department. Many residents wanted to participate in the sticker plan and expressed their support for it through their neighborhood associations. Some residents, however, preferred the status quo to having to pay for the privilege of using off-street parking in their neighborhoods. Until they realized that their neighborhoods were to be included in the plan, these latent opponents would probably have remained silent and unknown to the City Planning Department. Therefore, the City Planning Department was faced with the prospect of some local opposition when it made public the neighborhoods designated for participation. Viewing the dissatisfaction with the status quo on the part of the currently vocal residents as the behavior that would be the policy target, the analyst thought of a procedure that would allow them to seek participation. That way the City Planning Department would not be seen as imposing its preferences on the neighborhoods. Because there was already a procedure in place that allowed neighborhoods to self-select for designation as two-hour parking zones, the analyst specified an adaptation of that procedure as the way to structure the implementation of the NSP.

Thinking More Strategically about Policy Design

Backward mapping aside, we have so far considered strategic thinking primarily in the context of predicting and influencing the political and organizational feasibility of specific policy proposals. We now turn to strategic thinking in the context of policy design. In particular, we look at ways of making our policies less sensitive to errors in our assumptions about behavior and more effective in helping us learn about how to design better policies in the future.

Uncertainty and Error Correction

Policy analysis inherently involves prediction. Because the world is complex, we must expect to err. Our theories about human behavior are simply not powerful enough for us to have great confidence in most of our predictions. Changing economic, social, and political conditions can make even our initially accurate predictions about the consequences of adopted policies go far astray as time elapses. Our design of policies should acknowledge the possibility of error. In particular, can we design policies that facilitate the detection and correction of error?[43]

Redundancy and Slack. Duplication and overlap generally carry the negative connotation of inefficiency. In a world with perfect certainty, this connotation has validity: Why expend more than the minimum amount of resources necessary to complete a task? In our uncertain world, however, some duplication and overlap

[42]Arthur D. Fulton and David L. Weimer, "Regaining a Lost Policy Option: Neighborhood Parking Stickers in San Francisco," *Policy Analysis* 6(3) 1980, 335–48.

[43]For insights on error and error correction, see Aaron Wildavsky, "The Self-Evaluating Organization," *Public Administration Review* 32(5) 1972, 509–20.

can be very valuable. We don't consider redundant safety systems on airplanes as necessarily inefficient—even the best engineering and assembly cannot guarantee perfect performance from all primary systems. We should not be surprised, then, that redundancy can be valuable in many organizational contexts. Redundancy can provide a safety margin, serve as a source of resources for dealing with anomalous situations, and make available slack resources for organizational experimentation.[44] Thus, designing redundancy into policies can sometimes make them more feasible and robust.

Consider the problem of critical links in the implementation process. If one link in a chain of behaviors connecting the policy to desired outcomes seems especially tenuous, then you should look for ways to make the link redundant, recognizing the trade-off between costs and the probability of successful implementation. For instance, return to our earlier example of the program to ship nuclear wastes on railroads running through the state. Rather than simply asking mayors of cities along the most preferred route to prepare evacuation plans, you might simultaneously have evacuation plans prepared along a few alternative routes as well. If a mayor along the preferred route failed to comply, then you might be able to switch to one of the alternative routes without great loss of time. Whether the higher administrative (and probably political) costs of such a parallel approach were warranted would depend on the value of the reduction in expected delay it would provide.

Redundancy can also be useful in facilitating experimentation and the reduction of uncertainty. For example, imagine you are designing a county-funded program to purchase counseling services over the next year for 100 indigent drug abusers. Conceivably, a single firm could provide all the services. While the administrative costs of contracting with one firm for the entire 100 participants might be lower, hiring more than one firm would offer the potential for comparing performance. It also would enhance competition by increasing the chances that more than one firm will bid to provide services in future years.

Using redundant suppliers also makes it easier to cope with the unexpected loss of one supplier. For instance, one of the counseling firms may unexpectedly go bankrupt early in the year and default on its contract. It would probably be faster, and perhaps more desirable, to shift participants to other firms already under contract than to hire new firms.

Finally, building redundant resources (slack) into programs may be desirable if supplementing initial allocations during implementation will be difficult. For instance, if the credibility of the state transportation department's proposal to replace a series of bridges hinges critically on completing the first replacement in the promised six months, then the department would probably be wise to pad the budget for this first project with some reserve funds to deal with such unlucky circumstances as exceptionally bad weather or construction accidents. The political trade-off is between the lower initial support because of the higher budget and a reduced risk of lower future support due to loss of credibility.

Anticipating Evaluation. Often the effectiveness of adopted policies is not directly observable. For example, consider a program that provides intensive supervision for certain parolees. How would we determine if the participants had

[44]For a development of these ideas, see Martin Landau, "Redundancy, Rationality, and the Problem of Duplication and Overlap," *Public Administration Review* 29(4), 1969, 346–358; and Jonathan B. Bendor, *Parallel Systems: Redundancy in Government* (Berkeley: University of California Press, 1985).

lower recidivism rates? We could fairly easily observe the number of arrests and the number of months of street-time (time in community after release from prison) for the group. We could interpret the ratio of total arrests to total street-time as a crude measure of the recidivism rate for the participants. But how would we interpret this rate? We might compare it to the recidivism rate for a sample of nonparticipants. The comparison could be misleading, however, if participants differed substantially from the controls in terms of age, criminal history, education level, or some other factor potentially relevant to recidivism. We would have to worry that one of these factors may be confounding our results.

To guard against confounding, we might have designed the intensive supervision program as an experiment—randomly select participants and controls to increase the chances that the only systematic difference between the groups is the intensive supervision.[45] We could then more confidently attribute any measured differences in recidivism rates between the participant and control groups as due to the intensive supervision. Of course, the random selection of participants and controls must be part of the original program design.[46]

When randomized experiments are not possible, evaluators may turn to nonexperimental designs, such as *before-after comparisons*, which take measures on variables of interest before and after the policy is implemented, or *nonequivalent group comparisons*, which take measurements of the variable of interest for a group subjected to the intervention and a group not subjected to the intervention.[47] Even nonexperimental evaluations of policy effects generally require some forethought, however. For example, if we want to know whether improvements at a public park have increased use, then we had better plan on measuring use levels *before* the improvements are made so that we have a benchmark for comparing measurements made *after* the improvements. If we are worried that changes in the local economy over the period of the improvements may influence use, then we would be wise to take contemporaneous measurements at another park not being improved to help us spot any area-wide changes.

Building the prerequisites for evaluation into policy designs is not without cost. Such preparations as random selection of participants and collection of baseline data can involve substantial effort, perhaps consuming scarce managerial resources needed for implementation. Preparations for future evaluations can also delay implementation. So, before bearing these costs (or inflicting them

[45]We generally evaluate experiments in terms of their internal and external validity. *Internal validity* holds when the measured difference between the control and experimental groups can be reasonably attributed to the treatment. *External validity* holds when the measured difference can be generalized to some population of interest. For an excellent discussion of internal validity and external validity and the factors that jeopardize them, see Donald T. Campbell and Julian C. Stanley, *Experimental and Quasi-Experimental Designs for Research* (Chicago: Rand McNally, 1963), 5–6.

[46]Randomized selection from among the target population and randomized assignment to treatment and control groups greatly enhance the internal and external validity of evaluations. Implementing randomization, however, is often difficult. Administrators and professionals often do not want to give up discretion over assignment of subjects. For an illustration, see Leslie L. Roos, Jr., Noralou P. Roos, and Barbara McKinley, "Implementing Randomization," *Policy Analysis* 3(4) 1977, 547–59.

[47]Nonexperimental designs attempt to draw inferences about program effects when the use of randomly selected intervention and control groups is not possible. For more thorough treatments of nonexperimental designs, see Lawrence B. Mohr, *Impact Analysis for Program Evaluation* (Chicago: Dorsey Press, 1988); Harry Harty, Louis Blair, Donald Fisk, and Wayne Kimmel, *Program Analysis for State and Local Governments* (Washington, DC: Urban Institute, 1987); and Ann Bonar Blalock, ed., *Evaluating Social Programs at the State and Local Level* (Kalamazoo, MI.: W. E. Upjohn Institute, 1990).

on administrators), it is important to think carefully about the feasibility of actually carrying out the evaluation and the value of the resulting information.

Several questions are relevant to determining if planning for evaluation is likely to be worthwhile. First, can you imagine the results influencing a future decision? If the costs of the park improvements are sunk (there are no ongoing costs) and if no other park improvements are likely to be considered in the near future, then an evaluation is unlikely to be worthwhile. Second, will personnel with appropriate skills be available to conduct the evaluation? The parks department may be unable or unwilling to provide staff to collect and analyze data. Third, could the evaluation be completed soon enough to influence any decisions? Perhaps the county legislature will consider making similar improvements in another park next year—if an evaluation of the current improvements cannot be ready in time, then it will be irrelevant. Fourth, will the results of the evaluation be credible? If the county legislature does not trust the parks department to provide reliable information, then the evaluation is not likely to have much effect.

Short of evaluation requirements, it is sometimes desirable to build reporting requirements into policy designs.[48] Program administrators are commonly required to provide accounting data on expenditures and revenues. If activity levels (types of clients served, for instance) are routinely reported as well, then executive and legislative oversight may be better able to spot anomalous performance and perhaps take corrective action.

Reporting requirements may also have educational value; they let the administrator know of factors that are likely to be given attention by overseers.[49] For example, if you are concerned that the state employment office avoids trying to help parolees from prison, then you might require that, along with total clients, they report the number of clients with serious criminal records. If the administrator of the employment office believes that the budget committee or the governor's office is paying attention to the reports, then it is likely that more clients with criminal records will be served. Reporting requirements may also induce dysfunctional behavioral responses, say, by inappropriately shifting effort from highly valued but uncovered activities to less valued but covered ones. Consequently, reporting requirements themselves should be the subject of analysis and not imposed willy-nilly.

Facilitating Termination. Once policies are adopted, it is often difficult to repeal them. Even policies with large net social costs sometimes have vocal constituencies who benefit. Policies embodied in programs typically enjoy the support of their employees, clientele, and political sponsors. The public organizations that house programs tend to enjoy great longevity.[50] Even if we are fairly certain that a proposed policy is desirable, and will remain desirable for a long time, the inherent persistence of policies should give us some pause. When the consequences of

[48]For a conceptual discussion of the design of management control systems, see Fred Thompson and L. R. Jones, "Controllership in the Public Sector," *Journal of Policy Analysis and Management* 5(3) 1986, 547–71. With respect to the broader context of bureaucratic control, see William T. Gormley, Jr., *Taming the Bureaucracy: Muscles, Players, and Other Strategies* (Princeton, NJ: Princeton University Press, 1989).

[49]Janet A. Weiss and Judith E. Gruber, "Deterring Discrimination with Data," *Policy Sciences* 17(1) 1984, 49–66.

[50]Herbert Kaufman, *Are Government Organizations Immortal?* (Washington, DC: Brookings Institution, 1976), 70–77.

a policy are very uncertain, we should design it with the possibility of termination in mind.[51]

The most common way for policy designs to anticipate the possibility of termination is through *sunset provisions*, which set expiration dates for policies. Unless policies are legislatively renewed prior to their expiration dates, they automatically terminate. In this way, sunset provisions force explicit reconsideration of policies at specified times. We expect sunset provisions to be most effective when coupled with evaluation requirements that provide evidence on effectiveness during the consideration of renewal.

Given the limited capability of governments to conduct evaluations and the limited time available on legislative calendars, the widespread use of simple sunset provisions may not elicit serious reconsideration of policies. Garry Brewer argues that if they are to be effective in commanding attention in the legislative arena, then sunset provisions should be selectively employed. He further suggests that provisions be used in conjunction with *success thresholds*, which if not met, call for intensive evaluation.[52] Success thresholds alter the burden of proof somewhat during renewal decisions. While sunset provisions have the virtue of getting reconsideration of policies on the legislative agenda, even when coupled with evaluation requirements they do not directly affect the interests supporting them.

Support for continuation of policies should be expected from employees and other people whose livelihoods or careers depend on them. Furthermore others may oppose termination because they feel a moral repugnance against disrupting arrangements upon which such people have come to rely.[53] By designing organizational arrangements that keep the cost of termination to employees low, we reduce the likelihood of strong opposition. One approach to keeping costs of termination low is to avoid designing permanent organizations to implement and administer policies. Instead, consider using ad hoc groups like task forces that temporarily assign employees from elsewhere in the organization to the implementation of the policy.[54] If these employees see termination as simply a return to their former duties without loss of career status, they may be less likely to oppose it than if it involves the loss of jobs or status. Note that contracting out for services rather than producing them in-house also reduces the direct cost of termination to public organizations.

The use of temporary organizational structures is not without its disadvantages, however. Ad hoc groups of employees may not be willing to invest the extra effort

[51]See Mark R. Daniels, "Policy and Organizational Termination," *International Journal of Public Administration* 24(3) 2001, 249–62.

[52]Garry D. Brewer, "Termination: Hard Choices—Harder Questions," *Public Administration Review* 38(4) 1978, 338–44. For evidence on the effectiveness of sunset provisions, see Richard C. Kearney, "Sunset: A Survey and Analysis of State Experience," *Public Administration Review* 50(1) 1990, 49–57.

[53]Eugene Bardach, "Policy Termination as a Political Process," *Policy Sciences* 7(2) 1976, 123–31. Bardach also notes that people may oppose termination out of a reluctance to damage the existing program apparatus that may have future value. Also, on the psychological impediments to termination, see Peter de Leon, "Public Policy Termination: An End and a Beginning," *Policy Analysis* 4(3) 1978, 369–92.

[54]Robert P. Biller, "On Tolerating Policy and Organizational Termination: Some Design Considerations," *Polity Sciences* 7(2) 1976, 133–49. Biller offers a number of other provocative ideas about how to make policy termination more acceptable to members of organizations. He suggests the following sorts of institutional mechanisms: savings banks (allow organizations to keep part of the savings from terminated programs); trust offices (keep a skeleton crew to preserve institutional memory and provide a home for some program employees); and receivership referees (encourage organizations to reorganize voluntarily to eliminate ineffective programs).

needed for successful implementation if they do not associate their personal interests with the programs. Also, at some point ad hoc groups in effect become permanent as people become accustomed to new positions and lose interest in the old. Therefore, it probably makes sense to use ad hoc groups for implementing new programs only if any attempts at termination are likely to come in months rather than years.

What can we say about designing termination policies? A general strategy is to try to buy off the beneficiaries of the policy you hope to terminate.[55] In Chapter 10 we described "grandfathering" as one way of overcoming opposition to policy change. Another is to provide direct compensation to those who will bear costs as a consequence of the termination. For example, say we wanted to remove an agricultural price support that was becoming increasingly expensive and socially costly. We might be able to lessen opposition by proposing to pay current recipients at current levels for some period following removal of the price support.

Coping with Diversity

Analysts often face the problem of designing policies for diverse circumstances. Uniform policies that usually accomplish their goals may nevertheless fail badly with respect to specific localities, communities, categories of people, or firms. Central governments typically face the problem of diversity in connection with policies that influence the provision of local public goods or regulate local externalities. Sometimes such diversity can be accommodated by decentralizing certain aspects of policy. Other times diversity can be exploited in the design of implementation strategies.

Bottom-Up Processes. Rather than mandating participation in centrally established policies, it is sometimes advantageous to allow for self-selection. The implementation of sticker parking in San Francisco illustrates the use of a selection process as part of a policy design: neighborhoods had to apply for designation as sticker-parking areas. This bottom-up process avoided the opposition that might have arisen if the areas had been designated by the City Planning Department.

More generally, processes that permit the participation of interest groups in aspects of implementation may be valuable in forestalling political attacks on the entire policy. The basic idea is to provide a mechanism that permits the policy to be altered somewhat to accommodate local interests. Requiring public hearings, establishing local advisory boards, and providing resources for discretionary uses may offer opportunities for making policies more attractive to local interests. From the perspective of the policy designer, the trick is to structure such mechanisms so that they promote acceptable program adaptations and co-opt potential political opponents without creating bottlenecks or veto points that can threaten implementation.

Where local governments and organizations lack the capability to deal with local policy problems, higher levels of government may find it worthwhile to adopt long-run strategies of *capacity building*—that is, facilitate improvements in the managerial and analytical capabilities of local organizations so that they will be better

[55]For a discussion of this strategy and others, see Robert D. Behn, "How to Terminate a Public Policy: A Dozen Hints for the Would-Be Terminator," *Policy Analysis* 4(3) 1978, 393–413.

able to initiate bottom-up policies.[56] For example, if a state department of transportation were concerned that cities were failing to consider improved traffic control technologies, then it might adopt policies to make local personnel more aware of available technologies (through state-sponsored training, information networks, personnel exchanges, and direct information) and more capable of implementing them (through funding and technical assistance programs). Such programs are intended to increase the capability of local organizations to choose improvements that best fit local conditions.

Phased Implementation. Limited resources, including the time and attention of implementors, often make phased implementation desirable or necessary. How should the sites for the first phase be selected? One strategy is to select a representative set of sites so that the full range of implementation problems will likely be encountered. Seeking diversity in the first phase makes sense when the implementors are confident of their ability to deal with the problems that do arise. Assuming that the program survives the first phase, knowing the full range of problems that are likely to be encountered will permit reevaluation of its desirability and redesign of its implementation plan.

An alternative strategy for selecting sites for the first phase of implementation is to stack the deck in favor of the implementors by picking sites where the conditions for success seem most favorable. By starting with easier sites, the implementor is better able to avoid failure and build an effective staff for dealing with the later stages of implementation. Stacking the deck in the first phase makes sense when an early failure will make the program vulnerable to political attack. The trade-off is between more realistic information about future problems and better prospects for immediate success. Make a conscious choice.

Taking Account of Repeated Interaction

Our discussions of bureaucratic supply as a source of government failure (Chapter 8) and as a generic policy alternative (Chapter 10) emphasized formal incentives. Yet formal structures do not always fully explain organizational performance. Organizations with very similar formal structures can vary greatly in the way they perform.

Students of management and public administration have long recognized the importance of norms and leadership to organizational performance.[57] The absence of a theoretical framework for understanding these concepts has made it difficult to generalize about them. In recent years, however, the rational choice theory of in-

[56]See Bruce Jacobs and David L. Weimer, "Including Capacity Building: The Role of the External Change Agent," in Beth Walter Honadle and Arnold M. Howitt, eds., *Perspectives on Management Capacity Building* (Albany: State University of New York Press, 1986), 139–60.

[57]Chester I. Bernard, *Functions of the Executive* (Cambridge, MA: Harvard University Press, 1938); Herbert Kaufman, *The Forest Ranger* (Baltimore: Johns Hopkins University Press, 1960). For overviews of leadership, mission, and corporate culture in the public sector, see James Q. Wilson, *Bureaucracy: What Government Agencies Do and Why They Do It* (New York: Basic Books, 1989); and Mark H. Moore, *Creating Value: Strategic Management in Government* (Cambridge, MA: Harvard University Press, 1995). For an overview of the literature on private managers, see Sydney Finkelstein and Donald Hambrick, *Strategic Leadership: Top Executives and Their Effects on Organizations* (San Francisco: West, 1996).

stitutions,[58] which models social interactions as repeated games, has provided insight into social norms, leadership, and corporate culture. Although its practical application in policy analysis is still to be demonstrated, the rational choice theory of institutions offers some valuable general insights into policy design.[59]

Social Norms. People often exhibit behavior that appears to be consistent with certain *social norms* that involve people cooperating in ways that are immediately costly to them. For example, police officers often share a norm that requires them to rush to the aid of any fellow officer who appears to be in danger, even though doing so involves risks for those responding. Thus, if one adopts a myopic view of only the isolated situation, social norms appear to be irrational. From a less myopic perspective that incorporates future consequences, however, social norms can be seen to be individually rational.[60] Modeling social interaction as a repeated game provides a way of exploring the rational basis of social norms.

Consider Figure 11.1, which displays an abstraction of the Prisoner's Dilemma used to illustrate the problem of open access in Figure 5.6. The payoffs for combinations of the players' strategies, cooperate (C) and defect (D), are shown such that $a > 1$, $b > 0$, and $a - b < 2$, which defines the payoffs in a Prisoner's Dilemma game. The payoff from receiving unreciprocated cooperation, a, is larger than 1, the payoff from mutual cooperation; the payoff from providing unreciprocated cooperation is $-b$ which is less than the payoff of zero that results if neither player cooperates. In a single play of the game, sometimes referred to as the *stage game*, the only equilibrium is for both players to defect and receive a payoff of zero.

Now imagine that the players anticipate possibly playing the game against each other repeatedly. Specifically, imagine that each player believes that having completed a play of the game, there is a probability of δ of playing yet again. A δ close to 1 implies that the players believe that there is a very high likelihood of the game continuing for a long time; a low δ implies that they believe the game is likely to end soon.[61] As the players interact, they anticipate the probability of playing two times is δ (the current play for certain and a probability of δ of a second play), the probability of playing three times is δ^2, the probability of playing four times is δ^3, and so on.

Both players defecting in each round is one equilibrium in the repeated game. Another possible equilibrium involves both players using the following strategy: cooperate on the first play and continue to cooperate as long as the other player cooperated in the previous round; if the other player ever defects, then defect in all subsequent plays. Both players following this strategy will be in equilibrium if neither player can obtain a higher expected payoff from defecting. The expected payoff to each player of following the strategy if the other is playing it

[58] Andrew Schotter, *The Economic Theory of Social Institutions* (New York: Cambridge University Press, 1981).

[59] Randall Calvert, "The Rational Choice Theory of Institutions: Implications for Design," in David L. Weimer, ed., *Institutional Design* (Boston: Kluwer, 1995), 63–94.

[60] Edna Ullmann-Margalit, *The Emergence of Norms* (Oxford: Clarendon Press, 1977); and Michael Taylor, *Community, Anarchy, and Liberty* (New York: Cambridge University Press, 1982); Russell Hardin, *Collective Action* (Baltimore: Johns Hopkins University Press, 1982); and Robert Alexrod, *The Evolution of Cooperation* (New York: Basic Books, 1982).

[61] We can alternatively interpret δ as a discount factor for time preference in a game with an infinite number of plays. In terms of our discussion of discounting in Chapter 16, we would interpret δ as $1/(1 + d)$, where d is the individual's discount rate.

Stage Game

Player 2

$a > 1$ and $a - b < 2$

		Cooperate (C)	Defect (D)
Player 1	Cooperate (C)	(1, 1)	$(-b, a)$
	Defect (D)	$(a, -b)$	(0, 0)

Payoffs: (player 1, player 2)

Repeated Game: Stage game repeated with probability δ

Some possible equilibria in repeated game:

(1) Both players defect every play (only equilibrium in stage game repeated as long as game played)

Observed strategy pairs in equilibrium: (D, D), (D, D), ...

(2) Both players cooperate on first play and continue to cooperate as long as other player cooperated on previous play; if one player ever defects, then the other defects on all subsequent plays. Equilibrium if $\delta > (a - 1)/a$

Observed strategy pairs in equilibrium: (C, C), (C, C), ...

Figure 11.1 Equilibria in a Repeated Game

is $1 + \delta + \delta^2 + \delta^2 + \cdots = 1/(1 - \delta)$. In terms of deviating from this strategy, the largest possible gains come from defecting in the first play, so that if the other player were playing the strategy the payoffs would be $a + 0 + 0 + \cdots = a$. In other words, gaining the payoff a in the first play of the game would result in zero in all subsequent plays. Now neither player will wish to defect from the strategy if $a < 1/(1 - \delta)$, or, rearranging, if the probability of playing again, δ, is larger than $(a - 1)/a$. Thus, as long as this inequality holds, then both players following the strategy is an equilibrium that would appear as full cooperation between the players.

Even this simple example has some implications for the emergence of social norms like cooperation. The larger δ, and, therefore, the greater possible gain from mutual cooperation in the future, the larger can be the payoff from unilateral defection, a, without precluding the possibility of a cooperative norm. In other words, the more likely it is that the interaction will continue, the stronger the temptation for defection that can be possibly controlled by the social norm. In the context of organizational design, situations in which people interact more frequently (have a higher probability of playing another round of the game together) are thus more likely to support cooperative norms. Thus, building in the expectation of repeated interaction among organizational members offers the prospect for more cooperation. Of course, sometimes organizational designers wish to discourage cooperation that may not be socially desirable, as, say, between regulators and those being regulated. In such cases, inspection systems that avoid repeat interactions may be desirable from the perspective of discouraging the norm of corruption.[62]

This simple model suggests the importance of recruitment and socialization. Imagine that members of an organization did not know which specific person with whom they were playing the game, but they did know that they were all following strategies that involved cooperation in equilibrium. Now imagine that a person joined the organization, and that this new person assumed that everyone played the strategy of defecting, which is also an equilibrium. Individuals playing the game with the new member would encounter defections and thus defect in future rounds themselves. The result would be the movement from an equilibrium in which everyone cooperated on every play to one in which no one ever cooperated. Clearly, if the organization were able to do so, it would benefit from recruiting new members who would be predisposed to assuming that others played strategies consistent with cooperative equilibria. Socialization, through training or less formal interaction, would be valuable for increasing the chances that new members do not disrupt desirable equilibria.

Leadership and Corporate Culture. There are two obvious equilibria in the simple repeated game presented in Figure 11.1: each player defects on every play (the equilibrium in the stage game) and, assuming that the probability of repeated play is high enough relative to the payoff from defection, each player cooperates until encountering a defection and then defects in all future plays. But there are many other possible equilibria. For example, one might cooperate until one encounters a defection and then from then on play the strategy played by the other player in the previous round (the so-called tit-for-tat strategy). Indeed, repeated games generally have an infinite number of possible equilibria.[63] Those playing in a repeated game thus face the problem of coordinating on one of the desirable equilibria from among the many possible equilibria.

From this perspective, one function of *leadership* is to provide solutions to this type of coordination problem. Leaders may try to create *focal points,* or distinctive outcomes that attract attention, to help members coordinate.[64] For example, leaders may set clear examples by their own actions, by creating symbols, by identifying and rewarding exemplary behavior, or by making examples of those who violate social norms the leader is trying to promote. Creating and communicating a shared mission for the organization may also help the leader create expectations among members that facilitate coordination.

Yet leaders come and go. Members of the organization, who fear that their current cooperative efforts will not be rewarded by reciprocation from others because a change in organizational leadership might result in a new, and less cooperative,

[62]Small numbers of professional inspectors may necessitate repeated interaction. It may be desirable to increase the number of inspectors by recruiting volunteers. For a discussion of the use of volunteers from charitable organizations to monitor money flows in casinos in British Columbia, see Aidan R. Vining and David L. Weimer, "Saintly Supervision: Monitoring Casino Gambling in British Columbia," *Journal of Policy Analysis and Management* 16(4) 1997, 615–20.

[63]This is the implication of the so-called folk theorem. For a formal proof, see Drew Fudenberg and Eric Maskin, "The Folk Theorem in Repeated Games with Discounting or with Incomplete Information," *Econometrica* 54(3) 1986, 533–54.

[64]On the role of focal points in coordination games, see Thomas C. Schelling, *Strategy of Conflict* (Cambridge, MA: Harvard University Press, 1960).

equilibrium in the future, may be unreceptive to the coordinating efforts of the current leader. Here is where *corporate culture*, which is a set of norms associated with the organization itself rather than any particular leader, may come into play.[65] Organizations that have been able to establish reputations for consistently treating members in certain ways can draw on these expectations to maintain social norms among members even when leaders change.

Fully analyzing the impact of policy changes on organizations requires that attention be given to corporate culture. Functional corporate cultures are assets that should not be squandered. Externally imposed changes on organizations that force them to violate, and thereby undermine, valuable corporate cultures may result in reductions in performance that would not be predicted on the basis of changes in resources alone. For example, a unit of a public agency that allows its employees to take time off as rewards for intense or off-hour periods of work might be able to maintain a high level of morale and productivity that would be impossible if employees were required to work in strict compliance with the general rules of the agency.

Conclusion

Analysts who want to influence public policy should know the political environment. Clients are more likely to embrace policy proposals that promote their political interests. Strategies that take account of the interests of actors in the relevant political arenas can influence the likelihood that policies will be adopted. Anticipating and solving implementation problems requires an understanding of the interests of those who bear the consequences of the means and ends of policies. Thus, if analysts are to provide useful advice, then they cannot avoid paying attention to the political environment.

For Discussion

1. Imagine that a construction project will close a major parking lot on your campus for the next three years. As a consequence, some people currently parking on campus for a nominal fee will no longer be able to obtain permits. A member of the economics faculty has suggested raising the price substantially, from $25 per year to $200 per year, so that the number of permits demanded at the higher price will equal the number available. It would have to be approved by the transportation planning committee, which includes representatives from the faculty, the administration, unionized employees, and students. How would you assess the prospects for adoption of the proposal? What ideas do you have about how to improve the prospects?
2. Now imagine that the transportation planning committee adopts the policy of raising the parking fees. Sketch a brief implementation scenario.

[65]David M. Kreps, "Corporate Culture and Economic Theory," in James E. Alt and Kenneth A. Shepsle, eds., *Perspectives on Positive Political Economy* (New York: Cambridge University Press, 1990), 90–143; Gary J. Miller, *Managerial Dilemmas: The Political Economy of Hierarchy* (New York: Cambridge University Press, 1992).

12

Government Supply

Drawing Organizational Boundaries

Public policies usually require organizations for their implementation. Organizations, however, can take a variety of forms, ranging from government bureaus funded by lump-sum budgets and staffed by civil servants to for-profit privately owned firms. The analysis of organizational forms requires analysts to pay attention to the rules that govern various sorts of transactions. *Neoinstitutional economics (NIE)* retains the core assumptions of economic theory but explicitly considers the rules and information relevant to various sorts of transactions.[1] NIE concepts are useful in considering the appropriate boundaries for public organizations.[2]

A rationale for public provision, or financing, based on market failure or the achievement of other social goals, does not necessarily imply a rationale for

[1]One branch of this body of literature, sometimes referred to as the *new institutional economics*, relaxes the core assumption of the full rationality of economic actors. Instead, *bounded rationality*, in which actors do not use all the available information in their decision making, is assumed. See Oliver E. Williamson, *Markets and Hierarchies: Analysis and Antitrust Implications* (New York: Free Press, 1975). The factors we identify as relevant to the contracting-out decision apply whether or not full or bounded rationality is assumed.

[2]For a comprehensive review of NIE, see Thrain Eggertsson, *Economic Behavior and Institutions* (Cambridge: Cambridge University Press, 1990). For shorter surveys that relate NIE specifically to the public sector, see Brian Dollery, "New Institutional Economics and the Analysis of the Public Sector," *Policy Studies Review* 18(1) 2001, 185–211; and Aidan R. Vining and David L. Weimer, "Economics," in Donald F. Kettl and H. Brinton Millward, eds., *The State of Public Management* (Baltimore: Johns Hopkins University Press, 1996), 92–117.

government production or direct service delivery.[3] Government can finance provision of services so that they are delivered by either for-profit, private not-for-profit, or other public organizations. This process, typically described as *contracting out* or *outsourcing*, has grown in the United States, Great Britain, Australia, and other countries over the last two decades.[4] Increasingly, organizational forms for implementing public policy are hybrid mixtures, with traditional bureaus providing the "steering" for service provision with not-for-profit organizations or private firms that do some or all of the "rowing."

What factors should analysts consider in deciding when and how the rowing should be pushed beyond the organizational boundary of the bureau? The answer to this question is sufficiently important for policy analysts to warrant more in-depth treatment than was provided in Chapter 10 in the discussion of bureaucratic supply as a generic policy alternative. As we explain in more detail here, the major purpose of redrawing organizational boundaries of public agencies should be to improve the efficiency with which public services are delivered.[5] As we will see, the key challenge for policy analysts is to take account of all costs and benefits in assessing efficiency.

In order to address the meaning of efficiency, we draw from *transaction cost theory*, also known as *transaction cost economics*, a field of NIE economics that arose to explain why some economic activities organized as markets while others are organized as hierarchical entities. Transaction cost theory was pioneered by Ronald Coase and applied to organizations, and especially organizational boundaries, by Oliver Williamson.[6] Transaction cost theory recognizes that production costs are only part of the total costs of organizing the supply of a good or service. In addition, there are transaction costs associated with making and executing contracts among the entities engaged in the production process. In drawing organizational boundaries for policy alternatives, analysts should take account of transaction costs as well as production costs. The challenge is to find organizational arrangements that minimize the total costs of supply, including those associated with making, executing, and monitoring contracts.

Before examining issues relevant to determining total costs, it is useful to emphasize some of the fundamental ideas behind transaction cost theory. First, the theory uses "the transaction," whatever it may be in the particular context, as the unit of analysis. For example, the transaction could be a contemporaneous exchange in a spot market, the exercise of delegated authority in a hierarchy, an exchange between employees, or the execution of a contract specifying a sequence of actions to

[3]Aidan R. Vining and David L. Weimer, "Government Supply and Government Production Failure: A Framework Based on Contestability," *Journal of Public Policy* 10(1) 1990, 1–22.

[4]For recent reviews on the growth of contracting out in the United States, see Keon S. Chi and Cindy Jasper, *Private Practices: A Review of Privatization in State Government* (Lexington, KY: Council of State Governments, 1998); Elaine Morley, "Local Government Use of Alternative Service Delivery Approaches," in *The Municipal Year Book, 1999* (Washington, DC: International City/County Management, 1999), 34–44. For global evidence, see Graeme A. Hodge, *Privatization: An International Review of Performance* (Boulder, CO: Westview Press, 2000), at pp. 88–92.

[5]However, as we have emphasized throughout this book, we must also recognize the potential for government failure. On positive (rather than normative) reasons for privatization, closely related to contracting out, see Florencio Lopez-de-Silanes, Andrei Shleifer, and Robert W. Vishny, "Privatization in the United States," *RAND Journal of Economics* 28(3) 1997, 447–71.

[6]Ronald H. Coase, "The Nature of the Firm," *Economica* 4(16) 1937, 386–405. Williamson, *Markets and Hierarchies*.

complete an exchange occurring over a long period of time. Second, transaction cost theory recognizes that almost all production relationships involve contracts. Hierarchies, such as bureaus, nonprofits, or firms, are bundles of typically long-term contracts defining the responsibilities of employers and employees to each other. Markets involve contracts among hierarchies and individuals. In either case, the contracts can be formal, as in legal documents, or informal, as in, say, customary practice. Third, it recognizes that contracts are rarely, if ever, complete—the world is complex, and unforeseen contingencies can almost always arise. Fourth, it recognizes the ubiquity of informational asymmetries. As noted in the discussion of insurance markets in Chapter 6, asymmetries may arise either as hidden information, in which someone has relevant information unavailable to others, or as hidden action, in which someone can take relevant actions that are unobservable by others.

In summary, "transaction cost economics is concerned mainly with the governance of contractual relations."[7] The optimal organization of governance depends on a number of factors, including the nature of the goods and services that need to be produced and the characteristics (and especially incentives) of the parties engaged in contracting. We now turn to the set of cost factors that should, and do, influence the choice of institutional arrangements, or the governance, of the supply of goods to citizens.

Production Costs, Bargaining Costs, and Opportunism Costs

Three types of costs are relevant to the choice between direct production by public agencies and contracting out: production costs, bargaining costs, and opportunism costs.[8] Production costs are the costs associated with directly creating the good or service. Bargaining and opportunism generate the transaction costs of governance. Table 12.1 provides an overview of these costs and how they relate to the contracting decision.

Production Costs

Production costs are the *opportunity costs* of the real resources—land, labor, and capital—actually used to produce something, measured in terms of the value of the things that these resources would have produced in their next best alternative use. Economic theory suggests that competition pushes production costs to their lowest possible levels in *competitive environments*. The empirical evidence suggests that competition promotes technical efficiency.[9] Furthermore, in a competitive

[7]Oliver E. Williamson, "Transaction Cost Economics and Organization Theory," in Jennifer J. Halpern and Robert N. Stern, eds., *Debating Rationality: Nonrational Aspects of Organizational Decision Making* (Ithaca, NY: Cornell University Press/ILR Press, 1998), 155–94, at p. 159.

[8]This section draws upon the formulation presented in Steven Globerman and Aidan R. Vining, "A Framework for Evaluating the Government Contracting-Out Decision with an Application to Information Technology," *Public Administration Review* 56 (6) 1996, 577–86; and Aidan R. Vining and Steven Globerman, "Contracting-Out Health Care Services: A Conceptual Framework," *Health Policy* 46 (2) 1998, 77–96.

[9]For example, on the impact of competition on hospitals, see Emmett B. Keeler, Glenn Melnik, and, Jack Zwanziger, "The Changing Effects of Competition on Non-Profit and For-Profit Hospital Pricing Behavior," *Journal of Health Economics* 18(1) 1999, 69–86.

Table 12.1 *When Are Incremental Costs Likely to Favor Contracting Out?*

Production Costs	Bargaining Costs	Opportunism Costs
Unrealized economies of scale, so opportunities for gains in allocational efficiency.	Low task complexity, so relative certainty and less costly monitoring.	Low task complexity, so relatively little information asymmetry and more effective monitoring.
Lack of competition for agency product, so opportunities for reductions in X-inefficiency.	High contestability, so less bargaining leverage for contractee.	Low task complexity, so production externalities less likely.
Inflexibility in use of inputs in-house, so opportunities for reductions in X-inefficiency.	Low asset specificity, so less need to compensate contractee for risk.	High contestability, so less postcontract leverage for contractee.
		Low asset specificity, so less risk of holdup problem.

environment free from serious market failures, profit-oriented firms generally have lower costs than public or mixed-ownership organizations.[10] Production costs are likely to be lower with competitive contracting out, for three reasons.

First, in-house production may entail production at too low levels to be efficient;[11] that is, the public organization does not use enough of the good itself, or supply enough of the good to clients, to be able to produce it at the minimum efficient scale. Thus, in-house production may involve allocation inefficiency. An independent producer selling to multiple buyers may be able to achieve minimum efficient scale. These production costs should be conceived broadly—the most significant economies of scale might occur for intangible factors such as administrative systems and knowledge and learning. Scale economies alone, however, are not a sufficient argument for private sector production. Public organizations could engage in cooperative production that takes advantage of economies of scale. In practice, however, it is often difficult to design government organizations that can span political jurisdictions to achieve economies of scale. In addition, this cooperation also engenders bargaining and opportunism costs. On the other hand, large, jurisdiction boundary-spanning not-for-profit organizations may be able to achieve economies of scale.[12] Contracting out may provide a way of achieving economies of scale.

[10]Aidan R. Vining and Anthony E. Boardman provide a summary of the literature that compares the performance of firms to state-owned enterprises in competitive environments, "Ownership versus Competition: Efficiency in Public Enterprise," *Public Choice* 32(2) 1992, 205–39. For a review of the more recent literature that usually finds efficiency improvements after privatization, see William Megginson and John Netter, "From State to Market: A Survey of Empirical Studies on Privatization," *Journal of Economic Literature* 39(2) 2001, 321–89.

[11]Jonas Prager, "Contracting Out Government Services: Lessons from the Private Sector," *Public Administration Review* 54(2) 1994, 176–84.

[12]Howard P. Tuckman, "Competition, Commercialization, and the Evolution of Nonprofit Organizational Structures," *Journal of Policy Analysis and Management* 17(2) 1998, 175–94.

Second, as we discussed in Chapter 8, in-house production may not achieve the minimum costs that are technically feasible because of the absence of competition, resulting in X-inefficiency. Lack of competition usually blunts efficiency incentives because it eliminates comparative performance benchmarks for customers and overseers. Furthermore, the marginal costs of services are obscured, and monitoring by representatives and taxpayers difficult, when they are funded through lump-sum budget allocations to multiservice agencies rather than through sales to consumers. Contracting out may create efficiency incentives by competing with in-house production. It may also focus attention on the costs of particular goods and services.

Third, in-house production may be hampered by inflexibility in the choice of factor inputs that leads to X-inefficiency. Public agencies usually operate under civil service systems that make it difficult to hire and fire workers to obtain employees with the most appropriate skills for producing goods and services. Also, they often do not have direct access to capital markets, making it difficult to obtain or adjust equipment and other physical resources. Thus, even when the managers of public agencies have strong incentives to produce in the most technically efficient way, they may face constraints that prevent them from doing so. Contracting out may allow for more technically efficient uses of inputs.

There is considerable empirical evidence from a range of government activities that contracting out by government to private suppliers generally lowers production costs. A 1997 survey of the contracting-out experience of the sixty-six largest cities in the United States found that the annual cost savings were between 16 and 20 percent; respondents also estimated that contracting out improved service quality by between 24 and 27 percent.[13] A comprehensive meta-analysis based on "around three dozen studies" with "reasonable research integrity," concluded:

> This analysis has shown that contracting studies have typically reported real cost savings. … These effect sizes were found to be highly significant and were interpreted as being equivalent to an average cost saving of 8 to14 percent. Overall, the reliability of this average saving was beyond doubt. Cost savings differed between services and a general rule could not be applied to all.[14]

Two important caveats to the general findings of cost savings deserve note. First, studies that have examined the relative production costs of internal provision versus contracting out have not included bargaining and opportunism costs, which a priori might be expected to be higher with contracting out. Researchers are just beginning to turn their attention to this topic. One recent study finds that governments engage in more monitoring, and bear more monitoring costs, when the risks of opportunism are greater.[15] Additionally, not all forms of contracting out can be expected to lower production costs. In particular, *cost-plus contracts*, which guarantee the contractee a profit no matter how high the

[13]Robert J. Dilger, Randolph R. Moffitt, and Linda Struyk, "Privatization of Municipal Services in America's Largest Population Cities," *Public Administration Review* 57(1) 1997, 21–26.

[14]Graeme A. Hodge, *Privatization: An International Review of Performance* (Boulder, CO: Westview Press, 2000), at pp. 103 and 128.

[15]Trevor L. Brown and Matthew Potoski, "Managing Contract Performance: A Transactions Cost Approach," *Journal of Policy Analysis and Management* 22(2) 2003, 275–97.

measured costs of production, are unlikely to lead to low-cost production.[16] Second, cost comparison studies should control for quality differences. A few studies have done so,[17] but the great majority have not.

Bargaining Costs

Bargaining costs include the following components: (1) the costs arising directly in negotiating contract details, including identifying potential contractors, gathering information about their likely performance, and writing mutually acceptable contract provisions; (2) the costs of negotiating changes to the contract in the postcontract stage when unforeseen circumstances arise; (3) the costs of monitoring whether performance is being adhered to by other parties; and (4) the costs of disputes that arise if neither party wishes to utilize pre-agreed resolution mechanisms, especially "contract-breaking" mechanisms. Although only the first category of costs is experienced in the precontract period, the other categories of costs should be anticipated.

As an example, consider a social service agency attempting to contract out drug rehabilitation services to private organizations. After identifying relevant organizations, the agency would have to decide how many contracts to offer. For each contract, it would have to specify the quantities and characteristics of the services to be provided, the payments to be made for the services, and the circumstances that would allow the agency to terminate the contract. After the contract is put into effect, a contracted organization may discover that it cannot actually recruit enough clients of the types specified in the contract. The agency and organization must then reach agreement on how to deal with the changed circumstances, say, allowing substitution of client types or adjusting payments. Throughout, the agency must monitor the performance of the organization to make sure that it is providing the services specified in the contract. If the agency believes that the organization is not providing the specified services, then it must take actions to enforce or break the contract, actions that the organization may resist legally or politically if it believes that either the agency has made an incorrect assessment or unforeseen circumstances have arisen that preclude it from meeting contract terms.

Bargaining costs arise when both parties act with self-interest, but in good faith. The incremental bargaining costs of contracting out are relevant because a potential advantage of not contracting out is that the distribution of costs within the organization can be resolved by the existing arrangements of hierarchical authority. Nonetheless, bargaining within organizations, for example over wages, bonuses, internal transfer prices, or areas of responsibility, may also be costly;[18] thus, it is incremental bargaining costs of contracting out relative to agency production that are relevant.

[16]R. Preston McAfee and John McMillan, *Incentives in Government Contracting* (Toronto: University of Toronto Press, 1988).

[17]For example, see Randall G. Holcombe, "Privatization of Municipal Wastewater Treatment," *Public Budgeting and Finance* 11(3) 1991, 28–42; and Russell L. Williams, "Economic Theory and Contracting Out for Residential Waste Collection," *Public Productivity & Management Review* 21(3) 1998, 259–71.

[18]See Gary J. Miller, *Managerial Dilemmas* (New York: Cambridge University Press, 1992); and Aidan R. Vining and David L. Weimer, "Inefficiency in Public Organizations," *International Public Management Journal* 2(1) 1999, 1–24.

The Costs of Opportunism

Opportunism is behavior by a party to a transaction designed to change the agreed terms of a transaction to be more in its favor. Opportunism costs arise when at least one party acts in *bad faith*. Opportunism is more likely in the context of contracting out than in agency production, because the question of who gets rents (payments in excess of costs) is more relevant in the nonhierarchical relationships between organizations. Additionally, employees within organizations have better, and usually more frequent, opportunities to "pay back" (and, therefore, discourage) opportunistic fellow employees within the same organization. But just as there are bargaining costs within organizations, opportunism can occur within organizations. Therefore, as with bargaining costs, it is incremental opportunism costs that are relevant in choosing organizational arrangements. Opportunism is more often considered to occur *after* contracting has taken place, but some behaviors prior to contracting have opportunism-like characteristics.[19] One party may advance contract provisions that appear neutral but actually facilitate behavior inconsistent with the purposes of the contract. For example, the organization offering drug rehabilitation services may write a contract provision that ambiguously defines drug abuse so that it will be reimbursed for services to clients who the sponsoring agency does not intend to be the targets of treatment.

Opportunism can manifest itself in many ways. Returning to the contracting out of drug rehabilitation services, one can imagine ways that the contractee could take advantage of imperfect monitoring. For example, it may inappropriately count group sessions as individual services, treat canceled appointments as services delivered, shave time from sessions, use less qualified personnel than specified in the contract, or even simply not provide services, perhaps in collusion with clients who are receiving them involuntarily. If it would be very difficult for the agency to replace the contractee on short notice, then the contractee may be tempted to assert falsely that changed circumstances not covered in the contract make it unable to continue delivering services without additional payments or other more favorable contract terms.

While analytically it is possible to make a sharp distinction between bargaining and opportunism costs, they are difficult to distinguish in practice. It is in the interest of opportunistic parties to claim that their behavior results from an unexpected change in circumstances. Frequently the other party cannot tell whether the claim has genuinely arisen from unforeseen circumstances or not. An inability to distinguish between legitimate bargaining and opportunism itself raises contracting-out costs.

In summary, public policy should seek the governance arrangements that minimize the sum of production, bargaining, and opportunism costs across government, contractees, and third parties (citizens) for any given level and quality of service. This objective emphasizes that governments should be as concerned with the costs that they impose on contractees or third parties, as with the budgetary costs that they bear. However, at the organizational level (for example, an individual hospital), it is unrealistic to expect even nonprofit organizations to act with this

[19] Benjamin Klein, Robert G. Crawford, and Armen A. Alchian, "Vertical Integration, Appropriable Rents and the Competitive Contracting Process," *Journal of Law and Economics* 21(2) 1978, 297–326.

degree of altruism without appropriate incentives. Consequently, higher levels of government may have to set appropriate frameworks for contractual conditions (that is, design meta-contracts). For example, requirements for cost-benefit analysis to support decisions force attention on social costs, including the costs borne by third parties.

Predicting Bargaining and Opportunism Costs

Three major factors are likely to determine the sum of bargaining and opportunism costs in a specific contracting-out context: task complexity, degree of contestability, and degree of asset specificity. We discuss each of these in turn.

Task Complexity

Task complexity is the degree of difficulty in specifying and monitoring the terms and conditions of a transaction. For example, specifying and measuring the quality of food served by a contractee is relatively easy. Specifying and measuring the quality of complex medical services where patients have widely varying risk factors is relatively difficult. The degree of task complexity largely determines both the uncertainty surrounding the contract (this affects both contracting parties equally) and the potential for information asymmetry, or hidden information, in which one party to the contract has information that the other party does not have.

Complex tasks involve uncertainty about the nature and costs of the production process itself. Additionally, complex activities are more likely to be affected by various sorts of "shocks," or unforeseen changes in the task environment. Greater uncertainty raises bargaining costs, both during contract negotiations and execution. For example, a study of the aerospace industry found that more complex components were considerably likelier to be produced internally by firms than to be contracted out.[20]

Although information asymmetry does not always raise costs, usually it does, especially if a contract involves services where quality is only revealed considerably after the transaction occurs. High task complexity raises the probability that there will be information asymmetry, because it implies specialized knowledge or assets whose characteristics are only initially known to contractees or other external experts.[21] Consequently, information asymmetry is likely to create circumstances in which a party to the transaction can behave opportunistically. Opportunism arising from information asymmetry can occur either at the contract negotiation stage or at the postcontract stage, but is most likely to be significant postcontract. Either contractor or contractee may generate these costs. Higher task complexity also in-

[20]Scott E. Masten, "The Organization of Production: Evidence from the Aerospace Industry," *Journal of Law and Economics* 27(2) 1984, 402–17.

[21]John W. Crawford and Steven L. Krahn, "The Demanding Customer and the Hollow Organization," *Public Productivity & Management Review* 22(1) 1998, 107–18.

creases the potential for production externalities, that is, the potential for serious disruption to the rest of the public organization if the contracted service is withdrawn or degraded.[22]

Contestability

As discussed in Chapter 5, a contestable market is one in which even if only one organization is immediately available to provide a service, many others would quickly become available if the price offered by contract exceeded the average cost incurred by contractees. For example, markets for psychological assessment services are highly contestable, as many organizations have the capabilities to supply these services even if they are not currently doing so. The degree of contestability may, in some cases, be more important than the number of currently competing organizations providing the service.[23]

When the market for the service in question is highly competitive with a large number of organizations in the relevant (usually geographic) market producing the service, or very close substitutes, the public agency will likely be able to realize lower production costs without substantially higher negotiation and opportunism costs. Public agencies, however, may still be able to reduce production costs by contracting out activities even where there is no direct competition. Such goods may involve extensive scale economies and, as a result, there may be some degree of local, regional, or even national, natural monopoly. If providers are able to switch production to the good without sinking large up-front costs, however, then there is contestability.

The degree to which the activity being contracted for is contestable affects opportunism costs. If the market for the activity is contestable, then opportunism is reduced at the contract stage and, potentially, at the execution stage. Low contestability raises different issues in the two phases, however. During contract negotiations, a potential contractee in a market with limited contestability is tempted to offer services at a price above marginal cost (or average cost in circumstances where average cost is declining for the demanded good). This higher price can be thought of as a bargaining cost to the agency, because it must be paid to achieve the contract. If rent is fully realized by the contractee as profit, then it will represent a true social cost only to the extent that its financing from tax revenues involves a marginal excess burden (inefficiency related to the collection of revenue from the marginal tax source). More likely, however, some of the rent will be hidden by the contractor in nonproductive factor expenditures, such as excessive use of capital equipment, that do constitute social costs.

At the postcontract stage low contestability increases the risks of opportunism facing the other party and possibly third parties, for two reasons. First, the contractee cannot be quickly replaced (temporal specificity). Second, there is a heightened risk of "contract breach externalities."[24] This risk is especially relevant when

[22]Steven Globerman, "A Policy Analysis of Foreign Ownership Restrictions in Telecommunications," *Telecommunications Policy* 19(1) 1995, 21–28.

[23]William J. Baumol, John C. Panzar, and Robert D. Willig, *Contestable Markets and the Theory of Industry Structure* (New York: Harcourt Brace Jovanovich, 1982).

[24]See Globerman and Vining, "Framework for Evaluating the Government Contracting-Out Decision."

the contractee provides services that are related to a network of some kind. For example, a firm carrying out payroll operations might threaten to withdraw service, jeopardizing the payment of all payroll paychecks. This could effectively shut down a government. Situations where organizations fear breach externalities are often retained in-house. However, it is useful to emphasize that public agencies do not eliminate such externality problems by carrying out production themselves. Government employees can also opportunistically "hold up" their employer by withdrawing essential services (passive breach) or by picketing and various forms of sabotage (active breach).

Imperfect competition in the supply of many services attenuates the potential efficiency gains from contracting out. In particular, the presence of small and geographically dispersed populations, combined with the existence of economies of scale, typically limits the potential number of local contractees,[25] while high sunk costs act as a barrier to de novo entry of new suppliers. Further, the evidence suggests that governments often exacerbate the contestability problem. If potential contractees perceive that public agencies are soliciting unreasonably low bids or are arbitrarily requiring them to rebid at lower than originally contracted prices, then a competitive market may not emerge. Such behavior can thwart competition even in potentially competitive markets.

It may be possible for governments to enhance competition by expanding the size of the relevant geographic market through exchange agreements among themselves, whereby consumers could cross geographic jurisdictional boundaries to acquire services, with payments made to their suppliers from the agencies serving their home jurisdictions. For example, some states allow parents to send their children to school districts in which they do not live. A number of practical political obstacles can arise, however. In particular, governments are often loath to fund services that are provided outside their administrative boundaries, especially if it threatens the financial viability of provider organizations in their own localities.

Another potential approach to mitigating competition problems is for government contractors to own the (sunk cost) assets associated with service provision and for providers to own relatively fungible assets. As a practical matter, this requires governments to maintain ownership of buildings and relatively specialized and expensive equipment that would be leased to providers who successfully win the right to provide service. This strategy mitigates the need for entrants to make large sunk-cost investments and enhances contestability, though it requires that contracts be designed to provide appropriate use and maintenance of the assets.

Asset Specificity

An asset is "specific" if it makes a necessary contribution to the production of a good or service and has much lower value in alternative uses. There are various kinds of specificity, including physical, locational, human,[26] and temporal

[25]Brent S. Steel and Carolyn Long, "The Use of Agency Forces versus Contracting Out: Learning the Limits of Privatization," *Public Administration Quarterly* 22(2) 1998, 229–51.

[26]Williamson, *Markets and Hierarchies*, p. 55.

specificity.[27] Whatever the form of asset specificity, contracts that require either party to employ assets (usually physical capital assets but in some circumstances human capital assets) that have much less valuable or even no alternative use (that is, they are "sunk") raise the potential for opportunism. The contracting party that commits assets is vulnerable to holdup[28]—no matter what prices are agreed to in the contracting stage, the other party may be able to behave opportunistically by reneging and offering lower prices that only cover incremental costs. Asset specificity also reduces contestability at the time of contract renewal by creating a barrier to entry for potential bidders who have not accumulated specific assets. While the effects of asset specificity have not been studied systematically in the public sector context, extensive analogous private sector outsourcing evidence suggests that high asset specificity reduces contracting out.[29] The public sector evidence does suggest that governments engage in more monitoring when they contract out services that involve higher asset specificity.[30]

From a social efficiency perspective, government opportunism is as undesirable as contractee opportunism. Where contractees provide and own specific assets, such as highly specialized buildings, they have to worry about the potential for opportunistic behavior by public agencies. Governments can behave opportunistically once contractees have made asset specific investments.

It is important to emphasize that the costs that potentially arise from asset specificity are not totally exogenous. This point can be illustrated by thinking of this issue as a multiperiod game. Although bargaining and opportunism costs can occur either during contract negotiation (period 1) or postcontractually (period 2), it is feasible for government contractors to address both these costs at the contracting stage (that is, in period 1). The government player can anticipate what the optimal strategy in each period of the game will be for the other player (the contractee) and then by backward induction identify its own optimal strategy in each period. For example, suppose the government contractor is playing a game where contestability is high in period 1 but expected to be low in period 2 and subsequent periods once an initial bid winner makes sunk investments. Governments, therefore, should be able to predict that a contractee will behave opportunistically or generate bargaining costs in period 2 or some subsequent period. Governments should, therefore, incorporate this expectation into their period 1 strategy. To do so, government contractors must think through the factors influencing opportunism and bargaining costs as well as strategies to mitigate those costs.

[27]Scott E. Masten, James W. Meeham, Jr., and Edward A. Snyder, "The Costs of Organization," *Journal of Law, Economics and Organization* 7(1) 1991, 1–25, at p. 9; Steven Craig Pirrong, "Contracting Practices in Bulk Shipping Markets: A Transactions Cost Explanation," *Journal of Law and Economics* 36(1) 1993, 913–37.

[28]Two studies that demonstrate this are Howard A. Shelanski and Peter G. Klein, "Empirical Research in Transaction Cost Economics: A Review and Assessment," *Journal of Law, Economics and Organization* 11(2) 1995, 335–61; and Svein Ulset, "R&D Outsourcing and Contractual Governance: An Empirical Study of Commercial R&D Projects," *Journal of Economic Behavior and Organization* 30(1) 1996, 63–82.

[29]See, for example, Bruce R. Lyons, "Specific Investment, Economies of Scale, and the Make-or-Buy Decision: A Test of Transaction Cost Theory," *Journal of Economic Behavior and Organization* 26(3) 1995, 431–43.

[30]Brown and Potoski, "Managing Contract Performance."

In principle, then, contractual promises should be implemented in period 1 such that expected (social) opportunism and bargaining costs are minimized, even though they will only be triggered by (contingent) events that occur post-contractually. Thus, it is useful to distinguish between ex ante mechanisms and ex post mechanisms, emphasizing that in the case of the latter it is only the trigger that is ex post.

Can Opportunism Be Controlled by the Use of Not-for-Profits?

The not-for-profit sector includes many hospitals, museums, human service organizations, and, in the United States, many universities. The double market-failure rationale, introduced in Chapter 10, has been used to explain the role of not-for-profit organizations in the economy (although using somewhat different language). Not-for-profits typically provide public goods (the first market failure) in a context where potential contributors (governments or private individuals) do not have the information to assess whether their contribution is actually used to produce the public good (the second, or principal-agent, market failure). Henry Hansmann argues that as a result of the principal-agent problem (another prominent model within NIE) in such circumstances, profit-making firms are able to divert funds to owners because contributors have neither the incentive nor the information to monitor diversion. In addition, because of the difficulty of monitoring performance (that is, information asymmetry), the profit-making firm may provide inferior goods at excessive prices. In other words, donors may "trust" not-for-profits because they are not allowed to make a profit. Perhaps donors also see certain not-for-profits as having a strong sense of mission that leads them to maximize the output of desired goods. Against this must be set the possibility that not-for-profits, given the lack of information, may transfer or dissipate (for example, through higher salaries or less work) the excess of revenue over costs.[31]

One additional potential advantage of contracting with not-for-profits is that their form allows for voluntary contributions—those who value the supplied good can provide it or, where some level is provided by government, make additional contributions to expand its supply. Another is that it allows for great flexibility in the mix of services provided, a feature especially important where the recipients of the services have heterogeneous preferences.[32] Of course, the relative independence of not-for-profits sometimes makes it difficult for the government to mandate the exact set of services that will be supplied. Indeed, it may be difficult for government to stimulate the creation of not-for-profits where they do not already exist.

Governments may also wish to consider the consequences of contracting with not-for-profits on the not-for-profits themselves. Some opponents to providing publicly funded schooling through vouchers redeemable at private schools worry that

[31]Henry Hansmann. "The Role of Non-Profit Enterprise," in Susan Rose-Ackerman, ed., *The Economics of Non-Profit Institutions* (New York: Oxford University Press, 1986), 57–84.

[32]Burton A. Weisbrod, *The Nonprofit Economy* (Cambridge, MA: Harvard University Press, 1988), 25–31.

regulations imposed on participating schools will destroy the characteristics that make them attractive alternatives to public schools. Participation in contracting may also lead not-for-profits to change their organizational strategies, such as reducing their emphasis on fund raising from nongovernment sources.[33]

Assessing and Building Capacity

Public agencies may be able to make intraorganizational investments to increase the range of services for which contracting is feasible. Adding some personnel with relevant expertise may increase capacity for writing effective contracts for complex services and monitoring the performance of the services. Thus, the first step in upgrading to a more sophisticated computer system through contracting, for instance, may be to hire someone familiar with candidate systems. Building organizational capacity to monitor service quality may reduce opportunism once the contract is in place. More generally, the appropriate first steps for effective contracting out of services may be adding capacity to the central functions of public agencies. An agency is likely to be better able to steer effectively if it has personnel with rowing experience.

Managers may also be able to influence their external environments to promote more effective contracting. In situations in which the initial awarding of a contract may confer an advantage to incumbent contractees, it may be desirable to multi-source the task among several contractees to preserve competition in renewals. In other words, it might be worthwhile to bear higher contract administration costs and perhaps forgo some economy of scale to reduce future opportunism.[34]

Conclusion

All public agencies contract out the production of some goods—none that we know of make their own pencils. Deciding whether to contract out for more complex inputs to production, such as computer systems or highly specialized labor, or for final goods and services, such as refuse collection or special education, requires analysts to consider governance as well as production costs. These include the incremental costs of bargaining and opportunism over those that would result from in-house production. These incremental costs are likely to be high when the tasks to be completed by contractees are complex, contestability for the contracts is low, and production requires specific assets.

[33]Katherine O'Regan and Sharon Oster, "Does Government Funding Alter Nonprofit Governance? Evidence from New York City Nonprofit Contractors," *Journal of Policy Analysis and Management* 21(3) 2002, 359–79.

[34]For an example of this strategy, see Glenn R. Fong, "The Potential for Industrial Policy: Lessons from the Very High Speed Integrated Circuit Program," *Journal of Policy Analysis and Management* 5(2) 1986, 264–91.

For Discussion

1. Your city's highway department currently operates sidewalk snowplows. During major snowstorms the department gives top priority to clearing major streets. Consequently, sidewalks are often not plowed until several days after major storms. What factors should the mayor consider in deciding whether or not to contract out for sidewalk snowplowing?
2. You are the mayor of a medium-sized city in a developing country. A company is seeking a contract that would give it rights of way for installing cables to provide television and modem services within the city limits. The contract would specify subscription rates for the first three years of the contract. Should you be concerned about opportunism?

13

Gathering Information for Policy Analysis

Very few policy problems are truly unique. Invariably there is *some* information available somewhere that will assist you in some aspect of your policy analysis. Sometimes it is difficult finding any relevant information; other times, ever more frequently with the continuing expansion of the Internet, it is difficult to extract relevant information from among a great abundance of facts, data, and theories. Often you must tap data originally collected for some purpose very different from your own. In dealing with some policy analysis problems, however, you will have the mandate, time, and resources to conduct field research to gather directly relevant data yourself. Your field research may involve taking a firsthand look at some policy problem, or it may be limited to gaining expert advice about relevant theories and data sources. In this chapter we provide advice about how to begin gathering information in these various contexts.

In conducting policy analyses, you face the crucial tasks of developing explanations or models of what is going on and what will happen if any particular alternative is implemented. What, then, is the relevance of facts? Theories and models can tell us a great deal about broad trends and the general directions of expected impacts, but they can rarely tell us about magnitudes. For example, at any given moment, we can only observe a single point on a demand curve—almost always the current price but sometimes not even the current quantity. It is relatively easy and reasonable to predict that imposing a tax will decrease consumption of a good. It is basically an empirical question, however, about whether the reduction in the quantity demanded will be large (that is, if demand is elastic) or small (if demand is inelastic). Yet predicting the size of impacts is essential for evaluating alternative policies. In criminal justice, for instance, policymakers may be correct in assuming that increasing penalties for drug possession will decrease consumption of a given drug; but if demand for the drug is considerably more inelastic than they predict or hope, the policy may be ineffective, perhaps leading to more street crime to support more expensive habits.

Facts are relevant, therefore, in estimating the extent and nature of existing market and government failures and in predicting the impacts of policy alternatives. Data can often help us discover facts. For example, the total budgetary costs of a program might be calculated by identifying and summing all the expenditures for program elements. It can also enable us to make inferences that we are willing to treat as facts. Returning to the drug example, we might statistically infer the magnitude of the elasticity of demand with respect to punishment by analyzing data on drug consumption in jurisdictions with different levels of punishment. By using standard statistical techniques to make our inferences, we can generally say something about their probable accuracy through confidence bounds or significance levels. The facts we assemble, either through direct observation or inference, and organize by theories constitute our evidence for supporting our assertions about current and future conditions.

Two points warrant note. First, what one considers to be a fact will often depend upon the theory one brings to bear. The elasticity estimate we treat as a fact depends on the assumptions embedded in the statistical model we employed. A different, but perhaps equally plausible, model might have led to a very different inference. Second, virtually all the facts we bring to bear will to some extent be uncertain. Therefore, we are almost never in a position to prove any assertion with logic alone. Rather, we must balance sometimes inconsistent evidence to reach conclusions about appropriate assertions.

Gathering evidence for policy analysis can be usefully divided into two broad categories: document research and field research. Or, as Eugene Bardach puts it, "In policy research, almost all likely sources of information, data and ideas fall into two general classes: documents and people."[1] Within field research, we include conducting interviews and gathering original data (including survey research). Document research includes reviewing relevant literature dealing with both theory and evidence and locating existing sources of raw (primary) data.

Document Research

Relevant literature is generally easier to identify and more usable the greater the extent to which the policy problem is universal rather than particular, national rather than local, strategic (major) rather than tactical, and inherently important rather than unimportant. Thus, broadly speaking, the bigger the problem, the more likely it is that there will be an extant literature of potential usefulness. Unfortunately, we note one major caveat to this comforting assertion: often little relevant literature will be available on major but newly emergent problems. For example, one would have had difficulty finding literature on the policy aspects of acquired immune de-

[1]Eugene Bardach, "Gathering Data for Policy Research," *Urban Analysis* 2, 1974, 117–44, at p. 121.

ficiency syndrome until the late 1980s. when confronting such new problems or others with scarce literatures, you will be forced to be bold in the application of theory and creative in your search for analogous policy problems.

Literature Review

Four general categories of documents deserve consideration in the search for policy-relevant information: (1) journal articles, books, and dissertations; (2) publications and reports of interest groups, consultants, and think tanks; (3) government publications and research documents; and (4) the popular press.

If this text had been written twenty years ago, we would have recommended two approaches to accessing relevant journal articles and books: first, by topic, sector, or field (for example, housing, energy, or education); second, by discipline (for example, economics, political science, or sociology). Both approaches are still valid and, indeed, essential. In addition, however, there has arisen in the last two decades a literature with a direct public policy focus. This overtly public policy literature now overlaps with each of the other two approaches and, to some extent, supersedes them. For most purposes, it makes sense to look first at the policy literature in journals such as *Journal of Policy Analysis and Management*, *Policy Sciences*, *Policy Studies Review*, *Policy Studies Journal*, *Regulation Magazine*, *Canadian Public Policy*, *Journal of Comparative Policy Analysis*, and *Journal of Public Policy* (Great Britain). Many professional policy analysts find it worthwhile to subscribe to several of these journals. Many other journals deal with public policy in particular substantive areas. The *Journal of Health Politics, Policy and Law*, for instance, which concentrates on health-related issues, has a strong policy orientation. Similarly, many disciplinary journals have acquired a strong policy emphasis. For example, the *Yale Journal of Regulation* and *Law and Contemporary Problems*, normally found in law libraries, are among those law journals that have a particularly strong emphasis on public policy.

An obvious starting point for a literature review is the particular topic area of your problem: housing, energy, criminal justice, health, or transportation, for example. The major strength of topic-oriented journals and periodicals is also their weakness. They tend to be concerned with what is *unique* about the topic. In doing so, they can sometimes leave the impression that the topic is completely unique, thereby blinding the policy analyst to the possibilities of examining analogies and similarities in *other* policy areas. Keep in mind that this text—with its emphasis on market and government failure—asserts that many aspects of policy analysis are common across substantive areas. Another problem is that many topic-oriented journals have a specific disciplinary perspective that may be relatively hidden. It is important for you to understand whether a particular journal is primarily concerned with, say, the efficiency of employment issues rather than some other aspect.

Finally, one must distinguish between journals and periodicals. Journals are usually run by editorial boards with a high percentage of academics with scholarly norms, and their articles are usually refereed by experts or professional peers. While this does not eliminate, and may even contribute to, disciplinary bias, it does ensure that the vast majority of articles in such journals meet basic standards of competence and honesty. Periodicals, on the other hand, may be put out by individual firms, industry associations, and other interest groups, so that one must be cautious in using their articles as sources. Another major advantage of using journals is that they, unlike periodicals, usually provide extensive references. Thus, articles lead to other articles.

Simultaneously, the literature can be approached from a disciplinary perspective. With the growth of specialized professional schools devoted to such topics as education, social welfare, and criminology, the distinction between disciplinary and topical research has, to some extent, become blurred. Nevertheless, the distinction is still relevant for major disciplines such as economics, political science, sociology, psychology, and anthropology.

Because of the importance of efficiency considerations in almost any type of policy analysis, economics journals are an obvious starting point. Probably the most useful one is the *Journal of Economic Literature* (*JEL*). The *JEL* provides three useful services for the policy analyst. First, it provides literature reviews of both specific fields and theoretical issues. These reviews can save the analyst a tremendous amount of work in getting on top of an issue quickly and preparing comprehensive surveys of relevant literature. Second, it provides the titles of articles in recent issues of economic journals. Third, it provides a subject or topic index of recent articles in economic journals (fortunately for the analyst, broadly defined).

Not too long ago the index to the *JEL* was about the only means for easily searching the economics literature. The American Economic Association, the publisher of the *JEL*, now produces an electronic index to economics journals, books, dissertations, and selected working papers called *ECONLIT* (*www.econlit.org*). Most research libraries make it available on CD-ROM, and some commercial Internet services, such as *FirstSearch*, provide on-line access. *ABI/Inform*, a commercial service of UMI Company, also provides good coverage of business and applied economics sources with some full text coverage. *Worldwide Political Science Abstracts*, a service of Cambridge Scientific Abstracts, provides coverage of political science sources. Securing the full text of articles identified through searches is also becoming much easier. For example, articles from all but the most recent five years of most major economics journals are made available through *JSTOR* (*www.jstor.org*).

Other valuable guides to potentially relevant literature include *Public Affairs Information Service*, *The Reader's Guide to Periodical Literature*, *Ulrich's International Periodicals Directory*, *The Social Science Citation Index*, *Index to Legal Periodicals*, and *Simpson's Guide to Library Research in Public Administration*. There are also numerous specialized sources. In the criminal justice field, for example, the National Criminal Justice Research Service (NCJRS) of the National Institute of Justice provides an index and electronic access through its Website (*www.ncjrs.org*). The Educational Resource Information Center of the Department of Education provides an index to educational sources called *ERIC* (*www.ed.gov*). Many research libraries still maintain microfiche copies of most of the items indexed in ERIC. Although less policy oriented, the National Agricultural Library of the Department of Agriculture provides an index to agricultural sources called *AGRICOLA* (*www.nal.usda.gov*); Cambridge Scientific Abstracts provides an index to environmental sources called *Environmental Sciences and Pollution Management* (*www.csa.com*); and the U.S. National Library of Medicine provides an index to international journals of medicine called *MEDLINE* (*www.nlm.nih.gov*).

Analogous to journal articles are master's and doctoral dissertations. These are often extremely useful information sources because they usually delve into a problem in considerable detail and they often contain extensive bibliographies. Information on dissertations can be found in *Dissertation Abstracts International* and *Master's Abstracts*, and accessed on-line through the commercial service of UMI Company, *Dissertation Abstracts* (*www.umi.com*). A major problem with dissertations is that they are usually not available in libraries and, therefore, cannot be used for "quick and dirty" analyses. When time allows, copies of dissertations can often be obtained from University Microfilms in Ann Arbor, Michigan.

Apart from journals and theses, a large number of books are published annually on a wide range of public policy topics. These books are reviewed on a continuing basis in journals such as the *Journal of Policy Analysis and Management*. The *JEL* is again a valuable source of information on books published in economics. Each issue of the *JEL* provides brief reviews of thirty to forty of the more recent economics books. Computerized indexes, which often cover books as well as other material, are making it much simpler to conduct comprehensive searches for relevant books.

The second source of literature is interest groups, think tanks, and consulting firms. We consider these organizations together because they perform overlapping functions. *Interest groups* usually provide unsolicited information on policy issues, but they occasionally do contract research. *Consulting firms* mainly produce narrowly focused analyses, but sometimes they do policy research of more general scope. *Think tanks* tend to emphasize broader policy research, but many of the newer ones are closely tied to interest groups.

Even experienced analysts face difficulty in identifying and accessing the mass of potentially relevant material produced by interest groups, think tanks, and consulting firms. Some of this written material is published but is not easy to get hold of; some is not officially published but is reasonably accessible; and, most problematically, some is not published and not easily accessible, although it can be "dug up" (if you know where to dig). Of course, in the age of the word processor, desktop publishing, and the Internet, the distinction between "published" and "unpublished" is vanishing. For the policy analyst, the crucial considerations are accessibility and credibility.

Much of the interest group and think tank "action" in the United States is concentrated in Washington, D.C., although organizations producing policy-relevant studies can be found in most major cities such as New York and Los Angeles and in state capitals such as Sacramento, Austin, and Albany. In many other countries that have both concentrated political power and the seat of government in the largest city, almost all important policy organizations can be found in one place. London, Paris, and Rome fall into this category. Canada and Australia, in contrast, are federal systems with subnational governments and seats of government in relatively small cities (respectively, Ottawa and Canberra).

A valuable guide to the myriad interest groups and think tanks that are a potential source of policy-relevant analysis in Washington, D.C., is *The Capital Source*, published twice yearly by the *National Journal*. It provides relevant names of individuals and organizations, addresses, and telephone numbers. The *Research Centers Directory*, published by Gale Research Company, covers think tanks based in universities. The National Institute for Research Advancement provides access to the *Directory of Think Tanks 2002*, which provides brief descriptions of think tanks throughout the world, on its Website (*www.nira.go.jp*). Increasingly, a search of the Internet turns up Web pages maintained by think tanks and interest groups that provide information about, and sometimes electronic access to, their publications. Some examples of think tanks that provide access to working papers through their Websites include American Enterprise Institute for Public Policy Research (*www.aei.org*), Brookings Institution (*www.brook.edu*), Cato Institute (*www.cato.org*),

Center on Budget and Policy Priorities (*www.cbbp.org*), Rand (*www.rand.org*), Resources for the Future (*www.rff.org*), and, in Canada, Fraser Institute (*www.fraserinstitute.ca*) and C. D. Howe Institute (*www.cdhowe.org*).

Think tanks can be a major source of policy information, research, and analyses. Only a decade ago this would have been a relatively simple topic to discuss. A small number of think tanks—including the Brookings Institution, the Rand Corporation, and the American Enterprise Institute for Public Policy Research—dominated policy debate. The number of think tanks, including those at universities, has increased rapidly over the last decade. There appears to be a trend toward the proliferation of more specialized and more overtly ideological think tanks. Before this proliferation, analysts could generally presume that research from think tanks generally met the standards of accuracy and validity found in peer-reviewed scholarly research. Now that presumption is much weaker. Indeed, until one becomes familiar with the research standards employed by a particular think tank, it is probably prudent to treat it as one would an interest group.

Many organizations have sections that function as interest groups. Corporations, labor unions, trade and professional associations, and consultants often provide information to the political process. Often various government agencies operate in the manner of interest groups. For example, foreign embassies often do so in matters of international trade, and commerce offices at the state and local levels do so with respect to economic development.

A vast array of interest groups—corporate, consumer, professional, regional, political, issue-specific, and others—produces various kinds and quantities of policy analysis or at least policy-relevant information. These organizations range from Common Cause and the Sierra Club to the Conservative Caucus and the National Rifle Association. Among professional and trade associations can be found the Tobacco Institute, the Natural Gas Supply Association, and the Solar Energy Institute of North America. Information on many organizations like these can be found on their Web pages.

Why should the analyst consult these sources if their objectivity is suspect? A substantive reason is that these analyses almost always explicitly or implicitly propose public policy goals and policy alternatives. Therefore, they provide valuable sources of *potential* goals and alternatives for your analysis even if you ultimately decide to reject them. Another reason is that these sources may help you prepare for political opposition. If a particular interest group does not agree with the policy recommendations of your analysis, then it is likely to be a major critic. It is usually more effective to deal preemptively with these disagreements in your own analysis rather than to attempt to deal with them later.

The third major source of written material is government publications: national, state, regional, and local. The U.S. government is one of the world's most prolific publishers—on the order of 100,000 documents yearly. These documents are mainly published by either the Government Printing Office (GPO), which deals with congressional and agency materials, or the National Technical Information Service (NTIS), which deals with a wide range of technical and other reports. In addition, many state and federal agencies publish materials directly and often advertise their availability on Web pages. Studies from a variety of policy areas can be found on the Websites of the Congressional Budget Office (*www.cbo.gov*), the Council of Economic Advisers (*www.access.gpo.gov/eop/index.html*), and the General Accounting Office (*www.gao.gov*). With a little effort, the Web pages of other government agencies can be located with any of the popular search engines. You may find Fedworld (*www.fedworld.gov*) or the Federal Web Locator provided by the Villanova Center for Information, Law and Policy (*www.law.vill.edu/Fed-Agency/fedwebloc.html*) helpful as well.

The major government source for this material is the *Monthly Catalog of United States Government Publications*, now published electronically by the U.S. Superintendent of Documents (*www.gpo.gov*). This is essentially the government's "sales catalogue." The National Technical Information Service acts as a clearinghouse of government-funded research, including scientific, economic, and behavioral sciences material.

There are several valuable sources for tapping information about, and from, the U.S. Congress. The annual legislative products of the Congress are published in the *United States Statutes at Large*, and integrated into the *United States Code* by broad categories, or titles, about every six years. An excellent source of timely information about proposed legislation before the current and most recent Congress is *THOMAS* (*thomas.loc.gov*), a service provided by the Library of Congress. *THOMAS* allows one to search by keyword and retrieve the full text of bills. Other useful sources include *Congressional Quarterly Weekly Report*, for an overview of ongoing policy debates and politics; *Congressional Quarterly Almanac*, for yearly overviews and roll call votes; and *Digest of Public General Bills* (annual) and *Major Legislation of the Congress* (twice yearly), for information on new legislation.

Congressional committees routinely gather and make public information relevant to policy issues under their jurisdictions through committee reports. The reports typically present the record of hearings in which witnesses give testimony and submit written statements. Sometimes the reports provide background information collected by the committee staffs. The *CIS Annual*, published since 1970 by Congressional Information Services, Inc., provides a convenient way to search for information in hearing reports. One part of the *CIS Annual* has detailed indexes by subject and witnesses for all public hearings held during the year. The other part includes abstracts of testimony presented in the committee reports. The reports themselves are usually available at libraries that serve as depositories for government documents.

Rule making by federal executive agencies, especially those with explicit regulatory roles, such as the Environmental Protection Agency and the Food and Drug Administration, is likely at some time to be relevant to analysts working on policy issues at all levels of government. The official record of executive agency rule making is provided by the *Federal Register*, which is published each business day. Agencies announce proposed rules along with justifications, histories of related regulations already in force, and an invitation for interested parties to submit comments to the agency's docket on the proposed regulation. After the comment period, the agency publishes the regulation in final form, typically with responses to the comments it received in response to its proposed rule making. As the agencies must show reasonableness in rule making to avoid court challenges, the material they publish in the *Federal Register* is often detailed and therefore a valuable source for analysts working on related issues. Most libraries carry the *Federal Register*, and it can be accessed through a Website provided by the Government Printing Office (*www.access.gpo.gov/su_docs/aces/aces140.html*). The *Code of Federal Regulations* annually codifies the general and permanent rules published in the *Federal Register*.

Analysts dealing with issues at all levels of the U.S. government are also likely to confront federal constitutional issues on occasion. Decisions of the U.S. Supreme Court are published annually in *United States Reports: Cases Adjudged in the Supreme*

Court. Recent Supreme Court decisions, as well as information about cases decided in other federal and state courts, is made available by the Cornell Law School through a Website (*www.law.cornell.edu*). For those without training in legal research, it is usually best to search for articles in law school journals that put specific decisions into broader legal context. As articles in these journals customarily cite profusely, they often provide leads to nonlegal sources relevant to policy issues. Law journals and related sources can be searched through the *Index to Legal Periodicals*. A broader index to legal material is provided by the commercial service *LEXIS/NEXIS*, which also provides full text access to legal journals and case law.

Selected state and local government materials can be researched through the *Index to Current Urban Documents*, the *Municipal Yearbook*, the *County Yearbook*, *Council of Planning Librarians Bibliographies*, the *Monthly Checklist of State Publications*, and the Web page of the National Conference on State Legislatures (*www.ncsl.org*). State agencies are increasingly establishing Web pages that provide electronic access to reports, contact information for key personnel, and general information on administrative structure. Larger cities and counties now often provide Websites as well.

Finally, the popular press can be a valuable source of background information, especially when you are confronting a new issue. Newspaper and magazine articles rarely provide detailed information and analysis, but they often mention and quote experts, stakeholders, organizations, documents, and other sources of potential value. These leads are particularly valuable because they often appear in the popular press long before they do in other published sources. They also may be the only published references to many local issues. For these reasons, it is often useful to begin any new investigation with a quick search through the popular press.

Data and Statistical Sources

In many analyses it is useful to present and analyze new data. A major source of both raw and analyzed data is likely to be the articles, books, and documents described above. But you also may wish to examine primary data sources. Once again, an excellent source is the U.S. government. A very valuable desk reference is the *Statistical Abstract of the United States*, which is published annually by the U.S. Bureau of the Census. A particularly valuable and easy-to-use index is the *American Statistics Index: A Guide to the Statistical Publications of the U.S. Government*, which is published by the Congressional Information Service, Inc. Statistical information from many agencies can be accessed through the Federal Interagency Council on Statistical Policy Website (*www.fedstats.gov*).

The U.S. Census provides much useful demographic data. Several publications of the Bureau of the Census are especially useful for making comparisons across state and local jurisdictions: the *County and City Data Book*, the *Congressional District Data Book*, and the *State and Metropolitan Area Data Book*. The Website maintained by the Census Bureau provides on-line access to most census data (*www.census.gov*).

Once we move away from the federal government, even illustratively cataloguing the available data and statistics is impractical. *Statistical Reference Index: A Selective Guide to American Statistical Publications from Private Organizations and State Government Sources*, published by the Congressional Information Service, Inc., which also publishes the *Index to International Statistics: A Guide to the Statistical Publications of International Intergovernmental Organizations*, is the best general source for locating sources other than federal agencies. Research libraries often buy the accompanying fiche that provide all the cited data. Yet states, counties, municipalities, special districts, and local governmental departments all collect and, more or less, make available such data. While libraries sometimes catalogue annual reports and special studies from state and local agencies, usually such documents must be obtained directly from the agencies themselves. Keep in mind that the quality of such data varies widely.

Often universities and think tanks are important sources of data. For example, the Inter-University Consortium for Political and Social Research (ICPSR) at the University of Michigan archives data from surveys and other studies (*www.icpsr.umich.edu*), and the Urban Institute has established a data base with over 700 variables describing state social service systems through its Assessing the New Federalism Project (*www.urban.org*).

Finally, many social science journals now require authors to deposit the data they used for their statistical analyses in accessible archives. These data may be useful for addressing questions not directly addressed in the published research.

A Note on Documentation in the Age of the Internet

The sources listed here should make clear that the Internet, and especially the World Wide Web, has become a major source of information for policy analysts. This transformation has dramatically increased the amount of information that analysts can gather quickly. Fifteen years ago, when the first edition of this book was written, very few electronic tools were available, so gathering information mainly involved using reference books to find documents written on paper. This transformation raises important issues about documentation of sources.

There are three main purposes for documenting sources. First, it is right to give credit to others for the information and ideas that they have made available—this is especially important in academic settings where people are often judged by the intellectual contributions that they make. Second, documentation tells others how to find the sources that you have used—sometimes to be able to verify your claims but more often to explore in depth the information that you have found. Third, documentation provides an indication of the credibility and authority of the documents that you cite—why should we believe the sources?

The Internet has complicated all three of these purposes. As it is sometimes difficult to determine the original source of material found on Web pages, it is often difficult to give proper acknowledgment to those who produced the information. Clearly, for those following in your footsteps, it is important for them to have Web page addresses as part of the citation that you provide.[2] Although Web pages come and go, providing the address that worked for you gives other analysts at least a starting point for their search.

The most difficult issue concerns the role of your citation in communicating the credibility of your source. *Remember that almost anyone can put anything on a Web page.*

[2]For suggestions on formats for Internet citations, see Melvin E. Page, "A Brief Citation Guide for Internet Sources in History and the Humanities (Version 2.0)," *PS: Political Science and Politics* 29(1) 1996, 83–84. See also Xia Li and Nancy Crane, *Electronic Styles: A Handbook for Citing Electronic Information*, 2nd ed. (Medford, NJ: Information Today, 1996).

In contrast to articles in journals, which are subjected to peer review, or material in established periodicals, which at least receives consistent editorial review, appearance on a Web page lends no particular credibility to a source. It is important, therefore, that your citation provide as much information as possible about the source. Is it simply an electronic version of published material? If so, *provide a complete citation to the published source along with the Internet address where you found it*. If it is unpublished, can you provide any information relevant to assessing the author's credibility? For example, is the author writing as an individual or under the auspices of an organization? If as an individual, can you say anything about the author's professional status? If under the auspices of an organization that might not be well known, can you indicate its type?

Field Research

Field research consists of talking to people, gathering raw data, or finding unpublished reports, memoranda, or other organizational documents. These tasks are often related because it is usually difficult to find data without interviewing, and impossible to assess its reliability, validity, and comprehensiveness without talking to those who actually gathered it. Similarly, putting unpublished documents into proper perspective usually requires contextual information from those involved in their preparation.

How should you decide to whom to talk? Your literature review will often suggest some key people. Our discussion in the previous section, however, necessarily concentrated on the federal branches of government. If you work on state or local problems, then you should make sure that you have relevant directories and organizational charts. Such directories for the legislative and executive branches of government are usually readily available. Most analysts quickly develop their own directories of local interest groups, professional bodies, regulatory agencies, consulting firms engaged in policy research, quasi-public agencies, and law firms that deal with public issues. They also network with others working in the policy area.[3]

Do not limit your consideration to people currently in relevant organizations. In particular, recently retired employees are often valuable sources. Retired employees offer several advantages: they usually have time for interviews; they have had some time to reflect on their experiences; and they no longer have to worry about agency politics or retribution. Consequently, they may well be more forthright and more analytic. The only problem is that the "shelf life" of their information may be short.

Interviews need not be in person. Use the telephone or e-mail to check whether someone who appears to be an appropriate source (judging by title, department, or organizational role) is likely to be helpful. On projects with short time frames, you may be forced to do both preliminary spadework and interviewing over the telephone.

[3]Networks work best when those involved are willing to share, not just information but comradery as well. On effective networking, and more generally working well with colleagues, see Michael Mintrom, *People Skills for Policy Analysts* (Washington, DC: Georgetown University Press, 2003), 231–45.

We cannot provide here a comprehensive guide to interviewing—several complete books deal with this topic alone.[4] Instead, we give some basic advice on the major issues relating to interviewing: (1) What kind of information does interviewing elicit most effectively? (2) How can you judge the efficacy of the information you do get? (3) How do you get interviewees to talk? (4) How should you decide when to interview someone?

In the following list we reproduce, with some modification, the advice offered by other writers:[5]

1. *What information will interviewing elicit most effectively?*
   - **(a)** Historical background and context. The narrative of what has happened.
   - **(b)** Basic facts, whether directly through interviews or the raw data provided by interviewees.
   - **(c)** Political attitudes and resources of major actors. (These may not be written anywhere. Interviews may be the only source for this kind of information.)
   - **(d)** Projections about the future; extrapolations of current trends.
   - **(e)** Other potential interviewees and written materials.
2. *How can the efficacy of an interview be judged?*
   - **(a)** The plausibility, reasonableness, and coherence of answers.
   - **(b)** The internal consistency of answers.
   - **(c)** The specificity and detail of answers.
   - **(d)** Correspondence to known facts.
   - **(e)** Firsthand familiarity of the interviewee with the facts described.
   - **(f)** The interviewee's motivation, bias, and position.
   - **(g)** Reasons that the interviewee might withhold information.
   - **(h)** The self-critical nature of the interviewee.
3. *How do you get interviewees to talk?*
   - **(a)** The "energy" must come from the analyst, not the interviewee. Be prepared to ask questions.
   - **(b)** The analyst should not pretend to be neutral, but should avoid dogma and hostility.
   - **(c)** Demonstrate that you have other sources of information that interpret events differently from the current interview.
   - **(d)** Demonstrate reasonable tenacity on important questions.
   - **(e)** Point out other views on a topic and indicate that this is the interviewee's chance to tell her side of the issue.

[4]See Lewis A. Dexter, *Elite and Specialized Interviewing* (Evanston, IL: Northwestern University Press, 1970); and Jerome T. Murphy, *Getting the Facts: A Fieldwork Guide for Evaluators and Policy Analysts* (Santa Monica, CA: Goodyear, 1980). For an excellent treatment of gathering information through direct observation, see Richard F. Fenno, Jr., *Watching Politicians: Essays on Participant Observation* (Berkeley: IGS Press, University of California, 1990).

[5]Questions 1 and 2 are drawn (in a modified way) from Carl V. Patton and David Sawicki, *Policy Analysis and Planning* (Englewood Cliffs, NJ: Prentice Hall, 1986), 67–70; questions 3 and 4 (again modified) are from Bardach, "Gathering Data for Policy Research."

4. *How should you decide when to interview someone?*

Approach *early* in the interview sequence:

(a) Those who are likely to be rich sources of information.

(b) Individuals who have power. (They can provide access, either directly or indirectly, to other sources of information.)

(c) Knowledgeable persons who can give you information that will induce others to talk more freely.

(d) Friendly expert interviewees who will contribute to the credibility of the analysis.

(e) Potential opponents, to the extent that they can be assessed.

(f) Retired employees.[6]

Approach relatively *late:*

(a) Those interviewees who are likely to be hostile or defensive. (Use earlier interviews to acquire leverage.)

(b) Interviewees whom you may not be able to speak to again because they are busy, remote, or otherwise difficult to reach. (Especially if you want their reactions to policy alternatives that you cannot fully specify until the later stages of your project.)

(c) Powerful political opponents who could prevent you from gaining access to other interviewees.[7]

(d) Administrators who may not identify critical issues even though they have the requisite knowledge.

(e) "Expert" interviewees, especially academics, who may be more theoretically oriented.[8] (If you interview them too early, then you may not know enough to frame questions that take full advantage of their expertise.)

Most of these points speak for themselves, yet some additional considerations deserve mention. The responses to question 1 suggest that interviews are likely to be most useful for facts, history, and projections. As a corollary, they are likely to be less useful for either a theoretical explanation of what is going on (that is, a model) or a clear and reasoned delineation of goals. These must usually come from your own familiarity with theory and your literature review. There are two exceptions to this general observation, however. First, academic interviewees are usually more comfortable with models and theory. Indeed, they are unlikely to be familiar with program budgets, organizational structures, and institutional history. Second, many government agencies have their own analysts and researchers. These government employees are often more comfortable dealing with theoretical issues than are either program administrators or regular staff.

A major point to note with respect to the second question is that the reliability and value of an interview can often be judged only by conducting apparently redundant interviews. To the extent that the information from a particular interview is vital to your analysis, you should attempt to verify it with other interviews when possible.

Undoubtedly, the hardest issue to deal with is getting interviewees to talk (question 3). One general hint is to not demonstrate that you don't know what you're talking about. Why do we use the double negative? Because demonstrating that

[6]Added by authors, not on Bardach's original list.

[7]Bardach is aware of the contradiction of recommending both early and late interviews for potential opponents.

[8]Added by authors, not on Bardach's original list.

you are not ignorant is sometimes not the same as demonstrating knowledge. Put another way: if you know something, flaunt it subtly! If done skillfully, then your knowledge can be one way of introducing some reciprocity into the interview, something especially useful if you are likely to need additional interviews. This is just one aspect of the art of interviewing. More broadly, the trick, to paraphrase Bardach, is to be fair-minded, discreet, intelligent, and self-possessed and to avoid appearing to be partisan, a tale-bearer, a dope, or a dupe.[9]

In situations in which you think you have discovered information that is particularly important or controversial, you may want to write a follow-up letter or send an e-mail to the interviewee restating the information. Conclude with a request that the interviewee let you know if you have misinterpreted anything. Interviewees will sometimes respond with useful elaborations as well as corrections. The record of communication can also be useful in avoiding arguments about what was said. Always, common courtesy suggests that you send a brief note of thanks to people who have given you more than a few moments of their time.

Final practical tips on interviewing: Always do your homework plan a sequence of questions but be flexible in following it. Don't ask questions that you can answer from documents or from interviews with more accessible people. Make sure that you write up interview notes as soon as possible after an interview. When practical, do not schedule too many interviews in a given day. If you do, you're likely to appear flushed and rushed. It also makes it less practical to write up notes, and interviews start to merge into each other in your memory. Don't schedule lunch meetings if you expect to take extensive notes. Ask about other potential interviewees. And ask about potentially useful documents and data.

Putting Document Review and Field Research Together

Bardach suggests four basic ways of expanding the scope of information gathering: documents lead to documents, documents lead to people, people lead to people, and people lead to documents. Figure 13.1 sets out the one way in which Bardach's heuristics might unfold. The flowchart indicates that it is usually advisable to conduct a literature review initially, although starting with telephone interviews often is more appropriate for short-term projects. While the literature review may involve some searching, once you gain access to the relevant literature, the initial documents, references, and bibliographies will quickly lead you to other literature (that is, documents lead to documents). As the initial literature search progresses, it is likely to suggest specific people as potential interviewees or, at least, the role or type of potentially desirable interviewees (that is, documents will lead to people). The objective of the initial literature review is to give you enough background to conduct intelligent interviews. The gist of this advice can be boiled down to a simple heuristic: *know something before you talk to people.*

Once you have a broad sense of the issue, moving to an initial phase of field research is often productive. The first phase may productively consist largely of relatively brief telephone interviews. Alternatively, or additionally, it may consist

[9] Bardach, "Gathering Data for Policy Research," p. 131.

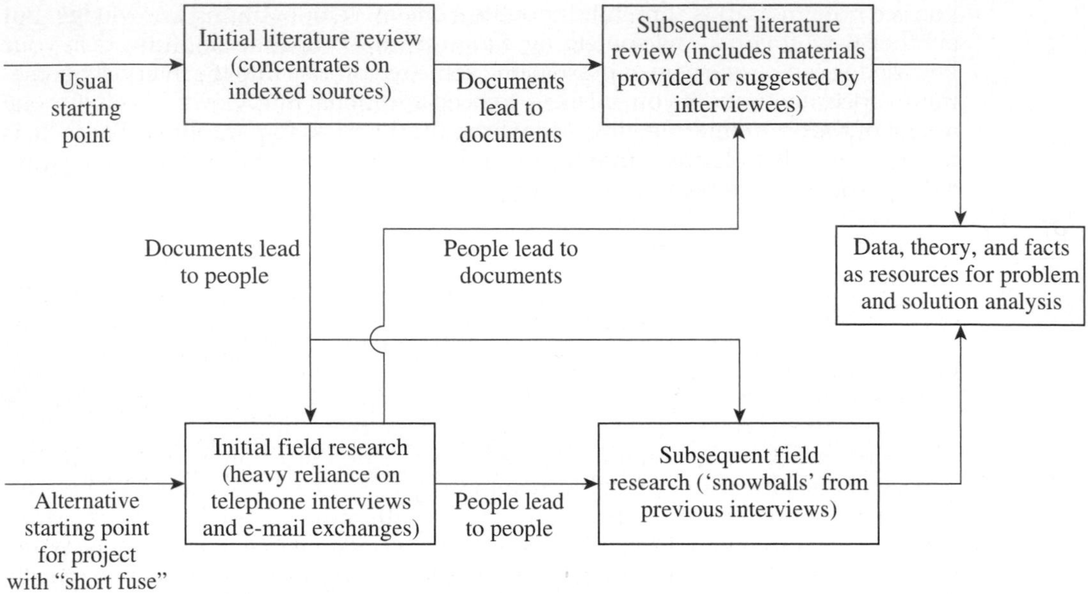

Figure 13.1 A Strategy for Combining Literature Review and Field Research

of interviews with potential early interviewees (for example, friendly experts). Especially attractive are potential interviewers who are located nearby. It is less costly (both in terms of time and money) to interview them than others farther away, and you can usually be much more flexible in scheduling the interviews.

Once the initial field research is completed, you should have enough direction to engage in both further literature reviews (that is, people have led to documents) and more extensive and systematic field research (that is, people have led to people and data).

Conclusion

In general, the more relevant information you can bring to bear on a policy problem, the greater will be your capability for producing good analysis. With the increasingly rich sources of information available, especially through the Internet, it is important to be thoughtful in your information-gathering efforts. Robert Behn and James Vaupel have pointed out that most students spend 99 percent of their time gathering and processing information (or conducting the literature review and field research).[10] They suggest instead that students should spend at least half their time thinking. The heuristic they suggest is *model simple*; think *complex*.[11] We agree. Yet,

[10]Robert D. Behn and James W. Vaupel, "Teaching Analytical Thinking," *Policy Analysis* 2(4) 1976, 661–92, at p. 669.

[11]Attributed by Behn and Vaupel, p. 669, to Gary Brewer from a talk given at Duke University on December 3, 1973, Robert D. Behn and James W. Vaupel, "Teaching Analytic Thinking," Policy Analysis 2(4) 1976, 663–92.

this is easier said than done. A critical point is to make sure that you don't get into a position where you can't see the forest for the trees. Keep in mind that the mass of data that you are collecting is useful only if it can be placed into an analytical framework. Always ask yourself where the facts you have fit in and what facts you would like to have.

For Discussion

1. Academic researchers in the United States must follow increasingly stringent guidelines for the protection of human research subjects. Although much research involving interviews with elected or appointed officials is often declared exempt, it must nevertheless be reviewed by Institutional Review Boards at universities and research organizations. The work of policy analysts is usually exempt from direct human subject regulation. Nonetheless, analysts have a responsibility to those who they rely on for information. What ethical principles do you think should guide analysts' information gathering from people?
2. The authors have heard policy analysts claim that "the telephone is one of the most important tools of the policy analyst." Should "the Internet is one of the most important tools of the policy analyst" replace this claim? Cite your reasons.

14

Landing on Your Feet

How to Confront Policy Problems

The previous chapters have been concerned with the conceptual foundations of policy analysis: how to diagnose problems, how to identify possible policy alternatives, how to think about efficiency and other policy goals, and how to measure some of the costs and benefits of either intervening in markets or altering existing public interventions. On these foundations the analyst must build a structure, one that is useful and appropriate for the context. In this chapter we focus on the construction process: how should one plan and execute a policy analysis? Our answer keeps central the notion that policy analysis as a process involves *formulating* and *communicating* useful advice to a client.[1]

Before you begin trying to do analysis, we suggest that you analyze yourself. Getting started on a written analysis is often difficult. We describe, therefore, how to go about developing a strategy for doing analysis (in other words, the "analysis of the analysis," or "meta-analysis").

[1]Pieces we find helpful on the *process* of policy analysis include Eugene Bardach, *The Eight-Step Path of Policy Analysis* (Berkeley, CA: Berkeley Academic Press, 1996); Christopher Leman and Robert Nelson, "Ten Commandments for Policy Economists," *Journal of Policy Analysis and Management* 1(1) 1981, 97–117; James M. Verdier, "Advising Congressional Decision-Makers: Guidelines for Economists," *Journal of Policy Analysis and Management* 3(3) 1984, 421–38; and Robert D. Behn and James Vaupel, "Teaching Analytic Thinking," *Policy Analysis* 2(4) 1976, 663–92.

Analyzing Yourself: Meta-Analysis

Your self-analysis should influence the way you go about doing policy analysis. You may base the self-analysis either on your first attempt at a policy analysis (the preferred method) or on your experience in writing academic papers (less preferable).

Students (and most others as well) tend to fall into one of two broad categories of thinkers and writers: linear and nonlinear.[2] Linear thinkers tend to solve problems by moving sequentially through a series of logical steps. Nonlinear thinkers tend to view problems configuratively, moving back and forth over steps as various pieces of the puzzle become apparent and begin to fall into place. We should stress that, for our purposes, neither is better or worse—*each* has its strengths and weaknesses.

Your particular weakness (or strength) may not have been revealed in other courses that were more structured and dealt with greater substantive certainty. This point is crucial. Your formal schooling has made you familiar with course assignments, especially problem sets in mathematics, statistics, and economics, where right and wrong answers can be specified. Policy analysis is never so certain. This does *not* mean that there are not good or bad analyses, but that your answer, the recommendation you make to a client, rarely by itself determines the quality of your analysis. Good analysis asks the right questions and creatively, but logically, answers them. The approach that you choose should allow you to eliminate, minimize, or at least mitigate your particular weaknesses in thinking and writing.

How can you diagnose your weaknesses? We have found that students who are linear thinkers and writers tend to suffer from "analysis paralysis." Linear thinkers, not surprisingly, like to start at the beginning of an analytical problem and then work step by step through to the end, following what is sometimes called a *rationalist approach*. If they cannot complete these steps sequentially, however, they tend to become paralyzed. In contrast, many others do not like to approach analysis sequentially. They have many ideas that they wish to get down on paper; yet they often have difficulty communicating these ideas in a well-organized, sequential mode, which, put bluntly, often results in written products that look like a regurgitated dog's dinner.

The first meta-analysis rule is that *linear thinkers should adopt nonlinear* ***thinking*** *strategies, while nonlinear thinkers should adopt linear* ***writing*** *strategies*. The format of this book should assist linear thinkers in adopting a nonlinear thinking approach because it compartmentalizes the analytical process. For example, you do not need to understand the problem fully to sketch out some generic policy alternatives. The previous chapters of the book, together with the next section, should also assist nonlinear thinkers in organizing analyses so that they can be communicated more clearly. Nonlinear thinkers can, and should, continue to think nonlinearly, but they must *write* linearly and comprehensively. Linear thinkers, on the other hand, will find that they will be more productive and less vulnerable to analysis paralysis if they also adopt nonlinear work strategies. Therefore, the second meta-analysis rule is that *analysts should simultaneously utilize linear and nonlinear modes when conducting policy analyses.*

[2]There is evidence that the distinction between the linear and the nonlinear corresponds to the differential abilities of the right and left sides of the brain: the left hemisphere is used for logical, sequential processes, while the right hemisphere is used for processes requiring intuition and creativity. Jan Ehrenwald argues that "geniuses" are those individuals best able to "shift gears" from one hemisphere to the other as required. See Jan Ehrenwald, *Anatomy of Genius: Split Brains and Global Minds* (New York: Human Sciences Press, 1984).

Subsequent sections of this chapter lay out the eight steps in the rationalist, or linear, mode. We label it the rationalist, rather than the rational, mode because *only* following this mode is unlikely to be optimally rational. Nonlinear, creative thinking can be very rational! Later, we return to how nonlinear strategies can be translated into practical techniques for conducting analysis. Before proceeding through these analytical steps, we wish to reiterate the importance of the client orientation in framing the analytical steps we subsequently discuss.

The Client Orientation

In the introductory chapters we have emphasized that policy analysis is client-driven, and considered some of the ethical issues relating to the relationship between analysts and clients. The concern here is more with the practical consequences of having a client. The first client heuristic may seem obvious, but it is often neglected: *you must address the issue that the client poses.* Academic experiences (especially in advanced courses) often do not prepare one for this reality because one has considerable discretion as to topic and approach. This is reasonable because when a professor is the client, he or she is most interested in your cognitive development. Real clients are only interested in getting their question answered. An important heuristic flows from this unpleasant fact: *it is almost always better to answer with uncertainty the question that was asked than to answer with certainty a question that was not asked.* Another heuristic follows as a corollary: *good analysis does not suppress uncertainty*, whether with respect to facts or theories.

We all like neatness, and most of us have been rewarded for unambiguous answers. In policy analysis, however, it is more effective to *highlight* ambiguities than to suppress them. Remember that if clients do not hear of these ambiguities from you, they will normally hear of them from analytical, or political, opponents—a much more unpleasant experience. As an analyst, you bear an essential responsibility to keep your clients from being blindsided as a result of your advice.

Highlighting ambiguity should not be seen as an excuse for vague, wishy-washy, or poorly researched analysis. Indeed, you will have to work harder to arrange the competing theories and facts intelligently. Additionally, highlighting ambiguity does not absolve you from drawing analytical conclusions. For example, if, for a given policy problem, it is unclear whether there is a market failure, you should succinctly summarize evidence on both sides of the issue and *then* reach your conclusion. Thus your client will be aware of both the arguments and your conclusion. It is particularly important to make your client aware of the weaknesses of the relevant data and evidence. Although the "facts" used in policy debates are often inaccurate or at least unverified, they nonetheless can remain unchallenged. This has been referred to as the "vitality of mythical numbers."[3] To pick one example, Douglas Besharov has demonstrated the wholesale deceptive use of statistics in analyses of the child abuse problem.[4]

[3]See Max Singer, "The Vitality of Mythical Numbers," *Public Interest* 23, 1971, 3–9. See also Peter Reuter, "The Social Costs of the Demand for Quantification," *Journal of Policy Analysis and Management* 5(4) 1986, 807–12.

[4]Douglas Besharov, "Unfounded Allegations—A New Child Abuse Problem," *Public Interest*, 83, 1986, 18–33.

What should you do if you become convinced that your client has asked the wrong question? We offer no definitive advice on how to deal with this difficult situation. One clear rule, however, is that you *must fully explain to your client why you believe that he or she has asked the wrong question.* Clients are often ambiguous about their goals, and they sometimes appear to have goals that you may consider inappropriate. You may be able to help your client ask a better question by identifying ambiguity and by indicating why you believe that certain goals are inappropriate. In general, you should try to do so at the early stages of your analytical effort rather than waiting until you deliver what your client expects to be the answer to the original question.

Clients often ask questions that are not wrong but just poorly formulated. Many times you will be presented "symptoms" that your client finds troubling. ("My constituents are complaining about the rising cost of day care.") Other times you may be presented with a policy alternative rather than a policy problem.[5] ("Should the state subsidize liability insurance for day-care centers?") Your task as an analyst is to reformulate expressions of symptoms and statements of policy alternatives into coherent analytical frameworks. ("Does the day-care industry under current regulations provide an efficient and equitable supply of services? If not, why not?") The following discussion of problem analysis provides guidance for doing so.

Steps in Rationalist Policy Analysis

The word *analysis* comes from the Greek word meaning to break down into component parts. Teachers of policy analysis usually specify the components of the analytical process as a series of steps along the lines of the following: define the problem, establish goals and valuation criteria, identify alternative policies, display alternatives and select among them, and monitor and evaluate the policy outcomes.[6] Such lists usually begin with "defining the problem" so that all the following steps can be described as "solving the problem." This formulation incorrectly suggests to the inexperienced student that defining, or explaining, the problem is a relatively short and simple part of the analytical process. In practice, analysts usually encounter the greatest difficulty and often expend the most time trying to define, explain, and model the problem in a useful way.[7] This task is important because the problem model largely determines the rest of the analysis, including which goals and methods should be used to judge the desirability of alternatives and the selection of policy alternatives.

Figure 14.1 provides a better perceptual picture of the policy analysis process. It divides the process into two major components: problem analysis and solution

[5]For a discussion of the importance of stripping away the prescriptive elements of problem definition, see Eugene Bardach, "Problems of Problem Definition in Policy Analysis," *Research in Public Policy Analysis and Management*, 1, 1981, 161–71.

[6]For example, Carl V. Patton and David Sawicki, *Basic Methods of Policy Analysis and Planning* (Englewood Cliffs, NJ: Prentice Hall, 1986), 26. Others provide lists that include implementation: Grover Starling, *The Politics and Economics of Public Policy: An Introductory Analysis with Cases* (Homewood, IL: Dorsey Press, 1979), 10.

[7]For a thoughtful treatment of problem definition in the organizational context, see David Dery, *Problem Definition in Policy Analysis* (Lawrence: University Press of Kansas, 1984).

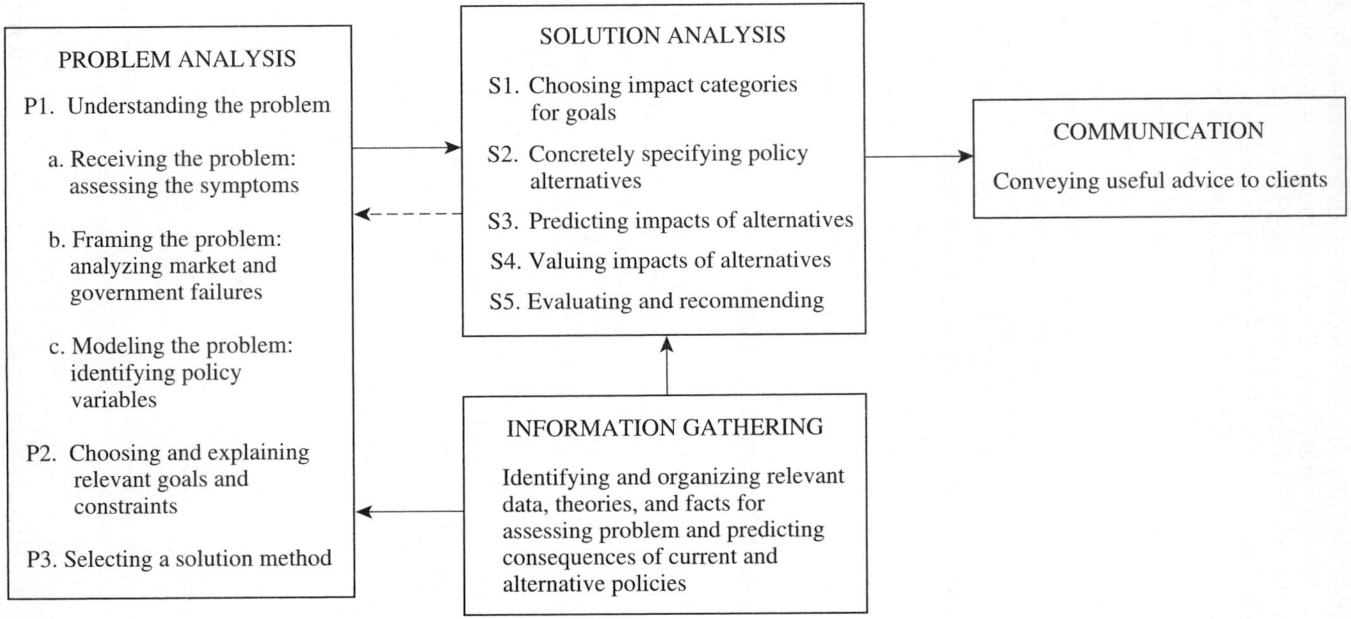

Figure 14.1 A Summary of Steps in the Rationalist Mode

analysis. Both are vital. For example, an analysis that devotes the great majority of its pages to analyzing the problem inevitably will not be credible in terms of the policy alternatives it presents or the reasons for choosing among them. Such an analysis may portray the nature of the problem convincingly, but its solution analysis will be deficient. Because most clients seek solutions, such an imbalance typically diminishes the value of an analysis. Conversely, your solution analysis and the resulting recommendation will carry little weight unless you convince the client that you have framed the problem correctly, thought carefully about the potentially relevant goals, and considered a range of alternatives.

Our experience suggests that quite a few students (and analysts) suffer in the extreme from looking only at solutions. They suffer from "recommendationitis," trying to cram their complete analysis into their recommendations. If you suffer from this syndrome (or the tendency to cram all your analysis into any one step of the analytical process), then you are probably a nonlinear thinker who should take especially seriously the need to structure your policy using the steps in the rationalist mode.

Problem Analysis

Problem analysis consists of three major steps: (P1) understanding the problem; (P2) choosing and explaining relevant policy goals and constraints; and (P3) choosing a solution method.

Understanding the Problem

Understanding a policy problem involves assessing the conditions that concern your client, framing them as market or government failures, and modeling the relationship between the conditions of concern and variables that can be manipulated through public policy.

Assessing Symptoms. Clients generally experience problems as conditions that some group perceives as undesirable. They tend to specify problems to analysts in terms of these undesirable symptoms, or impacts, rather than as underlying causes. The analyst's task is to assess the symptoms and provide an explanation (model) of how they arise.

Assessing symptoms involves determining their empirical basis. In a narrow sense, this means trying to locate data that help you put the symptoms in quantitative perspective. For example, if your client is concerned about automobile accidents in your county caused by drunk drivers, then you might try to locate data to help you estimate the number of such accidents, how the number has changed over time, what percentage of total accidents they comprise, and other measures that help you determine the magnitude, distribution, and time trend of the symptom. In a broader sense, you should become familiar with current public discussion about the symptom (read the newspaper!) and the history of existing policies that are generally perceived as being relevant to it. For example, you may find that, although there has been a steady decline in the number of alcohol-related accidents in recent years, a particularly tragic accident has focused public attention on the dangers of drunk driving. Viewed in the perspective of the favorable trend, drunk driving may seem less deserving of attention than other conditions of concern to your client.

Your description and assessment of symptoms generally appears as background in your problem analysis. It conveys the relative importance and urgency of the problem, and it begins to establish your credibility as someone who is knowledgeable about it. But the assessment of symptoms alone provides an inadequate basis for your analysis. You must identify causal relationships that link the symptoms to factors that can be changed by public policy. In other words, you must frame and model the problem.

Framing the Problem. Potentially any positive, or predictive, social science model can be used as the basis for problem analysis. The major focus of explanation here is a specification of the expected deviation between individual self-interest (utility maximization by individuals) and aggregate social welfare. Although we believe that this focus is usually the best starting point for framing policy problems, several caveats should be noted.

First, we must avoid the danger of reductionism in such an approach. Although for many purposes we can treat wealth maximization and utility maximization as synonymous, saying that people maximize utility is not the same as saying that people care only about money. Clearly, they care about many other things as well. Also, as we saw in the examination of nontraditional market failures, economics tends to treat preferences as fixed and, therefore, deals primarily with utility articulation rather than utility formation. Other social sciences have devoted considerably more effort to examining how preferences are formed. Consequently, much room exists for the other social sciences, including anthropology, psychology, and sociology, to play a part in framing the issues of market and government failures.[8]

Second, and this is obviously related, we have not claimed that efficiency is the only appropriate goal of public policy. Therefore, any realistic problem analysis framework must enable the analyst to integrate other goals or constraints into the analytical process. The framework should also allow the analyst to set out the goals in a coherent way: "... good policy analysis ... requires a clear statement and defense of the value judgments that combine with the analysis to lead to specific conclusions."[9] In the next section we suggest how to incorporate these goals into policy analysis. We believe, however, that you should begin by focusing your attention on efficiency.

The concepts of market and government failures provide the basis for framing policy problems in terms of efficiency. Chapter 9 offered a logical procedure for

[8]Amitai Etzioni eloquently argues that policy analysis should not be restricted to economic analysis. He offers, by way of comparison, medical knowledge, which eclectically incorporates political, social, cultural, psychic, and environmental factors. See "Making Policy for Complex Systems," *Journal of Policy Analysis and Management* 4(3) 1985, 383–95. See also Jack Hirschleifer, who argues, "There is only one social science. ... Ultimately, good economics will also have to be good anthropology and sociology and political science and psychology." In "The Expanding Domain of Economics," *American Economic Review* 75(6) 1985, 53–68, at p. 53.

[9]Helen Ladd points out that economic analysts often forget this: "The failure of some of the authors to spell out and defend their value judgments in some cases leaves the misleading impression that the policy conclusion follows logically from the analysis alone." Review of John M. Quigley and Daniel L. Rubinfeld, *American Domestic Priorities: An Economic Appraisal*, in *Journal of Economic Literature* 24(3) 1986, 1276–77, at p. 1277.

application of market and government failure concepts. As outlined in Figure 9.1, the starting point is a determination if there is an operational market. If there is, and there is neither evidence of market nor government failure, then there is no basis for intervention in the market to increase efficiency. If there is no operational market, or there is evidence of either market or government failure, then there is the opportunity for a policy change to increase efficiency. Framing in this way is likely to suggest some generic policy alternatives (review Table 10.6), as well as provide a starting point for more explicit modeling of the policy problem.

Modeling the Problem. The framing of problems in terms of market and government failures often leads directly to models linking policy variables to the conditions of concern. For example, consider a mayor concerned about the rising cost of land-filling solid waste. An analyst who viewed the problem in terms of market and government failures might frame the problem as one of an institutionally created negative externality: because residents pay for refuse collection based on the assessed value of their property rather than on the volume of refuse that they generate, they perceive the price that they pay to dispose of an additional unit of garbage (their marginal private cost) to be virtually zero rather than the actual cost that the city must bear to collect and landfill it (the marginal social cost). A model of the problem follows: the larger the marginal private cost of disposal seen by residents, the smaller the amount of garbage generated. Further elaboration of the model involves specifying the ways that marginal private cost can be increased and identifying effects of the increases. Simply charging residents fees in proportion to the amount of garbage that they generate, for instance, would directly internalize the externality but perhaps involve a number of undesirable impacts: high administrative costs and residents dumping illegally to avoid fees. Recognizing that these undesirable impacts might be less serious for some types of garbage, such as yard wastes, the analyst may decide to specify different models for different categories of garbage.

Sometimes modeling must go well beyond framing to identify important policy variables. Consider, for example, the problem of drug abuse. It can be easily framed as a negative externality problem. Some of the relevant impacts include street crime by addicts, the spread of diseases through the sharing of needles, child neglect and abuse by addicted parents, and crime associated with the distribution system. But identifying and evaluating the full range of policy variables requires a more explicit explanation of why people experiment with, and become addicted to, mood-altering drugs. Several hypotheses have been advanced: *contagion*—experimentation results from observation of, and pressure from, members of a peer group who are enjoying pleasures of early stages of use; *delinquency*—use by present-oriented young because it is risky, precocious, and pleasurable; *environmental escape*—use to escape reality of undesirable physical or social situation; *occupational hazard*—experimentation because of availability to those in the distribution system. Obviously, these models imply different policy variables. The contagion model suggests that anti-drug commercials by celebrities admired by the young may help counter peer pressure; the environmental escape model suggests a need for more fundamental changes in conditions and opportunities. The analyst seeks to determine the circumstances in which each of these behavioral models is most likely to apply.

In summary, understanding the problem involves investigating the symptoms that prompt client interest, framing the undesirable conditions in terms of market and government failures, and developing behavioral models that relate the conditions of concern to variables that can be manipulated by public policy. Each of these three tasks, but especially modeling, can only be done provisionally as the outset of an analysis. As we discuss below, each of the other steps in the rationalist mode forces reconsideration of the initial problem definition.

Choosing and Explaining Goals and Constraints

Probably the most difficult step in any policy analysis is deciding on appropriate goals. As Jeanne Nienaber and Aaron Wildavsky put it, "... of objectives [goals] it can be said that they invariably may be distinguished by these outstanding qualities: they are multiple, conflicting, and vague."[10] Only when you recognize this uncomfortable reality can you deal systematically and successfully with goals.

Even with the advice we offer, you are likely to find goal selection and delineation an inherently difficult task, as most of you will have had little experience in your academic careers in choosing goals. In most contexts you will have been given one or more goals to achieve. In policy analysis you face a much more difficult problem because you must determine the relevant goals. Specifying goals requires you to be normative: you often must decide what *should* be wanted. This is both difficult and inherently controversial. It is controversial because it means being overt about value systems. Nonetheless, we can suggest some ways that you may be able to assist your clients in establishing appropriate goals—ones that make trade-offs among policy alternatives apparent. Our advice falls under two headings: (1) accepting that goals are outputs of analysis as well as inputs to analysis, or, in other words, dealing with the vagueness, multiplicity, and conflict among goals as part of the analytical process; and (2) clarifying the distinction between goals and policies (and especially between goals and policy alternatives).

Goal Vagueness: Goals as Outputs. The problem analysis framework laid out in Figure 14.1, as well as the examples of actual policy analysis presented earlier in the book, should warn you to expect goal vagueness at the beginning of a policy analysis. Even if a particular client has clear goals, there may be good reasons why the client will not reveal them. Obviously, where clients do not have clear goals, they find it hard to structure the solution analysis for the analyst, whether it be the goals themselves or policy alternatives that might satisfy those goals. The revelation of this reality probably generates more analysis paralysis among novice analysts than anything else.

Novices often try to elicit goals from clients at the beginning of their efforts. Our advice: *resist this temptation*. You will notice that, for example, goals are not presented at the beginning of the salmon fishery policy analysis (Chapter 1) or the Madison taxicab policy analysis (Chapter 9). After you have provided your own initial explanation of the problem, eliciting goals from your client will probably be valuable and perhaps essential, but it is rarely so at the outset. There are two reasons why it is usually futile to ask for goals before starting the analysis: First, the client may not have decided on the appropriate goals in a particular policy context. As explained earlier, clients are usually driven by symptoms. Even if the client

[10] Jeanne Nienaber and Aaron Wildavsky, *The Budgeting and Evaluation of Federal Recreation Programs* (New York: Basic Books, 1973), 10.

has decided on the appropriate set of goals, he or she will almost certainly not have decided on the appropriate trade-offs between pairs of these goals. Second, a client may have goals but be unwilling to reveal them. Let us deal with each in turn.

Many observers argue that individuals preparing to make complex decisions do not have predetermined goals.[11] In fact, it may be desirable that decision makers not have rigid goals when dealing with complex, unstructured policy problems until after the problems have been analyzed. Put another way, it does not make sense to want something until you have some explanation of what is going on. For example, your client may not recognize the efficiency costs (and, therefore, the importance of efficiency as a goal) of a particular government intervention until you have explained it. However, clients are aware of specific impacts of the current situation or policy that concern them: "waiting times for taxis are too long," "too many young people are being killed in auto accidents involving alcohol," or "people are avoiding garbage pick-up charges by dumping on abandoned industrial sites." It is useful to get clients and others interested in the policy question to describe as many of these impacts as possible. As we will see, it is usually the analyst's job to translate these impacts into goal categories.

It may seem surprising that a client might not reveal goals to his or her policy analyst, but there may be good reasons for such a tactic. Wise decision makers realize that explicit goals often crystallize conflict and opposition. It may be that your client wishes to use you as a "stalking horse" in presenting and explicating controversial but worthy goals.

How should you formulate goals in these situations? Whether or not your client has suggested a particular goal or set of goals, you should explicitly consider the relevance of efficiency and equity. Clearly, this book's focus on both market and government failures suggests that policy analysis should always be centrally concerned with aggregate social surplus, or efficiency. Keep in mind that there is wide misunderstanding as to the meaning of efficiency, even among politicians and senior public managers. If asked directly whether they care about efficiency, some decision makers might answer negatively. But if the same individuals are asked if they are concerned that a current policy is resulting in death or injury or in extensive queuing by citizens, they would emphatically answer yes. Yet these are efficiency impacts.

Some policy analysts (mostly economists) argue that, in general, aggregate efficiency should be the primary concern of policy analysis and that distributional and other goals are rarely appropriate in evaluating alternative policies. They argue that seeking efficiency leads to the largest total of goods and therefore provides the greatest opportunity for redistribution. They advocate that distributional goals be met through explicitly redistributional programs, such as the tax system. Although we sympathize with the view that policy analysts should provide a voice for efficiency, especially because there is rarely an organized constituency in the political arena for maximizing aggregate social welfare, we presume that other goals are also usually important.

[11]See Henry Mintzberg, Gurev Raisinghani, and Andre Theoret, "The Structure of Unstructured Decision Processes," *Administrative Science Quarterly* 21(2) 1976, 246–75. As James March puts it, "… it seems to me perfectly obvious that a description that assumes goals come first and action comes later is frequently radically wrong. Human choice behavior is at least as much a process of discovering goals as for acting on them." James March, "The Technology of Foolishness," in James C. March and J. P. Olsen, eds., *Ambiguity and Choice in Organizations* (Bergen, Norway: Universitetsforlaget, 1976), 72.

Henry Rosen makes the case for routinely including equity considerations:

> Should equity issues be dealt with in each policy decision, or should they be dealt with through a separate income redistribution policy? ... In specific cases there usually is no way to identify all of the gainers and losers, and the information costs of attempting such identifications are often high. Moreover, the mechanisms for compensating losers are weak or nonexistent. ... An analysis which omits distributional effects and discusses only aggregate efficiency deals with a part of the decision maker's problem, and only a small part.[12]

Essentially similar arguments have been made for including other goals of public policy. We cannot tell you in general whether a particular goal should be included in your analysis, but we urge you to assume a priori that other goals as well as efficiency are relevant. This approach forces you to present reasoned arguments for either *including* or *excluding* a particular goal.

Whether or not you ultimately decide to include equity in the solution analysis, we also encourage you to take seriously the question of other appropriate goals, whether substantive or instrumental. Thus, if your analysis is not going to include goals that various stakeholders in the policy environment hold important, you should explain why. In the next section, we argue that equity, or any other goal, can be usefully viewed in terms of trade-offs with efficiency. Yet the fact remains that analytical technique cannot tell your client, or you, what you should want. Ultimately, the client, the analyst, and the political process must decide how much efficiency should be given up to achieve a given amount of redistribution or some other goal.

As introduced in Chapter 7, other goals can be broken down into two broad categories: substantive and instrumental. *Substantive goals* represent values, like equity and efficiency, that society wishes to secure for their own sake. These include considerations of human dignity, self-perception, and self-actualization. For instance, a Hastings Center report on organ transplants argued that, apart from efficiency, the relevant goals of public policy should include "the moral values and concerns our society has regarding individual autonomy and privacy, the importance of the family, the dignity of the body, and the value of social practices that enhance and strengthen altruism and our sense of community."[13]

Instrumental goals are conditions that make it easier to achieve substantive goals. Commonly relevant instrumental goals include political feasibility, increasing government revenues, and decreasing government expenditures (sometimes, more specifically, balancing budgets). As we explain later in this chapter, such instrumental goals often enter solution analysis as constraints rather than as goals. A constraint is simply a goal that must be satisfied up to some specified level, beyond which it has no value.

The appropriateness of including political feasibility as a policy goal is certainly disputable. As one perceptive commentator has put it: "[T]he motive may be defensive or offensive—to prevent the abuse of their analysis, or to make their analytic voices more influential—but analysts still need to increase their political

[12]Henry Rosen, "The Role of Cost-Benefit Analysis in Policy Making," in Henry M. Peskin and Eugene P. Seskin, eds., *Cost Benefit Analysis and Water Pollution Policy* (Washington, DC: Urban Institute, 1975), 367–68.

[13]The Hastings Center, *Ethical, Legal, and Policy Issues Pertaining to Solid Organ Procurement: A Report on Organ Transplantation*, October 1985, 2.

sophistication."[14] A clear example of political feasibility as an instrumental goal (or constraint) arose in debates over the 1986 U.S. tax reform bill. Although many analysts argued that mortgage interest deductibility is both inefficient *and* inequitable, it was undoubtedly retained because any attempt to eliminate the deduction would have made the whole concept of tax reform politically unfeasible.

Policy analysis is the art of the possible. Resource requirements, and especially resource constraints, therefore, are of central importance. As we will see in the next chapter, the Congressional Budget Office usually includes the impact of policy alternatives on net federal government revenues.

Resource constraints such as administrative infrastructure and availability of skilled personnel may also be critical in determining the viability of policy alternatives. Often this can be considered as a specific efficiency impact. Sometimes, it makes more sense to treat a resource constraint as a separate (instrumental) goal/constraint. Generally, *the constraint set should include any resources that are essential for either maintaining the status quo or implementing alternative policies.*

Your list of goals for a given problem might include efficiency, equity, human dignity, political feasibility, and budget availability. It is impossible, however, to describe the relevant goals for all policy problems. As you research a problem, you should always be aware of the importance of identifying potential goals. As you become familiar with specific policy areas you will become aware of the typical goals that are advocated. For example, in considering energy policy, security against the economic costs of oil supply disruptions is often an important policy goal that sometimes conflicts with short-run efficiency.

It should be becoming clear that an important heuristic is that the *specification of goals is an important output of policy analysis.* A clear elucidation of goals is fundamentally important to good policy analysis. Yet, in practice, it is the *trade-off* between goals that is especially difficult and controversial.

Clarifying the Trade-Offs between Goals. Selecting goals, per se, may be relatively noncontroversial. After all, it is easy to agree that distributional considerations should play *some* role in almost any policy problem. One complicating factor in goal trade-off is that the process of explaining relationships between goals and policies may itself alter the choice of goals.

Figure 14.2 illustrates a situation in which two goals, efficiency and equity, are represented on the axes. Assume that the decision maker wants both greater equity and efficiency but values additional units of each less at higher levels of attainment. He or she will have an indifference curve like I_A in the figure. Imagine that the decision maker is limited to choices of policy outcomes that lie within the feasible policy frontier indicated by the curve F_1E_1 so that the highest utility can be achieved by point X_1 on indifference curve I_A. At point X_1, the marginal trade-off between equity and efficiency equals the slope of the line *ac*, which is tangent to the indifference curve and the policy frontier at X_1.

In most analytical situations, the actual position of the policy frontier is not known until after considerable analysis has been done. For example, after information is gathered and analyzed, the policy frontier might be discovered to be F_2E_2 rather than F_1E_1. If F_2E_2 is the policy frontier, then the decision maker would choose

[14] Robert D. Behn, "Policy Analysis and Policy Politics," *Policy Analysis* 7(2) 1981, 199–226, at p. 216.

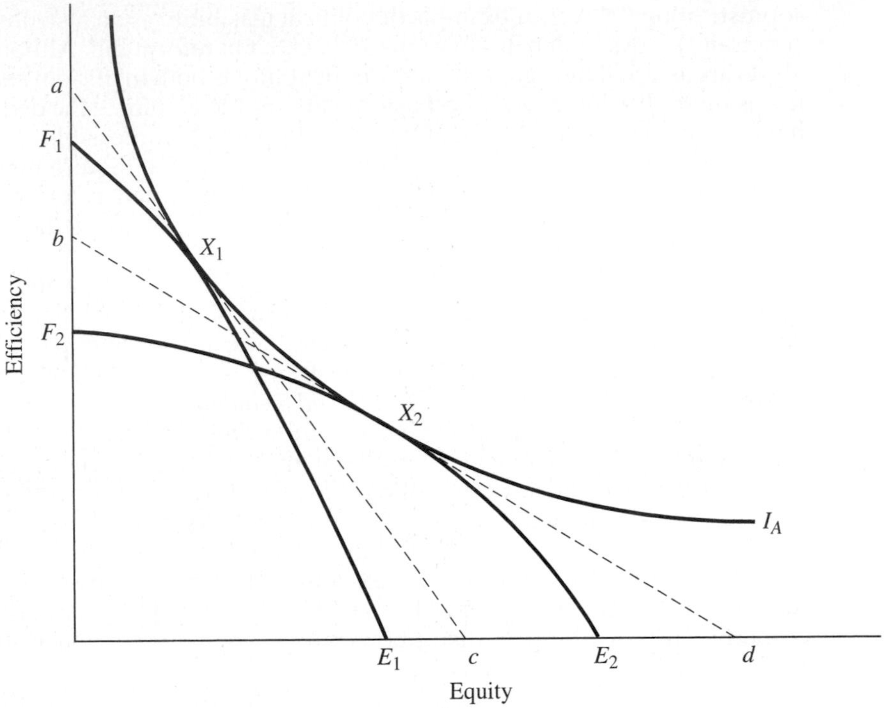

Figure 14.2 Goal Trade-Offs and Feasibility

point X_2 on I_A, implying a marginal trade-off between equity and efficiency given by the line *bd*. Thus, information on the nature of the policy frontier, which depends on the set of feasible policies identified, determines the marginal trade-offs that are possible between equity and efficiency. The focus of much public policy research and analysis is devoted to clarifying such issues. For example, in the area of welfare policy, an important consideration is the trade-off between benefit levels and work effort by recipients. Notice that preferences, per se, are not changed by providing such information (the decision maker's preferences are still represented by the indifference curve), but the levels of efficiency and equity selected do change, along with the rates at which the decision maker would be willing to make marginal trades between them.

The lesson is that the set of feasible policies, which usually must be identified by the analyst, determine the desirable trade-offs among goals. Therefore, we have an important heuristic: *the weights placed on goals (or impact categories) are more commonly an output of, rather than an input to, policy analysis.*

Clarifying the Distinction between Goals and Policies. Probably the most confusing semantic difficulty you will come across in policy analysis is making the distinction between goals (the values we seek to promote) and policies (the alternatives and strategies for promoting them). This semantic confusion arises because, in everyday language, policies (concrete sets of actions) are often stated as goals: "Our goal is to build 100,000 low income housing units," or "Our goal is to reduce class size to 18 students." Although this everyday use of such language is harmless, it derails many neophyte analysts. Goals should be used to *evaluate* alternative policies, but if a policy is stated as a goal, how can one evaluate it? Indeed, stated this way, any policy is self-justifying. In order to avoid this confusion, one must keep in mind a clear separation between goals and policies. We suggest that you do this by following another heuristic: *start by formulating goals as abstractly as possible and policy alternatives as concretely as possible.* Keep in mind that goals must ultimately be *normative*, a reflection of human values. Policy alternatives, on the other hand, are the concrete actions to achieve these goals. A policy alternative should seek to promote progress toward all the relevant goals, although, of course, in most cases a given alternative will do better on some goals, but worse on others, than some other alternative. The "Holy Grail" of policy analysis is the dominant alternative that does better than all other alternatives on *all* goals. It has been found a little more often than the Holy Grail, but not by much!

In the context of choosing implementation strategies, it is often reasonable to take already-decided policies as goals. For example, if the head of the state health department has already made a final decision that 90 percent of school-age children will be vaccinated against some disease this year, then this policy may be reasonably taken as a goal by those in the department who must decide how the vaccinations will be accomplished. Other goals, such as minimizing cost and maximizing population immunity, should be raised in connection with the choice of implementation strategies. Indeed, one might question the wisdom of the policy if it were made without consideration of these instrumental goals.

As an analysis proceeds, goals typically become less abstract as we identify specific impacts that help us to predict the aggregate impact each alternative would have in terms of goal achievement. For example, in cost-benefit analysis we are interested in the efficiency of each of the alternatives relative to the status quo. But the impacts that are relevant for efficiency may be quite varied. For example, the benefits of a new freeway might include both reduced driving time (time saved) and reduced accidents (lives, injuries, and property damage avoided). Similarly, the costs may include the (opportunity) cost of the construction workers' labor and the cost of the concrete. Ultimately each benefit impact category can be quantified (more specifically *monetized*) in terms of willingness to pay. Ultimately, each cost category can be quantified and monetized in terms of dollars of opportunity cost—in other words, dollars which can then be aggregated (a dollar is a dollar is a dollar). However, if we are not performing a cost-benefit analysis in which we actually do aggregate, it is easy to forget that these various impacts are, in fact, ways at getting at predicting the extent to which alternative will contribute to the achievement of a goal. These impacts can become goals in their own right. What is the problem? Well, certainly a "goal" of a highway project may be to reduce travel time. But it is dangerous not to realize that this is only one dimension of the efficiency impact of the project. Of course, often policymakers tend to focus on highly visible and, therefore, salient impact categories. Indeed, these may turn out to the only relevant categories, or at least the highly dominant ones, but they may not.

As we have stressed earlier in the chapter, you must overtly ask yourself what values (efficiency, equity, human dignity) lie behind the impacts that your client, or yourself, believe are important. As you become more experienced, you will begin to get better at doing this. When you observe impacts, you will be able to backward-map to a goal. For example, if a program uses real resources (employee time, building space, etc.), efficiency is inevitably relevant. If "who gets what" is an issue, as it almost always is, equity is *potentially* relevant, although inclusion should usually follow a considered analysis of the legitimacy of the equity claims. This usually requires identification of the groups (for example, license holders, Native fishers, and taxpayers in the salmon fishery analysis in Chapter 1) and their characteristics.

A note of warning: Getting, and then keeping, a focus on "big-picture" goals tends to become increasingly difficult as one moves to such nuts and bolts issues as sanitation, police patrol, and emergency services often found at the municipal and county levels. Clients at these levels of government sometimes claim that these sorts of issues are purely technical in nature and do not involve such value-laden considerations as efficiency and equity. Ultimately, good garbage collection is about efficiency (and perhaps equity and other goals in specific circumstances), even though it is easy to get mired in, well, the garbage.

Our experience suggests that almost all policy problems require an explicit goal framework to ensure that the impact categories comprehensively correspond to, and capture, appropriate values.

Choosing a Solution Method

Figure 14.1 shows that goal selection is a component of problem analysis. In other words, you must decide which goals are relevant to your analysis before you can begin to consider solutions systematically. This is because the nature and number of goals largely determine the appropriate solution method. Choosing *how* you will do the solution analysis is also a component of problem analysis.

Remember, policy analysis is an ex ante exercise. That is, we are interested in evaluating policies *before* they are introduced. Policymakers are also interested in ex post analysis, that is, the performance of policies *after* they have been put into operation. Assessments of such implemented policies are usually known as *program evaluation*. These evaluations may use a wide variety of techniques, including cost-benefit analysis, cost-effectiveness analysis, and qualitative multigoal analysis. (As we see, these same techniques are used in ex ante analysis.)[15] Policy analysis and program evaluation are distinct, although related, activities. They are related for several reasons. First, if an ex ante policy analysis has compared alternatives in terms of clearly specified goals, impacts, and valuation criteria, it usually makes sense to conduct the ex post program evaluation of the alternative actually implemented using the same goals, impacts, and criteria. Second, ex post evaluations of programs that are similar to the alternatives your analysis is considering are extremely useful inputs for ex ante analysis because they provide credible information on projected impacts. The crucial point is that we are interested in analytical techniques in an ex ante context where we have to predict, as well as value, impacts.

Figure 14.3 distinguishes three general goal circumstances: First, efficiency is the only relevant goal. Second, efficiency and one other goal are relevant. Third, efficiency and two or more other goals are relevant. The number of relevant goals determines the appropriate solution method.

There are five basic approaches to policy analysis: (1) formal ex ante cost-benefit analysis, (2) qualitative ex ante cost-benefit analysis, (3) modified ex ante

[15]For further elaboration on the distinction between ex ante and ex post analysis, see Anthony E. Boardman, Wendy L. Mallery, and Aidan R. Vining, "Learning from Ex Ante/Ex Post Cost-Benefit Comparisons: The Coquihalla Highway Example," *Socio-Economic Planning Sciences* 28(2) 1994, 69–84.

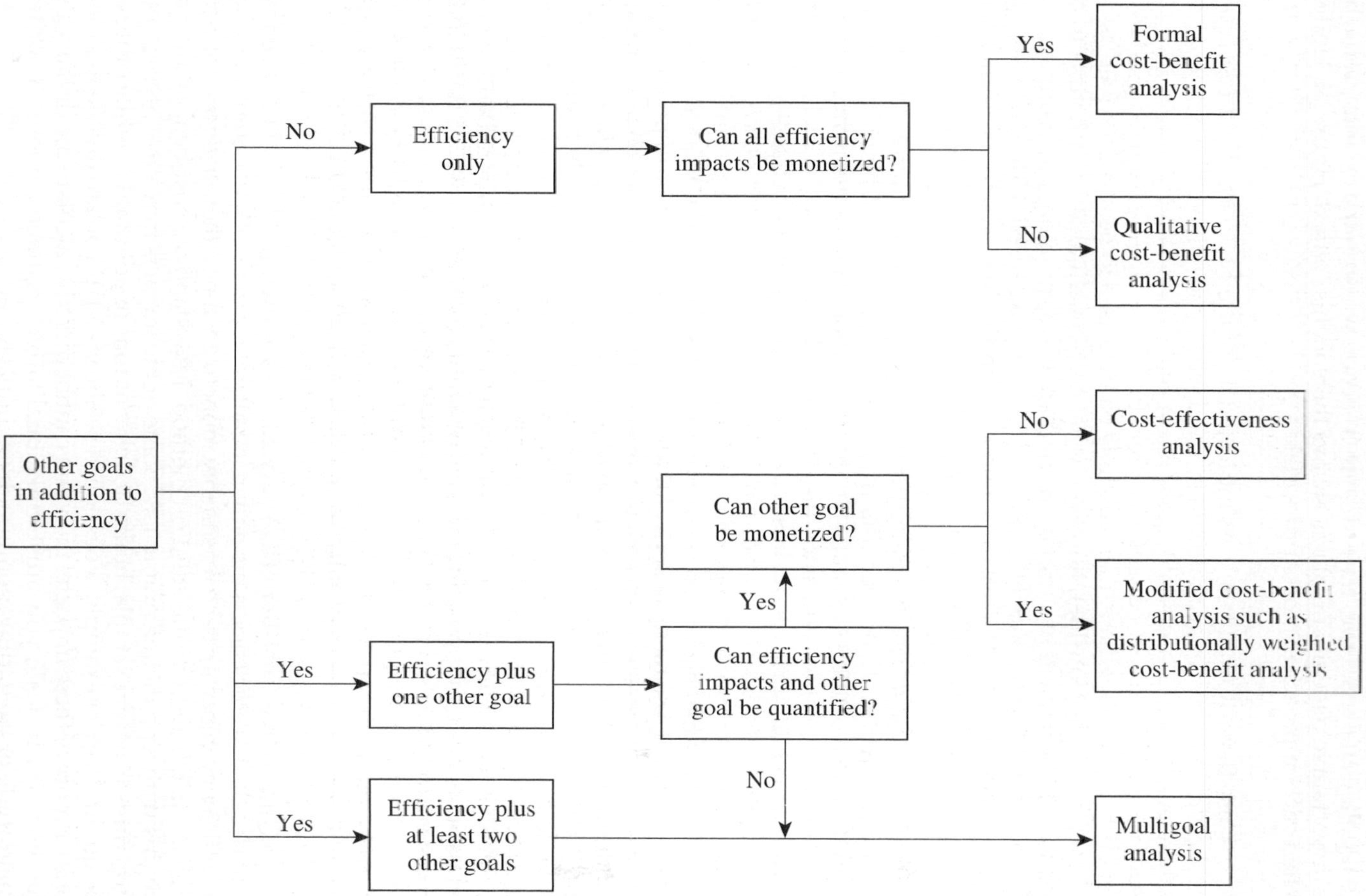

Figure 14.3 Choosing a Solution Method

cost-benefit analysis, (4) ex ante cost-effectiveness analysis, and (5) ex ante multigoal policy analysis. From now on in this section we drop the ex ante prefix, but it is important to remember that it is always there in this context. Figure 14.3 indicates when each approach is most appropriate.

Cost-Benefit Analysis. As indicated in Figure 14.3, *formal cost-benefit analysis* should be your primary solution method when you believe that efficiency is the only relevant goal. Conceptually, cost-benefit analysis is relatively simple. If you have read our chapter on cost-benefit (Chapter 16) or have already been exposed to cost-benefit analysis elsewhere, then you may be surprised to hear it described as being relatively simple. Consider, however, what cost-benefit analysis attempts to do. It reduces *all* the impacts of a proposed alternative to a common unit of impact, namely, dollars. Of course, once all impacts have been measured in dollars, they can be aggregated—a dollar is a dollar is a dollar. If individuals would be willing to pay dollars to have something, then presumably it is a benefit; if they would pay to avoid it, then it is a cost. Once all the impacts have been reduced to dollars, the evaluation rule is relatively straightforward: choose that alternative that generates the largest aggregate net benefits (in dollars). Thus, in cost-benefit analysis, although we have different "goals," in the conventional use of the word, they can all be reduced to positive efficiency impacts (benefits) or negative efficiency impacts (costs), which, in turn, can all be measured in dollars, or monetized.

Sometimes prices revealed in markets provide a basis for *monetization*. Often, however, market prices do not reflect marginal social costs or marginal social benefits because of the distortions caused by market failures and government interventions. There are also many classes of impacts, such as willingness of people to pay to preserve wilderness (existence value), that usually cannot be monetized through estimations based on direct observation of markets. Considerable skill and judgment must be exercised to assess the costs and benefits of these impacts plausibly.

Keep in mind that you will need some practice before you will feel comfortable deciding if all the relevant impacts that are called goals can really be viewed as elements of efficiency. Consider an example. You are confronted with a crowded freeway. Let us suppose for the sake of simplicity that your client states that her goals are to reduce commuting time and fuel consumption. Superficially, these appear to be different goals (and they certainly may differ in importance to different clients), but both can be translated into a common impact: dollar-cost savings. As we will see, this is conceptually straightforward, although in practice difficult.

Qualitative Cost-Benefit Analysis. As shown in Figure 14.3, even when you decide that efficiency is the only relevant goal, you must still determine whether all efficiency impacts can be reasonably monetized. If not, then *qualitative cost-benefit analysis* is the appropriate solution method. Like standard cost-benefit analysis, it begins with a prediction of impacts. Some of the impacts may be expressed in natural units (say, for example, hours of delay or tons of pollutants), while others may be qualitative (for example, a despoiled scenic view). If you are unable to monetize one or more of these impacts, then you cannot directly calculate the dollar value of net benefits. Instead, you must make qualitative arguments about the orders of magnitude of the various nonmonetized impacts.

Often impacts cannot be monetized because of technical difficulties in making valuations. When standard procedures do exist for inferring such values, limitations of time, data, and other resources frequently make monetization impractical. Even highly skilled professional economists sometimes resort to qualitative cost-benefit analyses when they write about policy issues. Rather than attempt difficult and time-consuming valuations, they fall back on theoretical arguments to assess orders of magnitude of efficiency impacts.

Ex post quantitative cost-benefit analyses are available in many policy areas.[16] Elements from these studies can often be used as a source for your ex ante quantitative estimates of costs or benefits, or at least as a guide for estimating their orders of magnitude. When you begin working in a new policy area, spending some time to become familiar with relevant cost-benefit analyses is likely to be a good investment.

When you cannot confidently monetize important efficiency impacts to within even orders of magnitude, you may find it useful to work with the nonmonetized impacts as if they were separate goals. For example, you may have to decide how to compare certain program costs with highly uncertain benefits, such as environmental or catastrophic failure risks. Thus, your qualitative cost-benefit analysis takes the form of the multigoal analysis we describe below.

Modified Cost-Benefit Analysis. It may seem reasonable to assume that if a client is only concerned with equity, or any other single, nonefficiency goal, then efficiency is irrelevant. Yet some thought should convince you that efficiency is almost certainly relevant. This can be most clearly illustrated for the case where equity is putatively the only goal. Any intervention in the market to finance redistribution (absent utility interdependence and market failure) must inevitably result in some deadweight loss. Even where we are primarily concerned with achieving a given redistribution, we should seek to minimize the deadweight loss; in other words, we should attempt to carry out the redistribution as efficiently as possible. In our conception of policy analysis, therefore, *analysis almost never involves a single goal unless that goal is efficiency.*

In a particular analysis you may conclude that efficiency and one other goal (most frequently, equity) are appropriate. As indicated in Figure 14.3, you can employ modified cost-benefit analysis if you are able and willing to monetize impacts on both efficiency and the other goal. In other words, you must be willing to assign dollar values to various levels of achievement of the other goal. For example, if the other goal is equality of the income distribution, modified cost-benefit analysis would involve weighting costs and benefits accruing to different income groups, resulting in *distributionally weighted cost-benefit analysis.*[17] The advantage of such an approach should be clear. By incorporating distributional issues into a cost-benefit analysis, you can come up with a single metric for ranking alternatives. This is obviously attractive. The major disadvantage should also be clear from our discussion above, namely, that the metric is only achieved by forcing efficiency and equity to be commensurable. Modified cost-benefit analysis, by assuming a particular set of distributional weights, also risks diverting attention from the trade-off between efficiency and distributional values in the ranking of alternatives, which merges both

[16] See "A Selected Cost-Benefit Analysis Bibliography," in Anthony E. Boardman, David H. Greenberg, Aidan R. Vining, and David L. Weimer, *Cost-Benefit Analysis: Concepts and Practice*, 2nd ed. (Upper Saddle River, NJ: Prentice Hall, 2001), 489–510.

[17] Ibid., pp. 411–27.

the distributional and efficiency assessments. When using modified cost-benefit analysis, it is usually desirable to present both the distributionally weighted net benefits and the unweighted net benefits of the policy alternatives.[18] A comparison of the weighted and unweighted net benefits makes clear the importance of the particular weights selected.

Cost-Effectiveness Analysis: Achieving Goals Efficiently. *Cost-effectiveness analysis* is appropriate when both efficiency and the other goal can be quantified but where the other goal cannot be monetized (see Figure 14.3). In contrast to modified cost-benefit analysis, where both goals are measured in dollars and thus commensurable, the two goals are treated as noncommensurable.

We can approach cost-effectiveness analysis in one of two ways. The first method, often called the *fixed budget approach*, is to choose a given level of expenditures (say, $10 million) and find the policy alternative that will provide the largest benefits (that is, the greatest achievement of the nonefficiency goal). The second method, which might be called the *fixed effectiveness approach*, is to specify a given level of benefit (however defined) and then choose the policy alternative that achieves the benefit as the lowest cost. Both of these methods are cost-effectiveness procedures.

Keep in mind the crucial distinction between cost-benefit analysis and cost-effectiveness analysis. Cost-benefit analysis can assess both (1) whether any of the alternatives are worth doing (that is, whether social benefits exceed social costs) and (2) how alternatives should be ranked if more than one generates positive net social benefits. Cost-effectiveness cannot tell the analyst whether a given alternative is worth doing (this requires a cost-benefit analysis), but if a decision is made to redistribute or achieve some other goal, it can help in deciding which policy alternative will do so most efficiently (with minimum losses of social surplus).

Edward Gramlich and Michael Wolkoff provide an excellent illustration of both this distinction and how to do cost-effectiveness studies. They suppose that the goal is equity: specifically, to raise the income of some group of people. They compare a negative income tax alternative, minimum wage legislation, and a public employment plan. Each intervention involves costs that may or may not exceed benefits. For example, the negative income tax is likely to discourage some individuals from working who would normally do so. The public employment plan is likely to *attract* low-income individuals. In short, all *may* generate net costs (that is, fail the cost-benefit test). If we are determined to go ahead with some program for redistributional purposes, however, which would make most sense? Gramlich and Wolkoff adopt the fixed budget approach and seek to find the most beneficial policy alternative, given a $5 billion expenditure. Notice, in this context, benefit is used in a special sense. It does not refer to aggregate social welfare but, rather, counts benefits going to specific low-income groups. The authors developed a weighting scheme that ranks these impacts. They found that the negative income tax was much more successful in redistributing income per $5 billion expenditure than either the higher minimum wage or public employment.[19]

[18]Arnold C. Harberger, "On the Use of Distributional Weights in Social Cost-Benefit Analysis," *Journal of Political Economy* 86(2) 1978, S87–S120.

[19]Edward M. Gramlich and Michael Wolkoff, "A Procedure for Evaluating Income Distribution Policies," *Journal of Human Resources* 14(3) 1979, 319–50.

Multigoal Analysis. When three or more goals are relevant, multigoal analysis is the appropriate solution method. As indicated in Figure 14.3, it is also the appropriate method when one of two goals cannot be quantified. It is usually the most appropriate solution method, and it should be the assumed approach until the explicit conditions set out in Figure 14.3 for one of the other methods are confirmed.

Because all of the other solution methods can be viewed as special cases of multigoal analysis, the remaining steps in the rationalist mode (all within the solution analysis phase) lay out how to conduct multigoal analysis. Specifically, they indicate how goal achievement can be estimated using impact categories, how alternatives can be formulated, and how the alternatives can be systematically compared in terms of the goals.

Solution Analysis

Policy problems rarely involve only one value. Multigoal policy analysis, therefore, usually serves as the appropriate solution method. As we have indicated, however, sometimes efficiency will appear to be the only relevant goal, so that you can evaluate current and alternative policies solely with cost benefit analysis. Other times, you may decide that only efficiency and one other goal are relevant, so that cost-effectiveness analysis seems appropriate. Yet even in these cases, it is usually best to begin with the presumption that some other goals may be relevant. If your initial assessment that either cost-benefit or cost-effectiveness analysis alone provides an appropriate evaluation rule remains unchanged, then you can easily treat either of these solution methods as a special case of multigoal analysis. Our discussion of solution analysis, therefore, deals with the general case of multiple goals.

Solution analysis (or choice) requires five steps: (S1) selecting impact categories for the relevant goals; (S2) generating a mutually exclusive set of policy alternatives; (S3) predicting the impact that each alternative would have in terms of goal achievement; (S4) valuing the predicted impacts, either using qualitative, quantitative, or monetized measures; and (S5) evaluating the set of alternatives against the goals and making a recommendation. At the heart of multigoal analysis is the systematic comparison of alternative policies (step S2) in terms of goals (step S1). As this and the next chapter make clear, we believe that a *goals/alternatives matrix* (or matrices) that displays the impacts of alternatives in terms of goals greatly facilitates this process.

Table 14.1 illustrates the usual structure of a goals/alternatives matrix. The leftmost column presents the goals determined during problem analysis. Step S1 involves *specifying the relevant impact categories* for assessing how well each policy alternative contributes to each of the goals. The column to the immediate right of the column of goals lists the impact categories determined in step S1.

Step S2 in solution analysis is the detailed *specification of policy alternatives* that can potentially promote the policy goals. In Table 14.1, the three policy alternatives label the rightmost columns. Note that policy I is identified as the status quo. It is almost always appropriate to include current policy as an alternative to avoid the risk of recommending a best alternative that is worse than the current policy.

Step S3 is *prediction*: What is your prediction as to how the alternative will do in terms of the goal or impact category? Step S4 is *valuation*: How desirable is the impact from a policy perspective? These two steps are often combined in a single

Table 14.1 *The Simple Structure of a Goals/Alternatives Matrix*

Goals	Impact Category	Policy Alternatives		
		Policy I (status quo)	Policy II	Policy III
Goal A	Impact A1	predicted impact and its valuation	predicted impact and its valuation	predicted impact and its valuation
	Impact A2	predicted impact and its valuation	predicted impact and its valuation	predicted impact and its valuation
	Impact A3	predicted impact and its valuation	predicted impact and its valuation	predicted impact and its valuation
Goal B	Impact B1	predicted impact and its valuation	predicted impact and its valuation	predicted impact and its valuation
	Impact B2	predicted impact and its valuation	predicted impact and its valuation	predicted impact and its valuation
Goal C	Impact C1	predicted impact and its valuation	predicted impact and its valuation	predicted impact and its valuation

goals/alternatives matrix by filling in all the cells of the matrix with valuations of the predictions of the impact of each policy alternative on each impact category. (However, it is often useful for the analyst to do *separate* prediction and valuation worksheet matrices.) These predictions and subsequent valuations will sometimes be quantitative, as when market information allows us to assess impacts of policies on efficiency in terms of changes in social surplus. Other times, the predicted impacts and their valuation will be qualitative and made in such terms as "poor," "good," or "excellent."

Step S5 involves *evaluation*: recommending one of the alternatives and explaining the basis for the choice. As one alternative rarely dominates the others in terms of all the goals, the explanation for the recommendation will almost always require an explicit discussion of trade-offs among goal achievements that the recommended alternative implies.

Table 14.1 emphasizes one crucial point, which can be summarized as a heuristic: *an analysis cannot be competent unless it comprehensively reviews all of the alternatives in terms of all of the goals*. The following sections elaborate on the five solution analysis steps.

Choosing Impact Categories for Goals

The first step in solution analysis involves moving from the goal or goals developed in problem analysis to more specific impact categories for evaluating the desirability of alternative policies in terms of the goals. For example, the general goal of equality in the distribution of some service might be operationalized as the impact category "the variance in service consumption across income groups." Sometimes a single impact category, perhaps even the initially specified goal itself, will provide an adequate basis for assessment. In Table 14.1 this is illustrated by goal C, which has only one impact category associated with it. For example, the goal might be "efficiency" and, if all efficiency impacts can be monetized, its associated impact category would be "net benefits." If the original goal were "pass constitutional test," it might reasonably serve as its own impact category. In most cases, however, more than one impact category is required to assess progress toward a goal adequately—goal A, for example, is shown as having three impact categories.

Specifying Policy Alternatives

We have already presented a set of generic policy solutions in Chapter 10. They provide templates for beginning the construction of policy alternatives. The specification of policy alternatives is one component of policy analysis where nearly everyone agrees one can, and should, be creative. When told this, many of our students have replied, "Give us a hint." Here we attempt to do so.

There are a variety of sources for developing policy alternatives: existing policy proposals; policies implemented in other jurisdictions; generic policy solutions, as outlined in Chapter 10; and custom-designed alternatives.

Existing policy proposals, including the status quo policy, should be taken seriously. Not because they necessarily represent the best set of alternatives, but rather because other analysts have found them to be plausible responses to policy problems. Proposals already on the table sometimes are the product of earlier analyses; other times they represent attempts by interest groups or by policy entrepreneurs to draw attention to policy problems by forcing others to respond to concrete proposals. (Indeed, you can sometimes work backwards from policy proposals to infer some of the perceptions and goals of the proposers.)

In some contexts we can borrow policy alternatives from other jurisdictions.[20] How have other cities, states, or countries handled policy problems similar to the one that your jurisdiction faces? In particular, have any parallel jurisdictions appeared to have handled a problem particularly well? If so, the policies adopted by those jurisdictions can be a source of policy alternatives.

Once you have identified a policy that appears to have been successful elsewhere, you can create many additional alternatives through the process of tinkering.[21] The idea behind tinkering is to decompose an alternative into its essential components, identify different designs for the components, reassemble the designs into alternatives, and then select those combinations that look most promising. For example, imagine that you found a recycling program in a neighboring city that appeared to be working well. It involves four components: (1) residents separating newspapers and metal cans from their regular refuse, (2) residents putting these materials at the curbside in a standard container provided by the city on regular refuse-collection days, (3) the city refuse department collecting these materials, and

[20]See Anne Schneider and Helen Ingram, "Systematically Pinching Ideas: A Comparative Approach to Policy Design," *Journal of Public Policy* 8(1) 1988, 61–80.

[21]See David L. Weimer, "The Current State of Design Craft: Borrowing, Tinkering, and Problem Solving," *Public Administration Review* 53(2) 1993, 110–20.

(4) the refuse department packaging and selling them to recyclers. It is easy to imagine variations on each of these components. Residents, for instance, could be required to separate only newspapers, or perhaps plastics and glass as well, from their regular refuse. They could be required to drop them off at a recycling center rather than placing them at the curb. The city could contract with a private firm to collect the materials. Reassembling the variations on the components, a new alternative would be to require residents to deliver only newspapers to a central location operated by a private recycler.

As discussed in Chapter 11, your efforts to predict the course of implementation of a policy alternative may require you to tinker in order to avoid problems that are likely to be encountered. Thus, in the course of your analysis, you are likely to identify new alternatives that result from tinkering with alternatives that you have subjected to substantial analysis.

It is rare, although not impossible, that you will end up considering a set of purely generic policy alternatives. Nonetheless, generic policy solutions often provide a good starting point for design. For example, if you frame the apparent overexploitation of a resource as an open-access problem, then it is natural to look first at such generic policy solutions as private ownership, user fees, and restrictions on access. Although the particular technical, institutional, political, and historical features of the problem may limit their direct applicability, the generic solutions can provide a framework for crafting and classifying more complex alternatives.

Once you develop a portfolio of generic alternatives, you can begin to modify them to fit the particular circumstances of the policy problem. For example, an open-access resource like salmon has value to both sport and commercial fishers. Selling exclusive harvesting rights to a private firm might create appropriate incentives for efficient long-term management of the salmon. The firm would probably find it difficult to control sport fishing, however, because it would face high transaction costs in using the civil courts to protect its property rights against individual poachers. A hybrid policy that reserved an annual catch of fixed size for licensed sportsmen might deal more effectively with the poaching problem by bringing the police powers of the government to bear. Modified alternatives of this sort can often be formed by combining elements of generic solutions or by introducing new features.

Finally, in the course of your analysis, you may come up with a unique, or custom-made, policy alternative. Its elements may be lurking in the literature or it may be the product of your imagination.[22] As we discussed in Chapter 11, "backward mapping" can sometimes be used to produce such custom-made designs. Certainly this is one area of policy analysis in which you should stretch your imagination. Much of the intellectual fun of policy analysis arises in trying to come up with creative alternatives.[23] Be brave! You can always weed out your failures when you begin your systematic comparison of alternatives. Indeed, you may not be able to identify your failures until you begin your comparative evaluation.

[22]For some examples of sources for such custom design, see David L. Weimer, "Claiming Races, Broiler Contracts, Heresthetics, and Habits: Ten Concepts for Policy Design," *Policy Sciences* (25)2 1992, 135–59.

[23]Often one can find ways of introducing well-known institutions into new contexts. For an example, see Richard Schwindt and Aidan R. Vining, "Proposal for a Future Delivery Market for Transplant Organs," *Journal of Health Politics, Policy and Law* 11(3) 1986, 483–500.

Be warned that your creative alternatives are likely to be controversial, so be prepared to take the heat! Sometimes you can launch trial balloons in order to get a sense of how hostile the reception will be. For example, you might try to get informal reactions to alternatives during interviews with people who have interests in the policy area.

Keeping these sources in mind, we can suggest some heuristics for crafting policy alternatives.[24] First, *you should not expect to find a perfect, or even dominant, policy alternative.* Policy analysis generally deals with complex problems and, most importantly, multiple goals. It is unlikely that any policy is going to be ideal in terms of *all* goals. Rarely is the best policy also a totally dominant policy.

Further, *do not contrast a preferred policy with a set of "dummy" or "straw person" alternatives.* It is often very tempting to make an alternative, which for some reason you prefer, look more attractive by comparing it to unattractive alternatives—almost anyone can look good if compared to Frankenstein's monster. This approach usually does not work and, moreover, it misses the very point of policy analysis. It rarely works because even relatively inexperienced clients are usually aware of the extant policy proposals advanced by interested parties. Your credibility can be seriously eroded if the client realizes that the alternatives have been faked. It misses the point of policy analysis because such an approach assumes that the critical component of analysis is the recommended alternative. As we have stressed, however, the *process* of policy analysis is equally important. You achieve the process goal of policy analysis by considering the best possible set of alternatives. Of course, comparing viable candidates makes determination of the best policy alternative more difficult and less certain, but, as we have already pointed out, it is better to have an ambiguous reality than a fake certainty.

Another heuristic may help you to avoid dummy alternatives: *don't have a "favorite" alternative until you have evaluated all the alternatives in terms of all the goals.* This may seem too obvious to state. Yet many neophyte analysts sprinkle their analyses with hints that they have accepted or rejected a policy alternative before they have formally evaluated it. The heuristic is, *make your primary ego and intellectual investments in the analysis and only marginally in the particular recommendation.*

Having ensured that your policy alternatives are not straw persons, you should *ensure that your alternatives are mutually exclusive;* they are, after all, *alternative* policies. Alternatives are obviously not mutually exclusive if you could combine all the features of alternative A with all the features of alternative B and come up with alternative C. In such circumstances, A and B may be too narrow and perhaps should be eliminated from the set of alternatives. For example, imagine a series of alternatives that specify fees for different classes of users of a public facility. If the adopted policy is very likely to set fees for all the classes, then it probably would be appropriate to combine the set of fees into a single alternative that can then be compared to other combinations that also cover all the classes of users.

You almost always face an infinite number of potential policy alternatives. If one of your policy alternatives is to build 10,000 units of low-income housing, mutually exclusive alternatives include building 9,999 units or 10,001 units. An infinite number of policy alternatives is a few too many. Given clients' limited attention

[24]Several of the ideas in this section are drawn from Peter May, "Hints for Crafting Alternative Policies," *Policy Analysis* 7(2) 1981, 227–44. See also Ernest R. Alexander, "The Design of Alternatives in Organizational Contexts," *Administrative Science Quarterly* 24(3) 1979, 382–404.

span (and analysts' limited time), *somewhere between three and seven policy alternatives is generally a reasonable number.*[25] Keep in mind that one of the alternatives should be current policy—otherwise you introduce a bias for change.

It is preferable to provide a reasonable contrast in the alternatives examined. Unless there are important discontinuities, it is analytically wasteful to make three of your alternatives 9,999 housing units, 10,000 housing units, and 10,001 housing units. *The alternatives should provide real choices.*

You should *avoid "kitchen sink" alternatives*—that is, "do-everything" alternatives. Such alternatives are often incomprehensible and unfeasible. If you find yourself proposing a kitchen sink alternative, take a close look at all the constraints your client faces. Does your client have the budgetary, administrative, and political resources it requires? If not, then it is probably not a valid alternative. You failed to recognize this because you omitted instrumental goals that encompass these constraints.

More generally, *alternatives should be consistent with available resources, including jurisdictional authority and controllable variables.* If your client is a mayor, then there is usually little point in proposing alternatives that require new federal resources. If you believe that such an alternative should be formulated, then you must recast it as a call for mobilization, coordination, or lobbying. In other words, it must be oriented around a set of steps that your client can take to generate the appropriate federal action.

Remember that *policy alternatives are concrete sets of actions.* (Remind yourself of the distinction between goals and policies.) Generic policy solutions are abstract statements. Thus, while it is useful for analytical purposes to think of a given alternative as the "demand-side subsidy alternative," this abstraction should be converted to a concrete proposal (for example, housing voucher worth X, going to target population Y) in your policy analysis. *You will not be able to predict consequences unless you provide clear and detailed specifications of your alternatives.* The alternatives should be clearly specified sets of instructions so that the client knows exactly what she is choosing and how it will be executed. To prepare these instructions, you must determine what resources will be needed during implementation and how these resources are to be secured from those who control them. In effect, as discussed in Chapter 11, you must be able to create a scenario that shows how the policy can be moved from concept to reality.

Predicting How Alternatives Will Do in Terms of Goals and Their Impact Categories

Once you have specified the relevant impact categories and policy alternatives, you must bring them together in a way that facilitates choice. The first task is to predict, or forecast, how each alternative will perform in terms of each goal and, if a goal has multiple impacts associated with it, all of the impacts. You should confront this task explicitly. By doing so, you make clear the predictions inherent in your analysis. This step is necessarily explicit in cost-benefit analysis: a prediction of impacts underlies the estimation of the stream of future costs and benefits. For ex-

[25]On the question of attention span, see George A. Miller, "The Magical Number Seven, Plus or Minus Two: Some Limits on Our Capacity for Processing Information," *Psychological Review* 63(2) 1956, 81–97.

ample, you may need to predict how many AIDS patients will use a clinic over the next fifteen years.

Your model of the policy problem (in problem analysis) is crucial to the prediction of impacts. Your model helped you understand and explain current conditions, which are observable. It should also help you predict what will happen in the future under current policy. For example, assume that the policy problem is rush-hour traffic congestion in the central business district (CBD), and that your model shows that crowding results because people base their commuting decisions on the private costs and benefits of the various transit modes. Because drivers do not pay for the delay costs that their presence inflicts on everyone else driving in the CBD during rush hour, too many people commute by automobile from the perspective of total social costs and benefits. Your model suggests that changing conditions, such as growing employment in the CBD, which alter the costs and benefits of various transit modes, will affect future congestion. By projecting changes in conditions, therefore, you can predict future congestion levels under current policy. You would make predictions about congestion under alternative policies by determining how they would alter the costs and benefits of different transit modes. Higher parking fees, for instance, would raise the private costs of commuting by automobile.

Consider how you might actually go about making the link between higher parking fees and congestion. Ideally, you would like to know the price elasticity of demand for automobile commuting in your city. That is, by what percentage will automobile use for commuting change as a result of a 1 percent change in price? Starting with estimates of the current price and level of automobile commuting, you could use the elasticity to predict levels under various parking fee increases. It is unlikely that you would have the authority, time, or resources to run an experiment to determine the elasticity. You may be able to take advantage of natural experiments, however. For example, your city may have raised parking fees for other reasons in the past. What effect did this have on automobile use? Do you know of any other cities that raised parking fees? What happened to their congestion levels? If you cannot find answers to these questions, then you might be able to find some empirical estimates of the price elasticity of automobile commuting in the literature on transportation economics. As a last resort, you might ask some experts to help you make an educated guess, or simply make a best guess yourself.

Policies almost always have multiple impacts. Use your model, your specification of the alternative, and your common sense to list as many different impacts as you can. For example, with respect to a parking fee increase: What will be the impact on automobile use for commuting? On the price and quantity of private parking in and near the CBD? On city revenues from parking fees and parking tickets? On the use of other transit modes? On off-peak driving in the CBD? On resident and commuter attitudes toward city hall? Sometimes, by thinking about one impact, you identify others. For instance, once you start thinking about how commuters might respond to the higher parking fees, you may realize that some will park in nearby residential neighborhoods and ride public transit to the downtown. If you had not already considered on-street parking congestion in nearby residential neighborhoods as an impact category, then you should add it to your list under the appropriate goal.

Once you have a comprehensive set of impacts associated with goals, you need to comprehensively link them to the alternatives. The key point is that *you should predict and value the effects of each alternative on every impact category*. After you have worked through all the alternatives, you will be able to compare them, either qualitatively or using explicit valuation criteria (the next step in solution analysis).

You can force yourself to be comprehensive in your prediction of impacts by constructing a separate goals/alternatives matrix. The cells of the matrix serve as a worksheet for making predictions. If a policy alternative does not seem to have an impact different from the current policy impact, then predict "no difference from current policy."

Table 14.2 shows what your worksheet might look like for the parking congestion problem. The columns are labeled with the three alternatives: current policy, a doubling of parking fees at city-owned lots in the CBD, and the establishment of bus-only lanes on certain major traffic arteries. Only by filling in all the cells do you make a complete set of predictions. As you gather more information, you can refine the cell entries until you are either satisfied with their accuracy or you have no hope of improving them further given the available time and resources.

Do not try to suppress the uncertainty in your predictions. You need not fill in cells with single numbers (point estimates). Instead, ranges (perhaps confidence intervals) may be appropriate. For example, you may be fairly confident that the average number of vehicles entering the CBD at rush hour on workdays will be very close to 50,000 under current policy over the next year because this has been the average over the last two years. In contrast, you may be very uncertain about the average number of vehicles that would enter if parking fees were doubled. Perhaps you believe it unlikely that the number would be either less than 45,000 or greater than 48,000. Rather than fill the appropriate cell with a specific number, you should indicate this range. Later you can use these upper and lower bounds to come up with "best" and "worst" cases for each alternative.

Many times your uncertainty will be so great that a qualitative rather than quantitative entry is appropriate. For instance, consider the criterion "Change in CBD business activity" in Table 14.2. Although it would be natural to measure this change in dollars, you probably have no basis for making quantitative predictions. Cell entries such as "Slight increase" or "Moderate decrease" may be the most realistic predictions you can make.

Remember predictions always depend on assumptions about the future (even predictions about what will happen tomorrow). Often, there are possible different "states of the world" that it is useful to include explicitly in the analysis. We can think of these sets of assumptions as *scenarios*, which we already encountered in Chapter 11 in the context of implementation analysis. The most likely state of the world is known as the *baseline scenario*, or the *baseline case*. For example, Robert Hahn makes a number of different assumptions about the costs of technology and fuel costs to compare the cost-effectiveness of a variety of policies intended to reduce emissions from vehicles.[26] For each set of assumptions (that is, for each scenario), he calculates the dollar cost of reducing the sum of emissions of reactive organic gases and nitrogen oxides by one ton. As fuel costs are directly relevant to most of the alternatives he considers, it make sense to assess the cost-effectiveness of each alternative in terms of an assumption about fuel prices. More generally, *when uncertainty about the future requires more than one scenario, it is necessary to produce a goals/impact matrix for each scenario considered*. This ensures that comparisons among alternatives are made under the same set of assumptions.

[26]Robert W. Hahn, "Choosing among Fuels and Technologies for Cleaning Up the Air," *Journal of Policy Analysis and Management* 14(4) 1995, 532–54.

Table 14.2 *Worksheet for Predicting Impacts of Alternative Policies for Dealing with Central Business District (CBD) Traffic Congestion*

Goals	Impact Category	Alternatives		
		Current Policy	**Double CBD Parking Fees**	**Create Express Bus Lane**
Access to CBD	1. Number of rush-hour vehicles (per workday)	50,000	45,000–48,000	44,000–48,000
	2. Average rush-hour delay for vehicles (minutes)	12	6–10	14–18
	3. Number of commuter-bus riders (per workday)	30,000	31,000–33,000	32,000–36,000
	4. Average rush-hour delay for bus commuters (minutes)	12	6–10	2–4
Fiscal Health	1. Revenues from parking fees and bus fares in excess of current policy (millions of dollars per year)	0	13.00–20.80	−0.52 to −0.13
	2. Direct costs in excess of current policy (millions of dollars per year)	0	0.12	3.50
Citywide Social and Economic Well-Being	1. Change in CBD business activity	None	Slight decrease?	Slight increase?
	2. Change in profits of private parking firms (millions of dollars per year)	0	13.0	−1.6 to −0.09
	3. Parking congestion in nearby residential neighborhoods	Moderate	High	Moderate
Public Acceptability	Public acceptability	Diffuse complaints	Drivers and CBD business owners oppose	Drivers oppose; bus riders favor

Valuing Alternatives in Terms of Goals and Their Impact Categories

Once you have made predictions of the consequences of each alternative for each impact category, the next step is to value the predictions in terms of their contributions to the goals. In some cases, the predictions themselves may already be appropriate valuations. For example, in an analysis with multiple impact categories for efficiency, many of which cannot be monetized, "lives saved" is an impact category that has a natural evaluative interpretation—more lives saved are better than fewer. In other cases, however, you must convert the impact categories into more evaluative forms. So, for example, if all other impacts can be monetized, it may be desirable to translate "lives saved" into a dollar estimate of how much an average member of society would be willing to pay for the corresponding reductions in risk.

If efficiency is the only relevant goal, and monetization is possible, then the choice rule is simply to select the alternative that gives the greatest excess of discounted benefits over discounted costs. If you have constructed a separate prediction matrix, it will typically express impacts in units that are not readily comparable. By introducing a common metric for several impacts, you can make them directly comparable. In this way, impacts can be aggregated into a smaller number of categories. Cost-benefit analysis serves as an extreme example—it requires that all impacts be valued in dollars. More generally, some, but not all, impacts can be expressed in the same units. *You should try to make the impact categories as comparable as possible without distorting their relationships to the underlying goals*. By combining impacts that are truly commensurate, you are likely to be able to make manageable comparisons across alternatives better.

When monetization is not appropriate or feasible, valuation must be applied to each impact category. For example, the impact category "variance in service consumption across income groups" can be operationalized for valuation as "minimize the variance in service consumption across income groups." Valuation can sometimes be best done by treating the achievement of some level of the impact category as a constraint. This same impact category might be operationalized as a constraint, such as "families with incomes below the poverty line should be given full access to the service."

Good valuation provides a basis for measuring progress toward achieving a goal. Not every goal can be reasonably quantified as a single objective or constraint, however. It is important that impact categories span all the important dimensions of the goal, and that incommensurate categories not be collapsed in the absence of an appropriate metric. For example, the goal of police investigation is to contribute to the arrest, conviction, and punishment of those who have committed crimes. Police departments often try to operationalize achievement of this goal by the valuation criterion, "maximize the number of reported offenses for which a suspect has been identified." These identifications, sometimes called *clearances*, accumulate with little cost to the police when someone arrested for one offense confesses to many others. If too much weight is placed on getting clearances, then investigators may help suspects get lenient sentences in return for admissions that clear reported offenses. The end result may be what Jerome Skolnick describes as a reversal of the hierarchy of penalties found in the substantive law, whereby those who have committed more crimes receive less severe punishments.[27] Further, investigators may also be tempted to make inappropriate arrests.

Rather than emphasize a single impact category that only measures one dimension of a goal, your valuation should cover all the important impact categories. With respect to investigation, for instance, maximizing the number of convictions and the sum of sentences given to those convicted as well as clearances might to-

[27]Jerome H. Skolnick, *Justice without Trial: Law Enforcement in Democratic Society* (New York: John Wiley, 1966), 174–79.

gether serve as an appropriate set of impacts. Of course, having three impacts rather than one forces you to consider the appropriate weights for deciding which policy is best for achieving the underlying goal. This added complexity is an unavoidable complication of trying to provide an appropriate basis for assessing progress toward a broad goal.

As these examples suggest, you should exercise considerable care in selecting and valuing impact categories to measure the achievement of goals. Always ask yourself: How closely do high scores in the impact categories correspond to progress toward goals? Asking this question is especially important because analysts and clients tend to focus attention on those impact categories that can be easily measured.[28] A sort of Gresham's law operates: *easily measured impact categories tend to drive less easily measured ones from analytical attention.* This tendency may lead us astray when the easily measurable impacts fail to cover all the important dimensions of the goal. For example, casualties inflicted on the enemy is one impact category for measuring success in war. It may be secondary to other impacts—the relative morales of the opposing sides, their respective capabilities for protracted struggle, or the control of disputed populations—for measuring progress toward the goal of ultimate victory. Yet, during the height of the Vietnam War, body counts became the primary measure of U.S. success because they could be easily reported as a number on a weekly basis. This emphasis made search-and-destroy missions appear relatively more effective than efforts to establish stable political control over the population, even though the latter might very well have contributed more to the chances of victory.[29]

We illustrate the valuation process by returning to the prediction matrix shown in Table 14.2. Four impact categories are associated with the goal, access to the CBD: the number of vehicles entering the CBD during rush hour and the average delay they face, and the number of commuter-bus riders and the average delay they face. As long as we consider an hour of delay faced by an automobile-commuter to be equivalent to an hour of delay faced by a bus-commuter, we can calculate the total commuter-hours of delay under each of the alternatives. We would thus have a single valuation criterion derived from the four impact categories associated with the general goal of access to the CBD. In other words, we might replace the four impact categories used in prediction with a single one for purposes of valuation. Depending on the complexity of prediction and valuation, it may be desirable to provide both the prediction and valuation goals/alternatives matrices, or simply the valuation matrix with an explanation of how the valuation was made. If only the valuation matrix is to be presented, then the initial set of goals and impact categories should be revised to be consistent with it.

The impact category, commuter-hours of delay, is still not directly comparable to the other categories in Table 14.2. Note that the impact categories under the goal "Fiscal Health" are measured in dollars and, therefore, could be combined using a single criterion we could call "net program costs." If we wanted to compare directly commuter-hours of delay with net program costs, then we would have to

[28]As Vincent N. Campbell and Daryl C. Nichols state, "... there is a tendency to undermine the purpose of stating objectives (to make clear what you want) by stating only those things that can be measured easily." "Setting Priorities among Objectives," *Policy Analysis* 3(4) 1977, 561–78, at pp. 561–62.

[29]Alain C. Entoven and K. Wayne Smith, *How Much Is Enough? Shaping the Defense Program, 1961–1969* (New York: Harper & Row, 1971), 295–306.

find a way of putting a dollar value on delay. One approach, often used by economists, is to assume that people value leisure time, which delay reduces, at about half of their wage rate.[30] You can make a dollar estimate of the value of improved access relative to current policy by multiplying the reduction in hours of delay by one-half of the average after-tax wage rate for the city. You might call the resulting criterion "monetized value of reductions in delays."

For example, using an average wage rate of $8 per hour, the dollar cost of delay would be $16.6 million per year under current policy (80,000 commuters per day times 0.02 hour per commuter per day times $4 per commuter per hour times 260 days per year), between $8.1 million and $14.1 million per year under alternative 2 (the doubling of parking fees), and between $11.8 million and $14.0 million per year under alternative 3 (the creation of express bus lanes). Compared to current policy, therefore, alternative 2 would reduce the monetized cost of delay by between $2.5 million and $8.5 million; alternative 3 would reduce the monetized cost of delay by between $2.6 million and $4.8 million.

You could next add your estimate of avoided delay cost impacts to net program costs to create a new valuation, "net monetized benefits," which implicitly assumes a one-to-one trade-off between the dollar measures of access to the CBD and fiscal health. Is "net monetized benefits" an appropriate amalgamation of the two impacts? From the perspective of the city government, the answer might very well be no, for a number of reasons: First, the delay encountered by bus commuters may not be as important to the city council as the delay encountered by drivers because a higher proportion of the latter are city residents. Second, the city council may be unwilling to trade program costs and revenues, which show up in the budget, dollar-for-dollar against monetized delay costs, which are diffuse and indirect. Indeed, if bus service were provided by an independent agency, the city council undoubtedly would want to see a separate listing of bus fares and parking fees in the revenue estimates.

"Net monetized benefits" would not be an appropriate valuation from the social welfare (efficiency) perspective. While program expenditures generally represent payments for real resources that could have been used to produce goods elsewhere in society, program revenues include transfers of money from parking fees to the city. These transfers would not be counted in a standard cost-benefit analysis done from the perspective of society as a whole. (We explore such issues in greater depth in Chapter 16.) These considerations thus suggest that "net monetized benefits" is an inappropriate valuation of the goals of "Access to the CBD" and "Fiscal Health." You might reasonably report it as one of your summary measures, however, as long as you keep "monetized value of reductions in delays" and "net program costs" as separate valuations.

In summary, you should look for ways to make impact categories comparable. In doing so, however, you should not lose sight of the underlying goals. Remember that your purpose in valuing impacts is to facilitate, rather than obscure, explicit comparison.

[30]Economists generally use 40 to 50 percent of the average after-tax rate as the value of an hour of commuting time saved. Reductions in losses of work time are usually valued at the after-tax wage rate. For an overview of the value of time and other common "shadow prices," see Anthony E. Boardman, David H. Greenberg, Aidan R. Vining, and David L. Weimer, "'Plug-In' Shadow Price Estimates for Policy Analysis," *Annals of Regional Science* 31(3) 1997, 299–324.

Evaluation: Comparing Alternatives across Incommensurable Goals

Choosing the best alternative is trivial when you have either a single goal with commensurate impact categories or an alternative that ranks highest on all impact categories. Unfortunately, reality is rarely so kind. Although you may sometimes be pleasantly surprised, you should expect to find different alternatives doing best in terms of achieving different goals. Your task is to make explicit the trade-offs among goals implied by various choices, so that your client can easily decide the extent to which she shares the values you brought to bear in choosing what you believe to be the best alternative. In other words, *you should continue to be overt about values in the final phase of evaluation.*

You should also be explicit about uncertainty. Rarely will you be able to predict and value impacts with great certainty. The scores you give alternatives for the impact categories usually constitute your best guesses. If your predictions are based on statistical or mathematical models, then your best guesses may correspond to sample means or expected values and you may be able to estimate or calculate variances as measures of your confidence in them. More often your best guesses and your levels of confidence in them will be based on your subjective assessment of the available evidence. In situations in which you are generally confident about your best guesses for the major evaluation criteria, a brief discussion of the range of likely outcomes may suffice.

We have already discussed some ways of organizing your evaluation when you are not very confident about your best guesses. When lack of confidence springs from uncertainty about relevant conditions in the future, you can construct a number of scenarios that cover the probable range. You can then choose the best alternative under each scenario. If one appears to dominate under all scenarios, then you can choose it with some confidence. If no alternative dominates, then you can make your choice either on the basis of the best outcomes under the most likely scenarios or on the basis of avoiding the worst outcomes under any plausible scenario. In either case, you should discuss why you think your approach is the most appropriate one.

Sometimes your confidence in your best guesses will vary greatly across alternatives. You may be very certain about your valuations to some alternatives, but very uncertain about others. One approach is to conduct a "best case," "most likely case," and "worst case" evaluation for each of the alternatives with very uncertain outcomes. You must then decide which case is most relevant for comparisons with other alternatives. Another approach is to create a new goal, perhaps labeled "minimize likelihood of regret," that gauges how probable it is that the actual outcome will be substantially less favorable than the best guess. You could then treat this new goal as just another incommensurable goal.

No matter from what source, as the number of goals or impact categories deserving prominence rises, the complexity of comparison becomes greater. In the face of such complexity, it may be tempting to resort to a more abstract decision rule. For instance, you might begin by scoring the alternatives on a scale of 1 to 10 for each of the criteria (say, ten points for fully satisfying the criterion, zero points for not satisfying it all). One possible decision rule is to select the alternative that has the highest sum of scores; another is to select the alternative with the highest product of scores.

Although rules such as these can sometimes be useful, we recommend that you *not* use them as substitutes for detailed comparisons of the alternatives. Simple decision rules tend to divert attention from trade-offs and the values implied in making them. Also, they invariably impose arbitrary weights on incommensurate goals. In other words, we urge caution in their use because they tend to obscure rather than clarify the values underlying choice.

One abstract decision rule that we believe is often appropriate for simplifying choice is the *"go, no go" rule*. To apply it, you must set a threshold level of acceptability for each goal. For example, if a goal (or impact category) is to "minimize SO_2 emissions," the threshold might be a reduction of at least 8.0 million tons per year from the levels in some base year. Once you have established thresholds for all the goals, you simply eliminate those alternatives that fail to pass any of the thresholds. If a single alternative remains, then you can accept it as the only one that has a "go" on every goal. If two or more alternatives remain, then you can focus your attention on them, making detailed comparisons in terms of trade-offs among goals. The difficult case arises when no alternative, including current policy, gets a "go" on every goal. You must then either develop better alternatives or lower some of the threshold levels!

In the decisions we make in our everyday lives, we often predict, value, and choose implicitly and incompletely. Indeed, our goals and alternatives often remain unspecified. When decisions are routine, our experience allows us to take these shortcuts with little risk of serious error. When the decision problems are novel or complex, however, we run the risk of missing important considerations when we do not explicitly value all of our alternatives in terms of all of our goals.

Presenting Recommendations

The final step in the rationalist mode of analysis is to give advice. Specifically, you should clearly and concisely answer three questions: First, what do you believe your client should do? Second, why should your client do it? And third, how should your client do it? Answers to the first two questions should come directly from your evaluation of alternative policies. Your answer to the third should include a list of the specific actions that your client must take to secure adoption and implementation of the recommended policy.

We offer several heuristics to help guide your presentation of recommendations. First, *your recommendations should follow from your evaluation of the alternatives (step S4)*. While this may seem obvious, we think it is worth stating. Sometimes what seem to be good ideas for policy solutions take form only as your deadline gets near. Resist the temptation to introduce these new alternatives as recommendations. The proper approach is to redo your specification and evaluation of alternatives so that the new candidate is systematically compared with the others. Otherwise you risk giving advice that you may later regret. One reason that we advocate working in a nonlinear way toward completion of the steps in the rationalist mode is that doing so increases the chances that good ideas arise early enough to be treated seriously.

Second, *you should briefly summarize the advantages and disadvantages of the policy that you recommend*. Why should your client accept your recommendation? What benefits can be expected? What will be the costs? Are there any risks that deserve consideration? By answering these questions, you appropriately draw your client's attention to the consequences of following your advice.

Finally, *you must provide a clear set of instructions for action*. Exactly what must your client do to realize the policy that you recommend? Sometimes the set of instructions can be very short. For example, if your client is a legislator, then the instruction "Vote for bill X" may be adequate. Often, however, adoption and implementation of your recommendation require a much more complex set of actions by your client. For example, imagine that you recommend to the director of the county social services department that funds be shifted from one day-care vendor to another. When and how should approval be secured from the county manager? Is it necessary to consult with the county's legal department? When and how should the vendors be notified? When and how should participating families be notified? Should any members of the county legislature be briefed in advance? Which staff members should be assigned to monitor the transition? These questions may seem mundane. Nonetheless, with a little thought, you should be able to imagine how failing to answer any one of them might jeopardize the successful implementation of the recommended policy. To do so systematically, you should prepare an implementation scenario as outlined in Chapter 11.

Communicating Analysis

The format of your policy analysis plays an important part in determining how effectively you communicate your advice to your client. Clients vary greatly in their levels of technical and economic sophistication; you should write your analysis accordingly. Generally, however, clients share several characteristics: (1) they usually want to play some role in shaping the analysis (but they do not want to *do* the analysis); (2) they are busy and they face externally driven timetables; and (3) they are nervous about using the work of untested analysis when they have to "carry the can" for it in the policy arena. These generalizations suggest some guidelines on how to present your work.

Structuring Interaction

Often you can productively involve your client in the analysis by sharing a preliminary draft. Do so early enough so that you can make use of your client's comments, but not so early that you appear confused or uninformed. By trying to prepare full drafts of your analysis at regular intervals over the course of your project, you force yourself to identify the major gaps that you must yet fill. Giving your client the opportunity to comment on one of these intermediate drafts will usually be more effective than ad hoc oral interactions. Of course, if you believe that your client is a better listener than reader (perhaps because you can only claim your client's time and attention through an appointment), you may find oral progress reports, perhaps structured by a prepared agenda, to be more effective. Be flexible. Use whatever type of communication that seems to work best in the particular context.

You can improve the effectiveness of your written interaction by carefully structuring your draft. You should follow two general guidelines: First, decompose your analysis into component parts; and second, make the presentation within the components clear and unambiguous. These guidelines are not only appropriate for your final product, but they also promote effective communication as intermediate stages by allowing your client to focus on those components that seem weak or unconvincing. Decomposition and clarity also tend to crystallize disagreement between you and your client. Although this may seem like a disadvantage, it usually is not. By crystallizing disagreement at an early stage in your project, your draft analysis helps you determine which of your client's beliefs might be changed with further evidence and which are rigid. In this way your preliminary drafts and other structured interaction with your client reduce the chances that your analysis will ultimately be rejected.

The steps in the rationalist mode, shown in Figure 14.1, provide a general outline for decomposing your analysis. While your final analysis must be written as if you began with the problem description (step P1) and moved sequentially to your recommendations (step S5), you should not necessarily try to write (as opposed to present) the components of your preliminary drafts in strict order lest you encounter the "analysis paralysis" we mentioned earlier. Obviously, the steps cannot be treated as if they were completely independent. For example, the impact categories you choose for evaluating your alternatives (step S1) cannot be finalized until you have specified the relevant goals (step P2). But very early in your project you should try to write a draft of each of the components as best you can. This effort forces you to think configuratively and anticipate the sort of information you will need to make the final draft effective. This may be particularly valuable in helping you move from problem to solution analysis so that you do not end up with an overdeveloped description of the status quo and an underdeveloped analysis of alternative policies.

Keeping Your Client's Attention

Clients are typically busy people with limited attention spans. Reading your analysis will be only one of many activities that compete for your client's attention. You bear the burden of producing a written analysis that anticipates your client's limited time and attention.[31]

While most of our suggestions stress presentational issues, timeliness is by far the most important element. If you are trying to inform some decision, then you must communicate your advice before the decision must be made. Sometimes clients can delay decisions. Often, however, the need to vote, choose a project, approve a budget, or take a public stand places strict deadlines on clients and, therefore, on their analysts. While you should always strive for excellence, keep in mind that an imperfect analysis delivered an hour before your client must make a decision will almost always be more valuable to your client than a perfect analysis delivered an hour after the decision has been made.

You can facilitate more effective communication with busy clients by following a few straightforward rules: provide an executive summary and a table of contents; set priorities for your information; use headings and subheadings that tell a story; be succinct; and carefully use diagrams, tables, and graphs.

Your analysis should not read like a mystery. Rather than holding your client in suspense, tell her your recommendations at the very beginning in an *executive*

[31]For an interesting discussion of policy communication in organizational contexts, see Arnold J. Meltsner and Christopher Bellavita, *The Policy Organization* (Beverly Hills, CA: Sage, 1983), 29–57.

summary. The executive summary should be a concise statement of the most important elements of your analysis including a clear statement of your major recommendations. In a short analysis of a few pages, your first paragraph can serve as an executive summary, with a statement of your recommendation at the end of the paragraph where one would normally look for a topic sentence. An analysis of more than a few pages should have a separate executive summary that stands on its own. It should generally be structured so that the last sentence of your first paragraph presents your recommendation and the subsequent paragraphs rehearse the analysis that supports it. Your objective should be to produce a concise statement that clearly conveys the essence of your advice and why you are offering it.

A *table of contents* enables your client to see at a glance where your analysis is going. It presents the structure of your decomposition so that your client can focus on aspects of particular interest. Together with the executive summary, the table of contents enables your client to skip portions of your analysis without losing the major points. While we all want people to read what we write, you should consider yourself successful (at least in a presentational sense) if your client takes your advice on the basis of your executive summary and table of contents alone.

You should arrange your material so that a client who reads sequentially through your analysis encounters the most important material first. Usually a ten-page analysis is not nearly as useful to the busy client as a five-page analysis with five pages of appendices. But doesn't the client still have to read ten pages of material? Only if she wants to! By breaking the analysis into five pages of text and five pages of appendices, you have taken the responsibility for prioritizing the information. As you and your client develop an ongoing relationship, your client may find it unnecessary to check the background facts and theoretical elucidations provided in the appendices.

Headings and subheadings allow your client to move through an analysis much more quickly. As a general rule, headings should approximately correspond to the steps in the rationalist mode. They should, however, be concise *and* tell a story. For example, rather than the heading "Market Failure," a section of your analysis might be titled "Smokers Do Not Bear the Full Social Costs of Smoking." Similarly, rather than "Government Failure," a preferable heading might be "Why State Price Ceilings Are Leading to Undersupply and Inefficiency." Use headings and subheadings freely—even a few pages of unbroken text can lose your client's attention.

Other presentational devices are also helpful in making your analysis readily useful to your client. Indenting, selective single spacing, numbering, and judicious underlining can all be used to highlight and organize important points in your analysis. The key is to make sure that they draw attention to the material that deserves it. A long series of points or "bullets," especially if expressed in sentence fragments without verbs, not only denies the reader adequate explanation but also fails to highlight the really important points. Even if you occasionally use bullets or other highlights for emphasis, continue to rely on the paragraph as the main unit of presentation.

Diagrams, graphs, and tables can be very useful for illustrating, summarizing, and emphasizing information. Use them, but use them sparingly, so that they draw attention to important information. Like headings, their titles should tell a story. All their elements should be labeled completely so that they can be understood with little or no reference to the text. Be sure you appropriately round all numerical

Table 14.3 *Communicating Policy Analyses*

Do	*Remember the client!* Keep in mind that your task is to provide useful advice. *Set priorities!* Organize your information carefully (essential material in the text, supporting material in appendices). *Decompose* your analysis into component parts. *Use headings that tell a story*. Avoid abstract headings such as "Market Failure." *Be balanced!* Give appropriate coverage to problem analysis and solution analysis. *Acknowledge uncertainty* but then provide your resolution of it. (Support your resolution with sensitivity analysis where appropriate.) *Be credible* by documenting as extensively as possible. *Be succinct*. *Avoid jargon* and clearly explain any technical terms. *Be value overt*. Make explicit arguments for the importance of goals. *Write crisp text*. Favor short and direct sentences; use the active voice.
Don't	*Write an essay!* The difference between an essay and a well-structured policy analysis should be clear to you by now. *Tell the client everything that you know as it comes into your head*. It's fine to think nonlinearly, but write linearly. *Write a mystery!* Instead, state your important conclusions up front in an executive summary.

information—the number of significant figures should be determined by your least accurate data rather than the number mechanically calculated by your computer. We offer Table 14.3 as a summary of our major suggestions on communication.

Be succinct! Keep the text focused on the logic of your analysis. Relegate tangential points and interesting asides to your files; or, if you think they might be useful in some way to your analysis, put them in footnotes or appendices. Be careful not to cut corners with jargon; use only technical terms that your client will understand. (Sometimes you might purposely include unfamiliar technical terms to prepare your client for debate with others—your task then is to explain the terms in the clearest possible manner.)

Try to write crisp text. Start paragraphs with topic sentences. Favor simple over complex sentences. Use the active rather than passive voice to keep your text lively: "I estimate the cost to be ..." rather than "The cost was estimated to be. ... " Allow yourself time to edit your own text, especially if you tend to be wordy.

Establishing Credibility

Until you have established a track record as a reliable analyst, you should expect your clients to be somewhat nervous about relying on your analysis. After all, they are the ones who will bear the political and career risks from following your advice. Therefore, if you want your advice to be influential, you must establish the credibility of your analysis.

You can enhance the credibility of your analysis in several ways. First, make sure that you cite your sources completely and accurately. Of course, you will find this easier to do if you have kept clear notes on your library and field research.

Second, flag uncertainties and ambiguities in theories, data, facts, and predictions. You do a great disservice to your client by hiding uncertainty and ambiguity, not just because it is intellectually dishonest but also because it may set your client up to be blindsided by others in the policy arena who have more sophisticated views. After flagging uncertainties and ambiguities, you should resolve them to the extent necessary to get on with the analysis. (Perhaps a "balance of evidence" will be the best you can do.) You should always check the implications of your resolution of uncertainty for your recommendations. Where your recommendations are very sensitive to the particular resolution, you should probably report on the implications of making a range of resolutions. For example, instead of just working through your evaluation of policy alternatives under your "base-case" assumptions, you might present evaluations under "best-case" and "worst-case" assumptions as well.

Finally, as we have already argued, you should be "value overt." Clearly set out the important goals and explain why you believe that they are important. Also, explain why you have rejected goals that others might believe important. Your explication of goals is especially important if you wish to argue to your client that she should alter her goals or give them different emphases.

Meta-Analysis Once Again: Combining Linear and Nonlinear Approaches

What we have called the rationalist mode of policy analysis consists of eight sequential steps, beginning with understanding the policy problem (step P1) and ending with presenting recommendations (step S5). These steps promote logical and comprehensive analysis. Rather than viewing them as the sequence that you should follow to produce analysis, however, you should think of them more as the outline for your final product. Someone who just reads your final report should be left with the impression that you followed the steps in sequence, even if someone else following your efforts from start to finish observed you jumping and iterating among them. Indeed, we believe that you generally should jump and iterate, working nonlinearly toward your linear product.

A brief reflection on our discussions of gathering information, specifying goals, and designing alternatives should make apparent why we urge you to work nonlinearly. Rarely do you know what information is available before you start gathering it—as noted in the previous chapter, one source leads to another. You may not be able to specify realistic goals until you have considered the range of feasible policy alternatives. Ideas for new alternatives may not emerge until you start to evaluate the ones you have initially designed. As we have noted, the policies advocated by interested parties can help you determine how they view "the problem," perhaps helping you to understand it better yourself.

We offer a practical hint for helping you combine the linear and nonlinear approaches: begin your analysis by starting a file (actually, both an electronic and a hard copy file usually help) for each of the steps in the rationalist mode—descriptions and models of the problem, goals, solution methods (though often this file can be closed very early), impact categories, alternatives, predictions, valuations, and recommendations. As you gather information, insights will come to you. Write them down in the appropriate file. Even if they do not survive in your final analysis, they not only help you get started but also provide a record of how your own thinking has progressed, something that may be useful when you think about how to communicate your analysis effectively to others.

Working with parallel files may have the added advantage of reducing the anxiety you face in writing to meet deadlines. If you already have a start on each of the components, then putting together the complete analysis will be less traumatic.[32] You can help yourself even more by occasionally going through the files to convert your insights and information into paragraphs. Doing so forces you to confront the weak links in your arguments, thereby helping you focus your attention on critical questions and required information. Also, some of the paragraphs may survive to your final draft, thus sparing you the anxiety of facing a blank page as your deadline approaches.

Once you have had some experience in doing policy analysis, take some time to reanalyze yourself. If you find yourself becoming paralyzed at one step or another, then you should probably try to force yourself to work more configuratively. (You may find it helpful to try to draft a full analysis about midway to your final deadline.) If you have trouble organizing and presenting your analysis, then you should probably try to follow the steps in the rationalist mode more closely.

Conclusion

Our focus in this chapter has been on policy analysis as the process of providing useful written advice to a client. We set out a series of sequential steps, the rationalist mode, that should help you structure your written product. We emphasized, however, that you should think configuratively about the steps as you gather information and work toward a final product. Although we have provided considerable practical advice, the analytical process cannot be reduced to a simple formula. That is why doing policy analysis is so interesting and doing good policy analysis is so challenging. Chapter 1 provides an example of a policy analysis in the format outlined in this chapter; Chapter 15 gives some examples of goals/alternatives matrices to illustrate this important focus of policy analyses.

For Discussion

1. Construct a goals/alternatives matrix for the Madison taxi regulation analysis presented in Chapter 9. How would your goals have to change if an alternative were added that involved the city organizing a common dispatching system for all taxi companies?
2. What goals might be relevant for assessing allocation systems for transplant organs?

[32] If you suffer from writer's block, then you might want to look at Martin H. Krieger, "The Inner Game of Writing," *Journal of Policy Analysis and Management* 7(2) 1988, 408–16.

15

Goals / Alternatives Matrices

Some Examples from CBO Studies

The rationalist approach set out in Chapter 14 provides a framework for doing comprehensive policy analysis. Among the various heuristics we offered for guiding the application of the rationalist approach, perhaps the most important and generally useful one is that *you should predict and value the effects of each alternative on **every** goal and **every** impact category relating to a goal.* The goals/alternatives matrix, or its variations, serves as a score sheet for helping analysts implement this heuristic. It also helps to communicate goals, alternatives, and their trade-offs to clients. In this chapter, we briefly discuss some examples of these types of matrices from policy analyses prepared by the Congressional Budget Office (CBO).

We draw on CBO studies for several reasons. First, CBO has a highly professional staff that has enabled it to establish a reputation of neutrality and nonpartisanship. Charges of partisanship from Republicans during the years following its creation in 1975 largely disappeared in the early 1980s, and it now seems to enjoy the same strong support under the Republican Congress that it enjoyed under predominantly Democratic Congresses during the first two decades of its operation. Second, CBO analysts do a variety of analytical tasks, ranging from answering questions raised by the staffs of congressional committees to major studies of policy issues. Among the latter are comprehensive policy analyses, though generally without explicit recommendations. Third, and ultimately most important for our purposes, CBO publishes many of its comprehensive analyses. Copies can be easily obtained from research libraries or directly from CBO. Many of the most recent studies, including three of the four discussed in this chapter, can be obtained from the CBO Web page (*www.cbo.gov*).

Limitations of space force us to restrict our discussion of the examples to brief sketches of the analyses from which they are drawn. Those attempting to do their first policy analyses may wish to refer to the complete versions of these studies, as well as to the sample analysis presented in Chapter 1, as models for presentation.

Setting Out Broad Options: Auctioning Radio Spectrum Licenses

The radio spectrum has immense value in the production of communication services. The Radio Act of 1912 (P.L. 62-204) claimed ownership of the radio spectrum for the federal government, but gave the secretary of commerce limited authority to regulate private users.[1] What was essentially a free good before radiobroadcasting technology replaced point-to-point transmissions became an open-access good during the early 1920s with broadcasters often interfering with each other as they strayed from allocated frequencies. The Federal Radio Act of 1927 (P.L. 69-632) established greater regulatory powers to be exercised for the "public interest, convenience, and necessity." The Federal Communications Act of 1934 (P.L. 73-416) gave these regulatory powers to the Federal Communications Commission (FCC), which soon began to use comparative hearings to allocate spectrum licenses when there were multiple applicants.

Since the beginning of spectrum regulation there have been proposals to allocate licenses by auctions rather than competitive hearings.[2] The potential for raising large sums of revenue gave the idea of auctions a boost in the early 1990s as both Congress and the executive branch looked for ways of reducing the federal deficit. In 1991, the House Committee on the Budget requested that CBO examine the arguments for and against auctioning licenses to the radio spectrum. CBO responded with *Auctioning Radio Spectrum Licenses* in March 1992.[3]

Although the CBO analysts were seeking to make a general comparison of auctions with comparative hearings and lotteries, it was necessary for them to specify an auction in sufficient detail so that predictions could be made. They created a "base case" that assumed that two licenses to 25 MHz (megahertz) would be offered, either nationally or locally, in the 1.7 to 2.2 Ghz (gigahertz) range for cellular and other personnel communications services (mobile telephones, two-way paging, portable fax machines, and wireless computer networks). The licensees would have the same property rights as those currently allocated through comparative hearings but would be required to cover the costs of relocating some private users who already had licenses that overlapped those being auctioned. The auctions themselves would be by first-price sealed bid, with the highest bid for the national license winning if it exceeded the sum of all the high local bids.

The analysts decided to compare auctions, comparative hearings, and lotteries in terms of three goals: economic efficiency, fairness, and federal revenue. Notice that the CBO analysts did not feel the need to resort to specific impact categories within these goals. Table 15.1 shows their assessment of the three alternative allocation methods in terms of the three goals. Several aspects of the table are worth noting.

[1]For a review of the early history of spectrum regulation, see Thomas W. Hazlett, "The Rationality of U.S. Regulation of the Broadcast Spectrum," *Journal of Law and Economics* 33(1) 1990, 133–75.

[2]Most notably, Ronald A. Coase, "The Federal Communications Commission," *Journal of Law and Economics* 11(2) 1959, 1–40.

[3]Congressional Budget Office, *Auctioning Radio Spectrum Licenses*, March 1992.

Table 15.1 *License Assignment Methods Compared*

Method	Efficiency	Fairness	Revenues
Comparative Hearing	Might not assign the license directly to the user who values it most. Secondary markets allow license sales to the users who value them most. Consumes substantial private resources in license-seeking activity and inflicts high administrative and delay costs on society.	Can ensure a specific distribution of licenses. Legal and administrative costs of the process give larger financial interests an advantage.	Revenues limited to license application fees. Total FCC fees for 1991 were $46.6 million, including renewals and fees for lotteries. New license fees range from $35 to $70,000. Comparative hearing fee for a new applicant for land-mobile services was $6,760 in 1991.
Lottery	A random process unlikely to assign the license directly to the user who values it most. Secondary markets allow license sales to the users who value them most. Less prone to delay than hearings, less prompt than auctions.	Allows applicants equal opportunity if they can pay the application fee. By awarding licenses to applicants who do not intend to provide services, grants lottery winners a windfall not shared by the public.	Lottery revenues are included in totals noted above. Fees for specific lotteries can be substantial. The digital electronic message service lottery, the 220–222 MHz filing of 1991, drew 60,000 applicants and total fees of $4.4 million.
Auction	Is likely to assign the license directly to the user who values it most. Should assign licenses more quickly and at a lower cost to society than alternatives.	Gives taxpayers a share of spectrum rents. Can be structured to accommodate small bidders.	CBO estimates that an auction of 50 MHz of spectrum for two additional land-mobile licenses could generate between $1.3 billion and $5.7 billion in fiscal years 1993 through 1995.

Source: Congressional Budget Office, *Auctioning Radio Spectrum Licenses,* March 1992, Table 2, p. 18.

First, the entries under efficiency and fairness are qualitative. Each entry provides a brief summary of the analysts' assessment of how a method contributes to a particular goal. The entries under efficiency are clearly comparative—auctions are best at allocating licenses quickly and at low cost to users who value them most. The entries under fairness, however, are less explicitly comparative. Instead, they simply summarize the important impacts of each method relevant to each of the goals. Establishing specific impact categories, such as the impact on access to licenses by smaller financial interests and the extent of scarcity rent capture for taxpayers, would have facilitated clearer prediction and ranking.

Second, entries under revenues provide some quantitative information. The figures for comparative hearings and lotteries are based on experience. The analysts' projected estimates of revenues from the base-case auction, $1.3 billion to $5.7 billion, dwarf the revenue from either of the other allocation methods. As the client, the House Committee on the Budget, was particularly interested in the revenue potential from license auctions, the analysts devoted considerable effort to estimating this range.

The analysts based their low estimate on the $210 million that Fleet Call, Inc., had paid mobile radio operators for the seventy-four licenses it obtained from them between 1987 and 1991 for conversion to cellular telephone service. On average, Fleet paid about $3.50 per person in the service areas it covered. Doubling this amount to take account of the two licenses, and scaling up to cover the populations of all the U.S. metropolitan statistical areas, gave the estimate of $1.3 billion.

The analysts' high estimate was based on a study conducted by Stanley Morgan, Inc., that estimated that a firm entering the land-mobile market could incur $35 to $37 per person in capital and start-up costs and still make an after tax return of 13 to 15 percent, even if prices fell by 35 percent from current levels and consumers made on average 20 percent fewer calls. The analysts estimated capital and start-up costs of $20 to $22 per person, so that $15 per person would remain available for bidding for licenses. Applying this $15 per person figure, which is consistent with the value financial analysts placed on Fleet Call's licenses when it went public in 1992, to the population of U.S. metropolitan statistical areas led to the high estimate of $5.7 billion.

In addition to making their own estimates of revenues, the analysts reviewed estimates made with other methods (acquisition costs and stock value changes), by other agencies (Office of Management and Budget), and from foreign experience (auctions in New Zealand and the United Kingdom). They also provided qualitative assessments of the implications of alternatives to the base-case assumptions.

Postscript: The Omnibus Budget Reconciliation Act of 1993 (P.L. 103-66) authorized the FCC to carry out a five-year experiment in auctioning licenses to spectrum. In order to take account of the fact that collections of adjacent licenses might be more valuable if held by a single firm rather than by different firms, the FCC ultimately selected a simultaneous ascending auction, a novel form of auction suggested by economists Paul Milgrom, Robert Wilson, and Preston McAfee.[4] In a simultaneous ascending auction, bids are made in rounds until no bidder wants to change a bid. Thus, bidders can change their bids as they see possibilities for assembling combinations of licenses covering desired geographic areas. In order to discourage bidders from holding back in early rounds, the FCC adopted rules that require bidders to post bonds that are forfeited if they fail to offer higher bids in successive rounds. In total, the rules established to guide the auctions covered more than 130 pages. The auction of three 30 MHz bands for personal communication services (A, B, and C blocks) in 1994 and 1995 elicited almost $18 billion in winning bids.

Quantitative Predictions: Restructuring the Army

The U.S. Army plans its force structure so as to be able to fight two, nearly simultaneous regional conflicts, usually assumed to occur on the Korean Peninsula and in the Middle East. These conflicts are assumed to require higher ratios of support to combat troops than the army maintained during the cold war to deter a conventional attack by the Soviet Union against North Atlantic Treaty Organization allies. Consequently, the army found itself with too few support personnel to carry out its new primary mission of responding effectively to regional conflicts. In order

[4]R. Preston McAfee and John McMillan, "Analyzing the Airwaves Auction," *Journal of Economic Perspectives* 10(1) 1996, 159–75.

Table 15.2 *Changes in Force Structure under the Army's Plan and Four Alternatives*

Option	Changes in Force Structure
Army's Plan: Reconfigure the National Guard	Convert 12 Guard combat brigades to support units
Alternative I: Increase reliance on host-nation support and civilian contractors	Eliminate four Guard combat divisions Rely on host nations and civilian contractors for the equivalent of 62,000 army support troops in two major regional conflicts
Alternative II: Create additional support forces in the active army	Convert two active duty heavy divisions and one Guard combat division to support units
Alternative III: Combine alternatives I and II	Convert two active duty heavy divisions to support units Eliminate four Guard combat divisions Cut 35,000 support troops from reserve component Rely on host nations and civilian contractors for the equivalent of 62,000 army support troops in two major regional conflicts
Alternative IV: Rely more heavily on the reserves to fight second major regional conflict	Eliminate three active duty divisions (two heavy and one light) and four Guard combat divisions Rely on host nations and civilian contractors for the equivalent of 62,000 army support troops in two major regional conflicts

Note: None of CBO's four alternatives (I to IV) would carry out the army's planned conversion of twelve Guard combat brigades to support units.

Source: Congressional Budget Office, *Structuring the Active and Reserve Army for the 21st Century* (Washington, DC: U.S. Government Printing Office, December 1997), Summary Table 1, p. xvi.

to restructure its forces to provide more support personnel, it proposed converting twelve National Guard brigades to support units.[5]

The Subcommittee on Personnel of the Senate Committee on Armed Services requested the CBO to examine alternatives to the army's plan. The resulting study, *Structuring the Active and Reserve Army for the 21st Century*, was completed in December 1997.[6]

The CBO analysts developed four alternatives to the army's plan; their elements are summarized in Table 15.2. Alternative I would rely on host nations (most likely the Republic of Korea and Saudi Arabia) and civilian contractors to provide services that would otherwise be provided by 62,000 support troops. It would also

[5]The army force structure has three elements: full time soldiers on active duty (active component), part-time soldiers in the Army Reserve who can be called up for active duty by the president (one part of the reserve component), and part-time soldiers in the National Guard who serve under state governors but can be federalized by the president in times of crisis (second part of the reserve component).

[6]Congressional Budget Office, *Structuring the Active and Reserve Army for the 21st Century* (Washington, DC: U.S. Government Printing Office, December 1997).

eliminate four combat divisions from the National Guard. Alternative II would convert two active duty combat divisions and one National Guard division to support units. Alternative III combines the main elements of alternatives I and II—note that the analysts make it an explicit alternative rather than implicitly combining the two alternatives during their analysis. Finally, alternative IV would rely on the host nation and civilian contractors, as in alternatives I and III, but would also rely on reserves to fight the second major regional conflict.

The CBO alternatives were designed so that they would cost less than the army's plan (the assumed status quo) but still provide deployment times to the theaters of operation that were at least as short. The summary table provided by the analysts, along with their discussion of the advantages and disadvantages of each alternative, suggests four policy goals: First, minimize the budgetary cost of the army. Second, minimize deployment times of forces similar in size to those deployed in the Persian Gulf war (Operation Desert Storm) to each of the theaters of operation. Third, minimize reliance on National Guard combat forces because use of these forces poses a risk in terms of delayed deployment. Fourth, minimize reliance on host-nation support because doing so poses risks in terms of the actual availability of appropriate support.

The top half of Table 15.3 provides quantitative predictions under a number of impact categories associated with each of these four goals. (The bottom half of the table provides a systematic summary of the force structures and personnel levels for each alternative.)

The "Average Annual Savings or Costs" impact category shows predicted budgetary impacts relative to the current army force structure. The direct savings result from reductions of personnel in deployable combat and support units, while total savings also include reductions of personnel who provide training and administrative services in nondeployable units based in the United States. These savings are further divided into those occurring through 2010, the restructuring period under the army's plan, and those occurring after 2010. Thus, total savings through 2010 and after 2010 serve as two valuation criteria for assessing progress toward the goal of reducing the budgetary cost of the army.

The "Deployment Times" impact category gives the predicted number of days after the start of the first conflict needed to deliver all the personnel and equipment needed to fight each of the regional conflicts. The three CBO alternatives that involve relying more heavily on host-nation support would permit faster deployments to each of the theaters than the army's plan by reducing the amount of matériel that would have to be transported.

The "Combat Forces from the Guard Needed for the Second Conflict" impact category predicts the performance of the alternatives in terms of the risk of deployment delays. The larger is the number of combat brigades from the National Guard required for deployment (all to second theater), the higher is the risk of delayed deployment. If the analysts had had a way of confidently translating reliance on National Guard combat brigades directly into risk estimates, then the latter could have been reported in the table as well.

The "Assumed Extent of Host-Nation Support" impact category predicts the risk of problems in the supply of support services. The greater is the number of soldier-equivalents of host-nation support, the greater is the risk that logistical problems will be encountered during deployment. As with the risks of reliance on

Table 15.3 *Effect of the Army's Plan and Four Alternatives on Annual Costs, Deployment Times, and Number of Forces*

	Army in 1998	Army's Plan[a]	Alternatives I	II	III	IV
Average Annual Savings or Costs (–) (millions of 1997 dollars)						
1998–2010						
Direct savings	n.a.	–200 to –400	700	–200	850	2,500
Total savings	n.a.	–200 to –400	1,200	–200	1,550	4,500
After 2010						
Direct savings	n.a.	0[b]	800	100	1,300	2,950
Total savings	n.a.	0[b]	1,400	100	2,150	5,250
Deployment Time (days after start of first conflict)[c]						
First theater	130	130	120	130	120	120
Second theater[d]	200	230	200	230	200	200
Combat Forces from the Guard Needed for the Second Conflict[e]						
Combat brigades	0	0	0	6	6	9
Assumed Extent of Host-Nation Support						
Soldier-equivalents	15,000	15,000	62,000	10,000	62,000	62,000
Changes in Deployable Forces						
Active Component						
Combat divisions	n.a.	0	0	–2	–2	–3
Combat personnel	n.a.	0	0	–33,000	–33,000	–44,000
Support personnel	n.a.	0	0	33,000	33,000	0
Reserve Component						
Combat divisions (Guard)	n.a.	–4[f]	–4	–1	4	4
Combat personnel (Guard)	n.a.	–42,700	–58,300	–15,000	–58,300	–58,300
Support personnel (Guard & Reserve)	n.a.	42,700	0	15,000	–35,000	0
Total Force Structure						
Combat Divisions						
Active component	10	10	10	8	8	7
Reserve component (Guard)	8	6[g]	4	7	4	4
Deployable Support Forces						
Active component	136,000	136,000	136,000	169,000	169,000	136,000
Reserve component	291,000	333,700	291,000	306,000	256,000	291,000
Total Personnel						
Active army	495,000	495,000	495,000	495,000	495,000	430,300
Army National Guard	367,000	367,000	305,000	367,000	287,100	305,000
Army Reserve	208,000	208,000	208,000	208,000	189,600	208,000

[a] Does not include personnel cuts recommended by the Quadrennial Defense Review.

[b] Some small savings in operation and maintenance costs may result from converting combat units to support units.

[c] Time required to deliver all troops and equipment needed to fight each of two major regional conflicts.

[d] Assumes the second conflict begins 45 days after the first.

[e] To form the equivalent of 5 1/3 divisions.

[f] Two divisions and six separate brigades.

[g] Although the army's plan would retain six combat divisions in the National Guard, it would reduce the number of separate brigades from 18 to 12, an additional reduction equivalent to two combat divisions.

Source: Congressional Budget Office, *Structuring the Active and Reserve Army for the 21st Century* (Washington, DC: U.S. Government Printing Office, December 1997), Summary Table 2, pp. xviii–xix.

National Guard combat brigades, the analysts had no way of confidently translating soldier-equivalents into a quantitative measure of risk.

Comparing across these impacts, it is clear that the CBO analysts constructed alternatives to the army's plan that trade higher levels of risk in the speed of deployment for reductions in budgetary costs. The alternatives also vary with respect to the source of added risk they involve. For example, alternative II involves greater risk from reliance on National Guard combat brigades but slightly smaller risk in terms of assumed host-nation support than the army's plan. In contrast, alternative I involves substantially higher risk in terms of assumed host-nation support but no greater risk than the army's plan from reliance on National Guard combat brigades.

Comparing Proposed Alternatives: Launching Digital Television

Digital communication technologies, which allow more information to be transmitted within a given bandwidth of electromagnetic spectrum than the older analog technologies, have created opportunities for new and enhanced uses of the spectrum, including the replacement of analog television with digital television. The switch to digital TV technology would allow broadcasters either to transmit much higher-quality pictures and sound or to squeeze as many as six programs of current quality into each 6 MHz channel. As digital signals are less prone to interference, the switch to digital TV would also allow the channels to be packed closer together, thereby freeing up spectrum for other uses. The transition to digital TV broadcasting also has its costs—consumers either would have to add adapters to their analog TVs or replace them with digital TVs.

In *Where Do We Go from Here? The FCC Auctions and the Future of Radio Spectrum Management*, a study requested by the House Committee on the Budget, CBO analysts assessed the FCC spectrum auctions that had already been held, projected revenues from planned auctions, and considered additional areas in which auctions might be used in the future.[7] With regard to the latter, the analysts compared a number of proposed alternatives, including several that involved auctions, for introducing digital TV.

The analysts took as a baseline, or status quo policy, the proposal that had been the primary focus of FCC proceedings on digital TV. The baseline assumes that the FCC gives each current broadcaster a second channel for digital broadcasting. After a transition period of about fifteen years, the FCC would reclaim the analog channels and reposition the digital channels to pack them more closely together. The freed-up spectrum would then be reallocated to general use through auctions.

The analysts compared the baseline to the five alternatives most prominently discussed during 1996. As shown in Table 15.4, the alternatives can be divided

[7]Congressional Budget Office, *Where Do We Go from Here? The FCC Auctions and the Future of Radio Spectrum Management* (Washington, DC: U.S. Government Printing Office, April 1997).

Table 15.4 *Summary of Plans for Introducing Digital TV*

Plan	Spectrum to Be Auctioned Licensees	Identity of Digital TV Broadcasting	Termination of Analog TV Use	TV Spectrum	
				Reallocated for General Use	Remaining
Baseline	Frequencies reclaimed and reallocated for general use	Current broadcasters	15 years after plan starts, subject to review	138 MHz	264 MHz for digital TV
Accelerated Use: Early Return	Frequencies reclaimed and reallocated for general use	Current broadcasters	2005	138 MHz	264 MHz for digital TV
Accelerated Use: 60–69	Overlay licenses on channels 60 to 69; other frequencies reclaimed later	Current broadcasters	15 years after plan starts, subject to review	138 MHz	264 MHz for digital TV
Up-Front Auction	Digital TV channels	Highest bidders	Upon decision of individual analog licensee and notification of service area	None	402 MHz for digital and analog TV; licensees may be allowed to offer other services
Full Overlay: Pressler	Overlay licenses on all TV frequencies	Current broadcasters willing to pay deposit	Upon decision of individual analog licensee and provision of free replacement service	402 MHz	None reserved for TV
Full Overlay: Right-to-Move	Overlay licenses on all TV frequencies	Current broadcasters	Upon decision of individual analog licensee and provision of free replacement service	402 MHz, except for frequencies locally occupied by digital TV licensees (average of 80 MHz)	No reserved blocks, but digital TV stations occupy an average of 80 MHz

Source: Congressional Budget Office, *Where Do We Go from Here? The FCC Auctions and the Future of Radio Spectrum Management* (Washington, DC: U.S. Government Printing Office, April 1997), Table 8, p. 52

into three categories. One category, which includes "Early Returns" and "60–69," has elements that would accelerate implementation of the baseline. The second category consists of the "Up-Front Auction," which would allow both broadcasters and nonbroadcasters to bid on new digital channels. The third category, including "Pressler" (named after its advocate, former Senator Larry Pressler) and "Right-to-Move," makes use of what is called "full overlay." Full overlay involves creating licenses for introducing digital services on existing channels. Within the existing channels, considerable unused spectrum is readily available for digital use. One source is the guard bands that are left unused in order to avoid interference between analog broadcasts. Other sources include frequencies held in reserve for future use and frequencies allocated to point-to-point transmissions, such as microwave links, that require use of only small geographic portions of their service areas. Overlay licenses are designed to transfer residual rights to channels from incumbent license holders to the holders of the digital overlay licenses; they may or may not require the holders of the overlay licenses to compensate current users displaced by the introduction of digital services.

Table 15.5 displays a goals/alternatives matrix for the introduction of digital TV. The analysts compared the six alternatives in terms of three policy goals: auction receipts, equity issues, and economic efficiency.

Two of the alternatives, Baseline and 60–69, involve auctions too far in the future for the analysts to be able to confidently predict the revenues likely to result from auctions. Two others, Pressler and Right-to-Move, are also insufficiently specified to allow predictions of auction revenues. Consequently, the analysts predicted auction receipts only for Early Return and Up-Front Auction. At least with respect to the overlay alternatives, the analysts could have provided their own specifications to make the comparison of alternatives more concrete.

The analysts addressed equity issues by describing the implications of each alternative for each of three groups (the relevant impact categories): broadcasters, viewers, and low-power stations. Broadcasters comprise commercial enterprises in large markets. Low-power stations, which include noncommercial stations and stations serving small markets, face potential problems in acquiring capital for the equipment needed for rapid conversion to digital broadcasting. They are also the most likely to be displaced by digital broadcasters during spectrum clearing or through overlay licenses. The analysts raised concerns about viewers served by these stations as well as the costs of adapting their TVs for digital reception.

The analysts provided qualitative descriptions of the implications of each alternative relevant to economic efficiency. In addition, they provided an estimate of the net benefits of Early Return relative to Baseline in a "Box," which can be thought of as an appendix embedded within the text. They estimated that the net benefits of earlier return ranged from zero to as much as $20 billion.

Table 15.6 summarizes the basis for the analysts' estimate of this range. They began estimating the benefits of earlier return by assuming that the benefits of the licenses to winning bidders equal the amount of their bids—$10 billion. Recognizing that this figure does not include gains to consumers, the analysts drew on an FCC study that estimated the ratio of social surplus to the economic gain accruing to a new television station owner to be 3.6. The analysts created a "Low-Case Estimate" assuming a ratio of 25 and a "High-Case Estimate" assuming a ratio of 4. They next assumed that private bids would be based on the present value of the anticipated stream of benefits discounted at a real rate of either 7 or 12 percent. (The distinction between real and nominal discount rates is discussed in Chapter 16.) Assuming that a 2 percent real discount rate is appropriate from the social perspective, the standard CBO assumption, then the social value of the earnings streams will be between 3.34 and 5.46 times higher than indicated by the private bids. The effect of Early Return would be to begin the digital licenses seven years earlier than in Baseline. Again, using the 2 percent real social discount rate, the early start date of the licenses would increase their value by 0.129 of their value under Baseline. Combining these steps led the analysts to estimate a range of benefits from Early Start of between $8.6 billion and $28.2 billion.

Offsetting these benefits, however, are three sorts of costs. First, the earlier start reduces the present value of the services of the existing stock of analog TVs. Second, low-power stations serving rural areas would be forced off the air sooner. Third, the present value of services from analog transmitters would be reduced. Combining these costs and subtracting them from the estimated benefits led the analysts to estimates of a net loss of $600 million in the low case to a gain of $22 billion in the high case. Taking account of the various uncertainties involved in arriving at these estimates, the analysts decided that the most plausible range of efficiency gains was the zero to $20 billion reported in Table 15.5.

Note how the analysts took advantage of an existing study to come up with a crucial piece of information, the likely ratio between bids and total social value, that they needed for their cost-benefit analysis. As they were appropriately cautious in extrapolating from this one study, the analysts created low and high cases to bracket the ratio the study reported. On the one hand, the wide range conveys the inherent uncertainty in the efficiency gains of Early Return over Baseline. On the other hand, the bottom end of the range suggests that Early Return would not be less efficient, and the high end of the range suggests that it could be considerably more efficient. In the real world of deadlines and limited information, finding rough estimates from existing studies and using them as guides for creating ranges of predictions is often the best one can do.

Postscript: On April 3, 1997, as the CBO report was about to be published, the FCC voted to adopt a plan that combined elements of Early Return and 60–69 (FCC Docket No. 87-268). Each of the nation's 1,600 television stations would receive a second channel for broadcasting digital versions of programs. Stations in the ten largest broadcast markets would be required to begin digital broadcasting within two years, and analog broadcasting would cease in 2006. As the broadcasting industry has begun lobbying Congress for legislation that would override provisions of the FCC plan, the analysis of alternatives provided by the CBO is likely to have an extended life.

Table 15.5 *Summary Evaluation of Plans for Introducing Digital TV*

	Auction Receipts		Economic Efficiency		Equity Issues		
Plan	**Estimate**	**Source**	**Main Implications**	**Relative to Baseline Plan**	**Broadcasters**	**Viewers**	**Low-Power Stations**
Baseline	Not estimated	Licensees for new services using cleared spectrum in about 2012	Licenses digital TV; eventually terminates analog TV and clears blocks of spectrum for new uses	Not applicable	Offered use of second 6 MHZ channel during transition period (15 years subject to review); must then surrender analog channel	New digital channels available; unadapted analog sets go dark after 15 years (subject to review)	Many displaced by digital channel assignment and spectrum clearing
Accelerated Use: Early Return	$10 billion in 2002, given other provisions of deficit-reduction plans that would auction another 120 MHz under 3 GHz	Same as baseline plan except receipts come in 2002	Same as baseline plan except transition ends in 2005	Probably more efficient; net gain estimated at roughly zero to $20 billion in 2002	Same as baseline plan except transition ends in 2005	New digital channels available; unadapted analog sets go dark in 2005; viewers of rural "translators" and other small budget stations may lose choices	Same as baseline plan except spectrum is cleared in 2005
Accelerated Use: 60–69	Not estimated	Same as baseline plan except overlay licenses for channels 60 to 69 are auctioned early	Same as baseline plan except some new services start early on channels 60 to 69	More efficient	Same as baseline plan	Same as baseline plan except some viewers of low-power stations on channels 60 to 69 may lose choices sooner	Same as baseline plan except some stations on channels 60 to 69 could be displaced sooner

Up-Front Auction	$12.5 billion in 1998 if all channels are auctioned, or $9.5 billion if noncommercial broadcasters are given digital channels for free	Digital TV licensees	Licenses digital TV; does not mandate termination of analog TV or clear spectrum	Unknown	Face more competition if outbid for digital channels; not obligated to cease analog service	New digital channels available; analog TV continues while sufficient market exists	Many displaced by digital channel assignments
Full Overlay: Pressler	Not estimated	Overlay licensees, plus interest on deposits and surrendered deposits from digital TV licensees	Licenses all TV spectrum; maximizes flexibility of licensees; does not require digital TV; protects free TV but allows it to move off the spectrum	Unknown	Must pay deposit for digital channels; may surrender deposit and keep two channels; need not use the digital channels for TV; may continue analog TV service and must arrange comparable free replacement service to end or reduce it	Digital TV may or may not be available on local broadcast channels; continued free TV on analog sets is guaranteed (but length of guarantee is not specified)	All are subject to displacement by overlay licensees
Full-Overlay: Right-to-Move	Not estimated	Overlay licensees	Similar to Pressler plan but requires digital TV	Probably more efficient	Offered use of second channel; must surrender analog channel to move digital channel if compensated by overlay licensee	New digital channels available; continued free TV on analog sets is guaranteed (but length of guarantee is not specified)	All are subject to displacement by overlay licensees, possibly with compensation required

Source: Congressional Budget Office, *Where Do We Go from Here? The FCC Auctions and the Future of Radio Spectrum Management* (Washington, DC U.S. Government Printing Office, April 1997), Table 9, pp. 57–58.

Table 15.6 *Estimated Benefits and Costs of a Shorter Transition to Digital TV*

	Low-Case Estimate	**High-Case Estimate**
Benefits		
Estimated auction receipts (billions of dollars)	10	10
Ratio of total social gains to licensee payoffs	2	4
Ratio of present values using social and private discount rates (based on social discount rate of 2 percent)	3.34 (Based on 7 percent private discount rate)	5.46 (Based on 12 percent private discount rate)
Share of present value attributable to seven-year head start	0.129	0.129
Estimated Economic Benefits (product of above terms, in billions of dollars)	8.6	28.2
Costs (billions of dollars)		
Value of lost service from analog TV sets	5	2
Value of lost service from rural translator stations	4	4
Depreciated value of analog transmitters	0.2	0.2
Estimated Total Costs	9.2	6.2
Estimated Net Benefits to the Economy (benefits minus costs, in billions of dollars)	–0.6	22

Source: Congressional Budget Office, *Where Do We Go from Here? The FCC Auctions and the Future of Radio Spectrum Management* (Washington, DC: U.S. Government Printing Office, April 1997), Box 4, pp. 60–61.

Combining Policy Alternatives: Improving Water Allocation

Agriculture in the western United States relies heavily on irrigation. During the twentieth century, the Department of the Interior, through its Bureau of Reclamation, spent billions of dollars to develop surface water supplies for western farmers. The allocation of this water at subsidized prices and with restrictions on resale has involved substantial costs for taxpayers who fund the subsidized projects, urban residents who must turn to higher-cost water sources, Native American water users who relied on now-diverted natural water systems, and ecosystems that have lost wetlands and other habitats for wildlife.

Recognizing these costs, in 1992 Congress passed and President George Bush signed into law the Central Valley Project Improvement Act (P.L. 102-575). The CVPIA requires the Bureau of Reclamation to implement a number of policies to increase the efficiency of water allocation and improve environmental quality in one of its largest projects, the Central Valley Project, in California. CVPIA provisions include the introduction of a water market that allows farmers to sell water to other users, allocations of project water for environmental purposes, surcharges on water sales to finance a fish and wildlife restoration fund, and tiered (increasing block-rate) pricing to raise the price of marginal water allotments to the U.S. Treasury's cost of provision.

At the request of the ranking minority member of the House Committee on Resources, CBO conducted a study of the impacts of the provisions of CVPIA with an eye toward assessing the implications of using similar policy tools to improve water allocation in other Bureau of Reclamation water projects. The result of the study, *Water Use Conflicts in the West: Implications for Reforming the Bureau of Reclamation's Water Supply Policies*, was published in August 1997.[8]

In order to investigate the effects of the CVPIA provisions, CBO analysts built a computer simulation model that estimated changes in crop revenues in a year of average rainfall that result from changes in water deliveries to each of three agricultural regions. Within the model, farmers were assumed to adjust crop mixes and acreages to maximize their profits in response to changing water prices, allocations, and resulting crop price changes. Parameters for the model were estimated statistically from crop and water use reports submitted by water districts over the period 1979 to 1991. The model also allowed estimates of the value to consumers of changes in water allocated to urban water districts.

Table 15.7 summarizes the impacts of various combinations of CVPIA provisions on crop revenues, revenues in water markets, and benefits to urban consumers. The row labeled "Baseline" estimates these quantities for a year of average rainfall under the pre-CVPIA allocation provisions. Successive rows add in cumulative succession "Water Markets," "Water Allocated for Environmental Purposes," "Surcharges," and "Rate Increases." It is interesting to note that if one takes reductions in crop revenues as social costs, then water markets alone would easily pass a cost-benefit test: the $17 million loss in crop revenues is exceeded by the $30 million gain in benefits to urban consumers. Further, the transfer of $18 million in the water market from urban consumers to farmers would result in positive net benefits for both farmers and urban consumers.

The analysts addressed the advantages and disadvantages of using reductions in crop revenues as an estimate of social costs. They noted that reductions in water use would also be accompanied by reductions in the costs of other inputs. As net revenues were about 54 percent of gross revenues in the Central Valley, the reductions in crop revenues were probably twice as high as economic costs. On the other hand, if one were concerned about regional economic impacts for distributional or political reasons, then one might apply a multiplier of 0.66 to translate dollars of crop reductions to additional dollars of lost economic activity in the region. Note that this loss in economic activity is not a cost from the national perspective except to the extent that it results in unemployed resources.

Although the analysts did not place an overall dollar value on the benefits of water allocated for environmental purposes, they considered four impact categories of possible benefit. For three of these impact categories—improvements in the commercial fishery, recreational fishing, and wetlands—the analysts extracted dollar per acre-foot estimates from previous studies. For the fourth category, nonuse value, which measures people's willingness to pay for preservation of endangered species, they noted some possibly relevant studies but also discussed the problems of using the dollar estimates they provided.

The analysts did not estimate net benefits of the full package of CVPIA provisions, yet one might proceed as follows to assess its implications for efficiency. The

[8]Congressional Budget Office, *Water Use Conflicts in the West: Implications for Reforming the Bureau of Reclamation's Water Supply Policies* (Washington, DC: Congress of the United States, August 1997).

Table 15.7 *Effect of the Central Valley Improvement Act on Agricultural Water Use, Urban Water Use, and Revenues*

Scenario	Total Agriculture		Water Market		Benefits to Urban Consumers (Millions of dollars)
	Water Use (Thousands of acre-feet)	Crop Revenues (Millions of dollars)	Water Transfers[a] (Thousands of acre-feet)	Water Revenues (Millions of dollars)	
Baseline	5,149	2,645	n.a.	n.a.	4,500
Change from Baseline					
Water markets	–243	–17	243	18	30
Change from Scenario with Water Markets and Water Allocated for Environmental Purposes					
800,000 acre-feet	–758	–62	–42	0	–3
1.2 million acre-feet	–1,134	–99	–66	0	–6
1.35 million acre-feet	–1,276	–113	–74	0	–7
Change from Scenario with Water Market and 1.2 Million Acre-Feet of Water Allocated for Environmental Purposes					
Surcharges	82	8	–82	–9	–10
Surcharges and rate increases[b]	110	11	–110	–11	–14
Change from Baseline					
Package of CVPIA provisions[c]	–1,266	–105	66	7	11

[a] To urban areas in Southern California.
[b] Tiered water prices and repayment rates.
[c] Includes 1.2 million acre-feet of water allocated for environmental purposes.

Source: Congressional Budget Office, *Water Use Conflicts in the West: Implications of Reforming the Bureau of Reclamation's Water Supply Policies* (Washington, DC: Congress of the United States, August 1997), Table 4, p. 44, and Table 5, p. 45. *Note*: Table 5 also includes columns that disaggregate "Total Agriculture" into the western San Joaquin Valley, the Sacramento Valley, and the Friant Region.

full package of CVPIA provisions, including the allocation of 1.2 million acre-feet for environmental purposes, reduces crop revenues by $105 million but increases benefits to urban consumers by $11 million. Thus, excluding environmental benefits and taking 50 percent of crop losses as social costs, the package involves net costs of about $41.5 million. This implies that the environmental benefits would have to be at least $43.75 per acre-foot for the full package to pass a cost-benefit test. As the upper bounds for the estimated ranges of commercial and recreational benefits are close to this level, the package of CVPIA provisions probably increases economic efficiency.

After assessing the likely impact of the CVPIA provisions in the Central Valley, the analysts turned to the question of whether these provisions should be applied to other Bureau of Reclamation projects. They noted three general considerations in this regard: First, policy problems differ across regions, so the goals and impact categories of reform may also differ. For example, environmental impacts may be less significant in some regions. Second, the sensitivity of farmers to changes in water prices may differ markedly across regions because of differences in feasible crops, the cost of irrigated land, and the availability of alternative sources of water. Third, the levels of the various provisions (specific prices and water policies) are as important as the type of provision (price increases, water markets, and allocations of water for environmental purposes). Predicting impacts requires a full specification of the provisions to be applied. Because of these considerations, the CBO analysts suggested that it may be desirable to allow Bureau of Reclamation managers to select from among the CVPIA provisions in reforming water allocations for their projects.

Conclusion

These sketches show how analysts actually apply elements of the rationalist approach in their work. In particular, variations of the goals/alternatives matrix help organize analysis and facilitate its presentation. Along the way we encountered several attempts to monetize the specific impacts of policies relevant to the goal of efficiency. In the next chapter, we set out the basic elements of cost-benefit analysis that provide principles for guiding monetization.

For Discussion

1. Comprehensive policy analyses in the rationalist mode are often done within executive agencies, though they are rarely published. What institutional factors do you think might contribute to publication of the CBO analyses?
2. Among the examples considered in this chapter, which goals/alternatives matrices did you find most effective in communicating the content of the analysis? Why?

16

Cost-Benefit Analysis

Cost-benefit analysis, a technique for systematically estimating the efficiency impacts of policies, came into common use in the evaluation of flood-control projects in the 1930s.[1] It has since been mandated and applied, with varying degrees of success, across the broad spectrum of public policies. Both President Reagan's Executive Order 12,291 and President Clinton's Executive Order 12,286 require U.S. federal agencies to prepare regulatory impact analyses for any regulations that are likely to result in a significant economic impact. The Clinton executive order requires that analyses identify social costs and benefits and attempt to determine if the proposed benefits of the regulation "justify" the costs to society. In the last decade, Congress has also begun to require cost-benefit-like analysis in a variety of legislation, such as the Unfunded Mandates Reform Act of 1995. Even the federal courts in the United States are now utilizing a form of "cost-benefit balancing" where legislation authorizes them to do so.[2] While the evidence suggests that many federal agencies have had difficulty in actually implementing cost-benefit practice, the requirement for such

[1]The U.S. Flood Control Act of 1936 required that water resource projects be evaluated on the difference between estimated benefits and costs. The Bureau of the Budget set out its own criteria in 1952 in *Budget Circular A-47*. For an overview, see Peter O. Steiner, "Public Expenditure Budgeting," in Alan S. Blinder et al., *The Economics of Public Finance* (Washington, DC: Brookings Institution, 1974), 241–357.

[2]For a review of the history of these executive orders, see Robert W. Hahn and Cass R. Sunstein, "A New Executive Order for Improving Federal Regulation? Deeper and Wider Cost-Benefit Analysis," *University of Pennsylvania Law Review* 150(5) 2002, 1489–552, esp. 1505–10.

analysis is now well entrenched.[3] Many states now also require that regulatory initiatives include some form of cost-benefit analysis.[4]

The appropriateness of cost-benefit analysis as a decision rule depends on whether efficiency is the only relevant value and the extent to which important impacts can be monetized. When values other than efficiency are relevant, cost-benefit analysis can still be useful as a component of multigoal policy analysis, which we discuss more fully in Chapter 14. When important impacts cannot be reasonably monetized, the first step of cost-benefit analysis—identifying impacts and categorizing them as costs or benefits—can, nevertheless, be embedded in a broader analytical approach. Thus, the value to analysts of familiarity with the basic elements of cost-benefit analysis goes beyond its direct use as a decision rule.

In this chapter we introduce the basic elements of cost-benefit analysis. A thorough treatment of all of the relevant theoretical and practical issues requires an entire text.[5] Here we focus only on the key concepts for doing and assessing cost-benefit analyses.

A Preview: Increasing Alcohol Taxes

Would a higher excise tax on alcohol be efficient? That is, would it increase aggregate social welfare? This is the sort of question that we try to answer with cost-benefit analysis. We compare an increased tax to the current, or status quo, tax regime. We begin by identifying all the impacts of the tax. Direct impacts include higher prices of alcohol for consumers and increased revenue for the government. But the higher price also leads to reduced consumption of alcohol. Lower levels of consumption produce several indirect effects: fewer fatalities and injuries and less property damage from alcohol-related automobile accidents, and perhaps better health and increased productivity for people who reduce their consumption of alcohol.

The next task in doing a cost-benefit analysis of an increased tax on alcohol is to put dollar values on its impacts. For example: How much money would we have to give consumers to make them willingly accept the higher price of alcohol? (The answer is one of the costs of the tax increase.) How much would people be willing to pay to reduce their risks of being in automobile accidents? (The answer is one of the benefits of the tax increase.) After answering questions such as these for all of the impacts, we then compare the marginal benefits of the tax increase with its marginal costs. If benefits exceed costs, then we conclude that the tax increase is *efficient*—that is, it would at least be possible to compensate fully all those who bear net costs and still have some excess left to make some people better off.

Later in this chapter we present an actual cost-benefit analysis of an increased tax on alcohol. First, however, we set out the basic concepts that help us correctly identify, measure, and compare costs and benefits. The following sections discuss

[3]On these difficulties, see Robert W. Hahn, Jason K. Burnett, Yee-Ho I. Chan, Elizabeth A. Mader, and Petrea R. Moyle, "Assessing the Regulatory Impact Analyses: The Failure of Agencies to Comply with Executive Order 12,866," *Harvard Journal of Law & Public Policy* 23(3) 2000, 859–85.

[4]Richard Whisnant and Diane DeWitt Cherry, "Economic Analysis of Rules: Devolution, Evolution and Realism," *Wake Forest Law Review* 31(3) 1996, 693–743.

[5]See, for example, Anthony E. Boardman, David H. Greenberg, Aidan R. Vining, and David L. Weimer, *Cost-Benefit Analysis: Concepts and Practice*, 2nd ed. (Upper Saddle River, NJ: Prentice Hall, 2001).

these concepts in terms of four basic steps: (1) identifying relevant impacts, (2) monetizing impacts, (3) discounting for time and risk, and (4) choosing among policies. We organize our discussion of the basic concepts underlying cost-benefit analysis according to these steps.

Identifying Relevant Impacts

The first step in cost-benefit analysis is to identify all the impacts of the policy under consideration and categorize them as either costs or benefits for various groups. This immediately raises a key issue: Who has standing?[6] That is, whose utility should we count when assessing costs and benefits? The question almost always arises in the context of choosing geographic boundaries. It also arises, however, when persons either cannot articulate their preferences or they articulate preferences that society considers invalid.

Geographic Extent

The most inclusive definition of society encompasses all people, no matter where they live or to which government they owe allegiance.[7] Analysts working for the United Nations or some other international organization might very well adopt such a universalistic perspective. Analysts employed by their national governments, however, would most likely view their fellow citizens, perhaps including residents of their countries who are not citizens, as the relevant societies for considering economic efficiency. Impacts that accrue outside national boundaries are typically ignored for purposes of measuring changes in economic efficiency. Of course, these external impacts may have political implications. For instance, Canadians would undoubtedly voice strong opposition to any U.S. policies that further exacerbate their acid rain problem. Because the political importance of externalities cannot always be readily determined, it is usually best to begin by listing *all* identifiable impacts, whether they are internal or external to the national society. Explicit judgments can then be made about which externalities should be ignored, which monetized (usually a heroic task!), and which highlighted as "other considerations."

The issue of geographic standing often arises for analysts working for subnational governments. For example, consider a city that is deciding whether to build a convention center. Assume that a cost-benefit analysis from the social perspective (giving standing to everyone in the country) predicts that the project will generate costs in excess of benefits of $1 million. Also assume, however, that the national government will pay $2 million of the costs of this particular project through an intergovernmental grants program. Because the residents of the city contribute a negligible fraction of the total taxes collected by the national government, the

[6]Our treatment of this topic benefited greatly from Dale Whittington and Duncan MacRae, Jr., "The Issue of Standing in Cost-Benefit Analysis," *Journal of Policy Analysis and Management* 5(4) 1986, 663–82. The term *standing* has its origins in the legal doctrine "standing to sue": plaintiffs have standing if they have a legally protectable and tangible interest at stake in the litigation. See *Black's Law Dictionary,* 5th ed., 1979, at p. 1260.

[7]Some would argue that even future generations should be included in the definition of society. We will address the implications of this view in our discussion of discounting.

grant appears to city residents as a $2 million benefit offsetting $2 million in costs. Thus, from the perspective of the city, the convention center appears to generate $1 million in net benefits rather than $1 million in net costs. The fact that national governments typically contribute large grants is one reason cities compete so enthusiastically for the right to host Olympic Games.

A variety of externalities, or spillovers, can cause a divergence between aggregate social welfare and the welfare of local governments. We can divide them into two broad categories: fiscal and economic. Fiscal externalities, like the intergovernmental grant in the example, transfer wealth, or rents, across the boundaries of local jurisdictions. In a cost-benefit analysis from the perspective of aggregate national social welfare, a *fiscal externality* appears as offsetting costs and benefits to different groups in society and, therefore, does not influence the final calculation of net benefits. For example, a program that lures a firm from one city to another typically involves costs for one city that offset the gross benefits accruing to the other.

Economic externalities, as discussed in Chapter 5, directly affect the capability of some persons outside the jurisdiction to either produce or consume. For example, if an upstream city upgrades its sewage treatment plant, then cities downstream enjoy cleaner water, which may enhance the recreational value of the river and perhaps reduce the cost of producing potable water. Although the upstream city might not count these downstream benefits in its cost-benefit analysis of the treatment plant, they should be included in a cost-benefit analysis from the perspective of social welfare.

How should analysts treat costs and benefits that are external to their clients' jurisdictions? We believe that analysts should estimate costs and benefits from the perspectives of their clients *and* society. The cost-benefit analysis from the perspective of society indicates what should be done in an ideal world. The cost-benefit analysis from the perspective of the local jurisdiction indicates what should be done to serve the direct interests of the client's constituency and, therefore, the political interests of the client. As an analyst, if you do not note significant externalities, you are failing in your duty to inform your client about appropriate values; if you do not clearly indicate the costs and benefits accruing to your client's constituency, you are probably failing in your responsibility to represent your client's interests.

Persons and Preferences

Should all persons within a jurisdiction have standing? Beyond citizens, almost everyone would agree that costs and benefits incurred by legal residents should be counted. What about those incurred by illegal aliens? The answer may depend on the nature of the costs and benefits. For example, if they result from direct changes in health and safety, we might be more inclined to count them than if they result from changes in incomes. The same reasoning probably applies to citizens convicted of serious crimes. Obviously, however, such questions about standing raise difficult ethical issues. Indeed, when such questions are central to the identification of relevant impacts, multigoal analysis, rather than cost-benefit analysis, is likely to be the more appropriate method.

The issue of standing also arises with respect to the expression of preferences. Do families and other institutions adequately articulate what would be the informed preferences of children, the insane, and other persons with limited ability to reason? Do markets and other institutions adequately express the preferences of future generations for such amenities as environmental quality? In other words, should we give special attention to impacts on any particular groups within society? Also, should we accept all preferences as valid? For example, burglars would undoubtedly view reductions in the monetary take from their crimes as a cost of an enforcement policy. Yet most analysts would not include this cost in their evaluation of the policy.[8] As with the other questions about standing, when these issues become central, we should carefully reconsider the appropriateness of cost-benefit analysis as the method of evaluation.

Reprise of Standing Issues

The first step in cost-benefit analysis is to identify all relevant impacts and classify them as either costs or benefits for various groups. It is best to start out by being inclusive of any affected groups. Reasoned arguments can then be made to exclude those groups that you believe should not have standing. When a client has a subnational constituency, it is usually desirable to estimate costs and benefits from the perspectives of both the national society and the constituency. If it appears that issues of standing will be central to your analysis, then you should consider switching from the cost-benefit framework to multigoal analysis.

Monetizing Impacts

The basic principle underlying cost-benefit analysis is the Kaldor-Hicks criterion: a policy should be adopted only if those who will gain could fully compensate losers and still be better off.[9] In other words, when efficiency is the only relevant value, a *necessary* condition for adopting a policy is that it have the potential to be Pareto improving. As we discussed in Chapter 4, policies that increase social surplus are potentially Pareto improving and, therefore, meet the Kaldor-Hicks criterion. Further, when considering mutually exclusive policies, the one that produces the greatest increase in social surplus should be selected because, if adopted, it would be possible through the payment of compensation to make everyone at least as well off as they would have been under any of the alternative policies.

Many economists treat the move from the Pareto-improving criterion to the *potentially* Pareto-improving criterion as if it were a minor step. It is not. Actual Pareto-improving exchanges are voluntary and, by definition, make someone better off without making anyone else worse off. Potential Pareto-improving moves do not guarantee that no one is made worse off—just that everyone could be made better off with appropriate redistribution following the move. Thus, while the

[8]Some analysts count part of the reduction in monetary returns from crime as a cost. See, for example, David A. Long, Charles D. Mallar, and Craig V. D. Thornton, "Evaluating the Benefits and Costs of the Job Corps," *Journal of Policy Analysis and Management* 1(1) 1981, 55–76.

[9]Nicholas Kaldor, "Welfare Propositions of Economics and Interpersonal Comparisons of Utility," *Economic Journal* 49(195) 1939, 549–52; and John R. Hicks, "The Valuation of the Social Income," *Economica* 7(26) 1940, 105–24. The principle can also be stated as suggested by Hicks: adopt a policy only if it would not be in the self-interest of those who will lose to bribe those who will gain not to adopt it. Although these formulations are not conceptually identical (Kaldor's is based on compensating variation; Hicks's is based on equivalent variation), they usually lead to the same result when applied in practical situations. Consequently, they are usually discussed as a single criterion.

Kaldor-Hicks criterion is ingenious in that it is Pareto-like, it is also controversial. As Richard Posner, among others, forcefully argues, cost-benefit analysis based on the Kaldor-Hicks criterion contains elements of utilitarianism ("the surplus of pleasure over pain—aggregated across all of the inhabitants of society") that the pure Pareto criterion avoids.[10] Most fundamentally, the aggregation underlying the Kaldor-Hicks criterion implicitly compares utility across individuals in terms of a money metric.[11] Nevertheless, the criterion provides a good test for determining if policies could be efficient, if not a fully acceptable rule, for choosing among policies.

In practice, two related concepts serve as guides for estimating changes in social surplus and, therefore, for applying the Kaldor-Hicks criterion: opportunity cost and willingness to pay. They provide ways of monetizing costs and benefits.

Valuing Inputs: Opportunity Cost

Public policies usually require resources (factor inputs) that could be used to produce other goods. Some examples: public works projects such as dams, bridges, and highways require labor, materials, land, and equipment; social service programs typically require professional services and office space; and wilderness preserves, recreational areas, and parks require at least land. The resources used to implement these policies cannot be used to produce other goods. The values of the forgone goods measure the costs of policies. In general, the *opportunity cost* of a policy is the value of the required resources in their best alternative use.

The nature of the market for a resource determines how we go about measuring its opportunity cost. Three situations arise: (1) the market for the resource is efficient (no market failures), and purchases for the project will have a negligible effect on price (constant marginal costs); (2) the market for the resource is efficient, but purchases for the project will have a noticeable effect on price (rising or falling marginal costs); and (3) the market for the resource is inefficient (market failure).

Efficient Markets and Negligible Price Effects. In an efficient market, the equilibrium price equals the marginal social cost of production. The amount that must be paid to purchase one additional unit exactly equals the opportunity cost of that unit. Because marginal cost is constant (the supply curve is perfectly elastic), we can continue to purchase additional units at the original price. The opportunity cost of the marginal units is simply the total amount we spend to purchase them.

Panel (a) in Figure 16.1 illustrates the opportunity cost of purchases in efficient factor markets with constant marginal cost. Purchasing Q' units of the factor for a public project can be thought of as shifting the demand schedule for the factor D to the right by a horizontal distance of Q'. (Strictly speaking, D is a derived demand schedule—it represents the marginal valuations of various quantities of the factor that derive from their use in producing goods that consumers directly demand.) Because the supply schedule S is perfectly elastic, and marginal cost (MC) is constant, price remains at P_0. The total amount spent on the factor used by the

[10]Richard Posner, *The Economics of Justice* (Cambridge, MA: Harvard University Press, 1983), 49. For a discussion of the same point from a very different perspective, see Steven Kelman, "Cost-Benefit Analysis: An Ethical Critique," *Regulation* January/February 1981, 33–40.

[11]For a fuller discussion of this issue, see Walter Hettick, "Distribution in Benefit-Cost Analysis: A Review of the Theoretical Issues," *Public Finance Quarterly* 4(2) 1976, 123–51.

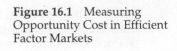

Figure 16.1 Measuring Opportunity Cost in Efficient Factor Markets

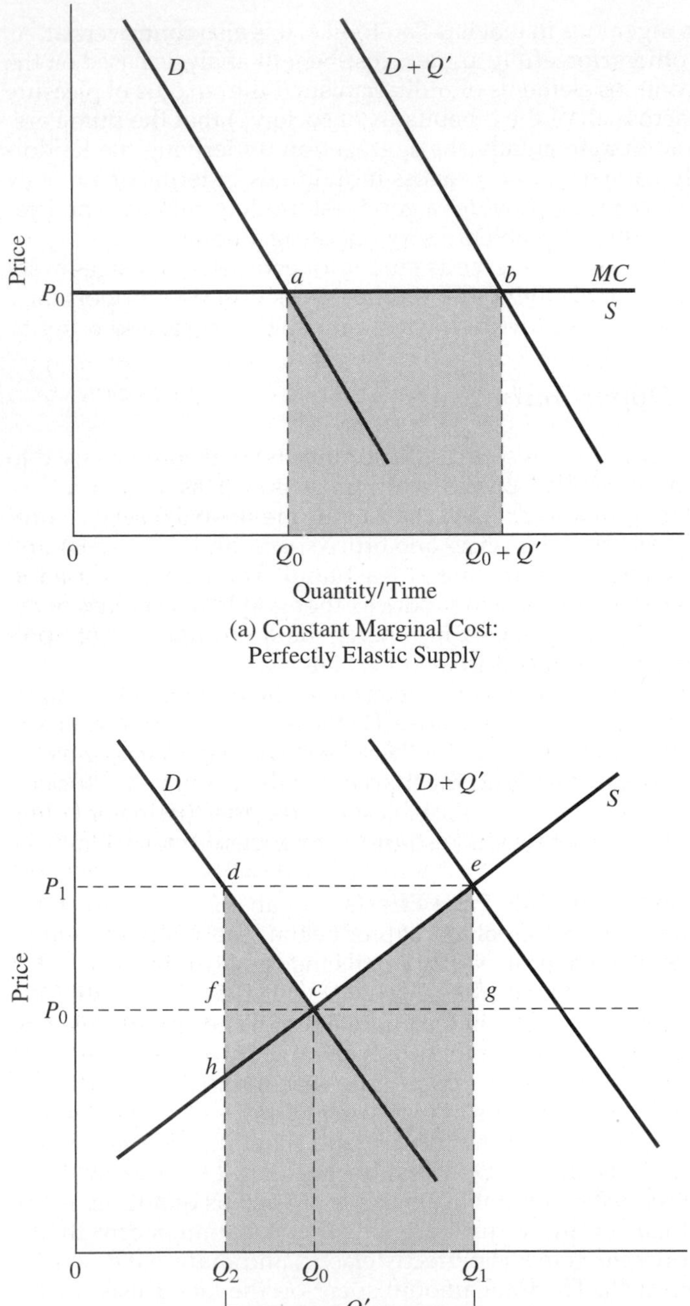

(a) Constant Marginal Cost: Perfectly Elastic Supply

(b) Rising Marginal Cost: Upward Sloping Supply

project is P_0 times Q', which equals the area of the shaded rectangle $ab(Q_0 + Q')Q_0$, the total social cost of using Q' units of the factor for the public project. If the Q' units are not used for the project, then P_0 times Q' worth of goods could be produced elsewhere in the economy. Thus, this public expenditure exactly equals the opportunity cost of using Q' units of the factor for the project.

Because most factors have neither steeply rising nor declining marginal cost schedules, interpreting expenditures as opportunity costs is usually reasonable when the quantity purchased makes a small addition to the total demand for the factor. For example, consider a proposed remedial reading program for a school district. The additional textbooks, which are purchased in a national market, undoubtedly represent only a small addition to total demand for textbooks and, hence, result in a negligible increase in their price. In contrast, to hire qualified reading teachers for the program in the local labor market may require higher salaries than those being paid to the reading teachers already employed.

Efficient Markets with Noticeable Price Effects. Panel (b) in Figure 16.1 illustrates the effect of factor purchases when marginal costs are increasing so that the supply schedule is upward sloping. As in panel (a), purchase of Q' units of the factor for use by the public project shifts the demand schedule to the right. Because the supply schedule S is upward sloping, the equilibrium price rises from P_0 to P_1. The total expenditure on the Q' units of the factor needed for the project is P_1 times Q', which equals the area of rectangle Q_2deQ_1.

Unlike the case in which marginal costs are constant, this expenditure is not the opportunity cost of using Q' units of the factor for the project. When purchases for a project induce a price change in a factor market, the effects of the price change on social surplus within the market must be taken into account when calculating opportunity cost. *The general rule is that opportunity cost equals expenditure less (plus) any increase (decrease) in social surplus occurring in the factor market itself.* In other words, expenditures do not accurately represent opportunity costs when purchases cause social surplus changes in factor markets.

Referring again to panel (b) in Figure 16.1, we can identify the changes in producer and consumer surplus that result from the increase in price from P_0 to P_1. Producer surplus increases by the area of trapezoid P_1ecP_0 (the increase of the area below price and above the supply schedule). At the same time, consumer surplus decreases by the area of trapezoid P_1dcP_0 (the decrease in the area above price and below the demand schedule). Subtracting the loss in consumer surplus from the gain in producer surplus leaves a net gain of social surplus in the factor market equal to the area of triangle *cde*. Subtracting this social surplus gain from the expenditure on the Q' units of the factor needed for the project yields the opportunity cost represented by the shaded area within the geometric figure Q_2dceQ_1. Note that calculation of this area is straightforward when the supply and demand schedules are linear—it is the amount of the factor purchased for the project, Q', multiplied by the average of the old and new prices, $1/2(P_1 + P_0)$.[12]

An alternative explanation may be helpful in understanding why the shaded area represents opportunity cost. Imagine that the government obtains the Q' units

[12]Exactly one-half of the area of rectangle *degf* is shaded (with a bit of geometry one can show that the area of triangle *cdf* plus the area of triangle *ceg* equals the area of triangle *cde*). Therefore, the total shaded area equals $1/2(P_1 - P_0)Q'$ plus P_0Q', which equals $1/2(P_1 + P_0)Q'$, the average price times the quantity purchased.

of the output by first restricting supply to the market from Q_0 to Q_2 and then ordering the firms in the industry to produce Q' for the government at cost. The social surplus loss resulting from restricting market supply to Q_2 is the area of triangle *cdh*, the deadweight loss. The total cost of producing the Q' units for the government is the area of trapezoid Q_2heQ_1. Adding these areas gives the same opportunity cost as calculated under the assumption that the government purchases the factor like any other participant in the market. It is interesting to note, however, that while public expenditures on the factor exceed opportunity cost when the government purchases it like everyone else, expenditure falls short of opportunity cost when the government obtains the factor through directives. In other words, *budgetary cost can either understate or overstate social opportunity cost.*

Inefficient Markets. In an efficient market, price equals marginal cost. Whenever price does not equal marginal cost, allocative inefficiency results. As we saw in Chapters 5, 6, 8, and 9, a variety of circumstances can lead to inefficiency: absence of a working market, market failures (public goods, externalities, natural monopolies, and information asymmetries), markets with few sellers, and distortions due to government interventions (such as taxes, subsidies, price ceilings, and price floors). Any of these distortions can arise in factor markets, complicating the estimation of opportunity cost.

Consider a proposal to establish more courts so that more criminal trials can be held. Budgetary costs will include the salaries of judges and court attendants, rent for courtrooms and offices, and perhaps expenditures for additional correctional facilities (because the greater availability of trial capacity may permit more vigorous prosecution). The budget may also show payments to jurors. Typically, however, these payments just cover commuting expenses. Compensation paid to jurors for their time is typically not related to their wage rate but, rather, set at a nominal per diem rate. Thus, the budgetary outlay for payments to jurors almost certainly understates the opportunity cost of the jurors' time. A better estimate of opportunity cost would be commuting expenses plus the number of juror-hours times either the average or the median hourly wage rate for the locality. The commuting expenses estimate the resource costs of transporting the jurors to the court; the hourly wage rate times the hours spent on jury duty estimates the value of goods forgone because of lost labor.

Assessing opportunity costs in the presence of market failures or government interventions requires a careful accounting of social surplus changes. For example, let us examine the opportunity costs of labor in a market where either minimum wage laws or union bargaining power keeps the wage rate above the market clearing level. In Figure 16.2, the pre-project demand schedule for labor D and the supply schedule for labor S intersect at W_E, the equilibrium wage in the absence of the wage floor, W_M. At the wage floor, L_S units of labor are offered but only L_D units are demanded so that $L_S - L_D$ units are "unemployed." Now imagine that L' units are hired for the project. This shifts the demand schedule to the right by L'. As long as L' is less than the quantity of unemployed labor, price will remain at the floor. The total expenditure on labor for the project is W_M times L', which equals the area of rectangle abL_TL_D. But trapezoid *abcd* represents producer surplus enjoyed by the newly hired and, hence, should be subtracted from the expenditure to obtain an opportunity cost equal to the shaded area inside trapezoid cdL_DL_T. Alternatively, we can think of the shaded area as the value of the leisure time (a good) given up by the newly hired workers.

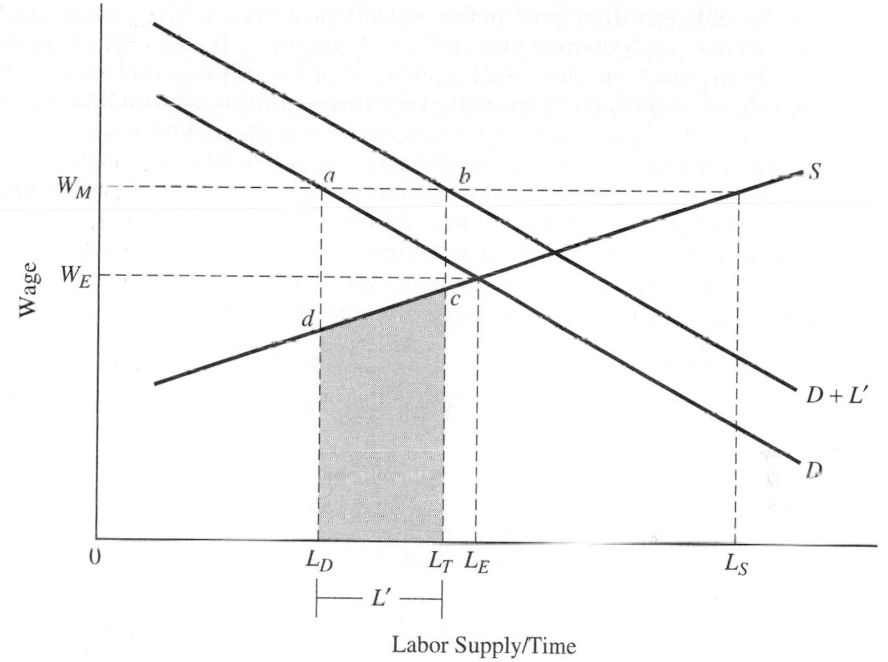

Figure 16.2 Opportunity Cost in a Factor Market with a Price Floor

The interpretation of cdL_DL_T as the opportunity cost of the labor depends on the assumption that the workers hired by the project place the lowest values on leisure among all those unemployed. (They have the lowest *reservation wages*, the minimum wages at which they will offer labor.) Note that this may not be a reasonable assumption because at wage W_M all those offering labor between L_D and L_S will try to get the jobs created by the project. Consequently, the shaded area in Figure 16.2 is the minimum opportunity cost; the maximum opportunity cost would result if the L' workers hired were the unemployed whose reservation wages were near W_M. Actual opportunity cost would likely be some average of these two extremes. In any event, the opportunity cost of the project labor would be below its budgetary cost.

Other market distortions affect opportunity costs in predictable ways. In factor markets where supply is taxed, expenditures overestimate opportunity costs; in factor markets where supply is subsidized, expenditures underestimate opportunity costs. In factor markets exhibiting positive externalities of supply, expenditures overestimate opportunity costs; in factor markets exhibiting negative externalities of supply, expenditures underestimate opportunity costs. In monopolistic factor markets, expenditures overestimate opportunity costs. To determine opportunity costs in these cases, apply the general rule: *opportunity cost equals expenditures on the factor minus (plus) gains (losses) in social surplus occurring in the factor market.*

A final point on opportunity costs: the relevant determination is what must be given up today and in the future, *not* what has already been given up, which are *sunk costs*. For instance, suppose that you are asked to reevaluate a decision to build a bridge after construction has already begun. What is the opportunity cost of the steel and concrete that are already in place? It is not the original expenditure made to purchase them. Rather, it is the value of these materials in the best alternative use—most likely measured by the maximum amount that they could be sold for as scrap. Conceivably, the cost of scrapping the materials may exceed their value in any alternative use so that salvaging them would not be justified. Indeed, if salvage is necessary, say for environmental or other reasons, then the opportunity cost of the material will be negative (and thus counted as a benefit) when calculating the net benefits *of continuing* construction. In situations where resources that have already been purchased have exactly zero scrap value (the case of labor already expended, for instance), the costs are sunk and are not relevant to our decisions concerning future actions.

Valuing Outcomes: Willingness to Pay

The valuation of policy outcomes is based on the concept of willingness to pay: *Benefits are the sum of the maximum amounts that people would be willing to pay to gain outcomes that they view as desirable; costs are the sum of the maximum amounts that people would be willing to pay to avoid outcomes that they view as undesirable.* Of course, estimating changes in social surpluses that occur in relevant markets enables us to take account of these costs and benefits. Three situations deserve consideration: (1) valuation in efficient markets, (2) valuation in distorted markets, and (3) valuation in secondary markets that undergo substantial price effects.

Efficient Markets. Valuation is relatively straightforward when the policies under consideration will affect the supply schedules of goods in efficient markets. A general guideline holds for assessing benefits: *The benefits of a policy equal the net revenue generated by the policy plus the social surplus changes in the markets in which the effects of the policy occur.* Note that the benefits can be either positive or negative. We generally refer to those that are negative as costs. Indeed, if we think of the use of factor inputs as an impact, then this statement of benefit calculation encompasses opportunity costs. In other words, depending on how we initially categorize policy impacts, we may measure any of them either as a cost or as a negative benefit.

Two situations are common: First, the policy may directly affect the quantity of some good available to consumers. For example, opening a publicly operated day-care center shifts the supply schedule to the right—more day care is offered to consumers at each price. Second, the policy may shift the supply schedule by altering the price or availability of some factor used to produce the good. For example, deepening a harbor so that it can accommodate large, efficient ships reduces the costs of transporting bulk commodities to and from the port.

Figure 16.3 shows the social surplus changes that result from additions to supply. The intersection of the demand schedule D and the supply schedule S indicates the equilibrium price P_0 prior to the project. If the project directly adds a quantity Q to the market, then the supply schedule as seen by consumers shifts from S to $S + Q$, and the equilibrium price falls to P_1. If consumers must purchase the additional units from the project, then the gain in consumer surplus equals the area of trapezoid P_0abP_1. Because suppliers continue to operate on the original supply schedule, they suffer a loss of surplus equal to the area of trapezoid P_0acP_1 so that the net change in social surplus equals the area of triangle abc, which is darkly

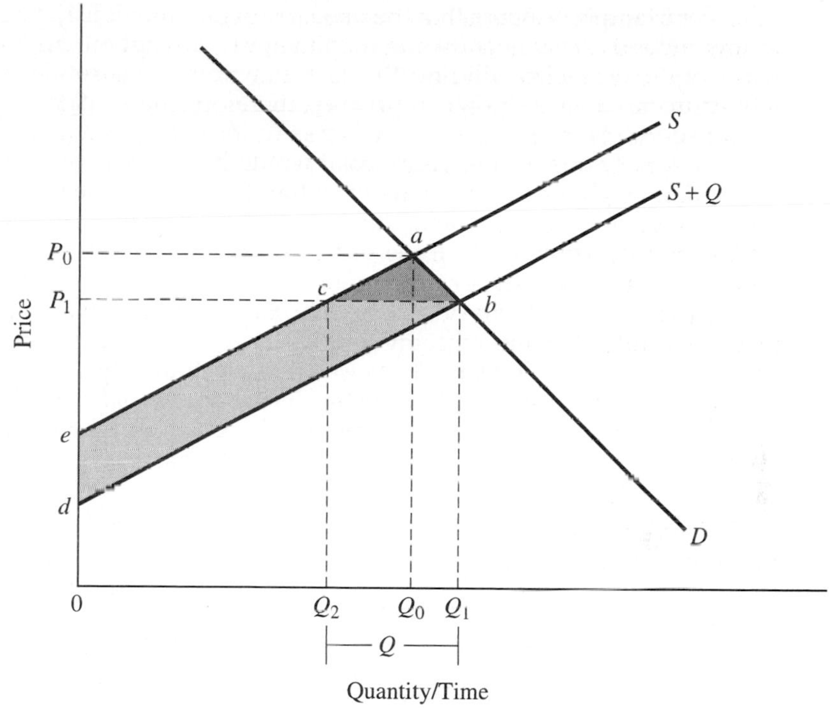

(a) Direct supply of Q by project: gain of *abc* plus project revenue Q_2cbQ_1
(b) Supply schedule shift through cost reduction: gain of *abde*

Figure 16.3 Measuring Benefits in an Efficient Market

shaded. In addition, however, the project enjoys a revenue equal to P_1 times Q, the area of rectangle Q_2cbQ_1. So the sum of project revenues and the change in social surplus in the market equals the area of trapezoid Q_2cabQ_1, which is the total benefits from the project selling Q units in the market.

What benefits accrue if the Q units are instead distributed free to selected consumers? If the Q units are given to consumers who would have purchased an identical or greater number of units at price P_1, then the benefit measure is exactly the same as when the project's output is sold. Even though no project revenues accrue, consumers enjoy a surplus that is greater by the area of rectangle Q_2cbQ_1, which exactly offsets the revenue that would accrue if the project's output is sold.

If the Q units are distributed to consumers in greater quantities than they would have purchased at price P_1, then area Q_2cabQ_1 will be the project's benefit only if these recipients can and do sell the excess quantities to those who would have bought them. If the recipients keep any of the excess units, then area Q_2cabQ_1 will overestimate the project's benefit in two ways. First, in contrast to the situation in which the Q units are sold, some consumers will value their marginal consumption at less than P_1. (If they valued it at or above P_1, they would have been willing to purchase at P_1.) Second, their added consumption shifts the demand schedule to the right so that the market price after provision of Q units by the project will not fall all the way to P_1. Even if the recipients do not keep any of the excess, the project's benefits may be smaller than the area of Q_2cabQ_1 because of transactions costs.

For example, suppose that the project provides previously stockpiled gasoline to low-income consumers during an oil supply disruption (an in-kind subsidy). Some of the recipients will find themselves with more gasoline than they would have purchased on their own at price P_1; therefore, they will try to sell the excess. Doing so will be relatively easy if access to the stockpiled gasoline is provided through legally transferable coupons; it would be much more difficult if the gasoline had to be physically taken away by the recipients. If the gasoline can be costlessly traded among consumers, then we would expect the outcome to be identical to the one that would result if the gasoline were sold in the market, with the revenue given directly to the low-income consumers.

Next suppose that the project, like the harbor deepening, lowers the cost of supplying the market. In this case, the supply schedule as seen by both consumers and producers shifts to $S + Q$, not because the project directly supplies Q to the market but, rather, because reductions in the marginal costs of firms allow them to offer Q additional units profitably at each price along $S + Q$. As with the case of direct supply of Q, the new equilibrium price is P_1 and consumers gain surplus equal to the area of trapezoid P_0abP_1. Producers gain surplus equal to the difference in the areas of triangle P_0ae (the producer surplus with supply schedule S) and triangle P_1bd (the producer surplus with supply schedule $S + Q$). Area P_1ce is common to the two triangles and therefore cancels, leaving the area *cbde* minus the area P_0acP_1. Adding this gain to the gain in consumer surplus, which can be stated as area P_0acP_1 plus *abc*, leaves areas *abc* plus *cbde*. Thus, the gain in social surplus resulting from the project equals the area of trapezoid *abde*. Because no project revenue is generated, area *abde* alone is the benefit of the project.

The straightforward measurement of willingness to pay illustrated in Figure 16.3 depends on two important assumptions: that the market is efficient and that effects in other markets can be ignored. We next relax these assumptions.

Distorted Markets. If market failures or government interventions distort the relevant product market, then the determination of the benefits and costs of policy effects is more difficult. Although the same general rule for measuring benefits continues to apply, complications arise in determining the correct social surplus changes in distorted (inefficient) markets. For example, a program that subsidizes the purchase of rodent extermination services in a poor neighborhood probably has an external effect: the fewer rodents in the neighborhood, the easier it is for residents in adjoining neighborhoods to keep their rodent populations under control. Thus, in Figure 16.4 we show the market demand schedule D_M as understating the social demand schedule D_S so that the market equilibrium price P_0 and quantity Q_0 are too low from the social perspective.

What are the social benefits of a program that makes vouchers worth v dollars per unit of extermination service available to residents of the poor neighborhood? When the vouchers become available, residents of the poor neighborhood see a supply schedule that is lower than the market supply schedule by v dollars. Consequently, they increase their purchases of extermination services from Q_0 to Q_1, and they see an effective price equal to the new market price less the per unit subsidy $(P_1 - v)$. Consumers in the targeted neighborhood enjoy a surplus gain equal to the area of trapezoid $P_0dc(P_1 - v)$; producers, who now see a price of P_1, receive a surplus gain equal to the area of trapezoid P_1edP_0; and people in the surrounding neighborhoods, who enjoy the positive externality, gain surplus equal to the area of figure

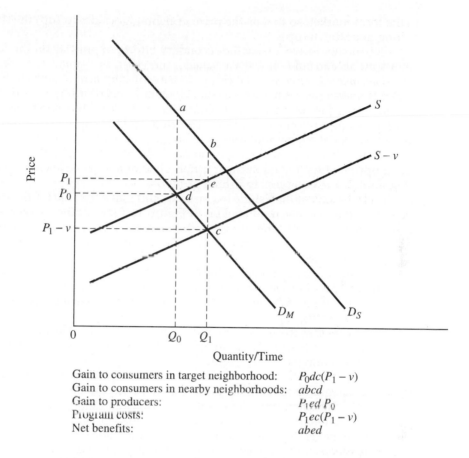

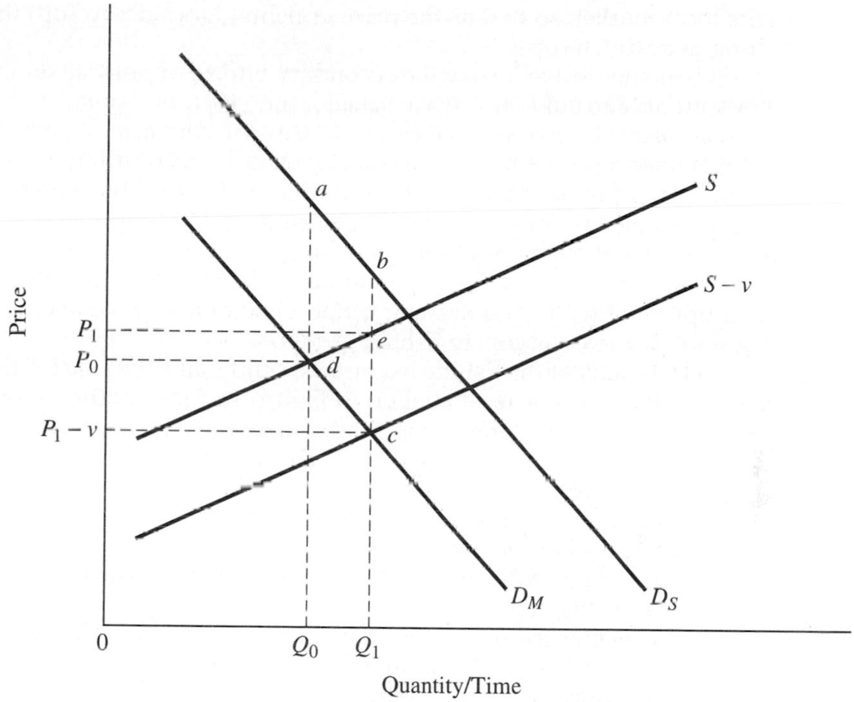

Gain to consumers in target neighborhood:	$P_0dc(P_1 - v)$
Gain to consumers in nearby neighborhoods:	*abcd*
Gain to producers:	$P_1ed\,P_0$
Program costs:	$P_1ec(P_1 - v)$
Net benefits:	*abed*

Figure 16.4 Social Benefits of a Subsidy for a Good with a Positive Externality

abcd, the area between the market and social demand schedules over the increase in consumption. Ignoring administrative costs, the program must pay out v times Q_1, which equals the area of rectangle $P_1ec(P_1 - v)$. Subtracting this program cost from the gain in social surplus in the market yields net program benefits equal to the area of trapezoid *abed*.

Effects in Secondary Markets. Many goods have important complements and substitutes. That is, a change in price of one good noticeably affects the demand for another. For example, stocking a lake near a city with game fish lowers the effective price of access to fishing grounds for the city residents. They will not only fish more but will also demand more bait and other fishing equipment. We say that access to fishing grounds and fishing equipment are complements because a decrease (increase) in the price of one will result in increases (decreases) in the demand for the other. In contrast, fishing might very well be a substitute for golfing in the local market, so that as the price of fishing goes down (up) the demand for golfing goes down (up).

When should we ignore the secondary effects of policies on the markets for complements and substitutes? *We should ignore effects in a secondary market when two conditions hold: (1) price does not change in the secondary market* ***and*** *(2) the secondary market is undistorted.* When these conditions hold, attributing costs or benefits to secondary markets leads to double-counting errors. If we have no reason to believe that the fishing equipment market is distorted, and the supply schedule for fishing equipment is flat so that the price of fishing equipment remains unchanged when the demand schedule for fishing equipment shifts to the right, then the increased consumption of fishing equipment is not relevant to our cost-benefit analysis of a program to increase access to fishing grounds.

A closer look at the fishing example should make the rule for the treatment of secondary markets clearer. Panel (a) in Figure 16.5 shows the market for "fishing days." Prior to the stocking of the nearby lake, the effective price of a day of fishing (largely the time costs of travel) was P_{F0}, the travel cost to a lake much farther away. Once fishing is available at the nearby lake, the effective price falls to P_{F1} and the number of days spent fishing by local residents increases from Q_{F0} to Q_{F1}. The resulting increase in social surplus equals the area of trapezoid $P_{F0}abP_{F1}$, the gain in consumer surplus. We measure this gain in consumer surplus using the demand schedule for fishing, D_F.

Now consider the market for fishing equipment. The decline in the effective price of fishing days shifts the demand schedule for fishing equipment from D_{E0} to D_{E1}, as shown in panel (b) of Figure 16.5. If the supply schedule is perfectly elastic, the likely case when the local market accounts for only a small fraction of demand in the regional or national market, then the shift in demand will not increase the price of fishing equipment. Does the shift in demand for fishing equipment represent any change in consumer welfare? The answer is no. The entire change is measured in the fishing market using the demand schedule for fishing days, which gives consumers' valuations of increasing levels of fishing while holding the price of other goods, including fishing equipment, constant. As long as price does not change in the equipment market, the social surplus change in the fishing market is the entire benefit from the stocking project.

Note that in situations in which we cannot measure social surplus changes in primary markets, we may try to infer them from the demand shifts in secondary markets. For example, imagine that we have no information to help us determine the demand schedule for fishing days, but we do have information to help us predict how the demand schedule for fishing equipment will change. For lack of a direct measure of benefits, we might take the difference between the social surplus in the fishing equipment market after the project (based on demand schedule D_{E1}) and the social surplus in the equipment market prior to the project (based on demand schedule D_{E0}). We would then apply some scaling factor to correct for underestimation that results from the fact that not all the consumer surplus from fishing will be reflected in the equipment market. (Some fishers will use old equipment and self-collected bait—their surplus will not appear in the equipment market.)

Now consider the situation in which the supply schedule in the secondary market is upward sloping. For example, in panel (c) of Figure 16.5, the supply schedule for fishing equipment is shown as S_E. (Perhaps the equipment is a special bait produced only in the local market.) Now price rises in the equipment market from P_{E0} to P_{E1}. This price is not taken into account in the consumer valuations represented in the demand

Figure 16.5 Valuation of Effects in Secondary Markets

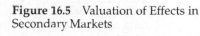

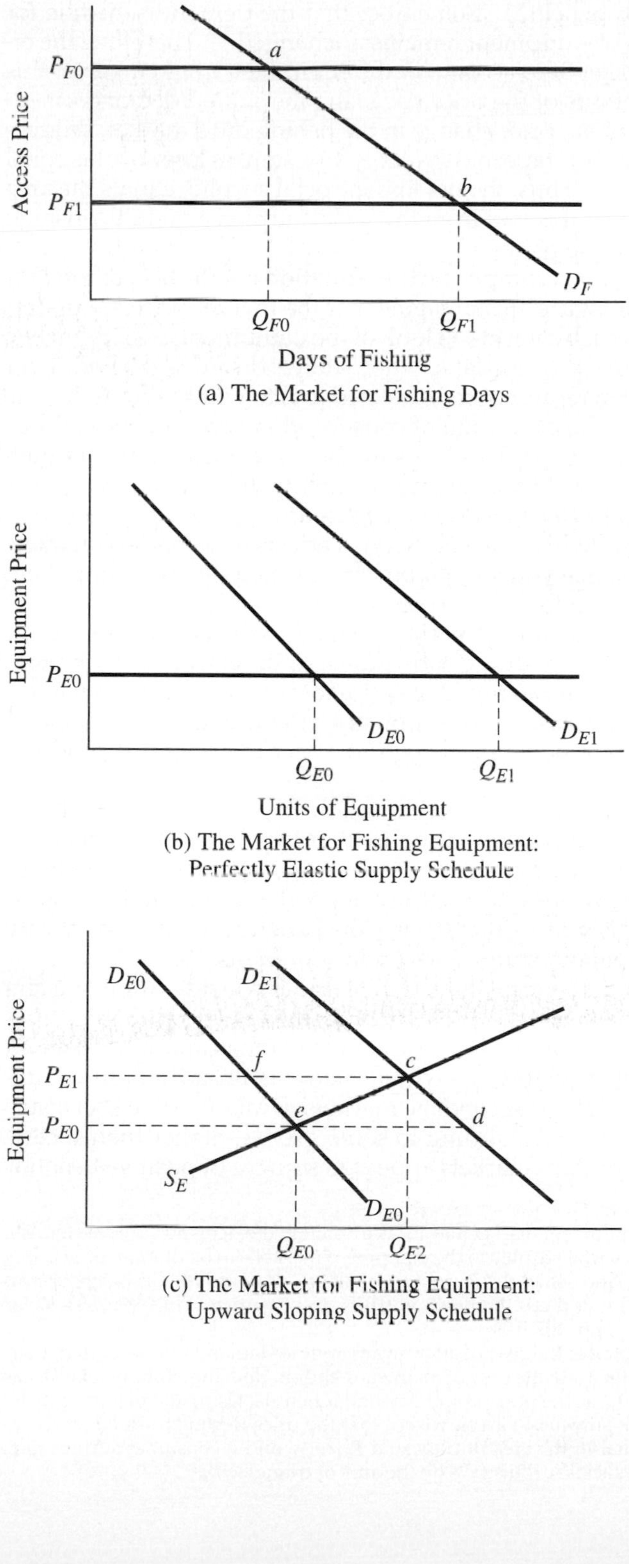

schedule for fishing shown in panel (a). (Remember that the demand schedule for fishing assumes that the price of equipment remains unchanged.[13]) Therefore, the effect of the price rise must be taken into account in the equipment market. We do this by measuring social surplus effects of the price rise using the shifted demand schedule D_{E1}, which takes account of the price change in the fishing days market. Producers gain surplus equal to the area of trapezoid $P_{E1}ceP_{E0}$. Consumers lose surplus equal to the area of trapezoid $P_{E1}cdP_{E0}$. Thus, the net loss in social surplus equals the area of triangle *cde*. We must subtract this loss from the social surplus gain in the fishing market to obtain the benefits of the project.

To see how market distortions complicate the valuation of effects in secondary markets, return to panel (b) of Figure 16.5. Imagine that the market price P_{E0} underestimates the marginal social cost by *x* cents. (Think of the equipment as lead sinkers, some of which eventually end up in the lake, where they poison ducks and other wildlife. The *x* cents would then represent the expected loss to wildlife from the sale of another sinker.) In this case, the expansion of consumption involves a social surplus loss equal to *x* times $(Q_{E1} - Q_{E0})$. This loss should be subtracted from the gain measured in the fishing market to obtain program benefits. In general, *quantity as well as price changes in distorted secondary markets are relevant in cost-benefit analysis.*

Despite these situations in which the valuation of effects in secondary markets is conceptually correct, in practice you should be very cautious in including them in a cost-benefit analysis. Our advice is based on several considerations.

First, price changes in the secondary market are likely to be small. Most goods are neither strong complements nor strong substitutes, so that large price changes in the primary markets are necessary to produce noticeable demand shifts in the secondary markets. Further, in the case of local policies, it is unlikely that demand shifts in secondary markets will be large enough to affect the prices of products sold in national markets.

Second, estimation problems usually preclude accurate measurement of welfare changes in secondary markets. Estimating own-price effects (how does the quantity demanded change as the price of the good changes?) is often difficult; estimating cross-price effects (how does the quantity of good *Y* demanded change as the price of good *Z* changes?) is more difficult yet. Consequently, we are rarely very confident of predictions of demand shifts in secondary markets.

Third, it is tempting for advocates of the policy under consideration to claim benefits in secondary markets because the difficulty of predicting effects in these markets gives leeway for optimistic claims. Ironically, such claims cannot be justified unless the secondary market is distorted—when society is broadly defined, demand shifts in undistorted (efficient) secondary markets *always* involve social surplus losses.[14] Only when we restrict standing to some group smaller than society as a whole do undistorted secondary markets appear as sources of positive benefits.

[13]The change in price in the equipment market may induce a shift in the demand schedule for fishing. Taking account of the change in social surplus in the equipment market can be thought of as a way of correcting for the shift in the demand schedule. For more details, see Edward M. Gramlich, *Benefit-Cost Analysis of Government Programs*, 2nd ed. (Englewood Cliffs, NJ: Prentice Hall, 1990), 83–87; or Boardman et al., *Cost-Benefit Analysis*, pp. 107–109.

[14]Panel (c) in Figure 16.5 illustrates the case of an outward shift in demand in a secondary market. We can use the same figure to illustrate the case of an inward shift in demand. Simply take D_{E1} as the original demand schedule and D_{E0} as the post-project demand schedule. Using the post-project demand schedule for measuring social surplus changes, we see that the price decline from P_{E1} to P_{E0} results in a producer surplus loss equal to the area of trapezoid $P_{E1}ceP_{E0}$ and a consumer surplus gain equal to the area of $P_{E1}feP_{E0}$ so that social surplus falls by the area of triangle fce.

For example, if you are evaluating the stocking project from the perspective of the local county, then you might include as a benefit increases in sales tax revenue resulting from nonresidents buying fishing equipment in the county. Keep in mind, however, that from the broader social perspective these revenues simply represent a transfer from nonresidents to residents and, therefore, appear in the social cost-benefit analysis as exactly offsetting costs and benefits.

Estimating the Demand for Nonmarketed Goods

Public projects often produce goods that are not traded in markets.[15] Indeed, market failures involving public goods provide the primary rationale for direct public supply. Consequently, we frequently encounter situations in which we cannot directly infer demand schedules from market data. There are a number of general approaches for assessing the demand for goods that are not traded in markets.[16] Here we briefly sketch three of these approaches: hedonic price models, survey assessments, and activity surveys.

Hedonic Price Models. Levels of nonmarketed goods sometimes affect the prices of goods that are traded in markets. For example, a housing price not only reflects the characteristics of the house but also such locational factors as the quality of the public school district, the level of public safety, and accessibility. (Remember the old saying: "There are three important factors in real estate—location, location, and location.") Now, if we could find houses that were identical in all these factors except, say, the level of public safety, then we could interpret any price difference as the value the market places on the difference in safety levels.

In practice, we are almost never fortunate enough to find groups that are identical in every way except for the particular characteristic of interest. Nevertheless, statistical techniques can often be used to identify the independent contribution of specific characteristics on price. The theoretical foundation for such estimation is known as the *hedonic price model.*[17] Later in this chapter we discuss use of the hedonic price model to estimate the value of life implicit in risk-wage trade-offs. Other applications include using intercity salary differences to estimate the benefits of air quality improvements[18] and using housing values to estimate the value of air quality improvements,[19] health risks,[20] and the quality of public schools.[21]

[15]For a summary, see Anthony E. Boardman, David H. Greenberg, Aidan R. Vining, and David L. Weimer, "'Plug-in' Shadow Price Estimates for Policy Analysis," *Annals of Regional Science* 31(3) 1997, 299–324, Table 1, at p. 304.

[16]See Boardman et al., *Cost-Benefit Analysis*, Chapters 11–14, for explanations of general approaches to benefit estimation.

[17]See Zvi Griliches, ed., *Price Indexes and Quality Change* (Cambridge, MA: Harvard University Press, 1971); and Sherwin Rosen, "Hedonic Prices and Implicit Markets: Product Differentiation in Pure Competition," *Journal of Political Economy* 82(1) 1974, 34–55.

[18]Mark Bayless, "Measuring the Benefits of Air Quality Improvements: A Hedonic Salary Approach," *Journal of Environmental Economics and Management* 82(1) 1982, 81–89.

[19]V. Kerry Smith and Ju-Chin Huang, "Can Markets Value Air Quality? A Meta-Analysis of Hedonic Property Value Methods," *Journal of Political Economy* 103(1) 1995, 209–27.

[20]Paul Portney, "Housing Prices, Health Effects, and Valuing Reductions in Risk of Death," *Journal of Environmental Economics and Management* 8(1) 1981, 72–78.

[21]David L. Weimer and Michael J. Wolkoff, "School Performance and Housing Values: Using Non-Contiguous District and Incorporation Boundaries to Identify School Effects," *National Tax Journal* 54(2) 2001, 231–53.

Lack of appropriate data severely limits the widespread applicability of the hedonic price model. Unless data describing all the major characteristics affecting price are available, a reliable estimate of the independent contribution of the characteristic of interest cannot be made. Even when data on all major characteristics are available, it may still be difficult to separate the independent effects of characteristics that tend to vary in the same pattern. Nonetheless, the hedonic price model offers a conceptually attractive approach even if its practical applicability is limited.

Opinion Surveys (Contingent Valuation). A direct approach to estimating the benefits of public goods is to ask a sample of people how much they would be willing to pay to obtain them in *contingent valuation surveys*.[22] By comparing the demographic characteristics of the sample to those of the general population, an estimate of the aggregate willingness to pay for specific levels of public goods can be made. A major advantage of this approach is that it permits estimation of the benefits of a wide range of public goods, including national ones like defense that do not vary at the local level. It also permits estimates of the benefits people derive from the provision of public goods to others. In some contexts, where there are no direct or easily observable indirect "behavioral traces," contingent valuation surveys may be the only feasible way to estimate willingness to pay.[23]

Obviously, this approach suffers from all the well-known problems of survey research: answers are sensitive to the particular wording of questions; nonrandom sampling designs or nonresponses can lead to unrepresentative samples; respondents have limited attention spans; and respondents often have difficulty putting hypothetical questions into meaningful contexts. There are also problems specific to valuing public goods. First, there is the practical difficulty of explaining the good being valued adequately to respondents. If respondents do not understand what is being valued, then it is not clear how to interpret estimates of their willingness to pay. Second, respondents may not treat the hypothetical choice they face as an economic decision. If this is the case, then they may ignore budget constraints and respond to gain "moral satisfaction," or what has been called a "warm glow."[24] Third, respondents may answer strategically. For example, because I know that I will not actually have to pay the amount that I state, I may inflate my true willingness to pay for public goods I prefer so as to increase the chances that the survey will value them highly. Although a conceptual threat to surveys, strategic behavior is probably not that serious in practice.[25] Further, it can be reduced by using referendum-type formats for valuation, typically with each respondent given a random dollar amount and asked if he or she would vote for provision of the public good if it were to cost that amount.

[22]For overviews, see Ronald G. Cummings, Louis Anthony Cox, Jr., and A. Myrick Freeman III, "General Methods for Benefits Assessment," in Judith D. Bentkover, Vincent T. Covello, and Jeryl Mumpower, eds., *Benefits Assessment: The State of the Art* (Boston: D. Reidel, 1986), 161–91; Robert Cameron Mitchell and Richard T. Carson, *Using Surveys to Value Public Goods: The Contingent Valuation Method* (Washington, DC: Resources for the Future, 1989).

[23]See Aidan R. Vining and David L. Weimer, "Passive Use Benefits: Existence, Option, and Quasi-Option Value," in Fred Thompson and Mark Green, eds., *Handbook of Public Finance* (New York: Marcel Dekker, 1998), 319–45.

[24]Daniel Kahneman and Jack Knetsch, "Valuing Public Goods: The Purchase of Moral Satisfaction," *Journal of Environmental Economics and Management* 22(1) 1992, 57–70.

[25]See Boardman et al., *Cost-Benefit Analysis*, pp. 377–79.

Despite concerns about relying on stated rather than revealed preferences, contingent valuation is now widely used. A blue-ribbon panel of economists has endorsed its limited use in environmental damage estimation.[26] It is also accepted as evidence in federal court cases.[27]

Activity Surveys: The Travel Cost Method. Some of the problems of opinion surveys can be avoided by questioning people about their actual behavior. The most common application of this approach is the estimation of the value of recreation sites from people's use patterns.[28] For example, imagine that we wish to estimate the value people place on a regional park. We could survey people who live various distances from the park about how frequently they visit it. We then would statistically relate the frequency of use to the travel costs (the effective price of using the park) and the demographic characteristics of the respondents. These relationships enable us to estimate the population's demand schedule for park visits so that we can apply standard consumer surplus analysis. Of course, the accuracy of the estimated demand curve depends on how well wage rates measure the opportunity cost of travel time; it will not be a good measure for people who view the travel itself as desirable.

Reprise of Monetization

Changes in social surplus serve as the basis for measuring the costs and benefits of policies. The concept of opportunity cost helps us value the inputs that policies divert from private use; the concept of willingness to pay helps us value policy outputs. The key to valuing outputs is to identify the primary markets in which they appear. When the outputs are not traded in organized markets, ingenuity is often needed to infer supply and demand schedules (remember the market for "fishing days"). Effects in undistorted secondary markets should be treated as relevant costs and benefits only if they involve price changes.

Discounting for Time and Risk

Policies often have effects far into the future. For example, deepening a harbor this year will allow large ships to use the harbor for perhaps a decade before dredging is again necessary. In determining the desirability of the harbor project, should we treat a dollar of benefit accruing next year as equivalent to a dollar of benefit accruing ten years from now? How should we take account of the possibility that dredging will be needed as soon as five years instead of the predicted ten? The concept *of present value* provides the basis for comparing costs and benefits that accrue at different times. The concept of *expected value* provides the commonly used approach to dealing with risky situations.

[26]Kenneth Arrow, Robert Solow, Paul Portney, Edward Leamer, Roy Radner, and Howard Schuman, "Report of the NOAA Panel on Contingent Valuation," *Federal Register* 58(10) 1993, 4601–14.

[27]Raymond J. Kopp, Paul R. Portney, and V. Kerry Smith, "The Economics of Natural Resource Damages after *Ohio v. U.S. Department of the Interior*," *Environmental Law Reporter* 20(4) 1990, 10127–31.

[28]See Marion Clawson and Jack L. Knetsch, *Economics of Outdoor Recreation* (Baltimore: Johns Hopkins University Press, 1966).

The Concept of Present Value

Most of us would be unwilling to lend someone $100 today in return for a promise of payment of $100 in a year's time. We generally value $100 today more than the promise of $100 next year, even if we are certain that the promise will be carried out and that there will be no inflation. Perhaps $90 is the most that we would be willing to lend today in return for a promise of payment of $100 in a year's time. If so, we say that the present value of receiving $100 next year is $90. We can think of the $90 as the future payment *discounted* back to the present. Discounting is the standard technique for making costs and benefits accruing at different times commensurate.

Imagine that you are the economics minister of a small country. The curve connecting points X_1 and X_2 in Figure 16.6 indicates the various combinations of current (period 1) and future (period 2) production that your country's economy could achieve. By using available domestic resources to their fullest potential, your country could obtain any combination of production on the curve connecting X_1 and

$$R_1 = PV(C_1, C_2) = C_1 + C_2/(1 + r)$$
$$R_1 = PV(Z_1, Z_2) = Z_1 + Z_2/(1 + r)$$

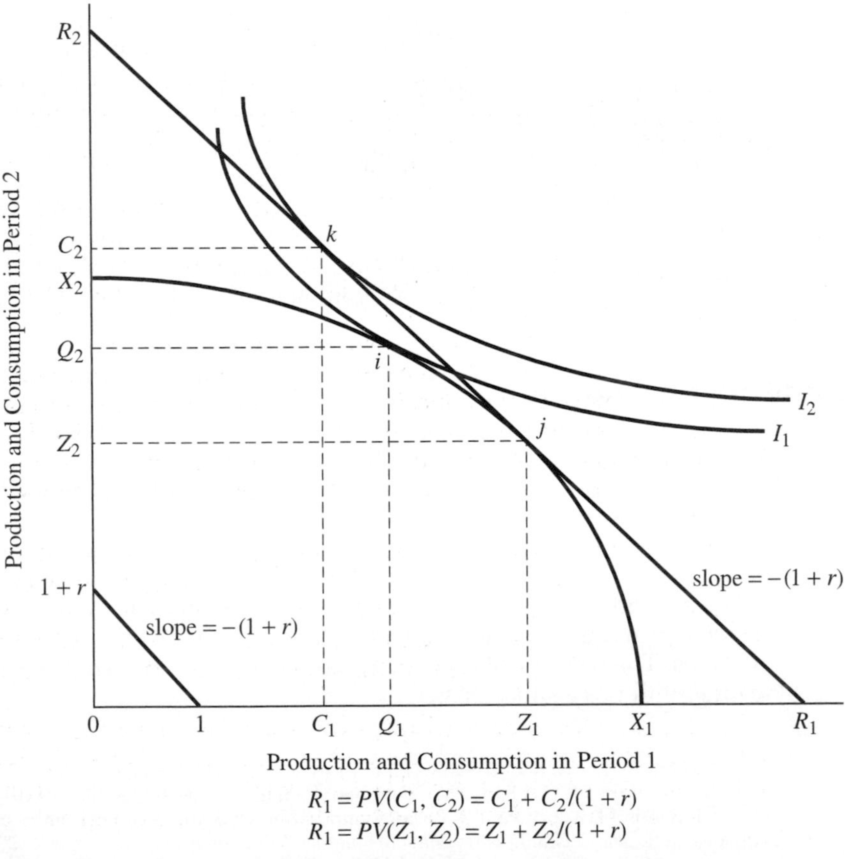

Figure 16.6 The Present Value of Production and Consumption

X_2. (The locus of these combinations is what economists call the *production possibility frontier* for your economy.) If all effort is put into current production, then X_1 can be produced and consumed in period 1, but production and consumption will fall to zero in period 2. Similarly, if all effort is put into preparing for production in period 2, then X_2 will be available in period 2, but there is no production in period 1. You undoubtedly find neither of these extremes attractive. Indeed, let us assume that you choose point *i* on the production possibility frontier as the combination of production and consumption in the two periods that you believe makes your country best off. The indifference curve labeled I_1 gives all the other hypothetical combinations of production and consumption in the two periods that you find equally satisfying to combination (Q_1, Q_2). You consider any point to the northeast of this indifference curve better than any point on it. Unfortunately, combination (Q_1, Q_2) is the best you can do with domestic resources alone.

Now suppose that you identify foreign banks that are willing to lend or borrow at an interest rate *r*. That is, the banks are willing to either lend or borrow one dollar in period 1 in return for the promise of repayment of $(1 + r)$ dollars in period 2. You realize that, with access to this capital market, you can expand your country's consumption possibilities. For instance, if you choose point *j* on the production possibility frontier in Figure 16.6, then you could achieve a consumption combination anywhere along the line with slope $-(1 + r)$ going through point *j* by either borrowing or lending. This line is shown as connecting points R_1 and R_2, where R_2 equals $(1 + r)R_1$. Each additional unit of consumption in period 1 costs $(1 + r)$ units of consumption in period 2; each additional unit of consumption in period 2 costs $1/(1 + r)$ units of consumption in period 1. Once these intertemporal trades are possible, your country's consumption possibility frontier expands from the original production possibility frontier connecting X_1 and X_2 to the discount line connecting R_1 and R_2.

The most favorable consumption possibility frontier results from choosing the production combination such that the discount rate line is just tangent to the production possibility frontier. This occurs at point *j*. The most desirable consumption opportunity is shown at point *k*, which is on your indifference curve I_2, the one with the highest utility that can be reached along the consumption possibility frontier (the line connecting R_1 and R_2). Thus, your best policy is to set domestic production at Z_1 and domestic consumption at C_1 in period 1, lending the difference $(Z_1 - C_1)$ so that in period 2 your country can consume C_2, consisting of Z_2 in domestic production and $(C_2 - Z_2)$, which is equal to $(1 + r)$ times $(Z_1 - C_1)$ in repaid loans.

Note that the most desirable point on the production possibility frontier gives us the largest possible value for R_1. But R_1 can be interpreted as the *present value* of consumption, which is defined as the highest level of consumption that can be obtained in the present period (period 1). We write the present value of consumption as $PV(C_1, C_2)$ and the present value of production as $PV(Z_1, Z_2)$. Each of these present values equals R_1.

We can arrive at an algebraic expression for the present value of consumption as follows: First, note that the present value of C_1 is just C_1. Second, note that the maximum amount that could be borrowed against C_2 for current consumption is $C_2/(1 + r)$. Third, adding these two quantities together gives

$$PV(C_1, C_2) = C_1 + C_2/(1 + r)$$

Similarly, we can express the present value of production as

$$PV(Z_1, Z_2) = Z_1 + Z_2/(1 + r)$$

The present value formula is easily extended to more than two periods. For example, consider the present value of consumption in three periods, $PV(C_1, C_2, C_3)$. If we are in the second period, the present value of future consumption is $A_2 = C_2 + C_3/(1 + r)$, the maximum quantity of consumption in the second period that can be obtained from C_2 and C_3. Now step back to the first period. The present value of consumption equals $C_1 + A_2/(1 + r)$, which by substitution gives

$$PV(C_1, C_2, C_3) = C_1 + C_2/(1 + r) + C_2/(1 + r)^2$$

In general, we can write the present value for N periods as

$$PV(C_1, C_2, \ldots, C_N) = C_1 + C_2/(1 + r) + \ldots + C_N/(1 + r)^{N-1}$$

The key to understanding the use of present value in cost-benefit analysis is to recognize that at point k in Figure 16.6 you are indifferent between having one additional unit of consumption in period 1 and $(1 + r)$ additional units in period 2. (The slope of I_2 at k, which gives your marginal rate of substitution between consumption in the two periods, equals the slope of the discount line.) Thus, in evaluating policies that make small changes to your consumption in the two periods, you should treat one dollar of change in period 1 as equivalent to $1/(1 + r)$ dollars of change in period 2. This is equivalent to taking the present value of the changes.

In an economy with a perfect capital market, all consumers see the same interest rate so that they all have the same marginal rates of substitution between current and future consumption. Because everyone is willing to trade current and future consumption at the same rate, it is natural to interpret the interest rate as the appropriate social rate for discounting changes in social surplus occurring in different periods so that they can be added to measure changes in social welfare. Later in this chapter we discuss the appropriateness of interpreting market interest rates as social discount rates.

When doing cost-benefit analysis, we apply the discounting procedure by converting benefits and costs to present values. So, for instance, if benefits B_t and costs C_t occur t periods beyond the current period, then their contribution to the present value of net benefits equals $(B_t - C_t)/(1 + d)^t$, where d is the social discount rate. The present value of net benefits equals the sum of the discounted net benefits that occur in all periods.

We illustrate discounting with a simple example. Consider a city that uses a rural landfill to dispose of solid refuse. By adding larger trucks to the refuse fleet, the city would be able to save $100,000 in disposal costs during the first year after purchase and a similar sum each successive year of use. The trucks can be purchased for $500,000 and sold for $200,000 after four years. (The city expects to open a resource recovery plant in four years that will obviate the need for landfill disposal.) The city can currently borrow money at an interest rate of 10 percent. Should the city buy the trucks? Yes, if the present value of net benefits is positive.

To calculate the present value of net benefits, we must decide whether to work with *real* or *nominal* dollars—either one will lead to the same answer as long as we use it consistently.

Real, or constant, dollars control for changing purchasing power by adjusting for price inflation. When we compare incomes in different years, we typically use the purchasing power in some base year as a standard. For example, nominal per capita personal income in the United States was $3,945 in 1970 and $9,503 in 1980. If you have ever listened to an older person reminisce, you know that a dollar purchased more in 1970 than it did in 1980. The consumer price index (CPI) is the most commonly used measure of changing purchasing power. It is based on the cost of purchasing a standard market basket of goods. The cost in any year is expressed as the ratio of the cost of purchasing the basket in the current year to the cost of purchasing it in some base year. For instance, using 1972 as the base year, real per capita personal income was $4,265 in 1970 and $5,303 in 1980. Thus, while nominal per capita personal income rose over the decade by 141 percent, real per capita income rose by only 24 percent.

In cost-benefit analysis, we are looking into the future. Obviously, we cannot know precisely how price inflation will change the purchasing power of future dollars. Nevertheless, if we take the nominal market interest rate facing the city as its discount rate, then we must estimate future costs and benefits in inflated dollars. The reason is that the market interest rate incorporates the expected rate of inflation—lenders do not want to be repaid in inflated dollars. Thus *one appropriate approach to discounting is to apply the nominal discount rate to future costs and benefits that are expressed in nominal dollars.*

The column of Table 16.1 on the extreme right shows nominal benefits assuming a 4 percent annual rate of inflation. Assuming that the projected annual savings of $100,000 in years 2, 3, and 4 represent a simple extrapolation of the savings in the first year, and that the $200,000 liquidation benefit is based on the current price of used trucks, we can interpret these amounts as being expressed in constant dollars. (We are implicitly assuming that wage rates, gasoline prices, and other prices that figure into the benefit calculations increase at the same rate as the general price level.) To convert from real to nominal dollars, we simply multiply the amount in each year by $(1 + i)^M$, where i is the assumed rate of inflation and M equals the number of years beyond the current year that the costs

Table 16.1 *Present Value of the Net Benefits of Investment in New Garbage Trucks*

		Yearly Net Benefits Based on Real Dollars	Yearly Net Benefits Assuming 4 Percent Annual Inflation
Year 1:	Purchase	–500,000	–500,000
	Savings	100,000	100,000
Year 2:	Savings	100,000	104,000
Year 3:	Savings	100,000	108,160
Year 4:	Savings	100,000	112,490
Year 5:	Liquidation	200,000	233,970
Present Value of Net Benefits		Real Discount Rate (d = .0577) $28,250	Nominal Discount Rate (r = .10) $28,250

Note: Let r = nominal discount rate, d = real discount rate, and i = expected inflation rate. Then $(1 + r) = (1 + d)(1 + i)$ or $d = (r - i)/(1 + i)$. If r = .10 and i = .04, then d = .0577.

and benefits accrue. For instance, the \$100,000 of real savings in the fourth year would be \$112,490 in nominal fourth-year dollars if the inflation rate held steady over the period at 4 percent. Using the 10 percent market interest rate seen by the city as the nominal discount rate, the present value of net benefits from purchasing the new trucks is \$28,250. Thus, as long as no alternative equipment configuration offering a greater present value of net benefits can be identified, the city should purchase the trucks.

An alternative method of discounting leads to the same present value of net benefits: *apply a real discount rate to future costs and benefits that are expressed in constant (real) dollars.* Projecting costs and benefits in constant dollars (that is, ignoring inflation) is natural. The difficulty arises in determining the appropriate discount rate. Nominal interest rates are directly observable in the marketplace; real interest rates are not. So when we decide that the interest rate facing the decision maker is the appropriate discount rate, we must adjust the observable nominal rates to arrive at real rates. This requires us to estimate the expected inflation rate just as we must if we decide to work with nominal costs and benefits. The real interest rate approximately equals the nominal interest rate minus the expected rate of inflation. More precisely:

$$d = (r - i)/(1 + i)$$

where d is the real discount rate, r is the nominal discount rate, and i is the expected rate of inflation.[29]

For our city, which sees a nominal discount rate of 10 percent and expects a 4 percent inflation rate, the real discount rate is 5.77 percent. Applying this real discount rate to the yearly real costs and benefits in the lefthand column of Table 16.1 yields a present value of net benefits equal to \$28,250. Thus, discounting real costs and benefits with the real discount rate is equivalent to discounting nominal costs and benefits with the nominal discount rate. As long as we use either real dollars and real discount rates or nominal dollars and nominal discount rates, we will arrive at the same present value.

The desirability of a policy often depends critically on the choice of the discount rate. Policies that involve building facilities, establishing organizations, or investing in human capital usually accrue costs before benefits: *when costs precede benefits, the lower the discount rate used, the greater is the present value of net benefits.* In the investment problem presented in Table 16.1, for example, the present value is over three times larger if a zero discount rate is used, and it becomes negative if a discount rate of over about 8.4 percent is used. Because analysts always have some uncertainty about the precise value of the appropriate discount rate, advocates of policies often argue for the lower discount rates than those who oppose them.

In situations in which there is likely to be controversy over the appropriate social discount rate, it is important to show the sensitivity of the present value of net benefits to the assumed social discount rate. When considering whether

[29]The real discount rate equals the nominal rate less the expected inflation rate when discounting is done continuously rather than by discrete period. (Think of the distinction between annual and continuous compounding of interest.) In discounting by discrete period, we can separate the nominal discount factor $(1 + r)$ into the product of the real discount factor $(1 + d)$ and the constant dollar correction $(1 + i)$. From the expression $(1 + r) = (1 + d)(1 + i)$, we can solve for $d = (r - i)/(1 + i)$.

or not to adopt a particular project, it may be informative to search for a breakeven rate, the lowest discount rate at which the policy under consideration offers positive net benefits.[30]

Determining the Social Discount Rate. We noted that lower discount rates generally make public investments appear more efficient. It should not be surprising, therefore, that the appropriate method for choosing the discount rate has been and continues to be hotly debated among theoretical and applied economists.[31] Unfortunately, policy analysts do not have the luxury of waiting until a clear consensus develops.

In a world with perfect capital markets, like the one illustrated in Figure 16.6, every consumer is willing to trade between marginal current and marginal future consumption at the market rate of interest. At the same time, the rate at which the private economy transforms marginal current consumption into marginal future consumption (the marginal rate of return on investment) also equals the market rate of interest. Thus, the market rate of interest would appear to be the appropriate social discount rate.

The situation becomes immensely more complicated when we relax our assumption of a perfect capital market.

First, because individual consumers have finite lives, they may not sufficiently take into account the consumption possibilities of future generations. Those yet unborn do not have a direct voice in current markets, yet we may believe that they should have standing in our cost-benefit analysis. The willingness of people to pass inheritances to their children and to pay to preserve unique resources gives indirect standing to future generations. Furthermore, future generations inherit a growing stock of knowledge that will compensate at least somewhat for current consumption of natural resources. Nevertheless, to the extent that the interests of future generations remain underrepresented in current markets, an argument can be made for using a discount rate lower than the market interest rate.

The argument is particularly relevant when evaluating projects, like the storage of nuclear wastes, that have consequences far into the future. Even very low positive discount rates make negligible the present value of costs and benefits occurring in the far future. Rather than trying to adjust the discount rate so that these far-off costs and benefits carry weight in a cost-benefit analysis, we believe that it is more appropriate to treat net benefits, discounted in the standard way, as the measure of one goal in a multigoal policy analysis.

[30]The discount rate at which the present value of net benefits equals zero is called the *internal rate of return*. Some analysts advocate the following decision rule: choose the project with the highest internal rate of return. Edward Gramlich gives reasons why this decision rule should *not* be used: First, it is possible that a project will have more than one internal rate of return, raising the question of which is the appropriate one for comparative purposes. Second, because the internal rate of return is not defined for projects that involve only current period costs and benefits, it does not always allow us to rank all alternative projects. Gramlich, *Benefit-Cost Analysis of Government Programs*, p. 93.

[31]For an introduction to the discount rate issues, see Robert C. Lind, "A Primer on the Major Issues Relating to the Discount Rate for Evaluating National Energy Projects," in Robert C. Lind et al., *Discounting for Time and Risk in Energy Policy* (Washington, DC: Resources for the Future, 1982), 21–94. Other articles in the same volume discuss particular conceptual issues. For assessments of current theory and practice, see *Journal of Environmental Economics and Management*, 18(2) 1990, Pt. 2 of 2 parts; and Anthony E. Boardman and David H. Greenberg, "Discounting and the Social Discount Rate," in Thompson and Green, eds., *Handbook of Public Finance*, pp. 269–318.

Second, taxes and other distortions lead to divergence between the rate of return on private investment and the rate at which consumers are willing to trade current and future consumption. Suppose that consumers are willing to trade marginal current and marginal future consumption at a rate of 6 percent, their *marginal rate of pure time preference*.[32] If they face an income tax of 25 percent and firms face a profits tax of 50 percent, then they will invest only in projects that earn a return of at least 16 percent. (The firm returns 8 percent to the investor after the profits tax is paid; the investor retains 6 percent after paying the income tax.)

Which, if either, of these rates should be interpreted as the social discount rate? Economists have generally answered this question in terms of the opportunity costs of the public project.[33] If the public project is to be financed entirely at the expense of current consumption, then the marginal rate of pure time preference is the appropriate discount rate. If the public project is to be financed at the expense of private investment, then the rate of return on private investment is appropriate. The *shadow price of capital approach* allows for financing at the expense of both consumption and private investment by first converting reductions in private investment to the streams of benefits that they would produce, and, once all financing is expressed in terms of lost consumption, discounting at the marginal rate of pure time preference.[34]

Controversy still remains, however, because economists disagree about whether public investment detracts primarily from current consumption or private investment. Arnold Harberger, for instance, argues that because marginal public expenditures are typically financed by borrowing, public investment fully displaces private investment.[35] Accepting this "crowding-out" hypothesis, we might use some market measure, such as the rate of return on corporate Aaa bonds, as the first approximation for the social discount rate.[36] Of course, we would adjust for expected inflation to arrive at a real social discount rate.

A discount rate based on the rate of return on corporate Aaa bonds would generally be considered riskless. Should a further adjustment be made for risk? Again, there is no clear consensus among economists on the answer.[37] In general, the answer depends on the expected correlation between the returns on the project and the level of national income. Upward adjustments to the riskless rate are in order if returns from the project are positively correlated with national income; downward adjustments, if returns are negatively correlated with national income. We very rarely have adequate information for making such adjustments, however.

What can we do in the absence of a consensus on the appropriate social discount rate? One approach is to report net benefits for a range of discount rates. Analysts should also explain why they believe the range they have used is reasonable. A related approach is to report the largest discount rate that yields positive net

[32]We take this example from Lind, *Discounting for Time and Risk in Energy Policy*, pp. 28–29.

[33]Ibid., pp. 32–33.

[34]Randolph M. Lyon, "Federal Discount Policy, the Shadow Price of Capital, and Challenges for Reforms," *Journal of Environmental Economics and Management*, 18(2), Pt. 2, 1990, S29–S50.

[35]Arnold C. Harberger, "The Discount Rate in Public Investment Evaluation," in *Conference Proceedings of the Committee on the Economics of Water Resource Development*, Report No. 17 (Denver, CO: Western Agricultural Economics Research Council, 1969).

[36]For a demonstration of how to move from market rates to the social discount rate under the Harberger hypothesis, see Steve H. Hanke and James Bradford Anwyll, "On the Discount Rate Controversy," *Public Policy* 28(2) 1980, 171–83.

[37]See Martin J. Bailey and Michael C. Jensen, "Risk and the Discount Rate for Public Investment," in Michael C. Jensen, ed., *Studies in the Theory of Capital Markets* (New York: Praeger, 1972), 269–93.

benefits. Clients can then be advised to adopt the project if they believe the correct discount rate is smaller than the reported rate.

Another approach is to use the same discount rate for all projects being considered by the decision-making unit. With this approach, at least all projects are evaluated using the same standard. The U.S. Office of Management and Budget adopted this approach in 1972, requiring all federal agencies to use a real discount rate of 10 percent.[38] Its 1992 guidelines lowered the generally used real discount rate to 7 percent.[39] Congress exempted water projects, however, because many politically favored projects needed a lower discount rate to show positive net benefits—even cost-benefit analysis itself can he subverted by government failure! Of course, there may be losses rather than gains in efficiency from using a common standard if it is far from the correct value. Most economists would agree that even the 1992 OMB standard is too high. In contrast, the real discount rate used by the Congressional Budget Office, 2 percent, is probably a bit on the low side.

Finally, there are some situations where market interest rates represent the opportunity cost of public investment and, therefore, are the appropriate discount rates. For example, if we are doing a cost-benefit analysis from the perspective of a local government, then the opportunity cost of public investment is the rate at which the local government can borrow. A similar argument can be made for small countries that borrow in international capital markets.

The Concept of Expected Value

Future costs and benefits can never be known with absolute certainty. Often, however, we know that certain future conditions, or contingencies, will influence costs and benefits. If we know which contingencies will arise, then we can make a much more accurate prediction. For example, if at least one major flood occurs in a river valley sometime over the next twenty years, then we might predict the present value of net benefits of building a dam to be, say, $25 million. If, on the other hand, a major flood does not occur, then we might predict the present value of net benefits of building the dam to be –$5 million. Of course, we do not know with certainty which of these contingencies will actually occur.

When dealing with contingencies in cost-benefit analysis, the standard approach is to assign probabilities to the various contingencies so that expected net benefits can be calculated. In common terminology, we convert the decision problem from one of uncertainty to one of risk by specifying contingencies and their probabilities of occurrence.

Once we have converted the problem to one of risk, we can apply the standard techniques of decision analysis.[40] Specifically, we follow a four-step procedure: First, identify a set of mutually exclusive contingencies that cover all possibilities.

[38] U.S. Office of Management and Budget, "To the Heads of Executive Departments and Establishments, Subject: Discount Rates to Be Used in Evaluating Time-Distributed Costs and Benefits," Circular A-94, March 27, 1972.

[39] U.S. Office of Management and Budget, "Guidelines and Discount Rates for Benefit-Cost Analysis of Federal Programs," Circular A-94 (Revised), October 29, 1992.

[40] For introductions to decision analysis, see Robert D. Behn and James W. Vaupel, *Quick Analysis for Busy Decision Makers* (New York: Basic Books, 1982); and Howard Raiffa, *Decision Analysis* (Reading, MA: Addison-Wesley, 1968).

For example, "one or more major floods in the next twenty years" and "no major floods in the next twenty years" are mutually exclusive and exhaust the possibilities. Second, for the policy being evaluated (the dam), estimate the present value of net benefits under each contingency ($25 million if one or more major floods, −$5 million if no major floods). Third, assign a probability of occurrence to each contingency such that the probabilities sum to 1. For instance, if over the last 100 years, there were two major floods in the river valley, then we might estimate the annual probability of a major flood occurring as .02, so that the probability of one or more floods in the next twenty years is .33;[41] the probability of a major flood not occurring would be 1 minus the probability of a major flood occurring, or .67. Fourth, multiply the present value of net benefits for each contingency by the probability that the contingency will occur and sum to arrive at the expected value of present net benefits. To find the expected value of the present net benefits for the dam, for example, we evaluate the expression

$$(.33)(\$25 \text{ million}) + (.67)(-\$5 \text{ million})$$

which equals $4.9 million.

In evaluating policies that have effects extending over a number of years, it is often appropriate to calculate the expected net benefits for each year and then discount to arrive at the present value of expected net benefits. For example, if we are evaluating a dam, we would almost certainly want our measure of net benefits to reflect when in the dam's twenty-year useful life the major flood would occur. (Only if we believe that the value of avoided loss from a major flood grows at a yearly rate exactly equal to the discount rate would the timing of the flood be irrelevant.) To do this, we use our estimate of the annual probability of there being a major flood (.02—two flood years in the last century) so that we can calculate the expected value of net benefits for the *i*th year as $ENB_i = (.02)NB_{Fi} + (.98)NB_{NFi}$, where NB_{Fi} equals the net benefits accruing in the *i*th year if a major flood occurs and NB_{NFi} equals the net benefits accruing in the *i*th year if a major flood does not occur. The present value of expected net benefits for the dam is the sum of these yearly expected values discounted back to the present.

When we calculate expected net benefits on a yearly basis, we can allow for changing probabilities. For instance, if we believe that deforestation accompanying population growth in the river valley will gradually increase the chances of a major flood above the historical frequency, we can estimate yearly probabilities on the basis of either a hydrological model or some expert opinion and use them in our yearly calculations. Obviously, the more speculative the probabilities that we use, the more important it is that we test the sensitivity of the present value of expected net benefits to changes in the probabilities.

For most of us, the use of expected net benefits makes intuitive sense. Is its use conceptually valid as well? Returning to the guiding principle of willingness to pay, the conceptually correct measure of benefits is the sum of the amounts that all

[41]The probability of no flooding in any year equals $1 - .02 = 0.98$. Assuming that the probability of flooding in any year is independent of the probability in any other year, then the probability of at least one flood in the next twenty years is $1 - .98^{20} = .33$.

those affected by the project would be willing to pay for the project *before* they knew which contingency occurs. So, for example, the total benefit of a dam would be the sum of the amount that each farmer would be willing to pay before he or she knew whether there would be a drought or normal rain in the subsequent years. These amounts are called *option prices*.[42] Although analysts sometimes attempt to elicit individuals' option prices through contingent valuation surveys, they more commonly rely on expected values of outcomes over the possible contingencies. So, for example, valuing the benefits of the dam would be done by estimating the farmers' producer surplus gains from the dam in a drought year, estimating their gains in nondrought years, and then finding an *expected surplus* applying the probabilities of drought and nondrought years to the surplus gains.

Option price can be either larger or smaller than expected surplus—the technical term for the difference is *option value. In cases of collective risk*, such as rainfall that affects the productivity of all farms in a river valley, *option price is the conceptually correct measure of benefits;* using expected surplus could result in either the adoption projects that do not increase efficiency or the rejection of projects that would have increased efficiency. Some theoretical progress has been made in determining the direction of option value, but only under fairly specific assumptions.[43] *In cases of individual risk*, such as death from automobile accidents, *the conceptually correct measure of benefits is the larger of option price and expected surplus;* using expected surplus is a conservative approach to measuring benefits that could lead to the rejection of projects that would have increased efficiency.

Although expected surplus is not a perfect measure of benefits in cases of uncertainty, in most cases it will be close to the conceptually correct measure. As the estimation of costs and benefits from market data inevitably involves errors, the likely small errors associated with the use of expected surplus should not be immobilizing. In other words, *the use of expected surplus is generally reasonable in practical cost-benefit analysis.*

Reprise of Discounting

People generally value a dollar today more than the promise of a dollar tomorrow; they generally prefer a certain dollar more than the chance of receiving a dollar. Therefore, cost-benefit analysis requires us to discount for time and risk. Costs and benefits accruing in different time periods should be discounted to their present values. We can use either the real discount rate with constant dollars or the nominal discount rate with nominal dollars to arrive at present values. When we are able to express our uncertainty about costs and benefits in terms of contingencies and their probabilities, we can calculate expected net benefits. Adopting only policies with positive expected net benefits will generally lead to increased aggregate efficiency.

[42]See Daniel A. Graham, "Cost-Benefit Analysis under Uncertainty," *American Economic Review* 71(4), 715–25.

[43]See, for example, Douglas M. Larson and Paul R. Flacco, "Measuring Option Prices from Market Behavior," *Journal of Environmental Economics and Management* 22(2) 1992, 178–98.

Choosing among Policies

Our discussion so far has largely considered the evaluation of single policies in isolation. If, after appropriately discounting for time and risk, a policy offers positive net benefits, then it satisfies the Kaldor-Hicks criterion and should be adopted (assuming, of course, that efficiency is the only relevant goal). A more general rule applies when we confront multiple policies that may enhance or interfere with each other: *choose the combination of policies that maximizes net benefits.* Physical, budgetary, and other constraints may limit the feasibility of generating such combinations.

Physical and Budgetary Constraints

Policies are sometimes mutually exclusive. For example, we cannot drain a swamp to create agricultural land and also preserve it as a wildlife refuge. *When all of the available policies are mutually exclusive, we maximize efficiency by choosing the one with the largest positive net benefits.* For example, consider the list of projects in Table 16.2. If we can choose any combination of projects, we simply choose all those with positive net benefits—namely, projects A, B, C, and D. Assume, however, that all the projects are mutually exclusive except C and D, which can be built together. By taking the combination of C and D to be a separate project, we can consider all the projects on the list to be mutually exclusive. Looking down the column labeled "Net Benefits," we see that project B offers the largest net benefits and therefore should be the one that we select.

Analysts sometimes compare programs in terms of their cost-benefit ratios. Note that project B, which offers the largest net benefits, does not have the largest

Table 16.2 *Choosing among Projects on the Basis of Economic Efficiency*

	Costs (millions of dollars)	Benefits (millions of dollars)	Net Benefits (millions of dollars)	Benefits/Costs
No Project	0	0	0	0
Project A	1	10	9	10
Project B	10	30	20	3
Project C	4	8	4	2
Project D	2	4	2	2
Projects C and D	7	21	14	3
Project E	10	8	–2	0.8

No Constraints: Choose **Projects A**, **B**, **C**, and **D** (net benefits = $43 million)
All Projects Mutually Exclusive: Choose **Project B** (net benefits = $20 million)
Costs Cannot Exceed $10 million: Choose **Projects A**, **C**, and **D** (net benefits = $23 million)

ratio of benefits to costs. Project A has a cost-benefit ratio of 10, while project B has a cost-benefit ratio of only 3. Nevertheless, we select project B because it offers larger net benefits than project A. This comparison shows that the cost-benefit ratio can sometimes confuse the choice process. Another disadvantage of the cost-benefit ratio is that it depends on how we take account of costs and benefits. For example, consider project B in Table 16.2. Imagine that the costs of $10 million consist of $5 million of public expenditure and $5 million of social surplus loss. We could take the $5 million of social surplus loss to be negative benefits so that costs would then be $5 million and benefits $25 million. While net benefits still equal $20 million, the cost-benefit ratio increases from 3 to 5. Therefore, *we recommend that you avoid using cost-benefit ratios altogether.*

Also note that projects C and D are shown as synergistic. That is, the net benefits from adopting both together exceed the sum of the net benefits from adopting each independently. Such might be the case if project C were a dam that created a reservoir that could be used for recreation and D were a road that increased access to the reservoir. Of course, projects can also interfere with each other. For instance, the dam might reduce the benefits of a downstream recreation project. The important point is that care must be taken to determine interactions among projects so that the combination of projects providing the greatest net benefits in aggregate can be readily identified.

Returning to Table 16.2, interpret the listed costs as public expenditures and the listed benefits as the monetized value of all other effects. Now assume that while none of the projects are mutually exclusive in a physical sense, total public expenditures (costs) cannot exceed $10 million. If project B is selected, the budget constraint is met and net benefits of $20 million result. If projects A, C, and D are selected instead, the budget constraint is also met but net benefits of $23 million result. No other feasible combination offers larger net benefits. Thus, under the budget constraint, net benefits are maximized by choosing projects A, C, and D.

Distributional Constraints

The Kaldor-Hicks criterion requires only that policies have the potential to produce Pareto improvements; it does not require that people actually be compensated for the costs that they bear. One rationale for accepting potential, rather than demanding actual, Pareto improvements for specific policies is that we expect different people to bear costs under different policies so that over the broad range of public activity few, if any, people will actually bear net costs. Another rationale is that even if some people do end up as net losers from the collection of policies selected on the basis of efficiency, they can be compensated through a program that redistributes income or wealth.

These rationales are less convincing for policies that concentrate high costs on small groups. If we believe that the losers will not be indirectly compensated, then we may wish to consider redesigning policies so that they either spread costs more evenly or provide direct compensation to big losers. We can think of limits on the size of losses as a constraint that must be met in applying the Kaldor-Hicks criterion. Alternatively, we can imagine applying weights to costs and benefits accruing to different groups—this would lead us to the modified cost-benefit analysis we discussed in Chapter 14. Using distributional constraints and weights obviously introduces values beyond efficiency.[44] We should be careful to make these values explicit. Indeed, the best approach would be to treat net benefits as the measure of efficiency within a multigoal analysis.

Of course, the inclusion of distributional values requires that costs and benefits be disaggregated for relevant groups. This entails doing separate cost-benefit analyses from the perspective of different income classes, geographic regions, ethnic groups, or whatever other categories that have distributional relevance. When you begin your analyses, err on the side of disaggregating too much. It may not be possible to gather necessary information to do distributional analysis at the end of a study. In addition, it may be that a distributional value will become important to you or your client only after you have seen the estimated distribution of net benefits. If efficiency does turn out to be the only relevant value, then aggregation is no more difficult than addition.

Disaggregation of net benefits by interest groups may be valuable in anticipating political opposition.[45] While the estimation of aggregate net benefits enables us to answer the normative question—Is the policy efficient?—the estimation of net benefits by interest groups helps us answer the positive question—Who will oppose and who will support the policy? For example, Lee S. Friedman estimated net benefits from several perspectives in his evaluation of the supported work program in New York City.[46] In addition to the social perspective, he estimated net benefits from the perspectives of taxpayers (Will the program continue to be politically feasible?), the welfare department (Will the program continue to be administratively feasible?), and a typical program participant (Will people continue to be willing to enter the program?). In this way, disaggregated cost-benefit analysis can serve as a first cut at predicting political and organizational feasibility.

Reprise of Policy Choice

When efficiency is the only relevant goal, we should choose the feasible combination of policies that maximizes net benefits. We should be especially careful in applying the net benefits rule when policies have interdependent effects. We should also anticipate the possible introduction of distributional values by developing disaggregated net benefit estimates where practical. Finally, disaggregating net benefits by interest groups may enable us to anticipate political and organizational feasibility.

We now return to the example of the analysis of the alcohol tax discussed at the beginning of the chapter. It illustrates the application of many of the concepts introduced so far.

[44]For a full discussion, see Boardman et al., *Cost-Benefit Analysis*, Chapter 18.

[45]For a general discussion, see Harold S. Luft, "Benefit-Cost Analysis and Public Policy Implementation: From Normative to Positive Analysis," *Public Policy* 24(4) 1976, 437–62.

[46]See Lee S. Friedman, "An Interim Evaluation of the Supported Work Experiment," *Policy Analysis* 3(2) 1977, 147–70.

An Illustration: Taxing Alcohol to Save Lives

Alcohol is a widely used, and abused, substance. While some evidence suggests that moderate use of alcohol actually improves health,[47] the medical literature reports that excessive use contributes to brain damage, cirrhosis of the liver, birth defects, heart disease, cancer of the liver, and a number of other adverse health problems.[48] These alcohol-related conditions play at least some role in over 100,000 deaths per year in the United States.[49] Yet the most dramatic consequence of alcohol abuse is the large number of highway fatalities caused by alcohol-impaired drivers. In 1980, for example, over 23,000 of the approximately 53,000 highway fatalities in the United States were caused by drivers who had been using alcohol.[50] Young drivers, who have higher accident rates than adults, are especially dangerous when they have been drinking. Drivers under the age of 22 years are 100 times more likely to die in fatal crashes when they are under the influence of six or more drinks than when they are sober.[51]

Not all of these adverse consequences of alcohol consumption fall on the drinker. On average, each 100 alcohol-impaired drivers who die in automobile accidents take with them about 77 victims. Nonfatal accidents caused by alcohol-involved drivers inflict injury and property damage on nondrinkers. Publicly subsidized health insurance programs pay for some fraction of the costs of the morbidity caused by alcohol abuse. These external effects suggest that the market price of alcohol does not fully reflect its marginal social cost.

Recognizing these adverse external effects of alcohol consumption, and seeing a potential for generating substantial public revenue, a number of economists advocate that federal excise taxes on alcoholic beverages be raised.[52] They note that per-unit taxes on beer and liquor have fallen greatly in real terms since the 1950s. The return of excise taxes to their previous real levels would not only raise revenue but would also internalize within the price of alcohol some portion of its external costs.

Evaluating the economic efficiency of any particular tax increase requires us to identify and monetize the external effects of alcohol consumption. One of the more important effects is highway fatalities. How many highway fatalities will be avoided if people consume less alcohol because increased taxes raise the retail price? Can these lives be reasonably monetized? We concentrate on these questions in the

[47] A. L. Klatsky, G. D. Friedman, and A. B. Siegleaub, "Alcohol and Mortality: A Ten-Year Kaiser-Permanente Experience," *Annals of Internal Medicine* 95(2) 1981, 139–45.

[48] National Institute on Alcohol Abuse and Alcoholism, *Fourth Special Report to the U.S. Congress on Alcohol and Health* (Washington, DC: U.S. Department of Health and Human Services, January 1981), 42–79.

[49] E. P. Nobel, *Alcohol and Health* (Washington, DC: Department of Health, Education and Welfare, 1978), 9–10.

[50] National Highway Traffic Safety Administration, *Alcohol Involvement in Traffic Accidents: Recent Estimates from the National Center for Statistics and Analysis* (Washington, DC: U.S. Department of Transportation, May 1982), DOT-HS-806-269, Appendix C.

[51] Charles E. Phelps, "Risk and Perceived Risk of Drunk Driving among Young Drivers," *Journal of Policy Analysis and Management* 6(4) 1987, 708–14.

[52] George A. Hacker, "Taxing Booze for Health and Wealth," *Journal of Policy Analysis and Management* 6(4) 1987, 701–708.

context of a cost-benefit analysis of an increase in the excise tax on alcohol. Our analysis relies heavily on Charles Phelps's estimates of the impact of tax increases on the highway fatality rates of young drivers.[53]

Estimating the Effects of a Tax on Alcohol

We consider the following impacts of an increase in alcohol taxes: social surplus losses in the alcohol markets (the major cost of the tax), reductions in fatalities caused by young and older drivers (benefits), reductions in the number of nonfatal highway accidents (benefits), and reductions in health and productivity losses (benefits). We discuss yearly effects with specific reference to a 30 percent tax on the retail prices of beer, wine, and liquor.

Social Surplus Losses in Alcohol Markets. In general, an excise tax reduces both consumer and producer surplus. If we assume that supply is perfectly elastic, however, the entire burden of the tax is borne by consumers. Figure 16.7 illustrates this case for the beer market. The 1988 retail price of beer averaged about \$0.63 per 12-ounce drink across the United States. At this price, 54 billion drinks are consumed annually in the United States. We assume that the beer industry would supply more or less at the same price; that is, the supply schedule is flat (perfectly elastic). If we impose a \$0.19 tax per drink (30 percent of the current retail price), the retail price seen by consumers would rise to \$0.82 per drink.

How will consumers respond? To answer this question, we must make assumptions about the demand schedule. Following the approach used by Phelps, we assume that demand is isoelastic. In particular, we assume that the demand schedule has the following form

$$q = ap^{-b}$$

where q is the quantity demand, p is the price, and a and b are parameters. The elasticity of this demand schedule equals $-b$, a constant. Relying on a review of the empirical literature, Phelps assumed that the price elasticity of demand for beer equals –0.5 (a 1 percent increase in the price leads to a 0.5 percent reduction in the quantity demanded).[54] As indicated in Figure 16.7, increasing the price to \$0.82 under these assumptions reduces consumption to 47.4 billion drinks per year. The shaded area in the figure equals \$9.538 billion, which is the loss in consumer surplus (equal to the sum of tax revenue and deadweight loss) in the beer market.[55] The area of the shaded rectangle equals \$8.951 billion, the portion of consumer surplus loss that is gained by the government as tax revenue. Thus, the net loss in social

[53]Charles E. Phelps, "Death and Taxes: An Opportunity for Substitution," *Journal of Health Economics* 7(1) 1988, 1–24.

[54]The empirical literature suggests a demand elasticity of between –0.3 and –0.4. Wishing to be conservative in his estimations of the costs of tax increases, Phelps selected –0.5 as his base case. (The higher the absolute value of the elasticity, the greater the consumer surplus loss in the beer market.) For a review of the empirical literature, see Stanley I. Ornstein, "Control of Alcohol through Price Increases," *Journal of Studies on Alcohol*, 41, 1980, 807–18. Given an elasticity ($-b$), the current price (p), and the current quantity (q), we can solve for the appropriate value of the constant (a) in the demand schedule, $q = ap^{-b}$.

[55]Mathematically, this area equals the integral of the demand schedule between the initial price (P_0) and the new price (P_1). For our isoelastic demand schedule, the area equals $(a/z)(P_1^{\,z} - P_0^{\,z})$, where z equals $(1 - b)$.

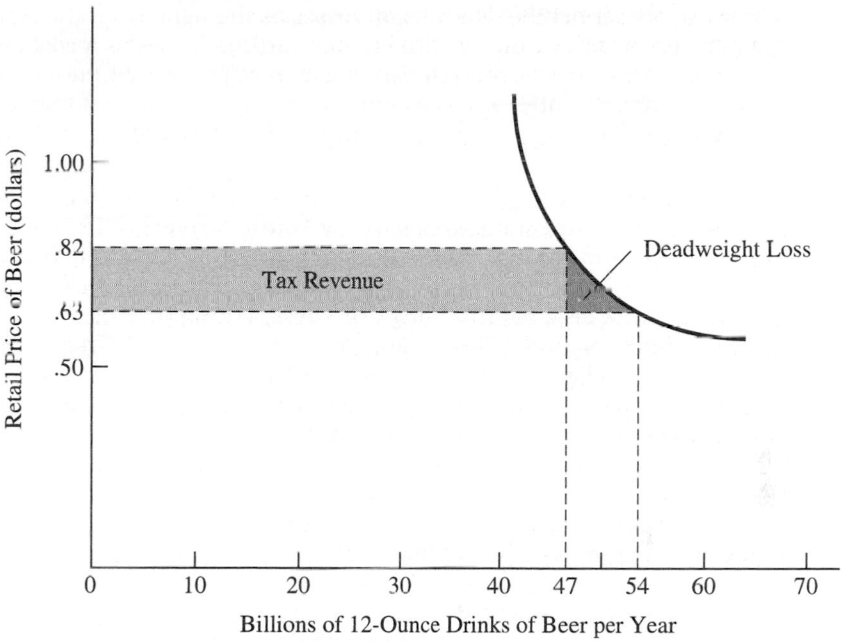

Figure 16.7 Social Surplus Loss in the Beer Market from a 30 Percent Tax

surplus in the beer market equals $0.586 billion, the difference between the consumer surplus loss and the government's revenue gain.[56] It is the deadweight loss we discussed in Chapter 4.

We follow the same procedure for estimating the social surplus losses in the wine and liquor markets.[57] For the wine market, we assume that the price elasticity of demand equals –0.75. Given the current average retail price of $0.46 per 5-ounce drink and current consumption of about 16 billion drinks per year, we find that a 30 percent tax on the current retail price yields a consumer surplus loss of $1.996 billion, a revenue gain of $1.814 billion, and a deadweight loss of $0.182 billion. Assuming an elasticity of –1.0 in the liquor market, a 30 percent tax on the average retail price of $0.63 per 1.5-ounce drink reduces annual consumption from 32 billion to 24.5 billion drinks and results in a consumer surplus loss of $5.205 billion, a revenue gain of $4.578 billion, and a deadweight loss of $0.627 billion.

Adding effects across the beer, wine, and liquor markets, we find that the 30 percent tax on retail prices reduces the consumption of alcoholic drinks by 16.6 percent, inflicts consumer surplus losses of $16.739 billion, generates tax revenue equal to $15.343 billion, and results in deadweight losses of $1.396 billion. We can

[56] If we were to assume a price elasticity of demand for beer of –.25 instead, we would find a social surplus loss of $0.306 billion. Assuming a demand elasticity of –.75 we would find a social surplus loss of $0.842 billion. When doing cost-benefit analyses, it is standard practice to test the sensitivity of our conclusions to changes in our assumptions. In other words, repeat the analysis, keeping all assumptions the same except the one under consideration. Given the consensus in the empirical literature, a range as large as –.25 to –.75 almost certainly covers the true value.

[57] We measure quantities in terms of drinks with approximately the same alcohol content: 12 ounces of beer, 5 ounces of wine, and 1.5 ounces of liquor.

either simply report the deadweight losses as the net cost of the policy in the alcohol markets or report the total consumer surplus losses as a cost and the total tax revenue as a benefit. Although the choice of approach will not alter our estimate of net benefits, the latter approach preserves information that may be relevant later if we decide that, along with economic efficiency, reducing the federal deficit is a relevant goal.

Reductions in Fatalities Caused by Young Drivers. The connection between alcohol taxes and fatal accidents caused by young drivers follows an intuitively straightforward chain: taxes raise the retail price of alcohol; higher prices lead young drivers to drink less; because they drink less, young drivers are involved in fewer fatal accidents. Michael Grossman, Douglas Coate, and Gregory M. Arluck estimated the price elasticity of youth drinking.[58] Phelps combined this information with data from autopsies on the blood-alcohol levels of drivers killed in automobile accidents to estimate the effect of consumption changes on accident risks.

Grossman, Coate, and Arluck analyzed data from the U.S. Health and Nutrition Survey to estimate the effects of price, the legal drinking age, and other variables on the frequency and intensity of drinking by youths aged 16 to 21. They found that the frequency and intensity of drinking were highly sensitive to price. Indeed, they estimated that a 7 percent increase in the price of beer and liquor would have about the same effect as raising the minimum legal drinking age by one year. (Wine consumption appeared not to depend on price.) Their estimates permit the calculation of the probability of drinking level i, $P(\text{drinking level } i)$, and the probability of drinking frequency j, $P(\text{drinking frequency } j)$, for any set of assumed alcohol prices. The levels of drinking intensity indicate the number of drinks taken on a typical drinking day: 6 and over, 3 to 5, 1 to 2. The level of drinking frequency indicates how often youths drink: every day, 2 to 3 times per week, 1 to 4 times per month, 4 to 11 times per year, and never (fewer than 3 drinks in previous year).

In order to calculate the number of driver fatalities, we need the probability of a young driver dying in an automobile accident conditional on drinking level, $P(\text{death}|\text{drinking level } i)$. That is, what is the probability that a youthful driver will be killed, given that he or she has had i drinks? Several states do autopsies, which measure blood-alcohol levels, on all highway fatalities.[59] Data from these states permit the estimation of $P(\text{drinking level } i|\text{death})$, the probability that a young driver killed in a highway accident was drinking at level i. Phelps realized that he could find the probability of death conditional on drinking level by using the following property of conditional probabilities:

$$P(\text{death}|\text{drinking level } i)P(\text{drinking level } i) = P(\text{drinking level } i|\text{death})P(\text{death})$$

where $P(\text{death})$ is the unconditional probability that a young driver will die in a highway accident. Because $P(\text{death})$ can be determined from aggregate statistics, it is possible to solve for the probability of death, given drinking level i:

$$P(\text{death}|\text{drinking level } i) = P(\text{drinking level } i|\text{death})P(\text{death})/P(\text{drinking level } i)$$

[58]"Price Sensitivity of Alcoholic Beverages in the United States," in H. D. Holder, ed., *Control Issues in Alcohol Abuse Prevention: Strategies for States and Communities* (Greenwich, CT: JAI Press, 1987), 169–98.

[59]National Highway Traffic Safety Administration, Appendix B.

which is simply a statement of Bayes' theorem.[60] These probabilities change as the tax on alcohol changes because P(drinking level i) depends on the price of drinks.

Phelps next used the conditional probabilities of death and the probabilities of drinking frequencies estimated by Grossman, Coate, and Arluck to calculate the reduction in the number of young drivers who would die as the tax on beer is increased. Phelps concentrated on beer for two reasons: first, it is by far the drink of choice of youths; and, second, the price elasticity for beer estimated by Grossman, Coate, and Arluck was much more statistically precise than their estimates for wine and liquor. As long as the tax is actually imposed on wine and liquor as well as beer, Phelps's approach leads to conservative estimates of the number of lives saved.

Phelps found that a 30 percent tax would result in 1,650 fewer drivers 16 to 21 years of age dying in highway fatalities per year. These driver fatalities are avoided because the tax decreases both the intensity and frequency of drinking. Because 77 nondriver fatalities are associated on average with each 100 driver fatalities, the 1,650 avoided driver deaths would result in an additional 1,270 lives saved per year. Thus, the 30 percent tax would reduce the number of highway fatalities caused by young drivers by about 2,920 per year.

Reductions in Fatalities Caused by Older Drivers. Unfortunately, no study comparable to that of Grossman, Coate, and Arluck is available for quantifying the behaviors of older drinkers in the United States. Consequently, we must use an ad hoc procedure that reflects two factors: first, on average, adults have a much less elastic demand for alcohol than do youths; and, second, for any given intensity of drinking, adults, on average, are less likely than youthful drivers to be involved in a fatal accident. As is often the case in cost-benefit analysis, we must do the best we can with available information.

We start by noting that the 30 percent tax reduces the number of alcohol-involved fatalities of young drivers by about 40 percent (a reduction of about 1,650 on a base of about 4,120). Ignoring that adults have less elastic demand for alcohol and that alcohol-involved adult drivers are less dangerous, we might simply assume

[60] A stylized example may be helpful to readers who have not encountered Bayes' theorem before: Imagine that you are playing a game that involves guessing the proportion of red (R) and white (W) balls in an urn. Assume that you know that the urn contains either 8 W and 2 R balls (Type 1 urn) or 2 R and 8 W balls (Type 2 urn). Also assume that you believe that the prior probability of the urn being Type 1 is one-half—that is, before you sample the contents of the urn, you believe that $P(\text{Type 1}) = P(\text{Type 2}) = .5$. Now imagine that you draw one ball from the urn and observe that it is white. What probability should you assign to the urn being type 1, *given* that you have observed a white ball? In other words, what is $P(\text{Type } I|W)$? Bayes's theorem tells you that

$$P(\text{Type 1}|W) = P(W|\text{Type 1})P(\text{Type 1})/P(W)$$

But you know that

$$P(W) = P(W|\text{Type 1})P(\text{Type 1}) + P(W|\text{Type 2})P(\text{Type 2})$$
$$= (8/10)(.5) + (2/10)(.5) = .5$$

(In other words, because the urn types are equally likely before you sample, you can assume that you are drawing from their combined contents of 10 W and 10 R so that the probability of drawing a white ball is .5.) Thus, applying Bayes' theorem gives

$$P(\text{Type 1}|W) = (8/10)(.5)/(.5) = .8$$

Thus, if you draw a white ball, then you should believe that the probability of the urn being Type 1 is .8.

that the 30 percent tax would reduce the number of alcohol-involved fatalities of older drivers by the same fraction. With about 8,000 alcohol-involved fatalities each year among drivers over 21, the simple estimate would be 3,200. Obviously, this approach would lead to an overstatement of the number of fatalities involving drivers over 21 that would be avoided by the 30 percent tax.

In order to take account of the less elastic demand of adults, we might scale the simple estimate by the ratio of the adult elasticity of demand to the youth elasticity of demand. Using the Grossman, Coate, and Arluck results, Phelps calculated the elasticity of demand for beer for those 16 to 21 years old to be –2.3. The elasticity of demand for older drinkers approximates the aggregate market elasticity because older drinkers constitute the large majority of the market. So the market elasticities we used in estimating effects in the alcohol markets (–0.5 for beer, –0.75 for wine, and –1.0 for liquor) are reasonable approximations for the elasticity of drinkers older than 21. The ratio of the weighted average of these elasticities to the youth elasticity equals 0.3. Applying this ratio to the simple estimate of 3,240 adult drivers saved yields an adjusted estimate of 972 per year.

A lack of relevant data makes it more difficult to adjust further for the lower propensity of older drivers to be involved in fatal accidents at any given drinking level. We do know that while those 21 and younger constitute about 13 percent of licensed drivers, they account for about 26 percent of all alcohol-involved accidents.[61] For lack of more relevant data, we assume that at any given drinking level, drivers over 21 are only 50 percent as likely to have fatal accidents as younger drivers. Adjusting for this factor reduces the estimate of adult drivers saved to 486. Applying the victim-to-driver ratio of 0.77 yields another 375 lives saved. Thus, we estimate the total number of lives saved due to changes in the behavior of drivers over 21 to be 861 per year.

Reductions in Injuries and Property Damage. Phelps estimated the injury and property damage costs of highway accidents involving alcohol-involved drivers to be about $3.75 billion per year, one-third of which is attributable to drivers 21 and younger.[62] To estimate the injury and property damage savings associated with changes in youth drinking behavior, we assume that nonfatal accidents fall in the same proportion as fatal accidents. Multiplying the percentage reduction in alcohol-related deaths of young drivers from a 30 percent tax (a 40 percent reduction) by the total costs of alcohol-involved nonfatal accidents ($1.25 billion) yields annual savings of $0.5 billion. Following the same procedure for older drivers (a 0.06 reduction times $2.50 billion) yields annual savings of $0.15 billion. Thus we estimate the total annual injury and property damage savings from imposition of the 30 percent tax to be $0.65 billion.

Health and Productivity Gains. We expect reductions in alcohol consumption to contribute to better health. We also expect reductions in alcohol consumption to increase productivity: better health and greater sobriety contribute to reductions

[61]National Highway Traffic Safety Administration, Appendix B, Table 6.

[62]Estimates of the percentage of accidents that involve alcohol-involved drivers can be found in National Highway Traffic Safety Administration, Appendix B. An earlier report provides estimates of the average cost of accidents, which can be inflated to 1986 dollars, the base year of the analysis. National Highway Traffic Safety Administration, *1975 Societal Costs of Motor Vehicle Accidents* (Washington, DC: U.S. Department of Transportation, December 1976). Phelps combined these estimates to arrive at the annual cost of injury and property damage caused by alcohol-involved drivers.

in absenteeism and workplace accidents. For lack of more appropriate information, we assume that health and productivity losses are proportional to alcohol consumption.[63] Therefore, because we expect the 30 percent tax to reduce alcohol consumption by 16.6 percent, we predict that health and productivity losses would also fall by 16.6 percent.

We must rely on previous studies for estimates of the yearly health and productivity costs associated with alcohol consumption. The best available estimates appear to be for the year 1975.[64] Converting these estimates to 1986 dollars gives annual health costs equal to $25.92 billion and annual productivity costs equal to $39.96 billion. Therefore, under our assumption of proportionality between consumption and costs, we estimate $4.29 billion in annual health savings and $6.61 billion in annual productivity savings from the 30 percent tax.

Monetizing and Interpreting Effects

We have measured all effects in dollars except lives saved. We might think, therefore, that our only remaining task is to assign a dollar value to lives saved. Unfortunately, we must also question whether all the effects we have quantified belong in our calculation of net benefits. Do any of the effects involve double counting?

Which Lives Count? We estimated lives saved in four categories: young drivers, victims of young drivers, older drivers, and victims of older drivers. We can think of the victims of alcohol-involved drivers as suffering an externality of the drivers' alcohol consumption. The costs borne by victims are not reflected in alcohol markets. In contrast, the costs borne by the drivers themselves may be reflected in their demand for alcohol. We expect that someone fully informed about the risks of driving under the influence of alcohol will consider these risks in deciding when and how much to drink. Other things equal, the higher the implicit values that drivers place on their own lives or the higher the probabilities of having fatal accidents after drinking, the less alcohol drivers will demand at any given price. To the extent that drivers are uninformed about the risks of driving under the influence of alcohol, their demand for alcohol will not fully reflect their risk of being an alcohol-involved driver fatality.

Think back to our earlier discussion of the measurement of costs and benefits in secondary markets. We can think of the alcohol markets as the primary markets and the "markets for victim and driver fatalities" as secondary markets. In the "fatality markets" people demand personal highway safety as a function of the "price" of safety, which can be thought of as the monetary equivalent of the level of effort expended on avoiding accidents. Now the market for victim fatalities is clearly distorted by the external effects of alcohol consumption. Therefore, we should count effects in the "victim market" in our cost-benefit analysis. The "driver market" is not distorted as long as drivers fully realize the increased risks they face from their alcohol consumption. If we believe that drivers are fully informed, then we should

[63]Proportional reduction would be unlikely if most of the reduction in alcohol consumption was by light rather than heavy drinkers. Evidence suggests, however, that even heavy drinkers do alter their behavior in the face of higher prices. See Hacker, "Taxing Booze for Health and Wealth."

[64]R. E. Berry, Jr., J. P. Boland, C. N. Smart, and J. R. Kanak, "The Economic Costs of Alcohol Abuse and Alcoholism, 1975," *Final Report to the National Institute on Alcohol Abuse and Alcoholism*, ADM 281-760016, August 1977.

not count reductions in their fatality rate as benefits—they are already counted in the alcohol markets. If we believe, however, that they do not fully take account of the increased risks, then the "driver market" is distorted by an information asymmetry and we should count all or part of the avoided fatalities as benefits.

We estimate benefits under three different sets of assumptions about how well young and older drivers are informed about the risks of drinking and driving. First, we assume that all drinkers are uninformed. (The belief of most parents!) Under this assumption, we count all avoided driver and victim fatalities as benefits. We can treat our estimate of benefits under this assumption as an upper bound on the true benefits. Second, we assume that all drinkers are fully informed. In this case, we count only avoided victim fatalities as benefits. This case provides a lower bound on benefits. Third, we make a "best guess" about the extent to which young and older drivers are informed. We assume that young drivers are only about 10 percent informed so that we count 90 percent of avoided young-driver fatalities as benefits.[65] We also assume that older drivers are about 90 percent informed so that we count 10 percent of avoided older-driver fatalities as benefits. As in the other cases, we count all avoided victim fatalities as benefits.

Monetizing the Value of Life. What dollar value should we assign to avoided fatalities? This question may strike you as crass, especially if you think about putting a dollar value on the life of a specific person. Many of us would be willing to spend everything we have to save the life of someone we love. But we all implicitly put finite values on lives when we make decisions that affect risks to ourselves and those we love. Do you always buckle your seat belt? Do you make all your passengers buckle theirs? Do you have a smoke detector on every floor of your house? Do you have a working fire extinguisher? Do you always wear a helmet when riding your bicycle? Do you always drive within the legal speed limit? If you answer No to any of these questions, you are implicitly saying that you do not put an infinite value on life—you have decided to accept greater risks of fatality in order to avoid small certain costs.

The key distinction is between actual and statistical lives. Most of us are willing to spend great sums to save the lives of specific persons. For example, we spare no cost in trying to rescue trapped miners. Yet we are less willing to take actions that reduce the probability of accidents—as a society we do not take all possible precautions to prevent miners from becoming trapped. Indeed, miners themselves sometimes knowingly accept higher risks by ignoring inconvenient safety rules. In other words, as long as we are dealing with probabilities rather than certainties, people seem willing to consider trade-offs between dollars and lives. By observing these trade-offs, we can impute a dollar value to a statistical life, the problem we face in our cost-benefit analysis of the alcohol tax.[66]

A number of studies have attempted to measure how much people implicitly value their lives by seeing how much additional wage compensation they demand

[65]Phelps reports that the college students he surveyed underestimated the increased risks of driving after heavy drinking by a factor of more than 10. Charles E. Phelps, "Risk and Perceived Risk of Drunk Driving among Young Drivers," *Journal of Policy Analysis and Management* 6(4) 1987, 708–14.

[66]The risk-premium approach is conceptually well grounded in the economic concept of willingness to pay. The other major approach, used by courts in deciding compensation in wrongful death cases, is to value life at the present value of forgone future earnings. While this approach provides abundant consulting opportunities for economists, it does not have as clear a conceptual basis in economic theory as the risk-premium approach and therefore should be avoided in cost-benefit analysis.

for working at riskier jobs.[67] Imagine two jobs with identical characteristics except that one involves a 1/1,000 greater risk of fatal injury per year. If we observe people willing to take the riskier job for an additional $2,000 per year in wages, then we can infer that they are placing an implicit value on their (statistical) lives of $2,000/(1/1,000), or $2 million. The validity of our inference depends on the jobs' differing only in terms of risk and the workers fully understanding the risk.

In practice, researchers use econometric techniques to control for a wide range of job and worker characteristics. In his review of major studies of wage-risk tradeoffs, W. Kip Viscusi found estimates of the value of life ranging from about $600,000 to over $8 million (in 1986 dollars).[68] We take $1 million, near the lower end of this range, as a conservative estimate of the value of life.[69]

Apportioning Other Effects. We must determine how much of the injury, property damage, health, and productivity effects to count as benefits under our uninformed demand, informed demand, and best guess cases. We follow the same line of argument that we used in deciding which avoided fatalities to count.

In the *uninformed demand* case, we assume that people do not consider the accident, health, and productivity costs of drinking so that we count the entire savings in these categories as benefits. This approach is consistent with treating the uninformed demand cases as an upper bound on benefits from the tax.

In the *informed demand* case, we assume that drinkers fully anticipate and bear these costs so that we do not count reductions in them as benefits. With respect to accident costs, for instance, we assume that the drinkers pay for the property damage and injuries they inflict on others through either higher insurance premiums or loss of coverage. Similarly, we assume that workers who are less productive because of their drinking bear most of the productivity losses in the form of lower wages. To the extent that insurance and wage rates do not fully reflect accident propensities, health risks, and productivity losses associated with drinking, our accounting will underestimate benefits—an approach consistent with treating the informed demand case as a lower bound on benefits.

In the *best guess* case, we apportion costs under the assumption that young drinkers are about 10 percent informed and older drinkers are about 90 percent informed of the health, productivity, and accident costs associated with their drinking. Because the majority of health and productivity losses accrue to older drinkers, we take 10 percent of the total savings in these categories as benefits. With respect to accidents, we count as benefits all the costs avoided by nondrivers as well as 90 percent of costs avoided by young drivers and 10 percent avoided by older drivers. Although lack of better information forces us to adopt these ad hoc assumptions, they probably provide a reasonable intermediate estimate of benefits.

[67]This approach was pioneered by Richard Thaler and Sherwin Rosen, "The Value of Saving a Life: Evidence from the Labor Market," in Nestor E. Terleckyj, ed., *Household Production and Consumption* (New York: Columbia University Press, 1976), 265–98.

[68]W. Kip Viscusi, "Alternative Approaches to Valuing the Health Impacts of Accidents: Liability Law and Prospective Evaluations," *Law and Contemporary Problems*, 46(4) 1983, 49–68. For a more recent review, see W. Kip Viscusi, "The Value of Risks to Life and Health," *Journal of Economic Literature* 31(4) 1993, 1912–46.

[69]A review of the reviews of estimates of the value of life suggests a range of $2.25 million to $3.5 million in 1994 dollars. Anthony E. Boardman, David H. Greenberg, Aidan R. Vining, and David L. Weimer, "'Plug-in' Shadow Price Estimates for Policy Analysis," *Annals of Regional Science* 31(3) 1997, 299–324, at p. 304.

Estimating Net Benefits

Having apportioned and valued effects, we are ready to estimate net benefits under each of the three cases. As long as we expect the same pattern of costs and benefits to persist over time, we need only look at the net benefits in the single year. If we think that costs and benefits will change substantially over time, then we should estimate net benefits for a number of years into the future and discount them back to the present. For instance, stricter enforcement of driving-while-intoxicated laws might reduce the frequency with which people drink and drive so that over time the number of lives saved from the tax will fall. When we expect costs and benefits to change over time, we should adopt a horizon equal in length to the period we expect the policy to be in effect.

Net Benefits of the 30 Percent Tax. Table 16.3 displays the costs and benefits of a 30 percent tax on the retail prices of beer, wine, and liquor. Note that the tax appears to offer positive net benefits in each of the three cases. We should be careful in our interpretation, however.

Table 16.3 *Costs and Benefits of a 30 Percent Tax on Alcohol (billions of dollars)*

		Uninformed Demand	**Best Guess**	**Informed Demand**
Lives Saved ($1 million/life)				
Young drivers		1.65	1.49	0
Victims of young drivers		1.27	1.27	1.27
Older drivers		.49	.05	0
Victims of older drivers		.37	.37	.37
Subtotal		**3.78**	**3.18**	**1.64**
Injury and Property Damage Avoided				
Young drivers		.50	.47	0
Older drivers		.15	.02	0
Subtotal		**.65**	**.49**	**0**
Health and Productivity Costs Avoided				
Health		4.29	.43	0
Productivity		6.61	.66	0
Subtotal		**10.90**	**1.09**	**0**
Tax Revenue				
Beer, wine, and liquor	**15.34**	**15.34**	**15.34**	
Consumer Surplus Change				
Beer, wine, and liquor	–16.74	–16.74	–16.74	
Net Benefits		**13.95**	**3.36**	**0.24**

First consider the net benefits in the informed demand case. The reported net benefits of $0.24 billion are quite small when compared to the size of the costs and benefits. If we have underestimated consumer surplus losses by as little as 2 percent, then the true net benefits under the informed demand case would be negative instead of positive. Because we have been conservative in counting benefits in this case, it is probably reasonable for us to conclude that the tax at least breaks even. Nevertheless, the general point is that we should not put false confidence in the accuracy of our specific estimates.

Next consider the uninformed demand case. Here we report large positive net benefits of $13.95 billion annually. In inspecting the benefit categories, we note that almost 80 percent of the net benefits come from benefits under the heading of avoided health and productivity costs. Yet the estimates underlying these benefits were pulled somewhat uncritically out of the literature. Lack of time and access to primary data forced us to take at face value the yearly health and productivity costs estimated by other analysts. Our uncertainty about the accuracy of these estimates should give us concern. We may be victim to what has been called the problem of "horse and rabbit stew." When we mix our fairly accurate estimates of avoided fatalities (rabbit) with the larger but less certain estimates of health and productivity savings (strong-flavored horse), our net benefits (stew) will be dominated by the less certain estimates (our stew will taste primarily of horse). The general point is that the uncertainty of the larger costs and benefits will largely determine the uncertainty of our net benefit estimate.

Fortunately, these problems are not as serious for the best guess case. Net benefits equal $3.36 billion, a fairly substantial amount even when compared to the large consumer surplus losses. Health and productivity benefits make up less than one-third of net benefits, reducing the danger that we have cooked horse and rabbit stew. Of course, whether or not our estimate of net benefits under the best guess is close to the true value of net benefits depends on the reasonableness of the various assumptions we have already discussed.

Net Benefits of Other Tax Rates. We focused on the 30 percent tax rate for purposes of exposition. Does the 30 percent rate offer the largest net benefits? Table 16.4 shows net benefits for lower and higher rates for each of the three cases. Under the

Table 16.4 *Net Benefits of Alcohol Taxes (billions of dollars)*

Tax Rate (tax revenue)	Uninformed Demand	Best Guess	Informed Demand
.10 (5.73)	6.24	2.09	0.63
.20 (10.80)	10.72	3.12	0.65
.30 (15.34)	13.95	3.36	0.24
.40 (19.46)	17.99	4.68	0.20
.50 (23.22)	21.60	5.79	0.03

informed demand case, net benefits peak at the 20 percent tax rate. Thus, if we see this case as the appropriate one (because either we think it is the most likely or we wish to be conservative), then we should recommend 20 percent as the most efficient rate.

Under either the uninformed demand or best guess case, net benefits continue to rise up to 50 percent, the highest rate analyzed. This indicates that an even higher rate than 50 percent may be optimal. Two considerations, one methodological and the other substantive, suggest caution in this interpretation. First, the farther we move from current policy, the less confidence we should have in our predictions of effects. Our assumption of isoelastic demand, for instance, may be quite reasonable for small, but not large, price changes. Second, as we move toward prohibitive taxes, we may encounter radically different behavioral responses. Think of the ways people responded to Prohibition in the United States during the 1920s: they smuggled alcohol into the United States from other countries; they formed criminal organizations, which corrupted officials and practiced violence, to supply alcohol to the illegal market; they made alcohol at home; they developed a taste for more concentrated, and therefore more easily smuggled, forms of alcohol.[70] Along with these sorts of behaviors, substantially higher taxes might induce greater use of other recreational drugs and perhaps trigger other important, but unanticipated, effects. Because we did not consider these possible effects, we should be cautious about advocating very high tax rates on the basis of our cost-benefit analysis alone.

Reconsidering the Value of Life: Switching to Cost-Effectiveness. If we are unwilling to assign a dollar value to lives saved, then we must abandon cost-benefit analysis because we have incommensurable goals: saving lives and increasing economic efficiency. As long as we have only two goals, we can apply cost-effectiveness analysis instead. We ask the basic question: How many dollars of economic efficiency must be given up for each life saved? For example, consider the informed demand case for the 30 percent tax. At a net cost of $1.4 billion, 1,645 lives can be saved, yielding a cost per life saved of $0.85 million.

We should compare the 30 percent tax rate with other tax rates in terms of cost per life saved. As the tax rate increases beyond 30 percent in the informed demand case, the number of lives saved goes up but so too does the cost per life saved. It is only when we compare alternatives that save the same number of lives that we can unequivocally say that the one with the lowest cost per life saved is best. Nevertheless, the cost per life saved indicates how high a dollar value of life we have to assume in a cost-benefit analysis to yield positive net benefits. As a rough comparison, a 1986 Office of Management and Budget review of health and safety regulations reported costs per life saved that ranged from approximately $100,000 to $72 million.[71] A more recent review of over 500 regulations and other actual or proposed policy interventions found that costs per life saved ranged from negative numbers (that is, the interventions actually saved resources as well as lives) to those costing over $10 billion (in 1993 dollars) per years of life saved.[72]

[70]For discussions of the costs of prohibition, see Irving Fisher, *Prohibition at Its Worst* (New York: Macmillan, 1926); and Malvern Hall Tillitt, *The Price of Prohibition* (New York: Harcourt, Brace, 1932).

[71]John F. Morrall, III, "A Review of the Record," *Regulation*, November/December 1986, 25–34.

[72]Tammy O. Tengs, Miriam E. Adams, Joseph S. Pliskin, Dana Gelb Safran, Joanna E. Siegel, Milton C. Weinstein, and John D. Graham, "Five-Hundred Life-Saving Interventions and Their Cost-Effectiveness," *Risk Analysis* 15(3) 1993, 364–90.

Valuing lives saved often arises in analysis of alternative health policies. Health researchers are often concerned not with prolonging life but also with the quality of the life enjoyed by those who live longer. They have developed a number of ways of estimating the values people place on various health states. Combining assessments of health states and duration of life leads to *quality adjusted life-years (QALYs)*, which are often used in cost-effectiveness analyses of alternative medical and health interventions.[73]

Reprise of Alcohol Tax CBA

Our analysis of alcohol taxation illustrates the basic craft and art of cost-benefit analysis. Basic concepts for measuring costs and benefits constitute the craft; drawing together fragmentary evidence from disparate sources to predict and monetize effects constitutes the art. Our conclusion that a 30 percent tax offers positive net benefits appears fairly robust to changes in assumptions about the measurement of benefits. Thus we could be fairly confident in concluding that it would increase economic efficiency if adopted. Yet we remain highly uncertain about whether 30 percent is close to the optimal rate.

Conclusion

Cost-benefit analysis provides a framework for evaluating the economic efficiency of policies. The calculation of net benefits answers the question: Does the policy generate sufficient benefits so that those who bear its costs could at least potentially be compensated so that some people could be made better off without making anyone worse off? In order to calculate net benefits, we must decide which effects are relevant and how they can be made commensurable. The general concepts of opportunity cost and willingness to pay guide us in the application of the craft of cost-benefit analysis. The art lies in making reasonable inferences from data that are usually fragmentary and incomplete. The art also lies in realizing when inadequate data or social values other than efficiency make the narrow cost-benefit approach inappropriate.

For Discussion

1. Consider a regulation that would ban the use of cell phones while driving automobiles. List the effects of the regulation and classify them as costs and benefits.
2. Cost-benefit analysis provides a method for identifying the most efficient alternative. Consider its relationship to distributional values from both a theoretical and a practical perspective.

[73]For a review, see Marthe R. Gold, Joanna E. Siegel, Louise B. Russell, and Milton C. Weinstein, eds., *Cost-Effectiveness in Health and Medicine* (New York: Oxford University Press, 1996).

17

Cost-Benefit Analysis in a Bureaucratic Setting

The Strategic Petroleum Reserve

Cost-benefit analysis alone rarely plays decisive roles in the resolution of important policy issues. Although cost-benefit analysis speaks to aggregate economic efficiency, the pluralistic and decentralized political systems of Canada, the United States, and most of the other Western democracies give voice to the organized interests that expect to be winners and losers. Lest aspiring analysts despair, however, they should realize that sound cost-benefit analysis can make important contributions to better policy by informing national and international leaders and by giving support to partisans whose interests happen to be consistent with aggregate economic efficiency. Thus, cost-benefit analysis may serve as a political resource as well as a normative guide.

In this chapter we look at the role cost-benefit analysis had in influencing decisions concerning the size of the Strategic Petroleum Reserve (SPR) program, a fundamental element of U.S. energy policy since the oil price shocks of the 1970s. Our story illustrates the use of cost-benefit analysis to evaluate programs whose future benefits are inherently uncertain. It also illustrates the process of doing quantitative analyses in bureaucratic settings and the role that such analyses can play in influencing political decisions. We hope to be both encouraging and sobering to aspiring analysts about the potential usefulness of their technical skills.

Background: Energy Security and the SPR[1]

After the Second World War, the United States became a net importer of crude oil. In 1959, the United States instituted mandatory quotas on oil imports to limit its growing dependence on foreign sources and to support higher prices for domestically produced oil. Throughout the 1960s, the Texas Railroad Commission stabilized domestic prices by regulating the quantity of oil produced in Texas, the major oil-producing state.[2] Thus, even though U.S. *dependence* on foreign oil continued to grow, the United States was not directly *vulnerable* to changes in the world oil market because the Texas Railroad Commission could adjust domestic production to compensate for shifts in import levels.

The picture had changed by the early 1970s. As countries asserted sovereignty over their natural resources during the 1960s, the international oil companies, anticipating eventual loss of control over oil reserves, favored high rates of current production that led to falling real prices. The years of falling real oil prices and a growing world economy contributed to a steady growth in world oil consumption. By the time national governments had achieved direct control over their domestic oil production, they were in a favorable position to exercise some market power through the Organization of Petroleum Exporting Countries (OPEC).

Meanwhile, in the United States two factors were contributing to greater dependence on imported oil and greater vulnerability to swings in the world market. Ceilings on wellhead prices of domestic crude oil had come into effect as part of the general wage and price controls instituted in August 1971 by President Richard Nixon. Although the ceilings had provisions to encourage the development of new oil fields, their overall effect was to slow the growth in domestic oil production and thereby increase import levels. By this time, the Texas Railroad Commission was allowing wells to produce at their maximum efficient rates, and therefore it no longer controlled excess capacity that could be used to increase domestic production rapidly.

Recognizing that a large fraction of oil supplied to the world market originated in the politically unstable Middle East, a small but growing number of analysts and political leaders in Congress and the executive agencies began to worry about the increasing vulnerability of the United States to disruptions of the world oil market. By the summer of 1973, there were several proposals that the U.S. establish petroleum stockpiles. For example, the National Petroleum Council, an industry advisory group to the Department of Interior, raised the possibility of protecting the United States from supply disruptions by storing ninety days of oil imports in salt dome caverns by 1978.[3] Senator Henry Jackson held hearings before the Interior and Insular Affairs Committee on legislation he had introduced that would establish government-owned petroleum stocks.[4] Although administration

[1]For a more detailed discussion of the U.S. stockpiling program, see David L. Weimer, *The Strategic Petroleum Reserve: Planning, Implementation, and Analysis* (Westport, CT: Greenwood Press, 1982). Our account here draws heavily on this source.

[2]For an overview of the contribution of the Texas Railroad Commission to price stability, see Arlon R. Tussing, "An OPEC Obituary," *Public Interest* 70(Winter) 1983, 3–21.

[3]National Petroleum Council, "Emergency Preparedness for Interruptions of Petroleum Imports into the United States," Proposed Interim Report, July 24, 1973.

[4]U.S. Congress, Senate, "Strategic Petroleum Reserves," Hearings before the Committee on Interior and Insular Affairs, 93rd Congress, 1st Session, May 30 and July 26, 1973.

witnesses offered cautious support for the idea of creating petroleum reserves, they argued that more time was needed to study the options.

Events did not allow much time for quiet study. On October 6, 1973, Egypt attacked Israeli positions along the Suez Canal. Led by Saudi Arabia, the Organization of Arab Petroleum Exporting Countries (OAPEC) tried to use the "oil weapon" in support of Egypt. When the United States began to resupply arms to Israel through bases in The Netherlands, OAPEC embargoed oil shipments to the two countries. More significantly, OAPEC members reduced their total oil production so that total world supply fell by about 5 percent in the last quarter of 1973 and the first quarter of 1974. The result was a quadrupling of oil prices. The spot price of Mideast light crude, for example, went from $2.70 per barrel in the third quarter of 1973 to $13.00 per barrel in the first quarter of 1974. This price shock triggered a deep recession that extended well into 1975. The "policy window" for energy security was clearly open.

Initiation of the SPR Program

In response to the Arab oil embargo, President Nixon announced Project Independence, a national effort to achieve energy self-sufficiency by the end of the decade. An interagency task force, eventually headed by the newly created Federal Energy Administration (FEA), began to analyze ways of implementing Project Independence. The task force eventually realized that reducing U.S. vulnerability to disruptions in the world oil market was a much more appropriate goal than self-sufficiency.[5] Yet most of the report was devoted to modeling domestic supply and demand to predict future import levels. Relying heavily on the earlier National Petroleum Council analysis, the Project Independence Report nevertheless suggested that petroleum stockpiles of a billion barrels or more might be justified on grounds of economic efficiency.

The creation of a strategic petroleum reserve was one of the few recommendations of the Project Independence Report included by the new Ford Administration in its legislative proposals of January 1975. Of all the proposals, it received the warmest reception in Congress. The Energy Policy and Conservation Act (P.L. 94-163), which was passed and signed into law in December 1975, gave the FEA administrator one year to submit to Congress a plan for the implementation of a Strategic Petroleum Reserve program that would have 150 million barrels of petroleum in storage within three years and eventually store up to 1 billion barrels. Although there was a presumption in the legislation that the SPR would hold about ninety days of petroleum imports (then about 500 million barrels) within seven years, the details of program design and implementation were left to the FEA administrator.

Basic Program Structure

The SPR plan, which was submitted to Congress in December 1976, called for 150 million barrels of oil to be in storage by December 1978, 325 million barrels by December 1980, and 500 million barrels by December 1982. The choice of 500 million barrels was the result of a compromise with the Office of Management and

[5]Federal Energy Administration, *Project Independence Report*, November 1974, p. 19.

Budget (OMB). OMB analysts favored a smaller reserve. Although FEA analysts believed that a larger reserve could be justified on efficiency grounds with reasonable assumptions about the likelihood of future disruptions, they did not wish to reopen the issue with OMB.

The SPR plan identified salt dome caverns and mines as the most desirable storage facilities. They were expected to be much cheaper than the major alternatives: steel tanks, floating tankers, and shut-in wells.[6] The writers of the plan anticipated that about 200 million barrels of salt dome storage capacity could be purchased from firms that had created caverns as a by-product of brine production and salt mining. Additional capacity would be created through solution mining (making caverns by dissolving salt with fresh water), which permitted new caverns to be filled with oil as they were being created. The salt dome formations were conveniently located along the Gulf Coast near existing transportation facilities so that oil taken out of storage could be easily distributed.

The SPR plan was generally well received in Congress. The only major criticism came from a few senators who wanted the plan to include the storage of petroleum products in regional locations as well as the storage of crude oil along the Gulf Coast. The FEA administrator under the new Carter Administration was able to deflect this criticism by promising further study. Consequently, the Senate and House allowed the plan to go into effect without amendment in April 1977.

Implementation Problems

The SPR program appeared to get off to a good start. Within one week of the plan's going into effect, three of the major sites for solution mining were acquired. Within a few months, oil was being injected into caverns at one site; by the end of the year, oil was being injected at all three sites and a conventionally mined site had been acquired. Soon, however, problems arose that frustrated efforts to keep the program on schedule and under budget. In 1979, when oil purchases were stopped in response to the increases in price growing out of the Iranian revolution, only 92 million barrels were in storage. The resulting general perception of failure, and some of the specific reasons for it, left the program vulnerable to later attempts to limit its size.

Here we briefly sketch some of the major sources of implementation failure at the outset of the SPR program.[7]

Problems Inherent in Program Design. The SPR plan was overly optimistic about how much existing storage capacity could be purchased and immediately put to use. Several caverns did not have as much capacity as expected.

[6]Storage on the form of surge capacity from shut-in oil wells is the most expensive of the alternatives. For each barrel of surge capacity, about eight barrels of proven reserves must be shut in. To have the capacity to increase production by 1 billion barrels per year would require 8 billion barrels of proven reserves, or about 25 percent of total U.S. proven reserves. Furthermore, transportation facilities and production crews would have to be kept at the ready. Whereas new solution-mined caverns were expected to cost between $1.35 and $2.15 per barrel (actual costs turned out to be closer to $3.00 per barrel) and new steel tanks between $8 and $12 per barrel, in situ storage was estimated to cost between $45 and $100 per barrel. Strategic Petroleum Office, "Strategic Petroleum Reserve Plan," December 15, 1976, Table IV-1, at p. 75.

[7]For a fuller discussion, see David L. Weimer, "Problems of Expected Implementation: The Strategic Petroleum Reserve," *Journal of Public Policy* 3(2) 1983, 169–90.

The capacity that was available required the disposal of a barrel of brine for each barrel of oil put in storage. Deep wells, which would eventually be replaced by planned pipelines to the sea, proved inadequate for disposing of the brine. The deficit of existing capacity, which necessitated more solution mining of new capacity, greatly exacerbated the problem of brine disposal—the mining of each barrel of new capacity produces seven barrels of brine as a by-product.

The SPR plan also failed to anticipate the difficulty of initiating and monitoring the large number of contracts—eighty-five major construction contracts alone during the first year—with a small staff based in Washington, D.C. The task was overwhelming. The eventual solution, a limited privatization of the contracting function, was to hire a prime contractor that in turn contracted for the necessary construction services and materials. Nevertheless, the initial contracting problem slowed implementation, contributed to cost overruns, and diverted attention from building a management infrastructure.

Should these problems have been foreseen by program planners? Undoubtedly, the limited technical experience of the planners contributed to their overly optimistic assumptions about the availability and feasible rate of developing storage capacity. But without taking time to do field experiments, it is not obvious how they could have made better estimates. In contrast, if they had prepared detailed implementation scenarios, then they might have anticipated the difficulty of administering so many contracts with such a small staff in an organization with no prior experience in procuring construction services.

Unrealistic Expectations. James R. Schlesinger, who later became secretary of the new Department of Energy, served as President Jimmy Carter's chief energy adviser in the early days of the new administration. He viewed reliance on Middle Eastern oil as a serious weakness in the U.S. defense posture. He also believed that the then "soft" world oil market would become "tight" in the early 1980s, so it would be better to accumulate oil for the reserve sooner rather than later. He therefore convinced the president that development of the SPR should be accelerated by two years and its ultimate size increased to 1 billion barrels.

These decisions were made, however, without consulting the SPR office about their feasibility. The SPR staff argued for a more modest acceleration; but Schlesinger insisted on changing the schedule so that 250 million barrels would be in storage by the end of 1978 and 500 million barrels by the end of 1980. So, at a time when the SPR office was straining to keep the implementation on the old schedule, it had to divert scarce managerial resources to devise a plan for meeting a more ambitious one. The plan was transmitted to Congress in May as an amendment to the original SPR plan.

Aside from using scarce managerial resources at a critical stage in the implementation, the acceleration decision forced the SPR office to take a number of gambles in order to meet the new schedule. For example, to avoid delays in deliveries of oil, purchases were made in anticipation of facilities being completed. When they were not ready, demurrage charges had to be paid for the unaccepted deliveries. The acceleration decision also contributed to a loss of credibility that hurt the program in its future efforts to secure needed resources. Thus, because of the failure to consider the feasibility of implementation, the acceleration decision actually decelerated the program. The decision to expand the size of the SPR to 1 billion barrels opened the bureaucratic battles that we discuss later in the chapter.

Lack of Organizational Support. When the SPR office was located within the FEA, it enjoyed a favored position. The head of the SPR office was an assistant administrator who reported directly to the FEA administrator. This access enabled the SPR office to obtain fast decisions from the administrator and elicit his support in securing cooperation from other agencies and other units within the FEA. For example, when the magnitude of the contracting problem became apparent, the administrator helped set up a special procurement board to expedite the signing of construction contracts.

All this changed with the creation of the Department of Energy (DOE) in October 1977. Instead of reporting directly to the FEA administrator, the director of the SPR office now reported to a deputy assistant secretary, who reported to an assistant secretary, who reported to the undersecretary, who reported to a deputy secretary, who reported to the secretary. No longer was it possible to get fast decisions. Furthermore, each substantive office within the department competed for the attention of the new hierarchy.

Three serious problems arose. First, the SPR office could not easily mobilize the DOE leadership to intervene with other agencies, such as the Environmental Protection Agency and the Army Corps of Engineers, whose procedures for issuing environmental and water use permits were slowing construction. Second, when the DOE was created by merging the FEA, the Federal Power Commission, and the Energy Research and Development Administration, the number of employees exceeded the limit for the new agency. The response was a department-wide hiring freeze—just at the time that the SPR office needed to add personnel with experience in contract administration. The director of the SPR office had to devote staff time to making special requests for new hires. Third, all procurement responsibilities were transferred to what had been the procurement office of the Energy Research and Development Administration. Its cumbersome procedures were designed to handle procurements for large and complex research and development projects. Contracts that the FEA would have processed in weeks or months now took as long as nine months. Indeed, a critical six-month period passed with virtually no contracts for the SPR being let.

These problems highlight the importance of considering organizational structure in designing new programs. Perhaps many of the problems could have been avoided if the SPR office had been established as either an independent agency or a unit reporting directly to the secretary. The necessity of winning support within the large DOE bureaucracy also became relevant in later battles with OMB over funding for program expansion.

Reprise of SPR Origins. The SPR program failed to meet either its original or accelerated schedule. At the end of 1978 only 68.5 million barrels were in storage—far less than the 150 million barrels called for by the old schedule or the 250 million barrels called for by the accelerated schedule. The 500-million-barrel mark was not reached until 1986, four years later than under the original schedule and six years later than under the accelerated schedule.

The implementation problems that led to these delays had been largely solved by 1980. But were (and are) the objectives of the SPR program appropriate? It is to this question that we turn next.

Analytical Approaches to the Size Issue

The intuitive logic behind stockpiling is simple: buy oil when prices are low (in normal markets) and sell oil when prices are high (in disrupted markets). Such speculation has the potential for generating profits, suggesting the possibility of private stockpiling. Why, then, should the government be involved in oil stockpiling? In other words, what market or government failure justifies publicly owned oil stocks? There are three major rationales for public stockpiling: two based on market failure and the other based on government failure.[8]

First, stockpiling involves external effects. Firms do not bear the full costs and benefits of their stockpiling decisions. When firms purchase oil stocks, they increase the world demand for oil, which may in turn increase the price. While the stockpilers must pay the higher price, so, too, must all buyers of oil. The economic costs of the higher prices, however, are external to the profit calculations of the stockpilers. Thus, the social costs of building stocks may be higher than the private costs. With respect to drawdowns that reduce price, the social benefits may be higher than the private benefits. Also, the mere existence of a large stockpile may provide political benefits, such as the deterrence of purposeful disruptions, that do not show up in the profits of private stockpilers. In general, we expect the positive externalities to be greater than the negative externalities. The reason is that stock accumulations usually occur gradually, so that small price increases with negligible economic effects result; drawdowns are likely to occur during price shocks, when even small price reductions can have noticeable economic benefits.[9]

Second, if firms are risk averse, then they may forgo stockpiling that reduces social risk. For an individual firm, stockpiling in anticipation of a major price shock is like gambling—if the price shock occurs, the firm profits; if it does not, the firm suffers a loss. Therefore, from the firm's perspective, stockpiling is like gambling—a sure payment is made in return for the small probability of a big gain. From the social perspective, however, stockpiling is like insurance—a sure payment is made in return for avoiding the small probability of a big loss.

Third, because of government price controls and mandatory petroleum allocations in the recent past, firms may anticipate the possibility that the government will prevent them from selling speculative stocks at market prices during future oil price shocks. In other words, past government actions have undermined the credibility of property rights to stockpiled oil. We can think of this as having created an institutional common property resource problem: because firms are not able with certainty to exclude others from using their stockpiled oil when it is most valuable, they will undersupply speculative stocks. Therefore, too little oil will be privately stockpiled for use during oil supply disruptions.

[8]George Horwich and David L. Weimer, *Oil Price Shocks, Market Response, and Contingency Planning* (Washington, DC: American Enterprise for Public Policy Research, 1984), 112–14.

[9]The major exception occurs in situations in which firms attempt to build their stocks once disruptions have already begun. Such behavior may be consistent with the maximization of profits if firms anticipate higher prices in the future, but it contributes to the magnitude of the price shock that the economy suffers.

These rationales suggest the desirability of a public role in oil stockpiling. But how big a role? Assuming that stockpiling is to be supplied directly by government, how big should the stockpile be? How quickly should it be built? And under what circumstances should it be used? The cost-benefit framework helps us begin to answer these questions.

Impacts of a Stockpiling Program

As shown in Table 17.1, we divide the impacts of a public stockpiling program into four categories: expenditure, direct market, political, and collateral effects.

Expenditure Effects. The most visible costs of an oil stockpiling program are the outlays that must be made to secure storage facilities and purchase oil. Estimates of the costs of building storage facilities can be based on engineering data or on the costs of similar facilities built in the past. Estimating the cost of oil requires projections of future prices, including the effects of the purchases themselves. Because purchases generally will not be made in disrupted markets, such projections can take the form of assumptions about long-run rates of price growth (or decline).

When the government sells oil from the stockpile, it realizes revenue. Large sales will depress the price of oil—the intended effect when stocks are used to counter a price shock caused by a disruption of the world oil market. We may assume that the program will be terminated at some future date by selling facilities and any remaining stocks at projected prices. These revenues constitute the anticipated scrap value of the program.

Market Effects. The left-hand panel of Figure 17.1 illustrates the market effects of a drawdown of stocks during a disruption of the world oil market. Prior to the disruption, the world price of oil is P_0, the price at which the supply schedule S_{WN}

Table 17.1 *Impacts of a Public Oil Stockpiling Program*

Expenditure Effects Outlays: oil purchases storage facilities Revenues: oil sales	Measured in benefit-cost analyses
Direct Market Effects Costs: price effects of purchases Benefits: price effects of drawdowns	Measured in benefit-cost analyses
Political Effects Deterrence against purposeful disruptions "Breathing space": foreign policy domestic policy	Not monetized
Collateral Effects Stockpiling displacement: private sector other countries	Adjustments to effective size of public stockpile

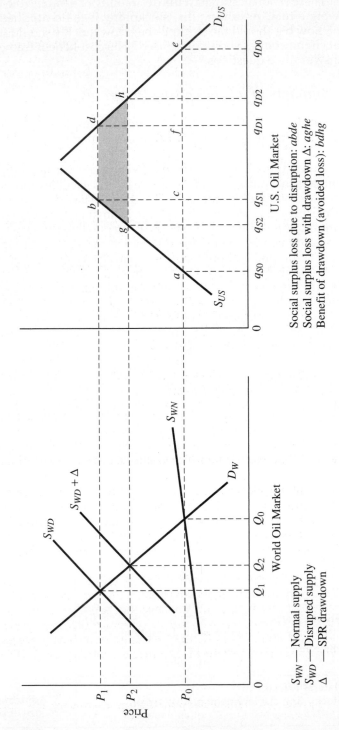

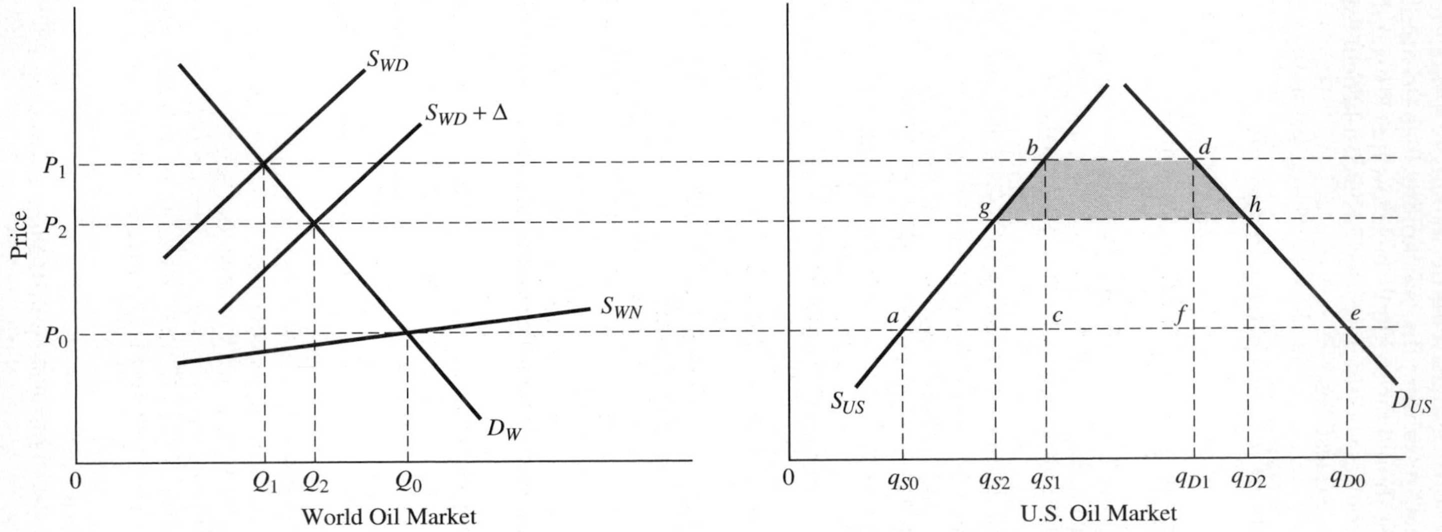

S_{WN} — Normal supply
S_{WD} — Disrupted supply
Δ — SPR drawdown

Social surplus loss due to disruption: *abde*
Social surplus loss with drawdown Δ: *aghe*
Benefit of drawdown (avoided loss): *bdhg*

Figure 17.1 Measuring the Direct Economic Benefits of an SPR Drawdown

and the demand schedule D_W intersect. A disruption, which suddenly removes supply from the market, shifts the supply schedule to S_{WD}. This shift causes price to rise to P_1. (The sudden jump in price from P_0 to P_1 is the *oil price shock*.) A drawdown of oil stocks shifts the supply curve back to the right. A drawdown of size Δ shifts the postdisruption supply schedule horizontally to the right by Δ units to $S_{WD} + \Delta$ so that price P_2 results. Thus, the drawdown keeps the postdisruption price from rising all the way to P_1. The difference between P_1 and P_2 is the source of the economic benefits of the drawdown for net oil importers like the United States.

A purchase of oil for the stockpile shifts the demand schedule in the world market to the right. If the supply schedule is horizontal over the range of the shifting demand schedule, then the purchase does not cause the price to rise. If the supply schedule is upward sloping, however, the shift in demand does cause price to rise. This rise in price results in economic losses for net oil importers that can be measured in the same way as the economic losses caused by the oil supply disruption.

Political Effects. A large stockpile may deter embargoes and politically motivated reductions in supply. The larger the stockpile, the more political opponents must reduce supply in order to impose any particular level of economic loss on importers. As long as the exporting countries anticipate that they also will suffer economic losses by reducing supply, the existence of a large stockpile will deter somewhat the use of supply disruptions for political purposes.

A large stockpile also expands the range of options that the United States can pursue in carrying out domestic and foreign policy. Because a stockpile drawdown provides "breathing space" between the time when supplies from an exporting region are disrupted and the time when the full impact of the resulting price increase is felt, diplomatic initiatives can be launched in a less politically volatile domestic environment than otherwise. If the disruption coincides with, or leads to, military intervention, the stockpile will enhance operational flexibility by reducing the costs to the United States and its allies of temporary damage that they might inflict collaterally to oil-producing facilities. In terms of domestic policy, drawdowns may lessen the political panic that can lead to price controls and mandatory allocations of the sort that exacerbated the economic costs of disruptions during the 1970s.[10]

Collateral Effects. Public stockpiling may discourage private stockpiling. The existence of a large stockpile controlled by the government may displace stockpiling that would otherwise be done by the private sector. Firms will expect government drawdowns during disruptions to reduce the price at which their own stockpiles could be sold. Although this price-reducing effect will tend to lower the size of private stockpiles, the marginal reduction is likely to be small if firms already anticipate that price controls and mandatory allocations of private stockpiles will be reimposed during disruptions large enough to trigger use of the government stockpile. Indeed, if firms believe that larger government stockpiles reduce the likelihood that price controls and allocations will be reimposed, increasing the size of the government stockpile may actually encourage private stockpiling. Overall, the displacement of private stockpiling is probably insignificant.

[10]For a discussion of the impact of the U.S. regulations during the 1970s, see Horwich and Weimer, *Oil Price Shocks*, pp. 57–110.

A large U.S. stockpile may also discourage the stockpiling efforts of foreign governments. Because oil consumers worldwide gain from drawdowns of the U.S. stockpile, other importing nations may take a "free ride" on large U.S. stocks. If this happens, then each barrel added to the U.S. stockpile will result in less than a barrel in net additions to world stocks. A factor that constrains free riding is the International Energy Agency. Its members, including the United States, Canada, Japan, Germany, and most of the other countries in Western Europe, have agreed to hold minimum levels of petroleum stocks for use during supply disruptions.[11] Even without such an agreement, fear that the United States may fail to use its reserves is likely to restrain countries somewhat from free riding.

The standard approach for taking account of these displacement effects in cost-benefit analyses is to assume that the public stockpile has a smaller effective, than physical, size. So, for example, if analysts believed that private stocks would be reduced by one barrel for each five barrels put in the public stockpile, then a 500-million-barrel reserve would have an effective size of only 400 million barrels.

Quantifying Costs and Benefits

We can employ the standard tools of economics to quantify the budgetary and market impacts of a stockpiling program. Unfortunately, the political and collateral effects are not as easily quantified. It is probably reasonable to assume that the displacement effects of a U.S. stockpiling program are small. Although the political benefits cannot be quantified, they nevertheless may be important, especially to a president who must make politically sensitive decisions, such as those concerning the resupply of Israel during a Middle East war or the use of military force to aid the government of Saudi Arabia against foreign-supported insurgents or an Iraqi invasion. In excluding political benefits from our cost-benefit analysis, we understate the net benefits of stockpiling. As we discussed in Chapter 16, the cost-benefit analysis becomes one component of a larger multigoal analysis.

We must also consider the issue of standing. As we have already mentioned, acquisitions and drawdowns affect the price of oil in the world oil market. One approach is to measure the costs and benefits accruing not just to the United States but also to its allies that import oil at the world price. Instead, the standard practice for analysts in the U.S. government has been to measure only costs and benefits accruing domestically. In other words, they give standing in their cost-benefit analyses only to U.S. residents.

Changes in Social Surplus. We return to Figure 17.1 to illustrate the measurement of the benefits of drawdowns and the costs of acquisitions.

The right-hand panel shows the effect of the rise in price from P_0 to P_1 on the U.S. oil market. At the predisruption price P_0, q_{D0} is domestically consumed (point *e* on the U.S. demand schedule, D_{US}) and q_{S0} is domestically produced (point *a* on the U.S. supply schedule, S_{US}). The difference between domestic consumption and domestic production equals the level of imports prior to the disruption. When the

[11]See Rodney T. Smith, "International Energy Agency Cooperation: The Mismatch between IEA Policy Actions and Policy Goals," in George Horwich and David L. Weimer, eds., *Responding to International Oil Crises* (Washington, DC: American Enterprise Institute for Public Policy Research, 1988), 17–103.

price rises to P_1, domestic consumption falls to q_{D1} and domestic production rises to q_{S1}. The resulting loss in social surplus equals the area of trapezoid *abde*; the area of triangle *def* represents the consumer surplus lost because less is being consumed; the triangle *abc* represents the real resource costs of increasing domestic production; and the area of rectangle *bdfc* represents the additional amount that consumers must pay to foreign suppliers for the imports that they continue to consume.

The postdisruption price with a drawdown of size Δ is only P_2. The social surplus loss of a rise in price from P_0 to P_2 equals the area of trapezoid *aghe*, which is smaller than the social surplus loss without the drawdown by the area of trapezoid *bdhg*. Thus, the avoided social surplus loss from the drawdown equals the area *bdhg* (which is shaded in the figure). Applying the rule developed in Chapter 12, we see that the benefits of the drawdown equal the realized revenue (Δ times P_2), plus the change in social surplus in the primary market (area *bdhg*).

Oil acquisitions that increase world price also cause a social surplus loss in the U.S. domestic oil market. Imagine that the rise in price from P_0 to P_1 had been caused by a very large oil purchase. It would cause the same loss in social surplus as the disruption. To calculate the costs of the acquisition, we would add expenditures for the purchased oil to the change of social surplus in the domestic market. Only if price did not rise as a result of the oil purchase would the cost of the acquisition just equal the budgetary cost.

What information is needed to calculate these direct social surplus changes? To locate the positions of the supply and demand schedules, we need projections of price, world consumption, domestic consumption, and domestic supply for the period of time during which the stockpiling program is to be in existence. Such long-run projections are typically based on historical trends. To measure the effect of supply interruptions on price, we need estimates of the price elasticities of supply and demand in the world oil market; to measure social surplus losses we need estimates of the price elasticities of supply and demand in the U.S. oil market. Econometric analyses of historical or cross-national data provide reasonable ranges for these elasticities.

Adjustment Costs. The social surplus analysis assumes that the economy can move from one equilibrium to another without cost. While this is a reasonable assumption for moderate price changes, it may not be for steep price changes in a commodity, such as oil, that is a basic input to important sectors of the economy. The higher price of oil requires that relative prices throughout the economy change to achieve efficient allocation at the new equilibrium. Not all prices are perfectly flexible, however. Nominal wages, for instance, tend to be downwardly sticky, so that during a large price shock we may see greater involuntary unemployment rather than an immediate fall in wages. Although inflation may eventually permit an appropriate adjustment by reducing real wages, the short-term consequences may be greater inefficiency than estimated by the direct changes in social surplus.

Similarly, sharp oil price shocks induce immense transfers in wealth from domestic consumers to domestic and foreign oil producers; this shifts demand schedules throughout the economy. Uncertainty about the new composition of demand can slow investment needed to produce a capital stock consistent with the new relative prices. Delayed investment and reduced aggregate consumption can lead to recession. The inefficiency of idle resources during recession and the loss in future output caused by delays in current investment are not reflected in the direct changes in social surplus.

In light of these adjustment costs, do cost-benefit analyses based on direct changes in social surplus have any systematic biases? Because adjustment costs grow disproportionately with the size of the price shock, direct measures of social surplus changes contribute more to an underestimation of the benefits of drawdowns than an underestimation of the costs of acquisitions. Therefore, cost-benefit analyses based on direct social surplus changes in the oil market generally underestimate the true net benefits of stockpiling.

Macroeconomic Simulations. Given that an oil price shock sets in motion price changes throughout the economy, a dynamic model of the entire economy would provide an attractive tool for estimating the full economic costs of oil price shocks and thereby the costs and benefits of stockpiling. Large-scale macroeconomic models employ hundreds of interrelated equations to represent various sectors of the economy and their interactions. A variety of these models are used in government and business for predicting GNP, inflation, unemployment, and other measures of aggregate economic performance. For example, the Department of Energy relied on the commercial forecasting models developed by Data Resources Incorporated (DRI) and Wharton Econometric Forecasting Associates in many evaluations of the SPR.

To measure the benefits of a stockpile drawdown, an analyst would employ the following procedure: First, specify a disruption scenario—the price path of oil over a number of three-month periods. Second, using the specified price path of oil, simulate the response of the economy and measure the present value of GNP over a period of several years. Third, specify a new price path of oil that reflects the assumed drawdown and measure the present value of GNP. Fourth, interpret the difference in the present value of GNP as the benefit of the drawdown.

Aside from the limitations of GNP as a measure of social welfare, already discussed in Chapter 7, two important practical problems inherent in this procedure make it analytically unattractive.[12]

First, the most commonly used macroeconomic models are not well designed to estimate the effects of supply-side shocks like oil supply disruptions. The models focus primarily on aggregate demand with only implicit accounting of supply flows; thus, they often produce internally inconsistent results that must be corrected with ad hoc procedures. Also, the econometrically estimated relationships in the models may not hold for large disruptions beyond the range of historical data.

Second, the great complexity of the models, and the numerous assumptions that must be made in using them to simulate something extraordinary like an oil price shock, provide a great opportunity for modelers to manipulate the results. For example, small changes in assumptions about government monetary and fiscal policies can have large effects on the estimated costs of disruptions. Because numerous ad hoc corrections are needed to achieve internal consistency, even well-trained macroeconomists may have difficulty in finding inappropriate assumptions hidden in the complexity. Given that the cost of using such models is high (in terms

[12]Exactly offsetting shifts in domestic consumption and exports would not change GNP. Yet the social surplus of U.S. residents would go down—foreigners now consume goods that they previously consumed. The measure of changes in economic efficiency should be the sum of changes in GNP and changes in foreign claims on GNP. For a comparison of GNP and social surplus welfare measures, see Horwich and Weimer, *Oil Price Shocks*, pp. 8–14.

of both human and computer time), it is often not feasible to test the sensitivity of all major assumptions. All these features invite analytical abuse by those already committed to policies.

Dealing with Uncertainty

Uncertainty about the timing, frequency, duration, and magnitude of oil supply disruptions provides an interesting challenge for anyone wishing to do a cost-benefit analysis of a stockpiling program. If no disruption occurs, or if one occurs before significant stocks can be accumulated, then the stockpiling program will almost certainly involve net costs. But this possibility must be weighed against the possibility that a drawdown during a major disruption will yield huge benefits that greatly exceed the costs of building the stockpile.

We briefly discuss here the two major approaches that have been used to deal with uncertainty in cost-benefit analyses of the SPR: scenario/break-even analysis and dynamic stochastic programming.

Scenario/Break-Even Analysis. Early cost-benefit analyses of the SPR were based on specified scenarios of program development and future market conditions. Each analysis compared two scenarios with identical program schedules: a disruption scenario with a specified supply interruption and a base-case scenario without it. After measuring the costs and benefits incurred under each scenario, the analysts then calculated how likely the scenario with the supply interruption would have to be for the program to barely pass the cost-benefit criterion with zero expected net benefits. For example, the scenarios might call for the addition of 60 million barrels of oil to the SPR in each of the next five years. The disruption scenario might then call for the drawdown of all 300 million barrels in response to a major supply interruption (say, the loss of 6 million barrels per day to the world market for a period of six months) in the seventh year. The base-case scenario might assume that oil would be held for another ten years and then sold. If the present value of the costs of acquiring and storing the oil under the base-case scenario equaled C, and if the present value of benefits from the drawdown during the disruption equaled a larger amount B, then the break-even probability, P_b, would equal C/B.[13] If the decision maker believes that the probability of an interruption similar to the one in the disruption scenario is greater than the break-even probability, then he would conclude that the proposed program schedule offered positive net expected benefits.

The scenario/break-even approach oversimplifies the stockpiling problem in a number of important ways. It does not allow for uncertainty over the timing,

[13]The break-even probability solves the following equation for zero net expected benefits:

$$0 = p_b(B - C) + (1 - p_b)(0 - C)$$

where B is the present value of benefits if the interruption occurs and C the present value of costs. Of course, this simple formulation implies a world with only two contingencies: the supply interruption in the scenario occurs and the supply interruption in the scenario does not occur. It also assumes that the costs of developing the reserve are identical with and without the supply interruption, or B is adjusted to make the costs equal. For example, B would equal the drawdown benefits plus the present value of the avoided costs of future acquisitions and minus the present value of forgone scrap value.

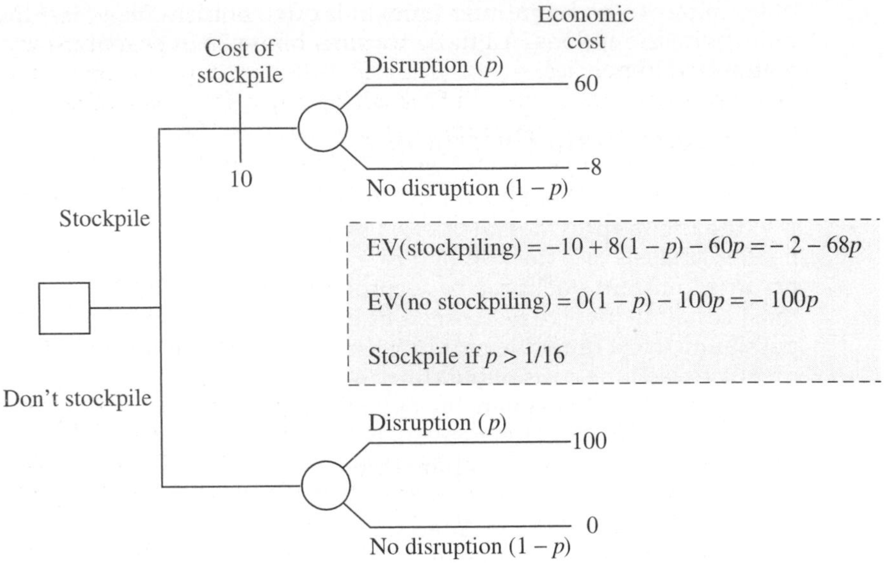

Figure 17.2 A Simple Decision Tree for the Stockpiling Problem

magnitude, and duration of disruptions. It ignores the possibility of there being more than one disruption over the life of the program. In considering the break-even probability, decision makers must subjectively account for these limitations in determining how large a probability to assign to the occurrence of the disruption. In addition, the scenario/break-even methodology provides little insight into the optimal timing of acquisitions and drawdowns.

Simple Decision Analysis

Decision analysis provides a framework for expressing the various dimensions of uncertainty in terms of combinations of simple risks.[14] The basic tool of decision analysis is the *decision tree*. Figure 17.2 illustrates a very simple decision tree that corresponds to a stylized break-even analysis. The tree consists of two types of nodes connected by lines representing outcomes. The square at the left of the tree is a *decision node*, where we begin by making one of two choices: adopt the proposed stockpiling program or do not adopt it. If we do not adopt it, then we move to the lower circle representing a *chance node*, which leads to a disruption (an economic cost of 100) with probability p and no disruption (an economic cost of zero) with probability $1 - p$. If instead we decide to adopt the proposed stockpiling program, then we pay for the program (an economic cost of 10) and move to the upper circle, which leads to a disruption (an economic cost reduced to 60 by drawdown) with probability p and no disruption (an economic cost of -8 because of liquidation of stocks) with probability $1 - p$.

[14]For an application of decision analysis within the context of cost-benefit analysis, see Anthony E. Boardman, David H. Greenberg, Aidan R. Vining, and David L. Weimer, *Cost-Benefit Analysis: Concepts and Practice*, 2nd ed. (Upper Saddle River, NJ: Prentice Hall, 2001), 156–91.

To calculate a break-even probability, we compare the expected value of stockpiling with the expected value of not stockpiling. These expected values are shown in the dashed box of Figure 17.2. By equating the expressions for the expected values and solving for p, we find that stockpiling offers positive net expected benefits if the probability of disruption is greater than 1 in 16.

Now imagine that we let the tree grow decision nodes at the end of each of the chance branches. We could interpret the resulting structure as representing two successive time periods. It would be possible to have no disruption over the two periods, one disruption lasting one period, or one disruption lasting the entire two periods. As we add more and more periods, the tree allows for the possibility of even more patterns of disruption. Thus, by constructing a multiperiod decision tree, we create a model that incorporates a large number of scenarios involving disruptions of varying length and frequency.

Also imagine that we expand the chance nodes to include several levels of disruption. Now the tree permits the possibility of scenarios with the magnitude of a disruption changing over time. We can allow for flexibility in the schedule of the stockpiling program by modifying the decision nodes to have multiple choices about increments and decrements to stocks.

Figure 17.3 shows a close-up of a small portion of an expanded decision tree for the stockpiling problem. As shown, we enter period t under normal market conditions with 50 million barrels of oil already in the stockpile. We are then faced with the decision of how much oil to acquire or drawdown. Eleven possible decisions are shown. They range in 10-million-barrel increments from drawing down the entire stockpile (-50 million barrels) to adding another 50 million barrels. If we add, say, 20 million barrels, then we move to the chance node with 70 million barrels in the stockpile. Now one of five possible market conditions occurs: a slack market in which some oil could be purchased without driving up that price; a normal market in which purchases drive the price up somewhat; a minor disruption; a moderate disruption; and a major disruption. The market condition and the stockpile size define the entering state at the beginning of period $t + 1$.

The decision tree for a stockpiling problem with, for instance, fifteen time periods, five market states, and stockpile increments of 10 million barrels would be literally impossible to draw or solve by hand. Fortunately, a general solution method called *stochastic dynamic programming* can be applied with the aid of a computer.

Stochastic Dynamic Programming. If we were to solve a decision tree by hand, we would start at the last period, calculating expected values over the outcomes of the last chance nodes. We would then replace the chance nodes with these expected values and prune off all but the chance node with the largest expected value for each decision node. We would then discount the dominant nodes back to the previous period. Continuing this process of taking discounted expected values and pruning off dominated chance nodes, we would eventually work back to the decision node in the initial period. As a result of this pruning process, we would be able to select the decision in the initial period that had the largest present value of expected net benefits. Reading through the pruned tree from the first to last period would give us the optimal strategy for any sequence of market conditions.

Stochastic dynamic programming employs a similar solution method, identifying the optimal sequence of drawdowns and acquisitions for any scenario of market conditions. Constraints on the allowable size of the stockpile in each period

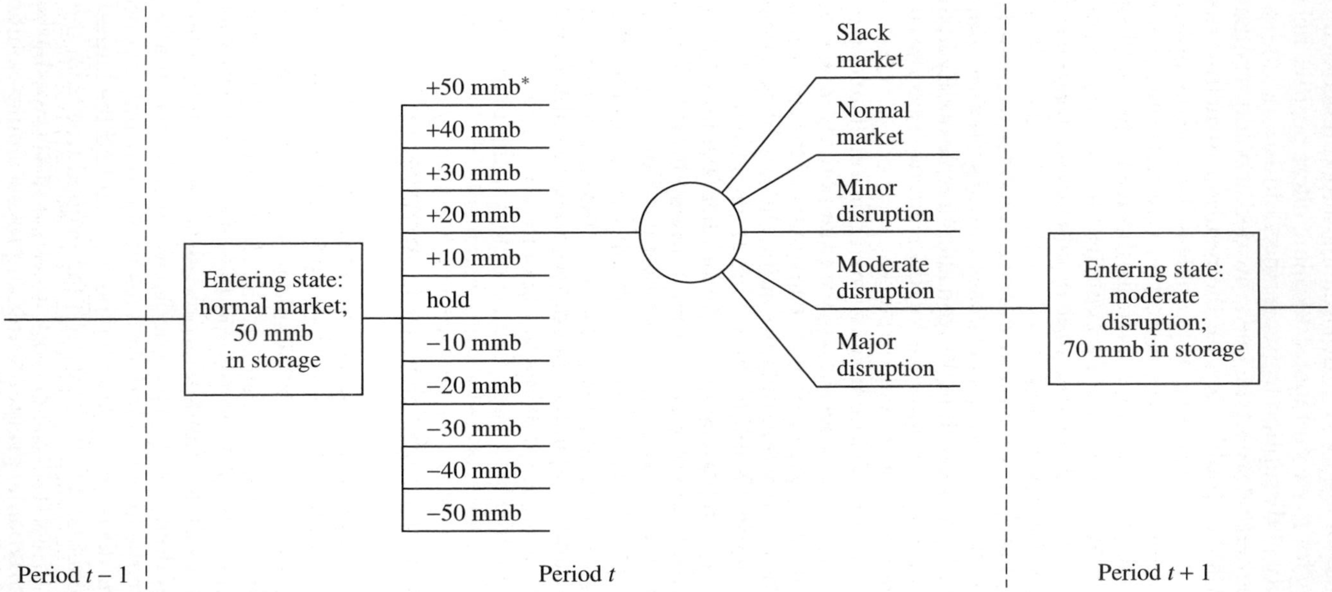

*mmb = million barrel increments

Figure 17.3 A Sample Node in the Expanded Decision Tree for the Stockpiling Problem

can be incorporated to model proposed schedules of storage capacity development. To compare alternative schedules, the stockpiling model would be solved for each schedule separately. The schedule offering the largest present value of expected net benefits would be selected as most efficient.

What assumptions must be made to employ stochastic dynamic programming? First, for each alternative program we require a specification of a schedule of storage capacity availability and the present value of the costs of providing it. Second, assumptions about prices, quantities, and elasticities for the world and U.S. oil markets are necessary for each period so that costs and benefits can be calculated. Third, a social discount rate must be selected. Fourth, the probabilities of each market condition arising in each period contingent on the market condition of the previous period are needed for calculating expected values. For example, given a normal market in the current period, what is the probability that the next period will also have a normal market?

The first three of these categories include the sorts of assumptions that we normally make in doing cost-benefit analysis. Therefore, we have fairly standard approaches for making them. Assumptions about the probabilities of market conditions are much more subjective. If we allow only two possible market conditions, for example, then we can easily do sensitivity analysis by varying the two assumed probabilities. For a model with five market conditions, however, sixteen independent probabilities must be specified. The greatest weakness in the stochastic dynamic programming approach is the difficulty analysts face in selecting these probabilities and communicating their significance to clients.

Stochastic dynamic programming was first applied to the oil stockpiling problem by Thomas J. Teisberg, then a member of the economics faculty at the Massachusetts Institute of Technology.[15] He worked with policy analysts in the DOE to develop a model that became the standard tool for evaluating economic costs and benefits of alternative stockpiling policies. In the story that follows, we look at the role played by this model in the debate between the DOE and the Office of Management and Budget over the appropriate size of the SPR.

The Role of Analysis in the SPR Size Controversy[16]

The Energy Policy and Conservation Act mandated the creation of an SPR of between 150 million and 1 billion barrels, with a strong presumption that the SPR would be sufficient to replace 90 days of petroleum imports (then about 500 million barrels). Although work completed by the Institute of Defense Analyses suggested that a much larger SPR was economically justified, the billion-barrel figure was selected as a round number larger than the largest size that the administration anticipated

[15]For a description of his model, see Thomas J. Teisberg, "A Dynamic Programming Model of the U.S. Strategic Petroleum Reserve," *Bell Journal of Economics* 12(2) 1981, 526–46.

[16]This section is based on Hank C. Jenkins-Smith and David L. Weimer, "Analysis as Retrograde Action: The Case of Strategic Petroleum Reserves," *Public Administration Review* 45(4) 1985, 485–94, which provides a full documentation of sources. Parts are reprinted with permission from *Public Administration Review*, 1985, by the American Society for Public Administration, 1120 G Street N.W., Washington, D.C. All rights reserved.

recommending to Congress in the SPR plan.[17] The lower level of 150 million barrels represented an estimate by the FEA of the amount of existing salt dome storage capacity that it could obtain for the program. The presumed size of 500 million barrels, consistent with the National Petroleum Council recommendation, was selected by President Ford as a compromise between the positions of the OMB and the FEA. Presaging later battles, the OMB had argued for a smaller SPR to reduce program costs, while the FEA had argued for the greater security that would be provided by a larger reserve.

The SPR plan submitted by the FEA to Congress in December 1976 included a cost-effectiveness analysis in support of the 500-million-barrel size.[18] The analysis concluded that under optimistic assumptions about import levels and the likelihood of disruptions, a reserve of 500 million barrels or larger was cost-effective. Agreement in favor of the 500-million-barrel size was tenuous, however. Analysts at OMB wanted to limit the size to 200 million barrels, but they could not gain sufficient support to override the legislative presumption for 500 million barrels. For their part, most FEA analysts believed that a larger size could be justified on economic grounds, but they decided not to press their case in view of anticipated opposition from OMB.

The Billion-Barrel Initiative

Development of the National Energy Plan, which called for expansion of the SPR to 1 billion barrels, was tightly controlled by James R. Schlesinger, President Carter's chief energy adviser. His staff tapped the agencies and departments for information but remained secretive about policy options. Operating efficiency was selected over "the more time-consuming process of consensus building."[19] The National Energy Plan draft was circulated within the administration for comments only a short time before President Carter released the final version on April 29, 1977. Consequently, OMB career staffers concerned with the SPR did not have time to convince their new director to seek presidential reconsideration of the billion-barrel goal included in National Energy Plan. In bureaucratic slang, Schlesinger had successfully "rolled" OMB on the SPR issue.

OMB found an opportunity to blunt the billion-barrel initiative during the preparation of the administration's FY 1979 budget proposals in the fall of 1977. Schlesinger, as secretary of the newly created Department of Energy, had requested funding for construction of the second 500 million barrels (Phase III would take the SPR to about 750 million barrels and Phase IV to 1 billion barrels) of storage capacity. When OMB cut these funds, Schlesinger appealed to the president. Schlesinger presented his case to the president at a White House meeting with the OMB director. OMB staffers, armed with flipcharts, began to make the case that a reserve size larger than 500 million barrels was unjustified. They were cut short by President Carter, however, who stated that the size of the SPR was not at issue: he

[17]Robert E. Kuenne, Gerald F. Higgins, Robert J. Michaels, and Mary Sommerfield, "A Policy to Protect the U.S. against Oil Embargoes," *Policy Analysis* 1(4) 1975, 571–97.

[18]The analysis employed an estimated relationship between oil import reductions and GNP. It is summarized in Randall Holcombe, "A Method of Estimating the GNP Loss from a Future Oil Embargo," *Policy Sciences* 8(2) 1977, 217–34.

[19]James L. Cochrane, "Carter Energy Policy and the Ninety-fifth Congress," in Craufurd B. Goodwin, ed., *Energy Policy in Perspective* (Washington, DC: Brookings Institution, 1981), 547–600, at p. 555.

was still committed to an ultimate reserve size of 1 billion barrels. The real issue was how much would be spent in FY 1979 for Phases III and IV. As a compromise, the president allowed planning funds to be included for only Phase III.

The results of this meeting might be viewed as a Pyrrhic victory for Schlesinger. He secured presidential reaffirmation of the billion-barrel goal. (Congress endorsed the expanded goal by approving an amendment to the SPR plan the following June.) In the process, however, OMB staffers, who would be involved in future budget fights over the SPR, were embarrassed in front of the president. It is possible that the incident influenced their attitudes toward the SPR program.

In these initial rounds, then, DOE analysts under Schlesinger had successfully mounted an initiative to expand the SPR size. Persistent opposition from OMB had been temporarily overcome. Given widespread support within both Congress and the administration, as well as the repeated analytic justification for a large SPR, how can the continued opposition of OMB be explained?

OMB analysts had legitimate reasons to question the analytical justification for the larger SPR size. The analysis presented in the SPR plan was unsophisticated in the way it measured the benefits of drawdowns and dealt with uncertainty. Within the analytical framework employed, ample room existed for disagreement over assumptions about future conditions. These assumptions, in turn, were critical to estimates of future SPR benefits. Thus, at this stage of the controversy, OMB opposition on analytical grounds was clearly defensible.

Institutional factors may also have contributed to opposition by OMB staffers. OMB is responsible for the overall budget and is concerned with limiting expenditures wherever possible. The SPR made an attractive target for several reasons: First, its benefits are diffuse, with no strong constituency to oppose budget cuts; its aggregate benefits may be large, but no politically active group anticipates a large enough share to make it worthwhile to take political action. Second, the SPR resembles an insurance policy in that the costs are certain but the full benefits accrue only from events that may not occur. Because the initial costs for SPR facilities and stock purchases are relatively large, those who are most responsible for the budget may be willing to accept higher levels of risk for reduced premiums. Third, the costs must be borne today while the benefits result sometime in the future. Those responsible for this year's budget may have a higher subjective discount rate than other decision makers. Thus the institutional mission of OMB, coupled with the diffuse benefits and high start-up costs of the SPR, made the initiative to expand the SPR a particularly attractive target for budget cutters.[20]

Analytical Trench Warfare, Round One: 1978

In February 1978, OMB organized an interagency task force to study contingency planning issues. It consisted of personnel from the Office of Contingency Planning in the Policy and Evaluation Office of DOE, the Special Studies Division for Natural Resources, Energy, and Science in OMB, and the Council of Economic Advisers (CEA). DOE agreed to consider alternatives for implementation of the expanded reserve, implicitly reopening the size issue.

[20]OMB staffers play the role of *guardians,* who seek to counter the efforts of *spenders* to obtain larger budgets. On the implications of these roles for the conduct of cost-benefit analyses in bureaucracies, see Anthony E. Boardman, Aidan R. Vining, and W. G. Waters II, "Costs and Benefits through Bureaucratic Lenses: An Example of a Highway Project," *Journal of Policy Analysis and Management* 12(3) 1993, 532 55.

By mid-April, participants reached tentative agreement on the assumptions that would be employed to measure the macroeconomic costs of oil supply disruptions. With these assumptions, DOE and CEA analysts used the Wharton and DRI macroeconomic models to estimate a relationship between reductions in oil imports and quarterly losses in GNP. The relationship was used by DOE analysts in a cost-benefit analysis of the fourth 250 million barrels (Phase IV) of the SPR. When OMB analysts discovered that the DOE analysis supported implementation of Phase IV, they began to attack the assumptions used—including some to which they had previously agreed. Although DOE made a number of concessions on assumptions, Phase IV still appeared to be justified. Finally, OMB presented its own analysis arguing against Phase IV in a memorandum to the president.

Secretary Schlesinger prepared to argue the issue with OMB during meetings on the FY 1980 budget. Schlesinger had been informed by his staff that OMB had argued that the probability of a severe disruption (the loss of approximately 60 percent of Persian Gulf exports for six months) would have to be between 10 and 25 percent per year over twelve years to justify Phase IV. With CEA concurrence, Schlesinger presented the DOE case that a yearly break-even probability of only 1 percent would justify Phase IV. When OMB agreed (its figures had been for the entire twelve-year period), Schlesinger seemed to be thrown off balance. Rather than threaten to take the issue to the president, he agreed not to press for Phase IV planning funds for FY 1980 and to recommend that the issue of ultimate size be referred to the National Security Council. One OMB analyst who attended the meeting believes that OMB would have backed down if Schlesinger had demanded a meeting before the president in which he would have asked the secretaries of Defense and State if they would be willing to assume that the probability of a major disruption would be less than 1 percent per year. Perhaps Schlesinger might have taken this approach if his analysts had not focused his attention on the apparent discrepancy between DOE and OMB conclusions.

Round Two: 1979

In January 1979, OMB began to pressure DOE to participate in another joint study of the economic costs and benefits of implementing the billion-barrel goal. DOE analysts who had been involved in the previous joint study argued against participation. They believed that the OMB analysts would not be satisfied with any analysis that supported SPR expansion. But institutional relationships within the federal bureaucracy make it difficult for a department to refuse an OMB request. Beyond its influence in a given budgetary dispute, OMB must be dealt with on numerous budget issues, and the costs of not cooperating can extend beyond the particular issue involved. DOE committed about twenty staff-months of professional time and approximately $80,000 for consultants to the project.

The first project task was to complete simulations of the macroeconomic effects of disruptions based on the DRI and Wharton macromodels. Although initially agreement was reached on a set of assumptions to be used, the OMB and CEA representatives continually required modifications of assumptions. This was frustrating for the DOE analysts who had to implement them, particularly because it appeared to them that OMB staffers were consistently looking for ways to make disruptions appear less costly and, hence, the SPR less valuable.

DOE completed a first draft of the study report in October 1979. It assumed that the first 550 million barrels of the SPR would be drawn down only for disruptions involving losses to the United States of over 1 billion barrels per year. It also assumed that private industry would draw down its stocks by 125 million barrels during a severe disruption. The expected benefits from SPR drawdowns were estimated for a number of disruption scenarios and their assumed probabilities of occurrence. The report concluded that the economically desirable reserve was 2.1 billion barrels or larger.

OMB staff participating in the study project were outraged. OMB had been preparing to argue not only against Phase IV but also against Phase III on grounds that new capacity should not be added while existing capacity was not being filled. (In light of the long lead time needed to construct storage facilities, the OMB position seemed to assume that the then-current tight market conditions caused by Iranian production reductions would prevail for five or six years.) Also, the revelations over the preceding year of cost overruns and schedule delays encountered during the implementation of Phases I and II made the SPR an even more tempting and perhaps more vulnerable target for budget cuts.

Focusing on the least certain (and, therefore, most vulnerable) techniques and assumptions included in the analysis, OMB raised four major objections to the draft report. First, the use of assumed probabilities for the disruption scenarios was attacked as arbitrary. DOE countered by arguing that, although arbitrary, the probabilities were viewed as conservative by most experts consulted. Second, OMB wanted the GNP loss function to be estimated on the basis of more accommodating monetary and fiscal assumptions that would yield lower real GNP losses but higher inflation rates. DOE responded that the more extreme the monetary and fiscal policy assumptions made, the more suspect the results of the macroeconomic models. Third, OMB objected to the assignment of a salvage value to SPR oil. DOE analysts thought it was obvious that the sale of remaining assets at the termination of the program should be counted as benefits. Finally, OMB argued that SPR drawdowns would not replace lost imports barrel per barrel—an objection that DOE analysts had to admit as valid. (Note that in Figure 14.1, the price effect of a drawdown depends on the price elasticities of supply and demand in the world market. Drawdowns of the SPR do not replace lost imports barrel for barrel.)

After it became clear that OMB was attempting to cut funds for Phase III from the budget, the DOE analysts decided to redo their analysis with a set of assumptions that OMB would not be able to attack. Successfully accomplished, such a move would reduce the opportunity for further delays based on demands for better analysis. The resulting new study, which even included an arbitrary across-the-board reduction of 25 percent of benefits to reflect possible inefficiencies in SPR use, found that expansion of the SPR to 750 million barrels was justified if one believed that the probability of a disruption of moderate size (less than 2 million barrels per day for one year) was greater than 3.5 percent per year.

This effort was to no avail. Not only did OMB cut funding for implementation of Phase III from the FY 1980 supplementary budget and the FY 1981 budget, but the DOE leadership decided not to appeal the decision to the president. Schlesinger, until then the strongest SPR supporter among the DOE leadership, was no longer secretary. The new secretary, Charles W. Duncan, and his assistant secretary for policy and evaluation, William Lewis, were not yet familiar with the issue. The remaining leadership in the past had emphasized long-run energy policy, such as conservation, over contingency planning measures, such as the SPR. Consequently, there was no one to lead a fight against OMB cuts. In fact, DOE Undersecretary John Deutch agreed to yet another joint OMB/DOE study to be conducted in 1980 for the FY 1982 budget decision on Phase III.

Round Three: 1980

While the Office of Contingency Planning was struggling with OMB over the 1979 study, the Office of Oil, also under the assistant secretary for policy and evaluation, was developing a methodology for investigating the optimal timing of oil acquisitions and drawdowns and of capacity expansions. Recognizing the weakness of methods previously used to handle the uncertainty about supply interruptions in prior studies, Lucian Pugliaresi, director of the Office of Oil, encouraged economist Thomas Teisberg to work on the problem.

Teisberg developed a stochastic dynamic programming formulation of the stockpiling problem. For each year of the SPR program, his model determines the oil acquisition or drawdown, subject to technical constraints, that minimizes the discounted sum of expected future net social surplus losses. Uncertainty is converted to risk by assuming probabilities of moving from each market condition to each of the other possible market conditions in future periods. Using the model to look ahead, at some point the stockpiling reaches a size at which additions are no longer optimal. This plateau level is an indication of the "optimal" stockpile size for planning purposes.

In December 1979, Glen Sweetnam, Steven Minihan, George Horwich, and other staff members in the Office of Oil completed a major study of acquisition and drawdown analyses using the Teisberg model. Over a range of assumptions, the plateau level was found to vary from 800 million to 4.4 billion barrels. More importantly, the study suggested that large net benefits were associated with rapid expansion of the SPR toward the plateau.

The new assistant secretary for policy and evaluation intensively reviewed the Office of Oil study and concluded that it employed a more appropriate methodology than that used in the joint OMB/DOE studies. He argued in a memorandum that future joint studies with OMB be based on modifications and extensions of the Teisberg model rather than on macroeconomic simulations.

Introduction of the new modeling technique added a fresh element to the struggle over the size of the SPR. On the one hand, the new technique was widely recognized as a more appropriate approach to the problem of public stockpiling than previously used methods. At the same time, however, introduction of the Teisberg model created opportunities for OMB to demand analysis as a delaying tactic.

In the spring of 1980, representatives from OMB and CEA objected to the use of the Teisberg model on a variety of grounds. Though some of the criticisms struck DOE analysts as gratuitous, and most of the others could easily be handled by revisions of the model, the most serious and fundamental objection concerned the probabilities assumed in the model. OMB complained that the assumed matrix of probabilities of going from each market condition to each of the others was "… so complex and theoretical as to have no meaning to policy-makers."[21] The DOE analysts admitted that the Teisberg model appeared complex, but argued that it was conceptually straightforward. They argued further that it provided a method to deal with uncertainty that was much more systematic than the scenario approach.

A compromise of sorts that permitted use of the Teisberg model was reached at a July meeting of the DOE assistant secretary for policy and evaluation, the OMB

[21]Chuck Miller, "Questions/Issues Regarding DOE (Teisberg) B/C Model: Memorandum of CEA and OMB Comments to Lou Pugliaresi, DOE," Office of Management and Budget, May 27, 1980.

assistant director for natural resources, energy, and science, a council member of CEA, and their respective staffs. The assistant secretary for policy and evaluation made it clear that DOE would include an analysis based on the Teisberg model in its FY 1982 budget request. He indicated that his staff would modify and run the model as requested by OMB but would not attempt to find mutually acceptable assumptions. He also committed $100,000 in contractor support (the former undersecretary had promised up to $1 million for the study) and four person-months of staff time to assist OMB and CEA in the proposed macroeconomic simulation study.

The DOE analysts provided energy projections and other advice as requested by OMB, but they refused to be drawn into battles about assumptions. Within a short time, it became apparent that the assumptions made by CEA and passively agreed to by OMB were going to yield results even more supportive of SPR expansion than the 1979 joint study. OMB and CEA never completed the proposed macroeconomic simulation study.

In the meantime, DOE had modified the Teisberg model to focus explicitly on the Phase III question. The results were presented in October at an OMB hearing on the SPR budget. Perhaps because the macroeconomic analysis had not turned out as they had expected, OMB finally expressed an interest in analyses from the Teisberg model. The analyses were completed with the understanding that DOE did not necessarily endorse the assumptions that OMB had requested.

To summarize the debate through 1980, the presidential decision in 1977 to expand the SPR to 1 billion barrels was not based primarily on economic analysis. In 1978, OMB forced DOE to evaluate the economic benefits of the expanded reserve with a somewhat more sophisticated methodology. Although the resulting analysis supported the expansion, OMB cut planning funds for Phase IV and secured agreement from DOE to reconsider the size issue in the next budget cycle. During 1979 OMB analysts attempted to force DOE to agree to combinations of assumptions in the previously used macroeconomic simulations that would lead to results not supporting expansion of the SPR. Even though fairly conservative assumptions were employed, the results favored expansion. Nevertheless, OMB delayed funding of Phase III from FY 1980 to FY 1982. In 1980, OMB analysts again attempted to draw DOE into a battle over assumptions in the macroeconomic approach. Failing, they reluctantly expressed interest in the stochastic dynamic programming model that DOE intended to use in support of its FY 1982 budget request.

Resolution

By mid-November 1980, it had become clear that OMB would not oppose funding in the Carter Administration's FY 1982 budget request for implementation of Phase III. Did analysis finally carry the day? Perhaps. In light of the extended fight over Phase III, however, a more plausible explanation is that analysis was a secondary factor. Most likely, the OMB staff anticipated that the assistant secretary for policy and evaluation, who enjoyed the confidence of the secretary, would recommend that the issue be taken to the president if Phase III funding was not included in the FY 1982 budget proposal. Unlike the previous two years, it appeared that the DOE leaders were confident of their analysis and willing to take OMB to the mat. At the time, the SPR program had begun to reestablish its managerial credibility, undercutting implied arguments that it could not handle implementation of Phase III. Finally, with hindsight, one cannot help but wonder if the presidential election were not a factor. As it turned out, President-elect Ronald Reagan appointed David Stockman, a strong congressional supporter of the SPR, as director of OMB. It may be that the career staff at OMB anticipated this possibility and did not wish to be seen by the new administration as being responsible for further delay of the SPR program. In fact, during the early months of the Reagan Administration, the same OMB staffers who had led the fight against expansion of the SPR throughout the Carter Administration directed a joint study with DOE of options for accelerating Phase III. Thus, it appears that changing political factors, as much as analysis, resolved the debate over the appropriate size of the SPR.

But analysis played an important role in several ways. First, if any of the cost-benefit studies conducted during the period of controversy had failed to find that expansion of the SPR was justified on economic grounds, then OMB would almost certainly have been able to stop Phase III. Second, without the Teisberg model, the Office of Oil staff probably would not have been able to convince the new assistant secretary to support SPR expansion. Absent his willingness to take the question of Phase III funding to the president, something usually done only for the most important issues, OMB might have continued to stall. Finally, the introduction of the Teisberg model drew attention to acquisition and drawdown strategies. One result was the consideration of acceleration options. Another was the later development within the Reagan Administration of a policy calling for early use of the SPR to counter oil price shocks.

Postscript

The SPR currently has capacity for holding 700 million barrels; it actually held 610 million barrels of crude oil in mid-2003. It is currently being filled with oil taken as in-kind royalties from oil leases on the outer continental shelf. The SPR can drawdown approximately 4.1 million barrels per day of crude oil for three months, with a declining rate in subsequent months. In coordination with the German Erdölbevorrantungsverband and the Japan National Oil Corporation, approximately 8.7 million barrels per day could be drawn down from government-controlled strategic reserves at the outset of a supply disruption.[22] In early 1991, an SPR drawdown of 17 million barrels was initiated to moderate prices during the first Gulf War.

Conclusion

Our story of the controversy over the size of the SPR should be both encouraging and sobering for aspiring analysts. It should be encouraging because it shows that participants in policy debates do consider the results of formal analyses to be important—at least sometimes—and because it demonstrates that new analytical insights can make a difference. It should be sobering because it shows analysis to be a political resource that can be abused.

[22]International Energy Agency, *Oil Supply Security: The Emergency Response Potential of IEA Countries in 2000* (Paris: OECD/IEA, 2001).

The opportunity for abuse is especially great in situations where no consensus exists about the reasonableness of analytical assumptions.[23] Political decision makers rarely have the time, inclination, or expertise to resolve analytical disputes. So when analysts disagree about assumptions and methods, analysis is unlikely to play a decisive, or perhaps even an informative, role. From a practical perspective, analysts should be prepared for attacks on their assumptions and methods by advocates of opposing policies. They should anticipate such attacks in choosing models, gathering supporting evidence, and eliciting support from neutral experts. From an ethical perspective, analysts should remember their responsibility to the value of analytical integrity in deciding whether to attack the analysis of others.

For Discussion

1. Analysts almost unanimously agree that strategic petroleum reserves should be used early during an oil supply disruption. The president, however, may hesitate initiating a drawdown out of concern that the disruption will outlast the reserves. Can you think of any institutional designs that might be employed to increase the chances of the use of the reserves at the outset of a supply disruption?
2. Imagine that you were an energy security analyst in the early 1970s. How might you expand the cost-benefit analysis of the strategic petroleum reserve into a multigoal analysis?

[23]Indeed, many complex simulation models have hidden assumptions that even experienced analysts have difficulty discovering. The situation is further clouded because there is relatively little effort expended in validating models—even those regularly used by government offices and consultants. See Constance F. Citro and Eric A. Hanushek, eds., *Improving Information for Social Policy Decisions: The Uses of Microsimulation Modeling*, Vol. I (Washington, DC: National Academy Press, 1991).

18

When Statistics Count

Revising the Lead Standard for Gasoline

Policy analysts must deal with many kinds of empirical evidence. Often the constraints of time and resources, as well as the nature of the policy problem under consideration, force analysts to rely on qualitative and fragmentary data. Sometimes, though, analysts can find data that enable them to estimate parameters that allow them to predict the magnitudes of the effects of policy interventions on social, economic, or political conditions. The estimates may permit the analysts to calculate the likely net social benefits of proposed policies or even apply formal optimization techniques to find better alternatives.

The effective use of quantitative data requires an understanding of the basic issues of research design and a facility with the techniques of statistical inference. Even when analysts do not have the resources available to do primary data analysis, they often must confront quantitative evidence produced by other participants in the policy process or extracted from the academic literature. If they lack the requisite skills for critical evaluation, then they risk losing their influence in the face of quantitative evidence that may appear more objective and scientific to decision makers. Well-trained analysts, therefore, need some facility with the basic concepts of statistical inference for reasons of self-defense if for no others.

The basics of research design and statistical inference cannot be adequately covered in an introductory course in policy analysis. Similarly, we cannot provide adequate coverage in this book. Yet we can provide an example of a policy change where quantitative analysis was instrumental: the decision by the U.S. Environmental Protection Agency in 1985 to reduce dramatically the amount of lead permitted in gasoline. The story of the new lead standard has a number of elements frequently encountered when doing quantitative analysis in organizational settings: replacement of an initial "quick and dirty" analysis with more sophisticated versions as more time and data become available; repeated reanalysis to rule out alternative explanations (hypotheses) offered by opponents of the proposed policy; and serendipitous events that influence the analytical strategy. Although our primary purpose is to tell what we believe to be an intrinsically interesting and instructive story about the practice of policy analysis, we hope to offer a few basic lessons on quantitative analysis along the way.

Background: The EPA Lead Standards

The Clean Air Amendments of 1970 give the administrator of the Environmental Protection Agency authority to regulate any motor fuel component or additive that produces emission products dangerous to public health or welfare.[1] Before exercising this authority, however, the administrator must consider "all relevant medical and scientific evidence available to him," as well as alternative methods that set standards for emissions rather than for fuel components.[2]

In 1971, the EPA administrator announced that he was considering possible controls on lead additives in gasoline.[3] One reason given was the possible adverse health effects of emissions from engines that burned leaded gasoline, the standard fuel at the time. Available evidence suggested that lead is toxic in the human body, that lead can be absorbed into the body from ambient air, and that gasoline engines account for a large fraction of airborne lead. The other reason for controlling the lead content of gasoline was the incompatibility of leaded fuel with the catalytic converter, a device seen as having potential for reducing hydrocarbon emissions from automobiles. The first reason suggests considering whether reductions in the lead content of all gasoline might be desirable; the second argues for the total removal of lead from gasoline for use by new automobiles equipped with catalytic converters.

Without going any further one might ask: Why should the government be concerned with the level of lead in gasoline? And why had the federal government already decided to require the installation of catalytic converters? The following analysis does not explicitly deal with the desirability of catalytic converters. As we have argued, however, it is always important to make sure that there is a convincing rationale for public action. The interventions at hand—the catalytic converter and the related lead restrictions—deal with market failures, specifically negative externality problems. In addition, another market failure may come into play with respect to lead: imperfect consumer information about the impacts of lead on health and the maintenance cost of vehicles. Because the health and maintenance impacts may not manifest themselves for many years (leaded gasoline is a post-experience good), markets may be inefficient because of information asymmetry. These apparent market failures make a case for considering government intervention.

Yet intervention itself may be costly. It is conceivable that the costs of intervention could exceed the benefits. Several questions must be answered before the

[1]The Clean Air Act Amendments of 1970, P.L. 91–604, December 31, 1970.
[2]Section 211(c)(2)(A), 42 U.S.C. 1857f-6c(c)(2)(A).
[3]36 *Federal Register* 1468 (January 31, 1971).

comparison of costs and benefits can be made: What are the impacts of gasoline lead additives on people, the environment, and property (including catalytic converters)? How do these physical impacts change under alternative public interventions? What are the dollar costs associated with these interventions, and what are the dollar benefits associated with the changes they produce? Finally, which alternative, including no intervention, appears to offer the greatest excess of benefits over costs?

The EPA explored these questions for a limited number of alternative lead regulations. About one year after raising the possibility of lead restrictions, the EPA administrator proposed formal regulations for lead reductions in 1972.[4] After an extended period of comment and several public hearings, the EPA was ready to issue final regulations requiring refiners to make available some unleaded gasoline for use by new automobiles, which, beginning with the 1975 model year, would be equipped with catalytic converters.[5] At the same time, the EPA re-proposed reductions in lead content for public health reasons.

The health-based standards were controversial. Refiners valued lead as a gasoline additive because it increased octane without affecting vapor pressure or other fuel properties that had to be balanced in the blending process. Refiners were joined in their opposition to the proposed regulations by manufacturers of the lead additives. Supporting the regulations were a number of environmental organizations, including the Natural Resources Defense Council, which successfully sought a court order that forced EPA to issue final regulations on November 28, 1973.[6]

The final regulations called for phased reductions over a five-year period in the average lead content of all gasoline sold. By 1979, the average would fall to 0.5 gram of lead per gallon (gpg) of gasoline. Implementation of the phase-down, however, was slowed, first by a court challenge to the regulation[7] and later by concerns about gasoline availability during the 1979 oil price shock following the Iranian revolution.[8] Consequently, the 0.5 gpg standard was not put into effect until October 1, 1980.

By 1982, some analysts in the EPA became concerned that as relatively more unleaded gasoline was sold to meet the demand from the growing number of automobiles in service with catalytic converters, refiners would be able to increase the concentration of lead in leaded gasoline and still meet the 0.5 gpg average. In February, the EPA announced a general review of the 1973 standards[9] and in August proposed new standards that would limit the content of lead in leaded gasoline rather than the average content of lead in all gasoline.[10] The final rules, issued in October 1982, set 1.10 grams per leaded gallon as the new standard.[11] (The new standard was roughly equivalent to the old standard in terms of total lead emissions—0.5 gpg on 100 percent of total gasoline sales versus 1.10 gpg on the approximately 45 percent of total gasoline sales that were leaded at the time. Because the quantity of leaded gasoline sold was expected to continue to decline,

[4]37 *Federal Register* 11786 (February 23, 1972).
[5]38 *Federal Register* 1254 (January 10, 1973).
[6]38 *Federal Register* 33734 (November 28, 1973).
[7]*Ethyl Corporation v. Environmental Protection Agency*, 541 F.2d 1 (1976).
[8]44 *Federal Register* 33116 (June 8, 1979).
[9]47 *Federal Register* 4812 (February 22, 1982).
[10]47 *Federal Register* 38070, 38072, 38078 (August 27, 1982).
[11]47 *Federal Register* 49331 (October 29, 1982).

corresponding reductions in lead emissions were projected.) Although implementation was slowed somewhat by the courts, the new regulations phased out special provisions that had been added to reduce the impact of the 1973 standards on small refiners. The regulations also allowed "trading" of additional reductions across refineries. For example, a refinery would be allowed to produce gasoline with 1.20 gpg if it "traded" with another refinery to produce an equivalent quantity with 1.00 gpg so that the pooled average would be 1.10 gpg.

Origins of the 1985 Standards

Several factors prompted reconsideration of the lead standard in the summer of 1983. EPA Administrator William D. Ruckelshaus and Deputy Administrator Alvin L. Alm were concerned that many cities would not achieve the 1987 ozone standards. Ozone, a major component of smog, results when emissions of hydrocarbons and nitrogen oxides chemically react in the atmosphere. Well-maintained catalytic converters greatly reduce these emissions from motor vehicles. The converters, designed to be used only with unleaded gasoline, lose their effectiveness when exposed to lead. Because leaded gasoline was both cheaper and offered higher performance than unleaded, many consumers were fueling their converter-equipped vehicles with leaded gasoline. A 1982 EPA survey estimated that 13.5 percent of vehicles were being misfueled.[12] Lowering the permissible level of lead in gasoline could reduce the misfueling problem in two ways. First, it would reduce the economic incentive to misfuel by raising the relative price of leaded to unleaded gasoline. Second, the lower lead levels would result in slower degradation of converters that were misfueled.

Another factor was continuing concern about the health effects of lead emissions. As new scientific evidence became available, the apparent connection between lead emissions and lead levels in blood became ever stronger. The growing evidence increased the chances that a more stringent standard could be adequately supported.

The external environment also seemed favorable. Many environmental groups had long advocated a total ban on lead; they would undoubtedly support further tightening of the standards. So, too, would alcohol fuel advocates, who hoped restrictions on lead would make alcohol more attractive as an octane-boosting fuel additive. In addition, the U.S. Court of Appeals for the District of Columbia District, in a case challenging the provisions of the 1982 lead standards, had given an opinion that currently available evidence "would justify EPA in banning lead from gasoline entirely."[13] Although not a guarantee of judicial acceptance of stricter standards, the opinion was encouraging.

The EPA leadership decided that another look at the lead standard would be worthwhile. Robert Wolcott, special assistant to the deputy administrator, was given the task of overseeing the project. He turned to Joel Schwartz, an analyst in the Economic Analysis Division who had worked on the 1982 regulations. Schwartz used

[12]U.S. Environmental Protection Agency, *Motor Vehicle Tampering Survey 1982* (Washington, DC: National Enforcement Investigation Center, EPA, April 1983).

[13]*Small Refiner Lead Phase-Down Task Force v. EPA*, 705 F.2d 506 (D.C. Cir. 1983), p. 531.

his accumulated knowledge from previous analyses to complete in two or three days a "quick and dirty" cost-benefit analysis of a total ban on lead additives.

Because a total ban was one of the options considered in 1982, it was fairly easy for Schwartz to come up with a reasonable estimate of cost. As is often the case in evaluating health and safety regulations, the more difficult problem was estimating the benefits of a total ban. Schwartz looked at two benefit categories: increased IQ scores of children due to lower levels of blood lead and the avoided damage to catalytic converters.

Schwartz used estimates from a variety of sources to piece together a relationship between lead emissions and the present value of lifetime earnings of children. The first step involved using estimates from the 1982 analyses of the relationship between lead emissions and blood lead levels in children. He next turned to epidemiological studies that reported a relationship between blood lead levels and IQs. Finally, he found econometric studies that estimated the contribution of IQ points to the present value of future earnings.

As a first cut at quantifying the benefits resulting from the more effective control of other emissions, Schwartz estimated the cost of catalytic converters being contaminated under the current standards that would not be contaminated under a total ban. He used the number of converters saved multiplied by the price per converter as the benefit measure. Assuming that converters themselves have benefit-cost ratios greater than 1, this benefit measure would be conservative.

These "back-of-the-envelope" calculations suggested that the benefits of a total ban on lead additives would be more than twice the costs. Schwartz discussed the results with his branch chief, G. Martin Wagner, who sent word to the office of the administrator that further analysis of a lead ban seemed worthwhile. A few weeks later Schwartz and fellow analyst Jane Leggett began a two-month effort to move from the back of an envelope to a preliminary report.

Pulling the Pieces Together

The most urgent task facing Schwartz and Leggett was to develop better measures of the benefits of a lead ban. The key to improving the measure of benefits from avoided converter poisonings was a more sophisticated accounting of the future age composition of the U.S. vehicle fleet. The key to improving the measure of benefits from reduced lead emissions was a better quantitative estimate of the relationship between gasoline lead and blood lead. Modeling and statistical analysis would be an important part of their work.

The age composition of the vehicle fleet continually changes as old vehicles, some of which have contaminated or partially contaminated converters, are retired and new ones, with fresh converters, are added. A ban on lead would have different effects on different vintage vehicles. For instance, a ban would be irrelevant for vehicles that already have contaminated converters but very important for vehicles that would otherwise be contaminated and remain in service for a long time.

The analysts developed an inventory model that tracked cohorts of vehicles over time. Each year a new cohort would enter the fleet. Each successive year a fraction of the vehicles would be retired because of accidents and mechanical failures. In addition, a fraction would suffer converter poisoning from misfueling. By following the various cohorts over time, it was possible to predict the total number of converters that would be saved in each future year from specified reductions in the lead content of leaded gasoline today and in the future. Avoided loss of the depreciated value of the catalytic converters (later avoided costs of the health and property damage from pollutants other than lead) could then be calculated for each future year. With appropriate discounting, the yearly benefits could then be summed to yield the present value of the lead reduction schedule being considered.

Two important considerations came to light during work on the vehicle fleet model. One was a body of literature suggesting that lead increases the routine maintenance costs of vehicles. Subsequently, a new benefit impact category, avoided maintenance costs, was estimated using the vehicle fleet model. The other consideration was the possibility that some engines might suffer premature valve-seat wear if fueled with totally lead-free gasoline. Although the problem was fairly limited (primarily automobile engines manufactured prior to 1971 and some newer trucks, motorcycles, and off-road vehicles), it suggested the need to consider alternatives to a total ban.

Efforts to quantify better the link between gasoline lead and blood lead focused on analysis of data from the second National Health and Nutrition Examination Survey (NHANES II). The NHANES II survey was designed by the National Center for Health Statistics to provide a representative national sample of the population between 6 months and 74 years of age. It included 27,801 persons sampled at 64 representative sites from 1976 to 1980. Of the 16,563 persons who were asked to provide blood samples, 61 percent complied.[14] The lead concentrations in the blood samples were measured, providing data that could be used to track average blood levels over the four-year survey period. The amount of lead in gasoline sold during the period could then be correlated with the blood lead concentrations.

A positive relationship between blood lead concentrations from the NHANES II data and gasoline lead had already been found by researchers.[15] The positive correlation is apparent in Figure 18.1, which was prepared by James Pirkle of the Centers for Disease Control to show the close tracking of blood lead concentrations and total gasoline lead.[16] Much more than the apparent correlation, however, was needed for the cost-benefit analysis. Schwartz used multiple regression techniques, which we will discuss in detail later in our story, to estimate the increase in average micrograms of lead per deciliter of blood (μg/dl) due to each additional 100 metric tons per day of lead in consumed gasoline. He also employed models that allowed him to estimate the probabilities that children with specified characteristics will have toxic levels of blood lead (then defined by the Centers for Disease Control as greater than 30 μg/dl as a function of gasoline lead. These probabilities could then be used to predict the number of children in the population who would avoid lead toxicity if a ban on gasoline lead were imposed.

In early November 1983, Schwartz and Leggett pulled together the components of their analysis and found a ratio of benefits to costs of a total ban to be greater than

[14] There appeared to be no nonresponse bias in the sample. R. N. Forthofer, "Investigation of Nonresponse Bias in NHANES II," *American Journal of Epidemiology* 117(4) 1983, 507–15.

[15] J. L. Annest, J. L. Pirkle, D. Makuc, J. W. Neese, D. D. Bayse, and M. G. Kovar, "Chronological Trends in Blood Lead Levels between 1976 and 1980," *New England Journal of Medicine* 308(23) 1983, 1373–77.

[16] Joel Schwartz, Jane Leggett, Bart Ostro, Hugh Pitcher, and Ronnie Levin, *Costs and Benefits of Reducing Lead in Gasoline: Draft Final Proposal* (Washington, DC: Office of Policy Analysis, EPA, March 26, 1984), V-26.

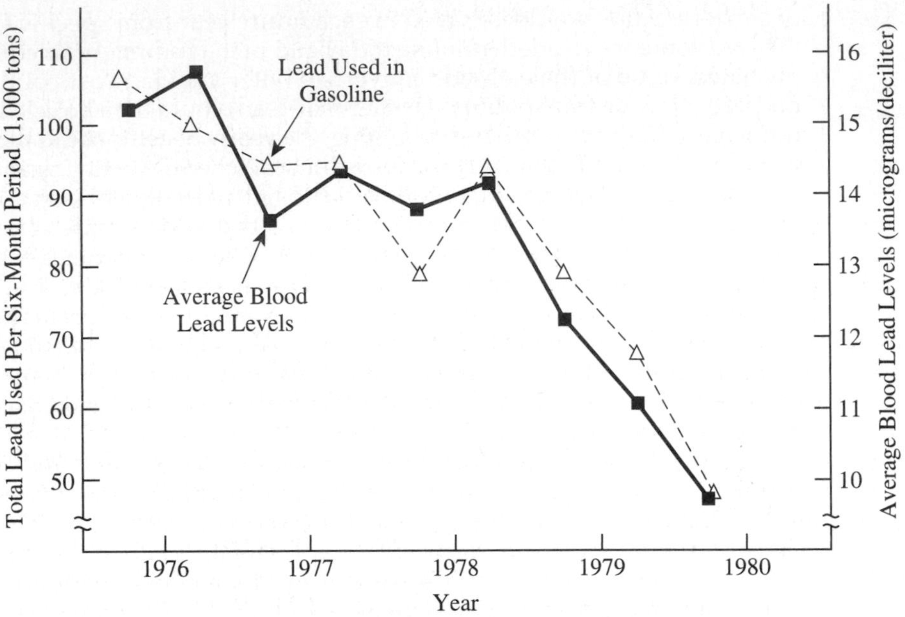

Figure 18.1 Lead Used in Gasoline Production and Average NHANES II Blood Lead Levels

Source: Joel Schwartz, Hugh Pitcher, Ronnie Levin, Bart Ostro, and Albert Nichols, *Cost and Benefits of Reducing Lead in Gasoline: Final Regulatory Analysis* (Washington, DC: U.S. Environmental Protection Agency, Office of Policy Analysis, February 1985), E-5.

Schwartz's original back-of-the-envelope calculation. Together with their branch chief, they presented their results to Deputy Administrator Alm, who found them encouraging. He gave the green light for the preparation of a refined version that could be presented to the administrator as the basis for a new regulation. Alm also wanted the various components of the refined study to be subjected to peer review by experts outside the EPA. At the same time, he urged speed in order to reduce the chances that word would get out to refiners and manufacturers of lead additives, the primary opponents of a ban, before the EPA had an opportunity to review all the evidence.

The branch chief expanded the analytical team in order to hasten the preparation of the refined report that would be sent to the administrator. Joining Schwartz and Leggett were Ronnie Levin, Hugh Pitcher, an econometrician, and Bart Ostro, an expert on the benefits of ozone reduction. In little more than one month the team was ready to send a draft report out for peer review.

The effort involved several changes in analytical approach. Because of the valve-head problem, the analysis focused on a major reduction in grams of lead per leaded gallon (from 1.1 gplg to 0.1 gplg) as well as a total ban. The available evidence suggested that the 0.1 gplg level would be adequate to avoid excessive valve-head wear in the small number of engines designed to be fueled only with leaded gasoline. At the same time, considerable effort was put into quantifying the maintenance costs that would be avoided by owners of other vehicles if the lead concentration were reduced. It soon appeared that the maintenance benefits consumers would enjoy would more than offset the higher prices they would have to pay for gasoline. Finally, the team decided that the benefits based on the blood lead (through

IQ) to future earnings relationship would be too controversial. Instead, they turned their attention to the costs of compensatory education for children who suffered IQ losses from high blood lead levels.

In late December, sections of the report were sent to experts outside the EPA for comments. The list included automotive engineers, economists, biostatisticians, toxicologists, clinical researchers, transportation experts, and a psychologist. During January 1984, the team refined their analysis and incorporated, or at least responded to, the comments made by the external reviewers.

Finally, in early February, the team was ready to present its results to Administrator Ruckelshaus. He agreed that their analysis supported a new standard of 0.1 gplg. He told the team to finalize its report without a proposed rule and release it for public comment. Ruckelshaus also directed the Office of the Assistant Administrator for Air and Radiation to draft a proposed rule.

The team's *Draft Final Report* was printed and eventually released to the public on March 26, 1984.[17] The team continued to refine the analysis in the following months. It also had to devote considerable time to external relations. Executive Order 12291 requires regulatory agencies to submit proposed regulations that would have annual costs of more than $100 million to the Office of Management and Budget for review. The team met with OMB analysts several times before securing their acceptance of the cost-benefit analysis of the tighter standard.

The political environment was taking shape pretty much as expected. Opposition would come from refiners and manufacturers of lead additives. The refiners, however, generally seemed resigned to the eventual elimination of lead from gasoline. Their primary concern was the speed of implementation. Some refiners seemed particularly concerned about the first few years of a tighter standard, when they would have difficulty making the required reductions with their existing configurations of capital equipment. In response, the team began exploring the costs and benefits of less stringent compliance schedules.

The manufacturers of lead additives were ready to fight tighter standards vigorously. In May, Schwartz attended a conference at the Centers for Disease Control in Atlanta, Georgia, on the proposed revision of the blood lead toxicity standard for children from 30 μg/dl to 25 μg/dl. Representatives of the lead manufacturers were also there. They openly talked about their strategy for challenging tighter standards. They planned to argue that refiners would blend more benzene, a suspected carcinogen, into gasoline to boost octane if lead were restricted. Schwartz investigated this possibility following the conference. He found that even if more benzene were added to gasoline, the total emissions of benzene would decline because of the reduction in the contamination of catalytic converters, which oxidize the benzene if not contaminated. The day that the proposed rule was published Schwartz put a memorandum in the docket covering the benzene issue, thus preempting the manufacturers' main attack.

The EPA published the proposed rule on August 2, 1984.[18] It would require that the permitted level of gasoline lead be reduced to 0.1 gplg on January 1986. The proposal stated the EPA assumption that the new standard could be met with existing refining equipment, but indicated that alternative phase-in schedules involving more gradual reductions also were being considered in case this assumption proved false. Finally, the proposal raised the possibility of a complete ban on gasoline lead by 1995.

[17]Ibid.

[18]49 *Federal Register* 31031 (August 2, 1984).

A Closer Look at the Link between Gasoline Lead and Blood Lead

Calculation of the direct health benefits of tightening the lead standard requires quantitative estimates of the contribution of gasoline lead to blood lead. The NHANES II data, combined with information on gasoline lead levels, enabled the members of the study team to make the necessary estimates. Their efforts provide an excellent illustration of how statistical inference can be used effectively in policy analysis.

The Need for Multivariate Analysis

A casual inspection of Figure 18.1 suggests a strong positive relationship between gasoline lead and blood lead. Why is it necessary to go any further? One reason is the difficulty of answering, directly from Figure 18.1, the central empirical question: How much does the average blood lead level in the United States decline for each 1,000-ton reduction in the total gasoline lead used over the previous month? Figure 18.1 indicates a positive correlation between gasoline lead and blood lead—changes in blood lead track changes in gasoline lead quite closely. But for the same correlation in the data, we could have very different answers to our central question.

Figure 18.2 illustrates the difference between correlation and magnitude of effect with stylized data. If our data were represented by the triangles, then we might "fit" line one as our best guess at the relationship between blood lead and gasoline lead. The effect of reducing gasoline lead from 500 tons per day to 400 tons per day would be to reduce average blood lead from 10.1 μg/dl to 10.0 μg/dl, or 0.1 μg/dl per 100 tons per day. An alternative sample of data is represented by the dots, which are plotted to have approximately the same correlation between gasoline lead and blood lead as the data represented by triangles. The slope of line two, the best fit to the dots, is 1.0 μg/dl per 100 tons per day—ten times greater than the slope of line one. That is, although the two data sets have the same correlation, the second implies a much greater contribution of gasoline lead to blood lead than the first.

Even after we display the data in Figure 18.1 as a plot between blood lead and gasoline lead, our analysis is far from complete because the apparent relationship (the slopes of lines one and two in our example) may be spurious. Blood lead and gasoline lead may not be directly related to each other but instead they may each be related to some third variable that causes them to change together. The classic illustration of this problem is the correlation sometimes found between the density of stork nests and the human birth rate. If one were to plot birth rates against the density of stork nests for districts in some region, then one might very well find a positive relationship and perhaps conclude that there might be something to the myth about storks bringing babies.

Of course, there is a more plausible explanation. A variable measuring the degree to which a district is rural "intervenes" between birth rate and nest density—rural areas have farmers who want a lot of children to help with chores as well as

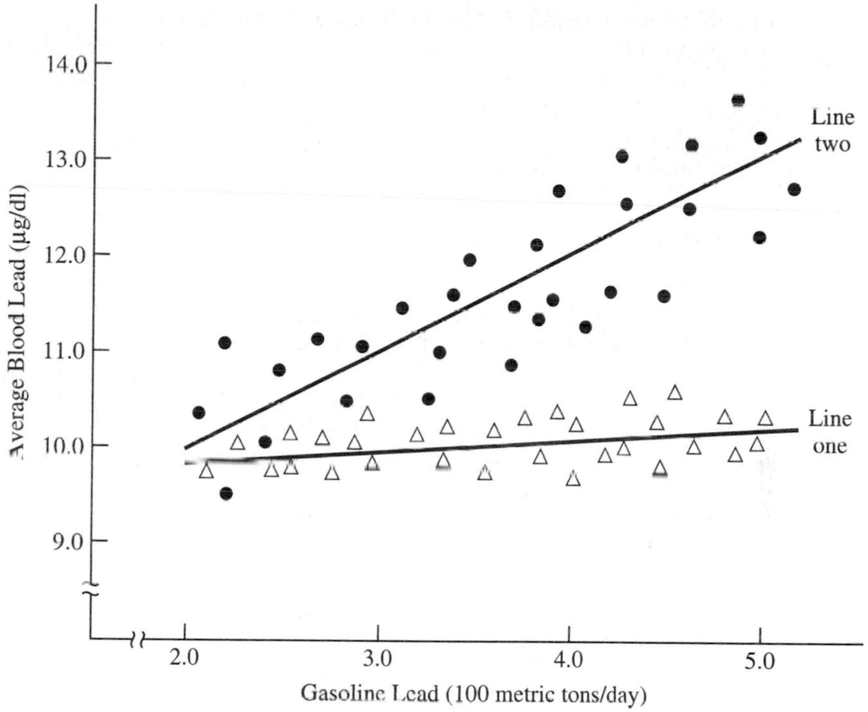

Figure 18.2 Data Samples with Identical Correlations but Different Regression Lines

a lot of open land that provides nesting grounds for storks; more urbanized areas tend to have people who want smaller families as well as less hospitable nesting grounds. Looking across a sample that included both rural and urban districts could yield the positive correlation between birth rate and nest density. If we were to "control" statistically for the intervening variable by looking at either rural or urban districts separately rather than pooled together, then we would expect the correlation between birth rate and nest density to become negligible.

As an illustration of the importance of intervening variables, consider a study based on a random sample of women living in 1972–1974 in Wickham, England.[19] After 20 years, 24 percent of those women in the sample who were smokers had died, while 31 percent of the women who had never smoked died, suggesting a naive inference that smoking reduces mortality risk! An obvious intervening variable to consider is each woman's age in 1972: age was correlated with mortality risk and negatively correlated with the propensity to smoke. When the researchers controlled for age by comparing death rates for women within six age groups, four

[19]David R. Appleton, Joyce M. French, and Mark P. J. Vanderpump, "Ignoring a Covariate: An Example of Simpson's Paradox," *American Statistician* 50(4) 1996, 340–41.

showed higher mortality rates for smokers, one showed lower mortality rates for smokers, and the group of oldest women showed no survivors among either smokers or nonsmokers. Looking just at women who were between 18 and 44 in 1972, 6.6 percent of smokers, but only 3.8 of nonsmokers, had died. Obviously, the surprising result in the overall sample was a consequence of aggregating different age groups rather than any longevity benefits of smoking.

Returning to our analysis of lead, we must be concerned that one or more intervening variables might explain the positive correlation between gasoline lead and blood lead. For example, there is some evidence that cigarette smokers have higher blood lead levels than nonsmokers. It may be that over the period the NHANES II data were collected the proportion of smokers in the sample declined, so that much of the downward trend in average blood lead levels should be attributed to reductions in smoking rather than reductions in gasoline lead.

To determine whether smoking is an intervening, or confounding, variable, we might construct separate diagrams like Figure 18.2 for smokers and nonsmokers. In this way, we could control for the possibility that changes in the proportion of smokers in the sample over time were responsible for changes in blood lead levels. If we fit lines with similar positive slopes to each of the samples, then we would conclude that smoking behavior was not an intervening variable for the relationship between gasoline lead and blood lead.

If the two lines coincided, then we would conclude that smoking did not contribute to blood lead. If the lines were parallel but not identical, then the difference between their intercepts with the vertical axis would represent the average effect of smoking on blood lead. If the lines were not parallel, then we might suspect that smoking interacted with exposure to gasoline lead so that their effects are not additive. That is, smokers were either more or less susceptible to exposure to gasoline lead than nonsmokers.

With unlimited quantities of data, we could always control for possible intervening variables in this way. Unfortunately, with a fixed sample size, we usually stretch our data too thinly if we try to form subsets of data that hold all variables constant (for example, everyone is a nonsmoker) except the dependent variable (blood lead levels) we are trying to explain and the independent variable (gasoline lead) we are considering as a possible explanation. For example, occupational exposure, alcohol consumption, region, and age are only a few of the other variables that might be causing the relationship in our data between gasoline lead and blood lead. If we selected from our sample only adult males living in small cities in the South who are moderate drinkers and nonsmokers and have no occupational exposure to lead, then we might have too few observations to reliably fit a line as in Figure 18.2. Even if we had adequate data, we would end up with estimates of the relationship between gasoline lead and blood lead from all of our subsets. (The number of subsets would equal the product of the number of categories making up our control variables.) We then might have difficulty combining these subset estimates into an overall estimate.

Of course, if the relationship truly varies across our subsets, then it would generally not make sense to make an overall estimate. As we will explain later, however, we never really observe the true relationship—our inference of it is always uncertain to some degree. Therefore, we may not be sure if it is reasonable to combine data from our subsamples. Because the variance of the error will be larger the smaller the size of our subsamples, the more we divide our data, the more difficult it is to determine whether observed differences reflect true differences.

The Basic Linear Regression Model

Linear regression provides a manageable way to control statistically for the effects of several independent variables.[20] Its use requires us to assume that the effects of the various independent variables are additive. That is, the marginal effect on the dependent variable of a unit change in any one of the independent variables remains the same no matter what the values of the other independent variables.

This assumption is not as restrictive as it might at first seem. We can create new variables that are functions of the original independent variables to capture nonlinearities. For example, if we thought smokers were likely to absorb environmental lead faster than nonsmokers, we might include in our linear regression model a new variable that is the product of the number of cigarettes smoked per day and the level of gasoline lead. This new variable, capturing the interaction of smoking and gasoline lead, would have an effect that would be additive with the other independent variables in the model, including the smoking and gasoline lead variables. The marginal effect of gasoline lead on blood lead would consist of the contribution from the gasoline lead variable and the contribution from the variable representing its interaction with smoking, which will change depending on the particular level of smoking.

We can express a linear regression model in mathematical form:

$$y = \beta_0 + \beta_1 x_1 + \beta_2 x_2 + \ldots + \beta_k x_k + \epsilon$$

where y is the dependent variable, $x_1, x_2, \ldots, x_k$ are the k independent variables, $\beta_0, \beta_1, \ldots, \beta_k$ are parameters (coefficients) to be estimated, and ϵ is an error term that incorporates the cumulative effect on y of all the factors not explicitly included in the model. If we were to increase x_1 by one unit while holding the values of the other independent variables constant, y would change by an amount β_1. Similarly, each of the coefficients measures the marginal effect of a unit change in its variable on the dependent variable.

Imagine that we set the values of all the independent variables except x_1 equal to zero. We could then plot y against x_1 in a graph like Figure 18.2. The equation $y = \beta_0 + \beta_1 x_1$ would represent the line fit to our sample of observations. The slope of the line is β_1, the magnitude of the change in y that will result from a unit change in x_1, other things equal. The actual observations do not lie exactly on the line, however. Their vertical distances from the line will be equal to the random error, represented in our model by ϵ, incorporated in each of the observations of y. As we do not know the true line, we must estimate it from the data. The vertical distances from the observed values to this estimated line we call e, the *prediction errors* of the estimated model. If the values of e are small, our line will fit the data well in the sense that the actual observations will lie close to it.

[20]For clear introductions, see Eric A. Hanushek and John E. Jackson, *Statistical Methods for the Social Sciences* (New York: Academic Press, 1977); and Christopher H. Achen, *Interpreting and Using Regression* (Beverly Hills, CA: Sage, 1982).

How should we go about fitting the line? The most commonly used procedure is the method of *ordinary least squares (OLS)*. When we have only one independent variable, so we can plot our data on a two-dimensional graph like Figure 18.2, the OLS procedure picks the line for which the sum of squared vertical deviations from the observed data is smallest. In order to distinguish our estimates of parameters from their true, but unobserved, values, we use the Latin (b) rather then Greek (β). So, for example, b_0 is the estimate of y-intercept, β_0, and b_1 is the estimate of slope, β_1.

When we have more than one independent variable, OLS determines the values of the coefficients ($b_0, b_1, \ldots, b_k$) that minimize the sum of squared prediction errors.[21] As long as the number of observations in our sample exceeds the number of coefficients we are trying to estimate, and none of our independent variables can be expressed as a linear combination of the other independent variables, the commonly available regression software packages will enable us to use computers to find the OLS fitted coefficients.[22]

The estimates of coefficients that we obtain from OLS will generally have a number of very desirable properties. If the independent variables are all uncorrelated with the error term, ε, then our coefficient estimators will be *unbiased*.[23] (*Note*: An *estimator* is the formula we use to calculate a particular estimate from our data.) To understand what it means for an estimator to be unbiased, we must keep in mind that our particular estimate depends on the errors actually realized in our sample of data. If we were to select a new sample, we would realize different errors and hence different coefficient estimates. When an estimator is unbiased, we expect that the average of our estimates across different samples will be very close to the true coefficient value. For example, if gasoline lead had no true effect on blood lead (gasoline lead had a true coefficient of zero), we would almost certainly estimate its coefficient

[21]The prediction error is the observed value of the dependent variable minus the value we would predict for the dependent variables based on our parameter estimates and the values of our independent variables. For the ith observation the prediction error is given by

$$e_i = y_i - (b_0 + b_1 x_{1i} + \ldots + b_k x_{ki})$$

The prediction error is also referred to as the *residual of the observation*. OLS selects the parameter estimates to minimize the sum of the squares of the residuals.

[22]When one independent variable can be written as a linear combination of the others, we have a case of *perfect multicollinearity*. A related and more common problem, which we can rarely do anything about, occurs when the independent variables in our sample are highly correlated. This condition, called *multicollinearity*, is not a problem with the specification of our model but with the data we have available to estimate it. If two variables are highly correlated, positively or negatively, then OLS has difficulty identifying their independent effects on the dependent variable. As a result, the estimates of the parameters associated with these variables will not be very precise. That is, they will have large variances, increasing the chances that we will fail to recognize, statistically speaking, their effects on the dependent variable. One way to deal with multicollinearity is to add new observations to our sample that lower the correlation. For example, if we had a high positive correlation between smoking and drinking in our sample, we should try to add observations on individuals who smoke but do not drink and who drink but do not smoke. Unfortunately, we often have no choice but to work with the data that are already available.

[23]Strictly speaking, we must also assume that our independent variables are fixed in the sense that we could construct a new sample with exactly the same observations on the independent variables. Of course, even if the independent variables are fixed, we would observe different values of the dependent variable because of the random error term. In addition, we must assume that the expected value of the error term is zero for all observations.

to be positive or negative rather than exactly zero. Repeating OLS on a large number of samples and averaging our estimates of the coefficient of gasoline lead, however, would generally yield a result very close to zero.[24] Indeed, by adding more and more samples, we could get the average as close to zero as we wanted.

Unfortunately, we usually only have a single sample for estimating coefficients. How do we decide if an estimate deviates enough from zero for us to conclude that the true value of the parameter is not zero? Making the fairly reasonable assumption that the error term for each observation can be treated as a draw from a Normal distribution with constant variance, the OLS estimators will be distributed according to the Student-*t* distribution.[25] That is, we can interpret the particular numerical estimate of a coefficient as a draw from a random variable distributed as a Student-*t* distribution centered around the true value of the coefficient. (The OLS estimator is the random variable; the actual estimate based on our data is a realization of that random variable.)

Knowing the distribution of the OLS estimator enables us to interpret the *statistical significance* of our coefficient estimate. We determine statistical significance by asking the following question: How likely is it that we would observe a coefficient estimate as large (in absolute value terms) as we did if the true value of the coefficient were zero? We answer this question by first assuming that the true value of the coefficient is zero (the null hypothesis) so that the distribution of our estimator is centered around zero. We then standardize our distribution to have a variance of one by dividing our coefficient estimate by an estimate of its standard error (a by-product of the OLS procedure). The resulting number, called the *t*-ratio, can then be compared to critical values in tabulations of the standardized Student-*t* distribution found in the appendix of almost any statistics text. For example, we might decide that we will reject the null hypothesis that the true value of the coefficient is zero if there is less than a 5 percent probability of observing a *t*-ratio (in absolute value sense) as large as we did if the null hypothesis is true. (The probability we choose puts an upward bound on the probability of falsely rejecting the null hypothesis.)[26] To carry out the test, we look in the standardized tabulations of the

[24]Our average will not be close to zero if gasoline lead is correlated with a variable excluded from our model that does have an effect on blood lead. In this case, gasoline lead stands as a proxy for the excluded variable. Other things equal, the stronger the true effect of the excluded variable on blood lead and the higher the absolute value of the correlation between gasoline lead and the excluded variable, the greater will be the bias of the coefficient of gasoline lead. We might not worry that much about the bias if we knew that it would approach zero as we increase sample size. (If the variance of the estimator also approached zero as we increased sample size, we would say that the estimator is *consistent*.) Although OLS estimators are consistent for correctly specified models, correlation of an independent variable with an important excluded variable makes its estimator inconsistent.

[25]The *Central Limit Theorem* tells us that the distribution of the sum of independent random variables approaches the Normal distribution as the number in the sum becomes large. The theorem applies for almost any starting distributions—the existence of a finite variance is sufficient. If we think of the error term as the sum of all the many factors excluded from our model, and further, we believe that they are not systematically related to each other or the included variables, then the Central Limit Theorem suggests that the distribution of the error terms will be at least approximately Normal.

[26]Falsely rejecting the null hypothesis is referred to as *Type I error*. Failing to reject the null hypothesis when in fact the alternative hypothesis is true is referred to as *Type II error*. We usually set the probability of Type I error at some low level like 5 percent. Holding sample size constant, the lower we set the probability of Type I error, the greater the probability of Type II error.

Student-*t* distribution for the critical value corresponding to 5 percent.[27] If the absolute value of our estimated *t*-ratio exceeds the critical value, then we reject the null hypothesis and say that our estimated coefficient is statistically significantly different from zero.

Fortunately, most regression software saves us the trouble of looking up critical values in tables by directly calculating the probability under the null hypothesis of observing a *t*-ratio as large as that estimated. To do a classical test of hypothesis based on the coefficient, we simply see if the reported probability is less than the maximum probability of falsely rejecting the null hypothesis that we are willing to accept. If it is smaller, then we reject the null hypothesis.

Consider the regression results presented in Table 18.1. They are based on data from 6,534 whites in the NHANES II survey for whom blood lead measurements were made. The analysts estimated similar models for blacks and for blacks and whites together. (Their estimates of the coefficient for gasoline lead never deviated by more than 10 percent across the different samples. To conserve space, they reported in detail only their regression results for whites. They chose whites because it was the largest subgroup and because it preempted the assertion that the relationship between blood lead and gasoline lead was due to changes in the racial composition of the sample over time.)

The dependent variable is the individual's blood lead level measured in μg/dl. The independent variables are listed under the heading "Effect." The independent variable of primary interest is the national consumption of gasoline lead (in hundreds of metric tons per day) in the month prior to the individual's blood lead measurement. The other independent variables were included in an effort to control statistically for other factors that might be expected to affect the individual's blood lead level. With the exception of the number of cigarettes smoked per day and the dietary factors (vitamin C, riboflavin, and so on), these other statistical controls are indicator, or "dummy," variables that take on the value one if some condition is met and zero otherwise. So, for example, if the individual is male, the variable "male" will equal one; if the individual is female, it will equal zero. The variables "vitamin C," "phosphorus," "riboflavin," and "vitamin A," which are included as proxy measures for dietary intake of lead, each measure dietary intake in milligrams. Otherwise, the other variables are intended to capture demographic, income, occupational exposure, drinking habit, and locational effects. The reported R^2 indicates that, taken together, the independent variables explain about 33 percent of the total variation in blood lead levels.[28]

The estimated coefficient for gasoline lead is 2.14 μg/dl of blood per 100 metric tons per day of national gasoline lead consumption. Dividing the coefficient

[27] The Student-*t* distribution is tabulated by degrees of freedom. In the basic OLS framework, the *degrees of freedom* is the total number of observations minus the number of coefficients being estimated. As degrees of freedom becomes larger, the Student-*t* distribution looks more like a standard Normal distribution. You should also note the difference between a one-tailed and two-tailed test. Because the standardized Student-*t* is a symmetric distribution centered on zero, a 5 percent test usually involves setting critical values so that 2.5 percent of area lies under each of the tails (positive and negative). A one-tailed test, appropriate when we are only willing to reject the null hypothesis in favor of an alternative hypothesis in one direction (either positive or negative, but not both), puts the entire 5 percent in the tail in that direction.

[28] R^2 is a measure of the *goodness of fit* of the model to the particular sample of data. It is the square of the correlation between the values of the dependent variable predicted by the model and the values actually observed. An R^2 of one would mean that the model perfectly predicted the independent variable for the sample; an R^2 of zero would mean that the model made no contribution to prediction.

Table 18.1 *Basic Regression Model for Estimating the Effects of Gasoline Lead on Blood Lead*[a]

Effect	Coefficient	Standard Error	P-Value
Intercept	6.15		
Gasoline	2.14	.142	.0000
Low income	0.79	.243	.0025
Moderate income	0.32	.184	.0897
Child (under 8)	3.47	.354	.0000
Number of cigarettes	0.08	.012	.0000
Occupationally exposed	1.74	.251	.0000
Vitamin C	-.004	.000	.0010
Teenager	-0.30	.224	.1841
Male	0.50	.436	.2538
Male teenager	1.67	.510	.0026
Male adult	3.40	.510	.0000
Small city	-0.91	.292	.0039
Rural	-1.29	.316	.0003
Phosphorus	-0.001	.000	.0009
Drinker	0.67	.173	.0007
Heavy drinker	1.53	.316	.0000
Northeast	-1.09	.332	.0028
South	-1.44	.374	.0005
Midwest	-1.35	.500	.0115
Educational level	-0.60	.140	.0000
Riboflavin	0.188	.071	.0186
Vitamin A	0.018	.008	.0355

[a] *Dependent variable*: Blood lead (μg/dl) of whites in NHANES II survey.

Source: Joel Schwartz et al., *Costs and Benefits of Reducing Lead in Gasoline: Final Regulatory Impact Analysis* (Washington, DC: Environmental Protection Agency, 1985), III-15. The original document reported incorrect standard errors; standard errors reported here were provided by Joel Schwartz.

estimate by its estimated standard error of 0.192 yields a *t*-ratio of about 11. The probability of observing a *t*-ratio this large or larger if the true value of the coefficient were actually zero is less than one chance in 10,000 (the 0.0000 entry in Table 18.1 under "*P*-value"). We would thus reject the null hypothesis in favor of the alternative hypothesis that gasoline lead does contribute to blood lead. In other words, we would say that gasoline lead has a *statistically significant effect* on blood lead.

After finding a statistically significant effect, the next question to ask is whether the size of the coefficient is *substantively significant*. That is, does the variable in question have an effect that is worth considering?[29] One approach to answering this question is to multiply the estimated coefficient by the plausible change in the independent variable that might occur. For example, by the end of the NHANES II survey, gasoline lead was being consumed at a rate of about 250 metric tons per day nationally. A strict policy might reduce the level to, say, 25 metric tons per day. Using the estimated coefficient of gasoline lead, we would expect a reduction of this magnitude to reduce blood lead levels on average by about 4.8 μg/dl (the reduction of 225 metric tons per day times the estimated coefficient of 2.14 μg/dl per 100 metric tons per day).

To get a better sense of whether a 4.8 μg/dl reduction is substantively important, we can look at the blood lead levels for representative groups at the 250 and 25 metric ton levels. For example, at the 250 metric ton level a nonsmoking (number of cigarettes equals zero), moderate drinking (drinker equals one; heavy drinker equals zero), nonoccupationally exposed (occupationally exposed equals zero), adult female (child, teenager, male, male teenager, and male adult equal zero), living in a large northeastern city (Northeast equals one; small city, rural, South, and Midwest equal zero), with moderate income (low income equals zero, moderate income equals zero), college degree (educational level equals one), and a high-nutrition diet (vitamin C, phosphorus, riboflavin, and vitamin A equal their mean levels in the sample) would be predicted to have a blood lead level of 10.6 μg/dl. We would expect the same person to have a blood lead level of only 5.8 μg/dl if the gasoline lead level were cut to 25 metric tons per day—a reduction of about 45 percent. Thus, the effect of gasoline lead on blood lead appears substantively as well as statistically significant.

The study team was especially interested in estimating the contribution of gasoline lead to blood lead in children. As a first cut, they developed a logistic regression model[30] for predicting the probability that a child between the ages of six months and eight years will have blood levels in excess of 30 μg/dl, the definition of lead toxicity used by the Centers for Disease Control at the time. *Logistic regression*, which assumes a nonlinear relationship between the dependent and the independent variables,[31] is usually more appropriate than linear regression when the dependent variable is dichotomous (Y equals one if the condition holds, and zero if it does not).[32] The study team found a strong relationship in the NHANES II data

[29]The standard errors of the coefficient estimates decrease as sample size increases. Thus, very large samples may yield large t-ratios even when the estimated coefficient (and its true value) are small. We refer to the power of a statistical test as one minus the probability of failing to reject the null hypothesis in favor of the alternative hypothesis. Other things equal, larger sample sizes have greater power, increasing the chances that we will reject the null hypothesis in favor of alternatives very close to zero.

[30]For an introduction to logistic regression, see Hanushek and Jackson, *Statistical Methods*, pp. 179–216.

[31]The logistic regression model is written:

$$P(Y) = e^Z/(1 + e^Z)$$

where $P(Y)$ is the probability that condition Y holds, e is the natural base, and $Z = b_0 + b_1x_1 + b_2x_2 + \ldots + b_kx_k$ is the weighted sum of the independent variables $x_1, x_2, \ldots, x_k$. The coefficients $b_0, b_1, \ldots, b_k$ are selected to maximize the probability of observing the data in the sample. Note that the marginal contribution of x_i to the value of the dependent variable is not simply b_i, as would be the case in a linear regression model. Rather, it is $b_i[1 - P(Y)]P(Y)$, which has its greatest absolute value when $P(Y) = 0.5$.

[32]The logistic regression model, unlike the linear regression model, always predicts probabilities that lie between zero and one (as they should).

between gasoline lead and the probability that a child has a toxic level of blood lead. In fact, they estimated that the elimination of gasoline lead would have reduced the number of cases of lead toxicity in the sample by 80 percent for children under eight years of age. The study team used logistic regression and other probability models to estimate how reductions in gasoline lead would change the number of children having various blood lead levels. These estimates were essential for their subsequent valuation of the effects of gasoline lead reductions on the health of children.

Reconsidering Causality

Finding that an independent variable in a regression model has a statistically significant coefficient does not by itself establish a causal relationship. That is, it does not guarantee that changes in the independent variable cause changes in the dependent variable. Even if the independent variable truly has no direct effect on the dependent variable, some other variable, not included in the model, may be correlated with both so as to produce an apparent relationship in the data sample (remember the apparent relationship between birth rates and the density of stork nests). Should the strong relationship between gasoline lead and blood lead be interpreted as causal?

The study team considered this question in detail. Although its demonstration was not legally necessary, they believed that adoption of the proposed rule would be more likely if a strong case for causality could be made. The approach was to apply the criteria commonly used by epidemiologists to determine the likelihood of causality. Not all of the criteria are directly applicable outside of the health area. Nonetheless, the way the study team applied the criteria illustrates the sort of questioning that is valuable in empirical research. Therefore, we briefly review the six criteria that they considered.

Is the Model Biologically Plausible? The study team noted that lead can be absorbed through the lung and gut. They pointed out that gasoline lead, the major source of environmental lead, is emitted predominantly as respirable particles in automobile exhaust. These particles can be absorbed directly through the lungs. They also contaminate dust that can be inhaled through the lungs and absorbed through the gut. Therefore, they argued, it is biologically plausible that gasoline lead contributes to blood lead.

Biological plausibility is the epidemiological statement of a more general criterion: Is the model theoretically plausible? Prior to looking through data for empirical relationships, you should specify a model (your beliefs about how variables are related). If you find that your data are consistent with your model, then you can be more confident that the relationships you estimate are not simply due to chance.[33]

[33]Imagine that you regress a variable on twenty other variables. Assume that none of the twenty independent variables has a true effect on the dependent variable. (The coefficients in the true model are all zero.) Nevertheless, if you use a statistical test that limits the probability of falsely rejecting the null hypothesis to 5 percent, then you would still have a 0.64 probability $[1 - (.95)^{20}]$ of rejecting at least one null hypothesis. In other words, if you look through enough data you are bound to find some statistically significant relationships, even when no true relationships exist. By forcing yourself to specify theoretical relationships before you look at the data, you will reduce the chances that you will be fooled by the idiosyncrasy of your particular data sample. For a brief review of these issues, see David L. Weimer, "Collective Delusion in the Social Science: Publishing Incentives for Empirical Abuse," *Policy Studies Review* 5(4) 1986, 705–708.

Is There Experimental Evidence to Support the Findings? The study team found reports of several investigations specifically designed to measure the contribution of gasoline lead to blood lead. One was an experiment conducted in Turin, Italy, by researchers who monitored changes in the isotopic composition of blood lead as the isotopic composition of gasoline lead varied.[34] They found that at least 25 percent of the lead in the blood of Turin residents originated in gasoline. Thus, the experiment not only confirmed the biological plausibility of the contribution of gasoline lead to blood lead but also suggested an effect on the order of magnitude of that estimated by the study team.

Being able to find such strong and directly relevant experimental support is very rare in policy research, much of which deals with the behavioral responses of people. Controlled experiments in the social sciences are rare, not only because they are costly and difficult to implement but also because they often involve tricky ethical issues concerning the assignment of people to "treatment" and "control" groups. Nevertheless, there have been a number of policy experiments in the United States over the last thirty years.[35] It is unlikely, however, that any of these experiments will be directly applicable to your policy problem. Therefore, you must typically broaden your search for confirmation beyond experiments to other empirical research.

Do Other Studies Using Different Data Replicate the Results? The study team reviewed several studies that also found relationships between gasoline lead and blood lead. These studies were based on data collected in conjunction with community-wide lead-screening programs funded by the Centers for Disease Control during the 1970s[36] and on data collected from the umbilical cord blood of more than 11,000 babies born in Boston between April 1979 and April 1981.[37] These studies reported statistically significant relationships between gasoline lead and blood lead, and thus supported the study team's analysis based on the NHANES II data.

Does Cause Precede Effect? The study team used information about the half-life of lead in blood to make predictions about the strengths of relationships between lagged levels of gasoline lead and blood lead that would be expected if gasoline lead contributes to blood lead. Lead has a half-life of about thirty days in blood. Noting that the average NHANES II blood test was done at mid-month, they predicted that the previous month's gasoline lead (which on average represents emissions occurring between fifteen and forty-five days before the test) should have a stronger impact on blood lead than that of either the current month (average exposure of zero to fifteen days) or the month occurring two months prior (average exposure of forty-five to seventy-five days). They tested their predictions by regressing blood lead levels on current, one-month-lagged, and two-month-lagged gasoline lead levels. As predicted, one-month-lagged gasoline lead was the most significant of the three. Also,

[34]S. Fachetti and F. Geiss, *Isotopic Lead Experiment Status Report*, Publication No. EUR8352ZEN (Luxembourg: Commission of the European Communities, 1982).

[35]For a review of the major policy experiments conducted in the United States, see David Greenberg and Mark Shroder, *The Digest of Social Experiments*, 2nd ed. (Washington, DC: Urban Institute, 1997).

[36]Irwin H. Billick et al., *Predictions of Pediatric Blood Lead Levels from Gasoline Consumption* (Washington, DC: U.S. Department of Housing and Urban Development, 1982).

[37]M. Rabinowitz, H. L. Needleman, M. Burley, H. Finch, and J. Rees, "Lead in Umbilical Blood, Indoor Air, Tap Water, and Gasoline in Boston," *Archives of Environmental Health* 39(4) 1984, 297–301.

consistent with the thirty-day half-life, two-month-lagged gasoline lead had a coefficient approximately one-half that of one-month-lagged gasoline lead. Thus, cause did appear to precede effect in the expected way.

Does a Stable Dose-Response Relationship Exist? The regression model used by the study team assumed a linear relationship between gasoline lead and blood lead. Did this relationship remain stable as the level of gasoline lead changed? To answer this question, the study team took advantage of the fact that, on average, gasoline lead levels were about 50 percent lower in the second half of the NHANES II survey than in the first half. If the relationship between gasoline lead and blood lead is stable and linear, then reestimating the regression model using only data from the second half of the survey should yield a coefficient for gasoline lead comparable to that for the entire sample. They found that the coefficients were indeed essentially the same. In addition, estimation of regression models that directly allowed for the possibility of nonlinear effects supported the initial findings of a linear relationship between gasoline lead and blood lead.

Is It Likely That Factors Not Included in the Analysis Could Account for the Observed Relationship? The study team considered several factors that might confound the apparent relationship between gasoline lead and blood lead: dietary lead intake, exposure to lead paint, seasonality, and sampling patterns.

The basic regression model included nutrient and demographic variables as proxy measures for the intake of lead in the diet. Yet these variables may not adequately control for a possible downward trend in dietary lead that could be causing the estimated relationship between gasoline lead and blood lead. Market basket studies conducted by the Food and Drug Administration over the survey period, however, showed no downward trend in dietary lead intake. Also, lead intake from drinking water is largely a function of acidity, which did not change systematically over the survey period. Evidence did suggest that changes in solder reduced the content of lead in canned foods over the period. But the study team was able to rule out the lead content in canned foods as a confounding factor when they added the lead content in solder as an independent variable, reestimated the basic regression model, and found that the coefficient of gasoline lead remained essentially unchanged.

The study team recognized changing exposure to lead paint as another potential confounding factor. They dismissed the possibility on three grounds.

First, paint lead is a major source of blood lead for children (who eat paint chips) but not for adults. If declining exposure to lead paint were responsible for the estimated relationship between gasoline lead and blood lead, then we would expect the reduction in blood lead to be much greater for children than for adults. In fact, the average reduction over the survey period for adults was only slightly smaller than that for children (37 percent versus 42 percent).

Second, the ingestion of paint lead usually results in large increases in blood lead levels. If reduced exposure to paint lead were responsible for declining blood lead levels, then we would expect to observe the improvement primarily in terms of a reduction in the number of people with very high blood lead levels. In fact, blood lead levels declined over the survey period even for groups with low initial levels.[38]

[38]The study team also used data from the lead-screening program in Chicago to estimate the probability of toxicity as a function of gasoline lead for children exposed and not exposed to lead paint. They found that gasoline lead had statistically significant positive coefficients for both groups.

Third, declining exposure to paint lead should be a more important factor in central cities than in suburbs because the latter tend to have newer housing stocks with lower frequencies of peeling lead paint. Yet the gasoline lead coefficient estimate was essentially the same for central city and suburban subsamples.

Blood lead levels in the United States are, on average, higher in the summer than in the winter. To rule out the possibility that seasonal variation confounds the relationship between gasoline lead and blood lead, the study team reestimated the basic model with indicator variables included to allow for the possibility of independent seasonal effects. The coefficients of the seasonal variables were not statistically significant when gasoline lead was kept in the model. Thus, it appeared that changes in gasoline lead could adequately explain seasonal as well as long-term changes in blood lead levels.

As already mentioned, the study team estimated the basic model on a variety of demographic subsamples and found no more than a 10 percent difference across any two estimates of the gasoline lead coefficient. They were also concerned, however, that changes in NHANES II sampling locations over the survey period might have confounded the estimation of the gasoline lead coefficient. Therefore, they reestimated the basic model with indicator variables for forty-nine locations and found that the gasoline lead coefficient changed by only about 5 percent. Furthermore, they found that, even when including variables to allow for different gasoline lead coefficients across locations, the coefficient representing the nationwide effect of gasoline lead was statistically and substantively significant. Together, these tests led the study team to dismiss the possibility of serious sampling bias.

The Weight of the Evidence

The study team produced a very strong case in support of an important causal relationship between gasoline lead and blood lead. In many ways its efforts were exemplary. It drew relevant evidence from a wide variety of sources to supplement the primary data analysis. It gave serious attention to possible confounding factors, considering both internal tests (such as subsample analyses and model respecifications) and external evidence to see if they could be ruled out. As a consequence, opponents of the proposed policy were left with few openings for attacking its empirical underpinnings.

Finalizing the Rule

The primary task facing the analytical team after publication of the proposed rule was to respond to comments made by interested parties. Team members participated in public hearings held in August and spent much of the fall of 1984 responding to comments placed in the public docket, which closed on October 1. During this process they became more confident that the proposed rule would produce the large net benefits they predicted. At the same time they discovered another benefit category—reductions in adult blood pressure levels—that could potentially swamp their earlier estimates of benefits.

In 1983, Schwartz chanced upon a research article reporting a correlation between blood lead and hypertension.[39] He began work with researchers at the Centers for Disease Control and the University of Michigan to determine if a relationship existed between blood lead and blood pressure levels. By the summer of 1984 their analysis of the NHANES II data suggested a strong link.[40] Because high blood pressure contributes to hypertension, myocardial infarctions, and strokes, the potential benefits from blood lead reductions were enormous. Although the final rule was ultimately issued without reference to quantitative estimates of the benefits of lower adult blood lead levels, the team provided estimates in the supporting documents.

The one remaining issue was the compliance schedule. The costs of various lead standards were estimated, using a model of the U.S. refining sector originally developed for the Department of Energy. The model represents the various types of refining capabilities that are available to convert crude oils to final petroleum products. It employs an optimization procedure for finding the allocations of crude oils and intermediate petroleum products among refining units that maximizes social surplus, the sum of consumer and producer surpluses. This allocation corresponds to that which would result from a perfectly competitive market operating without constraints on the utilization of available units. Cost was estimated by looking at the decline in social surplus resulting when the lead constraint was tightened—for instance, from 1.1 gplg to 0.1 gplg. The manufacturers of lead additives challenged these results on the grounds that the model assumed more flexibility in capacity utilization across different refineries than was realistic.

The analytical team held meetings with staffers from other EPA offices to consider alternative compliance schedules. Although a tentative decision was reached to set an interim standard of 0.5 gplg, to be effective July 1, 1985, and a final standard of 0.1 gplg, to be effective January 1, 1986, several staffers feared that some refiners would be unable to comply using their existing equipment. If these fears were realized, then the economic costs of the new rule would be higher than estimated and perhaps raise political problems.

A consultant to the project, William Johnson of Sobotka and Company, suggested a solution. If the physical distribution of equipment among refineries interfered with the flexibility in petroleum transfers assumed in the model, he reasoned, perhaps a secondary market in lead rights could be created to facilitate trading to get around specific bottlenecks. Taking the total permitted lead content from July 1, 1985 to January 1, 1988 as a constraint, the key was to create an incentive for refiners that could make the least costly reductions in lead additives below the interim 0.5 gplg standard to do so. Their additional reductions could then be used to offset excess lead in gasoline produced by refiners that could not easily meet the basic standards with the equipment they had in place. Because current reductions below the standard create a right to produce above the standard some time in the future, the trading process was called "banking of lead rights." Refiners would be free to

[39]V. Batuman, E. Landy, J. K. Maesaka, and R. P. Wedeen, "Contribution of Lead to Hypertension with Renal Impairment," *New England Journal of Medicine* 309(1) 1983, 17–21.

[40]The results of their research were later published in J. C. Pirkle, J. Schwartz, J. R. Landes, and W. R. Harlan, "The Relationship between Blood Lead Levels and Blood Pressure and Its Cardiovascular Risk Implications," *American Journal of Epidemiology* 121(2) 1985, 246–58.

buy and sell lead rights at prices that were mutually beneficial. As a result, the aggregate cost of meeting the new standard would be reduced.

Representatives from the various EPA offices involved with the lead rule agreed that banking seemed to be a good way to deal with concerns about the compliance schedule. Because it had not been discussed in the proposed rule published in August, banking could not be part of the final rule. Nevertheless, by moving quickly to propose banking in a supplemental notice, it would be available shortly after the new standard became final.[41]

The remaining task for the team was to prepare the *Final Regulatory Impact Analysis*, which would be published in support of the final rule.[42] The resulting document began by discussing the misfueling and health problems associated with lead additives along with alternatives (public education and stepped-up local enforcement to deal specifically with misfueling, pollution charges to deal generally with lead as a negative externality, and other regulatory standards) to the final rule. It then detailed the methods used to estimate the costs of tighter lead standards, the link between gasoline lead and blood lead, the health benefits of reducing the exposure of children and adults to lead, the benefits of reducing pollutants other than lead, and the benefits from reduced vehicle maintenance costs and increased fuel economy.

The present value of the net benefits of the final rule was presented with various assumptions about misfueling (the use of leaded gasoline in vehicles with catalytic converters). The lower level of permitted lead would reduce the price differential between leaded and unleaded gasoline, thereby reducing the economic incentive for misfueling. It was not possible to predict with confidence, however, how much misfueling would actually decline. Therefore, the reasonable approach was to consider net benefits over the range of possibilities. Table 18.2 presents the results of this sensitivity analysis. Note that net benefits were given both including and excluding the adult blood pressure benefits. Although the blood pressure benefits appeared huge, they were the last of the benefit measures considered and hence had the least developed supporting evidence. Nevertheless, even assuming that the standard would produce no reduction in misfueling and no health benefits for adults, the present value of benefits appeared to be more than double the present value of costs. Indeed, it appeared that maintenance benefits alone would more than cover higher refining costs.

The *Final Regulatory Impact Analysis* was released in February 1985. On March 7, 1985, the final rule was published in the *Federal Register*.[43] The 0.1 gplg standard would take effect on January 1, 1986, almost three years after work on the supporting analysis began. Subsequently, the Clean Air Act Amendments of 1990 mandated the elimination of lead from all motor fuel sold in the United States by

[41]50 *Federal Register* 718 (January 4, 1985); and 50 *Federal Register* 13116 (April 2, 1985).

[42]Joel Schwartz, Hugh Pitcher, Ronnie Levin, Bart Ostro, and Albert L. Nichols, *Costs and Benefits of Reducing Lead in Gasoline: Final Regulatory Impact Analysis*, Publication No. EPA-230-05-85-006 (Washington, DC: Office of Policy Analysis, EPA, February, 1985). By the time the final report was prepared, Jane Leggett left the project team. In the meantime, Albert Nichols, a Harvard University professor who was visiting the EPA as the acting director of the Economic Analysis division, began working closely with the team to produce the final document.

[43]50 *Federal Register* 9386 (March 7, 1985).

Table 18.2 *Present Value of Costs and Benefits of Final Rule, 1985-1992 (millions of 1983 dollars)*

	No Misfueling	Full Misfueling	Partial Misfueling
Monetized Benefits			
Children's health effects	2,582	2,506	2,546
Adult blood pressure	27,936	26,743	27,462
Conventional pollutants	1,525	0	1,114
Maintenance	4,331	3,634	4,077
Fuel economy	856	643	788
Total Monetized Benefits	37,231	33,526	35,987
Total Refining Costs	2,637	2,678	2,619
Net Benefits	34,594	30,847	33,368
Net Benefits Excluding Blood Pressure	6,658	4,105	5,906

Source: Joel Schwartz et al., *Costs and Benefits of Reducing Lead in Gasoline* (Washington, DC: Environmental Protection Agency, 1985), Table VIII-8, VIII-26.

January 1, 1996. In 1994, the United Nations Commission on Sustainable Development called upon governments to eliminate lead from gasoline; more than three dozen countries have already done so.

Conclusion

We have described a case where statistical analysis made an important contribution to changing policy. Is this case typical? Yes and No. You should not expect that such a confluence of skill, time, data, resources, and interest will often arise to produce such definitive empirical findings—regulatory analysis is not always done so well.[44] At the same time, you should expect to encounter empirical questions that at least can be approached, if not confidently answered, with the sort of statistical methods used by the EPA analysts. Consider a few prominent examples: Does the death penalty deter homicide?[45] Do higher minimum legal drinking ages and the 55-mile-per-hour speed limit reduce traffic fatalities?[46] Do smaller class sizes

[44]Robert W. Hahn, Jason K. Burnett, Yee-Ho I. Chan, Elizabeth A. Mader, and Petrea R. Moyle, "Assessing Regulatory Impact Analyses: The Failure of Agencies to Comply with Executive Order 12,866," *Harvard Journal of Law & Public Policy* 23(3), 2000, 859–85.

[45]See Isaac Ehrlich, "The Deterrent Effect of Capital Punishment: A Question of Life and Death," *American Economic Review* 65(3) 1975, 397–417; and Alfred Blumstein, Jacqueline Cohen, and Daniel Nagin, eds., *Deterrence and Incapacitation: Estimating the Effects of Criminal Sanctions on Crime Rates* (Washington, DC: National Academy of Science, 1978).

[46]See Charles A. Lave, "Speeding, Coordination, and the 55 MPH Limit," *American Economic Review* 75(5) 1985, 1159–64; and Peter Asch and David T. Levy, "Does the Minimum Drinking Age Affect Traffic Fatalities?" *Journal of Policy Analysis and Management* 6(2) 1987, 180–92.

improve student performance?[47] Do increases in the minimum wage actually produce theoretically predicted reductions in employment?[48] Although widely accepted answers to these empirical questions would not necessarily be decisive in resolving policy debates, they would at least move the debates beyond disputes over predictions to explicit considerations of values. Such highly controversial issues aside, you are likely to find that making empirical inferences and critically consuming those of others often contribute in important ways to the quality of your policy analyses.

For Discussion

1. Imagine that you wanted to estimate the price elasticity of demand for cigarettes in the United States. One approach might be to take advantage of the differences in prices across states due to differences in cigarette taxes. For example, you might regress per capita consumption of cigarettes in each state on the retail price of cigarettes in that state. What other variables might you want to include in your model?
2. We commend the EPA team for reestimating its model of the relationship between gasoline lead and blood lead in an effort to rule out alternative explanations for its initial finding of a strong positive relationship. Would we also commend them if they had initially found no relationship but continued to modify their models in an effort to find a positive effect?

[47]See Eric A. Hanushek, "Measuring Investment in Education," *Journal of Economic Perspectives* 10(4) 1996, 9–30.

[48]See David E. Card and Alan B. Krueger, *Myth and Measurement: The New Economics of the Minimum Wage* (Princeton, NJ: Princeton University Press, 1995); Richard V. Burkhauser, Kenneth A. Couch, and David C. Wittenburg, "'Who Gets What' from Minimum Wage Hikes: A Re-Estimation of Card and Krueger's *Myth and Measurement: The New Economics of the Minimum Wage*," *Industrial and Labor Relations Review* 59(3) 1996, 547–52; and Tom Valentine, "The Minimum Wage Debate: Politically Correct Economics?" *Economic and Labour Relations Review* 7(2) 1996, 188–97.

19

Doing Well and Doing Good

The preceding chapters set out what we believe to be the important elements of an introduction to policy analysis. As a faithful reader, you should now be ready to begin to produce your own analyses with some success. As you gain practical experience, we hope you will find it useful to return to some of the chapters for reference and reinterpretation. We conclude with a few thoughts about how you should view your role as a policy analyst.

Our first exhortation: Do well! Keep your client in mind! Policy analysts earn their keep by giving advice. Always strive to give useful advice by keeping in mind the range of actions available to your client. But, like a doctor, one of your guiding principles should be," Do no harm." This demands skepticism and modesty. Be skeptical about information provided by others and be modest about the accuracy of your own predictions so as to avoid leading your client into costly or embarrassing mistakes. As a professional advice giver, you should be prepared to allow your client to take credit for your popular ideas while keeping the blame for unpopular ones for yourself. Beyond the satisfaction of knowing that you have done a job well, you are likely to be rewarded with the trust of your client and the opportunity to continue to be heard.

But, as we tried to make clear in Chapter 3, your duties as a policy analyst go beyond responsibility for the personal success of your client. You have responsibilities to the integrity of your craft and to contributing to a better society. Thus our second exhortation: Do good!

Doing good requires some basis for comparing alternative courses of action. At the most general level, promoting human dignity and freedom are values widely shared in Western societies. Unfortunately, these values sometimes conflict, and they often do not provide direct guidance for dealing with the majority of issues that most analysts confront in their day-to-day work. As a practical matter, analysts must employ less abstract values in their search for good policy.

Throughout this book we have emphasized economic efficiency as an important goal in the evaluation of alternative policies. Aside from the intuitive appeal of efficiency—If we can make someone better off without making anyone else worse off, then shouldn't we do so?—we believe that it often receives too little attention in political arenas because it generally lacks an organized constituency. As a society we might very well be willing to sacrifice considerable efficiency to achieve distributional or other goals, but we should do so knowingly. Introducing efficiency as a goal in the evaluation of policies is one way that policy analysts can contribute to the "public good" (for once not used in the technical sense!).

Beyond raising efficiency as a goal, you can contribute to the public good by identifying other values that receive too little attention in political arenas. Are there identifiable groups that consistently suffer losses from public policies? Is adequate consideration being given to the future and the interests of future generations? Are dangerous precedents being set? Your social responsibility as an analyst is to make sure that questions such as these get appropriately raised.

Is raising politically underrepresented values consistent with providing useful, presumedly politically feasible, advice? Unfortunately, the answer is often no—self-interest often dominates. But at other times people, including politicians, respond to analysis in a public spirit, putting aside their narrow personal and political interests for the greater good.[1] Also, ideas that are not immediately politically feasible may become so in the future if they are repeatedly raised and supported with substantively sound analysis; witness the role of economic analysis in setting the stage for the eventual deregulation of the U.S. telephone, trucking, and airline industries.[2] Sometimes doing good simply requires analysts to advise their clients to forgo some current popularity or success to achieve some important value. You are doing exceptionally well when you convince your client to accept such advice!

[1]For a provocative development of this point, see Steven Kelman, "'Public Choice' and Public Spirit," *Public Interest* 87 1987, 80–94.

[2]See Martha Derthick and Paul J. Quirk, *The Politics of Deregulation* (Washington, DC: Brookings Institution, 1985), 246–52.

Name Index

A

Abraham, Kenneth S., 236
Abrams, Burton, 143
Achen, Christopher H., 463
Ackerman, Bruce A., 240
Adams, Miriam E., 424
Akerlof, George, 109
Albion, Mark S., 116
Alchian, Armen A., 179, 301
Alesina, Alberto, 175
Alexander, Ernest R., 347
Alexander, Ian, 239
Alexrod, Robert, 291
Alm, Alvin L., 455
Alm, James, 107
Alonso, William, 148
Alston, Lee, 4
Alt, James E., 294
Amy, Douglas J., 40
Anderson, Charles W., 40
Anderson, L. G., 19, 89
Anderson, Terry L., 215
Andreoni, James, 143
Annala, John, 14, 15, 17, 19, 20
Annest, J. L., 457
Anwyll, James Bradford, 406
Appleton, David R., 461
Arai, A. Bruce, 16
Arbogoss, Rebecca, 242
Arce, Daniel G., 81
Arluck, Gregory M., 416–18
Arnason, Ragnar, 14, 15, 19, 20
Arrow, Kenneth J., 110, 119, 122, 127, 159, 160, 227, 239, 399
Asch, Peter, 475
Averch, Harvey, 238
Axelrod, Robert, 115

B

Baden, John, 90
Bailey, Elizabeth M., 216
Bailey, Martin J., 406
Ball, Laurence, 129
Ballard, Charles L., 146
Bane, Mary Jo, 259
Banks, Jeffrey S., 179
Bardach, Eugene, 187, 225, 243, 244, 276, 279, 280, 288, 310, 319–21, 324, 327
Bardhan, Pranab, 165
Barnard, Chester I., 290
Barnett, Andrea, 230
Baron, David P., 166
Barr, Nicholas, 255
Barsh, Russell, 4
Barzel, Yoram, 73
Batuman, V., 473
Baumol, William J., 100, 247, 303
Bayless, Mark, 397
Bayless, Michael D., 138
Bayse, D. D., 457
Bazerman, Max H., 123
Becker, Gary S., 115, 116, 121
Beckman, Norman, 24
Beggs, Steven D., 257
Begun, James W., 245
Behn, Robert D., 177, 289, 322, 324, 335, 407
Behrens, William W., III, 28
Bell, Bruce, 222
Bellavita, Christopher, 358
Bendor, Jonathan B., 180, 285
Benker, Karen M., 232
Ben-Nur, Avner, 117
Bentham, Jeremy, 135
Bentkover, Judith D., 398
Benveniste, Guy, 52
Berglund, Mary, 196
Bergson, Abram, 136, 137
Berkowitz, Daniel, 214
Berliant, Marcus C., 145
Berliner, Diane T., 32, 223
Berman, Larry, 32
Bernstein, Marver H., 238
Berry, R. E., Jr., 419
Besanko, David, 114
Besharov, Douglas, 326
Bhagwati, Jagdish, 224
Biller, Robert P., 288
Billick, Irwin H., 470
Bimber, Bruce, 33
Biswas, B., 84

Black, Duncan, 159
Blair, Louis, 286
Blais, Andre, 163, 181
Blalock, Ann Bonar, 286
Blankenship, Jerry, 222
Blau, Julian H., 159
Blinder, Alan S., 380
Blomquist, William, 90
Blumstein, Alfred, 475
Boardman, Anthony E., 69, 179, 181, 214, 250, 251, 298, 338, 341, 354, 381, 396, 397, 398, 405, 412, 421, 440, 445
Bobb, David J., 200
Bohi, Douglas R., 223
Bohm, Peter, 225
Bok, Sissila, 48
Boland, J. P., 419
Bonchek, Mark S., 172
Borcherding, Thomas, 169, 251
Borenstein, Severin, 112
Borkin, B., 122
Bortolotti, Bernardo, 213
Boubakari, Nargess, 214
Bowman, James S., 52
Boxberger, Daniel, 5
Boyd, Colin C., 251
Boyd, Rick, 17
Bozeman, Barry, 228
Bradbury, Katharine L., 231
Bradford, David F., 145
Brams, Steven J., 173
Brander, James A., 222
Brandl, John E., 208
Brands, Richard B., 138
Bratton, W. Kenneth, 216
Brennan, Geoffrey, 138
Breton, Albert, 180
Brewer, Garry D., 24, 288
Brewer, Gary, 322
Bromley, Daniel W., 138, 153
Bronars, Stephen, 165
Brooks, Neil, 233
Brooks, Stephen, 25
Brown, Peter G., 40, 118, 153
Brown, Trevor L., 299, 305
Browning, Edgar K., 146
Brozen, Yale, 114
Buchanan, James M., 138, 167, 169, 172, 189, 252
Bueno de Mesquita, Bruce, 263
Bukszar, Ed, 136
Bulmer, Martin, 153
Burchell, Robert W., 28
Burkhauser, Richard V., 476
Burley, M., 470
Burnett, H. Sterling, 200
Burnett, Jason K., 381, 475
Burrows, James C., 257
Burrows, Paul, 220
Bush, George, 376

C

Cairns, Robert D., 194–96
Callahan, Daniel, 40
Calvert, Randall, 291
Camerer, Colin, 137
Campbell, Donald T., 286
Campbell, Vincent N., 353
Camrere, Colin, 117
Card, David E., 476
Cardilli, Carlo G., 212
Carroll, Lewis, 159
Carruthers, Norman, 189
Carson, Richard T., 84, 398
Carstensen, Peter, 194, 198, 202
Carter, Jimmy, 430, 444, 446
Casas-Pardo, Jose, 181
Casey, Keith, 14
Cebula, Richard J., 112
Chadwick, Edwin, 216
Chan, Yee-Ho I., 381, 475
Chappell, Henry W., Jr., 165
Charkravarty, Satya R., 150
Chechile, Richard A., 122
Cheit, Ross E., 109, 244
Cherry, Diane DeWitt, 246, 381
Chezum, Brian, 245
Chi, Keon S., 296
Chiappori, Pierre-Andre, 121
Cialdini, Robert B., 147
Citro, Constance F., 145, 451
Clawson, Marion, 399
Clements, Benedict, 226
Clinton, Bill, 380
Clotfelter, Charles T., 214
Coase, Ronald H., 96, 179, 296, 364
Coate, Douglas, 233, 416–18
Cochrane, James L., 444
Cohen, Bernard L., 274
Cohen, Fay, 5
Cohen, Jacqueline, 475
Cohen, Jessica L., 124
Cohen, Michael D., 115
Coleman, James S., 25
Comanor, William S., 116
Condorcet, Marquis de, 159
Cook, Brian J., 221
Cook, Paul, 252
Cook, Philip J., 121, 214
Cooke, Alan D. J., 122
Cooter, Robert, 136
Copithorne, Lawrence, 222
Cordes, Joseph J., 258
Corvisier, Andre, 247
Cossett, Jean-Claude, 214
Couch, Kenneth A., 476
Covello, Vincent T., 398
Cox, Louis Anthony, Jr., 398
Coyle, Dennis, 268
Crandall, Robert W., 240, 268
Crane, Nancy, 317
Crawford, John W., 302
Crawford, Robert G., 301
Creasy, Laura, 200
Crecine, John P., 246
Crowley, Brian Lee, 5
Cruise, Peter L., 48
Cummings, Ronald G., 398
Cummins, J. David, 120

D

Dales, John, 215
Dalton, Russell J., 146
Dana, Andrew, 90
Daniels, Mark R., 288
Danziger, Sheldon H., 147
Darby, Michael R., 110
Dave, Dhaval, 116
David, Martin, 145, 147
Davis, Douglas D., 84
Deacon, Robert, 4
De Alessi, Louis, 179, 250, 251
Debreu, Gerard, 119

DeJong, David N., 214
deLeon, Peter, 24, 288
Dempsey, Paul Stephen, 194, 197
Demsetz, Harold, 179
Derthick, Martha, 212, 478
Dery, David, 327
Deutch, John, 447
Devarajan, Shantayanan, 126
DeVoretz, Don, 6, 8, 16
Dewees, Christopher, 14, 17
Dexter, Lewis A., 319
Dickens, William T., 124
Dilger, Robert J., 299
Dion, Stephane, 181
Dobel, J. Patrick, 46, 53
Dodgson, Charles, 159
Dollery, Brian, 295
Domah, Preetum, 213
Dorosh, Gary W., 169
Downs, Anthony, 181, 231
Dranove, David, 114
Dror, Yehezkel, 28, 52
Drost, Helmar, 5
D'Souza, Juliet, 213
Duncan, Charles W., 447
Dunleavy, Patrick, 181
Dunn, William N., 20
Dupont, Diane P., 7, 11

E

Easterling, Douglas, 147
Eastland, James, 272
Eavey, Cheryl L., 136
Eggertsson, Thrainn, 4, 96, 295
Ehrlich, Isaac, 121, 475
Eisenberg, Daniel, 280
Eismeier, Theodore J., 232
Elkin, Stephen L., 221
Ellerman, A. Danny, 216
Elliott, Kimberly Ann, 223
Ellwood, David T., 259
Elmore, Richard F., 283
Entoven, Alain C., 353
Epstein, Richard A., 235
Erickson, E., 213
Erikson, Robert S., 176
Etzioni, Amitai, 138, 330
Evans, Nigel, 274
Evans, Robert G., 244

F

Fachetti, S., 470
Fama, Eugene F., 181, 251
Fantini, Marcella, 213
Farris, Paul W., 116
Fass, Murray F., 141
Faure, M. G., 245
Feenstra, Robert C., 241
Feldman, Martha, 31
Fenno, Richard F., Jr., 319
Ferman, Barbara, 279, 280
Finch, H., 470
Finkelstein, Sydney, 290
Fischer, Frank, 40
Fisher, Andrew, 194
Fisher, Anthony C., 126, 127
Fisher, Irving, 424
Fisher, Roger, 270, 271
Fisk, Donald, 286
Fixler, Philip E., Jr., 253
Flacco, Paul R., 409
Fleishman, Joel L., 40
Flowers, Marilyn R., 252
Fong, Glenn R., 307
Ford, Gerald, 444
Forester, John, 40
Forthofer, R. N., 457
Foster, Edward, 141
Foster, Vivien, 216
Fraas, Arthur G., 237
Francis, R., 20
Frank, Robert H., 117
Frankel, Jeffrey A., 224
Frankfurter, Felix, 269
Frantz, Roger S., 102
Fraser, Alex, 5
Frederickson, H. George, 30
Freeman, A. Myrick, III, 398
Freeman, Paul K., 255
French, Joyce M., 461
French, Peter A., 48
Frey, Bruno S., 118, 147, 218
Friedman, G. D., 413
Friedman, Lee S., 181, 246, 412
Friedman, Milton, 231, 245
Friedrich, Carl J., 276
Frohlich, Norman, 136
Fromm, Gary, 211
Fudenberg, Drew, 293
Fujii, Edwin T., 233
Fulton, Arthur D., 284
Furubotn, Eirik, 73

G

Gagnon, Alain-C., 25
Galal, Ahmed, 250
Gardner, B. Delworth, 90, 215
Gardner, Bruce L., 257
Gardner, Roy, 18
Garling, Tommy, 196
Garrett, Thomas A., 165
Gaunt, C., 196
Geiss, F., 470
Gibbard, Allan, 160
Gibbons, Robert, 262
Gibbs, Curtis, 225
Gidengil, Elisabeth, 163
Gilbert, D., 20
Ginsberg, R., 122
Glaser, Bonnie, 283
Globerman, Steven, 4, 8, 10 11, 256, 297, 303
Glover, T. F., 84
Goetz, Charles J., 189
Goetz, Linda, 84
Gold, Marthe R., 425
Goldberg, Victor, 217
Goldman, Alan H., 52
Gomez-Ibanez, Jose, 241
Goodfellow, Gordon, 255
Goodin, Robert E., 40, 126
Goodrich, Carter, 249
Goodwin, Craufurd D., 215, 444
Gordon, H. Scott, 4
Gordon, Michael R., 173
Gormley, William T., Jr., 243, 287
Grafton, R. Quentin, 3, 9, 14, 19
Graham, Daniel A., 121, 409
Graham, John D., 424
Gramlich, Edward M., 229, 342, 396, 405
Graymer, LeRoy, 167, 216

Green, Mark, 12, 127, 398, 405
Greenberg, David H., 69, 230, 341, 354, 381, 397, 405, 421, 440, 470
Greenberg, George, 36
Grenzke, Janet, 165
Griliches, Zvi, 397
Grinols, Earl, 214
Grossman, Gene, 222
Grossman, Michael, 233, 416–18
Grossman, Philip J., 183
Gruber, Judith E., 287
Gunton, Thomas, 222
Gutmann, Amy, 48

H

Hacker, George A., 413, 419
Hadden, Susan, 243
Hahn, Robert H., 216
Hahn, Robert W., 216, 237, 350, 380, 381, 475
Hall, Peter A., 25
Hall, Richard L., 165
Halpern, Jennifer J., 297
Hambrick, Donald, 290
Hamilton, Neil W., 249
Hamilton, Peter R., 249
Hanemann, W. Michael, 127
Hanf, Kenneth, 283
Hanke, Steve H., 406
Hanner, John, 90
Hansmann, Henry, 306
Hanushek, Eric A., 451, 463, 468, 476
Harberger, Arnold C., 62, 342, 406
Hardin, Russell, 138, 291
Hargrove, Erwin C., 279
Harlan, W. R., 473
Harrington, Joseph E., Jr., 114, 211, 238, 241
Harris, Richard, 272
Harris, Robert G., 212
Harsanyi, John C., 135, 139
Harty, Harry, 286
Hassler, William T., 240
Hausman, Jerry A., 230, 231
Haveman, Robert H., 85, 144
Hayek, F. A., 69
Hayes, Kathy J., 183
Hazlett, Thomas W., 238, 364
Head, J. G., 228
Heckathorn, Douglas D., 96
Heclo, Hugh, 32
Heinrich, Carolyn J., 30
Henriksson, Lennart E., 214
Hesterly, William S., 179
Hettick, Walter, 385
Hibbs, Douglas, 175
Hicks, John R., 384
Higgins, Gerald F., 444
Higgs, Robert, 4, 5
Hill, Carolyn J., 30
Hird, John A., 237
Hirschleifer, J., 120, 330
Hirschman, Albert O., 45
Hochman, Harold M., 229
Hodge, Graeme A., 213, 296, 299
Hodgson, Geoffrey, 138
Holcombe, Randall G., 300, 444
Holder, H. D., 416
Holt, Charles A., 84
Honadle, Beth Walter, 290
Hoos, Ida R., 28
Hope, Chris, 274
Horwich, George, 128, 152, 172, 223, 239, 257, 432, 435, 436, 438, 448
Hotelling, Harold, 126
Houghton, John, 240
Howard, Robert M., 245
Howe, Elizabeth, 52
Howell, William G., 231
Howitt, Arnold M., 290
Hoxby, Caroline Minter, 232
Huang, Ju-Chin, 97, 397
Hudson, Wade, 200
Hufbauer, Gary Clyde, 223
Huntington, Samuel P., 167, 238
Husock, Howard, 200

I

Ingram, Gregory K., 231
Ingram, Helen, 345
Irwin, Douglas A., 223
Irwin, Timothy, 239

J

Jackson, Henry, 427
Jackson, John E., 463, 468
Jacobs, Bruce, 145, 180, 290
Jasper, Cindy, 296
Jayaratne, Jith, 238
Jencks, Christopher, 148
Jenkins-Smith, Hank C., 41, 50, 184, 266, 443
Jennings, Bruce, 40
Jensen, Michael C., 181, 251, 406
Johnsen, Christopher, 173
Johnson, Leland L., 238
Johnson, Lyndon B., 29, 174
Johnson, Phillip E., 51
Johnson, Ronald N., 184
Johnson, William R., 146, 473
Johnston, Richard, 163
Jones, Bryan D., 174
Jones, Laura, 14, 15
Jones, L. R., 184, 287
Joskow, Paul L., 211, 216

K

Kagan, Robert A., 243, 244
Kagel, John H., 84
Kahn, Herman, 28
Kahneman, Daniel, 122, 123, 177, 398
Kaldor, Nicholas, 384
Kalt, Joseph P., 239
Kanak, J. R., 419
Kaplan, Thomas J., 281
Karier, Thomas, 103
Karni, Edi, 110
Katz, N., 122
Kaufman, Herbert, 287, 290
Kaufman, Jerome, 52
Kaufman, Jerome L., 28
Kearney, Richard C., 288
Keech, William R., 175
Keeler, Emmett B., 297
Keeler, Theodore E., 116

Kefauver, Estes, 272
Kehrer, Kenneth C., 258
Kelman, Steven, 221, 385, 478
Kennedy, John F., 272
Kettl, Donald F., 30, 295
Kim, Moshe, 213
Kimmel, Wayne, 286
Kingdon, John W., 175
Kirkley, James E., 3, 14
Kirkpatrick, Colin, 252
Klass, Michael W., 257
Klatsky, A. L., 413
Klein, Benjamin, 109, 301
Klein, Peter G., 305
Kleindoefer, Paul R., 218
Kleiner, Morris M., 245
Kneese, Allen, 221
Knetsch, Jack L., 123, 136, 398, 399
Knobeloch, William, 201
Koch, James V., 112
Kolko, Gabriel, 167
Kopp, Raymond J., 399
Kotlikoff, Laurence J., 255
Kovar, M. G., 457
Kraft, C. Jeffrey, 212
Kraft, John, 237
Krahn, Steven L., 302
Krashinsky, Michael, 232
Krehbiel, Keith, 160
Kreps, David M., 294
Krieger, Martin H., 281, 362
Krueger, Alan B., 476
Krutilla, John V., 127
Kudrle, Robert T., 245
Kuenne, Robert E., 444
Kuhn, Thomas S., 25
Kunreuther, Howard, 122, 218, 255

L

Ladd, Helen F., 231, 232, 330
Laitila, Thomas, 196
Lancaster, Kelvin, 69
Landau, Martin, 285
Landes, J. R., 473
Landy, E., 473
Larson, Douglas M., 409
Lasswell, Harold D., 25
Laurin, Claude, 179, 214, 250
Laux, Fritz M., 116
Lave, Charles A., 475
Lave, Lester B., 268
Law, Stephen M., 98
Leamer, Edward, 399
Lebow, David E., 141
Ledyard, John, 84
Lee, Robert D., Jr., 34
Leffler, Keith B., 109
Leggett, Jane, 456–58, 474
Leibenstein, Harvey J., 102
Leman, Christopher K., 249, 258, 324
Leone, Robert, 241
Lesher, Stephan, 269
Levin, Martin A., 279, 280
Levin, Ronnie, 457, 458, 474
Levy, David T., 475
Levy, Philip I., 224
Lewis, Tracy R., 221
Lewis, William, 447
Lewit, Eugene M., 233
Libecap, Gary D., 86, 184
Liebeskind, Julia, 179
Lilla, Mark T., 53
Lind, Robert C., 125, 405, 406
Lindblom, Charles, 276
Link, Albert, 228
Linsky, Martin, 273
Lipsey, R. G., 69
Liston Heyes, Catherine, 194–96
Littlechild, S. C., 118
Locke, John, 135
Long, Carolyn, 304
Long, David A., 384
Lopez-de-Silanes, Florencio, 296
Lott, John, 165
Ludwig, Jens, 231
Luft, Harold S., 412
Luken, Ralph A., 237
Lynn, Laurence, 258
Lynn, Laurence E., Jr., 30
Lyon, Randolph M., 218, 406
Lyons, Bruce R., 305

M

MacAvoy, Paul W., 167
MacCoun, Robert J., 213
MacFadyen, Alan, 222
Machiavelli, Niccolo, 274
Machina, Mark J., 122
MacRae, Duncan, Jr., 40, 118, 139, 382
Mader, Elizabeth A., 381, 475
Madison, James, 187
Madrian, Brigitte C., 124
Maesaka, J. K., 473
Magnuson, Warren, 272, 273
Majumdar, Sumit K., 239
Maki, Atsushi, 212
Makuc, D., 457
Malbin, Michael J., 33
Mallar, Charles D., 384
Mallery, Wendy L., 338
Manley, Irwin, 102
Mansfield, Edwin, 228
March, James C., 138, 333
Marell, Agneta, 196
Marini, Frank, 30
Marmor, Theodore R., 245
Marseille, Elliott, 225
Marshall, Melissa, 231
Martin, Stephen, 214
Marver, James D., 34
Maser, Steven M., 96
Mashaw, Jerry L., 147
Maskin, Eric, 293
Masten, Scott E., 302, 305
Mathios, Alan D., 238
Mavros, Panayiotis, 183
May, Peter, 347
Mayer, Connie, 253
Mayhew, David R., 276
McAfee, R. Preston, 16, 216, 217, 300, 366
McCaleb, Thomas S., 84
McCracken, Samuel, 274
McDaniel, Paul R., 226
McDaniels, Timothy, 177
McDonald, Karin, 283
McFetridge, Gordon, 227
McGrath, Connor, 263
McGuire, Martin, 224
McGuire, Thomas, 104
McKelvey, Richard D., 160

McKinley, Barbara, 286
McLean, Iain, 176
McLoughlin, Kevin, 232
McMillan, John, 16, 216, 217, 300, 366
Mead, Lawrence W., 259
Meadows, Dennis L., 28
Meadows, Donella H., 28
Mechanic, David, 277
Meckling, William H., 181
Meeham, James W., Jr., 305
Megginson, William, 214, 298
Melnik, Glenn, 297
Melnik, Mikhail, 107
Meltsner, Arnold J., 24, 33, 41, 264, 358
Mendeloff, John, 268
Merrill, Richard A., 268
Messick, David M., 123
Meyers, Marcia K., 283
Michael, Robert T., 145
Michaels, Robert J., 444
Mikesell, John, 175
Miles, Rufus E., Jr., 266
Milgrom, Paul, 109, 366
Mill, John Stuart, 135
Miller, Bradley, 223
Miller, Chuck, 448
Miller, Gary J., 189, 294, 300
Miller, George A., 348
Miller, L., 122
Mills, H. Quinn, 237
Milwood, H. Brinton, 30, 295
Minihan, Steven, 448
Mintrom, Michael, 318
Mintzberg, Henry, 333
Mitchell, Robert C., 84, 398
Moffitt, Randolph R., 299
Moffitt, Robert A., 258
Mohr, Lawrence B., 286
Montero, Juan P., 216
Montgomery, W. David, 223
Moore, Mark H., 290
Moore, Thomas Gale, 213
Morley, Elaine, 296
Morrall, John F., III, 424
Morrison, P. S., 196
Morrison, Steven A., 100
Morrow, James D., 89, 262
Mosher, Frederick C., 33
Moss, Milton, 140
Moyle, Petrea R., 381, 475
Mueller, Dennis C., 84
Mumpower, Jeryl, 398
Murphy, Jerome T., 319

N

Nagin, Daniel S., 147, 475
Nakamura, Robert, 275
Needleman, H. L., 470
Neese, J. W., 457
Negandhi, A. R., 251
Nelson, Harry, 9
Nelson, Philip, 106
Nelson, Richard R., 104, 227–28
Nelson, Robert H., 32, 324
Nemetz, Peter, 221
Netboy, Anthony, 4
Netter, John, 214, 298
Neustadt, Richard E., 40
Nevitte, Neil, 163
Newbery, David M., 234
Newman, David, 263
Nichols, Albert L., 458, 474
Nichols, Daryl C., 353
Nienaber, Jeanne, 332
Niskanen, William A., 47, 180
Nixon, Richard M., 29, 427, 428
Nixson, Frederick, 252
Nobel, E. P., 413
Nolan, James F., 98
Noll, Roger G., 190, 211, 216
Nordhaus, William D., 28, 140, 175
North, Douglass, 4

O

Oates, Wallace, 17, 187, 224
Oberholzer-Gee, Felix, 118, 147, 218
O'Connell, Stephen, 241
Oi, Walter, 106
Okun, Arthur M., 146
Olsen, John P., 138, 333
Olson, Mancur, 82, 172
Ooms, Van Doorn, 230
Oppenheimer, Joe A., 136
O'Regan, Katherine, 307
Ornstein, Stanley I., 414
Orphanides, Athanasios, 116
Osborne, Martin J., 89
Oster, Sharon, 307
Ostro, Bart, 457, 458, 474
Ostrom, Elinor, 14, 18, 86, 90
O'Toole, Laurence J., Jr., 280
Oum, Tae Hoon, 213

P

Page, Melvin E., 317
Palfrey, Thomas R., 176
Panagariya, Arvind, 224
Panzar, John C., 100, 303
Parker, David, 179, 214, 250
Pashigian, Peter, 246
Patton, Carl V., 319, 327
Pauly, Mark, 229
Payne, A. Abigail, 143
Payne, Bruce L., 40
Pearse, Peter H., 7–8, 14–17
Pejovich, Svetozar, 73
Pellechio, Anthony, 255
Peltzman, Sam, 104, 238
Pennock, J. Rolland, 164
Perroni, Carlo, 224
Peskin, Henry M., 334
Peters, Lon L., 251
Peterson, George E., 230, 231
Peterson, Paul E., 231
Phelps, Charles E., 413, 414, 417, 418, 420
Philipsen, N. J., 245
Pigou, Arthur Cecil, 220
Pirkle, James, 457, 473
Pirrong, Steven Craig, 305
Pitcher, Hugh, 457, 458, 474
Pivovarsky, Alexander, 214
Platen, William, 32
Pliskin, Joseph S., 424
Pollitt, Michael G., 213
Pollock, Richard, 257
Poole, Robert W., Jr., 102, 244, 253
Portney, Kent E., 147
Portney, Paul R., 17, 397, 399
Posner, Paul, 230

Posner, Richard A., 238, 385
Potoski, Matthew, 299, 305
Powell, Adam Clayton, 272
Prager, Jonas, 298
Pressman, Jeffrey L., 188, 275, 276
Price, Catherine Waddams, 239
Prichard, J. Robert S., 251
Priest, George, 235
Proudfoot, Stuart B., 232
Puchades-Navarro, Miguel, 181
Puelz, Robert, 121
Pugliaresi, Lucian, 32, 448
Putterman, Louis, 117

Q

Quade, E. S., 44
Quigley, John M., 330
Quirk, Paul J., 212, 478

R

Rabin, Matthew, 124
Rabinowitz, M., 470
Rabushka, Alvin, 263
Radin, Beryl A., 31
Radner, Roy, 399
Raiffa, Howard, 270
Raisinghani, Gurev, 333
Randers, Jorgen, 28
Ranney, Austin, 163
Rao, K. L. K., 251
Rappaport, Peter, 136
Rausser, Gordon C., 169
Rawls, John, 135–36
Ray, James Lee, 263
Razzolini, Laura, 183
Reagan, Ronald, 380, 450
Rees, J., 470
Reischauer, Robert D., 230
Reiter, Barry J., 244, 245
Rettig, R., 7
Reuter, Peter, 213, 326
Rhoads, Steven E., 218
Richards, John, 222
Riesel, Daniel, 242
Riker, William H., 159, 161, 173, 176, 177, 269, 271–73
Riley, John G., 120
Robbins, Ira P., 253
Roberts, Blaine, 237
Roberts, John, 109
Roberts, Russell D., 143, 229
Robinson, Kenneth, 102
Robyn, Dorothy, 212
Rodgers, James D., 229
Roe, Emery, 281
Rogers, Robert P., 238
Rogoff, Ken, 222
Rohr, John A., 45
Rolph, Elizabeth S., 215
Roos, Leslie L., Jr., 286
Roos, Noralou P., 286
Rose-Ackerman, Susan, 306
Rosen, Harvey S., 230
Rosen, Henry, 334
Rosen, Sherwin, 129, 397, 421
Rosenberg, Alexander, 115
Rosenthal, Howard, 175
Ross, Leola B., 183
Ross, Stephen M., 243
Roth, Alvin E., 84
Roth, Jeffrey A., 147
Rousseau, Jean Jacques, 135
Rousser, William, 168
Royston, Tom, 199
Rubenstein, Ariel, 89
Rubinfeld, Daniel L., 330
Rubinovitz, Robert, 238
Ruckelshaus, William D., 455, 459
Rudd, Jeremy B., 141
Rudd, Joel, 243
Ruggles, Patricia, 145
Russell, Clifford S., 221
Russell, Louise B., 425
Russett, Bruce, 263
Ryan, Alan, 135
Ryan, Philip, 53

S

Sabatier, Paul A., 266, 275
Sachs, Jeffrey, 3
Saffer, Henry, 116
Safran, Dana Gelb, 424
Sagi, P., 122
Salamon, Lester, 249
Salanie, Bernard, 121
Salisbury, Robert H., 170
Sallal, David, 179, 214, 250
Saloner, Garth, 112
Sampson, Gary P., 224
Samuelson, Paul A., 74
Sandler, Todd, 81
Sapolsky, Harvey M., 269
Sappington, David E. M., 179, 247
Satterthwaite, Mark, 160
Savas, E. S., 214
Sawhill, Isabel V., 231–32
Sawicki, David, 319, 327
Schaller, Bruce, 196
Schelling, Thomas C., 213, 221, 293
Scherer, F. M., 114
Schick, Allen, 29
Schlesinger, James R., 430, 444–47
Schmalensee, Richard, 216
Schmitz, Mark, 143
Schneider, Anne, 345
Schneider, Mark, 231, 242
Schneiderman, Mark, 230
Schoemaker, Paul J. H., 122
Schofield, Norman, 160
Scholz, John T., 147
Schotter, Andrew, 291
Schultze, Charles, 218, 221
Schuman, Howard, 399
Schwartz, Bernard, 269
Schwartz, Gary, 235
Schwartz, Gerd, 226
Schwartz, Joel, 455–59, 467, 473–75
Schwindt, Richard, 3–6, 8–11, 13, 14, 16, 346
Scitovsky, Tibor, 137
Scott, Anthony, 4
Seidl, John Michael, 258
Seidman, Harold, 250
Selznick, Philip, 269
Sen, Amartya, 136
Seskin, Eugene P., 334
Shanley, Mark, 114
Sharpe, Tom, 214
Shea, Dennis F., 124

Shelanski, Howard A., 305
Sheperd, William G., 101
Shepsle, Kenneth A., 172, 173, 294
Sherman, Roger, 100
Shin, Richard T., 213
Shleifer, Andrei, 296
Short, Helen, 251
Shoven, John B., 57
Shroder, Mark, 230, 470
Shulock, Nancy, 33
Shulte, Carl, 199
Siegel, Joanna E., 424, 425
Siegleaub, A. B., 413
Sigle, E., 213
Simon, Julian L., 28
Sinclair, Sol, 5, 6
Singer, Max, 326
Skolnick, Jerome H., 352
Slovic, Paul, 121, 122
Smallwood, Frank, 275
Smart, C. N., 419
Smeeding, Timothy M., 145, 147, 148
Smith, Adam, 234, 235
Smith, K. Wayne, 353
Smith, Lawrence B., 206
Smith, Richard A., 170
Smith, Rodney T., 436
Smith, Shannon L., 231–32
Smith, V. Kerry, 97, 397, 399
Smith, Vernon L., 216
Snavely, Keith, 147
Snow, Arthur, 121
Snyder, Edward A., 305
Snyder, Glenn H., 257
Snyder, James M., 176
Sobell, Russell S., 165
Solomon, R., 213
Solow, Robert, 399
Sommerfield, Mary, 444
Sorkin, Alan L., 100
Spavins, Thomas, 104
Spiller, Pablo T., 212
Spiro, Christopher, 230
Squires, Dale, 3, 14
Srinivasian, T. N., 224
Staffeldt, Raymond J., 34
Staley, Samuel R., 194, 200
Stanley, Julian C., 286
Starling, Grover, 327
Starr, Paul, 148
Staten, Michael E., 121
Stavins, Robert N., 216
Steel, Brent S., 304
Stein, Ernesto, 224
Stein, Herbert, 32
Steiner, Peter O., 380
Stern, Robert N., 297
Sternlieb, George, 28
Steuerle, C. Eugene, 147, 230, 231
Stigler, George, 167, 238
Stiglitz, Joseph E., 247
Stockman, David, 450
Stokes, Donald E., 266
Strauss, Robert P., 145
Struyk, Linda, 299
Sung, Hai-Yen, 116
Sunstein, Cass R., 380
Surrey, Stanley S., 226
Suyderhud, Jack P., 257
Sweetnam, Glen, 448
Switzer, Lorne, 228

T

Taylor, D. Wayne, 197–98
Taylor, Lori L., 183, 232
Taylor, Michael, 291
Taylor, Serge, 180
Teal, Roger F., 196
Teisberg, Thomas J., 443, 448–50
Teitenberg, Thomas H., 216
Tenbrusel, Ann, 123
Tengs, Tammy O., 424
Terleckyi, Nestor E., 421
Teske, Paul, 231
Thaler, Richard, 421
Thaler, Robert H., 117
Thatcher, Margaret, 263
Theoret, Andre, 333
Thomas, H., 251
Thomas, Patricia, 153
Thomas, Rich, 169
Thompson, Dennis F., 47, 48
Thompson, Frederick, 12, 127, 167, 184, 216, 287, 398, 405
Thompson, Lawrence H., 255
Thornton, Craig V. D., 384
Thurow, Lester C., 218, 234
Tiebout, Charles M., 189
Tillitt, Malvern Hall, 424
Tobin, Brian, 8
Tobin, James, 140
Tollison, Robert D., 167, 169
Toomen, Theo A. J., 283
Topel, Robert, 254
Townsend, Ralph, 7
Trebilcock, Michael J., 244, 245
Trebing, Harry M., 251
Triplett, Jack F., 141
Tropman, John F., 246
Tuckman, Howard P., 298
Tullock, Gordon, 167, 169, 172
Turris, Bruce, 14
Tussing, Arlon R., 427
Tversky, Amos J., 122, 123, 177

U

Uehling, Mark D., 169
Ullmann-Margalit, Edna, 291
Ulset, Svein, 305
Umbeck, John R., 121
Ury, William, 270, 271
Usher, Dan, 140

V

Valentine, Tom, 476
van den Berg, Caroline, 239
Vanderpump, Mark P. J., 461
Van Gaalen, Ronald, 180
Vannoni, Michael G., 216
Varian, Hal R., 92
Vaupel, James W., 322, 324, 407
Verdier, James M., 324
Vernon, John M., 114, 211, 238, 241
Vesvacil, Rick, 199
Vining, Aidan R., 3–5, 8–14, 69, 106, 127, 179, 181, 183, 185, 189, 214, 221, 246, 247, 250, 251, 256, 293, 295–98, 300, 303, 338, 341, 346, 354, 381, 397, 398, 421, 440, 445

Viscusi, W. Kip, 114, 122, 211, 238, 241, 242, 421
Vishny, Robert W., 296

W

Wade-Bensoni, Kimberly A., 123
Wagner, C. Martin, 456
Wagner, Richard E., 84
Walker, Michael, 14, 15
Wallace, Michael B., 86
Wallsten, Scott J., 252
Walsh, Ann-Marie H., 249
Walsh, Cliff, 118
Walters, Carl, 9, 15
Warner, Andrew, 3
Warner, Kenneth E., 242
Wassmer, Robert W., 183
Waters, Bill, III, 181
Waters, W. G., II, 445
Waverman, Leonard, 100
Weaver, R. Kent, 273
Wedeen, R. P., 473
Wei, Shang-Jin, 224
Wei Hu, 116
Weimer, David L., 3, 5, 9, 11–14, 69, 73, 106, 127, 128, 152, 167, 172, 179, 183–85, 188, 189, 222, 223, 239, 243, 244, 247, 257, 277, 278, 284, 290, 291, 293, 295, 296, 300, 341, 345, 346, 354, 381, 397, 398, 421, 427, 429, 432, 435, 436, 438, 440, 443, 469
Weinberg, Daniel H., 233
Weingast, Barry R., 173
Weinstein, Milton C., 424, 425
Weintraub, E. Roy, 56
Weisbrod, Burton A., 127, 258, 306
Weisman, Dennis L., 238
Weiss, Carol H., 33, 153
Weiss, Janet A., 287
Well, David, 242
West, Edwin G., 232
Westin, Kerstin, 196
Weyman, Frank W., 165
Weyman-Jones, Thomas, 239
Whalley, John, 57, 224
Whisnant, Richard, 246, 381
White, William D., 245
Whiteman, David, 33
Whittington, Dale, 118, 382
Wildavsky, Aaron, 27–29, 37, 180, 188, 268, 275, 276, 284, 332
Wilen, James, 14
Willey, W. R. Z., 216
Williams, Arlington W., 216
Williams, Russell L., 300
Williams, Walter, 24
Williamson, Oliver E., 179, 217, 251, 295–97, 304
Willig, Robert D., 62, 100, 303
Wilson, James Q., 176, 290
Wilson, Robert, 366
Wilson, Thomas A., 116
Wilson, Woodrow, 29, 30
Wimmer, Bradley S., 245
Winston, Clifford, 100, 212
Wintrobe, Ronald, 180
Wise, David A., 230, 231
Wiseman, J., 118
Witte, John F., 231
Wittenburg, David C., 476
Wittfogel, Karl, 248
Wolcott, Robert, 455
Wolf, Charles, Jr., 156
Wolkoff, Michael J., 206, 257, 342, 397
Wonnaccott, Ronald J., 224
Wright, Brian D., 257
Wright, John R., 165
Wu, Chi-Yuen, 28
Wykoff, Paul Gary, 189

X

Xia Li, 317

Y

Yarri, Menahem E., 135
Yetvin, Robert, 230
Ying, John S., 213
Yondorf, Barbara, 213
Young, H. Peyton, 136

Z

Zarnowitz, Victor, 129
Zeckhauser, Richard J., 120, 121, 242
Zenger, Todd R., 179
Zerbe, R., 250
Zervos, David, 116
Zhang, Yimin, 213
Zimbalist, Andrew, 190
Zwanziger, Jack, 297

Subject Index

A

Academic research, 25, 26
Activity surveys, 399
Actors, political, 264–67
Act-utilitarianism, 138–39
Addictive goods, 116
Adjustment costs, 128–29, 437–38
Administrative feasibility of policy alternatives, 16, 18–22
Adoption of policies
  vs. implementation, 261
  overview, 261
  political feasibility, 262–66
Adverse selection, in insurance, 120–21
Advertising, 108–9, 115–16, 175
Advocate for client, 42–43, 50
Agency, public. *See* Public agencies
Agency loss, 179–81
Aggregate social benefits, 23
Aggregate wealth of society, 142, 144
Alcohol tax analysis, 381–82
  cost-effectiveness, 424–25
  deadweight loss, 415–16
  estimating effects of tax, 414–19
  fatality reduction, 416–18
  health gains, 418–19
  ill-effects of alcohol, 413
  injury reduction, 418
  monetizing results, 419–21
  net benefit estimates, 422–25
  productivity gains, 418–19
  property damage reduction, 418
Allocation, 56
  through auction (*see* Auction)
  changes, 128
  of existing goods, 215
  of exploitation rights, 217
  inefficiency, 98–100
  institutional arrangements, 133
  intertemporal, 124–28
  through lottery, 215, 365
  on price basis, 172
  of property rights, 215
  social welfare perspectives, 138–39
Ambiguity, 326, 327
American Enterprise Institute for Public Policy Research, 34, 313, 314
Analytical integrity, 41–43
Analytical styles, 31
Area experts, 263
Army, U.S., restructuring analysis, 366–70
Asset specificity, 253, 304–6
Association for Public Policy Analysis and Management, 31, 52
Assumptions, during policy analysis, 10
AT&T breakup, monopoly agreements, 102
Auction
  advantages, 217–18
  disadvantages, 217
  of licenses, salmon fishery, 2, 8, 11, 13, 16–18
  of monopoly, 18, 19, 21
  of property rights, 215
  of radio licenses, 364–66
Axiom of independence, 160
Axiom of nondictatorship, 160
Axiom of Pareto choice, 160
Axiom of unrestricted domain, 159–60

B

Backward mapping, 281, 283–84, 346
Balance of payments, 141, 142
Bankruptcy laws, international, 125
Bargaining costs, 298, 300, 302–7
Baseline scenario, 350
Behavioral economics, 124
"Beltway bandit," 34
Benefit-cost analysis. *See* Cost-benefit analysis
Benefits
  in-kind, 148
  marginal, 73–74
  in real dollar, 402–3
Better Business Bureau, 109
Bias, perceptual, 177
Bliss point, 160–61
Break-even analysis, 439–40
British Telecom, privatization of, 214
Brookings Institution, 34, 313, 314
Budget
  deficit, 142
  derivation of, 55
  discretionary, 180–81
  limitations, 335
Bundling, 162–63
Bureaucratic failure, 185–86
Bureaucratic supply, 179–86, 191, 296
Business cycles, 129
Buy-back plan, salmon fishery, 6–11, 13, 17

C

Cable Television Consumer Protection and Competition Act of 1992, 237
Campaign finance reform, 176
Capital
  as budget factor, 55
  in-place, 100
  in natural monopolies, 100
  private, 11
  stock, 128
  stuffing, 7–9, 11, 15
  underinvestment in, 126
Capital markets, 125–28
Cartelization, 114, 236
Cash grants, 258–59
Cato Institute, 34, 313
Central economic planning, 27
Charity, 143
Choice, rational *vs.* irrational, 144
Civil service, 184–85. *See also* Public agencies
Classical planning, 26–29
Clean Air Act Amendments of 1970, 453
Clean Air Act Amendments of 1977, 240
Clean Air Act Amendments of 1990, 216, 474
Client
  advocate for, 42–43, 50
  -analyst relationship, 24, 34, 477
  attention span of, 358–60
  authority of, 40
  ethics (*see* Ethics)
  interaction with, 357–58
  issue advocacy, 42, 43, 50
  as necessary evil, 41
  objective technician (*see* Objective technicians)
  orientation, 27, 326–27
  sophistication of, 357
Club of Rome, 28–29
Coasian solution, 96, 97, 124, 215, 219
Collective action, 54
Collective risk, 120
Comparative statics, 128
Comparison of policy alternatives, 15–21, 350, 352–54
Compensation, 61
Competition
  as efficiency benchmark, 55–57
  equilibrium, 69
  imperfect, 114
  lack of, in public agencies, 182–83
  limiting, 167–68
  model, 63, 64, 65, 113, 115, 116, 128
  pricing, 66
Compliance, 277–78
Confidentiality, 42, 48, 51
Congestion, 72, 76–77, 91
Congressional Budget Office (CBO), 33, 34, 335, 363
  digital television launch analysis, 370–76
  radio license auction analysis, 364–66
  U.S. Army restructuring analysis, 366–70
  water allocation analysis, 376–79
  web site, 314, 363
Congressional Research Service (CRS), 33
Consequentialist philosophy, 135. *See also* Utilitarianism
Constant-income demand schedule, 62
Constant-utility demand schedule, 61
Constitutions, 146
Consumer
  behavior, 55
  benefits received, 73–74
  choice, 54
  cost of searching for purchases, 106
  frequency of purchases, 106
  price index, 139, 141
  surplus, 58–63
  uninformed *vs.* informed, 104–5
  valuation, 76
Consumer price index, 139, 141
Consumer Reports, 110
Consumer surplus, 58–63
Consumption
  externality, 83–84
  "free ride" incentive (*see* "Free ride")
  by households, 148, 150

in-kind subsidy, relationship between, 228–29
marginal costs, 83–94
overconsumption, 85–87, 90, 126
possibility frontier, 401
possibility mapping, 115
quality, relationship between, 106
relative limit, 117
rivalrous, 72
social cost, 85
Consumption possibility frontier, 401
Contestability, 253, 303–4
Contestable markets, 100–102
Contingent valuation surveys, 398–99
Contracting out, 296, 298
Control, *ex ante*, 184–86
"Cooked" results, 49–50
Corporate culture, 294
Cost
adjustment, 128–29, 437–38
average, 63–64, 87, 88, 100
bargaining, 298, 300, 302–7
curves, 63
future, 403
marginal, 63–64, 66, 76, 98, 100
marginal social (*see* Marginal social cost)
opportunism, 297, 298, 301–7
production, 297–300
search, 106–8, 112
social marginal, 221
Cost-benefit analysis, 338, 339
alcohol tax analysis (*see* Alcohol tax analysis)
of British Columbian salmon fishery, 10
vs. cost-effectiveness analysis, 342
expected value, 407–9
geographic extent, 382–83
modified, 338, 339, 341–42
monetizing impacts, 384–85
vs. multigoal analysis, 384
opportunity costs, 385–90
overview of technique, 380–81
present value, 400–405
qualitative, 338–41
quantitative, 341
relevant impacts, 382–83
of Strategic Petroleum Reserve Program (*see* Strategic Petroleum Reserve Program)
summary, 384
time/risk discounts, 399–409
Cost-effectiveness analysis, 338–40, 342
Cost-plus contracts, 299–300
Council of Economic Advisors (CEA), 32, 314, 445–46, 448, 449
CPI, 139, 141
Credibility, 360–61
Criminal sanctions, 242
Crowding, 72
Cushions, 210, 253
cash grants, 258–59
defining, 256
rainy day funds, 257–58
stockpiling, 256–58, 433–36, 441–43
transitional assistance, 258

D

Davis Plan, 6–7
Deadweight loss, 60, 65, 79, 94
in alcohol tax analysis, 415–16
in government-generated rent, 168
under price ceilings, 170–71
of social surplus, 168
due to uninformed consumer, 105
in X-efficiency, 103
Decentralization, 157
analysts, role in political system, 190
arguments for, 187
fiscal externalities, 189–90
implementation issues, 187–89
problems inherent in, 187–91
Decision making, 123–24
Decision tree, 110–12
Decriminalization, 213–14
Defense, national, as public good, 247
Demand
curve, 309
estimating, for nonmarketed goods, 397–99
expansion of, effect on natural monopolies, 101–2
and marginal social cost intersect, 94
price elasticity of, 97–98
for public goods, 76–77
range of, 114
schedule (*see* Demand schedule)
Demand curve, 309
Demand schedule, 65
"choke-off" point, 59
constant income type, 62
constant-utility type, 61
definition, 59
equilibrium, 59
as function of price, 61
marginal valuation schedule, 59
market type, 62
Marshallian, 62
price, 62
utility, 62
Democracy
as check on power, 163
direct, 157–63
district-based legislature, 172–74
interest groups (*see* Interest groups)
problems in, 163–78, 191
public policy, relationship between, 163–64, 166
self-interest in, 164
tyranny by the majority, 162, 187
voting (*see* Voting)
Department of Defense (DOD), 180

Department of Energy (DOE), 33, 188, 430, 431, 438, 444–50, 473
Department of Health and Human Services (DHHS), policy analysis guidelines, 35–37
Department of Housing and Urban Development (HUD), 230–31
Deregulation, 200–201, 211–13
"Desk officer," 36
Digital television launch analysis, 370–76
Dignity, human. *See under* Values
Disloyalty, 45–48
Disposable income, 148
Distributional consequences, 147–53
Distributional equity, 55
Double-market failure test, 247, 306
Drugs, as post-experience goods, 111
Drug testing, 270

E

Ease of enforcement, 12
Economic models, 55
Economics
  behavioral, 124
  central planning, 27
  neoinstitutional, 295, 306
  opportunity, 55
  transaction cost, 296
Economy
  benefits to, with government intervention, 167
  competitive (*see* Competition)
  equilibrium, 114
  preference, relationship between (*see* Preferences)
Efficiency
  of capital markets, 125–28
  dynamic, 241
  economic, 12
  market, 55–57, 78
  maximization, 410–11
  Pareto (*see* Pareto efficiency)
  of policy alternative, 15, 16, 18, 19, 21
  policy analysis, relationship between, 142–43
  in post-experience goods, 111
  as social value, 55
  X-inefficiency (*see* X-inefficiency)
Empirical evidence, 25
Enclosure movement, 90
Endogenous preferences, 115–16
Energy. *See* Fossil fuels
Environment, 153
  economists, 177
  emissions, tradable permits for, 215–16, 241
  regulations, 240
Environmental Protection Agency, 453–55
Equilibrium
  allocation of goods, 119
  competition, 69
  competitive, 114
  demand schedule, 59
  general economic model, 56, 69
  market, 94–95
  moving from one to another, 114
  Nash, 89
  pricing, 69, 105
  of wages, 388
Equitable distribution, 2
  case study, salmon fishery, 12
  fairness criteria, 12
Equity
  horizontal, 145, 182
  of policy alternative, 16–20
  vertical, 145, 182
Ethics. *See also* Values
  analysts' responsibilities, 41–43
  client's control over analyst, relationship between, 45, 47
  code of, 51–53
  common good *vs.* serving the client, 41–43
  confidentiality, 42, 48, 51
  framework, 40
Ethos, 53
Ex ante control, 184–86
Excludable ownership, 72
Exclusion, 4
Executive summary, 2–3, 358, 359
Existence value, 12, 127
Exit, 45–48
Expected utility hypothesis, 122
Expected value, 407–9
Experience goods, 106
  primary markets, 108–9
  secondary markets, 109–10
  summary, 110
Externalities
  adoption type, 92
  bargaining, relationship between, 96–97
  consumer type, 92–93
  correcting, 220–21
  definition, 83, 91
  efficiency consequences, 113
  efficiency losses, 93–95
  examples, 92
  fiscal, 189–90, 383
  market responses to, 96–97
  missing market, 92
  negative, 92–94, 219, 224, 240
  network type, 92
  organizational, 186
  positive, 92–93
  production type, 92–93
  taxes on, 219–21

F

Fact-finding, 51
Federal Communications Commission (FCC), 370, 373
  cable TV regulation, 237
  deregulation, 212

radio license allocation, 364, 366
Federal Energy Administration (FEA), 428, 429, 431, 444
Federal government, role of policy analysis within, 32–33
"Firefighting" function of policy analysis, 37
Fiscal policies, 129–30
"Fixers," 278–79
Fleet Call, 366
Foreign investment, 142
Forward mapping, 280–82
Fossil fuels
conservation for future, 126
oil embargo, 128, 152, 170, 428
overconsumption, 126, 427
policy goals, 335
price regulation, 170, 188
Project Independence, 428
Strategic Petroleum Reserve (*see* Strategic Petroleum Reserve Program)
Free goods, 4, 85–91
"Free ride," 83–84, 91, 110

G

General Accounting Office (GAO), 33, 314
General Agreement on Tariffs and Trade (GATT), 223, 224
General Possibility Theorem, 159–60
Generic policies
cushions (*see* Cushions)
defining, 209
vs. direct supply by government bureaus, 248–49
facilitating markets, 210–11, 215–16
freeing markets, 210–14
insurance (*see* Insurance)
nonmarket mechanisms for supplying goods (*see* Nonmarket mechanisms for supplying goods)
rules establishment (*see* Rules)
simulating markets, 210–11, 216–18
solutions (*see* Solution analysis)
subsidies to alter incentives (*see* Subsidies)
summary, 259–60
taxes to alter incentives, 210
Gini index of relative inequality, 150–51
Global warming, 153
GNP, 139–41
Goals/alternatives matrix. *See* Congressional Budget Office; Solution analysis
Goods
addictive, 116
allocation, 55–56
creation of new marketable goods, 215–16
experience (*see* Experience goods)
homogeneous, 108, 110
nonmarket mechanisms for supplying (*see* Nonmarket mechanisms for supplying goods)
organizational, public, 185–86
Pareto efficiency (*see* Pareto efficiency)
personal, 55
post-experience, 106, 110–12, 242
search, 106–8, 112
Government
complex, 187
decentralized (*see* Decentralization)
failure (*see* Government failure)
intervention, 210
state, role of policy analysis within, 34
subversive power of, 54
Government corporations, 250–52
Government failure, 37
bureaucratic supply, 185–86
cost-benefit analysis of, 407
decentralized government (*see* Decentralization)
direct democracy (*see* Democracy)
efficiency tradeoffs, 246
formal incentives, 290
framing the issues, 330–31
generic policies to correct (*see* Generic policies)
limited competition in, 182–83
market failure, relationship between, 204–8
output, value of, 182
passive, 206
prediction, 191
pricing, 182
representative government (*see* Representative government)
stockpiling as cushion against, 256–58
theory, 156–57
Grandfather clause, 258, 289
Grants-in-aid, 224
Greenhouse effect, 153, 240
Gresham's law, 353
Gross national product, 139–41

H

Harvesting royalties, 3, 13, 16–17
Hedonic price models, 397–98
Heresthetics, 271–73
Hidden action, 121
"Hired gun" analysts, 34
Hold harmless provision, 258
Human dignity, 55, 143–44, 478
Hyperinflation, 141

I

Implementation, 274
  vs. adoption, 261
  anticipating problems, 280–84
  decentralization, 187–89
  essential elements, securing, 276–78
  "fixers," 278–79
  reasonableness of theory, 275–76
  as series of adoptions, 262
Independence, axiom of, 160
Index of happiness, 115
Indifference curve, 61, 160, 401
Individual transferable quotas (ITQs), 2, 3, 14–15, 17, 19–20, 22
Infant industry argument, 222–23
Inferring, 52
Inflation, 141, 403
Information, 104
Information asymmetry, 180
  advertising, relationship between, 108–9
  consequence reduction, 236
  definition, 104
  diagnosing, 106–11
  efficiency consequences, 113
  experience goods (*see* Experience goods)
  inefficiency, 104–6, 183
  information policies, 242–43
  search goods, 106–8, 112
  summary, 110
Information gathering, 309–10
  data sources, 316–17
  document review, 321–22
  field research, 318–22
  Internet, 317–18
  literature review, 311–16
  statistical sources, 316–17
  strategies, 31
Institute for Defense Analyses, 34, 443
Institute for Research on Public Policy (Canada), 34
Institutional values, 139, 146–47
Insurance, 253
  adverse selection, 120–21
  complete, 118
  contingencies, 119
  designing, 254
  diversification, 120
  efficiency issues, 119
  fairness, 119, 121
  incomplete markets, 120–21
  law of large numbers, 120
  mandatory, 254–56
  against market failures, 210
  moral hazard, 121
  purchase, 254
  risk premium, 119, 120
  subsidized, 256
  underinsuring, 121
Interest groups, 165, 169–70, 313, 314
Interest rate, 125, 126
  market value, 127–28
  real, 404
  vs. risk, 127
Internet, 317–18
Interstate Commerce Commission (ICC), 167
ITQs. *See* Individual transferable quotas

J

Journalism, 25, 26, 30–31

K

Kaldor-Hicks principle, 135, 384–85, 410, 411
Kantian philosophy, 47

L

Land, as budget factor, 55
Law
  antitrust, 114, 235, 236
  of capture, 4, 86
  commercial, 235
  contract, 235, 236
  insurance, 236
  labor, 235
  of large numbers, 120
  liability, civil law, 235
  tort, 235, 236
Leadership, 293–94
Lead standard revision
  analytical approaches, 458–59
  background, 453–55
  benefits to cost ratio, 457–58
  causality, 469–72
  cause and effect, 470–71
  Environmental Protection Agency standards, 453–55
  linear regression model, 463–69
  modeling, 456, 457, 463–69
  multivariate analysis, 460–63
  origins of 1985 standards, 455–56
  rule finalization, 472–75
  statistical analysis, 456, 465–67
  surveys, 457, 460, 462, 466, 471, 472
Leaks, 45, 47, 49
Legislature
  co-optation strategies, 268–69
  geographic-based representation, 172–74
  role of policy analysis within, 33–34
Legitimacy, of political institutions, 146
"Lemons," 109
License auction, 2
Linear regression model, 463–69
Linear thinking, 325, 326, 361–62
Lobby groups. *See* Interest groups
Logistic regression, 468–69

Logrolling, 173, 252, 270
Lorenz curve, 150–51
Loss aversion, 123–24
Loyalty, 45–47

M

Madison taxicab policy analysis example, 192–208
Marginal excess burden, 219
Marginal revenue curve, 65–66
Marginal social benefit, 94
Marginal social benefit schedule, 87
Marginal social cost, 72, 87–88, 93–94
Marginal valuation schedule, 59
Market demand schedule, 62
Market failure, 37, 54–55, 71–112. *See also* Private goods; Public goods
  bureaucratic failure, relationship between, 185–86
  congestion, 76–77, 91
  efficiency tradeoffs, 246
  framing the issues, 330–31
  in free goods, 86
  generic policies to correct (*see* Generic policies)
  government failure, relationship between, 204–8
  of housing market, 206
  Madison taxicab example, 192–208
  nontraditional, 228
  privatization programs in response to, 214
  public goods (*see* Public goods)
  public intervention, relationship between, 157
  summary, 130
  theory, 246
  traditional (*see* specific market failure types)
Markets
  capital, 125–28
  competition, 70, 77
  contestable, 100–102
  distorted, 392–93
  efficiency, 55–57, 78
  facilitating markets, 210–11, 215–16
  freeing markets, 210–14
  inefficient, 388–90
  Pareto efficient (*see* Pareto efficiency)
  primary, 108–9
  rate of interest, 125
  responses to externality, 96–97
  secondary, 109–11, 393–97
  simulating markets, 210–11, 216–18
  supply, 66–67
  supply of public goods, 81–83
  surplus (*see* Social surplus)
  thin, 114
  traditional failures, 70
Market value, of licenses, salmon fishery, 6, 14
Marshallian demand schedule, 62
Media coverage of public office candidates, 175–76
Mifflin Plan, 9, 10, 15–16
Misrepresenting results, 50–51. *See also* Values
Missing market, 92
Model Cities program, 174
Monetary policy, 129–30
Monopoly
  AT&T breakup illustration, 102
  auction of, 18, 19, 21
  case study, salmon fishery, 4–5, 18
  natural (*see* Natural monopoly)
  pricing, 65–66
  rent, 65–66, 114, 167
Monopsony, 114, 223
Moral hazard, 121

N

Nash equilibrium, 89
National defense, as public good, 247
National Education Association (NEA), 170
National Institutes of Health (NIH), 242
National Organ Transplant Act, 241
National Rifle Association (NRA), 170
Natural monopoly
  allocative inefficiency under, 98–100
  declining average cost, 114
  definition, 97, 98
  dilemma of, 99–100
  efficiency consequences, 113
  policy considerations, 101–2
  social costs, 102–4
  technology, relationship between, 98
Negotiation, 270–71
Neoinstitutional economics, 295, 306
Net national product, 139–40
Net present value, 10–11, 15
  negative, 10
  positive, 11, 12
"New" public administration, 30
NNP, 139–40
Noncompliance, 242
Noncooperative games, 89
Nondictatorship, axiom of, 160
Nonlinear thinking, 325, 326, 361–62
Nonmarket mechanisms for supplying goods, 210, 246–48
  contracting out, 252–53
  direct supply by government bureaus, 248–49
  independent agencies, 249–50

Nonprofit organizations, analysts in, 23
Nonprofit sector, 306–7
Norms, social, 291–93
North America Free Trade Agreement (NAFTA), 223–24
Nuclear Regulatory Commission, hypothetical consultant to, 43

O

Objective technicians, 41–42, 49, 50
Occupational licensure, 244–46
Occupational Safety and Health Administration (OSHA), 240–41
Office of Management and Budget (OMB), 32, 34, 180, 407, 424, 428–29, 444–50, 459
Office of Technology Assessment (OTA), 33
Oil embargo. *See* Fossil fuels
"Old" public administration, 25, 26, 29–30
Oligopoly, 114
Omnibus Budget Reconciliation Act of 1993, 366
Open access, 4–6, 85–91
Operational market, 206–7
Operations research, 28
Opinion surveys, 398–99
Opportunism costs, 253, 297, 298, 301–7
Opportunity cost, 388–389
Opposition to policy change, 12
Option demand, 127
Ordinary least squares, 464
Organizational report cards, 243
Organization of Arab Petroleum Exporting Countries (OAPEC), 428
Organization of Petroleum Exporting Countries (OPEC), 427
Outsourcing, 296, 298
Overcapitalization, 6, 7
Ownership, excludable, 72
Ownership bans, 241–42

P

Pacific Salmon Revitalization Strategy, 9
Pareto efficiency, 56–57
  allocation, 66, 143
  allocation, relationship between, 133
  axiom of Pareto choice, 160
  of competitive equilibrium, 124
  conditions necessary, 71
  deadweight loss (*see* Deadweight loss)
  frontier, potential, 56, 57
  in goods allocation, 119
  improvement, 77, 115, 116
  intuitive interpretation of, 117
  Nash equilibrium, 89
  of a nonrivalrous good, 74
  in one-shot trials, 84
  of pollution on housing prices, 97
  pricing, relationship between, 128
  in referendums, 161–62
  vs. substantive values, 142
  thin market allocations, 114
  in traditional market failures, 112
  utilitarian view (*see* Utilitarianism)
Pearse Commission, 7–8, 13, 16–18, 22
Percentage ownership, 14
Pigovian tax solution, 220
Planning, classical, 26–29
Planning, programming, budgeting system (PPBS), 29
Policy
  adoption (*see* Adoption of policies)
  bottom-up design, 283–84, 289–90
  diversity, 289–90
  "dummy" alternatives same as trial, 347
  error correction, 284
  evaluating, 285–87
  goals, case study, salmon fishery, 11–13
  implementation (*see* Implementation)
  media influence, 176
  redundancy, avoiding, 284–85
  termination, 287–89
  valuation, 390–97
  window, 175–76
Policy alternatives. *See* Comparison of policy alternatives; Policy; Policy analysis; Values
Policy analysis. *See also* Policy
  adoption (*see* Adoption of policies)
  vs. business management, 24
  choosing from among multiple policies, 410–12
  vs. city planning, 24
  vs. classical planning, 26–29
  client orientation, 27, 326–27
  communicating, 328, 357–61
  compromise, 269–71
  credibility, 360–61
  defining, 1, 23–24
  ethical code or ethos, 51–53
  evaluation criteria, 327
  executive summary (*see* Executive summary)
  functions, 35–37
  generic policies (*see* Generic policies)
  implementation (*see* Implementation)
  vs. journalism, 25, 26, 30–31
  vs. law, 24

meta-analysis (*see* Self-analysis)
vs. policy research, 25–27
preparation, 37–38
problem analysis (*see* Problem analysis)
product of, 1
as a profession, 31–35
in profit-seeking firms, 35
public administration, relationship between, 25, 26, 29–30
vs. public health, 24
rationalism (*see* Rationalism)
recommendations, presenting, 356–57
vs. regional planning, 24
vs. social science research, 25, 26
in think tanks, 34–35, 313–14
within the U.S. Federal government, 32–33
written analysis (*see* Written analysis)
Policy analysts
bureaucracy, relationship between, 186
elected officials, relationship between, 178
Policy research, 25–27
Politics, 40. *See also* Representative government; Voting
activism, 166
actors in, 264–67
arena, choosing, 267–68
compromise, 269–71
co-optation, 268–69
corruption, 165
mobilizing support for policies, 276, 278
negative campaigning, 177
participation in, 55, 166
of policy analysis, 40
policy analysts, role in, 190
strategy, 264
Post-experience goods, 106, 110–12, 242
Poverty, 145, 148
Prediction errors, 463
Preferences
acceptability of, 115–18
addictive goods, 116
advertising influences, 115–16
endogenous, 115–16
fixed, 330
intensity, 161–62, 165
legitimacy of, 118
process-regarding, 117–18
relative consumption limit, 117
source of, 115–18
utility interdependence, 116–17, 139
Present value, 400–405
Price
ceilings, 170–72, 239
change, 61–62
controls, oil, 152
deadweight loss under, 170–71
elasticity, 233
equilibrium, 69
falling, 64
hedonic models, 397–98
peak-load, 234
producer surplus, relationship between, 63–66
regulation, 195–97, 237–39
relative, 219
supports, 168–69
utility, relationship between, 61–62
Pricing
competitive, 66
increases, 68–69
monopoly, 65–66
regulation, 170–72
setting, 55
sticky, 128, 141
Principal-agent relationship, 179–80
Prisoner's dilemma, 88, 89, 190, 262, 291
Private goods
characteristics, 72
rivalry, excludability, 77–78
Private ownership, 4–5
Probability assessment, 121
Problem analysis, 328
framing the problem, 330–32
goals, 331–38
modeling the problem, 331–32
solution analysis (*see* Solution analysis)
symptom assessment, 329–30
Producer surplus
measurement, 66–68
pricing, 63–66
Production, marginal cost of, 76–77
Production costs, 297–300
Production possibility frontier, 400–401
Professional sports, municipal subsidies for, 190
Profit
accounting, 64
definition, 64
economic, 64
-making firms, 252
Property
common, resource problems, 85–91
institutional, 90–91
structural, 90–91
Property rights
as basic public good, 236
common, 4–5
de facto, 73
defining, 73
de jure, 73
distribution, 215
established by usage, 97
exclusive, 6
as public good, 73
of resources, 126, 127
Prospect theory, 123
Protectionism, 223
Protest, 45, 47
Public agencies
civil service protections, 184–85
competition, lack of, 182–83
direct supply of goods, 248–49
double-market failure test, 247

Public agencies *(cont.)*
drawing organizational boundaries, 295–308
ex-post performance, 184
loss, 179–81
monitoring, 179
Public goods
ambient with consumption externality, 85
characteristics, 72, 77–78
classifications, 77–78
common property resources, 85–91
congestibility, 76–77
definition, 72
efficiency consequences, 113
excludability, 73
free goods, 85–91
intermediate group, 82, 91
market supply, 82–85
national defense, 247
nonrivalrous, 73–76
nonrivalry, nonexcludability, 81–86
open access, 85–91
organizational, 185–86
vs. private goods, 72
privileged group, 82–84, 91
property rights, 173
pure and ambient, 81–85
Public policy. *See also* Government
democracy, relationship between, 163–64, 166
forcing pricing, 99–100
government failure, relationship between (*see* Government failure)
rationales for, 54–55
Purchases, 106

Q

Qualitative benefit-cost analysis, 338–41
Quality
average, 108
consumption, relationship between, 106
heterogeneousness, 108
mean, 108
reliability, 109
uncertain, 110
variances, 106, 108
Quantitative benefit-cost analysis, 341
Quotas, 2, 3, 14–15, 241

R

Rand Corporation, 34, 314
Rationalism, 325–29, 361, 363, 379
Rational *vs.* irrational choice, 144
Rationing, 171
Rawlsianism, 133, 143
criticisms, 135–36
definition, 135
equality of outcome, 145
Redistribution, 117
of goods, 137, 145, 146
by government bureaus, 249
Regulations, 235
certification, 244
command and control principle, 237
criticisms, 238
direct information provision, 242–44
indirect information provision, 244–46
Madison taxicab example, 192–208
occupational licensure, 244–46
organizational report cards, 243
on price, 195–97, 237–39
privatizing, 257
quality, 243–44
quantity, 240–42
rate-of-return type, 238, 239
self-, 245
worker health and safety, 240–41
yardstick competition (price cap), 238–39
Regulator protection hypotheses, 197–98
Reliability, 109
Rent, 3
capture of, 222
control, 152
dissipation, 2–4, 9, 11, 12, 16, 20
economic, 3, 64
efficiency losses, 168
government-generated, 168
monopoly, 65–66, 114, 167
preservation of, 15–18, 20
price supports, 168–69
private, 11
rising, 170–71
scarcity (*see* Scarcity rent)
seeking, 166–72, 212
transfer, 8, 168–69
Rent dissipation, 2–4, 9, 11, 12, 16, 20
Representative government
analysts, relationship between, 178
campaign strategy, 175
cost monitoring, 179–80
exploitation of policy windows, 175–76
geographic-based election, 172–74
media, relationship between, 175–76
negative campaigning, 177
problems inherent in, 191
Research, policy, 25–27
"Resign and disclose," 48
Resignation, over value conflict, 46–47
Resources for the Future, 34, 314
Revenue, 64, 81
Rhetoric, 177, 273–74
Risk
collective, 120
premium, 119, 120
in setting interest rates, 127
subjective perception of, 121–22

Rules, 210
disadvantages, 234
efficiency of, 234
frameworks, 231–37
regulations (*see* Regulations)

S

Sabotage, 46, 49
Scarcity rent, 3, 67, 89, 90, 217, 219, 222
Scenario writing, 280–82
Search goods, 106–8, 112
Self-analysis, 324, 362
weaknesses, 325
writing strategies, 325
Shadow price of capital approach, 406
"Silent losers," 152–53
Sinclair Report/Davis Plan, 6–7
Single-market failure test, 250
Social choice, 157
Social consequences, 23
Social discount rate, 404–7
Social marginal rate of time preference, 124–27
Social norms, 291–93
Social surplus, 390
changes in, 139–40, 396, 402
consumer surplus, 58–63
definition, 57, 68
demand schedule (*see* Demand schedule)
as market efficiency yardstick, 57
maximumization, 69
net loss of due to underproduction, 99
producer surplus, 63–68
in Strategic Petroleum Reserve Program (*see under* Strategic Petroleum Reserve Program)
Social values, 23, 24
Social welfare
allocational perspective, 138–39
distribution issues, 138
functions, 133–38
institutional perspective, 138–39
maximization of, 330
multiplicative, 133
no-envy principle, 136
noneconomic indicators, 142
Rawlsianism (*see* Rawlsianism)
social indicators of change, 139–42
utilitarianism (*see* Utilitarianism)
as value, 133
Solution analysis, 328
alternatives, comparing, 355, 361–62
criteria choice, 343–44
goals/alternatives matrix, 343, 344, 363
policy alternatives, specifying, 345–48
predicting impacts, 348–51
recommendations, presenting, 356–57
valuing impacts, 351–54
Solution methods, 334
cost-benefit analysis (*see* Cost-benefit analysis)
cost-effectiveness analysis, 338–40, 342
multigoal analysis, 339, 340, 343, 383
Spatial stationarity, 91
"Speak out until silenced," 48
Special districts, 252
State government, role of policy analysis within, 34
Stationary goods, 91
Status quo effect, 123
Stochastic dynamic programming, 441, 443
Strategic behavior, 262
Strategic Petroleum Reserve Program, 188, 257, 426
adjustment costs, 437–38
analytical approaches, 432–33
collateral effects, 435–36
cost-benefit framework, 436
decision analysis, 440–43
direct market effects, 433–36
expenditure effects, 433
implementation problems, 188, 429–32
initiation of program, 428
macroeconomic simulations, 438–39
overview, 427–28
political effects, 435
scenario/break-even analysis, 439–40
size controversy, 443–50
social surplus changes, 436–37
stochastic dynamic programming, 441, 443
stockpiling, 257, 433–36, 441–43
structure of program, 428–29
Teisburg model, 443, 448–50
Strategic thinking, 262–63, 284–94
Subsidies, 148
to alter incentives, 210
to correct market failures, 218–19
demand-side, 219, 220, 228–33
food stamp program, 228–29
housing vouchers, 230–31
in-kind, 228–30
insurance, 256
intrusiveness, 218
maintenance-of-effort requirement, 225
matching grants, 224–26
in research and development, 227–28
school vouchers, 231–32
supply-side, 219, 220, 224–28
vouchers, 230–32
Success thresholds, 288
Sunk costs, 177
Sunset provisions, 288
Supply, bureaucratic, 179–86

Supply schedule, 66
of nonrivalrous goods, 74, 76
upward-sloping, 66, 74
Surplus. *See* Social surplus
Systems analysis, 28

T

Table of contents, of written analysis, 358, 359
Tariffication, 224
Tariffs, 167, 222–24, 241
Task complexity, 302–3
Taxes
commodity, 233
deadweight loss of (*see* Deadweight loss)
demand-side, 219, 220, 233–34
to discourage overcapitalization, 6
excise, 233, 414
expenditures, 226–28, 232–33
incentives, altering, 210
intrusiveness, 218
optimal rates, 221
output taxes, 219–21
Pigovian solution, 220
on pollutants, 221, 240
on profit, 128
raising, 174–75
royalty, 7–8, 13, 16–18
shares, 189
supply-side, 219–24
tariffs (*see* Tariffs)
trial-and-error experiments, 221
user fees, 233–34
Taxicab regulations, 192–208
Technical skills, 38
Think tanks, 34–35, 313–14
Thin markets, 114
Toll goods
market failures involving, 91
nonrivalry, excludability, 78–81
Trade
barriers, 224
deficit, 142
tariffs (*see* Tariffs)
Transaction cost theory, 296–97
Transitivity, 159–60
Travel cost method, 399
Trial balloons, 347

U

Ultimatum, issuing to client over value conflict, 47
Uncertainty
in basic competitive model, 119
insurance (*see* Insurance)
Underwriters Laboratory, 109
Unemployment, 141, 152
Unrestricted domain, axiom of, 159–60
Urban Institute, 34
Urban planning
impact, 28
master plan, 28–29
User fees, 233–34
U.S. Justice Department, 236
AT&T breakup and, 102
Utilitarianism
act-, 138–39
criticisms, 135
definition, 135
institutional, 138–39, 147
rule-, 138–39
Utilities, as monopoly, 102
Utility
articulation *vs.* formation, 330
declining marginal, 55
definition, 55
expected, 122
functions, 115
index of, 55
interdependence, 116–17, 139
levels, after price increase, 62
maximization, 122, 330
personal, 136
theory, 263

V

Valuation, 390–97
Value
consumer valuation, 76
existence, 12, 127
expected, 407–9
option, 409
social welfare, 133
Values, 40–41. *See also* Ethics
conflicts, 43–51
"cooked" results, 49–50
disloyalty, 45–48
distributional equity, 55
exit, 45–47
freedom, 478
human dignity, 55, 143–44, 478
institutional, 139, 146–47
instrumental, 153–54
Pareto efficiency (*see* Pareto efficiency)
substantive, 142–43
Voice, 45–48
Voluntary agreements, 54
Voting
agenda manipulation, 159–61, 172, 271–72
bliss point, 160–61
buying, 164–65
candidates (*see* Representative government)
costs incurred by voters, 164–65
cycles of, 160–61
district-based legislature, 172–74
electoral cycles, 174–75
fairness, 159–60
General Possibility Theorem, 159–60
indifference curve, 160
interest groups (*see* Interest groups)
opportunism in, 159
paradox of, 158–61
problems with system of, 158
referendums, 157–58, 161
self-interest in, 164

sophisticated, 159, 172, 272
tyranny by the majority, 162, 187
win sets, 160

W

Wage, 129
Warranties, 109
Water allocation analysis, 376–79
Wealth, 142, 144
Welfare economics, 70
Whistle-blowing, 48–49, 51
White House staffists, 43
"White market," 171
Willingness to pay, 392
World growth, limits on, 28–29
World Trade Organization (WTO), 223
Written analysis, 324
executive summary (*see* Executive summary)
headings, 359
simple *vs.* complex sentences, 360
structure, 359
table of contents, 358, 359
utilizing linear and nonlinear models, 325
writing strategies, 325

X

X-inefficiency, 102–4, 181–83, 251